Handbook of Gifted Education

Edited by

Nicholas Colangelo   *University of Iowa*

   and

Gary A. Davis   *University of Wisconsin, Madison*

Allyn and Bacon
Boston   London   Toronto   Sydney   Tokyo   Singapore

We dedicate this book
to
Kay and Joseph Colangelo
and Anthony Nicholas Pullano
and to
Cathy, Kirsten, Ingrid,
and Sonja Davis

Copyright © 1991 by Allyn and Bacon
A Division of Simon & Schuster, Inc.
160 Gould Street
Needham Heights, Massachusetts 02194

Library of Congress Cataloging-in-Publication Data

Handbook of gifted education / Nicholas Colangelo and Gary A. Davis,
  editors.
        p.   cm.
    Includes bibliographical references.
    ISBN 0-205-12652-9
    1. Gifted children—Education—Handbooks, manuals, etc.
    2. Talented students—Handbooks, manuals, etc.   I. Colangelo,
Nicholas, 1947–   II. Davis, Gary A., 1938–   .
    LC3993.H35   1990
    371.95—dc20
                                                          90-36623
                                                          CIP

Printed in the United States of America
10 9 8 7 6 5 4 3 2   94 93 92 91

Contents

Preface   vii

Contributors   ix

Guest Foreword   xv
Julian C. Stanley, Johns Hopkins University

PART I   INTRODUCTION   1

1   **Introduction and Historical Overview   3**
Nicholas Colangelo, University of Iowa
Gary A. Davis, University of Wisconsin, Madison

2   **Issues in the Education of Gifted Students   14**
James J. Gallagher, University of North Carolina, Chapel Hill

PART II   CONCEPTIONS AND IDENTIFICATION   25

3   **The Social Psychology of Giftedness   27**
Abraham J. Tannenbaum, Columbia University

4   **Giftedness According to the Triarchic Theory of Human
Intelligence   45**
Robert J. Sternberg, Yale University

5   **Giftedness from a Multiple Intelligence Perspective   55**
Valerie Ramos-Ford and *Howard Gardner,* Harvard University

6   **Toward a Differentiated Model of Giftedness and Talent   65**
Françoys Gagné, Université du Québec à Montréal

7   **Rampant Problems and Promising Practices in Identification   81**
E. Susanne Richert, Educational Resource Information Center (ERIC),
Sewell, New Jersey

PART III   INSTRUCTIONAL MODELS AND PRACTICES   97

8   **Enrichment and Acceleration: An Overview and New
Directions   99**
Shirley W. Schiever, Tucson Unified School District, Tucson, Arizona
C. June Maker, University of Arizona, Tucson

9   **The Schoolwide Enrichment Model: A Comprehensive Plan for the
Development of Creative Productivity   111**
Joseph S. Renzulli and *Sally M. Reis,* University of Connecticut,
Storrs

10   **The Autonomous Learner Model for the Gifted and Talented   142**
George T. Betts, University of Northern Colorado, Greeley

11 Mathematically Talented Childen: Can Acceleration Meet Their Educational Needs? 154
Camilla Persson Benbow, Iowa State University, Ames

12 Talent Searches 166
Sanford J. Cohn, Arizona State University, Tempe

√ **13 Ability Grouping and Gifted Students 178**
James A. Kulik and *Chen-Lin C. Kulik,* University of Michigan, Ann Arbor

14 Saturday and Summer Programs 197
John F. Feldhusen, Purdue University, Lafayette, Indiana

15 Special Residential High Schools 209
Penny Britton Kolloff, Cranbrook Schools, Bloomfield Hills, Michigan

PART IV CREATIVITY AND THINKING SKILLS 217

√ **16 The Assessment of Creativity 219**
Carolyn M. Callahan, University of Virginia, Charlottesville

√ **17 Teaching Creative Thinking 236**
Gary A. Davis, University of Wisconsin, Madison

√ **18 Developing Talent, Creativity, and Eminence 245**
Herbert J. Walberg, University of Illinois at Chicago
Manfred P. Herbig, Ruhr University of Bochum, Bochum, West Germany

√ **19 Creating Our Own Pathways: Teaching Students to Think and Become Self-Directed 256**
John Barell, Montclair State College, Upper Montclair, New Jersey

PART V PSYCHOLOGICAL AND COUNSELING SERVICES 271

√ **20 Counseling Gifted Students 273**
Nicholas Colangelo, University of Iowa, Iowa City

√ **21 Emotional Development and Emotional Giftedness 285**
Michael M. Piechowski, Northland College, Ashland, Wisconsin

22 Family Counseling 307
Linda Kreger Silverman, Gifted Child Develeopment Center, Denver, Colorado

23 Career Development 321
Philip A. Perrone, University of Wisconsin, Madison

24 Underachievement and Superachievement: Flip Sides of the Same Psychological Coin 328
Sylvia B. Rimm, Family Achievement Clinic, Oconomowoc, Wisconsin

PART VI SPECIAL TOPICS 345

√ **25 Extreme Precocity 347**
Martha J. Morelock and *David H. Feldman,* Tufts University

26 Young Gifted Children   365
Michael Lewis and *Barbara Louis,* Robert Wood Johnson Medical
School, New Brunswick, New Jersey

27 Gifted Adolescents   382
Thomas M. Buescher, Mid Coast Mental Health Center, Rockland,
Maine

28 Educating Gifted Girls   402
Barbara Kerr, University of Iowa, Iowa City

29 Ethnic and Cultural Issues   416
Alexinia Young Baldwin, University of Connecticut, Storrs

30 Gifted Handicapped   428
Merle B. Karnes, University of Illinois, Urbana-Champaign
Lawrence J. Johnson, University of Alabama, Tuscaloosa

PART VII   THE FUTURE   **439**

31 Future Goals and Directions   441
Donald J. Treffinger, Center for Creative Learning, Honeoye,
New York

Author Index   450

Subject Index   458

This book began with a vision—a vision of bringing together the thinking and writing of some of the most eminent authors in the field of gifted education, a vision of developing a scholarly handbook that would be at once a text for college senior and graduate courses and a sound resource for university educators and scholars/practitioners in the field.

The history of gifted education has shown an ebb-and-flow pattern in its prominence with both educators and the general public. Although the current "flow" was born in the 1970s, the decade of the 1980s witnessed a rapid expansion of interest in meeting the academic needs of gifted youngsters. The interest has been worldwide, with legislation and programs sprouting not only in the United States and Canada but also in the Dominican Republic, Costa Rica, Brazil, Russia, Australia, Egypt, India, mainland China, Hong Kong, Guam, South Africa, and many other countries.

The 1980s also brought a finer focus on social and psychological issues pertaining to gifted students—for example, issues concerning minority, female, handicapped, and very young gifted children; extraordinarily precocious children and youth; and even families of the gifted. The growth of the 1980s and into the 1990s is not simply a renewal of past efforts, such as the burst of math and science programs following Sputnik, but forays into fresh areas as well.

Support for the rapid growth of programs and services for the gifted and talented has been mostly enthusiastic and progressive. However, there also has been conflict: with critics in the general public, who see gifted education as an undemocratic and elitist movement that "gives to the rich"; with some teachers and principals, who install programs only in begrudging response to state mandates or community demands; and with the academic educational establishment, which has responded too slowly in providing course work and professional training for this pressing educational need.

Most of the strong interest in—indeed, demand for—college work in gifted education has come from teachers, counselors, and administrators who, after experiencing the realities of schools and classrooms, realize that gifted children present a unique and unmet challenge to the entire educational system. It is these educators who want a better understanding and a repertoire of strategies in gifted education. This book was conceived with this rapidly growing population of educators in mind. The book is divided into seven main sections: an introductory overview and presentation of issues; definitions and identification; program models and teaching practices; creativity and thinking skills; psychological and counseling services; special topics, which largely concern special populations of gifted students; and future trends. It is thus a comprehensive text, covering issues, problems, and practical strategies in all central components of gifted education.

Further, in view of the list of unusually authoritative authors, the book provides form and substance, in depth, for scholars who need an up-to-date resource. Those who study these chapters will become familiar with today's issues in the field, and with the seasoned ideas and unique insights expected of a resource volume. To help build the next decade of progress in gifted education is part of the vision that created this project.

We wish to thank secretaries Reta Litton, Virginia Travis, and Laurie Koch for their excellent typing and clerical assistance. We thank David Holling for his work as our graduate assistant. We also thank the staff at the Connie Belin National Center for Gifted Education for their proofreading and editorial assistance: Paula Christensen, Joanne Daggit, Kris Decker, Bryon Day, Glenda Droogsma, and Julie Sawyers. We wish to thank Allyn and Bacon editors Ray Short and Mylan Jaixen for their encouragement and support. Especially, we are grateful to all of our contributing authors, who enthusiastically endorsed this handbook and collaborated with us in realizing our vision.

We believe that teachers and counselors have the greatest direct impact on the day-to-day lives of gifted youngsters in schools. We hope this text will enrich the professional development of these and other readers, so that all can nurture the gifts of students. They have special talents and compelling needs that urgently require attention.

NC
GAD

Alexinia Young Baldwin is Professor and Head of Curriculum and Instruction at the University of Connecticut, with special research and writing interests in the education of the gifted child. She developed the Baldwin Identification Matrix and has focused much attention on the minority gifted child. Dr. Baldwin is a former president of the Association for the Gifted and currently serves as an elected board member of the National Association for Gifted Children. She served as associate editor and field editor for *Exceptional Children* and is a member of the advisory board of the *Gifted Child Quarterly*. She has written articles and chapters on educating gifted children, and is an active volunteer worker with ALTRUSA: International Service Organization for Executive and Professional Women.

John Barell is Professor of Curriculum and Instruction at Montclair State College. He formerly was coordinator of the Network on Teaching Thinking of the Association for Supervision and Curriculum Development, and currently conducts staff development workshops to help teachers foster thoughtfulness in students. He has authored many articles on teaching thinking skills, along with the books *Playgrounds of Our Minds, Opening the American Mind,* and *Pathways to Thoughtfulness: Enhancing Students' Thinking.*

Camilla Persson Benbow is Associate Professor of Psychology at Iowa State University (ISU) and Director of the Study of Mathematically Precocious Youth (SMPY) at ISU. She conducts a SMPY longitudinal study in which the development of 3,000 gifted individuals is studied throughout their adult lives. Dr. Benbow also directs the College for Youth–Talented and Gifted program at ISU, which provides educational programming to gifted students. Before moving to Iowa State University, she trained and worked for nearly a decade with Dr. Julian C. Stanley at Johns Hopkins University. She has published extensively on issues regarding acceleration, precocity in mathematics, and gender.

George T. Betts is Director of the Center for the Education and Study of the Gifted and Talented at the University of Northern Colorado. He is an elected board member of the National Association for Gifted Children and an international consultant in the areas of program development and counseling for the gifted and talented. Dr. Betts is a cofounder of the autonomous learner model, which has been adopted for grades K–12 in numerous school districts in the United States and Canada. He is author of the book *Autonomous Learner Model for the Gifted and Talented* and of articles on gifted education.

Thomas M. Buescher is Clinical Social Worker at Mid Coast Mental Health Center, Rockland, Maine. He was formerly a therapist and Research Scholar at the Center for Talent Development, Northwestern University. He holds an M.S.W. degree in clinical social work and a Ph.D. degree in special education and developmental psychology. Over his 20 years in education, he has served as an educational director, a middle school and high school teacher and counselor in programs for exceptional adolescents, and director of a middle school program for the gifted and talented. At Northwestern University he taught courses in special education and gifted education and administered university programs for talented adolescents. He has conducted research and written widely about the development and adjustment of gifted and talented adolescents and the concerns of their families. He writes for several publications and speaks frequently to teacher, counselor, and parent groups and adolescents in middle and high schools around the country.

Carolyn M. Callahan is Professor of Educational Studies at the University of Virginia. She has served as president of the Association for the Gifted and on the executive board of the National Association for Gifted Children. She also has served on the editorial boards of *Journal for the Education of the Gifted, Gifted Child Quarterly, Roeper Review, Exceptional Children,* and other journals. Her writings include *Scales for Rating the Behavioral Characteristics of Superior Children* (with Joseph S. Renzulli and Robert K. Hartman), the book *Developing Creativity in the Gifted and Talented,* and many articles and book chapters on gifted females and the evaluation of programs for the gifted and talented.

Sanford J. Cohn is Associate Professor of Special Education at Arizona State University, where he is the founder and director of the Center for Academic Precocity (formerly the Project for the Study of Academic Precocity). He has written many articles on educating the gifted and is coeditor (with Julian Stanley and William C. George) of *Educating the Gifted: Acceleration and Enrichment*. He is a productive researcher in the areas of program evaluation, verbal and mathematical reasoning abilities and information processing among the highly able, and culturally nonbiased identification measures. As a licensed psychologist, Dr. Cohn also works in a clinical setting with highly able youths and their families.

Nicholas Colangelo is the Myron and Jacqueline Blank Professor of Gifted Education and Director of the Connie Belin National Center for Gifted Education at the University of Iowa. He serves on the editorial boards of *Gifted Child Quarterly, Journal for the Education of the Gifted,* and *Roeper Review*. He is editor of the journal *Counseling and Values* and author of numerous research and theoretical articles on affective development and the counseling needs of gifted students. He has edited three books, including *New Voices in Counseling the Gifted* (with Ronald T. Zaffrann).

Gary A. Davis is Professor of Educational Psychology at the University of Wisconsin, Madison, where he teaches courses in creativity and gifted education. He is author of numerous articles in the areas of creativity, moral education, and effective schooling, and of many books, including *Education of the Gifted and Talented* (with Sylvia Rimm), *Creativity Is Forever, Psychology of Problem Solving, Training Creative Thinking, Creative Teaching of Values and Moral Thinking,* and *Effective Schools and Effective Teachers*. He is a reviewer, consulting editor, and editorial board member for several creativity and gifted education journals.

John F. Feldhusen is the R. B. Cane Distinguished Professor of Education at Purdue University and Director of the Gifted Education Resource Institute. He has been instrumental in the creation of many programs for the gifted at Purdue University, which are described in his present chapter. He has authored many articles and books on teaching the gifted, including *Creative Thinking and Problem Solving* (with Donald J. Treffinger). He is editor of the *Gifted Child Quarterly* and former president of the National Association for Gifted Children.

David H. Feldman is Professor of Developmental Psychology in the Eliot-Pearson Department of Child Study at Tufts University. He also directs the Jessie Smith Noves Fellows Program in Gifted Education, has served as national chairman of the Social Science Research Council's Committee on Research on Giftedness and Creativity, and was the 1988 Scholar of the Year of the National Association for Gifted Children. He is author of *Beyond Universals in Cognitive Development* and *Nature's Gambit*.

Françoys Gagné is Professor of Psychology at the Université du Québec à Montréal, where he organized a uniquely French-speaking research laboratory on giftedness. He was founder and president of Giftedness Québec, an advocacy group for teachers and parents, and gives lectures and conducts workshops on giftedness. His earlier work focused on college teaching and the psychometrics of student course evaluations, offering computer and consulting services to over forty Canadian colleges.

James J. Gallagher is Kenan Professor of Education at the University of North Carolina at Chapel Hill. He has worked in gifted education for over thirty years. Dr. Gallagher has served as president of the World Council for Gifted and Talented Children, as president of The Association for the Gifted, and as chair of the Illinois Governor's Council on the Gifted. He is the author of *Teaching the Gifted Child* and a number of research articles and monographs on productive thinking in the classroom. He currently serves as editor of the *Journal for the Education of the Gifted*.

Howard Gardner is Professor of Education and Co-director of Project Zero at the Harvard Graduate School of Education. He also is a research psychologist at the Boston Veterans Administration Medical Center and adjunct professor of neurology at the Boston University School of Medicine. His research focuses on human cognitive capacities, particularly those central to the arts, in normal children, gifted children, and brain-damaged adults. He is the author of numerous articles in professional journals and wide-circulation periodicals. Among his nine books is the well-known *Frames of Mind,* along with *The Quest for Mind; The Shattered Mind; Art, Mind and Brain; The Mind's New Science;* and *Developmental Psychology*. In 1981 he was awarded the MacArthur Prize Fellowship.

Manfred P. Herbig is Professor and Director of the Department of Teaching and Instruction at Ruhr University, Bochum, West Germany. He was awarded a Fulbright Scholarship at the University of Illinois, where he collaborated with Herbert Walberg on several research and writing projects. He has published primarily in the areas of educational measurement, experimental design, personal development, and learning and teaching.

Lawrence J. Johnson is Associate Professor and Chair of Early Childhood Special Education at the University of Alabama. He is on the executive board of the Teacher Education Division of the Council for Exceptional Children and is chair of the research task force of the early childhood division of CEC. Dr. Johnson serves as associate editor of the *Journal of Early Intervention,* editor of the Research Notes section of the *Journal of Early Intervention,* and on the editorial boards of *Remedial and Special Education, Journal for the Education of the Gifted,* and *Teacher Education and Special Education.* He is author (with Merle B. Karnes) of *Identifying and Programming for Young Black Gifted Children.*

Merle B. Karnes is Professor of Special Education at the University of Illinois. She has a long history of work in gifted education. Dr. Karnes is best known for her work with young gifted children, especially those who are handicapped or from low-income homes or minority populations. She has conducted research and written extensively about these populations. She is editor of *The Underserved: Our Young Gifted Children,* to which she contributed several chapters, and (with Lawrence Johnson) of *Identifying and Programming for Young Black Gifted Children.* Currently she is conducting research on and programming for gifted children who are mainstreamed in regular classrooms.

Barbara Kerr is Associate Professor of Counselor Education and Associate Director of the Connie Belin National Center for Gifted Education at the University of Iowa. She is author of *Smart Girls, Gifted Women; Career Education for Gifted and Talented;* and a number of articles related to the career development of gifted and talented students. She has a strong research focus on the educational and counseling needs of gifted girls.

Penny Britton Kolloff received her Ph.D. degree from Purdue University, where she served as Assistant Director of the Gifted Education Resource Institute, and aided John Feldhusen with the development of the Program for Academic and Creative Enrichment (PACE) and the Purdue three-stage enrichment model. Until 1990 she served as director of the Center for Gifted and Talented Programs at the Burris Laboratory School at Ball State University, coordinated follow-up activities for Indiana participants in the Midwest Talent Search, and taught graduate courses in gifted education. Dr. Kolloff

worked toward the establishment of the Indiana Academy of Science, Mathematics, and Humanities, a residential high school for gifted students, and was instrumental in the development of the first Indiana Governor's Scholars Academy. She currently is Director of Curriculum at Cranbrook Schools, Bloomfield Hills, Michigan.

Chen-Lin C. Kulik is Assistant Research Scientist at the University of Michigan Center for Research on Learning and Teaching. Her research specialties include psychological measurement and the application of statistical methods in education and the health sciences. She is coauthor of the monograph *Meta-Analysis in Educational Research,* published in the *International Journal of Educational Research.*

James J. Kulik is Research Scientist at the University of Michigan Center for Research on Learning and Teaching. At Michigan he has taught psychology courses, directed university-wide programs of teacher evaluation and student testing and placement, and conducted research in education. He is author of the book *Undergraduate Education in Psychology* and of numerous articles. His major interest in recent years has been the quantitative integration of research findings in education, a topic covered in his coauthored monograph *Meta-Analysis in Educational Research,* published in the *International Journal of Educational Research.*

Michael Lewis is Professor of Pediatrics, Psychiatry, and Psychology, and Chief of the Institute for the Study of Child Development at the University of Medicine and Dentistry of New Jersey in New Brunswick, New Jersey. He is coauthor of the book *Children's Emotions and Moods* and coeditor of *The Handbook of Developmental Psychopathology.* He is currently completing a book titled *The Exposed Self.*

Barbara Louis is a graduate student in psychology at Rutgers University in New Brunswick, New Jersey, where she also is coordinator of the Gifted Child Clinic. She is also coordinator of assessment for the Inner City Gifted Project at the Institute for the Study of Child Development at the University of Medicine and Dentistry of New Jersey. She is preparing a manuscript entitled *Giftedness in Young Children: Parental Beliefs.*

C. June Maker is Professor of Special Education at the University of Arizona, Tucson, where she coordinates graduate degree programs in the education of the gifted. She has held national offices in several organizations, including the National Association for Gifted Children. She has been a teacher, a regional supervisor for a state department of education, and an administrative intern in the federal office for the gifted, and has consulted with local school districts, state departments of education, and other public and private agencies. Dr. Maker is author of *Curriculum Development for the Gifted, Providing Programs for the Gifted Handicapped, Teaching-Learning Models for Gifted Education, Training Teachers for the Gifted and Talented: A Comparison of Models,* and numerous articles pertaining to gifted handicapped, teacher training, developing the talents of exceptional children, and teaching learning-disabled students.

Martha J. Morelock is a doctoral student in the Eliot-Pearson Department of Child Study at Tufts University, where she is Jessie Smith Noves Fellow in Gifted Education. She has published several articles on gifted and prodigious children and is a column editor for the national newsletter *Understanding Our Gifted.*

Philip A. Perrone is Professor of Counselor Education at the University of Wisconsin, Madison. His teaching and research focus on counseling the gifted in decision making and career planning, and on guidance needs of at-risk students. He is the author of *Developmental Education and Guidance of Talented Learners, Guidance and the Emerging Adolescent, Programmed Instruction in the Use of Tests in Counseling,* and journal articles, and has produced ten educational films. He consults with school districts regarding guidance programs and improving the education and guidance of gifted students.

Michael M. Piechowski is Associate Professor of Education and Psychology at Northland College in Ashland, Wisconsin. He has taught at the University of Illinois (where he received two teaching awards) and Northwestern University. Dr. Piechowski has published many research and theoretical articles on emotional development, the theories of Jung and Dabrowski, development of gifted adolescents and adults, and self-actualizing people.

Valerie Ramos-Ford holds the title of Researcher with Project Spectrum, a collaborative project between David H. Feldman at the Eliot-Pearson Department of Child Study at Tufts University and Howard Gardner at Project Zero at the Harvard Graduate School of Education. Project Spectrum is an innovative approach to preschool and early school curriculum and assessment that addresses a broad range of cognitive capabilities in young children. Prior to her involvement in educational research,

Ms. Ramos-Ford was a preschool teacher and educational consultant in the Boston area.

Joseph S. Renzulli is Professor of Educational Psychology at the University of Connecticut, and Director of the National Research Center on the Gifted and Talented. His list of books includes *The Enrichment Triad Model, The Revolving Door Identification Model* (with Sally M. Reis and Linda H. Smith), *Psychology and Education of the Gifted* (with Walter B. Barbe), *Systems and Models for Developing Programs for the Gifted and Talented.* He is a former president of the Association for the Gifted and currently serves on the editorial boards of *Exceptional Children* and the *Gifted Child Quarterly.* He has served as consultant to numerous schools districts and agencies, including the Office of Gifted and Talented (U.S. Office of Education) and the White House Task Force on the Education of the Gifted.

Sally M. Reis is Project Director and Instructor at the University of Connecticut. She is a staff member of the Teaching the Talented Program at the University of Connecticut and is coordinator of the Young Scholars Saturday Semester, a regional program based on the Enrichment Triad Model. She has been a teacher of the gifted at the elementary, junior high, and high school levels. She is coauthor of the *The Revolving Door Identification Model* (with Joseph S. Renzulli and Linda H. Smith) and author of numerous articles on gifted education. She serves on the editorial boards of *Roeper Review* and the *Gifted Child Quarterly.*

E. Susanne Richert is Director of the National Clearinghouse for Gifted Resources at the Educational Information and Resource Center in Sewell, New Jersey. She coauthored the *National Report on Identification* (with James J. Alvino and R. C. McDonnel), as well as many articles and training manuals on gifted education. She also is coauthor (with James J. Alvino) of a forthcoming book *Gifted Boys, Gifted Girls.* She has served as an educational consultant to the U.S. Supreme Court; to the departments of education of the United States, Israel, Hungary, Nigeria, and Canada; to over twenty state departments of education in the United States; and to several hundred school districts throughout the United States and Canada. She serves on the editorial boards of the *Gifted Child Quarterly, Journal for the Education of the Gifted, Roeper Review,* and *Gifted Children Monthly.*

Sylvia B. Rimm is a licensed psychologist and director of the Family Achievement Clinics in Wisconsin. She gives workshops and speaks widely on the topics of underachievement and giftedness. She is the author of *Underachievement Syndrome: Causes and Cures, Guidebook to Underachievement Syndrome: Causes and Cures, Education of the Gifted and Talented* (with Gary A. Davis), *How to Parent So Children Will Learn,* and articles on the topics of gifted education, creativity, and underachievement. She also developed the creativity inventories PRIDE, GIFT, and (with Gary A. Davis) GIFFI I and II, and the underachievement inventories AIM, GAIM, and AIM-TO.

Shirley W. Schiever is At-Risk Coordinator at a fine arts magnet middle school in Tucson, Arizona. She has served as coordinator of a research project focusing on identifying gifted minority students, elementary teacher, teacher of the gifted, curriculum specialist, district gifted coordinator, and university instructor. She is a board member and past president of the Arizona Association for Gifted and Talented, and is cochair of the Curriculum Studies Division of the National Association for Gifted Children. She has published many articles and book chapters on the gifted, has written the recent book *A Comprehensive Approach to Teaching Thinking,* and coedited a book (with C. June Maker) entitled *Critical Issues in Gifted Education, Volume 2, Defensible Programs for Cultural and Ethnic Minorities.*

Linda Kreger Silverman is Director of the Gifted Child Development Center in Denver, Colorado, specializing in assessment and counseling services for gifted children and their families. She previously was a faculty member of the University of Denver, where she taught courses in gifted education and counseling. She has published widely on the education of the gifted and lectures throughout the country. She is the editor of *Advanced Development,* a new professional journal on giftedness in adults, and *Understanding Our Gifted,* a newsletter for parents, teachers, and counselors.

Julian C. Stanley is Professor of Psychology and director of the Study of Mathematically Precocious Youth (SMPY) at Johns Hopkins University, Baltimore, Maryland. He specializes in identifying boys and girls 12 years old or less who reason extremely well mathematically, and helping them find the special, supplemental educational opportunities they need. He began the SMPY at Johns Hopkins University in 1971. He is a past president of the American Educational Research Association, the National Council on Measurement in Education, and two divisions of the American Psychological Association: Educational Psychology, and Evaluation and Measurement. His work has led, since 1979, to large talent searches conducted by Johns Hopkins, Duke University, Northwestern University, and the University of Denver and to many residential academic summer programs for intellectually talented young people.

Robert J. Sternberg is IBM Professor of Psychology and Education at Yale University. He is author of *The Triarchic Mind,* editor of *The Nature of Creativity,* and coeditor (with Janet Davidson) of *Conceptions of Giftedness.* He has written extensively on the nature of intelligence and is the originator of the componential and triarchic theories of intelligence.

Abraham J. Tannenbaum is Professor Emeritus of Education and Psychology at Teachers College, Columbia University. At Columbia University he directed programs in the education of the gifted and of the behaviorally disordered. From 1975 to 1980 he directed the federally sponsored Graduate Leadership Education Project, which involved seven universities in an effort to produce leaders in gifted education. He served as president of the Metropolitan Association for the Study of the Gifted and as president of the Council for Children with Behavior Disorders. In 1981 he received the Hollingworth Award for research on the gifted, and in 1985 the National Association for Gifted Children's Distinguished Scholar Award. His most recent major book is *Gifted Children: Psychological and Educational Perspectives.*

Donald J. Treffinger is Director of the Center for Creative Learning at Honeoye Lake, New York, and Professor of Creative Studies at the State University College at Buffalo. He is author or coauthor of over a dozen books, including *Creative Problem Solving: The Basic Course* (with Scott G. Isaksen), *Handbook of Creative Learning* (with Scott G. Isaksen and Roger L. Firestien), and *Teaching Creative Thinking and Problem Solving* (with John F. Feldhusen), and a number of articles on creative learning, problem solving, and gifted education.

Herbert J. Walberg is Research Professor of Education at the University of Illinois at Chicago. He has served as an advisor on educational research and improvement to government and private agencies in the United States and many foreign countries. He has written or edited 35 books, including *Research on Teaching* (coedited with Penelope L. Peterson), and was instrumental in the preparation of the government booklet *What Works: Research About Teaching and Learning.* He has authored several hundred articles on giftedness and talent development, educational productivity, international comparisons, classroom instruction, and parent education. He chairs the scientific committees of the National Assessment Governing Board and the Paris-based Organization for Economic and Cooperative Development.

Guest Foreword: So Important a Book, I Wish It Were Even Longer

JULIAN C. STANLEY
Study of Mathematically Precocious Youth (SMPY)
Johns Hopkins University
Baltimore, Maryland

Nicholas Colangelo and Gary Davis have rendered the field of educating the gifted a great service. Perhaps no one who has not served as editor of such a volume can realize how exquisitely difficult, time-consuming, and challenging it can be to work with 37 different authors, besides oneself, in getting a book ready for press. Colangelo and Davis, however, are highly experienced writers and editors, and their product is well worth the effort involved. Not only do they have 31 chapters, but these were prepared by a most impressive variety of specialists in giftedness, intelligence, ability grouping, creativity, thinking skills, counseling, and other aspects of gifted education. Many of the greatest names in the field are represented.

Much of the most interesting and important landscape is covered, some of it with desirable overlap among several chapters. One cannot do everything in one book of manageable size. With inevitable limitations of space, time, and energy, Colangelo and Davis are to be congratulated for their product. If the book could have been longer, however, perhaps it would have been well to include several more chapters. The alert instructor using this volume as a textbook for graduate courses may want to assign reading on general intelligence (g). The foundation that Binet, Spearman, Terman, and Leta Hollingworth gave us is too precious not to be treated in more depth. Also, while the history of gifted children and adults is treated as part of the first chapter, a whole chapter on history might have enriched the volume. The instructor can readily provide some of that from Oden (1968) or Goodenough (1949).

Several perplexing problems are attacked in the various chapters. One of these is the question of what is meant by the terms *giftedness* and *gifted,* and whether or not they obstruct our thinking and prejudice many laypersons against efforts on behalf of high-ability young people. Being "gifted" seems to imply having been *given* intellectually valuable potential without having had to work for it. An egalitarian society does not take kindly to the notion that some are "born with a silver spoon in their mouths."

In addition, using the noun *giftedness* connotes that there is a *single* dimension, perhaps bipolar ("gifted" versus "not gifted"). Yet most of the chapters speak strongly against that implied idea. Perhaps we should change the term to *aptitude* or *potential,* as in "musical aptitude," "mathematical potential," "dramatic promise," and the like. In my own work I have usually tried to avoid *giftedness* and *gifted* and, instead, employ longer expressions such as "youths who reason exceptionally well mathematically" for those who score at least 500 on the mathematical part of the College Board Scholastic Aptitude Test (SAT-M) before age 13. They are approximately the ablest one percent of their age group in presumed potential for learning mathematics and related subjects such as physics and computer science rapidly and well. For those who score at least 700 before age 13, the top 1 in 10,000 of their age group, the adverb *exceptionally* is upgraded to *extremely.* This is a rough-and-ready way to try to convey in words some of the operational meaning of the high scores.

One proof of a good book is that it stimulates discussion and alternative formulations. Certainly, this one has already done that for me. I feel confident that it will be used widely and will help upgrade the caliber of thinking of many graduate students, their teachers, and others concerned with high-ability, high-promise, high-potential, "gifted" boys and girls.

REFERENCES

Goodenough, F. L. (1949). *Mental testing: Its history, principles, and applications.* New York: Rinehart.

Oden, M. H. (1968). The fulfillment of promise: 40-year follow-up of the Terman gifted group. *Genetic Psychology Monographs, 77* (1st half), 3–93.

Introduction

Introduction and Historical Overview

NICHOLAS COLANGELO   *University of Iowa*
GARY A. DAVIS   *University of Wisconsin, Madison*

■ Giftedness is one of the most exciting and at the same time most controversial issues facing education today. The base of the controversy is society's subtle (and sometimes not so subtle) love–hate relationship with giftedness and talent. On the one hand we applaud the individual who has risen from a humble background. We value and admire his or her talent and drive. On the other hand, as a nation we have a strong commitment to egalitarianism, as reflected in that mighty phrase "All men are created equal." The dynamics of the love–hate relationship with giftedness and talent have been documented by a number of educators (e.g., Colangelo, 1982, 1987; Davis & Rimm, 1989; Gallagher & Weiss, 1979; Gardner, 1961).

Ambivalence toward gifted education has contributed to an ebb-and-flow pattern in its development for at least the last 50 years. Society swings back and forth between the goals of equity and excellence (Gallagher, Weiss, Oglesby, & Thomas, 1983). When excellence is a major concern, programs for the brightest receive attention and priority. Two examples of times when excellence has taken precedence are the reaction to Sputnik in the late 1950s and the present turmoil in education as highlighted by the jolting government report *A Nation at Risk* (National Commission on Excellence in Education, 1983). When equity has been the primary concern, for example, in the 1960s and early 1970s, then gifted education becomes a minor issue. "Equity" is associated with meeting the needs of average and, more typically, below average and disadvantaged students, who are perceived as needing help so they can become equal. Treating issues of equity and excellence as mutually exclusive (indeed, as antagonistic) has been destructive

to the development of sound and stable educational practices.

It seems that people either enthusiastically defend or attack gifted education—often without any, or at best with minimal, factual information. The following are some themes that help account for the ambivalent or even hostile reactions to gifted education.

Perceiving Giftedness as Effortlessness

For some, the word *gifted* smacks of "getting something for nothing." If people hold this view (even on a subliminal level), they will resent efforts in gifted education, since they do not want to give more to those already basking in privileges. In fact, however, and regardless of native ability, achieving excellence in any field takes hard work. Bloom's excellent studies emphatically highlight the effort and commitment required to develop talent to a high degree (Bloom, 1985; Bloom & Sosniak, 1981). It is unfortunate that there is a misperception of equating giftedness with effortlessness, since this is not borne out in studies or biographies of eminent individuals. We believe it is more accurate to paraphrase a saying attributed to Thomas Edison, "When it comes to great achievement, the perspiration outweighs the inspiration."

Egalitarianism and Giftedness

A core difficulty in thinking clearly about meeting the educational needs of gifted youngsters is that providing such special opportunities runs counter to the idea of a democratic or egalitarian society. John Gardner's (1961) book *Excellence: Can We Be Equal and Excellent Too?* delineates the confusing tension that has existed between encouraging and restraining individual performance. It is, as previously mentioned, essentially a love–hate phenomenon. People believe in individual opportunity and in the idea of excellence, yet many fear elitism—this connotes the belief that one person or group is inherently better or of more value than others. In order to allay this fear, there arises a belief that if equality, or "the same for everyone," is enforced, then elitism will be defeated.

People have very strong personal feelings about elitism. However, the recognition of differences is not the same as holding an elitist point of view. Recognizing the skill of a piano virtuoso does not indicate a belief that this skill somehow makes the person better than others as a human being.

Youngsters can act elitist (self-centered, self-important) for a variety of reasons, such as outstanding athletic abilities, good looks, or family wealth. However, elitism in these areas somehow is not as important an issue as it is with children who are gifted. Remarkably, as a group, gifted youngsters have been found to be more understanding and modest than most other youngsters (Goldberg, 1965). Also, we have found no research that supports the belief that gifted youngsters themselves hold more elitist attitudes than do other groups of students.

While society in general and educators in particular drift back and forth between emphasizing and restraining individual performances, youngsters of all ability levels are caught in the middle. There is need for more critical thought about what is meant by "democracy in education" and the perceived incompatibility between equality and individual differences.

In fact, if the matter is cast as "equality of opportunity," the incompatibility disappears.

Anti-Intellectualism

In his excellent book *Anti-Intellectualism in American Life,* Richard Hofstadter (1963) argued that, as a group, Americans and many others are hostile to intellectual pursuits and those who are seen as intellectually gifted. Hofstadter traces the roots of this phenomenon

to the founding of the colonies and the settling of the frontier.

Currently, if a youngster excels in sports, dance, art, or even music, the problem of anti-intellectualism does not seem to arise. However, if a youngster is labeled *intellectually gifted,* then it is another matter. Although society can allow and applaud certain areas of talent, high intellectual ability spurs considerable ambivalence. It seems that intellectual giftedness threatens the self-esteem of others, both youngsters and adults, in a way that most other talents do not.

"They will make it on their own"

One common argument against any special educational considerations is that gifted students by virtue of their giftedness will make it on their own. Davis and Rimm (1989) review studies indicating that many students labeled gifted indeed do *not* make it on their own. An inadequate and unchallenging curriculum, social and emotional difficulties, inadequate parenting, and peer pressures all can extinguish the high potential accomplishment of gifted children and adolescents.

The Excitement of Educating Gifted Students

While we have discussed problems confronting gifted education and gifted students themselves, and more difficulties will be discussed in later chapters, there nonetheless is tremendous excitement about giftedness. It is a phenomenon that has intrigued virtually all societies in recorded history. As Sternberg and Davidson (1986) state, "Giftedness is arguably the most precious natural resource a civilization can have" (p. ix). Children who produce and create well beyond our expectations invigorate us and show us the possibilities of human potential. Adults of eminence have left their mark in helping societies develop morally, technologically, and aesthetically. In our own experience we have never met teachers more excited about teaching than when they work with gifted children.

[handwritten margin note: it is worse for a gifted student to act elitist than an athlete]

Historical Overview of Giftedness and Gifted Education

The focus on giftedness is by no means a recent happening. A brief historical summary of how societies have responded to giftedness will help put our modern challenges in perspective. Also, it will indicate that our concern with giftedness and gifted education is deeply rooted in the human experience.

Giftedness Around the World

A capsule history of recognizing and providing differentiated training for gifted children might begin in ancient Sparta. There, military skills were so exclusively valued that all boys beginning at age 7 received schooling and training in the fine art of combat and warfare. Giftedness emerged and was fostered in terms of fighting skills and military leadership (Meyer, 1965).

In Athens, upper-class Greeks sent their boys to private schools that taught reading, writing, arithmetic, literature, history, the arts, and physical fitness. When the boys became older, professional teachers (sophists) were hired to teach the young men mathematics, logic, rhetoric, politics, grammar, general culture, and "disputation." Plato's famous academy selected both young men and young women, based on intelligence and physical stamina rather than social position, and charged no fees.

Roman education emphasized architecture, engineering, law, and administration. Both boys and girls attended first-level (elementary) schools, and some girls attended grammar (second-level) schools. Higher education was not permitted for females. However, some gifted women emerged who greatly affected Roman society, for example, Cornelius, Roman matron and mother of statesmen Gaius and Tiberius Gracchus (Good, 1960).

The renaissance in Europe (1300–1700) produced remarkable art, architecture, and literature, and for good reason. Strong and wealthy governments rewarded their creatively gifted with wealth and honor. Such brilliant and aesthetically talented persons as Michelangelo, da Vinci, Boccacio, Bernini, and Dante were sought out and supported well.

Early China, beginning with the Tang Dynasty (618 A.D.), valued its gifted children and youth highly. Child prodigies were sent to the imperial court, where their gifts were recognized and cultivated. China at this time anticipated four principles of modern gifted education. First, they accepted a multiple-talent concept of giftedness, valuing literary ability, leadership, imagination, reading speed, memory capability, reasoning, and perceptual sensitivity. Second, they recognized that some apparently precocious youth would grow up to be average; some seemingly average youth would later show gifts; and true child prodigies would show gifts and talents throughout their lives. Third, they realized that abilities of even the most gifted would not fully develop without special training. Support was considered especially important because of the belief that these children were weak and unhealthy and would not live long. Fourth, they believed that education should be available to children of all social classes, but that they should be educated differently according to their abilities.

During the Tokugawa Society period in Japan from 1604 to 1868, poor village children were taught loyalty, obedience, humility, and diligence. However, Samurai children received training in Confucian classics, martial arts, history, composition, calligraphy, moral values, and etiquette. A few individual scholars established private academies for the intellectually gifted, both Samurai and common (Anderson, 1975).

In early America, concern for the gifted was virtually nonexistent. Some gifted youth were accommodated in that attending secondary school and college was based on both academic achievement and the ability to pay the fees (Newland, 1976).

With compulsory school attendance laws, education became available to all children, but there remained little attention to the gifted and talented. There were a few noteworthy exceptions: Some schools in Elizabeth, New Jersey, began tracking gifted and slow learners as early as 1866; St. Louis initiated tracking in 1871. Special classes for gifted children began in Los Angeles and Cincinnati in 1916; in Urbana, Illinois, in 1919; and in Manhattan, New York, and Cleveland, Ohio, in 1922.

Contemporary History of Gifted Education

A contemporary history of gifted education does not require a long account. It is a story of four people and one Russian satellite.

English scientist Sir Francis Galton (1822–1911), younger cousin to Charles Darwin, is credited with the earliest significant research and writing on intelligence and intelligence testing. Highly impressed by Cousin Charles's *Origin of the Species,* Galton reasoned that evolution would favor persons with keen senses—persons who could sense approaching danger and detect food sources. He concluded that intelligence was related to the keenness of one's senses, and his efforts to measure intelligence therefore involved tests of visual acuity, auditory acuity, tactile sensitivity, and reaction time. The hereditary basis of intelligence appeared to be confirmed by his observation that distinguished persons seemed to come from succeeding generations of distinguished families, a conclusion reported in his most famous book *Hereditary Genius* (Galton, 1869).

While his intelligence tests failed, Galton's emphasis on the high heritability of intelligence is today shared by many psychologists but disputed by others who point to obvious learning and environmental factors.

Alfred Binet, with his colleague T. Simon, was hired by government officials in Paris to devise a test to identify which dull children would not benefit from regular classes and therefore would receive special training. At the time, some children were placed in schools for the retarded because they were too quiet, too aggressive, or had problems with speech, hearing, or vision. A direct test of intelligence was sorely needed.

A number of Binet's tests—hand-squeezing strength, hand speed in moving 50 cm, the amount of forehead pressure that causes pain, detecting differences in hand-held weights, and reaction time to sounds or in naming colors—failed. However, scores on tests of memory, judgment, reasoning, comprehension, and the ability to pay attention tended to concur with the criterion, teachers' judgments of intelligence.

Binet gave us the concept of *mental age,* the notion that children grow in intelligence and that any given child may be measurably ahead of or behind the typical intellectual stage for his or her actual age. A related notion is that at any given chronological age, children who learn the most do so partly because of greater intelligence.

In 1911, Henry Goddard summarized his evaluation of 2,000 normal children (Stanley, 1976). The transition from using the Binet tests with below-average children to employing them with normal and above-average children thus was complete and successful.

Stanford psychologist Lewis Terman made two historically significant contributions to the field of gifted education. First, he supervised the modification and Americanization of the Binet-Simon tests, producing in 1916 the grandfather of all American intelligence tests, the *Stanford-Binet Intelligence Scale.* The test was revised in 1937, 1960, and again in 1986.

Terman's second contribution was his identification and long study of 1,528 gifted children, about 800 boys and 700 girls. They have been the most studied group of gifted individuals in the world. In the 1920s Terman and Melita Oden (1925) administered the Stanford-Binet test to students initially identified by teachers as highly intelligent. The final sample consisted almost entirely of those who scored 140 or higher, the upper 1%. The subsequent field studies in 1927–1928, 1939–1940, and the late 1950s, interspersed with occasional interviews and mailings, traced the personal and professional activities of the subjects for over half a century. Davis (1990) noted that for many of these subjects death has been the only escape from Terman's project.

According to Stanley (1976), Galton was the grandfather of the gifted-child movement, Binet the midwife, Terman the father, and Columbia University's Leta Hollingworth the nurturant mother. Her pioneering contributions to gifted education consisted of personal efforts supporting gifted education and gifted students in the New York City area, from about 1916 until her death in 1939, and the publication of two major books, *Gifted Children: Their Nature and Nurture* (Hollingworth, 1926) and *Children above 180 IQ Stanford-Binet: Origin and Development* (Hollingworth, 1942). Hollingworth argued that it is the business of education to consider all forms of giftedness in pupils in regard to how unusual individuals may be trained for their own welfare and that of society at large.

The last significant historical event to predate the mid-1970s resurgence of interest in gifted education was the launching in 1957 of the Russian satellite Sputnik. To many, this represented an obvious and shocking technological defeat: The Soviet Union's scientific minds had outperformed ours. Earlier reports criticizing American education and, particularly, its ignoring gifted children suddenly became very popular. For example, a 1950 Educational Policies Commission report had noted that mentally superior children were being neglected, which would produce losses in the arts, sciences, and professions. A book entitled *Educational Wastelands* (Bestor, 1953) charged that "know-nothing educationists" had created schools that provided "meager intellectual nourishment or inspiration, particularly for bored gifted students."

Following the launch, more reports compared the quality and quantity of American versus Russian education. A 1959 report entitled *Soviet Commitment to Education* (First Official U.S. Education Mission to the USSR, 1959) claimed that the typical Soviet high school graduate had completed 10 years of math, 5 years of physics, 4 years of chemistry, 1 year of astronomy, 5 years of biology, and 5 years of a foreign language.

The aftermath of Sputnik was described by Tannenbaum (1979) as a "total talent mobilization." Academic coursework was telescoped (condensed) for bright students; college courses were offered in high school; and foreign languages were taught in elementary schools. Acceleration and ability grouping were used, and efforts were made to identify gifted and talented minority children. New math and science curricula were developed, most notably the *School Mathematics Study Group* math materials, the *Physical Science Study Committee* physics program, and the *Biological Science Curriculum Study* biology materials. In high school there was a newfound concern for high scholastic standards and career mindedness. Bright students were expected to take the tough courses—to fulfill their potential and submit their developed abilities for service to the nation (Tannenbaum, 1979).

Both the scare of Sputnik and the keen interest in educating gifted and talented students wore off in about 5 years.

Handbook of Gifted Education

The present volume is divided into seven sections. We believe they cover the major topic areas and issues in gifted education. In the remainder of this chapter we shall briefly summarize and integrate the 31 chapters that make up these seven sections.

Part I: Introduction

This first section provides an introduction to the background, topics, and issues in the field of gifted education.

In the present chapter we have highlighted some continuing and pressing issues and provided a brief historical context. We continue with previews and integrations of the remaining chapters.

In Chapter 2, James J. Gallagher provides an overview of issues and trends at the forefront of attention in the education of gifted students. He focuses on new conceptualizations of intelligence, interactions of genetic and environmental forces, and special subpopulations of gifted students, particularly underachievers, minorities, and females. In recent decades Gallagher has been a leader in formulating public policy regarding giftedness. He therefore ends his chapter with a discussion of three national priorities that need attention:

1. Underserved gifted students, including gifted minorities, handicapped, and very young children
2. The formation of a support network to improve program quality
3. Collaborative efforts with professionals from other disciplines

Part II: Conceptions and Identification

Part II focuses on the different ways "giftedness" is conceptualized and ways gifted students are identified. Two themes emanate from this section. The first is that there are diverse and competing conceptualizations of giftedness; there is no agreed upon definition, nor does it seem likely we shall have one in the near future. The second theme is the recognition that identification procedures are not always tied to theoretical constructs.

In Chapter 3, Abraham J. Tannenbaum argues that it is futile and naive to expect a satisfactory definition of giftedness to emerge purely from studies of cognitive powers or processes. He maintains that intellect is often the sole focus of behavioral scientists studying giftedness. Tannenbaum argues for a social-psychological perspective that takes into account comprehensive and subtle interrelationships among personal and situational factors that have proved relevant to giftedness. He discusses five such factors: superior general intellect, distinctive special aptitudes, facilitating nonintellective attributes (i.e., motivation, self-concept, metalearning), a challenging environment, and favorable elements of chance.

In Chapter 4, Robert J. Sternberg sets forth his triarchic theory of human intelligence, a revolutionary milestone among theories of intelligence. The chapter is divided into four main parts. The first discusses three kinds of intellectual giftedness: analytic, synthetic, and practical. *Analytic* giftedness is exhibited by people who tend to do well on conventional intelligence and aptitude tests. These people are good problem solvers and reasoners. *Synthetic* giftedness is displayed by people who are unconventional thinkers: They are insightful, intuitive, and creative. *Practical* giftedness is displayed by people who are unusually adept at coping with the problems of everyday life, whether in the home or in the workplace. The second part of the chapter argues that gifted people are those who capitalize upon their strengths and compensate for their weaknesses. The third part of the chapter briefly describes the forthcoming Sternberg Triarchic Abilities Test, which measures each of the three kinds of giftedness. The last part of the chapter takes the position that giftedness is not a fixed attribute, but rather an attribute capable of being developed. Sternberg clearly focuses on cognitive processes and probably would be faulted by Tannenbaum for not including social psychological factors.

Valerie Ramos-Ford and Howard Gardner in Chapter 5 challenge the notion of "general intelligence." They suggest that it is possible for individuals to be "gifted" in any of at least seven separate and somewhat independent intellectual domains: linguistic, logical-mathematical, spatial, musical, bodily-kinesthetic, and interpersonal and intrapersonal understanding. Ramos-Ford and Gardner argue that most current tests of intelligence measure only the linguistic and logical-mathematical domains and thus "giftedness" has been narrowly circumscribed. They end the chapter with applications of the theory of multiple intelligences, which has been used to identify the intellectual strengths, interests, and training styles of children as young as preschool. The critical reader may wish to compare Sternberg's triarchic conception with Gardner's seven intelligences.

Françoys Gagné in Chapter 6 offers a "differential model of giftedness and talent." He distinguishes *giftedness* as natural abilities and aptitudes, while *talent* comprises developed abilities or skills. He thus defines giftedness as *competence* that is distinctly above average in one or more domains of human aptitude. Talent is *performance* that is distinctly above average in one or more fields of human activity. In Gagné's model, aptitudes are subdivided into four categories (intellectual, creative, socioaffective, and sensorimotor) and talents into five categories (academic, technical, artistic, interpersonal, and athletic). He considers talents—performances—to be the developmental product of interactions between aptitudes and intrapersonal and environmental catalysts. Gagné's model describes two types of catalysts: intrapersonal (e.g., curiosity, motivation, autonomy) and environmental (e.g., parents, peers, schools). Gagné proposes that his model can enhance the percentage of people identified as gifted and talented, and that his model should assist in designing useful curricula and programs.

In the seventh and final chapter of Part II, E. Susanne Richert reveals major gaps between research and practice in identification of the gifted. She analyzes what she considers to be the errors made in identification and proposes specific recommendations to school districts for eliminating them. Richert's chapter ends with a lengthy list of identification instruments, with recommendations for their use, taken from the *National Report on Identification* (Richert, Alvino, & McDonnel, 1982), a study commissioned by the U.S. Department of Education.

Part III: Instructional Models and Practices

In Part III, the chapters focus on various ways the educational needs of gifted youngsters may be addressed. There is an array of programs and practices designed to meet these educational needs. Enrichment programs allow students to broaden their school experiences by pursuing topics in greater depth or by studying topics not offered at all in the regular curriculum. Enrichment typically is viewed as a *lateral* process in that exploration and depth are the main characteristics.

Acceleration programs provide opportunities for students to progress through material or a program at faster rates or younger ages than is conventional. Acceleration thus means covering material faster than the usual grade-level sequence. Acceleration is considered a *vertical* process, since it is based on moving through material rapidly and on to material at a higher level.

In Chapter 8, Shirley W. Schiever and C. June Maker contend that a false dichotomy has been made between acceleration and enrichment of curriculum for gifted students. After a brief survey of past and existing practices related to enrichment and acceleration, the authors argue that curriculum for the gifted must include *both* enrichment and acceleration components. Schiever and Maker discuss their spiral model of thinking, which offers a structure for integrating enrichment and acceleration principles into the curriculum of programs for the gifted and talented.

In Chapter 9, Joseph S. Renzulli and Sally M. Reis present their schoolwide enrichment model (SEM) as a comprehensive plan designed to overcome many of the problems that have hindered special programs for gifted students in the past. The SEM is based on research into the characteristics of creative and productive individuals, which underlies their three-ring definition of giftedness, and Renzulli's earlier enrichment triad model. The authors place emphasis on the development of gifted behaviors and the labeling of programs and services rather than students.

George T. Betts, in Chapter 10, presents his autonomous learner model (ALM). The ALM divides into five dimensions (orientation, individual development, enrichment activities, seminars, and in-depth studies) designed to meet the diversified cognitive, emotional, and social needs of gifted students. A central point is that as the gifted have their needs met, they will develop into autonomous learners, with the ability to be responsible for the development, implementation, and evaluation of their own learning.

Both the Renzulli and Reis SEM and Bett's ALM are examples of enrichment models. They are both also total programming plans. While the SEM has a longer developmental history and a more detailed implementation structure, at this point in the history of gifted education there are no data regarding their comparative effectiveness.

In Chapter 11, Camilla Persson Benbow presents the Study of Mathematically Precocious Youth (SMPY) model for identifying and providing educational services to mathematically talented students. Benbow makes the case that giftedness can be viewed as intellectual precocity. Accordingly, she argues that *acceleration* is the most effective and defensible curricular practice with gifted students, especially in the area of mathematics. Benbow concludes that acceleration has not been shown to be detrimental to social and emotional development, as some believe.

In Chapter 12, Sanford J. Cohn presents an overview of the talent search concept and proceeds toward specific details that would allow someone to initiate a talent search program. Like SMPY, talent searches base selection on high Scholastic Aptitude Test—Mathematics (SAT-M) scores, and also on high SAT-Verbal scores. One can legitimately ask about creatively and artistically gifted students, who may be ignored by both SMPY and talent searches. Cohn's chapter closes with an analysis of possibilities proffered by the continued spread of talent search programs.

Chapter 13 by James A. Kulik and Chen-Lin C. Kulik is an analysis of research on ability grouping. Kulik and Kulik use the statistical method of meta-analysis to summarize findings from more than 100 independent studies of ability grouping. Their analysis provides clear evidence that high-aptitude and gifted students do indeed profit from separate grouping in schools. The authors conclude that academic benefits are striking and large in programs that provide accelerated instruction for gifted students.

In Chapter 14, John F. Feldhusen presents Saturday and summer programs for the gifted as activities for enhancing their cognitive and affective growth. Such programs allow gifted youth to interact with one another and pursue special interests and talents. Feldhusen believes that such interactions serve to confirm and strengthen their talents and support the development of a positive self-concept.

In Chapter 15, the last of Part III, Penny Britton Kolloff discusses the growing trend of special residential high schools as a means of meeting the needs of highly gifted teenagers. She describes several specific schools and shows how and why they are successful.

Part IV: Creativity and Thinking Skills

Creativity and higher level thinking skills are among the most complex concepts in the field. The focus of Part IV is on understanding these concepts and how they can be taught.

In Chapter 16, Carolyn M. Callahan discusses the use of the construct of creativity in defining and identifying gifted students. She then presents an overview of the desired psychometric characteristics of instruments designed to measure creativity and the issues surrounding their use in identification. Callahan concludes her chapter with recommendations for the appropriate use of creativity assessment tools.

Gary A. Davis, in Chapter 17, focuses on teaching creative thinking skills. He describes

five core goals of creativity training (raising creativity consciousness, fostering a metacognitive understanding of creativity, strengthening creative abilities, teaching techniques of creative thinking, and involving students in creative activities) and strategies for achieving them. Davis recommends that all the activities and approaches he describes be included in a comprehensive creativity training program.

In Chapter 18, Herbert J. Walberg and Manfred P. Herbig isolate factors that promote learning and thus aid talent development. They synthesize research demonstrating that the quantity and quality of instruction have strong effects on achievement, which they argue is continuous with creativity and eminence. Walberg and Herbig apply research from educational psychology to developing talent, creativity, and eminence. On the basis of studies of eminent adults, they conclude that general knowledge and/or disciplined mastery of special fields are required for special performances.

In Chapter 19, John Barell defines thinking as an exploratory process that does not guarantee success but might result in getting out of a rut or opening one's eyes to undisclosed meanings and realities. He further describes thinking as figuring something out for oneself by a heuristic process of "saying things tentatively to oneself" in an attempt to solve a dilemma. Many major aspects of thinking are presented in this chapter: problem solving, critical and creative thinking, and the overarching reflective process of metacognition.

Part V: Psychological and Counseling Services

A unique feature of the current focus on gifted attention is a strong emphasis on psychological needs of the gifted. Gifted students are viewed no longer simply as extraordinary and efficient learners, but as complex personalities with exceptional sensitivities and often vulnerabilities.

In Chapter 20, Nicholas Colangelo traces the recognition of counseling needs of the gifted to the pioneering work of Leta Hollingworth from the early 1900s to the 1940s. However, it is only in the last decade that counseling has been viewed as a highly important component in programs for the education of the gifted and talented. Colangelo reviews research on social and emotional needs of the gifted and concludes with a proposal for school counseling programs that is developmentally grounded.

In Chapter 21, Michael M. Piechowski indicates that virtually none of the current approaches to emotional development address directly the emotional development of the gifted. One exception is Dabrowski's theory of emotional development, which was formulated in response to developmental crises of talented youth and adults. Piechowski addresses two key concepts in Dabrowski's theory: developmental potential, which includes the characteristic emotional intensity of the gifted and talented, and the concept of developmental levels, which addresses differences in types of personal growth. A preliminary study by Piechowski shows that in one type of emotional growth the individual follows the path of adaptation to the status quo and prizes social usefulness. A second type of emotional growth is introspective and displays the distinctive features of emotional giftedness that take the person beyond mere social usefulness.

In Chapter 22, Linda Kreger Silverman explains why it is not easy to raise a gifted child. Families of gifted children face several unique issues with very little support; their needs are not taken seriously. Silverman addresses the issues through a combination of research analysis and the author's clinical experience. Suggestions are provided to enhance counselors' skills in serving gifted students.

Philip A. Perrone in Chapter 23 focuses on career development needs of the gifted and talented. Perrone discusses Gottfredson's theory, which describes how career aspirations are formed, and Holland's theory, which explains career decision making. These theories provide an excellent basis for identifying the unique career seling needs of the gifted and talented.

Section V ends with Chapter 24, in which Sylvia B. Rimm demonstrates how underachievement and high achievement are "flip sides of the same psychological coin." Based on her successful clinical efforts, she explains the

dynamics of underachievement and an effective model for correcting them.

Part VI: Special Topics

Part VI includes special areas that are important foci in today's educational concern for giftedness, topics that have received only passing attention in most earlier works. For example, identifying and meeting the educational needs of the culturally diverse, handicapped, and preschool gifted are pressing yet neglected issues. Understanding child prodigies and idiot savants takes us into terrain that is largely unmapped.

In Chapter 25, Martha J. Morelock and David H. Feldman present research and discussion on three types of extremely precocious children: the child of extraordinarily high IQ, the prodigy, and the savant. The extraordinarily high IQ child demonstrates extremely high verbal-conceptual abstract reasoning ability. Prodigies, by definition, perform at the level of an adult professional in some cognitively demanding field. They display anywhere from above-average to extraordinarily high abstract reasoning ability. The fascinating "prodigious savant," on the other hand, is seriously mentally handicapped, yet possesses spectacular islands of ability that stand in stark contrast to the handicap.

Morelock and Feldman suggest that extreme precocity presents particular developmental issues. Extraordinarily high IQ children and prodigies, for example, share similar problems in establishing peer relationships and also in dealing with the frustration inherent in possessing a profile of widely disparate abilities. Generally, because of the peaks and valleys seen in the ability profiles of extremely precocious children, individualized programs are essential components of their educational planning.

In Chapter 26, Michael Lewis and Barbara Louis focus on giftedness in the preschool period, from 2 to 6 years of age. The first issue addressed is the constituents of giftedness in young children. This involves the measurement of giftedness from either a general intelligence or a specific skills perspective. The next issue is a process-oriented question that concerns genetic and environmental influences. Genetic predispositions are seen to impose constraints on the level of developmental attainment, while environmental forces influence the course of development. The development of intelligence is a result of the interaction of these forces. Environmental influences are elaborated, including the effects of environmental deprivation on early giftedness. The final issue addressed is the stability of early giftedness—that is, whether gifted preschoolers maintain their position and become gifted schoolchildren and adults. Major stress events in the lives of children are discussed in light of their potential impact on the stability of intelligence. The issue of the "invulnerable child" is also considered.

Thomas M. Buescher, in Chapter 27, discusses the peculiarities and unique needs of gifted adolescents. Buescher explores some of the major challenges confronting gifted adolescents, not so much because of their remarkable abilities, but because of their developmental stage. He provides a road map of the passage from childhood to adolescence and the demands for gifted adolescents to balance their abilities with their emerging identities. Buescher concludes the chapter with suggestions for parents and educators regarding how to understand and work effectively with gifted adolescents.

In Chapter 28, Barbara Kerr discusses how gifted girls differ from girls in general and from gifted boys in their academic behavior, aspirations, and social adjustments. Kerr reviews research findings related to characteristics and needs of gifted girls that have implications for identification and curriculum. She advocates shaping expectations, enhancing exploratory behaviors, and encouraging gifted girls to "fall in love with an idea."

In Chapter 29, Alexinia Young Baldwin indicates how inadequate attention to ethnic and cultural issues has resulted in a lack of proportional representation of ethnic/cultural minorities in programs for the gifted. Baldwin offers a perspective on current identification processes and argues for content in college-level gifted courses that is relevant to minority students.

In Chapter 30, Merle B. Karnes and Lawrence J. Johnson focus on a neglected subgroup of gifted children, the handicapped. They emphasize that it is a staggering waste of human resources if the gifted handicapped are overlooked and deprived of the opportunity to develop their potential. Karnes and Johnson provide a brief historical overview of work with the gifted handicapped and describe a model program at the University of Illinois for preschool gifted handicapped children. The authors take a definite stand against the deficit model, whereby handicaps are emphasized, and advocate emphasizing instead the strengths of the gifted handicapped.

Part VII: The Future

This final section concludes the book with an article by Donald J. Treffinger on future directions. He asserts that the current paradigm in gifted education focuses on distinguishing gifted from nongifted students and then providing the identified group with specialized curriculum and services. He contends that this paradigm is rooted in the psychometric tradition, drawing primarily on ability and achievement measures for distinguishing gifted students. Treffinger criticizes the conceptualization of giftedness as fixed and quantifiable. He proposes a shift to a new paradigm that conceptualizes giftedness as more flexible, inclusive, and instructionally oriented. He concludes his chapter with implications of his new paradigm for future research and practical applications.

Summary

This *Handbook* provides a journey through the terrain of giftedness. The chapters in this text provide a comprehensive view of this terrain. The reader will know the pitfalls and excitement.

Giftedness is an intensely dynamic concept that eludes categorization and quantification. This exciting dynamic gives the field its vibrancy and uniqueness.

REFERENCES

Anderson, R. S. (1975). *Education in Japan: A century of modern development*. Washington, DC: U.S. Government Printing Office.

Bestor, A. E. (1953). *Educational wastelands*. Urbana: University of Illinois Press.

Bloom, B. S. (1985). *Developing talent in young people*. New York: Ballantine.

Bloom, B. S., & Sosniak, L. A. (1981). Talent development vs. schooling. *Educational Leadership, 39,* 86–94.

Colangelo, N. (1982, May). *Counseling issues in gifted education*. Keynote address, Minnesota Council for Gifted and Talented Conference, St. Paul.

Colangelo, N. (1987). Issues in gifted education. *The Oregon Counseling Association Journal, 101,* 7–12.

Davis, G. A. (1990). *Creativity is forever* (3rd ed.). Dubuque, IA: Kendall/Hunt.

Davis, G. A., & Rimm, S. B. (1989). *Education of the gifted and talented* (2nd ed.). Englewood Cliffs, NJ: Prentice-Hall.

First Official U.S. Education Mission to the USSR. (1959). *Soviet commitment to education*. Bulletin 1959, No. 16. Washington, DC: Office of Education, U.S. Department of Health, Education and Welfare.

Gallagher, J. J., & Weiss, P. (1979). *The education of gifted and talented children and youth*. Washington, DC: Council for Basic Education.

Gallagher, J. J., Weiss, P., Oglesby, K., & Thomas, T. (1983). *The status of education for gifted students in the United States: An examination of needs, practices, and policies*. Chapel Hill: Frank Porter Graham Child Development Center, University of North Carolina.

Galton, F. (1869). *Hereditary genius*. London: Macmillan.

Gardner, J. W. (1961). *Excellence: Can we be equal and excellent too?* New York: Harper & Row.

Goldberg, M. L. (1965). *Research on the talented*. New York: Bureau of Publications, Columbia University.

Good, H. G. (1960). *A history of Western education* (2nd ed.). New York: Macmillan.

Hofstadter, R. (1963). *Anti-intellectualism in American life*. New York: Knopf.

Hollingworth, L. S. (1926). *Gifted children: Their nature and nurture*. New York: Macmillan.

Hollingworth, L. S. (1942). *Children above 180 IQ Stanford-Binet: Origin and development*. New York: World Book.

Meyer, A. E. (1965). *An educational history of the western world*. New York: McGraw-Hill.

National Commission on Excellence in Education. (1983). *A nation at risk: The imperative for educational reform*. Washington, DC: U.S. Department of Education.

Newland, T. E. (1976). *The gifted in historical perspective*. Englewood Cliffs, NJ: Prentice-Hall.

Richert, E. S., Alvino, J. S., & McDonnel, R. C. (1982). *National report on identification: Assessment and recommendations for comprehensive identification of gifted and talented youth*. Washington, DC: Educational Information Resource Center, U.S. Department of Education.

Stanley, J. C. (1976). Concern for intellectually talented youths: How it originated and fluctuated. *Journal of Clinical Child Psychology, 5,* 38–42.

Sternberg, R. J., & Davidson, J. E. (Eds.). (1986). *Conceptions of giftedness*. New York: Cambridge University Press.

Tannenbaum, A. J. (1979). Pre-Sputnik to post-Watergate concern about the gifted. In A. H. Passow (Ed.), *The gifted and the talented* (pp. 5–27). Chicago: National Society for the Study of Education.

Terman, L. M., & Oden, M. H. (1925). *Genetic studies of genius: Mental and physical traits of a thousand gifted children*. Stanford, CA: Stanford University Press.

Issues in the Education of Gifted Students

JAMES J. GALLAGHER   *University of North Carolina, Chapel Hill*

■ Over a decade ago I wrote a chapter in the yearbook for the National Society for the Study of Education entitled "Issues in Education for the Gifted" (Gallagher, 1979). At that time the major concerns in the field were the definition of *gifted;* the balance between special curriculum and the stimulation of special skills such as creativity; the special subgroups of the underachiever and the culturally different; the need for an effective support system for training, research, technical assistance, and dissemination; and finally, as mentioned by Colangelo and Davis in Chapter 1, America's love–hate relationship with the gifted.

Many of these problems remain today, 10 years later, even though they may have changed somewhat in perspective and direction. However, there have been other problems added as well in the intervening 10 years, so that this chapter is more than just a restatement of our failures to cope with the issues of the late 1970s.

This chapter will focus on issues that seem to be at the forefront of current concerns: the changing perception of intelligence, the increased sensitivity to the needs of subgroups of gifted students, the sought-for balance between knowledge organization and creativity, and the uses of public policy to further the programs for gifted students.

Education for gifted students is merely a small part of the larger enterprise called American education. Any force that has an impact on the whole of American education affects education for the gifted. The major impact in the past decade has been the cry for educational reform. The publication of the report *A Nation at Risk* (National Commission on Excellence in Education, 1983) stirred a wide variety of concerns about the viability of American education to produce students who could help our country be economically competitive with other nations in the 21st century.

One tangible result of the educational reform movement has been the establishment of residential secondary schools for gifted and talented students in mathematics and science (Eilber, 1987; see Chapter 15 by Kolloff in this volume). Another is the increased interest in curriculum development and the extensive use of educational technology, such as the computer, as a strategy to reestablish America's leadership through increased intellectual and technological sophistication.

What Is Intelligence?

Earlier generations rather smugly defined intelligence as "what intelligence tests measure" (Weinberg, 1989). Decades of experience have diminished our confidence in the works of Binet, Terman, and Wechsler. Although their tests remain superb predictors of school performance, *school aptitude tests* might be a better term for them than intelligence tests.

One area in which our ideas have gradually changed has been our realization of the complex intertwining of the influences of genetics and environment in intellectual development.

Genetics and Environment

One major attitudinal shift has been in the increasing realization of the role played by the environment in the development, or *crystallization,* of intellectual abilities. Although evidence gathered from twin studies and sibling and adoptive studies has clearly established the role of genetics in intellectual development (Plomin, 1989), it has become increasingly clear that the early environment of the child influences substantially the full development of those abilities.

Eysenck (1986) presented evidence supporting the role that genetics plays in the development of such basic skills as immediate memory span and reaction time. However, the development of more sophisticated problem-solving and problem-finding skills, as well as the motivation to put them to use, seems clearly influenced by environment.

Bloom (1985) described a retrospective study on world-class athletes, musicians, and scientists. Interviews with the gifted individuals themselves (declared world-class performers by their colleagues) and their relatives indicated the strong influence played by early family stimulation and enthusiasm for the development of the child's special talents. This family enthusiasm often took the practical form of seeking out special opportunities for the development of these skills, such as obtaining special tutors, that allowed these young people to develop their talents to a fuller degree. Such a finding also naturally raises the question of what talents might exist in families or subcultures in which potentially gifted students could not reach full crystallization because of the lack of opportunity to develop basic intellectual skills.

This strong interactive relationship between environment and genetics (Sameroff & Chandler, 1975) helps to explain some otherwise puzzling bits of information about the development of gifted youngsters. For example, it can explain the disproportionate number of males who are achieving well in mathematics (Stanley & Benbow, 1986), the disproportionately heavy incidence of giftedness in some ethnic groups in which learning and language development are especially stressed, such as in Jewish and Asian populations (Adler, 1978; Terman & Oden, 1959), and why there is a smaller proportion of minority group representation when measures of intellectual ability are taken at school age (Baldwin, 1987; Frasier, 1987). These findings also suggest that we are far short of reaching the full potential of our population, since the environmental setting for the full development of intellectual abilities is not positive in the case of many children.

Information Processing

The introduction of information-processing models in discussions of intellectual abilities has helped spur interest in decision-making functions of the intellect (Gardner, 1985; Perkins & Simmons, 1988; Sternberg & Davidson, 1986). Previous models such as Bloom, Englehart, Furst, Hill, and Krathwohl (1956) and Guilford (1977) had not included a decision-making function (executive function) that would allow us to understand how it is possible to make choices between options. Since good judgment (the appropriate choice between competing options) is one of the hallmarks of gifted individuals, the questions for educators are how this intellectual process functions and what instruction can do to enhance it.

Perkins and Simmons (1988) believe that intellectual competence on a given task depends on three major factors: the power of one's neurological computer, the tactical repertoire one can bring to bear, and a stock of context-specific content and know-how. Perkins and Simmons conclude that there is great importance in teaching tactics, since intellectual power is strongly genetic and the content is there in the standard curriculum.

Perkins and Simmons contend that several things have to be explicitly taught because they will not occur under ordinary circumstances. Tactics have to be explicitly instructed because they will not automatically be picked up or "soaked up" by the student, and extensive practice in the use of tactics must be provided so that the skill becomes automatic. Deliberate planning has to be made for conceptual transfer, since transfer occurs far less often or readily than one might think.

The translation of new findings on intellectual functioning into educational curricula and strategies has begun, but a great amount of transformation of thinking by educators will have to take place before the translation is fully completed.

Subgroups of Gifted Students

It is somewhat trite these days to announce that there is considerable heterogeneity within the category of students we call gifted. It is more important to focus on meaningful subgroups within the larger construct to see what special education problems and opportunities exist there.

Gifted Underachievers

One of the subgroups in the gifted domain that has received very little attention over the past decade has been those students referred to as *gifted underachievers,* students who appear to possess considerable intellectual potential but who are performing in a mediocre or worse fashion in the educational setting. In part, this lack of attention would seem to be due to the tendency of many communities and states to accept the definition of *gifted* student as one who is productive and effective (see Renzulli, 1982). Such a definition legislates the underachiever out of the gifted category. Still, there are many educators who would wish to find some ways of stimulating and encouraging such youngsters to use the vast potential that they would seem to have (see Rimm, 1987; see also Chapter 24 by Rimm in this volume).

Janos and Robinson (1985) in a recent review concluded that underachieving students are distinctly different from achieving gifted students in their family characteristics and social relations, being inferior in emotional maturity, social adjustment, self-image, and school motivation.

The few educational interventions that are reported to be successful for gifted underachievers (Whitmore, 1980) have stressed programs of intense and consistent intervention over an extended period of time. It is clear that we are dealing with complex behavior patterns, established over a long period of childhood, and that these will not be turned around without substantial effort. We do not have available at present a menu of programmatic possibilities to attack that problem of underachievement. This was an issue 10 years ago, and it remains an issue today.

Cultural and Ethnic Minorities

One of the increasing concerns addressed during the last decade has been the particular needs of racial subgroups of gifted children (see Maker & Schiever, 1989). Cultural and ethnic minorities are some of those subgroups, and their differential membership in programs for the gifted has become a source of concern in the field. Data are now available to suggest that black, Hispanic, and Native American children appear in gifted programs at only about one half their prevalence in the larger society, while Asian Americans appear at twice their percentage in the American population (Zappia, 1989).

Considerable attention is being paid to the possible bias of measuring instruments that are held responsible for these differential prevalence rates (Baldwin, 1987; Frasier, 1987). However, an alternative explanation is, in fact, available to us. Instead of clinging to the discredited idea that intelligence is totally genetically based and impervious to environmental effects, which would be the only reason we might expect equal prevalence of giftedness across ethnic and racial groups, we should consider whether such differential prevalence rates could be easily explainable through the differential environmental advantages or disadvantages that such subpopulations have had in our society (see Gallagher, 1985; Perkins & Simmons, 1988). Of course, it is easier to change the identifying tests than to change the uneven societal playing field upon which our children must compete.

Maker (1989) summed up the changes in identification practices designed to maximize the discovery of minority children with special talent: Use objective and subjective multiple assessment procedures; include culturally and linguistically appropriate instruments; and use a case study approach in which decisions are made by a team of qualified individuals.

A further question now being explored is what kind of special program would be desired for these minority gifted students, once identified. A number of observers have pointed out that the special needs of these subgroups call for differential educational approaches (Baldwin, 1987; Sisk, 1989; Udall, 1989).

R. Gallagher (1989) and Wong and Wong (1989) pointed out that the Asian American gifted, despite the manifestly high performance of many of these students, have many adaptation problems in American society and are in need of special attention. Problems resulting from, for example, bilingualism, cultural identity, and career choice of lower level occupations, call for increases in counseling and support, and there remains the special issue of gifted Asian American girls in a subculture in which males appear to be highly favored.

Sparling (1989) reported on the favorable use of the integrative education model and the shared responsibility model in working with black gifted students, stressing that such methods seem to fit well with the special learning needs of black students.

Maker (1989, p. 301) summarized program suggestions from a wide variety of specialists concerned with Hispanic, black, Native American, and Asian American gifted children as follows:

1. Identify students' strengths and plan a curriculum to develop these abilities.
2. Provide for the development of basic skills and other abilities students may lack.
3. Regard differences as positive rather than negative attributes.
4. Provide for involvement of parents, the community, and mentors or role models.
5. Create and maintain classrooms with a multicultural emphasis.

While these precepts would seem to be good advice for any student and teacher, increased attention and emphasis should be considered for these factors when planning for multicultural gifted students. We are sure to see an increase in such differential planning in the future as our sensitivity to the special needs of these subgroups becomes intensified.

Gifted Girls

One subgroup of gifted students that is attracting more and more attention is that of gifted girls and women. The first major indicator of differences between gifted girls and women, compared with gifted males, was found in the longitudinal study of Lewis Terman and his colleagues (Terman & Oden, 1947). From a career perspective, the women in the sample were much less productive than the men.

Although there are clearly complicating factors that explain such differences, particularly the multiple responsibilities of homemaking and child rearing for women, there remains some concern that there are a number of other inhibiting factors influencing negatively the full intellectual developmental of gifted girls and women in our society as well (Jacklin, 1989).

Reis and Callahan (1989) asked whether women have come such a long way forward from earlier times:

> Why, for example, are less than 2 percent of American patentees women? . . . Why are there only two females in the United States Senate, one female on the Supreme Court, and one female cabinet member? Why do women constitute less than 5 percent of the House of Representatives, own only 7 percent of all businesses in this country, [constitute less than] 2 percent of all school superintendents, . . . occupy only 5 percent of executive positions in American corporations, hold none of the leading positions in the top five orchestras in the United States. . . . (pp. 101–102)

Eccles (1985) pointed out that women are "underrepresented in almost all advanced educational programs and in the vast majority of high-status occupations" (p. 261). It is the progressive limiting of options for girls, particularly in fields such as math and science, that has caught the attention of educators.

Although some still believe that there may be a constitutional difference between males and females in such specific aptitudes as mathematics (Leroux, 1985; Stanley & Benbow, 1986), the mainstream of thought today is focused upon the social environment and how it can be modified to encourage the gifted female student. One such suggestion for a more encouraging environment has been to design programs that exclude boys (Fox, 1977; Rand & Gibb, 1989), since research has pointed to the fact that boys dominate classroom discussion, monopolize computer facilities, and so forth (Sadker & Sadker, 1985; Sanders & Stone, 1986). A great deal of research and creative program development on how to create a facilitating school and societal environment must be done before we are likely to know how far the gifted girl can progress, given a more favorable chance to achieve than in the past.

There are many other subgroups of gifted children, of course. For example, some children are both *gifted and handicapped,* such as learning disabled gifted students (Whitmore & Maker, 1985). Because of the uniqueness of each of these children, the educational strategy often employed is to develop an individual case study or an Individual Education Plan (IEP) to meet their needs.

Another subgroup is *preschool gifted* children, who are not receiving very much attention from formal educational systems (Gallagher, 1985). There also are students with special abilities in art, music, dance, and so forth. Bachtel-Nash (1984) has produced an extensive directory of programs for the artistically gifted.

Pedagogical Issues in Gifted Education

The ebbs and flows of educational philosophy at one time focused on *where* the gifted student is educated (should it be in a special school, resource room, regular classroom, etc.?). Recent discussions have focused much more upon the nature of the content to be presented and the *problem finding* and *problem solving* strategies that these students are supposed to master.

There has probably never been a more intensive effort in gifted education than the focus upon stimulating creative thinking. It has consumed the field's interest over the entire last generation of special educators (see Feldhusen & Treffinger, 1985; Maker, 1982; Meeker, 1969; Parnes, 1972; Torrance, 1979).

Despite a continuing interest in the development of such strategies for gifted students, there has grown a new realization that such strategies cannot, and should not, be considered apart from the knowledge base of the student. There is an increasing realization that you cannot just be creative in the abstract, you must be creative in something, in mathematics or art or historical research, and to do that you must have some organization of knowledge in that field.

Rabinowitz and Glaser (1985) pointed out that the presence of an associative network of concepts and facts about a given topic is what separates the expert from the novice in special fields and what allows the expert to see the full significance of new information and to use it to solve problems. Rabinowitz and Glaser concluded that:

> Experts, however, are able to base their representations on high-level principles—information that is not explicitly stated within the problem. They can quickly retrieve from memory, functional or principled relations among concepts. (p. 86)

One other mental operation that has received attention recently is the process by which controlled mental processes are made automatic (Rabinowitz & Glaser, 1985; Sternberg, 1984). Whether in athletics or intellectual striving, the ability to make complex processes automatic allows easy accessibility to relevant knowledge and frees up attentional resources that can then be directed toward other aspects of the task. A strong knowledge base allows more effective automaticity.

In short, cognitive skills or strategies are most useful when they are combined with an effective associative network of concepts and systems of ideas. Such a network increases the effectiveness of memory, allows a better organization of a hierarchy of ideas, and makes it easier to access the information upon demand. Obviously, the educational question of moment is how to develop most effectively such an associative network.

Some investigators have raised the issue that *creativity,* instead of being an exclusively internal process, may be better thought of as an interaction between an environment and internal thought (Greeno, 1989). Such interactions can cause individuals to reorganize their existing concepts and produce unique results without necessarily adding to their knowledge base.

The increasing popularity of the topic of thinking strategies (Belmont, 1989) reflects an attempt to reorganize environmental elements and internal concepts in ways more conducive to a useful product. As Belmont points out, the

Vygotsky idea of the "embeddedness of the developing mind in society" has taken hold. Thinking, while ultimately internalized, must operate within an influential and responsive social context. This is encouraging for educators since it raises the possibility that education can focus on the creation of interactive environments that can maximize the individual's capabilities.

Environmental Settings

Along with an increasing emphasis on thinking strategies, there remains a concern for the appropriate setting for the program for gifted students. There has been an increasing willingness to call into question some of the standard models for education of gifted students. One of the most popular of these models has been the *resource room,* or pullout, program in the elementary school. Now there is a substantial debate in progress (see Renzulli, 1987; Van Tassel-Baska, 1987) about the merits of such a procedure.

Secondary programs for gifted students also are receiving renewed attention. The generic concept of giftedness does not fit well with the specific content organization of the secondary school, and the middle school as well.

What Is the Appropriate Secondary Education for the Gifted?

One of the unresolved issues is what to do about secondary education for gifted students. Most of the current efforts to provide special education for gifted students have concentrated on the elementary school. Programs for gifted students have focused on the device of the resource room or special classes taught by teachers with special expertise in teaching gifted students. In about 10 states, special teacher certification is required to teach gifted children, but such certification standards are rarely imposed or implemented at the secondary level.

If a teacher has expertise in a content field and is teaching an *Advanced Placement* class, few questions are raised about whether he or she has the correct training to be working with gifted children. Few persons trained in the specific disciplines of language arts or history or chemistry feel it is necessary for them to learn the pedagogical skills deemed important to educate gifted students at the elementary level. Nor do certification guardians of the states bother much about it.

In gifted education we must come to some agreement among ourselves and our secondary education colleagues on what the most desirable approach should be. If we believe that pedagogical instruction in problem solving or stimulating creative thought is important in the sixth grade, why does it become unimportant in the eighth grade? Does the answer lie in an unwillingness to go into professional combat with the content area organizations that could be counted upon to frown on any additional requirements, particularly requirements that stress the nature of the student rather than the conceptual organization of the content field? The issue is complicated by the absence of any evidence to suggest that the teaching skill of the content specialist is improved by going through a gifted education preparation program.

Public Policy for Gifted

One of the major issues of concern in the field of gifted education is the degree to which public policies at the state and federal level will provide additional assistance for special education for this target group of students. The allocation of public funds to some group of citizens but not to others always requires extensive explanation. In the case of children in poverty, or children with handicapping conditions, the argument is straightforward. We believe, as a society, that children who are in trouble, or at risk for not developing in an effective way, should receive special help. This is a concept well established in programs such as Head Start and in much legislation providing special education assistance to handicapped children (Kirk & Gallagher, 1989).

The situation is somewhat different when the issue of special education for gifted children arises. Here one cannot appeal to the sorry state in which such children find themselves. Often as not, they are doing well in school, relatively speaking, and do not seem to be having many academic or personal difficulties.

Yet, even with these inhibiting factors, as of 1986 gifted education had special state-level legislation in 47 states, and over $289 million was provided annually to local school systems to help them provide additional educational services to gifted students (O'Connell, 1986). At present, all 50 states have enacted special legislation.

In addition, there has been a modest federal initiative that will provide funds for research, personnel preparation, demonstration, and a National Research Center for the Gifted and Talented (Reis, 1989). Such federal help is designed to add to the state investment, since states generally prefer to spend money on direct services rather than on research and personnel preparation.

In the instance of gifted children it is not their individual troubles that concern us, but rather the societal trouble in which we find ourselves. There have been a wide variety of reports announcing the poor performance of American students relative to foreign students in mathematics, science, and technology (Coleman & Selby, 1983; Gallagher, 1988; National Commission on Excellence in Education, 1983).

The argument for special attention to gifted children is that many of these youngsters will become the leaders of the next generation in science, politics, the arts, and humanities. If we are to maintain our superior position, from an economic standpoint, over other rapidly developing countries in the world, we will have to rely heavily on the capabilities of such students. The evidence available to the present time is that these gifted students are not performing up to their potential and certainly not performing competitively with their opposite numbers in other cultures.

Unlike the argument that it is our duty, as a caring member of western civilization, to provide help for the handicapped child, the argument for special attention to gifted students centers upon a degree of "enlightened selfishness" on the part of the citizenry. Such an argument brought forth major resources to this area in the Sputnik era (Bruner, 1960; Goodlad, 1964) and seems to have the potential for doing the same again while our concern is high regarding our economic viability versus Japan, Korea, Taiwan, West Germany, and so forth.

I recently identified three major national priorities that I believe should receive urgent attention (Gallagher, 1988). The first of these is the need to serve a variety of subgroups of gifted students that are currently *underserved* and need specific educational attention. These include the underachieving gifted, culturally different gifted, handicapped gifted, early childhood gifted, and female gifted students. A second major priority is the need for a *support network* that would improve program quality in the field of gifted education. Included in such support networks would be investments in research and development, personnel preparation, demonstrations of program excellence, and program evaluation efforts.

The third major priority is in the area of *collaborative efforts,* in which those professionals engaged in gifted education are urged to work closely with colleagues from other disciplines on such topics as understanding the nature of intelligence, developing differentiated curricula with specialists in content fields, and making full use of the developing technology with the computer and its multifaceted potential for differential instruction.

Other Issues

There are many specific issues of importance not covered in this broad sweep of major issues, for example, the social and emotional status of gifted students. Are gifted students prone to suicide and suicide attempts?

What is the nature of the differential curriculum that should be presented to gifted students? Should the content and the skills or strategies presented be unique or merely a variation of those presented to the average child? Are there methods of instruction that will allow the gifted student to prosper in the regular classroom? Space does not permit an extensive review of every aspect of this complex educational puzzle.

Ten Years from Now?

What can we expect to see at the start of the 21st century as issues in the education of gifted students? Surely some continued advance can be expected in the understanding of intelligence itself, which may further redefine what we refer to as gifted students. The decision-making processes in intelligent behavior are sure to come under more extensive scrutiny. Some additional measuring instruments built upon information-processing models also would be likely products to emerge.

One of the real advantages of science is to teach us how to ask better questions. One question that we have been asking, whether giftedness is genetically determined, has turned out to be the wrong question. Much better questions are directed at what factors in the environment interact with the neurological computer in a person's head to create a productive individual, and how these effects are experienced at various ages. We should be seeing considerable work along those lines in the 1990s.

How far we may progress in educational methods may very well be determined by the final results of the reform movement in American education generally. If it lasts long enough to generate better curricula and more insights into the virtues of certain instructional strategies, then gifted students will likely profit more from such innovations than any other group of students.

In any event, there is good reason to expect continued research and instructional interest in the fate of gifted students in this decade. The needs of the country are too visible and of too much concern to expect otherwise.

REFERENCES

Adler, M. (1978). A study of the ethnic origins of giftedness. *Gifted Child Quarterly, 1,* 98–101.

Bachtel-Nash, A. (1984). *National direction: Programs for K–12 artistically gifted and talented students.* Paramount, CA: Tam's.

Baldwin, A. (1987). Undiscovered diamonds. *Journal for the Education of the Gifted, 10*(4), 271–286.

Belmont, J. (1989). Cognitive strategies and strategic learning: The socio-instructional approach. *American Psychologist, 44,* 142–147.

Bloom, B. S. (1985). *Developing talent in young people.* New York: Ballantine.

Bloom, B. S., Englehart, M. D., Furst, E. J., Hill, W. H., & Krathwohl, D. R. (1956). *Taxonomy of educational objectives, handbook I: Cognitive domain.* New York: McKay.

Bruner, J. (1960). *The process of education.* Cambridge, MA: Harvard University Press.

Coleman, W., Jr., & Selby, C. (1983). *Educating Americans for the 21st century.* Washington, DC: National Science Board Commission on Precollege Education in Mathematics, Science, and Technology.

Eccles, J. (1985). Why doesn't Jane run? Sex differences in educational and occupational patterns. In F. Horowitz & M. O'Brien (Eds.), *The gifted and talented developmental perspectives* (pp. 251–295). Washington, DC: American Psychological Association.

Eilber, C. (1987). The North Carolina School of Science and Mathematics. *Phi Delta Kappan,* June, 773–777.

Eysenck, H. (1986). Toward a new model of intelligence. *Personality and Individual Differences, 7,* 731–736.

Feldhusen, J. F., & Treffinger, D. J. (1985). *Creative thinking and problem solving in gifted education.* Dubuque, IA: Kendall/Hunt.

Fox, L. H. (1977). *The effects of sex role socialization on mathematics participation and achievement* (Contract No. FN17400-76-0114). Washington, DC: National Institute of Education.

Frasier, M. (1987). The identification of gifted black students: Developing new perspective. *Journal for the Education of the Gifted, 10*(3), 155–180.

Gallagher, J. J. (1979). Issues in education for the gifted. In A. H. Passow (Ed.), *The gifted and the talented: Their education and development* (pp. 28–44). Chicago: University of Chicago Press.

Gallagher, J. J. (1985). *Teaching the gifted child* (3rd ed.). Boston: Allyn and Bacon.

Gallagher, J. J. (1988). A national agenda for educating gifted students: A statement of priorities. *Exceptional Children, 55*(2), 107–114.

Gallagher, R. (1989). Are we meeting the needs of gifted Asian-Americans? In C. J. Maker & S. Schiever (Eds.), *Critical issues in gifted education: Defensible programs for cultural and ethnic minorities* (Vol. 2, pp. 169–173). Austin, TX: Pro-Ed.

Gardner, H. (1983). *Frames of mind: The theory of multiple intelligences*. New York: Basic.

Gardner, H. (1985). *Frames of Mind* (2nd ed.). New York: Basic.

Goodlad, J. (1964). *School curriculum reform in the United States*. London: H. M. Stationery Office.

Greeno, J. (1989). A perspective on thinking. *American Psychology, 44,* 105–111.

Guilford, J. P. (1977). *Way beyond the IQ*. Buffalo, NY: Bearly.

Jacklin, C. (1989). Female and male: Issues of gender. *American Psychologist 44,* 127–133.

Janos, P., & Robinson, N. (1985). Psychosocial development in intellectually gifted children. In F. Horowitz & M. O'Brien (Eds.), *The gifted and talented developmental perspectives* (pp. 149–195). Washington, DC: American Psychological Association.

Kirk, S. A., & Gallagher, J. J. (1989). *Educating exceptional children* (6th ed.). Boston: Houghton Mifflin.

Leroux, J. (1985). *Gender differences influencing gifted adolescents: An ethnographic study of cultural expectations*. Unpublished doctoral dissertation, University of Connecticut, Storrs.

Maker, C. J. (1982). *Curriculum development for the gifted*. Rockville, MD: Aspen.

Maker, C. J. (1989). Programs for gifted minority students: A synthesis of perspectives. In C. J. Maker & S. Schiever (Eds.), *Critical issues in gifted education: Defensible programs for cultural and ethnic minorities* (Vol. 2, pp. 311–328). Austin, TX: Pro-Ed.

Maker, C. J., & Schiever, S. (Eds.) (1989). *Critical issues in gifted education: Defensible programs for cultural and ethnic minorities* (Vol. 2). Austin, TX: Pro-Ed.

Meeker, M. (1969). *The structure of intellect*. Columbus, OH: Merrill.

National Commission on Excellence in Education. (1983). *A nation at risk: The imperative for educational reform*. Washington, DC: U.S. Department of Education.

O'Connell, P. (1986). *The state of the states gifted and talented education*. Augusta, ME: Counsel of State Directors of Programs for the Gifted.

Parnes, S. (1972). *Creativity: Unlocking human potential*. Buffalo, NY: D.O.K.

Perkins, D., & Simmons, R. (1988). The cognitive roots of scientific and mathematical ability. In J. Dreyden, G. Stanley, S. Gallagher, & R. Sawyer (Eds.), *The Proceedings of the Talent Identification Programs/National Science Foundation Conference on Academic Talent*. Durham, NC: Duke University Talent Identification Program.

Plomin, R. (1989). Environment and genes: Determinants of behavior. *American Psychologist, 44,* 105–111.

Rabinowitz, M., & Glaser, R. (1985). Cognitive structure and process in highly competent performance. In F. Horowitz & M. O'Brien (Eds.), *The gifted and talented: Developmental perspectives* (pp. 75–98). Washington, DC: American Psychological Association.

Rand, D., & Gibb, L. (1989). A model program for gifted girls in science. *Journal for the Education of the Gifted, 12,*(2), 142–155.

Reis, S. (1989). Reflections on policy affecting the education of gifted and talented students: Past and future perspectives. *American Psychologist 44,* 399–408.

Reis, S., & Callahan, C. (1989). Gifted females: They've come a long way or have they? *Journal for the Education of the Gifted, 12,* 99–117.

Renzulli, J. S. (1982). What makes a problem real? *Gifted Child Quarterly, 26,* 147–156.

Renzulli, J. S. (1987). The positive side of pull-out programs. *Journal for the Education of the Gifted, 10*(4), 245–254.

Rimm, S. B. (1987). Creative underachievers: Marching to the beat of a different drummer. *The Gifted Child Today, 48,* 2–6.

Sadker, M., & Sadker, M. (1985). Sexism in the schoolroom of the 80's. *Psychology Today, 19*(3), 54–57.

Sameroff, A., & Chandler, M. (1975). Reproductive risk and the continuum of caretaking casuality. In F. Horowitz (Ed.), *Review of child development research* (Vol. 4, pp. 187–244). Chicago: University of Chicago Press.

Sanders, J., & Stone, A. (1986). *The neuter computer*. New York: Neal-Schuman.

Sisk, D. (1989). Identifying and nurturing talent among the American Indians. In C. J. Maker & S. Schiever (Eds.), *Critical issues in gifted education: Defensible programs for cultural and ethnic minorities* (Vol. 2, pp. 128–132). Austin, TX: Pro-Ed.

Sparling, S. (1989). Gifted black students: Curriculum and teaching strategies. In C. J. Maker & S. Schiever (Eds.), *Critical issues in gifted education: Defensible programs for cultural and ethnic minorities* (Vol. 2, pp. 259–269). Austin, TX: Pro-Ed.

Stanley, J., & Benbow, C. (1986). Youths who reason exceptionally well mathematically. In R. Sternberg & J. Davidson (Eds.), *Conceptions of giftedness* (pp. 361–387). New York: Cambridge University Press.

Sternberg, R. J. (1984). *Advances in the psychology of human intelligence* (Vols. 1 & 2). Hillsdale, NJ: Erlbaum.

Sternberg, R. J., & Davidson, J. E. (Eds.). (1986). *Conceptions of giftedness*. New York: Cambridge University Press.

Terman, L., & Oden, M. H. (1947). *The gifted child grows up: Twenty-five years follow-up of a superior group* (Vol. 4). Stanford, CA: Stanford University Press.

Terman, L. M., & Oden, M. H. (1959). *Genetic studies of genius: The gifted group at midlife* (Vol. 5). Stanford, CA: Stanford University Press.

Torrance, E. P. (1979). *The search for satori and creativity*. Buffalo, NY: Creative Education Foundation.

Udall, A. (1989). Curriculum for gifted Hispanic students. In C. J. Maker & S. Schiever (Eds.), *Critical issues in gifted education: Defensible programs for cultural and ethnic minorities* (Vol. 2, pp. 41–56). Austin, TX: Pro-Ed.

Van Tassel-Baska, J. (1987). The ineffectiveness of the pull-out program model in gifted education: A minority perspective. *Journal for the Education of the Gifted, 10*(4), 255–264.

Weinberg, R. (1989). Intelligence and IQ: Landmark issues and great debates. *American Psychologist, 44,* 98–104.

Whitmore, J. R. (1980). The etiology of underachievement in highly gifted young children. *Journal for the Education of the Gifted, 3*(1), 38–51.

Whitmore, J., & Maker, C. (1985). *Intellectual giftedness in disabled persons*. Rockville, MD: Aspen.

Wong, S., & Wong, P. (1989). Teaching strategies and practices for the education of gifted Cantonese students. In C. J. Maker & S. Schiever (Eds.), *Critical issues in gifted education: Defensible programs for cultural and ethnic minorities* (Vol. 2, pp. 182–188). Austin, TX: Pro-Ed.

Zappia, I. (1989). Identification of gifted Hispanic students. In C. J. Maker & S. Schiever (Eds.), *Critical issues in gifted education: Defensible programs for cultural and ethnic minorities* (Vol. 2, pp. 19–26). Austin, TX: Pro-Ed.

Conceptions and Identification

3

The Social Psychology of Giftedness

ABRAHAM J. TANNENBAUM *Columbia University*

It takes no more than plain common sense to realize that it takes much more than extraordinary brainpower for a person to become *demonstrably* gifted. Of course, brainpower is necessary for achievement, but it isn't sufficient. At best, it figures boldly in how well an individual *may* fare in a variety of tasks, without guaranteeing how well he or she *will* fare, and in *what* specific domain of excellence. Making the leap from promise to its fulfillment requires not only ability, but also ancillary personal attributes, along with enriching and opportunistic life experiences, all of them reinforcing each other in a rare and subtle combination. Some of these internal and external contributors to gifted behavior are already known to behavioral scientists; others have yet to be explicated. Still others are of a fortuitous nature, materializing often as strokes of luck that spell the difference between success and failure. Yet despite the self-evident truism that "brains alone do not giftedness make," psychologists and educators keep looking for new and better ways to assess children's abilities in order to find *the* perfect predictor of future accomplishment. Their narrowly focused perseveration is reminiscent of the blind man's struggle to discern the shape of the proverbial elephant by examining ever more closely and gingerly only one of its limbs.

Psychometrists, of all people, are modestly aware that ability per se is only part of the puzzle of giftedness. They are less sanguine about the predictive validity of the tests they construct than are their "customers" who use or critique the tests (Messick, 1989). And for good reason: Empirical evidence is clearly on the side of caution. Attempts at locating gifted children solely through measures of thinking abilities have a history of unrealistic hopes and meager outcomes. The onetime confidence in the high IQ proved overblown when it was discovered that while many children who were dubbed gifted on this basis went on to "A" status by qualifying for careers in various high-level professions, others with equally high IQs had to settle for a "C" label because of lapsing into relative mediocrity (Oden, 1968).

Critics of IQ tests also have argued that a single metric cannot reveal much about multiple, discreet intelligences (Gardner, 1983; Guilford, 1967). They have not improved matters by advocating probes into special aptitudes, considering the bleak outcomes of longitudinal research on the validity of such measures (Thorndike & Hagen, 1959). Furthermore, separate cross-validation studies of three batteries of widely used aptitude tests showed that a single general ability factor usually predicted criterion performance in each of a number of educational subjects and in job requirements at least as well as did the best single aptitude subtest in the respective batteries (Thorndike, 1985). Granted, the *essence* of a theoretical construct cannot be captured completely by tests designed to assess it; still, the choice of tests and what they purport to measure reflects fairly faithfully what the essence is purported to be. If clues to giftedness are diagnosed strictly by cognitive power measures, it is a good bet that the diagnostician expects to find all the signs of giftedness in cognitive power.

The recent shift of emphasis from proficiency to processes of thinking promises to yield better clinical insights into giftedness (Sternberg, 1986), but again the sole stress is on mental functioning while ignoring other vital facilitators in the psyche and in the environment. Despite the considerable advantages of deep explorations into *how* (not just *how well*) the gifted find and solve problems, such efforts lack a broad perspective that takes into its sweep the *social* as well as some other psychological dimensions of high potential.

Finally, if childhood proficiency were the only meaningful early sign of maturing giftedness, what better harbinger could there be than early prodigious behavior? The child prodigy already has a proven record of excellence, not just the promise of a great future. Yet there are many instances of early brilliance fizzling out by the end of the prodigies' adolescent years. This is true not only for young violinists, as in Bamberger's (1986) studies, but for budding geniuses in other fields as well. Bamberger hypothesized that a musical prodigy's "midlife crisis" is characterized by what she calls "serious cognitive reorganization" in the child and a simultaneous demand from audiences for more mature instrumental interpretations. Too often, these wonder children fail to measure up as they grow into a new stage of life because "there can be neither return to imitation and the unreflective, spontaneous 'intuitions' of childhood, nor a simple 'fix-up'" (Bamberger, 1986). When the mismatch between internal developments and external expectations are uncorrectable, the prodigy remains just a "has-been," or a "might-have-become," and again early ability alone proves inadequate to define giftedness.

After his detailed study of six young geniuses—two whizzes in chess, one each in music, math, and creative writing, and a young polymath labeled "omnibus prodigy"— Feldman (1986, p. 235) reported follow-up information that "only one of the six prodigies . . . has gone more or less in a straight line from where he started to where he is now." Why the turnaway? Perhaps partly because of what Feldman calls "four time frames," or the social-historical contexts within which the prodigy's talent operates and which define the meaningfulness of that talent. The first is the child's individual history, how it is different from that of most contemporaries and how he or she functions productively in the era in which he or she lives. The second pertains to the existence and stage of sophistication of a domain or discipline in which the child can excel. For example, it is impossible for a bril-

liant classical ballerina to burst into the world of dance if there is no longer any public admiration of classical ballet as a performing art. The third time frame reflects a nation's cultural and political priorities and how much society is willing to invest in order to nurture talents that are compatible with these priorities. Finally, the fourth frame is broader than the other three, referring to the evolution of human thought and culture in which the individual prodigy fits.

Both Bamberger and Feldman offer heady speculations about the mix of ingredients needed to actualize giftedness even among child prodigies, whose abilities early in life are openly manifested. How much more critical are such ingredients, and others, too, in cases where children's potentialities are not nearly so obvious, but have to be inferred from performance on tests designed to "dig" for relatively hidden promise. If such tests fail to predict individual excellence unerringly, no matter how much effort is dedicated to refining and redesigning them, the best advice to educators of the gifted is to lower their expectations rather than to fulminate against the testing movement. This is not an evasion of scientific responsibility; quite the contrary, it is a plea to stop wasting precious time in search of simplistic solutions to an intricate problem, namely, determining what contributes to the making of a gifted person.

Essentials of Giftedness: A Filigree of Factors

In their edited collection of theories of giftedness, Sternberg and Davidson (1986) present a comprehensive array of definitions, which range from the purely cognitive (Sternberg, 1986) to a blend of the intellectual and motivational (Renzulli, 1986) to the primarily social (Csikszentmihalyi & Robinson, 1986). Still, a decision must be made whether children can be regarded as gifted at all, inasmuch as they qualify only by childhood standards. Except for a one-in-a-generation young Mozart or Mendelssohn, children stand out only in comparison to other children, not relative to adult achievers. It is nevertheless fashionable to equate giftedness with accelerated early development, even in the professional literature on the subject. A student earns the label by being a precocious learner and is thus prepared for a faster-paced education.

An alternative approach, and the one preferred here, is to recognize the facts that gifted adults do not necessarily have histories of childhood precocity and that early accelerated development does not necessarily eventuate in adult giftedness. It is therefore preferable to consider individuals who show early promise as *potentially* gifted, not *manifestly* so, since they usually shine in comparison to age-mates, rarely by universal adult standards. Furthermore, as noted earlier, both common sense and research evidence argue for hedging bets on the fulfillment of early promise.

Recognizing children selected by any criteria as unequivocally gifted runs the risk of including a few who do not qualify and excluding some who do. But even settling for the vagaries of potential giftedness leaves open the need to specify the *forms* of giftedness in which promise is shown. In response to this need, it may be argued that excellence reveals itself in one of two broad categories of ability: (1) skills in *producing* new ideas or material inventions that enhance the moral, physical, emotional, social, intellectual, or aesthetic life of humanity, or (2) skills in *performing* brilliantly before appreciative audiences or in the service of various kinds of clientele who benefit from such service. Excluded in favor of innovators are the masters of trivia—the straight A retrievers and dispensers of other people's knowledge, who masquerade as gifted even though they can never generate a worthwhile idea of their own. Also excluded are the appreciators of great performance who are incapable of performing brilliantly themselves.

In order for a child to become truly gifted, five factors have to interweave most elegantly: (1) *superior general intellect*, (2) *distinctive special aptitudes*, (3) *a supportive array of nonintellective traits*, (4) *a challenging and facilitative environment*, and (5) *the smile of good fortune at crucial periods of life*. Each of these elements is required, though not adequate in and of itself, if a person is to achieve excellence in any publicly valued area of activity. No combination of four qualifiers can compensate for

the absence or insufficiency of the fifth. The minimal essentials, or threshold levels, for all five vary with every talent domain. For example, giftedness in theoretical physics requires higher tested intelligence and fewer interpersonal skills than do the social service professions. Obviously, no single set of measurement criteria can be equally effective and efficient for identifying, for example, both potential "hard" scientists and politicians. Nor is it meaningful to suggest that either the scientist or the politician is the "smarter" of the two because of differences in their general intelligence or in their special aptitudes. The five factors interact in different ways for separate talent domains, but they *all* are represented in some way in every form of giftedness.

Superior General Intellect

General intellectual ability can be defined roughly as the *g* factor, which is itself defined roughly as some kind of mysterious mental strength denoting abstract thinking ability and shared by a variety of specific competencies. (See Chapters 4 and 5 for an elaboration of general intellective processes.) It is usually reflected in measures of general intelligence and in the common variance among tested special aptitudes.

The *g* factor, as revealed in tested general intelligence, figures on a sliding scale in all high-level talent areas. This means that different threshold IQs are required for various kinds of accomplishment, higher in academic subjects than, for example, in the performing arts. There is no basis for making extreme assertions about the IQ, such as discounting its relevance to giftedness entirely or accepting without reservation Terman's (1924) hypothesis that high-IQ children constitute the only pool out of which all geniuses inevitably emerge. Instead, positions along this continuum should be adjusted according to the talent area, which means taking a stance closer to one extreme for some kinds of giftedness and nearer the opposite extreme for others.

Although Terman never quite persuaded every behavioral scientist that high IQ is indispensable for giftedness, his work undoubtedly contributed to the current popularity of intelligence testing for identifying giftedness. In a survey of expert opinion on intelligence and aptitude tests, Snyderman and Rothman (1987) found that psychologists and educators knowledgeable in areas related to intelligence testing generally agreed that the instruments are valid and useful in measuring some of the most vital aspects of intelligence. More important, Terman's longitudinal study of more than 1,500 high-IQ children revealed much of what is now known about this special population.[1] He found that these children had an exemplary record not only in school and later in career accomplishments, but also in psychosocial development.

Serious mental illness and personality problems were reported less often in the high-IQ sample than one would expect among average-IQ peers, and relatively few of them had any kinds of criminal records. On the contrary, most of the men and women found time to participate actively in civic welfare efforts and generally in fulfilling the obligations of good citizenship. In 1968 Oden summarized her follow-up findings with these words: "Now, after forty years of careful investigation, there can be no doubt that, for the overwhelming majority of subjects, the promise of youth has been more than fulfilled" (Oden, 1968, p. 51). There was, however, a striking absence of geniuses of Shakespeare, Mozart, or Picasso stature in Terman's population. Perhaps the reason is that the California districts where he assembled his population in the early 1920s did not spawn and nurture any immortals, at least not at that time in history.

In a study complementary to Terman's scrutiny of high-IQ subjects from childhood to adulthood, Cox (1926) reviewed the lives of 279 eminent men and 3 eminent women who had

---

[1] The multivolume *Genetic Studies of Genius* reports research conducted by Lewis M. Terman and his associates (Burks, Jensen, & Terman, 1930; Cox, 1926; Terman & Oden, 1925, 1947, 1959). Terman helped prepare the 1959 volume but died 2 years before its publication. Several additional follow-up studies have been prepared by Melita Oden (1968), Pauline S. Sears and Ann Barbee (1977), Robert R. Sears (1977), and Pauline S. Sears (1979).

achieved fame sometime between the mid-15th and the end of the 19th century. Evaluating their biographical data, she concluded that, indeed, these personages would have scored extremely high in IQ just as Terman had expected. More recently, Walberg (1969, 1982) reported findings similar to Cox's on the basis of his retrospective studies of artists and scientists (see Chapter 18). Wallace and Walberg (1987) also estimated a mean IQ of 162 for a group of 42 essayists who lived and achieved renown before the turn of this century.

From the bulky evidence on relationships between high IQ and giftedness, it is easy to appreciate why intelligence testing is so popular in screening for able children and why superior general intellectual ability is one of the signs of high potential and one of the links to its fulfillment. Terman never proposed a theory of intelligence; he merely developed the IQ instrument as a practical device for assessing abstract thinking ability in much the same way that a medical aide uses the blood pressure cuff to measure systolic and diastolic levels without caring much about theory and research on how blood circulates in the body. True, Terman's belief in the supremacy of hereditary factors in IQ seems antiquated today, but he bequeathed at least two enduring legacies to the behavioral sciences. One of them was his conviction that the gifted are not mutants who possess some kinds of freakish powers bestowed upon them by biological accident. Instead, the gifted differ from the nongifted in degree rather than in kind, which means that all humans are "brothers and sisters" under the normal curve of the IQ distribution. Those who find themselves at the upper extreme merely have more powerful versions of the same attributes possessed by those who are closer to average in ability.

A second enduring outcome of Terman's work was his conclusion that potential giftedness reveals itself even in childhood. "Early ripe, early rot" is a once-popular platitude that he helped turn into a canard by his studies of high-IQ children growing up. Despite the many cases of aborted genius, his data provide some assurance that children with high potentialities and reasonably stable personalities who are given the right opportunities to hone their skills stand a better-than-average chance to excel eventually in their careers. Because greatness does not materialize suddenly and unaccountably in adulthood, but instead has its roots in the early years of growth, schools are in a key position to help children realize their potential. Terman's work confirms the need for special educational programs for the gifted, an idea that would be irrelevant if there were no developmental connection between early promise and later fulfillment.

Inasmuch as Terman conducted his longitudinal study in a single generation of high-IQ subjects, it is important to consider whether his results are timebound or generalizable from one era to the next. The issue takes on important meaning in light of Flynn's (1987) large-scale study of intergenerational gains in IQ in countries where such data were available. He found that present-generation 20-year-olds in Holland scored about 20 points higher in IQ than did their counterparts some 30 years earlier. Both groups were compared on the same test, using the same norms. An increase of such dramatic magnitude means that, in his sample at least, the number of persons with an IQ of 150 and above has increased proportionately by a factor of almost 60 from the previous to the present generation. Yet, the number of patents granted has actually diminished, with the 1980s showing only 60 to 65% of the yearly rate for the 1960s. This may mean that IQ is no longer as relevant to the world of invention as it once was, or perhaps as scientific knowledge accumulates and inventions become more and more sophisticated, the threshold IQ has to rise in order to qualify a child as a potential producer of ideas.

In the last analysis, high IQ is a boon or a bust in the configuration of factors that make up giftedness, depending on how much confidence is invested in it. For example, Feldman (1984) studied the careers of 19 men with IQs of 180 and above and compared them with those of a sample of 15 men representing the IQ 150 range, all of them taken from the Terman population. Although the majorities of both groups pursued careers as professionals or as business executives, he found "only" 4 of the 19 IQ 180+ men (versus none of the IQ 150 men) could be described as "distinguished." Disappointed, he

concluded that "the overall impression is one of lower achievement than the traditional view of IQ would have predicted . . ." (p. 520). Here is a case of choosing to describe a container of liquid filled to the halfway mark as either half empty or half full. Feldman was obviously disappointed by the 15 "failures" in a group of 19; others may consider 4 "successes" out of only 19 cases a rousing endorsement of the high IQ—or, more precisely, whatever intellective strengths the IQ measures—as constituting part of the makeup of giftedness, especially since the scores were obtained some *60* years before Feldman's follow-up. Again, if we moderate our expectations of the IQ, it can be useful in helping define high potential.

As an approach to the understanding of intellectual giftedness, the investigators of thought processes in Sternberg's triarchic theory may eventually help to pinpoint the extraordinary strengths needed to achieve excellence (see Chapter 4). This is an obvious advantage to the educator who appreciates diagnostic data in order to design a curriculum that is prescribed to accommodate the individualities of gifted children. However, like the psychometric tradition from which it tries to depart, it focuses on intellect almost exclusively, as if this were virtually the only important requisite for gifted behavior. It ignores the nonintellective and situational antecedents that interact in many subtle and powerful ways with the processes of cognition. Furthermore, measures of these processes have not yet been validated in long-range studies to determine whether they forecast future achievement any better than do IQ or special ability test scores. The chances are that the predictive validity of such instruments is no better than those coming out of the psychometric tradition, because both types focus on cognitive power while largely neglecting other aspects of the psyche and their interaction with the environment.

Special Aptitudes

Some behavioral scientists who are critical of the importance of a *g* factor, or even deny its existence, argue strongly in favor of defining giftedness as extraordinary special ability.

Robinson (1977) pointed to the absurdity of declaring children gifted even though they have no noticeable gifts at all, except for the knack of scoring well on an IQ measure. A fairly similar sentiment was expressed by Stanley and Benbow (1986) in justifying the use of aptitude tests rather than the IQ in identifying precocity in mathematics. Although they acknowledge the IQ to be "perhaps the best *single* index of general learning rate" (p. 364), they found it impossible using only IQ scores to organize a group that was reasonably homogeneous in a single subject area, be it mathematics or history or English literature. This kind of reasoning makes sense in light of the fact that follow-up studies of Terman's high-IQ children (Oden, 1968) showed how wide-ranging the disciplines in which his population excelled were and how futile it would have been to predict the nature of eventual careers from childhood IQs. True, as Thorndike (1985) pointed out, a general factor may predominate in the development of specific skills, but it is likely that special aptitudes not only particularize the area of an individual's competence but also help determine the individual's degree of success in a particular area of competence. In other words, the *g* factor may explain more of the variance in achievement than does an aptitude measure, but both together can be more valid than either one separately.

Ever since Spearman (1927) recognized the *g* factor as a necessary intellectual force for every kind of problem solving and discovered specific abilities that share common variance with the *g* factor, yet are partly independent of it, the nature and number of special abilities have been subject to wide speculation. Vernon (1950), for example, divided *g* into two major *group factors,* one of them denoting verbal, educational aptitudes, including word and number skills, and the other representing practical aptitudes, such as mechanical information and spatial and psychomotor skills. The use of factor analysis to demonstrate the existence of distinguishable special abilities was developed and applied originally by Thurstone (1947), whose studies led him to recognize seven special abilities, including verbal meaning, reasoning, word fluency, number facility, memory, spatial relations, and perceptual speed.

Also as a result of factor analytic verification, Guilford (1967, 1977) proposed a structure-of-intellect model of as many as 150 factors in which five operations (i.e., cognition, memory, divergent production, convergent production, and evaluation) convert five types of content (i.e., figural [visual and auditory], symbolic, semantic, and behavioral) into six types of products (i.e., units, classes, relations, systems, transformations, and implications). More recently, Gardner (1983) abandoned factor analysis in favor of clinical and neurological insights into the variety of intelligences (see Chapter 5).

Whatever number of special aptitudes may exist in the psyche, in order for any of them to be actualized into giftedness, they have to undergo nurturing experiences that crystallize and enrich them. Yet, it is doubtful if any one aptitude by itself can amount to much no matter how ingeniously it is cultivated. As McNemar (1964) remarked caustically, fractionating and fragmentizing ability into what he called "more and more factors of less and less importance" may reflect nothing more than some special sign of "scatterbrainedness."

Gifted behavior probably involves an orchestration of several aptitudes rather than relying on the performance on what amounts to a "one-string fiddle." Furthermore, general ability comes into play in an important way. As Benbow, Stanley, Kirk, and Zonderman (1983) demonstrated in their study of mathematically precocious children who were in the top 0.03% of their age group in general intellectual ability, whereas *g* can account for as much as 50% of the variance on a battery of special ability tests administered to a random population, it figures less strongly in a high-functioning group. Thus, special aptitudes take on particular importance at elevated levels of *g* in accounting for the variance in achievement.

Multiple Aptitudes—Singular Achievements

An association between artistic and scientific abilities may seem farfetched at first blush. However, an attempt has been made to provide some supportive evidence. Root-Bernstein (1987a, 1987b) cites a long list of famous scientists, such as Louis Pasteur and Joseph Lister, who were also graphic artists, Johannes Kepler and Max Planck, who were musicians, and J. Robert Oppenheimer and George Washington Carver, who wrote poetry. More important, he is convinced that creativity in the arts and sciences is so highly correlated that genius in science cannot develop in the absence of high-level proficiency in the arts, since one enhances the other. He therefore hypothesizes that several "tools of thought" are common to both, including:

> perceptual acuity, pattern recognition, pattern forming, analogizing, abstracting, and imagining . . . also transforming skills: learning to "see" what a mathematical equation looks like, or to "hear" what data sounds like; or learning to "feel" like the molecule or "act" like the machine that one would like to comprehend. All of these skills are absolutely essential to scientific and technological curricula. All of them, intrinsically at least, already exist in the fine arts. (1987a, p. 18)

Far more obvious than the connection between artistic and scientific aptitude is the association between science and mathematics, and for this there is fairly hard evidence. Benbow and Minor (1986) conducted a follow-up study of 1,996 seventh and eighth graders who qualified for special acceleration programs in mathematics on the basis of their scores on the *Scholastic Aptitude Tests* (SATs), (Verbal and Mathematics Portions). The researchers found that the SAT-Math scores obtained in junior high school were strongly associated with science achievement in senior high school for both sexes.

There also appears to be a relationship between mathematical and verbal precocity. In her investigation of mathematically precocious children, Fox (1974) found that performance on verbal reasoning tests, when adjusted for age, related positively to learning rates in mathematics. Those with lower verbal scores tended to progress at a lower pace than those with equivalent math aptitude scores but with higher verbal ratings. In fact, Aiken (1972) cited several studies to show that problem-solving abilities relate more closely to reading comprehension than to computational facility. However, the correlation of mathe-

matical and verbal skills may decrease when their relationship to general intelligence is held constant. This is understandable, since IQ is heavily saturated with abstract reasoning, which figures prominently in both mathematical and verbal comprehension.

How Effective and Efficient Are Measures of Aptitudes?

From the little evidence gathered thus far, it would seem that aptitude measures generally are valid with high-functioning students, provided the students receive appropriate educational stimulation. For example, Stanley and Benbow (1986) cite several follow-up investigations of children identified as superior in mathematical aptitude who had benefited from radical acceleration in mathematics as part of the SMPY program. The results showed that participants in the program were much more advanced in their education than were nonparticipants. There also appeared to be no reason to fear that accelerating the rate of learning would produce gaps in knowledge or poor retention. Equally important, differences among children in initial scores on the mathematical aptitude measure were associated with subsequent differences in mathematical achievement among those in the program.

Less impressive are the results of post hoc studies of adults in a variety of occupations, since the data are far more enlightening for their retrospective insights than for prospective forecasting. One of the best known investigations is Roe's (1953) retrospective research on 67 biologists, physical scientists, and social scientists between ages 31 and 60 who had been judged by their peers as distinguished contributors to their fields. The three subgroups seemed to show marked variations in their personal development, including both intellective and nonintellective attributes. Differences in visual aptitudes, auditory-verbal skills, imageless thought, and kinesthetic abilities were directly relevant to the type of science fields or subjects they pursued. For example, geneticists and biochemists obtained higher scores on nonverbal tests than did the physiologists, botanists, and bacteriologists who made up the rest of the biological sciences sample. Also, anthropologists were relatively low in mathematical ability compared with the psychologist and social science group. As for the physicists, those dealing more with theory in their respective fields scored higher on verbal tests, in comparison with the experimentalists, who excelled on the spatial measures.

Although Roe's data showed some relationship between specific cognitive strengths and areas of specialization in science, it would be difficult to justify counseling young students about which branches of science they should enter, or even whether they should concentrate on science at all, on the basis of cognitive measures alone, for several reasons: (1) Existing tests seem to be more adequate in retrospective analyses than in making accurate forecasts; (2) even though special aptitudes probably do exist in young children, they are more easily measured in adolescence for purposes of making prognoses; and (3) under the best of circumstances, tests of cognition can only reveal whether the person has the intellectual power to qualify for careers in a particular field, but whether such careers *will* be pursued is only partly associated with intellect.

In the last analysis, special aptitudes can help a child excel in a particular domain, *if* she or he also shows evidence of superior general ability. But to bring giftedness fully to life, these cognitive faculties have to be energized by an encouraging disposition, an enriching environment, and timely elements of chance.

Nonintellective Factors

Relating personality traits to giftedness is basically a chicken-and-egg problem. Nobody knows for sure whether, and to what extent, these attributes are *causes, concomitants,* or *consequences* of successful achievement. Of the many nonintellective factors that figure in achievement, motivation, self-concept, and metalearning are among the most important.

Motivation

Of all personality traits, none has drawn more attention than motivation to achieve. Renzulli

(1978) counts high *task commitment* as one of only three major factors that characterize giftedness, the other two being creativity and above-average ability. It also appears that the origin of desires to achieve make a difference in outcomes. For example, Amabile (1983) makes a strong distinction between intrinsic and extrinsic motivation and shows evidence that children and adults perform more creatively when the urge to excel comes from within rather than from without.

The importance of autonomously oriented achievement is probably what characterizes Piechowski's (1979) concept of *overexcitability,* which he defines as an intense personal reaction to an experience. There are five modes of overexcitability: (1) the *psychomotor* mode, characterized by excessive physical energy, movement, restlessness, and action, (2) the *sensual* mode of comfort and sensory delectation, (3) the *intellectual* mode of logic, questioning, and the search for truth, (4) the *imaginational* mode of dreams, fantasies, and images, and (5) the *emotional* mode of attachments to other people, empathy, and love. He points out that "at times the inner tensions and conflicts may be overwhelming. [See Chapter 21.] Still, the process of development must go on—an arduous passage from a lower to higher level—from external to internal control, from impulse to reflection, from sociability to empathy and compassion, from social norm to the norm of the ideal, from relative to universal values, from competition to service to others, from possessive and security-seeking love to all-embracing love" (p. 29). Research seems to show that not only are elevated levels of achievement associated with elevated overexcitability profiles, but there is also a relationship between types of overexcitability and the domains in which superior achievement is demonstrated (Piechowski, Silverman, & Falk, 1985).

A closer look at the nature of achievement motivation helps clarify how high-ability children make the most use of their potentialities. According to Rosen (1956), the achievement syndrome consists of several elements, among them at least three specific beliefs along the following continua:

1. *Activistic-passivistic orientation,* denoting one's perception of control of self. Those who are activistic, or internally oriented, reject the fatalistic view that success is in the cards, but are instead convinced that they can manipulate the environment and shape their destinies.

2. *Individualistic-collectivistic orientation,* which offers the choice between self-sufficiency as against dependency on collaboration. The potentially gifted often choose to work at a task they like, even in the company of people they dislike, rather than to work with people they like at a task they dislike.

3. *Present-future orientation,* denoting the choice between immediate gratification versus planning for the future, even if it means sacrificing present gains for eventual compounded gains. The highly motivated take a more optimistic view of their chances of eventual success, whereas the less motivated tend to believe that things hardly ever work out, so why make long-range plans?

Although achievement orientation helps in understanding achievement outcomes, some investigators have suggested that it is situational. This means that a child may be motivated to achieve on the ball field but not at school, and possibly even on the ball field today but not tomorrow (Katz, 1969; Maehr, 1974).

In a study of more than 300 eighth graders, Castenell (1983) attempted to distinguish among three situations in which achievement motivation could manifest itself: at school, among peers, and at home. He also investigated race, sex, and social class differences in each of the three settings. Results showed the importance of specifying the circumstances in which desires to perform well are expressed. For example, whereas whites seem to manifest their achievement motivation along traditional channels, such as schooling, blacks seem to express theirs in several contexts. Also, boys seem to be more interested in achieving success among peers than are girls, for whom sharing an experience with other girls may be more important than outperforming them. But the major finding was that not all adolescents perceive academic achievement as being necessary for success in life; many have stronger desires to achieve status at home or among peers. The gifted child, whose need to excel at school can make the difference between what he or she perceives as success and failure, may be faced with a dilemma in choosing between school demands for heavy commitment to academics as against peer pressure to conform to a more conventional adolescent lifestyle.

Self-Concepts

A strong drive among the gifted to excel, and succeeding at it, should provide them with better self-concepts. However, from a review of the literature on the subject, Olszewski-Kubilius, Kulieke, and Krasney (1988) concluded that the evidence is equivocal. They suggested several possible reasons for the inconsistent findings. One problem has to do with results varying according to sample size, social class, and ethnicity. In studies showing better self-images among the gifted, experimental subjects were generally in special classes for the gifted, whereas the comparison groups were in regular classrooms. The visibility of special classes may have attracted greater recognition among adults that, in turn, helped some experimentals to feel better about themselves than did the relatively neglected controls.

Another possible explanation for the sometimes-lower, sometimes-higher self-concepts among gifted children has to do with their willingness to take risks. Beery (1975) and Covington and Beery (1976) proposed a theory of achievement behavior in which students protect their self-concepts of high ability by exercising little effort to learn. They refuse to submit themselves to a test in which the demands are high, in order to avoid the risk of failure and the implication that their potential is not as high as they think it is. In a study of 360 college freshmen, Covington and Omelich (1979) presented evidence to support the theory that school achievement behavior is affected by feelings of personal competency and efforts to preserve a sense of self-worth. In pressured problem-solving situations, the students tended to give up their pursuit of solutions with the attitude that "nothing ventured, nothing lost."

It appears, therefore, that high self-regard has to be actualized through risk-taking behavior; otherwise, it amounts to little more than empty bravado or self-delusion. Sometimes, the gifted who are endowed with strong egos pay social penalties for appearing to be arrogant, but if they did not believe that their abilities were exceptional, they could never prime themselves for maximum effort when they were called upon to confirm their giftedness through yet another extraordinary accomplishment.

Metalearning

The highly motivated gifted child is also reinforced by more acute metalearning orientations. As used here, the term *metalearning* is an adaptive mechanism of sensing the name of the game of success in school situations and elsewhere. It is therefore different from "metacognition," which is basically a cognitive process of understanding one's own thinking. The gifted constantly tune in to what teachers, mentors, or critics expect of them, and they direct their considerable abilities accordingly. If earning academic honors means absorbing huge gobs of facts, remembering them, organizing them, and laying them out in neat and abundant piles, the child will conform if she or he has the desire and intellective power to do so. On the other hand, when originality is required in the classroom, and students are threatened with failure if they simply regurgitate ideas they have absorbed, there is a redirection of energy toward creating new and meaningful ideas. The gifted make the switch quickly, though not always easily. Some may qualify as gifted by one set of expectations and not by the other. But unless they make the effort to sense the expectations quickly and accurately, they may not be able to activate their abilities to fulfill their potential, even if the abilities are intact.

Metalearning is therefore a kind of mastery of ground rules rather than of complex, abstract reasoning skills. In the process of fine-tuning their readiness for success in an achievement-oriented society, potentially gifted children realize quickly and clearly that before they initiate problem-finding or problem-solving behavior, they have to determine in advance whether they are dealing with semantic, symbolic, or figural material. They see the advantages of making preliminary estimates about parameters within which solutions will be located and beyond which there can only be bizarre or impossible solutions. They have to assume in advance that, in the case of solving differential equations, for example, single, exact, or multiple relevant solutions are expected, not general approximations. They understand that it is helpful to try to reduce data to manageable proportions by eliminating facts and ideas that can only delay or spoil outcomes. They also develop the habit of deferring judgment until all the relevant data are sifted, rather than jumping to hasty solutions. In other words, they are aware of the need to know the road to excellence before testing their ability to make the journey.

If metalearning rituals are followed, achievement will depend on whether the student has the requisite kinds and amounts of cognitive power and willpower; if the rituals are not followed, then cognitive power alone cannot mobilize a person toward high-level productivity or performance. Sometimes it is tragic that children with exceptional mental strength, particularly those coming from socially disadvantaged backgrounds, are demeaned or pitied for cognitive deficits when in reality that fault is traceable to poor metalearning habits that prevent proper release of potential.

The Environment

Giftedness requires social contexts that enables it to mature. These contexts are as broad as society itself and as restricted as the sociology of the classroom. Human potential cannot flourish in an arid cultural climate; it needs nurturance, urgings, encouragement, and even pressures from a world that cares. The child lives in several environments, the closest of which are the family, peer group, school, and community, while the remotest are the various economic, social, legal, and political institutions. They all help to determine the *kinds of talent* that society is willing to honor as well as the *amount of investment* that it is willing to make in cultivating these talents. Societal conditions are therefore critical in stimulating the potentially gifted child's pursuit of excellence.

Broad Social Perspectives

It is misleading to characterize talent as rare brainpower operating without temporal or cultural discipline. Talent needs to fit into its own *Zeitgeist* (spirit of the times) in order to be recognized and appreciated. Otherwise, it will remain stillborn or will mature to serve an unappreciating audience that may regard it either as anachronistic if it is a throwback to earlier times or as too avant-garde if the times are not yet ready for it.

For the 20th century, and probably beyond, Phenix (1964) asserted that Western society rewards talent in six general domains:

1. *Symbolics,* including basic forms of communication through ordinary language, mathematics, and such nondiscursive symbolic forms as gestures, rituals, and rhythmic patterns
2. *Empirics,* comprising the sciences of the physical and living world
3. *Aesthetics,* including the various arts, such as music, painting, theater, and literary creation
4. *Synnoetics,* signifying insightful relationships between people or psychological understandings about people
5. *Ethics,* which emphasizes moral meanings that are concerned with obligation instead of fact, what ought to be rather than what was, is, or will be
6. *Synoptics,* which embraces meanings that integrate history, religion, and philosophy comprehensively

These categorizations do not preclude radical changes within single domains. Quite the contrary, Branscomb (1986) forecasts major reintegrations of the sciences by the early part of the 21st century. For example, he expects the social and the natural sciences to work more collaboratively than ever before, sees a growing association of science and the arts, and envisions a resurgence of pure mathematics as the handmaiden of science. In the music world others anticipate major changes, including speculation as to whether the symphony orchestra, as it is now constituted, will survive the 20th century or will soon be replaced by instruments producing synthetic sounds. But the domains of science, art, music, and the rest will probably remain basically unchanged, even if the form in which they appear and the giftedness they require for their furtherance are altered radically.

In his insistence on breaking away from understanding creativity solely through the study of creative persons and processes, Csikszentmihalyi (1988) argues that creativity is the product of three main shaping forces: (1) the *domain* in which productivity or performance is acceptable and which undergoes substantive and stylistic change from one period in history to another, so that, for example, creating music in the Mozartean idiom is not "revelant" to 20th-century composition; (2) the *field* of teachers, critics, patrons, and creative peers who judge individual contributions to each domain; and (3) the *person* who creates within the limits of an acceptable domain and sometimes revolutionizes it to the satisfaction of the field. Thus, giftedness does not develop in an environmental vacuum but rather interacts with the particular domain and field in a sensitive and dynamic partnership.

Social Class and the Family

In his study of environmental correlates of IQ and achievement in a wide-range ability population of children, Wolf (1966) concluded that the *status variables,* which define socioeconomic levels, correlate only about .40 with children's IQ scores. *Process variables,* on the other hand, refer to various means through which parents encourage and provide opportunities for their children to engage in learning experiences outside school. These motivators include (1) parental pressures on children to achieve at school and away from school, (2) parental pressures on children to develop sophisticated language usage, and (3) parental provisions for enhancing children's learning opportunities outside school. Wolf measured the process variables through a questionnaire administered to mothers of his sample population. Results showed a startlingly high correlation of .69 between mothers' response to the total instrument and the targeted children's Henmon-Nelson IQ scores. An even more impressive coefficient of .80 was obtained in relation to *Metropolitan Achievement Test* results. In a subsequent replication of this study, Trotman (1977) noted similarly high correlations between the process variables and IQ for white as well as black ninth graders in a middle-class suburban school system.

Whereas Wolf and Trotman focused on children ranging widely in ability, Sloane (1985) looked at the home influences of children who grew up to excel individually as Olympic swimmers, world-class tennis players, concert pianists, sculptors, research mathematicians, and research neurologists. These subjects were interviewed in their mid-30s and asked to recall the nature and extent of their parents' encouragement to fulfill their early promise. Generally, the respondents described a nurturing, challenging home environment. Parents wanted them to be involved in learning activities as often as possible, to do their best, to make productive use of time, and to measure up to high standards of performance. Homework was checked regularly at home, and children quickly learned the family's code that work had to be finished before play could be started. Little time was allowed for idling, as parents arranged for a steady stream of constructive activities for their children. In the early years of talent development, parents introduced the children to their respective talent fields. Often, older siblings or relatives, as well as parents, taught the children informal lessons in these disciplines, but at a later stage of development, special instructors were brought in to raise the challenges to new heights. Later still, the parents' own direct roles in the children's lessons and practice disappeared entirely as the outside tutors took complete charge. These tutors were carefully selected to provide often costly services at advanced levels.

Although Sloane's results probably described the home experiences of most gifted children who eventually succeed in fulfilling their potential, the picture she presents is by no means universal. Goertzel and Goertzel (1962) and Goertzel, Goertzel, and Goertzel (1978) provided descriptions of geniuses who had to overcome the ill effects of living with smothering or dominating mothers, failure-prone fathers, or generally troubled families whose offspring strove for excellence possibly as a sign of protest against parental oppression. Therefore, whatever seems *logically* essential in child-rearing practices for the nurturance of giftedness often fails to be confirmed *empirically*. The inconsistency of the picture suggests that perhaps there are no generalizations, except that much depends on the special chemistry between person and parent. For one child, a particular nurturance at home may inspire creative work; for another child, the same parental influence may have an adverse effect, or none at all. This would imply a need to determine what kinds of home environments and childhood individualities constitute the best matches in fostering extraordinary potential in children.

The School

One widespread myth about potentially gifted children is that they excel with or without special education. People who argue against enrichment programs claim they aren't worth the investment because "talent will out anyway," as if full-blown from Zeus' head. To reinforce their doubts, they cite familiar cases of immortals, such as Churchill, Edison, and Einstein, who apparently suffered no ill effects from mediocre schooling in their early years of life. According to this popular claim, talent incubates strictly from an individual's innate resources, and the only real help schools can give is to clear away obstacles that stand in the way of great achievement.

But empirical evidence suggests that schools can make a difference. In a follow-up investigation of children selected in 1976 and in 1978 to participate in several acceleration programs sponsored by SMPY, Brody and Benbow (1987; see Chapter 11) report long-term positive effects of this form of enrichment.

The children showed impressive academic achievements, participated widely in extracurricular activities, expressed ambitious goals and aspirations, and showed no unusual signs of social or emotional maladjustment. These results confirm an earlier meta-analysis by Kulik and Kulik (1984; see Chapter 13) involving a combination of the data taken from previous experimental studies, half of them with same-age controls, and half with older-age controls. In all of the 13 studies with same-age control groups, the accelerates outperformed the comparably able elementary and secondary school students. The authors' conclusion is unequivocal: "Acceleration contributes to student achievement" (p. 415). As for the comparisons with older pupils, the results were also impressive, inasmuch as "talented youngsters who were accelerated into higher grades performed as well as the talented, older pupils already in those grades" (p. 421).

In an earlier meta-analysis of the educational impact on high-functioning students, focusing this time on ability grouping, Kulik and Kulik (1982) combined the results of 14 studies and concluded that the children "apparently benefited from the stimulation provided by other high-aptitude students and from the special curricula that grouping made possible" (p. 425). However, a subsequent study of ability grouping by Slavin (1987) using a best-evidence synthesis technique combining features of meta-analytic and narrative reviews found "little support . . . for the assertion that high achievers benefit from ability grouping" (p. 301). This review touched off a controversy regarding the procedures used in reaching such pessimistic conclusions (Gamoran, 1987; Hiebert, 1987).

From all indications, it would seem that ability grouping alone does not guarantee improvements in school performance; there must be some curriculum adjustments in these special classes in order to produce positive results. What, indeed, does happen when qualified students enroll in enriched honors programs? According to Kulik (1985), the outcomes are clearly salutary. In fact, in this meta-analysis of 25 studies, enrichment enabled the students to raise their test scores by as much as a third of one standard deviation.

All in all, there is enough compelling evidence to show that well-conceptualized, well-designed plans to challenge potentially gifted children to the limits of their abilities produce advantages in achievement and in other aspects of personal growth. The real question is not whether special education makes a difference; instead, educators should concern themselves with more refined experimentation aimed at determining *which* able children benefit from *what kinds* of special education.

The Peer Group

All children are affected by the learning atmosphere at school. The peer culture can affect the social climate in a classroom to make it comfortable or unbearable for individual children to do their best. Unfortunately, the record in many schools has not been encouraging on that score. In a study of stereotypes adolescents attach to academic brilliance (Tannenbaum, 1962), it was discovered that being brilliant per se was no more (or less) acceptable than being average at school. But woe unto the brilliant adolescent who was described as studious or who got homework assignments in on time! Worse still, being brilliant, studious, and uninterested in sports was disastrous to one's reputation. The teenagers were saying, in effect, that it is all right to earn the highest marks at school if those who earn them don't show too much effort in climbing to the top and if they share America's love affair with sports. Conversely, those students who are uninterested in sports but are interested in studying hard and handing in homework on time can curry favor with age-mates far more easily by being average in schoolwork than by performing brilliantly. This study was replicated in Canada (Mitchell, 1974) with the same results.

Do such attitudes affect students' academic performance? Coleman (1960) addressed this question and discovered that high school students with superior potential were less likely to underachieve in school settings in which students had positive feelings about scholastic pursuits. Evidently, in educational settings in which negative feelings about being brilliant were relatively strong, students who had it in them to excel scholastically chose to hide their lights under a bushel.

On the positive side, the school environment for promoting excellence need not be so bleak. In another replication of the Tannenbaum study, this time in a community where special efforts were made to emphasize educational achievement for all children and to provide special opportunities for the potentially gifted, Morgan (1981) discovered a more positive feeling about academic brilliance and studiousness among 11th graders. Apparently, communities can make a difference in creating a fertile soil for the cultivation of talent.

However, the problem seems to persist in too many schools, not only in the peer culture but also among instructors. In still another replication of the Tannenbaum study, Cramond and Martin (1987) solicited reactions from pre- and in-service teachers rather than from students. Sadly, the results showed no difference between the two teacher samples or between the total teacher group and the adolescent sample investigated by Tannenbaum 25 years earlier. However, potentially gifted students sometimes swim against the mainstream. In a study of attitudes toward live potentially gifted students, not the hypothetical variety as in the previously described investigations, Colangelo and Kelly (1983) obtained better results. Despite the fact that general students rated academic activities, including special classes for the gifted, much lower in importance than athletics, their attitudes toward the gifted were "neutral." Although this is a far cry from giving potentially gifted children the kind of boost they need from peers, at least they were tolerated as members of the adolescent culture. In such a tolerable climate the potentially gifted students showed strong desires to be part of the special program designed for them. How much more strongly might they have been attracted to this program if academics were rated higher in importance than athletics and the academically talented were respected for their accomplishments? Such a question can be asked in too many schools in America.

Chance Factors

The influence of the unexpected and unpredictable on the course of human development is largely a neglected subject in studies of giftedness. Apparently, behavioral and social scientists prefer to deal with phenomena that are manageable rather than mysterious. This aversion is understandable, because what is there to say about luck, except that it exists and that it can make the difference between success and failure? Nobody knows what forms it will take, or when or how often it will strike. It is treated almost as if it were a supernatural force, inscrutable and therefore outside the pale of science. Nonetheless, nobody can deny its power to actualize or inhibit, to direct or redirect a creative act.

The question of how much of the variance in great accomplishment is attributable to chance has rarely been addressed by researchers, and the little evidence that does exist is hardly more than speculative. A rare exception to the relative neglect of chance factors is Simonton's (1984) use of a method he calls *historiometry* to estimate more objectively the contributions of *Zeitgeist,* genius, and chance to the emergence of immortal figures in history. According to his preliminary findings, chance factors play an important role, contributing perhaps as much as 80% of the variance in achieving tactical victory on the battlefield. Much work remains yet to be done in other domains of excellence, but it seems likely that when that work is done chance factors will figure more prominently than was ever suspected.

Perhaps the most daunting obstacle to dealing with chance is that it is unpredictable and therefore introduces an element of mystery in forecasting the fulfillment of early promise. It is hard for educators, parents, and members of the helping services to realize that their best laid plans and actions for potentially gifted students can be enhanced or nullified by circumstances over which they have no control. Even when a person seems to be a sure bet for success or failure, the smile or the frown of fortune can turn matters around completely. Getzels (1979) discovered this in his longitudinal study of talented young adult art students.

After collecting considerable data on backgrounds, abilities, personalities, and processes by which his subjects executed a creative work of art, he conducted a follow-up study 5 to 6 years after their graduation to see how well earlier signs of talent led to subsequent success in the field.

Of the 31 former fine arts students, 7 could not be located and were considered either as having abandoned a career in art or as not being visibly successful in it. Of the 24 who could be found, 8 had abandoned art as a career, 7 were only marginally involved, and the remaining 9 had achieved various levels of success as fine artists. Consider the important part chance played in the careers of his subjects, as per his own words: "There were idiosyncratic accidents and exigencies determining each artist's life and achievement that could not be reflected in the group data" (p. 385). Yet, despite the fact that chance factors probably had a good deal to do with the shrinking of his sample from 31 to only 9 subjects, his report was mainly concerned with showing an impressive predictive validity of the instrument used in assessing the students' artistic talent before they launched their careers. What the study should have taught the researcher is that whatever information he gathered about the subjects during their years in art school could reveal only a little about their prospects for future success in the field, since so much depended on the unpredictable.

Is chance simply a stroke of luck, a random event experienced by an individual and totally unrelated to the lawful functioning of the psyche or the environment? From all indications, it is more complicated than one may expect. According to Austin (1978), there are four kinds of chance factors. The first is simply luck, good or bad, that befalls a person who is basically in a passive state. This is the familiar example of the unforeseen situation in which someone is in the right (or wrong) place at the right (or wrong) time.

At the second level of chance, a person increases the likelihood of being struck with good fortune by setting the mind and body into constant motion, although the activity is ill defined, restless, and aimlessly driven. While it is mostly wasteful, such behavior gives the person an edge in stumbling upon a good idea. The basic task is to overcome inertia by stirring the "pot of random ideas" constantly so that they can collide. They mostly repel each other, but perhaps a few will connect in new unanticipated combinations. This constant motion helps produce what Simonton (1988) calls "configurations . . . a chance confluence of multiple determinants [which] seem to hang together in a stable arrangement or patterned whole of interrelated parts" (p. 390).

The third level of chance connects an unforeseen experience with a person who is uniquely equipped to grasp its significance. In such a situation, social and psychological factors interact profoundly to illustrate Louis Pasteur's dictum that "chance favors the prepared mind." Luck strikes rarely, and it is a rare person who can make the most of it; how much less probable it is that the two rarities should come together at all, much less with prodigious effect! As an example of a one-in-a-generation person experiencing a once-in-a-millennium event, Austin describes the sequence of developments leading up to Sir Alexander Fleming's discovery of penicillin as follows: (1) He noticed that a mold had accidentally fallen into his culture dish, (2) the staphylococcal colonies residing near it stopped growing, (3) he therefore suspected that a mold must have secreted something to destroy the bacteria, (4) this brought to mind a similar experience he once had, and (5) he began to suspect that this mysterious ingredient—the mold—could be used to destroy staphylococci that cause human infections.

It is interesting to note that the "similar experience" Fleming remembered was his suffering from a cold some nine years earlier, when his own nasal dripping accidentally fell on a culture dish, killing the bacteria around the mucus. He followed this lead with further experimentation but got nowhere until the accident with the mold reminded him of the nasal drippings, but this time he was onto a most celebrated medical discovery. Several intriguing questions come to mind. What if Fleming had worked in squeaky-clean laboratories all of his life, where after-hours clean-up and maintenance were impeccable? What if he were in the habit of wiping his runny nose rather than allowing it to drip? Would mankind then have been blessed with the miracle drugs that now adorn medical practice?

Finally, there is a fourth level of chance, which involves more focus than initiative and personal idiosyncrasy, compared with the first three levels. Austin calls it *altamirage,* a facility for becoming lucky because of the highly individualized action taken by a person. He describes it piquantly as the kind of good fortune "experienced by only *one* quixotic rider cantering in on his own homemade hobbyhorse to intercept the problem at an old angle" (p. 77). Such rare individuals are not only distinctive but often eccentric in their hobbies, personal lifestyles, and motor behaviors. When they succeed in some spectacular way, it seems as if fate has smiled upon them unexpectedly, when in truth they were somehow able to force a smile by tickling fate. "What makes them tick" in such a special way is hidden from view at all times except when they make the great leap forward to discovery.

In an even more embracing characterization of chance, Atkinson (1978) seems to ascribe all human behavior and accomplishment to "two crucial rolls of the dice over which no individual exerts any personal control: the accidents of birth and background. One roll of the dice determines an individual's heredity; the other his formative environment" (p. 221). The happenstances of a person's birth to a particular race, gender, type of family, neighborhood, and school all contribute in many ways to growth and development.

No matter how chance factors are defined, one truism seems irrefutable: Luck interacts with inspiration and perspiration in a mutually dependent way. Without intimations of high potential, no amount of good fortune can help the person achieve greatness; conversely, without some experience of good fortune, no amount of potential can be truly realized.

Final Thought

Several important topics have been omitted from this chapter but are elaborated in other chapters, specifically, definitions of *gifted, tal-* *ented,* and *creativity;* underachievement; and gender differences in accomplishment. To repeat my main underlying theme, it is naive to characterize giftedness strictly from a psychological perspective. Only a psychosocial approach is comprehensive enough to help us understand the multifaceted nature of giftedness and talent.

REFERENCES

Aiken, L. R. (1972). Ability and creativity in mathematics. *Review of Educational Research, 42,* 405–434.

Amabile, T. M. (1983). *The social psychology of creativity.* New York: Springer-Verlag.

Atkinson, J. W. (1978). Motivational determinants of intellective performance and cumulative achievement. In J. W. Atkinson & J. D. Raynor (Eds.), *Personality, motivation, and achievement* (pp. 221–242). New York: Wiley.

Austin, J. H. (1978). *Chase, chance, and creativity.* New York: Columbia University Press.

Bamberger, J. (1986). Cognitive issues in the development of musically gifted children. In R. J. Sternberg & J. E. Davidson (Eds.), *Conceptions of giftedness* (pp. 388–413). New York: Cambridge University Press.

Beery, R. (1975). Fear of failure in the student experience. *Personnel and Guidance Journal, 54,* 190–203.

Benbow, C. P., & Minor, L. L. (1986). Mathematically talented males and females and achievement in the high school sciences. *American Educational Research Journal, 23,* 425–436.

Benbow, C. P., Stanley, J. C., Kirk, M. K., & Zonderman, A. B. (1983). Structure of intelligence in intellectually precocious children and in their parents. *Intelligence, 7,* 129–152.

Branscomb, L. M. (1986). Science in 2006. *American Scientist, 74,* 649–657.

Brody, L. E., & Benbow, C. P. (1987). Accelerative strategies: How effective are they for the gifted? *Gifted Child Quarterly, 31,* 105–110.

Burks, B. S., Jensen, D. W., & Terman, L. M. (1930). *The promise of youth: Follow-up studies of a thousand gifted children.* Stanford, CA: Stanford University Press.

Castenell, L. A. (1983). Achievement motivation: An investigation of adolescents' achievement patterns. *American Educational Research Journal, 20,* 503–510.

Colangelo, N., & Kelly, K. R. (1983). A study of student, parent, and teacher attitudes toward gifted programs and gifted students. *Gifted Child Quarterly, 27,* 107–110.

Coleman, J. S. (1960). The adolescent subculture and academic achievement. *American Journal of Sociology, 65,* 337–347.

Covington, M. V., & Beery, R. (1976). *Self-worth and school learning.* New York: Holt, Rinehart, & Winston.

Covington, M. V., & Omelich, C. L. (1979). Effort: The double-edged sword in school achievement. *Journal of Educational Psychology, 71,* 169–182.

Cox, C. M. (1926). *The early mental traits of three hundred geniuses.* Stanford, CA: Stanford University Press.

Cramond, B., & Martin, C. E. (1987). Inservice and preservice teachers' attitudes toward the academically brilliant. *Gifted Child Quarterly, 31,* 15–19.

Csikszentmihalyi, M. (1988). Society, culture, and person: A systems view of creativity. In R. J. Sternberg (Ed.), *The nature of creativity* (pp. 325–339). New York: Cambridge University Press.

Csikszentmihalyi, M., & Robinson, R. E. (1986). Culture, time, and the development of talent. In R. J. Sternberg & J. E. Davidson (Eds.), *Conceptions of giftedness* (pp. 264–284). New York: Cambridge University Press.

Feldman, D. H. (1984). A follow-up of subjects scoring above 180 IQ in Terman's genetic studies of genius. *Exceptional Children, 50,* 518–523.

Feldman, D. H. (1986). *Nature's gambit.* New York: Basic.

Flynn, J. R. (1987). Massive IQ gains in 14 nations: What IQ tests really measure. *Psychological Bulletin, 101,* 171–191.

Fox, L. H. (1974). A mathematics program for fostering precocious achievement. In J. C. Stanley, D. P. Keating, & L. H. Fox (Eds.), *Mathematical talent: Discovery, description, and development* (pp. 101–125). Baltimore, MD: Johns Hopkins University Press.

Gamoran, A. (1987). Organization, instruction, and the effects of ability grouping: Comment on Slavin's "Best evidence synthesis." *Review of Educational Research, 57,* 341–346.

Gardner, H. (1983). *Frames of mind.* New York: Basic.

Getzels, J. W. (1979). From art student to fine artist: Potential, problem finding, and performance. In A. H. Passow (Ed.), *The gifted and talented: Their education and development* (The 78th Yearbook of the National Society for the Study of Education, pp. 372–387). Chicago: University of Chicago Press.

Goertzel, V., & Goertzel, M. G. (1962). *Cradles of eminence.* Boston: Little, Brown.

Goertzel, M. G., Goertzel, V., & Goertzel, T. G. (1978). *300 eminent personalities.* San Francisco: Jossey-Bass.

Guilford, J. P. (1967). *The nature of human intelligence.* New York: McGraw-Hill.

Guilford, J. P. (1977). *Way beyond the IQ.* Buffalo, NY: Bearly.

Hiebert, E. H. (1987). The context of instruction and student learning: An examination of Slavin's assumptions. *Review of Educational Research, 57,* 337–340.

Katz, I. (1969). A critique of personality approaches to Negro performance, with reseach suggestions. *Journal of Social Issues, 25,* 13–27.

Kulik, C. C. (1985, August). *Effects of inter-class ability grouping on achievement and self-esteem.* Paper presented at the American Psychological Association Convention, Los Angeles.

Kulik, C. C., & Kulik, J. A. (1982). Effects of ability grouping on secondary school students: A meta-analysis of evaluation findings. *American Educational Research Journal, 19,* 415–428.

Kulik, J. A., & Kulik, C. C. (1984). Effects of accelerated instruction on students. *Review of Educational Research, 54,* 409–425.

Maehr, M. (1974). *Sociological origins of achievement.* Monterey, CA: Brooks/Cole.

McNemar, Q. (1964). Lost: Our intelligence—Why? *American Psychologist, 19,* 871–882.

Messick, S. (1989). Meaning and values in test validation: The science and ethics of assessment. *Educational Researcher, 18*(2), 5–11.

Mitchell, J. O. (1974). *Attitudes of adolescents towards mental ability, academic effort, and athleticism.* Unpublished master's thesis, University of Calgary, Alberta, Canada.

Morgan, H. (1981). *Adolescent attitudes toward academic brilliance in the suburban high school.* Unpublished doctoral dissertation, University of Colorado, Boulder.

Oden, M. H. (1968). The fulfillment of promise: 40-year follow-up of the Terman gifted group. *Genetic Psychology Monographs, 77,* 3–93.

Olszewski-Kubilius, P., Kulieke, M. J., & Krasney, N. (1988). Personality dimensions of gifted adolescents: A review of the empirical literature. *Gifted Child Quarterly, 32,* 347–352.

Phenix, P. H. (1964). *Realms of meaning.* New York: McGraw-Hill.

Piechowski, M. M. (1979). Developmental potential. In N. Colangelo & R. T. Zaffrann (Eds.), *New voices in counseling the gifted* (pp. 25–27). Dubuque, IA: Kendall/Hunt.

Piechowski, M. M., Silverman, L. K., & Falk, R. F. (1985). Comparison of intellectually and artistically gifted on five dimensions of mental functioning. *Perceptual and Motor Skills, 60,* 539–549.

Renzulli, J. S. (1978). What makes giftedness? Reexamining a definition. *Phi Delta Kappan, 60,* 180–184.

Renzulli, J. S. (1986). The three-ring conception of giftedness: A developmental model for creative productivity. In R. J. Sternberg & J. E. Davidson (Eds.), *Conceptions of giftedness* (pp. 53–92). New York: Cambridge University Press.

Robinson, H. B. (1977). *Current myths concerning gifted children* (Gifted and Talented Brief No. 5). Ventura, CA: National/State Leadership Training Institute.

Roe, A. (1953). *The making of a scientist.* New York: Dodd, Mead.

Root-Bernstein, R. S. (1987a, March 16). *Education and the fine arts from a scientists' perspective.* A "white paper" written for the College of Fine Arts, University of California, Los Angeles.

Root-Bernstein, R. S. (1987b). Tools of thought: Designing an integrated curriculum for lifelong learners. *Roeper Review, 10,* 17–21.

Rosen, B. C. (1956). The achievement syndrome: A psychocultural dimension of social stratification. *American Sociological Review, 21,* 203–211.

Sears, P. S. (1979). The Terman studies of genius, 1922–1972. In A. H. Passow (Ed.), *The gifted and the talented: Their education and development* (The 78th Yearbook of the National Society for the Study of Education, pp. 75–96). Chicago: University of Chicago Press.

Sears, P. S., & Barbee, A. H. (1977). Career and life satisfaction among Terman's gifted women. In J. C. Stanley, W. C. George, & C. H. Solano (Eds.), *The gifted and the creative: A fifty-year perspective* (pp. 28–65). Baltimore: Johns Hopkins University Press.

Sears, R. R. (1977). Sources of life satisfactions of the Terman gifted men. *American Psychologist, 32,* 119–128.

Simonton, D. K. (1984). *Genius, creativity, and leadership: Historiometric inquiries.* Cambridge, MA: Harvard University Press.

Simonton, D. K. (1988). Creativity, leadership, and chance. In R. J. Sternberg (Ed.), *The nature of creativity* (pp. 386–426). New York: Cambridge University Press.

Slavin, R. E. (1987). Ability grouping and student achievement in elementary schools: A best-evidence synthesis. *Review of Educational Research, 57,* 293–336.

Sloane, K. D. (1985). Home influences on talent development. In B. S. Bloom (Ed.), *Developing talent in young people* (pp. 439–476). New York: Ballantine.

Snyderman, M., & Rothman, S. (1987). Survey of expert opinion on intelligence and aptitude testing. *American Psychologist, 42,* 137–144.

Spearman, C. E. (1927). *Abilities of man: Their natures and measurement.* New York: Macmillan.

Stanley, J. C., & Benbow, C. P. (1986). Youths who reason exceptionally well mathematically. In R. J. Sternberg & J. E. Davidson (Eds.), *Conceptions of giftedness* (pp. 361–387). New York: Cambridge University Press.

Sternberg, R. J. (1986). A triarchic theory of giftedness. In R. J. Sternberg & J. E. Davidson (Eds.), *Conceptions of giftedness* (pp. 223–243). New York: Cambridge University Press.

Sternberg, R. J., & Davidson, J. E. (Eds.). (1986). *Conceptions of giftedness.* New York: Cambridge University Press.

Tannenbaum, A. J. (1962). *Adolescents' attitudes toward academic brilliance.* New York: Bureau of Publications, Teachers College, Columbia University.

Terman, L. M. (1924). Editor's introduction. In L. M. Stedman, *Gifted children: Their nature and nurture.* Yonkers-on-the-Hudson, NY: World Book.

Terman, L. M., & Oden, M. H. (1925). *Mental and physical traits of a thousand gifted children.* Stanford, CA: Stanford University Press.

Terman, L. M., & Oden, M. H. (1947). *The gifted child grows up.* Stanford, CA: Stanford University Press.

Terman, L. M., & Oden, M. H. (1959). *The gifted group at midlife.* Stanford, CA: Stanford University Press.

Thorndike, R. L. (1985). The central role of general ability in prediction. *Multivariate Behavioral Research, 20,* 241–254.

Thorndike, R. L., & Hagen, E. (1959). *Ten thousand careers.* New York: Wiley.

Thurstone, L. L. (1947). *Multiple factor analysis: A development and expansion of "the vectors of the mind."* Chicago: University of Chicago Press.

Trotman, F. K. (1977). Race, IQ, and the middle class. *Journal of Educational Psychology, 69,* 266–273.

Vernon, P. E. (1950). *The structure of human abilities.* London: Methuen.

Walberg, H. J. (1969). A portrait of the artist and scientist as young men. *Exceptional Children, 36,* 5–11.

Walberg, H. J. (1982). Childhood traits and environmental conditions of highly eminent adults. *Gifted Child Quarterly, 25,* 103–107.

Wallace, T., & Walberg, H. J. (1987). *Gifted Child Quarterly, 31,* 65–69.

Wolf, R. (1966). The measurement of environments. In A. Anastasi (Ed.), *Testing problems in perspective* (pp. 491–503). Washington, DC: Council on Education.

4

Giftedness According to the Triarchic Theory of Human Intelligence

ROBERT J. STERNBERG *Yale University*

T hroughout most of this century, intellectual giftedness has been defined as a unidimensional construct. The most frequently used measure of that dimension has been the IQ. Underlying the use of this measure is the belief that intelligence is a single thing and that IQ provides a reasonably good, although not perfect, measure of it. Sometimes, achievement test scores as well as IQ test scores are used in the identification of children as gifted. However, achievement test scores tend to be highly correlated with IQ test scores and measure almost the same thing. The basic thesis of this chapter is that we ought to define intellectual giftedness in a broader way that goes beyond what is measured by either IQ or achievement tests.

Kinds of Intellectual Giftedness

In my *triarchic theory of human intelligence* (Sternberg, 1985, 1988b), there are multiple loci of intellectual giftedness. Giftedness cannot possibly be captured by a single number. Unless we examine the multiple sources of giftedness, we risk missing identification of large numbers of gifted individuals. The three main kinds of giftedness are in terms of *analytic, synthetic,* and *practical* abilities.

Analytic Giftedness

Giftedness in analytic skills involves being able to dissect a problem and understand its parts. People who are strong in this area of intellectual functioning tend to do well on con-

ventional tests of intelligence because these tests place a premium on analytic reasoning. For example, analogy items require analysis of relations between pairs of terms and pairs of relations; synonym items require analysis of which of several answer options most closely corresponds to a given target word; reading comprehension involves analysis of reading passages; matrix problems involve analysis of interrelations among rows and columns of figures, numbers, or whatever. In other words, analytic giftedness is the kind best measured by existing tests.

I frequently give the example of one of my past students, "Alice," who was a prime example of analytic giftedness. Her test scores were excellent, her undergraduate grades were excellent, her teachers thought that she was extremely smart, and she did well in almost all the things that are traditionally viewed as part of intellectual giftedness. However, Alice proved to have difficulty in her later years of graduate school. Although she was excellent at analyzing ideas, she was not nearly so good at coming up with clever ideas of her own.

Synthetic Giftedness

Synthetic giftedness is seen in people who are insightful, intuitive, creative, or just adept at coping with relatively novel situations. People who are synthetically gifted do not necessarily do well on conventional measures of intelligence. Indeed, if they see more in a problem than did the test constructor or read different things into the problem, they may get answers wrong because they don't see things the way

[margin handwritten note: these students have difficulty (coming up w/ their own ideas)]

Preparation of this chapter was supported by a grant from the Spencer Foundation, a grant from the McDonnell Foundation, and Contract MDA90385K0305 from the Army Research Institute.

see things in different ways

many others do. Thus, people with synthetic giftedness may not be the ones with the highest IQs. But they may be the ones who ultimately make the greatest contributions to various pursuits, such as science, literature, art, drama, and the like. Synthetic giftedness is important not only in science and the arts. People who make money in the stock market tend to be contrarians: They can see market phenomena in ways different from that of others analyzing the market. Similarly, people who make money in business tend to be those who see a need for a new product or service or see a new way of delivering such. Synthetic giftedness is important for success in the world but is hardly measured at all by existing tests.

I sometimes give as an example of synthetic giftedness my graduate student "Barbara," who did not do well at all on tests but who was recommended to us at Yale as having unusual creative and insight skills. Despite her low test scores, Barbara proved herself to be enormously creative in producing ideas for new research. Thus, although she may not have been as strong as Alice in analyzing problems, she was much better at coming up with new problems of her own.

Practical Giftedness

A third kind of intellectual giftedness is practical giftedness, which involves applying whatever analytic or synthetic ability you may have to everyday, pragmatic situations. The practically gifted person is one who can go into an environmental setting, figure out what needs to be done to succeed in that setting, and then do it. Many people have strong analytic or synthetic abilities but are unable to apply these abilities to negotiating successful relations with other people, or to getting ahead in their careers. The practically gifted person specializes in these uses of abilities.

I sometimes give as an example of a practically gifted individual my graduate student "Celia," who had neither Alice's analytic ability nor Barbara's synthetic ability, but who was highly successful in figuring out what she needed to do in order to succeed in an academic environment. She knew what kind of research was valued, how to get articles into journals, how to impress people at job interviews, and the like. In other words, although she did not have the skills of an Alice or a Barbara, she could turn the skills she had to her advantage in practical settings.

Combining Analytic, Synthetic, and Practical Giftedness

Of course, people do not possess just one of these different kinds of skills; rather they have some blend of the three. Moreover, this blend can change over time because intelligence can be developed in various directions. People who are extreme in just one of these kinds of giftedness without having at least some skill in the others may tend to be less successful in ultimately convincing people of their worth. For example, someone who is very creatively gifted but cannot demonstrate it in practical settings and cannot convince people of the worth of his or her ideas may encounter frustration at every turn. Thus, an important part of giftedness is being able to coordinate these three aspects of abilities, and knowing when to use which. Giftedness is as much a well-managed balance of these three abilities as it is a high score on any one or more of them. I therefore sometimes refer to a gifted person as a good "mental self-manager."

Loci of Intellectual Giftedness

The kinds of intellectual giftedness described above are general categories of superiority. In order to understand giftedness more fully, one would wish to understand the loci of information processing that contribute to the kinds of giftedness described above.

Components of Intelligence

Metacomponents. In the triarchic theory, executive processes used to plan, monitor, and evaluate problem solving and decision making are referred to as *metacomponents*. Metacomponents are essential to successful problem solving and decision making. I usually refer to eight of them, although I do not believe the list necessarily to be exhaustive.

1. *Problem recognition.* One cannot solve a problem of which one is unaware. Some people excel in problem solving because they are quick to recognize when they have problems or else are good at generating important problems to study. Problem recognition therefore precedes the normal problem-solving cycle in that it is prerequisite for it.

2. *Problem definition.* It is not enough to recognize a problem: One also has to figure out the nature of the problem being confronted. Problem definition involves figuring out just what a given problem is. Some people may be good problem solvers but frequently are solving the wrong problem. People who excel in problem definition are those who, when confronted with a set of environmental contingencies, can figure out exactly what the problem is that needs to be solved. I believe it somewhat ironic that schools tend to present children, even gifted children, with the problems that they are supposed to solve. In everyday life, and in the contributions of great discoverers and inventors, problem recognition and problem definition are key. Therefore, I believe we should give more emphasis to having students figure out problems rather than having us define the problems for them.

3. *Selection of lower order components for problem solving.* This metacomponent involves the choosing of a set of processes to solve a problem. We have a large array of mental processes at our disposal. No matter how well we may execute any one or more of these processes, the processes may not be effective for us if we don't know when to use them. Good problem solvers tend to be people who know which processes to use when.

4. *Ordering of lower order processes into a strategy.* Having chosen a set of processes, it is necessary to sequence them in a way that will lead from the formulation of the problem to its solution. One may choose the correct processes but misorder their execution, with the result that a problem proves to be insoluble. Individuals who excel in this metacomponent are able to sequence steps correctly.

5. *Mental representation of problems.* In order to solve a problem, one needs somehow to represent it mentally. Alternative forms of mental representation are available. For example, linear syllogisms such as "John is taller than Mary. Mary is taller than Susan. Who is tallest?" are soluble through either a linguistic representation of information, a spatial representation of information, or a combination of the two (Sternberg, 1985). Thus, in this and other problems, options are available for the representation of information. However, not all representations of a given problem are equally useful, and how useful a given representation is depends not only on the problem but on the strengths and weaknesses of the individual in exploiting different representations. Hence, someone who excels in mental representation is not someone who is necessarily the best utilizer of every representation, but rather someone who knows what representations to use when, given the constraints of the problem, the time to solve the problem, and that person's abilities.

6. *Allocation of processing resources.* In life, we often have too many things to do in the amount of time we have to do them. Thus, it is necessary to allocate our time and mental processing resources to make as effective use as possible of the time and resources we have at our command. People who excel in this metacomponent are able to set aside the amounts of time and processing resources that best suit a particular problem. Other people may be good problem solvers but spend too long on problems that do not deserve a lot of time and not enough time on problems that deserve more. Effective resource allocation is extremely important, I believe, for successful performance in the complex stream of everyday life.

7. *Solution monitoring.* Solution monitoring refers to keeping track of how problem solving is going as one is solving a particular problem. In other words, it often happens that we start going down a garden path in our problem solving, or else start on a path that may ultimately lead to solution but only after a long uphill battle. Good solution monitors keep track of where their problem solving is leading them, and as they see that the path they are on is not taking them where they want to go, they consider using an alternative strategy.

8. *Solution evaluation.* After one is done solving a problem and has found a solution, the problem-solving cycle is not complete. One still needs to evaluate the quality and appropriateness of the solution. Students in various levels of schooling often make errors in their work because their solutions are unacceptable. They may never bother to check whether they even make sense, much less whether they are exact. We need to evaluate our solution against the original constraints of the problem. People who excel in this metacomponent are not necessarily the best in the other metacomponents. However, they recognize when a solution isn't what it should be and therefore can persevere until they come up with a solution that fits the constraints of the problem.

The metacomponents are interactive with each other. In my experience, it is almost impossible to measure them singly, as almost any task that requires one of them also requires at least several others. We have had some success in measuring metacomponents (Sternberg, 1985), but I doubt that any of our measures or anyone else's are pure. An important locus of giftedness is not only in how adept a person is at executing each of the metacomponents but in how adept the person is at combining them and utilizing them in a well-integrated way.

Performance Components. Performance components are the processes used to solve a problem. Thus, the metacomponents decide what to do, whereas the performance components actually do it. The number of performance components is quite large, as somewhat different performance components are used in the solution of different problems. Nevertheless, there is overlap within classes of tasks. Here, I will discuss some of the performance components involved in inductive reasoning. It is important to note, however, that they represent only a small subset of the total number of performance components in human information processing.

1. *Encoding.* In order to solve a problem, one first has to perceive the terms of the problem and retrieve information in long-term memory relevant to those perceptions. The

process involved is encoding. My own work as well as that of others (e.g., Siegler, 1978) suggests that encoding is a particularly important process in the solution of problems. If one misencodes the terms of a problem, it doesn't matter how well one operates on the encodings: The answer will be wrong, because the problem is incorrectly perceived. Excellent encoders tend to be people with large knowledge bases, who see more in the terms of a problem than might a novice. Expert encoders do not always encode more quickly than novices. Indeed, some of our research suggests that expert encoders may encode the terms more slowly, in part because they have more knowledge to call on, and in part because strong encoding can facilitate later operations on those encodings (see Sternberg & Rifkin, 1979; S. Sternberg, 1969).

2. *Inference.* Inference is involved in seeing the relation between two terms or objects. It is used in a large variety of tasks. Excellent inferrers are good at compare-and-contrast tasks, in that they easily see relations between different things. The inferences that are made depend in part on how well the relevant objects are encoded. One may not be able to infer a relation between two objects if one doesn't know the relevant attributes about which the inference needs to be made.

3. *Mapping.* This process is used to determine relations among relations. For example, it forms the basis for analogical reasoning. We have found that mapping appears somewhat later than other components of performance, perhaps because it involves second-order relations (Sternberg & Rifkin, 1979). It is possible to map relations of successively higher orders, and work with adolescents shows that the acquisition of mapping of successively higher order relations continues throughout adolescence (Case, 1978; Sternberg & Downing, 1982).

4. *Application.* Application is the carrying over of a relation from one set of terms to another. For example, in analogies, it is used to apply a relation previously inferred (Sternberg, 1977; see Mulholland, Pellegrino, & Glaser, 1980, for an alternative point of

knowledge base

view). Good appliers are able to carry over relations they have inferred in one setting to another setting.

Knowledge Acquisition Components.

Knowledge acquisition components are used to learn new information. Gifted individuals are often particularly effective in the use of these components because they are so often adept at learning new information. We have proposed that there are three knowledge-acquisition components that are particularly important in learning (Sternberg & Davidson, 1983).

1. *Selective encoding.* Selective encoding is used to separate information that is relevant to one's purposes from information that is not relevant. For example, when a scientist receives a computer output of data from an experiment, the person often is confronted by a bewildering array of numbers. The good selective encoder knows which of these numbers are important to the particular scientific purposes. Indeed, selective encoding is important in all walks of life. For example, a business executive needs to know which factors are relevant in making a management decision and which factors are of less consequence. A writer needs to know which details to include in an article or a book and which details are of little or no interest. An artist must decide how detailed to make a particular painting or sculpture. Selective encoding, therefore, is important to giftedness in many different walks of life.

2. *Selective combination.* Often, it is not enough just to decide what details are relevant for a particular purpose. One needs to know how to put those relevant pieces of information together. For example, in doing a mathematical proof, the greatest difficulty often is not in figuring out which postulates or theorems are relevant, but in figuring out how to sequence them together to reach the desired conclusion. In any aspect of science, one frequently needs to put together the pieces of a difficult puzzle, much as a detective would when trying to analyze clues at the scene of a crime. Similarly, a doctor needs to figure out how a set of symptoms can be used in combination to help him or her understand the particular presenting syndrome.

3. *Selective comparison.* Selective comparison is the use of old information for new purposes, for example, recognizing how information one has used in one experiment could be carried over to another experiment. Kekulé's dream about a snake dancing around and biting its tail was a selective comparison in that it provided the basis for his figuring out the structure of the benzene molecule. Good selective comparers not only see analogies between present problems and past ones, they also see sources of disanalogy between sets of problems. In other words, they see the dissimilarities as well as the similarities between the old situation and the new one.

The Role of Experience

The components of intelligence described above are always applied in a task that is either relatively *novel* or relatively *familiar*. In some cases, the components of problem solving change as the problem solver becomes more familiar with the task and sees better ways of doing it. But my research has shown that more often the components are executed more rapidly or efficiently but these components do not change as one becomes more familiar with the problem-solving tasks.

Two regions of experience for the application of components to tasks are particularly relevant for understanding intelligence.

1. *Relative novelty.* Insightful people are often particularly adept at applying components of information processing to problems that are relatively novel. They can take a problem that is quite different from ones they have solved before and see a new way of solving it that most other people would not see. The student Barbara, described above, would be a case in point. Coping with relative novelty is an important part of synthetic intelligence. I emphasize the word *relatively* because problems that are extremely novel do not measure intelligence well at all. For example, it would be pointless to give calculus problems to second graders. The region of interest for measuring synthetic ability is the region in which a problem is new, but not completely so. In assessing these skills, we use insight problems (Davidson

& Sternberg, 1984), nonentrenched conceptual projection problems (Sternberg, 1982), and counterfactual analogies (Sternberg & Gastel, 1989). People who are gifted in coping with relative novelty often tend to be our most creative contributors to society.

2. *Relative familiarity.* The region of relative familiarity is the region in which task performance starts to be automatized. Automatization is a critical part of intelligence in that many of the problem-solving behaviors we need to perform are executed again and again and can be executed much more efficiently if they do not consume many resources and even can be executed in parallel. For example, reading is initially a difficult and halting process but becomes smooth and rapid once the bottom-up processing of words and sentences becomes automatized. Driving, speaking, and writing are all processes that can become increasingly automatized with practice. People who are good automatizers have an edge in problem solving over people who are not, in that their automatization frees processing resources that can be used to cope with novelty. People who do not automatize need to devote processing resources to the basics of a problem, with the result that these resources are not free for dealing with the more novel aspects of a given problem.

There is no guarantee that people who are good at coping with relative novelty will be good automatizers. In other words, giftedness does not necessarily apply at all levels of the experiential continuum. A person might be gifted at one level of this continuum or at several levels. I suggested earlier that superior automatization frees resources for coping with novelty. However, there can also be costs associated with automatization. Sometimes, as experts become more and more routinized in their solution of a problem or a class of problems, they lose flexibility. They begin to have difficulty seeing things in new ways. Our research has even found that this loss of flexibility can impede experts more than novices when a task that is familiar to the experts is changed in its essential aspects (Sternberg & Frensch, in press).

Contextual Functions

The components of intelligence are applied to various levels of experience in order to serve three different functions in everyday contexts. Understanding of practical giftedness of the kind demonstrated by Celia requires understanding of the three functions that intelligent thinking and behavior can serve.

1. *Adaptation.* Adaptation refers to the adjustment of one's self and one's behavior to the environment in order to provide a good fit to that environment. When one takes on a new job, a new school, a new relationship, or any kind of new environment, it is usually necessary to adapt in some degree. Our research suggests that practically intelligent people are often good adapters (Wagner & Sternberg, 1985). People who are practically gifted are not necessarily those who are the most superior in executing the components of intelligence. Rather, their superiority is in exploiting these components in practical settings. Others may be better at executing the components in the abstract but do not know how to apply them in everyday life.

Our research suggests that a critical aspect of environmental adaptation is the acquisition and utilization of tacit knowledge (Wagner & Sternberg, 1985). Tacit knowledge is what one needs to know in order to adapt to an environment when that knowledge is not explicitly taught and often not even verbalized. In other words, tacit knowledge comprises the tricks of the trade or the rules of thumb that lead to successful performance in a given domain. It is possible to identify the tacit knowledge within a given domain (see, e.g., Sternberg, 1988b, for an identification of tacit knowledge relevant to business management). Practically intelligent people are adept at picking up this knowledge. The ability to pick up and also to exploit the knowledge does not appear to be much related to conventional IQ.

2. *Selection.* It is not always practically intelligent to adapt to an environment. Sometimes, the smart thing is to get out. If you can see that a job, problem, relationship, or whatever is not one that is suitable for you, it may be best to put it behind you. Practically intelligent people know when to get out. The practically intelligent person is someone who achieves a balance between adaptation and selection. He or she knows when to try to conform to an environment but also when to leave it.

3. *Shaping.* One does not always leave an environment when it is not just so. For example, one may be in a job that is nonideal but see ways to make the job better. Relationships are almost never just what one wants, but it is often possible to shape them into something better. I believe that if there is a pinnacle of practical intelligence, it is in the ability of an individual to shape an environment. Practically intelligent people balance not only adaptation and selection but shaping as well. They have a knack for turning environments into what they want them to be. Often, they are able to convince others to work in the environments that they set up. Great scientists, artists, writers, politicians, and others are people who succeed in shaping their environments. They set the paradigms that others follow, rather than merely following those paradigms. Hence, a practically gifted person is able to set standards, not just conform to them.

Capitalization on Strengths and Compensation for and Remediation of Weaknesses

The main point of this chapter has been that there are many different kinds and loci of giftedness. It is naive to assume that intellectual giftedness can be captured through a single number. However, I do believe that there is one thing that people who are intellectually gifted throughout their lives have in common: They are people who know what they are good at, know what they are not good at, and are able to capitalize on their strengths and compensate for their weaknesses. They also may remediate their weaknesses to the point where these weaknesses no longer get in their way. Over short periods of time, it is possible to appear gifted without knowing and exploiting strengths and without knowing and finding ways around weaknesses. But over the long term, in order maximally to exploit the abilities one has, capitalization and compensation become key.

This view of giftedness is quite different from the standard one. It suggests that people who are intellectually gifted are not necessarily good at lots of things. One cannot add up the scores on a bunch of subtests or items and measure giftedness simply in terms of the number of items correctly answered. A person may show up as far more gifted being good in one thing than being good in a large number of things. The big question is not how many things a person is good at, but how well a person can exploit whatever he or she is good at and find ways around the things that he or she is not good at.

Measurement of Intellectual Giftedness

The kinds of skills described here are not measured well by conventional tests of intelligence or other cognitive abilities. At best, such tests measure analytic skills, but they do not measure synthetic and practical skills. They often do not even measure analytic abilities that well (Sternberg, 1984). Conventional tests of creativity attempt to measure divergent thinking abilities, but they do not measure synthetic intelligence in a way that I consider adequate. Apparently, I am not alone in this perception (see chapters in Sternberg, 1988a). At the time this chapter is being written, I am developing a test, the *Sternberg Triarchic Abilities Test,* that will be published by the Psychological Corporation in 1991 and will measure the various abilities described in this chapter. It will provide separate scores for analytic, synthetic, automatization, and practical abilities, as well as separate scores for verbal, quantitative, and figural processing. The test is being devised at nine levels ranging from kindergarten to adult, and in two forms. I view one special use of the test as for identifying gifted individuals. The advantage to the use of a test such as this one is that intellectual giftedness is defined much more broadly than would be the case if one used only a single IQ score. In this test, there are seven subscores rather than just one global score or just two or three subscores. The idea is that someone may be gifted with respect to some aspects of the theory but not others. Indeed, few people will be gifted with respect to all aspects of the triarchic theory.

How does the newly developed test differ from a conventional intelligence test? It differs in several respects.

First, it is broader, providing measurement of synthetic and practical skills as well as analytic skills. Moreover, separate scores are provided for verbal, quantitative, and figural processing. Thus, it can potentially identify as gifted some children not now being so identified.

Second, even for measuring conventional analytic abilities, the test is, I believe, more progressive than most existing ones. For example, many existing tests measure vocabulary. However, vocabulary is highly dependent on background. It is a measure of the products rather than the processes of learning. Students from diverse backgrounds may do unequally well not because of differences in abilities but because of differences in opportunities provided by diverse environments. In the triarchic test, verbal analytic abilities are measured by learning words from context. Students receive unknown words (neologisms) embedded in context and need to use the context to figure out the meanings of the words. In this way, we measure the precursor to vocabulary—learning from context—and hence zero in on the processes rather than the products of learning.

Third, only the automatization subtest is severely timed. Current tests confound speed with quality of information processing. I believe it is more effective to separate the measurement of mental speed from the measurement of power. Hence, the measurement of speed is through automatization, while other subtests are liberally timed so that the children will have enough time to finish the items.

Fourth, the test is based on a theory of intelligence, rather than being wholly empirically derived. Most existing intelligence tests are atheoretical, or only weakly based on a theory of intelligence. As a result, it is not even clear what they are measuring. We have become stuck with an operational definition of intelligence—whatever it is that the tests test—without really understanding the construct. The triarchic test is an attempt to undergird

the measurement of intelligence with a theory, rather than to proceed entirely on an empirical and atheoretical basis.

How does one actually measure some of the new kinds of abilities not covered on previous tests? Consider, for example, coping with novelty. In the verbal subtest, subjects are given reasoning problems preceded by either factual or counterfactual statements. For example, a verbal analogy might be preceded by a statement such as "Balloons are filled with air" or, in contrast, "Balloons are evil." Subjects have to solve the reasoning problems, assuming that the preceding premise is true. Half the premises are true and half are not. We have found that whereas "Alice types" are better at solving standard verbal analogies, "Barbara types" are better at solving these novel analogies, in that they can more freely assume something that is counterfactual to be true. Alice types have trouble escaping their everyday presuppositions. The quantitative test consists of number matrices in which some of the entries are conventional numerals and some are numbers represented by new numeration systems. Examinees are given the equivalences between the old and new number systems and have to convert back and forth between them in order to solve the matrix problems.

Practical abilities are measured by a variety of item types as well. For example, the verbal subtest consists of informal reasoning items in which examinees must recognize inferential fallacies in advertisements, political slogans, everyday statements, and the like. The idea is for students to show their skill in reasoning with everyday formal reasoning material rather than with academic formal reasoning material. The figural test consists of maps and diagrams, for example, a subway map or a map of the city, and subjects must use the information in the maps to plan efficient routes. Again, the idea is to assess the application of the components of intelligence to practical settings.

Thus, the idea of testing is to expand our notion of giftedness and then be able to identify as gifted those individuals who may be adept in skills that are not measured by conventional tests. These individuals may actually be the ones who later in life make the more important contributions. Analytic abilities alone are generally not enough to enable one to make important contributions. There is a need for synthetic and practical thinking as well.

Developing Intellectual Giftedness

I do not believe that intellectual giftedness is necessarily something with which one is born. It is generally accepted by psychologists that there is some hereditary component to intelligence; at the same time it is accepted that there is more to intelligence than just the effects of heredity. Although one probably cannot take a mentally retarded individual and turn him or her into a budding genius, I believe that it is possible to increase our intellectual skills, and we have now collected evidence that suggests as much (Davidson & Sternberg, 1984; Sternberg, 1987). I have developed a program for teaching intellectual skills at the high school and college levels (Sternberg, 1986) and have worked as well with younger children. The idea of development ought to be combined with the idea of testing: One gives a first form of an intelligence test, then training, then a second form of the intelligence test in order to assess improvement.

What abilities, exactly, should be tapped? My answer to this question is based on my notion that practical intelligence involves capitalization on strengths and compensation for (or remediation of) weaknesses. I believe we need to teach students to make the most of their strengths and to find ways around or ways to improve their weaknesses. We cannot render enormous changes for everyone. What we can do is help students more effectively exploit their intellectual abilities at the same time that they increase those abilities in need of enhancement.

Our experience is that the teaching of intellectual skills does not eliminate individual differences. We will not end up with everyone performing at the same level. To the contrary, when we have trained both children identified as gifted and children not so identified, almost all the children will have improved, but the amount of difference at the end of training is about the same as the amount of difference at the beginning. In other words, the learning curves for gifted and nongifted children are roughly parallel. Everyone improves, but individual differences are maintained. In some cases, there are changes in rank orders of individuals, but we have never found an instance in which we have eliminated differences in performance across individuals.

I do not believe that intelligence is the whole story to giftedness. Creativity is important (see Sternberg & Lubart, in press), as are personality dispositions and motivational states. Hence, when I have talked about giftedness in this chapter, I have focused mainly on its intellectual side, not on all sides. We should not believe that the only possible kind of giftedness is with respect to intelligence.

To conclude, it is possible to understand intellectual giftedness in a way that transcends the bounds of our usual conceptions of intelligence. I propose in this chapter one model of extending these bounds, the triarchic theory of human intelligence. I believe this theory provides us with a firmer and broader base for understanding intellectual giftedness than we have through existing theories and tests designed to measure intellectual excellence.

REFERENCES

Case, R. (1978). Intellectual development from birth to adulthood: A neo-Piagetian interpretation. In R. Siegler (Ed.), *Children's thinking: What develops?* (pp. 37–71). Hillsdale, NJ: Erlbaum.

Davidson, J. E., & Sternberg, R. J. (1984). The role of insight in intellectual giftedness. *Gifted Child Quarterly, 28,* 58–64.

Mulholland, T. M., Pellegrino, J. W., & Glaser, R. (1980). Components of geometric analogy solution. *Cognitive Psychology, 12,* 252–284.

Siegler, R. S. (1978). The origins of scientific reasoning. In R. S. Siegler (Ed.), *Children's thinking: What develops?* (pp. 109–149). Hillsdale, NJ: Erlbaum.

Sternberg, R. J. (1977). *Intelligence, information processing, and analogical reasoning: The componential analysis of human abilities.* Hillsdale, NJ: Erlbaum.

Sternberg, R. J. (1982). Nonentrenchment in the assessment of intellectual giftedness. *Gifted Child Quarterly, 26,* 63–67.

Sternberg, R. J. (1984). What should intelligence tests test? Implications of a triarchic theory of intelligence for intelligence testing. *Educational Researcher, 13*, 5–15.

Sternberg, R. J. (1985). *Beyond IQ: A triarchic theory of human intelligence.* New York: Cambridge University Press.

Sternberg, R. J. (1986). *Intelligence applied: Understanding and increasing your intellectual skills.* San Diego, CA: Harcourt Brace Jovanovich.

Sternberg, R. J. (1987). Most vocabulary is learned from context. In M. G. McKeown & M. E. Curtis (Eds.), *The nature of vocabulary acquisition* (pp. 89–105). Hillsdale, NJ: Erlbaum.

Sternberg, R. J. (Ed.). (1988a). *The nature of creativity.* New York: Cambridge University Press.

Sternberg, R. J. (1988b). *The triarchic mind.* New York: Viking.

Sternberg, R. J., & Davidson, J. E. (1983). Insight in the gifted. *Educational Psychologist, 18*, 51–57.

Sternberg, R. J., & Downing, C. J. (1982). The development of higher-order reasoning in adolescence. *Child Development, 53*, 209–221.

Sternberg, R. J., & Frensch, P. A. (in press). A balance-level theory of intelligent thinking. *Zeitschrift für Pädagogische Psychologie.*

Sternberg, R. J., & Gastel, J. (1989). If dancers ate their shoes: Inductive reasoning with factual and counterfactual premises. *Memory and Cognition.*

Sternberg, R. J., & Lubart, T. I. (in press). An investment theory of creativity and its development. *Human Development.*

Sternberg, R. J., & Rifkin, B. (1979). The development of analogical reasoning processes. *Journal of Experimental Child Psychology, 27*, 195–232.

Sternberg, S. (1969). Memory-scanning: Mental processes revealed by reaction-time experiments. *American Scientist, 4*, 421–457.

Wagner, R. K., & Sternberg, R. J. (1985). Practical intelligence in real-world pursuits: The role of tacit knowledge. *Journal of Personality and Social Psychology, 49*, 436–458.

5

Giftedness from a Multiple Intelligences Perspective

VALERIE RAMOS-FORD and HOWARD GARDNER   *Harvard University*

Introduction: The Traditional Approach to the Assessment of Intelligence

There exists an extensive history of approaches to the identification of gifted and talented individuals. One of the most widely implemented methods has been the administration of a standardized measure of intelligence, the "IQ test." As is widely known, the use of such measures can be traced to the work of Alfred Binet. In the light of the expansion of public education in Paris at the turn of the century, this pioneering psychologist and his colleagues were asked to devise measurements that could assist in identifying students who were likely to succeed or fail in elementary school (Binet & Simon, 1905). In response, they created the first measure of scholastic intelligence and its influential byproduct, the intelligence quotient (or IQ). Binet's ideas made their way swiftly across the Atlantic and were embraced particularly by Lewis Terman and his colleagues at Stanford University, who created the most widely used standardized intelligence instruments (Terman, 1925). Although these measures were indisputably of some value, they led by a perhaps unintended sequence to a narrow view of intelligence—one inextricably tied to those skills most valued in the schools of the time, logical-mathematical and linguistic skill.

Nearly a century later, many educators, scientists, and laypersons still subscribe to this limited view of intelligence. Consequently, hundreds, perhaps thousands of tests of this nature have been developed to measure individuals' capabilities and readiness for a range of academic and professional situations. The testing industry has become an increasingly powerful decision maker in our society. Results of such tests determine who will be admitted into academic settings from preschool to law school and into professions ranging from police work to teaching. While many of these tests are useful as means to specific ends, their proponents often describe the instrument as revealing far more about an individual's capabilities and characteristics than they actually do. Many, if not most, of these tests rely heavily on the test taker's performance on a series of rapid-fire, short-answer or multiple-choice questions anchored in the linguistic and logical-mathematical domains. What results is a snapshot of the individual's capabilities at a precise point in time, in a limited range of intellectual spheres, as discerned in the often-stressful test-taking situation.

The testing community has had a particularly strong impact on the identification and education of the "gifted" and "talented" in our society. In part because of Terman's widely known longitudinal study of California children with high IQs, the terms *giftedness* and *high IQ* had become virtually synonymous by the 1930s. Despite the efforts of many individuals over the last several decades to broaden the definition and assessment of intelligence (Feldman, 1980; Gardner, 1983; Guilford, 1967; Thurstone, 1938), a majority of children who participate in specialized programs for the gifted and talented today are still admitted on the basis of IQ; a score of 129 might keep one child out of such a program while a score of 130 allows another child in.

In response to this situation, we and our colleagues at Harvard Project Zero have set

The work described in this chapter was supported in part by grants from the Spencer Foundation, the W. T. Grant Foundation, and the Rockefeller Brothers Fund.

forth a theory-based, pluralistic view of human cognition: the *theory of multiple intelligences* (MI theory). Based on this view, we are now developing alternative methods of assessment for children from preschool to high school, some of whom are considered to be "at promise" in one or more of the intelligences. In the following pages, we will explore MI theory and examine in detail one of the new approaches to the assessment of intelligence that it has spawned.

A New Look at Intelligence: The Theory of Multiple Intelligences

The MI or "multiple intelligences" theory, which was first presented by Gardner in *Frames of Mind* (1983; see also Walters & Gardner, 1985, 1986) challenges the notion of general intelligence, or *g,* on which most current models of intelligence testing are based. MI theory questions the idea that an individual's intellectual capacities can be captured in a single measure of intelligence; instead, it suggests an approach to assessment that actively seeks to identify what is possibly unique about an individual's proclivities and capabilities in a number of domains of knowledge. As the term *multiple intelligences* suggests, we believe that human cognitive competence is better described as a set of abilities, talents, or mental skills that we have chosen to call *intelligences.*

In our inquiry, we defined *intelligence* as an ability or set of abilities that permit an individual to solve problems or fashion products that are of consequence in a particular cultural setting. Beginning with this definition, we outlined a number of criteria for what constitutes an intelligence. The criteria were drawn from several disparate sources: exploration of trajectories of development in normal and gifted individuals; the breakdown of skills under conditions of brain damage; exceptional populations including prodigies, idiot savants, and autistic children; cross-cultural accounts of cognition; psychometric studies; and studies on the training and generalization of particular skills. From these sources, we arrived at seven

candidate intelligences: *linguistic, logical-mathematical, spatial, musical, bodily-kinesthetic,* and two areas of person-related understanding, *interpersonal* and *intrapersonal.* This list should not suggest that the seven intelligences are the only acceptable candidates. There may well be other intelligences. Moreover, most if not all of these intelligences can be broken down further into subcomponents of skill and understanding. The seven intelligences proposed so far are intended to support the notion of a pluralistic view of intelligence, not to restrict its scope or define it in its entirety.

A common critique of MI theory has focused on the use of the word *intelligence* to describe the competences addressed. Many would suggest that some of the intelligences (for example, musical or bodily-kinesthetic) would more accurately be labeled *talents* or *gifts.* Whereas there is no reason that these competences must be called intelligences, we have deliberately chosen to do so as a challenge to those who consider logical-mathematical and linguistic capability to be on a different plane from other capacities considered in MI theory. As far as we are concerned, one could (and perhaps should) drop the word *intelligence* entirely and speak instead of *linguistic talent* and *logical-mathematical talent.* What we have attempted to do is remove language and logic from the pedestal that they have occupied for generations in western society; instead, we believe we have taken a step toward the "democratization" of the range of human cognitive capabilities.

The Seven Intelligences

Let us briefly summarize each of the seven intelligences. The first we will consider, *linguistic intelligence,* is one of the most studied human competences. In addition, it is one of the two fundamental competences tapped by traditional measures of intelligence. Linguistic intelligence can be broken down into subcomponents including syntax, semantics, and pragmatics as well as more school-oriented skills such as written or oral expression and understanding. It is exemplified in the novelist, lecturer, lawyer, and lyricist, to name but a few adult roles that exploit linguistic intelligence. In children, a capability in the domain might manifest itself in the ability to tell rich and coherent stories or to report with accuracy on experiences they have had—not simply in the ability to repeat sentences and define words on a standardized measure of intelligence.

Logical-mathematical intelligence has also been the subject of considerable scholarly inquiry, particularly in the research of the eminent developmental psychologist Jean Piaget (1983). Logical-mathematical intelligence can also be divided into an inventory of subcomponents: deductive reasoning, inductive reasoning, computation, and the like. Logical-mathematical intelligence is exemplified in the adult role of mathematician or physicist. In children, an ability in the domain might be demonstrated through facility with counting, calculations, and the ability to create useful notations.

Logical-mathematical and linguistic intelligence represent the skills most addressed and valued in traditional school settings. These forms of intelligence are considered to be the archetypes of "raw intelligence," and include those skills that purportedly cut across all domains. Skills in these two domains continue to form the basis of a great majority of standardized measures of intelligence, even though their prominence outside the school setting can be challenged. We list them first not because we consider them to be of greater importance or value than the intelligences yet to be discussed, but rather because they are the two domains of intelligence primarily probed in traditional school and testing situations. Indeed, we propose that all seven intelligences should have equal claim to priority.

Spatial intelligence can be observed in a wide array of vocations and avocations in our and other cultures. It entails the capacity to represent and manipulate spatial configurations. The architect, engineer, mechanic, navigator, sculptor, and chess player all rely upon spatial intelligence in the work they undertake, although perhaps they do not employ that intelligence in exactly the same way. Mechanics rely on their understanding and interrelation of various parts of a machine; painters demonstrate spatial intelligence through their use of space when applying pigments to a canvas; land surveyors must be able to recognize features of a piece of land from a number of different perspectives. In the young child, a capability in this domain might be seen as a facility with puzzles or other spatial problem solving, or an attention to elements of design "all the way around" a clay sculpture. Spatial intelligence is not as highly valued or supported in our current educational system as linguistic and logical-mathematical intelligence, but it is clearly a significant constituent of success in a number of valued adult roles.

The fourth intelligence to be considered is a *bodily-kinesthetic* form. Bodily-kinesthetic intelligence refers to the ability to use all or part of one's body (like one's hands or one's mouth) to perform a task or fashion a product. For example, it is manifest in the dancer, athlete, mime, and surgeon. The child with bodily-kinesthetic intelligence can be seen moving expressively in response to different musical and verbal stimuli, or demonstrating keen athletic ability in organized sports or on the playground.

Musical intelligence is also included in the seven candidate intelligences. It includes pitch discrimination; the ability to hear themes in music; sensitivity to rhythm, texture, and timbre; and in its most integrated forms, the production of music through performance or composition. The musical child can be seen singing to himself as he tells a story, noticing the different sounds in his environment, and so on.

Finally, MI theory recognizes two domains of intelligence about persons. *Interpersonal intelligence* entails the ability to understand other individuals—their actions and their motivations. In addition, it includes the ability to act productively based on that knowledge. In most cases, an individual's interpersonal intelligence is the knowledge that guides her through the social interactions of daily life. In more developed forms, this intelligence can be seen in teachers, therapists, and salespersons as well as religious and political leaders. Children skilled in this domain can be perceived as leaders and organizers in the classroom, as cognizant of how and where other children spend their time, and as sensitive to the needs and feelings of others.

The companion to interpersonal intelligence is *intrapersonal intelligence*. Intrapersonal intelligence refers to a person's understanding of self. It includes knowledge and understanding of one's own cognitive strengths, styles, and intelligences, as well as one's feelings and range of emotions. In addition, it entails the ability to put that knowledge to use in planning and carrying out successful activities. Since this is the most private of the intelligences, it is usually necessary to gain evidence of it through language, music, visual art, or some other form of expression. The young child who demonstrates intrapersonal intelligence might be heard saying to his teacher, "I feel a little sad because my mother didn't bring me to school today. Is it okay if I stay with you until I feel better?", or, "Drawing is my favorite activity, even though I don't draw as well as I want to."

The Autonomy of the Intelligences

According to MI theory, each intelligence is a relatively autonomous intellectual potential that is capable of functioning independently of the others. Particularly convincing support for this claim has been found in the neuropsychological literature. For example, research with brain-damaged adults has repeatedly demonstrated that particular faculties can be lost while others remain relatively or even wholly untouched (Gardner, 1975). To be sure, we are not suggesting that normally functioning individuals will demonstrate intelligences that work completely independently of one another. In fact, it can be assumed that in most cases the intelligences work in consort with one another. What differs among individuals is their *profile* of intelligences. Theoretically, there could be individuals who perform at the same level across intelligences, or even excel in all the intelligences. In most cases, however, individuals exhibit a more jagged profile of abilities, exhibiting relative strengths and weaknesses across domains. A high level of ability in one domain does not, and should not, foretell a similarly high level in another.

The notion of the autonomy of intelligences has significant implications for the gifted and talented community. Armed with research from a variety of sources, this notion supports the often-voiced claim that the concept of a measurable *g* is at best limited and at worst educationally misleading. For example, it cannot be presupposed that an individual who demonstrates exceptional linguistic and logical-mathematic skills on a standardized measure of intelligence will also display exceptional ability (or even interest) in all other domains. Neither can it be presupposed that a child who performs poorly on such a measure will fail to excel in one of the other domains of intelligence. There are many examples that can be given in support of each of the preceding claims: the child with an overall IQ of 130 who has a great deal of difficulty understanding spatial problems; the 10-year-old violin prodigy who has difficulty with her academic subjects; or the poet who has little skill or understanding in the logical-mathematical domain.

The existence of differences within an individual's levels of capability supports the notion that each intelligence proceeds along its own developmental trajectory. In other words, each intelligence is organized in terms of a physical or societal content to which it is particularly attuned; it is capable of developing independently of other intelligences, and independently of an all-encompassing "general intelligence." It follows from these statements that individuals will differ in regard to the areas in which they are considered to be at promise (or at risk), and the extent to which they are considered to be so in each domain.

A Multiple Intelligences Approach to Assessment

There are clearly many areas of human endeavor that contemporary constructs of intelligence fail to explain. Take, for example, the piano virtuoso, the world-class athlete, or the skilled architect. It is likely that the particular intelligences involved in each of these individuals' areas of expertise would not be evident in the results of a measure of intelligence limited to logical-mathematical or linguistic capabilities. While we do not dispute the value of considering IQ as one factor in the identification and placement of a gifted individual, we do suggest that other factors deserve to be taken into account as well. For example, we suggest considering the quality of products that a child has already fashioned; his or her desire for membership in a program and stated goals for participation; his or her performance during a trial week or two with other gifted children; and other such unobtrusive measures. Such a combination of approaches would undoubtedly uncover more gifted individuals with more diverse capabilities than any standardized measure could be reasonably expected to identify.

An MI approach to assessment makes a conscious move away from the traditional testing methods. Toward this goal, we have incorporated a number of features into our current approach to assessment.

Assessment versus Testing. What distinguishes assessment from testing is the former's preference for methods and measures that elicit information in the course of ordinary performances rather than in the decontextualized setting of formal testing. An examination of progress and learning (or lack thereof) should occur every time an individual is involved in a domain and not merely at specified (and often artificial) points during the year. In our view, educators, and the students under their charge, should engage in regular and appropriate reflection on their goals, the various means to achieve them, the success (or lack thereof) in achieving these goals, and the implications of this assessment process for rethinking goals and procedures (Gardner, in press).

Ecological Validity. An essential criterion in our approach is that the assessment be ecologically valid. In other words, we believe that an assessment of a person's capabilities is most informed and useful if it takes place in a situation that closely resembles the individual's actual working conditions. In the case of school-age children, the assessment best occurs in the classroom with materials or instruments that take into account a child's previous experience. This goal can be achieved by supplying classrooms with engaging and enjoyable materials and activities in each of the seven domains of intelligence outlined above. Doing so maximizes the teacher's opportunities to observe a particular child's strengths and interests while simultaneously maximizing the child's opportunity to discover and develop her capabilities and interests in a variety of domains. By directly involving teachers and children in the assessment process, the evaluation of various capabilities can become an ongoing, unobtrusive part of the child's natural learning environment.

Intelligence-Fair Assessment. Another criterion in our approach is that the assessment instruments be "intelligence fair." As already mentioned, most testing instruments rely heavily on the test taker's linguistic and logical-mathematical capabilities as a means of tapping capability in other domains. To as great an extent as possible, our assessment instruments do not confound intelligences; instead, they look directly at the intelligence in operation. For instance, if we are interested in assessing a young child's understanding of numbers, we would not ask her to express her understanding through a verbal response to a verbally presented problem that involves numbers, for example, "If Jeff has 2 apples and Karen has 3, how many apples do they have altogether?" Instead, we might ask the child to play a board game in which she could demonstrate her skill and understanding of numbers and number concepts through the manipulation of various props. Similarly, if we were interested in finding out about a child's social understanding, the assessment would include observing the child as her particular social skills emerge during naturally occurring interactions in the classroom.

Working Styles. In addition to looking at individuals' capabilities in all domains, the MI approach to assessment also considers an individual's approach, or *working style,* in each domain. For example, we consider the level of engagement, persistence, and distractibility of an individual as she interacts with a variety of materials. Such information helps to explain why certain individuals are much more likely than others to develop in a given domain, or to utilize lessons learned in one domain as they attempt to master another pursuit. Gaining information about an individual's working style enables the observer to compare a child's mode of attack across tasks. One can determine if the individual has a consistent working style across domains; whether the individual has working styles that emerge in some domains but not others; and whether there is a connection between particular working styles and the individual's success or failure in a given domain. This information, when coupled with that gained about the individual's particular profile of intelligences, will yield rich information regarding the most effective pedagogical approach for a given individual.

The information yielded from this approach to assessment differs from that yielded by most standardized measures. Whereas the latter usually results in a series of subtest scores and/or an IQ score, the former is best communicated in the richer format of a narrative profile. Such profiles present a more balanced and more holistic view of an individual's intelligence, one that addresses all domains of knowledge and capability as well as the individual's approach to each. In addition, the profile serves as a guide to the kinds of activities that can nurture and support the particular array of capabilities exhibited by the individual. In this way, the assessment process gathers and presents information in a way that is of use to parents, teachers, and the children themselves.

In summary, our approach strives toward making assessment as engaging and enjoyable for the child as it is informative for the adults who interact with the child. It stresses the notion of assessment as an ongoing process, the importance of previous exposure to materials, and the importance of a meaningful context in which the assessment takes place. The integration of assessment into everyday classroom activities in this way also serves to expand and individualize the curriculum, thereby creating an environment that allows all children to discover and explore their special interests and capabilities.

MI theory is a new contribution to the debate about human cognitive potentials and remains largely unstudied and untested. Yet it has proved possible over the last few years to

undertake a number of educational experiments that attempt to develop, and also assess, the broad spectrum of intelligences. At the middle school and high school levels, we are engaged in Arts Propel, a collaboration with Educational Testing Service and the Pittsburgh public schools. Propel represents a large-scale effort to stimulate artistic learning and to assess its level of competence (Gardner, 1989; Wolf, 1988; Zessoules, Wolf, & Gardner, 1988). In middle school we have begun an examination of the practical intelligences needed for success in school; in elementary school a number of teachers in Indianapolis have developed a curriculum that seeks to nurture all of the child's intelligences (Olson, 1988). Because one project is furthest along at this point, we will now describe in some detail our effort with preschool children.

Project Spectrum: An Innovative Approach to the Assessment of Intelligences at the Preschool Level

Project Spectrum is a collaborative project undertaken by several researchers at Harvard Project Zero, David Feldman at Tufts University, and the staff and students at the Eliot-Pearson Children's School. Spectrum was originally designed to identify the different cognitive strengths and interests in a representative group of 4-year-old children. We were interested in whether, during the preschool years, children could be reliably distinguished from one another in terms of their cognitive profiles. However, over its initial 4 years of development, the project evolved into an approach to preschool curriculum with assessment aspects integrated into it at various points (for further details, see Hatch & Gardner, 1986; Malkus, Feldman, & Gardner, 1988; Ramos-Ford, Feldman, & Gardner, 1988; Wexler-Sherman, Gardner, & Feldman, 1988).

Using Feldman's notion of domain-specific development in nonuniversal domains (Feldman, 1986) and the seven domains of intelligence set forth in MI theory as points of departure, and through a series of close observations of preschoolers in the context of the classroom, we identified what we perceived to be the core abilities of this age group in each domain of intelligence. It was soon apparent that there were subcomponents of each domain that also warranted examination; that the intelligences ought to be described in terms of meaningful cultural activities or domains; and that, as mentioned earlier, it was equally important to look at the children's working styles in each domain. What resulted was a general philosophy and approach to preschool curriculum; the development of 15 measures that more formally tap 4-year-olds' cognitive capabilities in the seven domains of intelligence and their subcomponents; and the identification of over a dozen working styles seen in children of this age (see Tables 5.1 and 5.2).

The Spectrum Classroom

A Spectrum classroom contains a rich and diverse set of materials, games, puzzles, and learning areas that are designed to engage and

Table 5.1
Domains of Knowledge Examined in Project Spectrum

Language
  Narrative measure: Storytelling board
  Descriptive measure: Reporter task
Movement
  Creative movement measure: Biweekly
    movement curriculum
  Athletic measure: Obstacle course
Music
  Production measure: Singing activities
  Perception measure: Pitch discrimination
Numbers
  Counting measure: Dinosaur game
  Calculating measure: Bus game
Visual Arts
  Art portfolios (including structured drawing
    activities)
Social
  Social analysis measure: Classroom model
    activity
  Social roles measure: Peer interaction checklist
Science
  Hypothesis-testing measure: Water activity
  Logical inference measure: Treasure hunt game
  Mechanical measure: Assembly activity
  Naturalist measure: Discovery area

Table 5.2
Measures of Working Style Examined by Project Spectrum

Child is:
  Easily engaged/reluctant to engage in activity
  Confident/tentative
  Playful/serious
  Focused/distractible
  Persistent/frustrated by task
  Apt to reflect on own work/impulsive
  Apt to work slowly/apt to work quickly
  Conversational/quiet
Child:
  Responds to visual/auditory/kinesthetic cues
  Demonstrates planful approach
  Brings personal strength/agenda to task
  Finds humor in content area
  Uses materials in unexpected ways
  Shows pride in accomplishment
  Is curious about materials
  Shows concern over "correct" answers
  Focuses on interaction with adult
  Transforms task/materials

interest preschoolers. For example, art materials, musical instruments, a dramatic play area, puzzles and games that stimulate numerical and logical thinking, and a natural science corner are made available to the children. In addition, there are regularly scheduled activities such as creative movement sessions, and a class newspaper in which children can regularly demonstrate their oral language skills by reporting on the events of their weekends and vacations. Through careful observations in such a setting, one can gain considerable information about the profile of interests and abilities of individual children.

The 15 measures we have developed (see Table 5.1) are intended as a complement to the enriched classroom environment. They have been designed to look specifically at a child's capability when there is some uncertainty about her level of understanding or skill in a particular domain based on the less formal, everyday observations in the classroom. The more formal nature of these measures should not suggest that they be used in isolation; the information gained from them should always be used in concert with other available sources of information. In addition, the information gained should be treated as a measure of the child's ability in a domain at a precise point in time, not as a measure of the child's overall potential in a domain. The only way to find out how a child's capability in a domain will evolve is to reassess the child on a regular and reliable schedule.

Criteria for Developing Spectrum Materials

A main criterion in the development of Spectrum materials is that they be stimulating and enjoyable to the preschool-age child. Our materials are made to be sturdy, engaging, and inviting so that children are comfortable working in many content areas regardless of their levels of skill. Themes within the activities are geared toward the preschooler's world of experiences and interests.

For example, in a popular Spectrum activity in the area of logical-mathematical intelligence, or number skills, the child plays a board game in which her game piece, a small dinosaur, must escape from the hungry mouth of a large dinosaur. The number and direction of moves are determined by two dice, one that displays numbers and another that features plus and minus signs. Through a series of random and deliberate placements of the dice, the child attempts to maneuver her dinosaur to safety. This activity results in a quantified account of the child's ability working with the number concepts embedded in the game.

In the storyboard activity, a measure of narrative language skills, a child is presented with an enticing assortment of characters, props, and creatures that can be incorporated into a story. The materials provide the child with a stimulating basis for telling a fanciful story, while simultaneously providing the teacher with an opportunity to look at the child's use of vocabulary and sentence structure, as well as the child's ability to tell a thematically coherent story. For children who are more comfortable using descriptive language, a complementary reporting activity taps many of the same components measured by the storytelling activity.

Recording Information Gathered through the Spectrum Approach

The Spectrum approach provides teachers (and others associated with the preschool-age child) with a means of organizing and recording their observations of individual children. Spectrum measures use a range of different methods for recording and scoring a child's performance in the various domains. Depending on the nature of the activity and the domain it focuses on, these methods range from the use of fully quantified score sheets to more holistic and subjective checklists. An example of the former would be the scoring system used for the aforementioned dinosaur game. An example of the latter would be the checklists we have devised for recording a child's engagement and production in the visual arts and creative movement activities. We expect that most teachers will not find it practical, or even possible, to administer formally all 15 measures to all children in their class, nor will they use all the methods of recording that we provide. (This procedure has been done in the past, but chiefly for research purposes; see Feldman et al., 1989). Nonetheless, our materials and measures are invaluable for those times when more structured observation and methods of recording are deemed necessary.

The Spectrum Profile

By the end of a school year, through the implementation of the Spectrum approach, teachers should have gathered a wealth of information about the intellectual strengths and working styles of each child under their direction. This information becomes the basis of *Spectrum profiles*. The profile is a relatively brief individualized written report generated from the child's formal and informal engagement with Spectrum materials over the course of the school year. The profile, in straightforward language, describes the particular pattern of intellectual capabilities and working styles exhibited by each child. It addresses relative strengths and weaknesses within a child's own range of capabilities, and occasionally it records "absolute" strengths when the child's performance stands out in relation to the larger population of preschoolers.

Consistent with our belief that assessment should be in service of individuals and not simply a means of ranking them, the profile provides concrete yet informal suggestions for follow-up activities for each child. For example, if a child demonstrates a strength or interest in the bodily-kinesthetic domain, suggestions are made for activities in the home and community that might serve to support the child's capabilities in the domain. Similarly, if a child demonstrates difficulty with number skills, the report suggests activities that could assist in the child's remediation in the domain; for example, additional counting and calculating games might be suggested and described.

In summary, the profile aims to present information that can be put to use in service of an individual's future involvement and success in a range of intellectual undertakings. The Spectrum profile is intended as a guide to the individual's profile of cognitive capabilities and working styles and to the specific needs and opportunities that accompany such a profile.

Toward a More Capacious View of Giftedness

Project Spectrum serves as one model that incorporates key elements of the new approach to assessment we are suggesting. We believe that it is an ecologically valid, "intelligence-fair," and unobtrusive approach to assessment that yields rich information about a child's distinctive profile of capabilities, interests, and styles of learning across the many domains of human cognition. In addition, Spectrum presents multiple opportunities to assess a child's evolving profile of intelligences by bringing the assessment process out of the testing room and into the classroom.

It is particularly important during the preschool and early elementary years that opportunities be maximized for children's exploration across a range of domains. While the discovery of particular interests and abilities can be quite spontaneous for some gifted children, specifically designed activities, materials, or situations may be needed to instigate such a discovery in many children, even those who are considered to be "at promise." A Spectrum classroom presents all children with opportunities to explore their interests and abilities across domains, while simultaneously providing their teacher with a systematic way of assessing and, more importantly, responding to each child's needs. Thus, assessment becomes an ongoing process embedded within the learning environment instead of a decontextualized task that occurs at an unmotivated time during the year.

The MI approach to assessment strives toward identifying the gift in every individual. We have suggested that the first step toward achieving this goal is to address capabilities in the many domains of human cognition discussed above, instead of focusing exclusively on those in the logical-mathematical and linguistic domains. In addition, we suggest broadening the focus of assessment to include the identification of *relative strengths* (those an individual exhibits in relation to her own profile of cognitive capabilities) as well as *absolute strengths* (those an individual exhibits in relation to the wider population of his peers). Should this procedure be adopted, informed educational and extracurricular decisions can be made that are based on the learner's complete profile of intellectual capabilities, not simply on her strengths (or weaknesses) in isolation.

It is likely that the MI approach to assessment will identify many more children as being "at promise" than the traditional methods of the past. The identification of a wider array of capabilities in a wider population of individuals presents a challenge not only to the schools but also to families and communities to create opportunities in which these diverse capabilities can be supported and developed. To the extent that children so identified can be included in official gifted programs, both the children and the programs will be beneficiaries. But even if it is not possible to include every gifted child in an official program, the very exercise of recognizing gifts and laying out options can be expected to have beneficial effects for each child, and perhaps also for the surrounding culture.

REFERENCES

Binet, A., & Simon, T. (1905). Méthodes nouvelles pour le diagnostic du niveau intellectuel des anormaux. *L'annee Psychologique, 11,* 245–336.

Feldman, D. H. (1980). *Beyond universals in cognitive development.* Norwood, NJ: Ablex.

Feldman, D. H. (1986). *Nature's gambit.* New York: Basic.

Feldman, D. H., Gardner, H., Adams, M., Hatch, T., Goldman, J., Krechevsky, M., Ramos-Ford, V., & Viens, J. (1989). *Project Spectrum: July 1987–June 1989.* Final Annual Report to the Spencer Foundation, Chicago.

Gardner, H. (1975). *The shattered mind.* New York: Knopf.

Gardner, H. (1983). *Frames of mind: The theory of multiple intelligences.* New York: Basic.

Gardner, H. (1989). Zero-based arts education: An introduction to Arts Propel. *Studies in Art Education, 30*(2), 71–83.

Gardner, H. (in press). Assessment in context: The alternative to standardized testing. In B. Gifford (Ed.), *Report of the Commission on Testing and Public Policy.* Boston: Kluwer.

Guilford, J. P. (1967). *The nature of human intelligence.* New York: McGraw-Hill.

Hatch, T., & Gardner, H. (1986). From testing intelligence to assessing competences: A pluralistic view of intelligence. *Roeper Review, 8,* 147–150.

Malkus, U., Feldman, D. H., & Gardner, H. (1988). Dimensions of mind in early childhood. In A. Pellegrini (Ed.), *The psychological bases of early education* (pp. 25–38). Chichester, England: Wiley.

Olson, L. (1988). Children flourish here: Eight teachers and a theory changed a school world. *Education Week, 7,*(1), 18–19.

Piaget, J. (1983). Piaget's theory. In P. Mussen (Ed.), *Handbook of child psychology* (pp. 21–27). New York: Wiley.

Ramos-Ford, V., Feldman, D. H., & Gardner, H. (1988). A new look at intelligence through Project Spectrum. *New Horizons For Learning, 8* (Spring), 6, 7, 15.

Terman, L. M. (1925). *Genetic studies of genius* (Vol. 1). Stanford, CA: Stanford University Press.

Thurstone, L. (1938). *Primary mental abilities.* Chicago: University of Chicago Press.

Walters, J., & Gardner, H. (1985). The development and education of intelligence. In F. Link (Ed.), *Essays on the intellect* (pp. 1–21). Washington, DC: Curriculum Development Associates.

Walters, J., & Gardner, H. (1986). The theory of multiple intelligences: Some issues and answers. In R. Sternberg & R. Wagner (Eds.), *Practical intelligences* (pp. 163–182). New York: Cambridge University Press.

Wexler-Sherman, C., Gardner, H., & Feldman, D. H. (1988). A pluralistic view of early assessment: The Project Spectrum approach. *Theory into Practice, 28,* 77–83.

Wolf, D. P. (1988). Opening up assessment. *Educational Leadership, 45*(4), 24–29.

Zessoules, R., Wolf, D. P., & Gardner, H. (1988). A better balance: Arts Propel as an alternative to discipline-based arts education. In J. Burton, A. Lederman, & P. London (Eds.), *Beyond DBAE: The case for multiple visions of art education* (pp. 117–130). North Dartmouth, MA: University Council on Art Education, Southeastern Massachusetts University.

6

Toward a Differentiated Model of Giftedness and Talent

FRANÇOYS GAGNÉ   *Université du Québec à Montréal*

Definitions of giftedness abound. Among the better known are those of the U.S. Office of Education (USOE) and of Joseph S. Renzulli. The USOE definition presents giftedness as follows:

> Gifted and talented children are those identified by professionally qualified persons who by virtue of outstanding abilities, are capable of high performance. Children capable of high performance include those with demonstrated achievement and/or potential ability in any of the following areas singly or in combination: 1. general intellectual ability; 2. specific academic aptitude; 3. creative or productive thinking; 4. leadership ability; 5. visual and performing arts; 6. psychomotor ability (Marland, 1972, p. 5).[1]

In his 1979 monograph, Renzulli criticizes the above definition and then defines giftedness as the conjunction of three characteristics: above-average ability, high creativity, and high task commitment (motivation). This trio of abilities expresses itself in various fields of human activity.

In spite of the popularity of the above definitions, many experts in the field of giftedness continue to propose their own definitions. In fact, there are so many of them that an entire volume (Sternberg & Davidson, 1986), as well as a classification system (Stankowski, 1978), has been devoted to the question. Two terms appear regularly in most of these definitions: *giftedness* and *talent*. The odd thing is, few experts have stopped to compare the two terms and to determine whether they represent fundamentally distinct concepts. In most texts they are synonyms, although a few authors do associate giftedness with intellectual abilities

and talent with nonintellectual abilities, such as artistic, technical, or athletic skills (Gagne, 1985). A few others see a continuum, with *talented* at a lower point than *truly gifted*.

I propose that the terms *giftedness* and *talent* be given distinct significations that are quite close to those used in popular language, and easily operationalized. In the next section, by way of an introduction, I have gathered together a few observations gleaned from diverse sources. Try to identify which two phenomena will define the two concepts of giftedness and talent, respectively, in the examples below.

Preliminary Observations

1. When Greg Louganis, Olympic and world champion diver, was only 18 months old, he accompanied his mother to his older sister's dance class. During this short visit he showed a great sense of balance and a precocious mastery of muscular control by learning to do a headstand and a somersault. At the age of 9 he began a more systematic training in diving and had confirmed the international caliber of his talent in this field by the age of 15 (Michelmore, 1988).

2. "The strength of the East Europeans is hard earned. Their rigorous training practices are legendary. In Rumania, for instance, tots are singled out as young as age four for training at one of the country's elite sports schools. To gain admission, the tumbling tykes not only have to excel at tests that demonstrate speed, flexibility, and abdominal strength, but they must also convince coaches that they possess

The author expresses his most sincere thanks to Michel Ferrari, MA student at Université du Québec à Montréal, for his translation work.

that unquantifiable drive that makes for champions. Once admitted, they find that their academic schedules and lives revolve around training" (Smolowe, 1988, p. 56). Only 10 years later, the more talented will find themselves members of their country's national and Olympic teams.

3. Recently, at a picnic, I observed the oldest son of a friend of mine. This child, barely 11 years old, brilliantly led the games of about a dozen children, most much younger than himself. I pointed out to his mother that his behavior with these younger children (a mixture of leadership, concern, and gentleness) impressed me greatly, considering his age, and that he seemed to have a real aptitude for interpersonal and social relations. His mother replied that ever since the age of 2 he had shown an interest in other children, especially those younger than himself.

4. One of my colleagues, a psychologist at an elementary school, recently told me that of the 20 or so children (mostly boys) referred to her over the previous months because of repeated failure in school and social inadaptation in class, more than half had turned out to be decidedly above average in terms of intellectual giftedness (IQ scores over 130). Not only that, they were both interested and very cooperative during the interview and the testing.

5. Some years ago, Laval University, located in the provincial capital of Québec, set up a program to evaluate the physical condition of the local population, made up mostly of civil servants. They discovered that some of them had a competence (in terms of physical force, flexibility, cardiovascular capacity, and other characteristics of fitness) that was far above average, and this without practicing any particular sport.

6. Perhaps you know of people who astound their friends with the ease and rapidity with which they improve, no matter what new type of activity they become involved in. Whether it is an academic subject, an artistic activity, an administrative task, or a sport, these people quickly outdistance other novices and rapidly achieve a level of performance that attests to their undeniable talent, all the while gaining

the envy of those who have to "slave away" in order to achieve a comparable level of skill.

The Differentiated Giftedness-Talent Model

The above examples serve to distinguish two sets of behavior that are uncommon or extraordinary. On the one hand, there are those behaviors that are naturally easy, in other words, that are not the result of systematic training in a particular field of activity. This spontaneous ease is particularly evident in young children, since no one doubts the absence of training. It is important to realize, however, that one may find this type of gift in adults who take up a new type of activity for the first time and show progress that is well above average. On the other hand, some of the examples given above describe an exceptional level of mastery in a particular field of human activity that is the result of systematic training wherein the environment plays an especially important role. Essentially, what I propose to distinguish by using the terms *giftedness* and *talent* are *natural* abilities, or *aptitudes,* and *developed* abilities, or *skills.* Here is a more formal definition of these two concepts.

> *Giftedness* corresponds to competence that is distinctly above average in one or more domains of human aptitude. *Talent* corresponds to performance that is distinctly above average in one or more fields of human activity.[2]

As to their different types, I propose to subdivide aptitudes (gifts) into four categories (intellectual, creative, socioaffective, and sensorimotor) and talents into five categories (academic, technical, artistic, interpersonal, and athletic). Both sets of categories are illustrated in Figure 6.1. As shown in the figure, talents are considered to be the developmental product of an interaction between aptitudes and intrapersonal and environmental catalysts.

How do aptitudes and talents differ from one another? Not all of the six differentiating characteristics presented below refer to differences in the intrinsic nature of the two constructs. Moreover, in order to maximize their

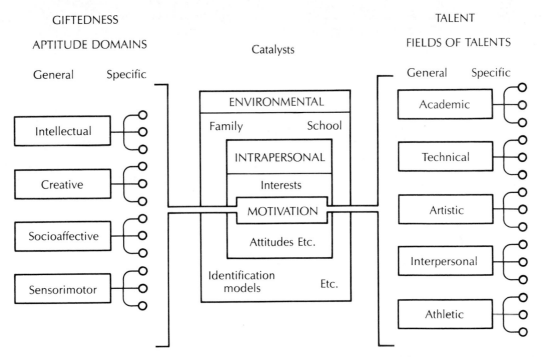

Figure 6.1 The differentiated giftedness-talent model.

differences, I have sometimes a bit exaggerated the descriptions. However, additional nuances will be presented later in the chapter.

1. *Person/context.* Aptitudes are named for personal characteristics (e.g., intelligence, sociability, empathy, strength, visual acuity, etc.), whereas talents are named for a field of human activity (e.g., mathematics, literature, science, dance, swimming, etc.).

2. *Adverb/indirect complement.* It is generally easier to label an aptitude by using an adverb (e.g., intellectually, creatively, socially, or physically gifted). Talents are best described using an indirect complement of place (e.g., To be talented in the visual arts, computer programming, crafts, music, fencing, hockey, etc.).

3. *Process/product.* In any given activity, aptitudes usually specify the process or the way in which the activity is realized, whereas talents correspond to the product of that activity. Thus, the realization of a painting (the product of an artistic talent) calls upon ap-

titudes that are brought into play during its production: probably cognitive ones, sometimes creative ones, and certainly sensorimotor ones.

4. *Nature/nurture.* Because they describe characteristics of the individual, aptitudes have a significant hereditary component. This explains the impression of ease, natural grace, and spontaneity, commonly called *natural talent.* Of course, heritability by no means implies immutability, although the genetic baggage does impose certain constraints; in particular, it places a ceiling on learning. Talents, on the other hand, depend much more on the environment for their development; this is due mostly to the important role of the catalysts and of systematic training.

5. *Potential/actualization.* As a corollary to the previous characteristic, one might say that aptitudes constitute a *potential* in the popular meaning of the word. Talents correspond to the actualization of this potential in one or more fields of activity. Put another way, this implies that aptitudes are only useful in everyday life to the extent that they contribute to the development and the expression of particular talents.

6. *Testing/performing.* Although aptitudes can be directly observed in action, the best way to precisely measure a person's level of aptitude in a given domain is to use standardized tests (for example, intelligence or creativity tests, tests that evaluate flexibility or visuomotor coordination, etc.). Talents, on the contrary, are best measured in a real-life context and by using the actual activity that serves to define the talent. Thus, it is on the ice that the hockey player's talent is evaluated, with an instrument for musical talent, and in the workshop for a handyman.

This model always generates questions when I present it as part of a university course or in workshops with educators. Some questions concern the nature of the model's components or their interaction; others have to do with the concrete implications of the model for the description, screening, and servicing of students considered gifted or talented. The following series of comments are aimed precisely at providing answers to these diverse questions, to "put some meat on the bones," so to speak. They have been grouped together according to the three major components of the model: aptitudes, catalysts, and talents (see Figure 6.1). A few words will also be said about the dynamic interaction among them.

About the Aptitudes Component

As previously stated, *aptitudes* are the building blocks of talents. Now, let us examine some of their characteristics more closely.

The Term Aptitudes

Abilities was used in the original presentation of this model to designate this component related to gifts. At that time I hesitated to employ the term *aptitudes* because of the controversy among psychometricians surrounding its use (Mehrens, 1982). For example, Anastasi (1980) claims that this term has acquired "misleading

surplus meanings" (p. 2), and that the very high correlations between measures of aptitudes and those of performances make any distinction between the two purely artificial. She suggests using the combinatory expression *developed abilities* instead. On the other hand, Cronbach and Snow (1977) defend the conceptual usefulness of a distinction between potential and performance and define aptitude as "any characteristic of a person that forecasts his probability of success under a given treatment" (p. 6). Snow (1980) notes that the high correlations observed only confirm the good predictive power of aptitude tests as indicators of greater ease and speed of subsequent learning. One wonders why Anastasi so emphatically rejects the word *aptitude* while accepting the word *capacity,* a clear synonym for aptitudes. She defines *capacity* in the following way: "Only in the sense that a present behavior can be used as an indicator of other, future behavior can we speak of a test measuring 'capacity'" (1988, p. 25). In this context, the term *aptitudes* appears to be an appropriate description of the abilities that constitute giftedness. This also permits using the term *abilities* in more general fashion as an indicator of both aptitudes (natural abilities) and talents (developed abilities).

The Taxonomy

Figure 6.1 proposes four general aptitude domains: intellectual, creative, socioaffective, and sensorimotor. When I first described this taxonomy (Gagné, 1985), I had reservations about its exhaustiveness. I even went so far as to create a category *other* as an "expansion port" for adding any categories that might have been missed. Since then I have watched for other categories of aptitudes and analyzed taxonomic systems and dozens of lists of characteristics and nomination forms in the hope of finding new categories. I found nothing that could not be classified within one or another of the four domains. There are other indications that these four general domains cover the spectrum of human aptitudes. For instance, Bloom (1985) also identifies four general areas of "talent" quite similar to mine: athletic or psychomotor, artistic, cognitive or intellectual, and interpersonal relations. In the literature on personality structure (Rapaport, 1959) one also finds a distinction between three major dimensions of behavior: *cognitive* (thoughts), *affective* (emotions), and *conative* (goal-directed actions).

The Subcategories

Owing to important differences among authors, and because of insufficient research, it is not possible to specify clearly the particular subdomains of aptitudes. Subcategories can vary considerably in the intellectual domain alone. Using factor analysis many researchers have tried to identify relatively independent groups and subgroups of intellectual aptitudes. Work by Thurstone, Kelly, Guilford, Vernon, and many others, synthesized by Anastasi (1988, Chapter 13), suggest a large variety of plausible candidates for specific intellectual abilities (e.g., verbal, spatial, numerical, perceptual, mechanical, and mnemonic ability). Others, starting from different theoretical frameworks, have proposed their own personal taxonomy of intellectual aptitudes (see, for example, Sternberg's triarchic theory of intelligence [Sternberg, 1985], Gardner's theory of multiple intelligences [Gardner, 1983], and Chapters 4 and 5 in this volume). How does one choose from among this "cafeteria" of propositions?

A similar problem arises with creativity. In fact, the list of creative aptitudes goes well beyond the classic four of fluency, flexibility, originality, and elaboration proposed by J. P. Guilford and E. P. Torrance. Not only does it include a large number of thinking skills deemed essential to efficient creative problem solving (e.g., analogical reasoning, synthesis, visualization, etc.), but some even suggest that "some personality traits could be viewed as 'creative abilities,' for example, sense of humor, curiosity, artistic interests or talent, tolerance for ambiguity, spontaneity, and perhaps others" (Davis & Rimm, 1989, p. 209). How can a limited number of nonoverlapping subcategories be extracted from such diversity?

As for the socioaffective domain, while recent work (see especially Ford & Tisak, 1983) seems to confirm the construct validity of certain instruments used to measure social ap-

titudes, this area of research is still much too embryonic for experts to start mapping its outlying areas.

Finally, undoubtedly because of the social importance of sports and athletics, the domain of sensorimotor aptitudes appears better charted, for example: abilities related to the various senses; precision and speed of visuomotor coordination; gross motor abilities (strength, speed, flexibility, etc.); balance or kinesthetic abilities; and so forth (Bruininks, 1978). Still, the classification systems remain numerous.

Refinement of a taxonomic system is of great scientific interest—and not only heuristic—as attested by the utility of the classification system of living things in the natural sciences and of the periodic table of elements in chemistry. Nevertheless, we are far from reaching a consensus on the nature of these subcategories of aptitudes.

The Role of Creativity

The present model gives a much more modest role to creativity than that which the majority of experts reserve for it. For instance, Renzulli (1979; see also Chapter 9 by Renzulli and Reis in this volume) makes creativity one of three essential components of giftedness. The literature that Renzulli cites to justify this inclusion appears convincing at first glance. However, the apparent preeminence of creativity may stem from a bias in the fields selected for study (architecture, arts, sciences) and in the types of expertise studied. For example, Renzulli extensively cites MacKinnon's (1964) study in which a panel of judges identified a group of prominent architects on the basis of originality of thought, ingenuity, and the rejection of established conventions, among others. It is hardly surprising that creative individuals were identified using criteria such as these. True, "It is usually the originality, novelty, or uniqueness of a person's contribution that brings him or her to the attention of the public" (Renzulli, 1979, p. 15). However, this statement refers to individuals who can be considered agents of change, innovators, inventors, and the like. What about celebrated athletes, whose accomplishments make international headlines; musicians of international repute; teachers or professors who have positively influenced their students; and many others who have attained a certain prominence, if not absolute renown, by means of interpretive performances or other skills, and not principally through creative aptitudes? Creativity may be regarded as a major determinant of exceptional performance in certain fields, but not in all. It should be considered one sphere of aptitudes in which giftedness can express itself, but not among others.

Nature versus Nurture

Aptitudes, because they represent personal characteristics, depend in part on heredity. There was once a time (not so long ago!) when there were many defenders of a purely environmentalist position, as many as those who maintained a strictly hereditarist one. However, numerous studies conducted over the last 20 years, and not only concerning intellectual aptitudes, have clearly shown the untenability of these two extremes. An interactionist position, in which these two developmental principles are recognized as being joint agents, appears to have greater validity. One of the foremost specialists in this field of study synthesizes the major findings to date as follows:

> Not only my own work but research by many others also supports the modest conclusion that we are different from one another on both genetic and environmental bases—not only in intellectual ability but also in personality, cognitive style, gestural and postural communication, linguistic style, and probably all other measurable characteristics. I am hard pressed to think of any aspect of human behavior for which genetic as well as environmental differences will not explain part of the variability. Studies that have addressed the possibly different amount of genetic and environmental variability have failed to find consistently different degrees of "heritability" among any measured behavioral traits. Everything seems to have moderate "heritability." (Scarr, 1981, pp. 526–527)

The first message of behavioral genetic research is that genetic influence on individual differences in behavioral development is usu-

ally significant and often substantial. Genetic influence is so ubiquitous and pervasive in behavior that a shift in emphasis is warranted: Ask not what is heritable, ask what is not heritable (Plomin, 1989, p. 108).

The interactionist position allows for a certain malleability of aptitudes, confirmed through everyday experience. This means that aptitudes can and do develop, not only through maturation but also as a result of systematic training. However, this malleability remains within limits fixed by heredity; time and again research has shown that programs aimed at developing intellectual aptitudes attain modest though statistically significant results (Snow, 1982). The hereditary element also explains the precocious spontaneous experience of certain behavior. This is often called "natural talent," but seen through the lens of the present model, it is the expression of a natural aptitude in a particular field of talent. Recall Observation 2 at the beginning of this chapter: If there were no hereditary component to aptitudes, no selection process would be necessary, only efficient training.

Aptitudes and Constitution

Figure 6.1 retains only those elements needed to show the difference between giftedness and talent. One ingredient of talent that is absent, apart from systematic training or learning, is physical *constitution* as distinct from physical aptitudes. Ballet specialists will tell you, for example, that there exists an ideal ballerina's physique and that the various constitutive elements of this physique are actively sought out when selecting candidates for advanced training in ballet. In the same way, finger length of pianists will, to an extent, determine the range of their repertoire. This phenonmenon is even more evident in sports, to the point where in eastern block countries young athletes are frequently directed toward certain athletic disciplines depending on the strengths and weaknesses of their physical constitution. These constitutive elements are not aptitudes per se, but they are constraints that inevitably limit the level of maximal performance that an individual may aspire to attain.

Diversified Giftedness

When we speak of "giftedness" in general we refer to a group of persons who are much too heterogeneous to be easily characterized. Furthermore, research has shown that intragroup variability among *intellectually* gifted people is much larger than their commonalities (Roedell, Jackson, & Robinson, 1980). Imagine, then, the differences between these individuals and those who are physically or socially gifted! Thus, I feel it is imperative not to speak of "gifted people" in general, except to designate the large target population that constitutes our professional area of interest. In every other case, we should specify the particular type of giftedness to which we refer by using the appropriate adverb. By so doing, we will probably notice that we almost always speak of *intellectual* giftedness. Maybe we will also realize that we often confuse intellectual and creative giftedness in our screening instruments. Finally, perhaps we will differentiate our interventions so as to better adapt them to the specific needs of those who have different gifts, as we usually do for persons who manifest different talents.

About the Catalysts Component

As their name indicates, the *catalysts* act as positive (or negative) moderators that transform (or do not transform) aptitudes into talents. I find it useful to distinguish between two general types of catalysts: *intrapersonal* (e.g., curiosity, motivation, perseverance, autonomy, etc.) and *environmental* (e.g., parents, siblings, peers, school, identification models, etc.).

Intrapersonal Catalysts

In most lists of characteristics of the gifted, descriptions of aptitudes are interspersed with descriptions of intrapersonal catalysts. This is partly understandable inasmuch as both contribute to the emergence of talents, but this interpenetration of the two categories maintains an ambiguity concerning their respective roles. In fact, aptitudes are involved as *constituent* elements of talents, whereas the catalysts (both intrapersonal and environmental) provide a framework that *supports the development* of talents. Two intrapersonal catalysts seem to play a particularly important role: *interest* and *motivation*. Interests help steer a person toward a field of talent in which his or her energies will be invested, while motivation determines how much energy will be applied to learning activities in the chosen field of talent. All things being equal (especially the level of aptitude), the degree of motivation should be directly related to the level of observable talent.

The Role of Motivation

In his model, Renzulli (1979) considers motivation (what he calls "task commitment") to be one of the three essential ingredients of giftedness. When I analyzed this definition (Gagné, 1985), I said that it posed a major problem for explaining underachievement, in which we usually find a lack of motivation for academic tasks in spite of greatly superior intellectual capacity.[3] How can one say that a boy or a girl with an IQ of 130 or more is not gifted because, for one reason or another, this aptitude is not confirmed by academic achievement? It is important to distinguish the *potential* indicated by psychometric instruments from observed *performance* in a given field, in this case academic studies. The same problem also presents itself in other aptitude domains. For example, Bloom (1982) in reporting the preliminary results of his important study on the process of ascent to preeminence in six distinct talent areas—concert pianists and sculptors in the arts; mathematicians and research neurologists in the sciences; Olympic swimmers and tennis players in sports—noted a similar problem.

> In homes where other children were also interested in the talent area, the parents sometimes mentioned that one of the other children had even greater "gifts" than the individual in the sample, but that the other child was not willing to put in the time and effort that the parents or the teacher expected and required. (pp. 512–513)

If one accepts the premise that gifted underachievers really are gifted, then giftedness needs to be redefined in a way that allows motivation to play a different role. Yet a central role for this construct is essential since, as Renzulli's (1979) review of the literature clearly demonstrates, exceptional performance in a particular field stems largely from an intense and prolonged investment of energy in tasks relevant to that field. This is precisely why I have placed motivation at the heart of the catalysts. However, some individuals who possess a very high level of aptitude in a given domain may attain very high levels of performance (talent) with a minimum of "task commitment." For example, consider those children who easily remain at the head of their class without any apparent effort, right through their high school or even college education, all the while getting involved in a stream of cultural, social, or sports activities. You probably have met, during your school years, a student whose multiple talents made you realize that no one is totally immune to that forbidden feeling of envy! In short, motivation in my model is not a constituent of giftedness, but a constituent of talent.

Nature/Nurture

Scarr's and Plomin's statements presented earlier, clearly indicate that partial heritability extends to all human characteristics and, consequently, to the intrapersonal catalysts as well. The recent work of Bouchard and his colleagues (Bouchard, 1984) comparing identical twins separated during infancy and raised in different family environments largely confirms Scarr's position. This implies that an individual's level of motivation, for example, not only is the result of experience or education, but also is due in part to the genetic endowment received from parents.

The Environmental Catalysts

I have given little attention to this aspect of my model because many experts in the field of giftedness have studied the supportive (or impeding) role played by significant others (parents, teachers, peers, siblings, etc.) who surround the gifted or talented child. There is no need to

repeat what has already been described in depth in most textbooks. I will limit myself to three comments. First, when we think of environmental catalysts, *people* spontaneously leap to mind. Figure 6.1 clearly illustrates this bias. However, the contributing role of physical environments should not be forgotten: Do not expect great talent in surfing or downhill skiing to be nurtured in the midwest! Second, I include *chance,* a special causal agent about which almost no one—except Tannenbaum (1983; see Chapter 3)—has spoken, among the environmental catalysts. Finally, I have doubts about the apparent primacy, in the eyes of a majority of educators, of the environmental catalysts. I will have more to say on this subject later.

About the Talents Component

The fifth characteristic that differentiates aptitudes from talents—potential versus actualization—gives away my definite preference for focusing on *talents* rather than *aptitudes.* In fact, this talent component constitutes the heart of my model. This preference will be discussed in the last part of the chapter, which is devoted to some practical applications of the model. For now, let us examine the talent component in more detail.

The Taxonomy

When this model was first presented (Gagné, 1985), I abstained from suggesting a taxonomy of talents. At the time I argued that hierarchizing talents into general and specific fields is almost impossible given the interrelatedness of fields of human activity. For example, the inventor of a new artificial heart works in the medical domain, applying to it principles and techniques of the physical or biological sciences and of engineering. Where is this talent to be placed?

Since then, my own research on peer nominations (Gagné, 1989; Gagné & Bégin, 1988) has necessitated the elaboration of a taxonomy of talents, if only to provide a logical grouping of the 40 prototypes of aptitudes or talents submitted to pupils. The system of five categories that we finally decided upon stems from the bibliographic search mentioned earlier. This system of categories does not take into account talents that emerge only in adulthood. In fact, it was conceived only to measure talents that appear during late childhood (from about the age of 7 or 8) and that therefore can be included in a peer nomination form. As shown in Figure 6.1, the system contains five general categories of talent, some of which were given temporary subcategories: *academic* (literature, social science, science, mathematics); *technical; artistic* (visual arts, crafts, drama, music, singing, dance); *interpersonal* (leadership, administration, sales); *athletic*. This taxonomy does not pretend to represent correctly the entire range of possible talents. What it does is integrate all the talents found in our literature review into a useful structure.

Borderline Cases

Some behavior is difficult to classify as a subdomain of aptitudes or as a subfield of talent. This is the case with leadership, for example, which changes category depending upon one's theoretical framework (see Foster, 1981). Some models present leadership as a trait inherent in only certain individuals; others define leadership as a set of behaviors brought about by particular environmental characteristics. An analogous problem occurs for certain athletic talents that so directly refer to a single narrowly circumscribed aptitude (e.g., speed and sprinting, strength and weight lifting, etc.) that we ask ourselves whether one of the two categories is not redundant. Due to their technicality, these classification problems will not be discussed further in the present text. However, I believe that their existence, or the final decision concerning them, will not change the verdict concerning the validity of the general structure of this model.

Hidden *and* Natural *Talents*

By definition, this model does not recognize the existence of *hidden talents,* since the development of talent necessarily implies systematic training of some sort; this is why I used the term *performance* in its definition. However, *hidden talent* can refer to the fact that some youngsters might not manifest their talent(s) in a particular environment or in front of certain people. For example, young adolescent girls sometimes hide (at least partly) their academic talent so that peers, mainly those of the other sex, will not reject them. Also, the school environment, at least in the primary grades, does not offer young handymen many occasions to express their talent in mechanics. On the other hand, it is quite possible for a person to possess hidden aptitudes that no one has ever noticed, maybe not even he or she. For example, the intellectual giftedness of underachieving students is often only discovered when the child is referred to a psychologist for socioaffective, not intellectual, evaluation. The physically gifted civil servants mentioned in the fifth preliminary observation are another example of such hidden aptitudes.

I emphasized earlier that the concept of *natural talent* is not incompatible with our model. It is indeed possible for someone who has an aptitude that is far above average to become rapidly familiar with the basics of a field of talent. The habitual floundering of the novice is avoided, and, at least compared with other beginners, the performance is almost immediately above average. The younger the person, the harder it is to distinguish between giftedness and talent, since natural ease transfers almost effortlessly into a performance that is well above average for beginners. Think of those children who in just a few hours have mastered the rudiments of downhill skiing, while others remain novices for weeks or months! Natural talent is usually noticed in very precocious young children, because of the obvious lack of formal learning. In short, the manifestation of natural talent is nothing more than the expression of exceptional natural *aptitude* in a given field of talent, which, as mentioned earlier, depends in part upon heredity. Note that if most people tend to spontaneously associate the phenomena of hidden or natural abilities with talents rather than with aptitudes, it is quite simply because aptitudes are almost never expressed in their pure state, in other words, outside a given field of talent.

The Heritability of Talents

In the introduction to his recent volume on the development of talents, Bloom (1985) stated that talent involves a close interaction between various environmental agents. The text gives the impression that, with appropriate training, almost anyone may attain any developmental objective. However, the careful selection made by talent scouts, often of very young children (see the second preliminary observation), confirms the fact that talent (in athletics, art, or academic disciplines) does not start with a *tabula rasa,* nor is it independent of an individual's underlying aptitudes. I believe that few sports, music, or dance teachers would agree with Bloom on this point. In sum, if talents by definition have nothing hereditary about them, the fact that they are based on aptitudes and catalysts that are partially hereditary means that they depend indirectly on genetic influences.

About the Relationships Between the Components

This section brings together a series of comments on the interactions among the three components of the differentiated giftedness-talent model, as well as some related questions.

The Dynamics of Talent Development

Figure 6.1 partly illustrates the dynamics of the development of talents. Talents T stem from the interaction between aptitudes A that are necessarily above average but not necessarily exceptional, and the facilitating action of the intrapersonal and environmental catalysts C. The dynamic between them is represented by the following equation: $T = f (A \times C)$. From this equation, it follows that a given level of talented performance in a particular field may be due to a lesser degree of aptitude correlated with a proportionally greater intervention of the catalysts. It is well known, for example, that a greater proportion of the variance in academic results is explained by taking both motivation and intellectual abili-

ties into account than by considering only the latter (Corno & Snow, 1986). What Figure 6.1 does not show is that talent is also the direct result of more or less systematic learning, the intensity of which depends, among other things, on (1) the level of excellence a person wishes to attain, (2) the initial level of aptitude, (3) the strength of the intrapersonal catalysts, and (4) the level of support from the environmental catalysts.

Multifaceted Relationships

Figure 6.1 shows a certain semantic correspondence between certain aptitude domains and fields of talent, as can be seen by the labels given to both sets of categories (intellectual–academic, creative–artistic, etc.). However, this apparent one-to-one relationship is only superficial. My hypothesis is that (1) each specific talent is expressed by a particular profile of aptitudes, somewhat different from the profile characteristic of any other talent, and (2) each aptitude may contribute to the development of many distinct talents. It is because of these multifaceted relationships between aptitudes and talents that I use brackets to relate the giftedness component to the talent component.

Talent Implies Giftedness, but Not Vice Versa

It logically follows from this model that where there is a talent there necessarily is a set of underlying aptitudes, whether or not they are visible to the untrained eye. No matter what the talent, it must find its source in one or, probably, several aptitudes. On the other hand, a gift is not necessarily actualized in a specific field of talent. The example of *potentially athletic* civil servants clearly shows that giftedness is necessary but not sufficient for talent to emerge.

Intensity and Stability

Level of skill in an aptitude or in a talent is a *normative* concept; thus, there is no absolute threshold of talent. One becomes talented in so far as one's performance is well above average in a reference population, whatever the size of that population. For example, if you complete a marathon, no matter how long it takes you do do so, you will instantly become *the* talented runner in your neighborhood! Moreover, since all fields of talent have a developmental component, age almost always is a consideration. This is due to both the progressive maturation of underlying aptitudes and the considerable length of learning time needed to develop a talent, hence the notion of *precociousness*. Because of this normative aspect, a talent manifested at a particular stage of development may disappear, or at least may diminish, if not maintained by learning and practice. Take, for example, a young girl of 5 or 6 who does not develop her budding talent in swimming through rigorous practice and the constant support of parents and teachers. She probably will not be considered talented 10 years later. She may remain more talented than the average person, but at age 15 she probably will not emerge at the local, state, or national level as one judged to be exceptionally talented. I clearly distance myself from popular language, according to which the label *talented* sticks with a person for life, whether or not one continues to show above-average performance in his or her field of talent. This is an idea expressed in the familiar adage, "What a waste of talent!"

Causal Preponderance

If you ask most artists or athletes to what they owe their talent, they will inevitably answer that it is due to one or more of the catalysts mentioned earlier. They often even put greater emphasis on the environmental catalysts than on the intrapersonal ones. The impression gathered from these people is that the level of their natural abilities played only a secondary role in the emergence of their talent. Reading Bloom's (1985) volume, one gains the same impression, an impression reinforced by the position taken by Bloom himself in favor of environmental factors. This is especially evident when he states that "there must be an enormous potential pool of talent available in the United States. It is likely that some combinations of the home, the teachers, the schools, and

the society may in large part determine what portions of this potential pool of talent become developed" (p. 5).

I believe that what we have here is a case of perceptual bias due to a selection bias. Once the precociously talented are grouped together for special training, the range of differences in aptitudes within the group becomes relatively minor while the components of the learning environment are made clearly visible. So it becomes easy to conclude: "Anyone can do it if they are motivated to put in the time and effort." We forget the selection steps that led to the progressive elimination of candidates who reached their limit due to their (normatively) lesser aptitudes or their insufficient interest or motivation.

Implications for Identification and Programming

In the field of gifted education, the two most important areas of practice are identification and intervention through enrichment. In this last section, let us look at a few practical implications of the differentiated giftedness-talent model.

Better Awareness of Diversity

Almost 20 years ago, the U.S. Commissioner of Education stated that giftedness and talent could take a variety of forms. He was not the first to remind educators that there is much more than intellectual giftedness or academic talent, even in very young children. In spite of this, most often, school districts in the United States as well as in Canada continue to identify an undifferentiated group of talented or gifted youngsters. True, traditional instruments do not permit much differentiation, since they are usually oriented toward intellectual aptitudes and academic talent. A recent survey of more than a thousand school boards in most states provides evidence of this: It revealed that the most frequently used identification techniques were teacher nominations (91% of school boards); achievement tests (90%); IQ tests

(82%); and grades (50%) (Cox, Daniel, & Boston, 1985, p. 189). Yet, we should interest ourselves in the emergence of talent in the visual arts, in computer programming, in particular academic disciplines, in various interpersonal talents, and so forth, early on. A model that includes a taxonomy of gifts and talents might help to better visualize how diversity can express itself.

Identification Instruments

This model can have a direct impact on identification instruments. First of all, it can provide a framework for classifying the contents of the instruments that professionals intend to use and thus allow them to become aware of the particular type(s) of aptitude(s) or talent(s) that they will highlight. At the same time, this classification might bring about the realization that some instruments actually are *pluri-thematic* in the sense that their contents are spread over several domains or fields. This is frequently the case with questionnaires or checklists for teachers and parents, as well as many peer nomination forms (PNFs).

A typical example of this last type of instrument is *The Muffs* (Delisle, Gubbins, Ciabotti, Salvatore, & Brucker, 1984), the only PNF on the market. The 12 items of this instrument propose prototypes as diverse as *banker, inventor,* and *director* (of a play). Yet the choices are added together into a single global score corresponding to the total number of nominations received. Thus, the all-round talented youngsters find themselves advantaged in the identification process to the detriment of those whose talents are more focused, albeit of comparable or higher levels. It would seem more fair to substitute a profile of strengths and weaknesses, knowing that *all-roundness* would reappear in the particular form of the profile. We would use all the various sources of information (dossiers, tests, teachers, parents, peers, etc.) in a more efficient way if we asked those making the evaluation to specify a particular type of aptitude or talent rather than a general category, a category that we know will be heavily saturated with intellectual giftedness and academic talent.

The idea of differentiating talents by means of a profile is not new. For example, when they developed their Scales for Rating the Behavioral Characteristics of Superior Students (SRBCSS) (Renzulli, Smith, White, Callahan, & Hartman, 1976), covering 10 domains of ability and of talent, the authors warned the users not to add up the scores obtained, but to create instead a profile of strengths and weaknesses. I wonder how many were able to resist the temptation to add them all up. Another peculiarity of the SRBCSS is that most people use only the first four scales (Learning, Motivation, Creativity, and Leadership), ignoring the six categories dealing with nonacademic talents (Visual Arts, Music, Dramatic Art, Communications-Precision, Communication-Expression, and Planning). This is still more proof of the predominance of educators' attention to intellectual aptitudes and academic talent.

Finally, our model may sensitize the authors of future screening instruments to the need to organize contents into more homogeneous categories, allowing the calculation of specific scores for particular talents; or to create instruments that are specifically oriented toward one category or another. At the same time, those who create lists of characteristics of gifted or talented individuals may find that their lists contain a jumble of aptitudes, talents, and intrapersonal catalysts, to which are sometimes added behavioral characteristics presumed to be associated with (intellectual) giftedness, such as "likes to read," "is preoccupied with existential questions," or "likes discussing things with adults!"

Reassessment of Prevalence

It is impossible to say with certainty how prevalent giftedness is among the general population. Yet the answer to this question has important implications if only in terms of the size of the client population funded and serviced. There are two major points of view on this subject. On one hand, those who maintain a restrictive position limit the prevalence of giftedness or talent to less than 5% of the population, that is, those beyond approximately two standard deviations above the mean on a typical ability measure. On the other hand, those who maintain a more liberal position (see, for example, Reis & Renzulli, 1982) argue that at least 15 to 20% of the population distinguish themselves sufficiently from the general population to benefit from an academic program somewhat different from that of the average student.

Even if these percentages are attributed to a general category of talented or gifted people, there can be no doubt that implicitly we are discussing the *intellectually* gifted and the *academically* talented. What happens when one considers many other domains of aptitudes or fields of talent? Is it always the same people who excel in all these various domains or fields? One must expect a certain overlap, but as some studies have shown (see especially Feldman & Bratton, 1980; Hainsworth, 1978; Pearce, 1983; Taylor, 1975), when one adds more criteria of what constitutes giftedness and talent, more people qualify for inclusion.

Our research team has made an attempt to quantify this phenomenon. We obtained raw data from a PNF administered to over 60 fourth- to sixth-grade classes in a local school district. The PNF evaluated six aptitudes or talents separately: intelligence, creativity, leadership, athletics, visual arts, and music. Two questions were asked concerning each domain or field. We identified all the students in each class who, because of the number of nominations received, were among the three highest of their class ($N = 25$ on average, so about the top 12%) on *any one* of the six categories. Following the hypothesis of complete overlap of talents, we should have selected only 3 pupils per class. According to the opposite hypothesis of complete lack of overlap of aptitudes or talents, we should have found 18 pupils per class (3 pupils × 6 categories). In fact, the actual number of children found varied between 8 and 11 in most cases, just about midway between the two extremes. In other words, with only six distinct criteria and a rate of selection of 12% per category, we managed to select about 40% of the pupils in any given group. Similarly, Feldman and Bratton (1980), with a rate of 8% and with 18 distinct (but probably moderately correlated) criteria, selected a full 92% of a group of 63 elementary school children. In this light, the 15 to 20% of the "liberals" becomes very conservative!

A Better Fit Between Clientele and Program

It is important not to forget an obvious principle: The specific objectives of the program should determine the definition of the appropriate clientele (Feldhusen, Asher, & Hoover, 1984). For example, a program that wishes to develop a given artistic talent should be offered first of all to children who show promise in this particular field. A program that promotes the development of mathematical talent should screen candidates, as the Study of Mathematically Precocious Youth (Stanley, 1976) did so well, with instruments specifically tailored to this field of talent. It would be extremely unjust to deny obviously talented youths access to a program in their field of talent under the pretext that their IQ scores fall below some arbitrary cutoff point established at the state or local level.

This proposal does not mean that we cannot begin the intervention process by first becoming interested in a specific target population and then trying to imagine a range of intervention methods appropriate to the particular aptitudes or talents of this clientele. In fact, that is exactly how Professor Stanley (1977) first got the idea of the SMPY project. But the screening process itself should not precede one's planning of the structure and contents of the enrichment activities for a particular target clientele. In other words, we should not say: "Let's identify our gifted; then we will decide what to do with them!" We should look to most athletic programs and most music conservatories for guidance; they both show quite clearly what is meant by a good fit between specific talent and specific enrichment. The more we are aware of the diversity of gifts and talents, the more we will diversify our enrichment activities in order to offer specific answers to specific needs.

The Priority of Talent over Giftedness

Should the priority be placed on the development of aptitudes or talents? I answered this question earlier by stating my clear preference for talents over aptitudes. This preference is essentially related to the immediate utility of talents as stepping-stones either for careers or for fulfilling hobbies. Developing talents is working on something concrete, which also will be more easily perceived as such by children. Furthermore, there does not appear to be as much of a problem of justice in selecting a small percentage of talented youngsters for a special program in talent development compared with selecting high-aptitude pupils for general or cultural enrichment. Finally, at least in the area of intellectual reasoning, the development of "pure" thinking skills seems less profitable in terms of transfer than its development as part of the acquisition of specific school-related knowledge (Glaser, 1984). This preference has a direct impact on identification procedures, specifically on the choice of criteria and, consequently, of instruments. This means, for example, that I am not in favor of using IQ tests in every identification process, only in situations in which that specific aptitude has been shown to be pertinent to success in the enrichment program. Moreover, in the decision-making process I would give clear preference to demonstrations of performance in the talent field over formal tests of underlying aptitudes.

Conclusion

While the differentiation of the concepts of giftedness and talent is an important step to further our knowledge of this population, the elaboration of a taxonomy of gifts and talents appears no less important. In fact, in terms of impact on programs, the second objective is clearly more important. There are at least two reasons for this. First, as aptitudes and talents grow in number so does the percentage of gifted and talented people. As I believe that a majority of people possess at least one domain or field of excellence, we maximize our chances of finding and recognizing these areas of excellence. Second, the more specific we become in identifying aptitudes and talents, the better are our chances of conceiving programs that meet the specific needs of these subgroups of gifted or talented people. I would like to think that we will see in the near future more effective mapping strategies of the aptitude and talent profiles of all children as soon as they enter the school system, and regularly afterward.

NOTES

1. Psychomotor ability was removed in the 1978 revision.

2. In order to keep ambiguity between the two concepts at a minimum, I have avoided using identical terms in both definitions. I thus use the term *domains* for aptitudes and the term *fields* for talents. For the same reason, *competence* is distinguished from *performance,* even though, strictly speaking, any competence is assessed by a performance of some kind.

3. Renzulli (1988) answers this critique by citing the following sentence in his original 1978 explanation: "Gifted and talented children are those possessing *or capable of developing* this composite set of traits and applying them to any potentially valuable area of human performance" (p. 19). He states that the words in italics cover gifted underachievers. I recognize not having noticed this nuance; but the author himself does not mention it anywhere else in his text. Further, the sentence remains ambiguous because of the nondifferentiation between giftedness and talent, as well as between potential (capable of . . .) and performance (possessing, applying).

REFERENCES

Anastasi, A. (1980). Abilities and the measurement of achievement. In W. B. Schrader (Ed.), *Measuring achievement: Progress over a decade* (pp. 1–10). San Francisco: Jossey-Bass.

Anastasi, A. (1988). *Psychological testing* (6th ed.). New York: Macmillan.

Bloom, B. S. (1982). The role of gifts and markers in the development of talent. *Exceptional Children, 48,* 510–522.

Bloom, B. S. (1985). *Developing talent in young people.* New York: Ballantine.

Blouchard, T. J., Jr. (1984). Twins reared together and apart: What they tell us about human diversity. In S. W. Fox (Ed.), *Individuality and determinism: Chemical and biological bases* (pp. 147–184). New York: Plenum.

Bruininks, R. H. (1978). *Bruininks-Oseretsky test of motor proficiency: Examiner's manual.* Circle Pines, MN: American Guidance Service.

Corno, L., & Snow, R. E. (1986). Adapting teaching to individual differences among learners. In M. C.

Wittrock (Ed.), *Handbook of research on teaching* (3rd ed., pp. 605–629). New York: Macmillan.

Cox, J., Daniel, N., & Boston, B. O. (1985). *Educating able learners: Programs and promising practices.* Austin: University of Texas Press.

Cronbach, L. J., & Snow, R. E. (1977). *Aptitudes and instructional methods.* New York: Irvington.

Davis, G. A., & Rimm, S. B. (1989). *Education of the gifted and talented* (2nd ed.). Englewood Cliffs, NJ: Prentice-Hall.

Delisle, J., Gubbins, E. J., Ciabotti, P., Salvatore, L., & Brucker, S. (1984). *The Muffs: Peer identification instrument.* Monroe, NY: Trillium.

Feldhusen, J. F., Asher, J. W., & Hoover, S. M. (1984). Problems in the identification of giftedness, talent, or ability. *Gifted Child Quarterly, 28,* 149–151.

Feldman, D. H., & Bratton, J. C. (1980). Relativity and giftedness: Implications for equality of educational opportunity. In J. S. Renzulli & E. P. Stoddard (Eds.), *Gifted and talented education in perspective* (p. 20). Reston, VA: Council for Exceptional Children.

Ford, M. E., & Tisak, M. S. (1983). A further search for social intelligence. *Journal of Educational Psychology, 75,* 196–206.

Foster, W. (1981). Leadership: A conceptual framework for recognizing and educating. *Gifted Child Quarterly, 25,* 17–25.

Gagné, F. (1985). Giftedness and talent: Reexamining a reexamination of the definitions. *Gifted Child Quarterly, 29,* 103–112.

Gagné, F. (1989). Peer nominations as a psychometric instrument: Many questions asked but few answered. *Gifted Child Quarterly, 33,* 53–58.

Gagné, F., & Bégin, J. (1988, November). *Do peers agree when nominating the more talented?* Paper presented at the meeting of the National Association for Gifted Children, Orlando, Florida.

Gardner, H. (1983). *Frames of mind: The theory of multiple intelligences.* New York: Basic.

Glaser, R. (1984). Education and thinking: The role of knowledge. *American Psychologist, 39,* 93–104.

Hainsworth, J. (1978). A teacher corps projection of multiple talents. In C. W. Taylor (Ed.), *Teaching for talents and gifts* (pp. 85–89). Salt Lake City: Utah State Board of Education.

MacKinnon, D. W. (1964). The creativity of architects. In C. W. Taylor (Ed.), *Widening horizons in creativity* (pp. 359–378). New York: Wiley.

Marland, S. P. (1972). *Education of the gifted and talented: Report to the Congress of the United States by the U.S. Commissioner of Education.* Washington, DC: US Government Printing Office.

Mehrens, W. A. (1982). Aptitude measurement. In H. E. Mitzel (Ed.), *Encyclopedia of educational research* (5th ed., pp. 137–145). New York: Free Press.

Michelmore, P. (1988, June). Greg Louganis: High diver with a heart. *Readers' Digest,* pp. 163–170.

Pearce, N. (1983). A comparison of the WISC-R, Raven's progressive matrices, and Meeker's SOI-Screening form for the gifted. *Gifted Child Quarterly, 27,* 13–19.

Plomin, R. (1989). Environment and genes: Determinants of behavior. *American Psychologist, 44,* 105–111.

Rapaport, D. (1959). The structure of psychoanalytic theory: A systematizing attempt. In S. Koch (Ed.), *Psychology: A study of a science: Vol. 3. Formulations of the person and the social context* (pp. 55–183). New York: McGraw-Hill.

Reis, S. M., & Renzulli, J. S. (1982). A case for a broadened conception of giftedness. *Phi Delta Kappan, 63,* 619–620.

Renzulli, J. S. (1978). What makes giftedness? Reexamining a definition. *Phi Delta Kappan, 60,* 180–184, 261.

Renzulli, J. S. (1979). *What makes giftedness: A reexamination of the definition of the gifted and talented.* Ventura, CA: Ventura County Superintendent of Schools Office.

Renzulli, J. S. (1988). A decade of dialogue on the three-ring conception of giftedness. *Roeper Review, 11,* 18–25.

Renzulli, J. S., Smith, L. H., White, A. J., Callahan, C. M., & Hartman, R. K. (1976). *Scales for rating the behavioral characteristics of superior students.* Mansfield Center, CT: Creative Learning Press.

Roedell, W. C., Jackson, N. E., & Robinson, H. B. (1980). *Gifted young children.* New York: Teachers College, Columbia University.

Scarr, S. (1981). *Race, social class, and individual differences in IQ.* Hillsdale, NJ: Erlbaum.

Smolowe, J. (1988, September 19). Sprite fight: Which of the extraordinary tumbling pixies will become the Seoul sweetheart? *Time,* pp. 56–57.

Snow, R. E. (1980). Aptitude and achievement. In W. B. Schrader (Ed.), *Measuring achievement: Progress over a decade* (pp. 39–59). San Francisco, CA: Jossey-Bass.

Snow, R. E. (1982). The training of intellectual aptitude. In D. K. Detterman & R. J. Sternberg (Eds.), *How and how much can intelligence be increased* (pp. 1–37). Norwood, NJ: Ablex.

Stankowski, W. M. (1978). Definition. In R. E. Clasen & B. Robinson (Eds.), *Simple gifts* (pp. 1–8). Madison: University of Wisconsin-Extension.

Stanley, J. C. (1976). Use of tests to discover talent. In D. P. Keating (Ed.), *Intellectual talent: Re-*

search and development (pp. 3–22). Baltimore: Johns Hopkins University Press.

Stanley, J. C. (1977). Rationale of the study of mathematically precocious youth during its first five years of promoting educational acceleration. In J. C. Stanley, W. C. George, & C. H. Solano (Eds.), *The gifted and the creative: A fifty-year perspective* (pp. 75–112). Baltimore: Johns Hopkins University Press.

Sternberg, R. J. (1985). *Beyond IQ: A triarchic theory of human intelligence.* New York: Cambridge University Press.

Sternberg, R. J., & Davidson, J. E. (Eds.). (1986). *Conceptions of giftedness.* New York: Cambridge University Press.

Tannenbaum, A. J. (1983). *Gifted children: Psychological and educational perspectives.* New York: Macmillan.

Taylor, C. W. (1975). Cultivating new talents: A way to reach the educationally deprived. In W. B. Barbe & J.S. Renzulli (Eds.), *Psychology and education of the gifted* (2nd ed., pp. 424–430). New York: Irvington.

7

Rampant Problems and Promising Practices in Identification

E. SUSANNE RICHERT   *Educational Resource Information Center (ERIC),*
Sewell, New Jersey

National studies such as the Marland (1972) report, the *National Report on Identification* (Richert, Alvino, & McDonncl, 1982) and the Richardson study (Cox, Daniel, & Boston, 1985) reveal major gaps between research and practice in identification of the gifted. One of the participants on the panel of experts for the *National Report on Identification* called problems in identification "an epidemic of errors." Yarborough and Johnson (1983) and others have pointed to the gap between theory and practice. A disturbing trend is the widening of this gap with the proliferation of the following major errors that distort identification:

1. Elitist and distorted definitions of giftedness
2. Confusion about the purpose of identification
3. Violation of education equity
4. Misuse and abuse of tests
5. Cosmetic and distorting use of multiple criteria
6. Exclusive program design

This chapter will analyze these errors and offer recommendations in the following areas:

1. Principles of identification
2. Defensible defintions
3. Appropriate use of test data
   a. Selection of tests and instruments
   b. Use of tests with groups disadvantaged in identification
   c. Using data to identify special populations
4. Appropriate use of data from multiple sources
5. Other procedures and sources of information
   a. Teacher, parent, and peer nominations
   b. Self-nominations
   c. Data on student progress
6. Developmental curriculum
7. Comprehensive low-cost programs

Rampant Problems in Identification of Gifted Students

Elitist and Distorted Definitions of Giftedness

Many districts and states are using elitist definitions of giftedness that include only certain kinds of gifted students, most often those who are white, middle class, and academically achieving. A major purpose of the federally legislated definition was to expand the concept of giftedness beyond IQ (Marland, 1972). Yet in practice, much more limited definitions are applied. Some state or local definitions distort the intention of the federal definition by inappropriately distinguishing between *gifted* and *talented,* creating a hierarchy by using the former for general intellectual ability measured primarily by intelligence tests and the latter for the other gifted abilities referred to in the federal definition: specific academic aptitude, and creative, visual and performing arts, and leadership abilities.

Some state departments of education, that of New York, for example, distort J. S. Renzulli's conception of giftedness as the intersection of above-average ability, creativity, and motivation by designating as *gifted* (and thereby eligible for programs) those students who demonstrate all three, and as *talented* those students who exhibit only two (New York State Department of Education, n.d., p. 2). Such distinctions ignore the differences between the full manifestations of giftedness studied in adults and the potential of children that gifted programs are designed to develop.

Many distinctions are made among students with gifted potential that are not predictors of adult gifted achievement but are rather indices of present performance on test instruments. It is important to remember that giftedness in test taking is not yet a recognized field of human endeavor to which original contributions can be made. False distinctions between *talented* and *gifted* among children, or designating degrees of *giftedness* ("highly," "severely," "profoundly," or "exotic" gifted) rather than specifying the identification procedures used (high IQ or high achievement) creates implicit hierarchies, engenders elitism within programs, and excludes many students with gifted potential. Such implicit hierarchies ignore the fact that giftedness *emerges,* as Renzulli (1978), Richert (1986), Richert et al. (1982), Tannenbaum (1983), and others assert, through the interaction of innate abilities and learning or experience.

There are a variety of reasons for such elitism. The major bias that impels such practices is the prevalent myth that academic achievement is related to adult giftedness. Repeated studies (Baird, 1982; Holland & Richards, 1965; Hoyt, 1965; Munday & Davis, 1974; Price, Taylor, Richards, & Jacobsen, 1964; Taylor & Ellison, 1967; Taylor, Albo, Holland, & Brandt, 1985) have revealed no correlation, or sometimes a small negative correlation, between academic achievement and grades and adult giftedness in a broad range of fields. This should not be surprising since many of the evaluation criteria for determining grades, such as propensity for convergent thinking, conformity to expectations of teachers or test makers, and meeting externally determined deadlines, are inversely correlated with adult eminence or original contributions to most fields. These studies demonstrate that test scores predict test scores; grades predict grades. Giftedness, or original contribution to

a field, requires nonacademic abilities unrelated or inversely related to school achievement, such as creativity and intrinsic motivation.

Confusion about the Purposes of Identification

There are various kinds of confusion about the purposes of identification. Identification is not, as too many people assume, a mere categorization of gifted abilities already fully manifest. If it were, educational programs would be unnecessary. Identification is actually a needs assessment for the purpose of placing students into educational programs designed to develop their latent potential. Some parents, out of a desire to have their children reaffirm their own self-esteem, want a label for the innate abilities their children inherited from them (see Miller, 1981, *Prisoners of Childhood,* about parents of gifted children using them to meet their narcissistic needs).

Teachers, administrators, and often parents feel that entry into a program for the gifted should be a reward for achievement or "good" behavior, operationally defined as conformity to school or test-maker expectations. Many educators seem to want the identification procedure to reaffirm the values inherent in the school systems to which they have committed their own abilities. This is a distortion of the purpose of programs for the gifted, which are necessary precisely because the standard curriculum rarely maximizes exceptional potential.

Giftedness requires originality, risk taking, and intrinsic motivation. It could well be argued that conformity to school expectations and external rewards such as grades or test scores may inhibit giftedness. Extracurricular activities beyond the required curriculum are therefore probably the best predictors of adult gifted achievement (Goleman, 1984; Guilford, 1977). The only defensible rationale in our democratic society for additional expenditures is student need, not reward for conformity to teacher or test-maker expectations, which is essentially how students become academic achievers.

Violation of Educational Equity

Some gifted students are consistently being screened out by present prevalent practices. In national figures published by the U.S. Department of Education's Office of Civil Rights, minority groups such as blacks, Hispanics, and Native Americans are underrepresented by 30 to 70% in gifted programs (U.S. Department of Education, 1979). These figures are collected each year but are evidently considered so controversial that they have not been published since 1979.

While most states formally subscribe to the comprehensive federal definition of giftedness, in practice many local districts tend to seek— and to find—white, middle-class academic achievers. Measures of academic achievement that are most often used by schools, including teacher recommendations, grades, and most especially standardized tests, have been amply demonstrated to have cultural biases (Black, 1963; Davis, Gardner, & Gardner 1941; Goolsby, 1975; Hoffman, 1962; Kamin, 1974; Klineberg, 1935; Miller 1974; Nairn & Associates, 1980; Samuda 1975).

The *National Report on Identification* (Richert et al., 1982) reveals that measures of academic achievement, which are not very good predictors of adult gifted achievement, are often screening out the following subpopulations:

- Underachieving, learning-disabled, handicapped, and minority students who most need programs to develop their potential
- The most creative and divergent thinkers who, as Torrance (1979) has pointed out, will be excluded by IQ tests

Even if there is cultural homogeneity within a school district, there is always a range of economic differences. A significant finding of the *National Report* is that it is the poor who are most consistently screened out of gifted programs because their disadvantage cuts across every other subpopulation (Richert et al., 1982).

Because one pernicious effect of the "excellence" reforms has been even greater reliance on standardized tests for assessment, this discrimination has not only persisted but seems to have increased since 1979. This shocking inequity is a problem not only for those excluded from gifted programs but also for those included, since it makes programs vulnerable to charges of elitism.

Misuse and Abuse of Tests

Identification instruments are being misused. The *National Report on Identification* revealed that there are major discrepancies between reported practices and the intended use of various tests and instruments for the five areas of giftedness in the federal definition. Tests are being used in ways that test makers never intended, sometimes to measure abilities that they were not designed to determine. For example, achievement and IQ tests are used almost interchangeably, thereby confusing the categories of specific academic and general intellectual ability. They are also being inappropriately used to identify creativity and leadership (national survey of identification practices reported in *National Report on Identification,* Richert et al., 1982, Chap. 2, pp. 23–39).

Instruments and procedures are being used at inappropriate stages of identification. Instruments and procedures are being used at inappropriate stages of identification. Diagnosis is not the purpose of initial screening procedures. However, the use of diagnostic tests, such as the Stanford Achievement Test (reading and math) and the Woodcock Reading Mastery Tests, for screening is common. Such tests are only useful for determining placement in a particular course or to measure progress once students are placed in a program option (*National Report on Identification,* Richert et al., 1982, pp. 35, 62).

Another problem occurs when data from parents are gathered only *after* students are nominated by teachers or after they qualify for a talent pool through a test score. Under such procedures disadvantaged students have already been screened out. The same error occurs when teachers assess the creativity or motivation of students only *after* they qualify for a talent pool with a standardized achievement test score, or when individualized IQ tests are given only to students after they qualify through a group IQ test or are referred by teachers. Most of these efforts are merely cosmetic since they often simply reinforce the exclusion of the same disadvantaged groups of students.

Cosmetic and Distorting Use of Multiple Criteria

One of the few apparently positive trends is the collection of data from a variety of sources for identification. Practitioners in many states are typically using test scores (IQ, achievement, or both), teacher observations, and sometimes even parent observations.

The intent of collecting a variety of data may be to make the procedure appear more defensible or more inclusive. However, the data are often misused in several ways: The data may be unreliable, used at an inappropriate stage of identification, weighted in indefensible ways, or invalidly placed in a matrix containing other data.

Unreliable Data. Some data that are not very reliable are collected. In most districts, teachers tend to be involved in identifying students for programs. There is ample evidence from several studies that teachers without training in characteristics of the gifted are often unreliable sources of identification data (Baldwin, 1962; Barbe, 1964; Ciha, Harris, Hoffman, & Potter, 1974; Cornish, 1968; Gear, 1976, 1978; Holland, 1959; Jacobs, 1971; Pegnato & Birch, 1959; Wilson, 1963). Other questionable sources of information include locally designed checklists or observation forms that are not research based.

Inappropriate Combination of Data. The statistically unsound practice of combining data from multiple sources in various matrices or other weighted-scoring procedures, which may obscure a variety of important indicators of potential, was strongly criticized by a national panel of experts (Richert et al., 1982).

While the combination of creativity, productivity, and task commitment are indisputable requisites for manifestations of adult giftedness, the relative importance and the developmental patterns of each of these in children has not yet been demonstrated. Adding the results of various procedures or measures is also questionable since it is the statistical equivalent of adding apples and oranges. The range, standard deviations, reliability, and construct and content validity of different measures, whether formal or informal, are not necessarily equivalent, and simply adding the various scores together or arbitrarily determining weightings is highly problematic (Richert et al., 1982).

Furthermore, combining data inappropriately also tends to identify jacks-of-all-trades, or students who develop ability, creativity, and motivation concurrently, but may eliminate the "masters of some," who especially need a gifted program to develop their potential, for example:

- Students with a very high IQ who may be underachieving in school because of the extreme inappropriateness of the regular curriculum and therefore lack teacher or parent nominations
- Exceptionally intellectually creative students, who are often screened out by IQ or achievement measures (Torrance 1979)
- Creative students who are independent, rebellious, and nonconforming, who tend not to get teacher or even parent recommendations

Furthermore, most of the identification procedures used, such as standardized tests, teacher recommendations, and grades (often used for such secondary program options as honors, AP, or accelerated courses), are really measures of conformity to middle-class academic values and achievement. The national survey of practices reported in the *National Report on Identification* (Richert et al., Chap. 2) revealed that even when multiple measures are used, standardized test scores tend to be given disproportionate weight. The more measures that are used and *combined* inappropriately, the more likely it becomes that disadvantaged students (poor, minority, creative, and others who tend to be underachievers in schools) will be excluded. Therefore, the use of multiple measures, which merely reinforce a narrow concept of giftedness, may create the appearance of inclusiveness but can actually exacerbate elitism in identification.

Exclusive Program Design

Because of the limited resources, there have been several counterproductive trends among theoreticians and groups vying for services. Parents whose children are being served through present identification practices defend the status quo because they fear their children will be excluded if other groups, such as the disadvantaged, are included. Many administrators argue that because of limited resources only small numbers of students can be served, with the result that the same white middle-class students are identified.

One unfortunate outcome of educational reforms trying to foster "excellence" has been the reinforcement of elitist programs that serve as few as 2 to 5% of students. Program models that delineate a hierarchical pattern (*pyramids* or *ladders*), rather than an egalitarian model that simply acknowledges various kinds of gifted potential that may require different programmatic provisions, create unnecessary forms of elitism. No one knows how many students have gifted potential, since no one has made an effort to elicit giftedness from all students. Luis Machado, Minister for the Development of Intelligence in Venezuela, comes close to attempting to do so. Machado (1980) has embarked on an ambitious venture to develop maximum intellectual potential in *all* segments of Venezuelan society. While programs for the gifted, by definition, cannot serve all children, serving fewer than 25% of students will exclude too many students with gifted potential.

Although many states and districts use broad written definitions, in practice primarily students with a single pattern of manifestation of giftedness are served, that is, high-achieving, conforming students. In addition, considerable effort by writers in the field is being expended in debates as to which are the single best program models, rather than in the development of practical inexpensive program models that could serve more students.

Promising Practices in Identification

Principles of Identification

Principles for assessing identification procedures emerged through the deliberations of the national panel of experts that met as part of the *National Report on Identification* (Richert et al., 1982). They should be heeded by practitioners. They are as follows:

1. *Defensibility.* Procedures should be based on the best available research and recommendations.
2. *Advocacy.* Identification should be designed in the best interests of all students. Students should not be harmed by procedures.
3. *Equity:*
   - Procedures should guarantee that no one is overlooked.
   - The civil rights of students should be protected.
   - Strategies should be specified for identifying the disadvantaged gifted.
   - Cutoff scores should be avoided since they are the most common way that disadvantaged students are discriminated against. (High scores should be used to include students, but if students meet other criteria, through self or parent nominations, for example, then a lower test score should not be used to exclude them.)
4. *Pluralism.* The broadest defensible definition of giftedness should be used.
5. *Comprehensiveness.* As many gifted learners as possible should be identified and served.
6. *Pragmatism.* Whenever possible, procedures should allow for the modification and use of instruments and resources on hand.

Defensible Definitions

The *National Report on Identification* (Richert et al., 1982) analyzed a strong trend in the United States toward a broadening of definitions over the last century to include multiple abilities and factors of giftedness. A few of the contributors to that direction have been Guilford in his multifactored structure of intellect model (1977), Torrance (1964) in creativity, Renzulli (1978) in elaborating some of the motivational factors in giftedness, Tannenbaum (1983) in stressing the nonintellective and experiential variables in manifestations of giftedness, Roeper (1982) in suggesting that it might be necessary to develop a concept of *emotional giftedness* and Piechowski and Colangelo's (1984) elaboration of Dabrowski's conceptualization of a developmental potential intrinsic to giftedness.

In the area of cognitive science, the publications of Gardner (1983; see Chapter 5) and Sternberg (1985; see Chapter 4), as well as the special issue of the *Roeper Review* (Silverman, 1986b), emphasize the recognition of diverse, discrete cognitive abilities in the identification of giftedness. In addition, I have argued for a comprehensive and pluralistic definition that not only acknowledges the existence of various exceptional abilities but is ethical in that it will not harm or limit the potential of exceptional students (Richert, 1986, 1987). Definitions used should not harm students. Students who are labeled *gifted* resent the label with good reason (Colangelo & Brower, 1987; Kerr, Colangelo, & Gaeth, 1988). Often, inappropriate expectations for consistently high academic performance are projected onto identified students by educators or parents. It is much more defensible, in terms of the research, and more acceptable, in terms of students' self-concepts, to view the identification process as a *needs assessment* that targets untapped gifted potential. Districts should use broad, pluralistic definitions, such as the federally legislated definition that includes diverse abilities. Such definitions may identify up to 25% of the students as requiring a program to help develop their diverse gifted potentials.

Appropriate Use of Test Data

Selection of Tests and Instruments. The misuse of tests can be avoided by considering the cautions and recommendations of the panel of experts for *The National Report* (Richert et al., 1982), which are summarized on the list of tests and recommendation for use in Table 7.1.

The list indicates the appropriateness of tests for different abilities, populations, and stages of identification. Practitioners should follow these precautions in the use of tests:

1. Select different measures and procedures to identify each diverse gifted ability.
2. Address these issues before using any test:
   - Is the test appropriate for the ability being sought?
   - Is the test being used at the appropriate stage of identification (i.e., nomination into a broad talent pool; assessment for a specific program option; evaluation within a program)?
   - Is the test appropriate for any disadvantaged subpopulations in the district that are typically discriminated against in measures of academic achievement (i.e., poor, minority, creative, underachieving, etc.)?

Equitable Procedures for Identifying Groups Disadvantaged in Identification

Avoiding Discrimination. Discrimination against disadvantaged students should be assiduously guarded against both for the purpose of equity and to avoid charges of elitism. The special procedures described below are required in order to find students with gifted potential among the social groups that are most disadvantaged in an identification process that relies heavily on measures of academic achievement (such as teacher recommendations, grades, or standardized tests), particularly such groups as:

- The poor (students meeting federal standards for qualifying for free or reduced-price lunch)
- Minority races or cultures
- Students with minimal proficiency in English
- Males (when identifying verbal ability below the fifth grade)
- Females (when identifying mathematical ability)

Regardless of students' social background, special efforts are necessary to identify these students with gifted potential who also tend to be excluded from programs that rely primarily on measures of academic achievement:

- The intellectually creative
- The academically underachieving
- The handicapped or learning disabled

Equitable Use of Academic Achievement Data. If in using actual test data or teacher recommendations to identify students, the outcome is more than a 5 to 10% underrepresentation of any individual subpopulation (the poor, minority races or cultures, students with minimal proficiency in English, males or females) within a school district, then the following procedures guaranteeing equity should be used.

When selecting standardized tests, only those tests deemed appropriate by the national panel of experts for disadvantaged students should be considered. *The National Report* (Richert et al., 1982) lists more than 12 tests that have been assessed as appropriate for the subpopulations in various school districts. These are indicated on the list of instruments in Table 7.1. If a school district is not already using an approved test, there are several problems in selecting different tests for various populations. It is certainly a more costly and complicated choice than using existing test data. Questions may also be raised as to whether the instruments are measuring the same abilities or whether comparisons across tests are valid.

If a district is using a test that is not approved for one of its disadvantaged subpopulations, the most practical approach is to use existing test data but to renorm it to overcome test bias. In a procedure approved by the U.S. Office of Civil Rights, the scores may be disaggregated (i.e., broken down) by various populations in order to factor out the inherent bias in most standardized tests (Angoff, 1971; Hansen, Hurwitz, & Madow, 1953; Sudman 1976; Wood & Talmadge, 1976). Renorming allows the selection of the same percentage of students from each subpopulation to ensure equal representation from each group. The purpose of renorming is, however, not merely to achieve equity. Rather than relying solely on school achievement, which is skewed by social and economic environmental differences, the major objective of renorming is to identify inherent and latent gifted potential in all populations.

These are the steps for renorming test scores or teacher nominations.

1. Determine whether the existing procedure underidentifies any of the disadvantaged subpopulation in the district by more than 5 to 10% to determine whether the following steps should be taken.
2. Determine the percentage of students that will be identified for each program option. (For example, a district may chose to select 25% of its students for program options in mathematics and reading in grades K–6.)
3. Disaggregate the scores. Determine in which of these categories students belong:
   - Economic:
     Disadvantaged (use federal guidelines for free or reduced-price lunch)
     Advantaged (*not* needing free or reduced-price lunch)
   - Races or cultures:
     Black
     White
     Hispanic
     Other
   - Sex:
     Male
     Female
4. Rank-order the disaggregated scores from the various populations *within* each group.
5. The same percentage of the top-scoring students from *each* subpopulation as from among advantaged students is selected. If the district has resources for serving, for example, 25% of its students grades K–8 in homogeneously grouped classes in reading, then based on achievement subtest scores in reading, the top 25% of the white students, top 25% of the black students, top 25% of the Hispanic students, top 25% of the boys, and top 25% of the girls should be selected for services. Students will, of course, fall into several categories (economic, social, sex), but a balance can be worked out so that the outcome is a group representative of the district's entire school population.

Table 7.1
Alphabetical Listing of Instruments and Recommendations for Use

INSTRUMENT	General Intellectual	Specific Academic	Creativity	Leadership	Visual and Performing Arts	Advantaged	Disadvantaged	Early Childhood	Grades 4–8	High School to Adult	K–12	Nomination	Assessment	Evaluation
	CATEGORY					POPULATION		AGE				ID STAGE		
ASSETS	●	●	●		●	●						●	●	
Barron-Welsh Art Scale					●	●		●	●	●	●	●		
Biographical Inventory-Form U		●	●	●	●	●			●	●			●	
California Achievement Tests		●			●					●	●	●		
California Psychology Inventory					●				●	●		●		
Cartoon Conservation Scales	●					●	●	●				●	●	
Cattell Culture Fair Intelligence Series	●					●	●	●				●		
CIRCUS	●	●				●	●	●				●	●	
Cognitive Abilities Test	●				●		●	●				●	●	
Columbia Mental Maturity Scale	●				●	●	●	●				●	●	
Comprehensive Tests of Basic Skills		●			●					●	●	●		
Cornell Critical Thinking Tests					●					●		●		●
Creativity Assessment Packet			●		●	●	●	●				●		
Creativity Tests for Children			●		●	●	●	●				●		
Design Judgment Test				●	●			●	●			●		
Differential Aptitude Tests	●	●			●				●	●		●		●
Early School Personality Questionnaire					●	●	●	●				●		
Gifted and Talented Screening Form	●	●	●	●	●	●		●	●	●		●		
Goodenough-Harris Drawing Test	●				●	●	●	●	●			●		
Group Inventory for Finding Creative Talent (GIFT)			●		●	●	●	●				●	●	
Group Inventory for Finding Interests (GIFFI)			●		●					●		●	●	
Guilford-Holley L Inventory					●					●		●		
Guilford-Zimmerman Aptitude Survey	●				●					●		●		
Henmon-Nelson Tests of Mental Ability	●	●			●				●	●	●	●		
High School Personality Questionnaire					●				●	●		●		
Horn Art Aptitude Inventory				●	●	●				●		●		
Iowa Tests of Basic Skills		●			●		●	●	●			●	●	
Kaufman—ABC	●	●			●	●		●				●	●	
Khatena-Torrance Creative Perception Inventory			●		●			●	●	●		●	●	
Lorge-Thorndike Intelligence Tests	●				●		●	●	●			●		
Maier Art Judgment Tests				●	●			●	●			●		
Metropolitan Achievement Tests		●			●							●	●	
Multidimensional Screening Device	●	●	●	●	●	●						●		
Musical Aptitude Profile				●	●	●	●		●	●	●	●	●	
Otis-Lennon Mental Ability Test	●					●						●	●	

If data from teachers do not differ markedly from test scores, rather than offering complementary information, such data may have a similar bias. In that case, data from teachers may be renormed in the same manner. The scores from teacher nomination forms can be disaggregated and ranked within each of the various subpopulations, and a fixed top percentage from within, rather than across, each subpopulation may be selected.

INSTRUMENT	CATEGORY					POPULATION		AGE				ID STAGE		
	General Intellectual	Specific Academic	Creativity	Leadership	Visual and Performing Arts	Advantaged	Disadvantaged	Early Childhood	Grades 4–8	High School to Adult	K–12	Nomination	Assessment	Evaluation
Peabody Individual Achievement Test		●				●					●	●		
Pennsylvania Assessment of Creative Tendency			●			●		●	●			●		
Piers-Harris Children's Self-Concept Scale						●		●	●			●		
Preschool Talent Checklist	●	●	●	●	●	●	●	●				●		
Primary Measure of Music Audiation					●	●	●	●				●		
Progressive Matrices—Advanced	●					●				●		●		
Progressive Matrices—Standard	●					●						●		
Remote Associates Test						●		●				●	●	
Ross Test of Higher Cognitive Processes	●					●		●				●		●
Scales for Rating Behavioral Characteristics of Superior Students	●		●	●	●	●	●				●	●		
Seashore Measures of Musical Talents					●	●	●		●	●		●		
The Self-Concept and Motivation Inventory (SCAMIN)						●	●	●	●	●		●		
Sequential Tests of Educational Progress (STEP)		●				●	●		●	●		●		●
Short Form Test of Academic Aptitude	●	●				●	●		●	●		●		
Slosson Intelligence Test	●					●		●		●		●		
SOI Gifted Screening Form		●	●			●	●	●	●	●		●	●	
SOI Learning Abilities Test		●	●			●	●	●	●	●		●	●	
SRA Achievement Series		●				●					●	●	●	
Stallings' Environmentally Based Screen	●					●	●					●		
Stanford Achievement Test		●				●	●	●	●			●	●	
Stanford-Binet Intelligence Scale	●					●		●	●			●		
System of Multicultural Pluralistic Assessment (SOMPA)	●					●	●					●		
Tennessee Self-Concept Scale						●		●				●		
Test of Creative Potential			●			●		●	●			●	●	
Tests of Achievement and Proficiency		●				●				●		●	●	
Torrance Test of Creative Thinking—Verbal			●			●			●					
Torrance Test of Creative Thinking			●				●		●	●		●	●	
Torrance Test of Creative Thinking—Figural										●		●	●	
Vane Kindergarten Test	●	●				●						●	●	
Watson-Glaser Critical Thinking Appraisal	●					●			●	●		●		●
Weschler Intelligence Scale for Children Revised (WISC-R)	●					●		●	●	●		●		
Weschler Preschool and Primary Scale of Intelligence	●					●		●				●		

Alternative Test Procedures for Learning-Disabled or Handicapped Students. Tests that are not affected by specific handicapping conditions should be used to assess the exceptional potential of learning-disabled and handicapped students. These students may also be identified by using non-standardized data, such as parent, self, or teacher nominations.

Appropriate Use of Multiple Sources of Data

Recent work in the field of cognitive science, as reviewed above in the discussion of defensible definitions, presents a very strong case for multiple and discrete kinds of intelligence (rather than single-factored intelligence), each of which requires different assessment measures.

Precautions should be taken when using data from various measures. Districts should not add apples and oranges when collecting formal and informal data. The purpose of using data from different sources is *not to validate or confirm* one source with another (parent nomination and teacher nomination, or IQ and achievement test scores, for example). The goal is to have a variety of measures *complement each other* in order to find diverse indicators of potential that a single measure cannot reflect.

Data from different sources should be used *independently,* and each source should be sufficient to include a student in a program. High scores should be used only to *include* students. *Cutoff scores should not be used* since they tend to exclude creative, underachieving, and disadvantaged students. Intellectually creative or disadvantaged students should not be excluded from a program solely on the basis of a test score if there are other indicators of exceptional potential, such as teacher, parent, or self-nominations. In other words, a high score on a nonstandardized measure *or* a standardized test should be enough to offer entry into a program for at least 1 year. Students should be able to qualify for a program by scoring high on *any* of several measures, rather than on most or all.

Other Procedures and Sources of Information

Data from Parents, Teachers, and Peers. Checklists and other informal data from parents, teachers, and peers should be used appropriately to *complement* rather than confirm tests or other data about school achievement at appropriate stages of an ongoing assessment. They are especially important to ensure identification of the disadvantaged populations cited above. At the primary (K–3) level, parents are good sources of information about a child's strengths and intrinsic motivation demonstrated by extracurricular activities outside school. At all grade levels, teachers *trained* in negative characteristics of the gifted are particularly good sources of observations about creative behaviors. A list of some negative characteristics associated with high levels of creativity, critical thinking, or intrinsic motivation is presented in Table 7.2. Without such training, data from teachers may offer information even less useful than a standardized test (Gear, 1976, 1978). Checklists provide opportunities for seeking information about students' activities beyond the required curriculum.

Peer nominations are useful especially to find leadership potential, for it is from peers that leaders emerge and by peers that leaders must first be recognized. Peer nominations also have some utility in the area of creativity, since peers have a good basis for judging the exceptionality, imaginativeness, and uniqueness of a fellow student's ideas.

The panelists for the National Report (Richert et al., 1982) stressed that the following standards should be used for such instruments:

- Characteristics listed should be *research based,* not just the product of a well-intentioned local committee (several are included in Chapter 6 of the *National Report*).
- The list should include negative or unexpected characteristics indicated by the research.
- Teachers using such instruments must be *trained* to observe especially the negative behaviors.

In addition, nomination forms should produce different scores for diverse abilities. For example, a minimum requirement would be for teacher observation checklists to evaluate both specific academic abilities that the program addresses and intellectual creativity. Because achievement and IQ tests tend to screen out the most creative students and teachers often have biases against the nonconforming student, nominations for creativity are especially cru-

Table 7.2
Characteristics of the Gifted That Tend to Screen Them Out of Programs

BEHAVIORS	ASSOCIATED WITH:
Bored with routine tasks, refuses to do rote homework. Not interest in details; hands in messy work. Makes jokes or puns at inappropriate times.	CREATIVITY • High tolerance of ambiguity • Independent, divergent thinking • Risk taking • Imaginative, sensitive
Refuses to accept authority; nonconforming, stubborn. Difficult to get her to move onto another topic.	MOTIVATION • Persistence in interest areas
Emotionally sensitive—may overreact, get angry easily, or be ready to cry if things go wrong.	• Intensity of feelings and values • Independence
Tends to dominate others. Often disagrees vocally with others or with the teacher about ideas or values.	CRITICAL THINKING • Sees discrepancies between real/ideal truth/expression
Is self-critical, impatient with failures. Is critical of others, of the teachers.	• Sets high standards • Capable of analysis and evaluation

cial. With the exception of the Torrance Tests of Creative Thinking (the Figural version is especially useful with all populations including the disadvantaged) (Torrance & Ball, 1984) and the Structure of the Intellect—Learning Abilities test (Meeker, Meeker, & Roid, 1985), there are very few readily available standardized tests that will elicit scores in creativity.

Self-Nominations. Starting at about grade 4, self-nominations have been used very successfully in many programs. Students are informed about the curriculum and objectives or invited to visit various program options. They apply for those that interest them. This method taps into the intrinsic motivation and intense interests of the gifted. Table 7.3 includes an interview protocol for self-nominations. Table 7.4 is a form for assessing interviews in terms of student motivation, interests, creativity, and quality of efforts beyond the required curriculum.

Use of Data on Student Progress. The last stage of identification is evaluation. If a program for the gifted offers effective, trained staff, an appropriate curriculum, and enough time within each program option, then identification should be not only an ongoing process. Students should be assessed annually to determine *not* whether they are "gifted," but whether they should remain in a particular program option or would be better served in another option or in the regular classroom. The same data being gathered to evaluate individual students may be used in aggregate for program evaluation and improvement.

Table 7.3
Interview Protocol for Self-Nominations

1. On what do you spend most of your time outside school when *you* can choose the activity?
2. How much time do you spend on this activity or interest?
3. From whom or where did you learn about this activity or interest?
4. What have you done or produced as a result of your interest?
5. How would you evaluate the quality, effectiveness, or originality of your achievement?
6. What more would you like to know about your interest?
7. Would you like to talk with people who are experts on your interest, or read more about it?
8. If you had help in getting the information, materials or contacting experts, would you want to prepare a project, paper, model, slide tape, talk, artwork, and so on, or use your new information for some real problem you or someone else wants to solve?
9. What problems have you had in trying to study or work independently? In using your time? In finding information? In completing your project?
10. Would you like help in improving in these areas?

Richert et al. (1982) and Hagen (in an interview by Silverman, 1986a), among others, point out that criteria used to place students into programs are not necessarily appropriate for exiting them. The real challenge in evaluating student progress in a program for the gifted is the development of standards for evaluation that correlate with adult original contributions to a field, so that the present low or inverse correlation between school performance and later original contributions will be defeated and more students will be able to develop their gifted potential. Data on student progress in a program option (related to the program's curriculum objectives, which should be designed to develop not only higher level cognitive abilities, both creative and critical-thinking, but also higher level emotional and ethical potential), rather than any changes in standardized test scores that may have provided students entry into the program, should determine whether a student continues in the

Table 7.4
Assessment of Interview

	Not at All	Somewhat	To a Great Degree
1. Does the student initiate his or her own activities?			
2. Is the student's interest *intense* enough so he or she has sought or will seek to learn more?			
3. Does the student show motivation to apply what he or she may learn to produce something?			
4. Does the student indicate commitment to use his or her abilities and be productive?			
5. Do activities, products, or achievements indicate an original or creative approach?			
6. Does the student have problems in initiating or completing independent activity?			
7. Are there areas such as time management that require attention?			
8. Does the student need assistance in developing research skills?			

program each year. (See Richert, 1986, for analysis of the higher levels of cognitive, affective, and ethical taxonomies appropriate for curriculum objectives.)

The few standardized tests appropriate at this stage are specified in the "Evaluation" column on the list of test instruments included in Table 7.1. These tests may provide some assessment of progress in critical thinking. However, teacher, self, and peer *product and process evaluations* are very useful indicators of progress. Product evaluations should include assessments of higher level cognitive skills such as creativity, complexity, and pragmatism (does it work?) as well as critical thinking. Process evaluation by self and teacher should address, in addition to cognitive skills used, higher level affective and social skills such as independence, intrinsic motivation, risk taking, persistence, decision making, cooperation, and so forth. Process and product evaluation may be carried out through the use of various criterion-referenced scales and checklists that address the goals of the program. Many have been collected in an evaluation handbook (Richert, 1978).

Developmental Curriculum

Elsewhere, I point out that the regular classroom is a de facto identification procedure (Richert, 1987). If the regular classroom develops only those abilities that can be measured by tests or recognized by teachers, then many underachieving or disadvantaged students will be missed in identification. If, however, the regular class does indeed develop higher level cognitive and affective abilities, then it can offer what may be called a *developmental curriculum* that can evoke gifted potential (Richert, 1987). The long-range educational goal of all districts should be to train all teachers in methods that maximize the potential of all students. Then whatever their background, characteristics, or diverse potential, students could be identified because their abilities would become manifest. Another immeasurable benefit of this approach would be the improvement of the quality of education for all students. This is one of the ways that the goal of Machado (1980), to develop maximum intel-

lectual potential in all segments of Venezuelan society, could be applied in our society.

Comprehensive Low-Cost Programs

Because of the inevitable competition for resources, an inexpensive program design is necessary to serve the 20 to 25% of students with gifted potential who require programs to develop their abilities. A crucial advocacy issue to consider is that identifying much fewer than 20% of students will tend to polarize parents of high-achieving students and disadvantaged or minority parents in the competition for places in a program. In order to develop a high-quality program that can serve the diverse needs of up to 25 or even 30% of a student population, I have recommended a five-step plan for modifying a diversity of existing district resources (including homogeneous grouping in required subject areas, the regular classroom, cocurricular activities, and electives, among many others; Richert, 1985a, b, c). Two of the most crucial steps in this approach are equitable identification and intensive staff development for those faculty who will be teaching the various program options. Without a pragmatic and comprehensive program design, broad-based and equitable identification cannot be carried out.

Conclusion

Pluralism, or the celebration of diversity, as Alexis de Tocqueville observed, is the hallmark of American democracy. Rather than developing identification procedures and programs that are elitist and exclusive, programs for the gifted should reflect American pluralism. Educators should also adopt the Hippocratic injunction to "do no harm" by avoiding errors and distortions that exclude some students from programs that they need or impose impossible expectations on students. Programs for students with gifted potential can be defensible and equitable if the following practices are followed:

- Adoption of a comprehensive and pluralistic definition that includes diverse abilities and emphasizes potential rather than labeling

- Recognition that the purpose of identification and programmatic provisions for the gifted is not to label or to reward achievement or conformity to school expectations, but to find and develop exceptional potential
- Use of data about cognitive (especially creative) and noncognitive abilities from various sources beyond academic achievement to identify diverse, discrete gifted abilities
- Appropriate assessment of data from multiple sources
- Equitable use of academic achievement data by renorming test scores to overcome bias against various disadvantaged groups, particularly the poor and minority groups
- Identification of up to 25% of a district's population so that if errors are made they are errors of inclusion rather than exclusion
- Development of cost-effective multiple program options to serve the diverse needs of a heterogeneous gifted population
- Funding of appropriate staff development

This pluralistic approach incorporates the expanding conceptualizations of giftedness and provides equitable, comprehensive, defensible, and pragmatic identification procedures and programs that can serve the needs of both students and our society.

REFERENCES

Angoff, W. H. (1971). Scales, norms and equivalent sources. In R. L. Thorndike (Ed.), *Educational measurement* (pp. 514–515). Washington, DC: American Council on Education.

Baird, L. L. (1982). *The role of academic ability in high level accomplishment and general success* (College Board Report No. 82). New York: College Board Publications.

Baldwin, J. W. (1962). The relationship between teacher-judged giftedness, a group intelligence test and an individual test with possible gifted kindergarten pupils. *Gifted Child Quarterly, 6,* 153–156.

Barbe, W. B. (1964). *One in a thousand—A comparative study of moderately and highly gifted country elementary school children.* Columbus: Ohio State Department of Education, Division of Special Education.

Black, H. (1963). *They shall not pass.* New York: Morrow.

Ciha, T. E., Harris, R., Hoffman, C., & Potter, M. (1974). Parents and identifiers of giftedness, ignored but accurate. *Gifted Child Quarterly, 18,* 202–209.

Colangelo, N., & Brower, P. (1987). Gifted youngsters and their siblings: Long-term impact of labeling on their academic and personal self-concepts. *Roeper Review, 10,* 101–103.

Cornish, R. C. (1968). Parents', teachers', and pupils' perception of the gifted child's ability. *Gifted Child Quarterly, 12,* 14–47.

Cox, J., Daniel, N., & Boston, B. O. (1985). *Educating able learners.* Austin: University of Texas Press.

Davis, A., Gardner, B., & Gardner, M. R. (1941). *Deep South.* Chicago: University of Chicago Press.

Gardner, H. (1983). *Frames of mind.* NY: Basic.

Gear, G. H. (1976). Teacher judgment in identification of gifted children. *Gifted Child Quarterly, 10,* 478–489.

Gear, G. H. (1978). Effects of training on teachers' accuracy in identifying gifted children. *Gifted Child Quarterly, 12,* 90–97.

Goleman, D. (1984, July 31). Style of thinking, not IQ, tied to success. *New York Times,* pp. 14, 15, 18.

Goolsby, T. M. (1975). *Alternative admissions criteria for college: Nontraditional approaches to assess the academic potential of black students.* Atlanta, GA: Southern Regional Education Board.

Guilford, J. P. (1977). *Way beyond the IQ.* Buffalo, NY: Bearly.

Hansen, M., Hurwitz, W., & Madow, W. (1953). *Sample survey methods and theory* (Vol. 1). New York: Wiley.

Hoffman, B. (1962). *The tyranny of testing.* New York: Crowell-Collier.

Holland, J. L. (1959). Some limitations of teacher ratings as predictors of creativity. *Journal of Educational Psychology, 50,* 219–223.

Holland, J., & Richards, J. M. (1965). *Academic and non-accomplishment: Correlated or uncorrelated?* (ACT Research Report No. 2.). Iowa City: The American College Testing Program.

Hoyt, D. P. (1965). *The relationship between college grades and adult achievement: A review of the literature* (ACT Research Report No. 7.). Iowa City: The American College Testing Program.

Jacobs, J. C. (1971). Effectiveness of teacher and parent identification of gifted children as a function of school level. *Psychology in the Schools, 8,* 140–142.

Kamin, L. J. (1974). *The science and politics of IQ.* New York: Wiley.

Kerr, B., Colangelo, N., & Gaeth, J. (1988). Gifted adolescents' attitudes toward their giftedness. *Gifted Child Quarterly, 32,* 245–247.

Klineberg, O. (1935). *Race differences*. New York: Harper & Row.

Machado, L. A. (1980). *The right to be intelligent*. Elmsford, NY: Pergamon.

Marland, S. P., Jr. (1972). *Education of the gifted and talented: Report to the Congress of the United States by the U.S. Commissioner of Education*. Washington, DC: Department of Health, Education, and Welfare.

Meeker, M. N., Meeker, R., & Roid, G. (1985). *Structure-of-intellect learning abilities test (SOI-LA)*. Los Angeles: Western Psychological Services.

Miller, A. (1981). *Prisoners of childhood: How narcissitic parents form and deform the emotional lives of their gifted children*. New York: Basic.

Miller, L. P. (Ed.). (1974). *The testing of black students: A symposium*. Englewood Cliffs, NJ: Prentice-Hall.

Munday, L. S., & Davis, J. C. (1974). *Varieties of accomplishment after college: Perspective of the meaning of academic talent* (ACT Research Report No. 7.). Iowa City: The American College Testing Program.

Nairn, A., & Associates (1980). *The reign of ETS: The corporation that makes up minds* (the Ralph Nader report on the Educational Testing Service). Washington DC: Ralph Nader.

New York State Department of Education. (n.d.). *Guidelines for the identification of the gifted and talented*. Albany: The State Education Department.

Pegnato, C. C., & Birch, J. W. (1959). Locating gifted children in junior high schools: A comparison of methods. *Exceptional Children, 25,* 300–304.

Piechowski, M. M., & Colangelo, N. (1984). Developmental potential of the gifted. *Gifted Child Quarterly, 8,* 80–88.

Price, P. B., Taylor, C. W., Richards, J. M., & Jacobsen, T. L. (1964). Measurement of physician performance. *Journal of Medical Education, 39,* 203–211.

Renzulli, J. S. (1978). What makes giftedness: Reexamining a definition. *Phi Delta Kappan, 60,* 108–184.

Richert, E. S. (Ed.). (1978). *Evaluation handbook for gifted programs*. Sewell, NJ: Educational Information and Resource Center.

Richert, E. S. (1985a). Using existing resources for programs for the gifted and talented. In Richert, E. S. (Ed.), *Administration handbook for gifted programs* (pp. 37–70). Sewell, NJ: Educational Information and Resource Center.

Richert, E. S. (1985b). Identification of gifted children in the United States: The need for pluralistic assessment. *Roeper Review, 8,* 68–72.

Richert, E. S. (1985c). The state of the art of identification of gifted students in the United States. *Gifted Education International, 3,* 47–51.

Richert, E. S. (1986). Toward the Tao of giftedness. *Roeper Review, 8,* 197–204.

Richert, E. S. (1987). Rampant problems and promising practices in the identification of disadvantaged gifted students. *Gifted Child Quarterly, 31,* 149–154.

Richert, E. S., Alvino, J., & McDonnel, R. (1982). *The national report on identification: Assessment and recommendations for comprehensive identification of gifted and talented youth*. Sewell, NJ: Educational Information and Resource Center, for US Department of Education.

Roeper, A. (1982). How the gifted cope with their emotions. *Roeper Review, 5,* 21–24.

Samuda, R. J. (1975). Alternatives to traditional standardized tests, introduction. In R. J. Samuda (Ed.), *Psychological testing of American minorities* (pp. 131–157). New York: Dodd, Mead.

Silverman, L. K. (1986a). An interview with Elizabeth Hagen: Giftedness, intelligence and the new Stanford-Binet. *Roeper Review, 8*(3), 168–171.

Silverman, L. K. (Ed.). (1986b). The IQ controversy (special issue). *Roeper Review, 8*(3).

Sternberg, R. (1985). *Beyond I.Q.* Cambridge: Cambridge University Press.

Sudman, S. (1976). *Applied sampling*. New York: Academic.

Tannenbaum, A. J. (1983). *Gifted children: Psychological and educational perspectives*. New York: Macmillan.

Taylor, C. W., Albo, D., Holland, J., & Brandt, G. (1985). Attributes of excellence in various professions: Their relevance to the selection of gifted/talented persons. *Gifted Child Quarterly, 29,* 29–34.

Taylor, C. W., & Ellison, R. L. (1967). Biographical predictors of scientific performance. *Science, 155,* 1075–1080.

Torrance, E. P. (1964). *Education and the creative potential*. Minneapolis: University of Minnesota Press.

Torrance, E. P. (1979). *The search for satori and creativity*. Buffalo: Creative Education Foundation.

Torrance, E. P., & Ball, O. E. (1984). *Torrance tests of creative thinking: Streamlined* (Revised manual, Figural A and B). Bensenville, IL: Scholastic Testing Service.

United States Department of Education. (1979). *Office of Civil Rights report*. Washington, DC: U.S. Government Printing Office.

Wilson, C. (1963). Using test results and teacher evaluation in identifying gifted pupils. *Personnel and Guidance, 41,* 720–721.

Wood, C. T., & Talmadge, G. K. (1976). *Local norms: ESEA Title I evaluation and reporting systems* (Technical paper No. 7). Mountain View, CA: RMC Research.

Yarborough, B. H., & Johnson, R. A. (1983). Identifying the gifted: A theory–practice gap. *Gifted Child Quarterly, 27,* 135–138.

PART III

Instructional Models and Practices

Enrichment and Acceleration:
An Overview and New Directions

SHIRLEY W. SCHIEVER   *Tucson Unified School District, Tuscon, Arizona*
C. JUNE MAKER   *University of Arizona, Tucson*

■ The question "Is this an enrichment or an acceleration program?" is indicative of two of the problems associated with these terms. First, the implication is made that no program could be both enriched and accelerated, that one mode must be chosen and adhered to, and that never the twain shall meet. Second, by referring to enrichment or acceleration *programs,* confusion is created. Does enrichment refer to the curriculum or the service delivery of the program? Does an acceleration program deliver an accelerated curriculum, or does it provide for the (grade) acceleration of students? The purpose of this chapter is to clarify the confusion that exists and to make a case for the complementary nature of enrichment and acceleration and the necessity for inclusion of both in curriculum for gifted students. To this end, a brief overview of enrichment and acceleration practices will be provided, an application of catastrophe theory to curriculum for the gifted offered, and a model of thinking presented as a structure for developing and examining curricula.

Enrichment

The term *enrichment* is used to refer to curriculum as well as program delivery services. *Enriched curriculum* refers to richer, more varied educational experiences, a curriculum that has been modified or added to in some way (Davis & Rimm, 1989; Howley, Howley, & Pendarvis, 1986). These modifications or additions may be in content or in teaching strategies, and ideally they are based on the characteristics of the learners for whom they are designed.

An *enrichment program* goal is to offer students curriculum that is greater in depth or breadth than that generally provided. After-school or Saturday classes, resource rooms, additions to regular-classroom curriculum, or special interest clubs may be used as ways to implement an enrichment program. The key element for an enrichment program should be a *systematic* plan for extended student learning.

Renzulli's enrichment triad (1977) is designed to provide a variety of enrichment experiences. This model provides for three levels of enrichment that offer stimulating experiences and process training to all or most students in a school, with the gifted (those with above-average intelligence, creativity, and task commitment) responding to these experiences by tackling real problems (such as local pollution) and developing real products (such as letters to the editor or presentations to the town council).

While the triad model offers advantages such as enrichment for all students and services for a relatively large number of qualified students, it has inherent disadvantages as well. These include (1) the exclusion of underachieving or unmotivated gifted students from the in-depth explorations of real problems, (2) the difficulty of ensuring relatively consistent enrichment across the school population, and (3) the logistic and liability problems associated with students' conducting research in, and interacting with, members of the community.

Howley, Howley, and Pendarvis (1986) describe three approaches to enrichment: process oriented, content oriented, and product oriented. Each of these approaches will be considered briefly as it applies to curriculum.

The process-oriented approach to enrichment is designed to develop students' higher mental processes and, in some cases, their creative production as well. Students usually are taught the steps of components of one or more models, such as Bloom's taxonomy of cognitive objectives (Bloom, Englehart, Furst, Hill, & Krathwohl, 1956), creative problem solving (Parnes, 1981), the structure of intellect (Guilford, 1967), or strategies for thinking and feeling (Williams, 1972) and are required or encouraged to apply the focus skills through using learning centers, engaging in discussions, and/or conducting an independent study on a topic of interest to them.

One concern regarding this approach is that frequently the thinking processes are taught and/or practiced in isolation from content, or subject matter. The resulting fragmentation is not likely to promote the transfer of the higher thinking skills to other content areas or to daily problems or situations. Many times, games that require strategic planning or problem solving are used to "teach thinking," and this results in justified criticism. Thinking processes are best taught and practiced using substantive content. If students are expected to think, they need something to think *about*.

Content-oriented approaches to enrichment stress the presentation of a particular content area. Generally, the curriculum for mathematics, science, language arts, or the social sciences is treated with a greater breadth and depth than is possible in the regular curriculum. Offerings may be in the form of minicourses, museum and science center programs, college options for precollege students, and mentorships (Howley et al., 1986). For example, at the elementary level, students might be offered a minicourse in prealgebra; at the junior high level students could be offered a mentorship with an astronomer; or at the high school level students might enroll in either Advanced Placement (AP) biology, calculus, chemistry, English, or American history or in classes held on a college campus. (AP classes also are considered to be a content-acceleration method.)

The disadvantage of minicourses and special programs is that usually the enrichment is separated from the curriculum students are exposed to on a consistent basis in the regular class or classroom. This violates developmental and curricular principles. From a developmental standpoint, learning experiences should be sequential if skills and the information base are to develop in a logical progression and rest on a solid foundation. Such detached offerings also violate the curriculum principle of *organization* (Maker, 1982a, 1982b); that is, all or major portions of instruction and learning experiences should be organized around basic concepts or abstract generalizations that enable students to learn efficiently and see the interconnectedness among concepts and disciplines.

Product-oriented enrichment programs emphasize primarily the *result* or *product* of instruction rather than the content or processes involved. Products may be tangible, such as a report, painting, novel, or presentation, or intangible, such as improved mental health (Howley et al., 1986) or coping skills. Commonly, enrichment programs purportedly emphasize processes (the higher levels of thinking), but in reality, process instruction is directed toward demonstrating the processes learned by developing products. This situation may result from the pressure exerted on teacher and student alike to show what happens in the program for the gifted, that is, to produce evidence that learning *is* occurring and that it *is* different from regular class activities.

The criticism of product-oriented enrichment is that frequently it results in a "make it and take it" system, in which students churn out products without establishing a knowledge base or striving for accuracy and excellence in the product. Quantity becomes the yardstick rather than quality. Such situations represent a lack of understanding of the necessity for, and role of, process, content, *and* product in curriculum enrichment for gifted students.

Acceleration

The term *acceleration* is commonly used to denote models of both service delivery and curriculum delivery. Acceleration as a service-delivery model includes early entrance to kindergarten or to college; grade skipping; or part-time grade acceleration, in which a student enters a higher grade level for part of the school day to receive advance instruction in one or more content areas. Service-delivery acceleration offers standard curricular experiences to students at a younger-than-usual age or lower-than-usual grade level. Acceleration as a curriculum model involves speeding up the pace at which material is presented and/or expected to be mastered. Such acceleration may occur in a regular classroom, a resource room, or special classes. It may take the form of telescoping, so that students complete 2 or more year's work in 1 year, or self-paced studies. While each type of acceleration has advantages, certain disadvantages also exist; both will be discussed briefly.

Early entrance to kindergarten or first grade allows children who are ready for the academic rigors and the structure of school to encounter learning that may be challenging. Early entrance also allows students to complete schooling at a relatively young age, leaving more time for career and professional development. However, early entrance may tax the physical maturity of some children. They may tire before older students or experience frustration with the level of their psychomotor development. That is, their fine motor coordination may be underdeveloped by kindergarten standards, and they may have difficulty manipulating crayons or pencils. Additionally, this placement does not provide intellectual peers for the gifted child; average 5-year-old children do not think in the same ways or about the same topics as gifted 4-year-old children. Early entrance to college usually holds fewer perils than early entrance to kindergarten, unless the gifted students hope to socialize with college students of normal college age. However, the intellectual stimulation and challenges of good college courses may override this disappointment.

Full-time grade acceleration (grade skipping) is an economical way to provide for gifted students. For some students, usually those in the primary grades, parents and students may find grade skipping offers sufficient challenges, and therefore is a viable placement. However, grade skipping may put older gifted students at a maturational disadvantage similar to that of the young kindergartener. This disadvantage becomes more pronounced during the middle and high school years, when physical maturation determines athletic prowess and influences heavily an individual's self-confidence.

Acceleration as a service-delivery model fails to provide a differentiated curriculum for gifted learners. Students receive instruction and have learning experiences that are designed for average students who are *older* than the gifted students, but the curriculum is not changed to match the needs of the gifted. The pace and content remain unchanged; the learner merely experiences them at an earlier age than usual.

Telescoping curriculum content so that gifted students may cover more material in less time and self-paced learning are types of curriculum acceleration. Bright students may master material rapidly and feel good about their accomplishments in this type of acceleration, and it is an economical plan. Telescoping and content acceleration generally present more problems to teachers and administrators than to students. Teachers need the requisite skills and time to telescope curriculum, and self-paced content acceleration for individual students also requires planning time and special management techniques.

As with acceleration as a service-delivery model, acceleration as a curriculum model offers "the same but sooner and/or faster" to gifted students. The content, learning processes, and expected products remain the same for students, whether they are gifted or not; only the onset and pace change.

Research on Acceleration

Researchers have studied acceleration of the various types and at different grade levels and generally have reported academic achievement and social adjustment equal to or better than nonaccelerated, similar-ability peers, with no discernible negative effects from the acceleration. Reported advantages of acceleration include (1) improved motivation, confidence, and scholarship; (2) prevention of lazy mental habits; (3) early completion of professional training; and (4) reduction of the cost of education (Van Tassel-Baska, 1986).

In spite of evidence supporting the efficacy of acceleration for gifted students, widespread resistance to the concept and practice exists. The current organizational structure of most schools is geared to average students, with few provisions for the gifted; teachers and administrators are reluctant to allow or create variances for individual students. Service-delivery acceleration or individually paced learning also challenges the purpose of school, in terms of the democratic ideal and the concept of socialization with age peers. Additionally, acceleration as it has been practiced frequently has meant only covering more material faster, and the belief exists that acceleration is responsible for social maladjustment or that it creates skill gaps in core areas (Van Tassel-Baska, 1986).

Enrichment and Acceleration as Complementary Program Components

Combining or integrating enrichment and acceleration for gifted students is not a revolutionary idea. In practice, meeting the needs of gifted students as determined by their learning characteristics requires that abstract and complex concepts be taught (enrichment) and that students proceed at a pace that is more rapid than that of the average learner (acceleration). Additionally, support for such integration may be found in the literature. Fox (1979) believes that acceleration means the adjustment of learning time to meet student capabilities and that this adjustment will lead to higher levels of abstraction, more creative thinking, and mastery of more difficult content. Van Tassel-Baska (1981) stated that the term *enrichment* has no meaning for the gifted unless it is inextricably bound to good acceleration practices. Davis and Rimm (1989), in asking whether a special math, computer, or foreign language class in the elementary school is considered enrichment or acceleration, implied that in many cases the dichotomy is a false one.

As evidenced by practice and the literature, enrichment and acceleration are complementary components of comprehensive curriculum for gifted learners. In the remainder of this chapter, using the concept of catastrophe theory as rationale and organizer, we will make a case for the necessity of including both enrichment and acceleration components in curriculum for gifted students.

Catastrophe Theory and Curriculum for Gifted Students

As explained by Berliner (1986), catastrophe theory is a mathematical system to account for abrupt changes in the nature of objects. It was invented by René Thom, a topological mathematician, and first published in 1968 in France. The theory may be applied to phenomena that are discontinuous, sudden, and unpredictable, wherein change occurs imperceptibly or gradually to a point and then suddenly a new state occurs. The simplest example from the physical world is the change of water into steam. As water heats, at some point (depending on the interaction of temperature, volume, pressure, and chemical particles), the water changes from liquid to gas. More heat has become the agent of a qualitative change; an interaction among factors has occurred. In Berliner's (1986) words, "More leads to different" (p. 34).

When applying the catastrophe theory to curriculum, the critical factors are curriculum content, process, and product, and acceleration and enrichment. Curriculum content, processes, and products must be accelerated and enriched to that point at which *more* becomes *different*. This is the point at which an interaction occurs; the curriculum becomes *qualitatively differentiated*. Further discussion and examples of this concept follow.

One recommended modification to the *content* of curriculum for gifted students is an increase in the level of abstractness (Maker, 1982a). The concepts selected to be taught should be abstract rather than concrete; thus they should be concepts such as culture, values, and mathematical patterns. Choosing abstract concepts *enriches* the curriculum, but the presentation and exploration of the concepts also must be *accelerated* if the dynamic of catastrophe theory is to be activated, if the curriculum is to become qualitatively different. For example, a regular sixth-grade curriculum might include a study of the eastern hemisphere. Gifted students need to establish a factual information base, just as others do. However, gifted students should spend the majority of their time dealing with abstract concepts such as culture, cause–effect relationships, or political and economic systems. The abstractness of the content provides a type of enrichment, as this is beyond the regular curriculum, but the pace of presentation also must be accelerated.

The *processes* of instruction and learning included in curriculum for gifted students should be modified in a variety of ways, including an emphasis on the higher levels of thinking (Maker, 1982a). For example, gifted students should spend the majority of their time critically examining, synthesizing, and evaluating ideas, rather than memorizing and applying information and procedures. Focusing on the higher thought processes enriches the curriculum; these skills should be taught and practiced at an accelerated rate as well. The acceleration involves teaching the skills to students at younger-than-usual ages as well as pacing the instruction more rapidly than normal.

Student *products* reflect content learned and processes engaged in before and during the creation of the product. Products of gifted students should demonstrate the results of enrichment and acceleration of content and process instruction by the sophistication of the concepts included and the presentation, form, or format of the finished product. For example, average fourth-grade students, on completion of a unit of study on their state of residence, might submit reports of factual information about the state and include a map and drawings of the state flag, flower, and bird. A more abstract approach suitable for gifted fourth-grade students might focus on the effects of political forces on their state's government and economic climate. After examining and evaluating these forces, these students might develop and give presentations to state legislators regarding the effect of, for example, underfunding educational programs or the attraction of new industry to the state.

Applying catastrophe theory to the acceleration and enrichment of the content, processes, and products of the curriculum for gifted students provides a conceptual framework for differentiating such curriculum. The critical point is that all three factors—content, process, and product—must be both enriched *and* accelerated. Without both acceleration and enrichment, more is simply more; the point of the interaction that produces a quali-

tative difference is not reached. Acceleration and enrichment are necessary but not sufficient factors in developing and presenting curriculum to gifted learners. The catastrophic change that produces differentiated curriculum only occurs when all factors are present to a sufficient degree.

The Spiral Model of Thinking

Schiever (1990) has developed a model of thinking that provides a framework within which to examine the role of acceleration and enrichment in curriculum development. A brief explanation of the spiral model of thinking follows.

Schiever envisions thinking skills and the development of thinking as a spiraling continuum of skills, maturation, and experiences. The continuum of thought originates with *enabling skills* and includes *developmental processes, complex thinking strategies*, and *solving undefined or real-life problems*.

In the spiral model, the most basic building block of cognition is the *enabling skills*. These skills drive and make possible all thinking; they feed directly into the developmental processes, but are present in complex thinking strategies and in solving undefined or real-life problems. While all the enabling skills are basic and relatively simple, some of these skills are more complex than others. For example, encoding or remembering are relatively simple cognitive operations; determining relevance and comparing and contrasting are more complex skills. As with all thinking, the enabling skills vary depending on the task at hand or the problem to be solved, as well as the maturity and cognitive sophistication of the thinker. For example, comparing and contrasting concrete objects, such as buttons, is a lower level operation than comparing and contrasting thought systems.

The *developmental processes* develop from simplest to most complex—*classification, concept development, deriving principles, drawing conclusions*, and *making generalizations* (see Figure 8.1). Any of the developmental processes may be transformed and applied to complex thinking tasks *at the level of the thinker's maturity and experience*. For example, young children may classify blocks accord-

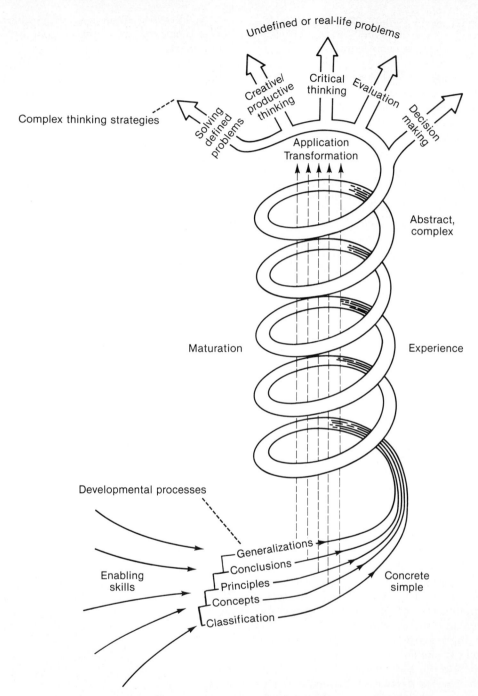

Figure 8.1 Spiral model of thinking.

ing to shape and/or color to make a pattern (solve a defined problem). As thinkers mature and incorporate more experiences into their cognitive bank, they are able to, for example, classify increasingly abstract and complex ideas. They move from the concrete (objects and experiences) to high levels of abstraction and complexity (concepts such as love, altruism, or infinity).

The developmental processes spiral through developmental stages and life experiences, gradually spiraling upward toward *transformation* and *application*. The developmental processes are transformed, that is, selectively adapted to the situation at hand, and then applied to the complex thinking strategies of (1) *defined problem solving,* (2) *decision making,* (3) *critical thinking,* (4) *creative/productive thinking,* and (4) *evaluation.* The complex thinking strategies are interrelated and make possible the solving of undefined or real-life problems (see Figure 8.1), which Schiever sees as the ultimate goal of all formal and informal cognitive instruction and development.

Curriculum for the Gifted

Experts in the field (e.g., Clark, 1983; Kaplan, 1979; Maker, 1982a) agree that curriculum for gifted students should be differentiated according to the characteristics and needs of the gifted. A number of models and checklists have been developed as ways to approach developing such differentiated curricula (Feldhusen & Wyman, 1980; Kaplan, 1974; Maker, 1982a; Sato & Johnson, 1978). Based on current research, preferred practices, a reconceptualization of the thinking process, and catastrophe theory, we offer a new approach. This approach illustrates the interdependent and interactive nature and roles of enrichment and acceleration in developing curricula for gifted students.

Problem Solving and the Curriculum

As educators focus more intensely on thinking skills and the thinking process, problem solving is mentioned frequently. Anderson's (1980) definition of problem solving as any goal-directed sequence of cognitive operations is very broad, but he is not alone in believing that thinking *is* problem solving. This belief leads to a natural progression of examining and/or planning curriculum for gifted students from a problem-solving perspective.

Types of Problems

Getzels (1964) makes a distinction between a *presented problem situation* and a *discovered problem situation.* A presented problem has a known formulation, method of solution, and solution. A discovered problem situation does not yet have a known formulation and therefore has no known method of solution and no known solution. Based on this concept, Getzels and Csikszentmihalyi (1967) developed a conceptual distinction between types of problems. According to these researchers, one can distinguish problem situations on the basis of (1) how clearly and completely the problem is stated at the beginning, (2) how much of the method for reaching the solution is available to the solver, and (3) how general the agreement about an acceptable solution is. Two ends of a continuum can be identified. At one end is a situation in which the problem, method, and solution are known to the presenter. The problem solver only needs to employ the appropriate steps to arrive at the correct solution. At the other end of the continuum is a situation in which the problem is not formulated and no known method of solution or solution exists. Most problems, or tasks and projects, in people's personal and professional lives are of the latter type.

Maker (1986) expanded a model produced by Getzels and Csikszentmihalyi (1967, p. 81), producing four problem types, and Schiever (1990) identified a fifth type. These problem types differ in what is known both to the problem presenter and the problem solver:

I The problem and the method of solution are known to the problem presenter and the problem solver, but the solution is known only to the problem presenter.

II The problem is known by the presenter and the solver, but the method of solution and the solution are known only to the presenter.

III The problem is known to the presenter and the solver, more than one method may be used to solve the problem, and the solution or range of solutions is known to the presenter.

IV The problem is known to the presenter and the solver, but the method and the solution are unknown to both the presenter and the solver.

V The problem is unknown or undefined, and the method and the solution are unknown to both the presenter and the solver (see Table 8.1). In the classroom setting, problems of this type may be presented so that students use skills necessary to solve real-life problems.

If thinking is considered to be problem solving, the utility of this conceptualization for curriculum development is readily apparent. School learning experiences typically consist primarily of Type I problems, wherein students are presented a clearly defined problem (such as in math) and taught the steps necessary to reach a solution. However, if one believes that the goal of curricula is to prepare students to be adults who successfully cope with and solve both personal and career problems, curricula also must include solving problems of types II, III, IV, and V if the necessary skills are to be taught and practiced. If gifted students are to become leaders and professionals with the capabilities society wants and needs and/or self-fulfilled adults, their school experiences must prepare them to be effective solvers of undefined, real-life problems.

Problem Solving, the Spiral Model, and Curriculum

Viewing the spiral model in terms of problem types provides a useful approach to curriculum development. The developmental processes each can be considered in light of problem types; that is, in what ways can, for example, classification be taught as a Type I, II, III, IV, or V problem? Curriculum content provides the context for teaching the developmental processes within the problem-solving perspective. Examples of such an approach to curriculum development follow. These examples are based on the belief that requiring students to memorize the results of other people's thinking is not a preferred teaching practice. Rather, students should be allowed and enabled to develop their own classification categories, concept delineations, principles, conclusions, and generalizations.

A social studies curriculum designed to teach the three key concepts of *difference, interdependence,* and *societal control* (Taba, Durkin, Fraenkel, & McNaughton, 1971) will be used to illustrate how content and process (thinking skills) can be taught within a problem-solving framework. Content objectives for the concept *differences* in Grade 1 encompass differences in (1) family composition

Table 8.1
Types of Problem Situations

	Problem		Method		Solution	
Type	Presenter	Solver	Presenter	Solver	Presenter	Solver
I	K	K	K	K	K	U
II	K	K	K	U	K	U
III	K	K	R	U	R	U
IV	K	K	U	U	U	U
V	U	U	U	U	U	U

Source: Adapted with permission from *The Creative Vision* by J. W. Getzels and M. Csikszentmihalyi, 1976, page 80, Table 6.1. Copyright © 1976 by John Wiley & Sons, New York.

Note: K = Known, U = Unknown, R = Range.

and size, (2) family responsibility, and (3) family lifestyle. The teaching of these dimensions of *difference* can be organized according to the developmental processes and the problem types. For example, to teach the skill of classification as a Type I problem in the context of *differences,* the teacher might ask students to find out how many children are in each family represented in the classroom. The families then could be classified according to teacher-provided categories related to size. This classification experience would be within the parameters provided by the teacher and would serve primarily as a foundation for the development of the concept of *differences*. The students would be solving a defined problem (a complex thinking strategy), but the Type I structure would dictate the low level of the classification behaviors and the limitations on level and frequency of use of other developmental processes or complex thinking strategies. Increasing the pace (acceleration) of experiences would not result in differentiated curriculum, since neither content nor processes would be enriched.

A Type II activity might require students to classify families according to whether they are the same as or different from the (individual) student's family, according to teacher-provided criteria. The problem again would be defined by the teacher and known to him or her and the students, but only the teacher would know how the students should structure and accomplish classification if they were to reach the preferred (or "right") solution. For example, categories such as type of pet(s), language(s) spoken, or length of time living in the current house might be established. The teacher could collect and record the necessary data on the chalkboard and then ask students individually or in small groups to put their families in the appropriate categories. Type II structure keeps the classification behaviors at a relatively low level, since the criteria or categories are provided. However, some low-level evaluation and decision making may be required, such as whether to count a parent's knowledge of a language or Hebrew lessons as a second (or third) language. Again, students have solved a defined problem and may have used developmental processes and complex thinking strategies infrequently and at a low level. Nei-

ther content nor processes have been enriched, so acceleration will not result in differentiated curriculum.

The Type III problem might be presented like this: Group the families represented in our class into three groups that are equal or nearly equal in size. The problem is stated, but a range of possible methods and solutions exists. Students would evaluate and make desicions regarding categories and classification, develop concepts, and reach conclusions. Content and processes are enriched in this example, so acceleration of pacing would result in differentiation.

The Type IV problem might be defined through a question such as, "How can we find and group the differences between our families?" The problem would be known to teacher and students, but the method and solution would be unknown and probably would evolve as the process unfolded. Students must generalize about observed differences between families, decide on which differences they will focus, and determine categories and levels of differentiation (e.g., by number in family, such as 2, 3, 4, etc., or small [2–3], medium [4–6], or large [7 or more]). Information must be processed prior to classification, and therefore the classification behaviors will be at a higher level of abstraction than for types I and II, and more complex categories are likely to be developed. In this example, content and processes are enriched. If accelerated pacing is included, as well as enriched and accelerated student products, the interaction that produces a differentiated curriculum may be expected to occur.

The key question for a Type V classification activity could be, "In what ways are families different from each other?" Students therefore would need to define the problem in some way that gave them a direction in which to move toward solution. Conceivably, students could engage in most or all of the developmental processes and complex thinking strategies as they solved the problem. For example, students would have to (1) make conclusions and arrive at decisions before they gathered data, (2) examine critically and evaluate the data, (3) derive the principles of *familyness,* and (4) generalize from their sample to families in general.

Drawing on their individual concepts of *family* and *different,* students might attempt to derive the principles that would enable them to select (draw conclusions, make decisions) and convey the essence of what they had generalized about familial differences. The developmental processes would be transformed as needed to fit the content and the task to be performed. As in the Type IV task, when families are classified within this activity, the levels of thinking will reflect the prior processing of information. The structure of this Type V problem may lead to the discovery and processing of information related to differences between family responsibilities and lifestyles (other learning objectives for this unit). As with the Type IV problem, curriculum content and processes have been enriched. Accelerated pacing and enriched and accelerated products may be expected to result in qualitatively different learning experiences.

At the middle school or junior high level, the context for expanding the concept of differences is the United States—its people and development (Taba et al., 1971). Content objectives include differences in (1) regional economics and points of view and (2) goals, such differences resulting in conflicts.

Using a Type I approach and the classification process, students might be required to learn about and classify geographic regions of the United States according to economic characteristics or the industry base, as defined by the teacher. The problem and its solution are well defined, and enabling skills and a low level of classification behavior are the primary cognitive requirements. In this example, neither the processes nor the content of the curriculum have been enriched.

A Type II problem might require students to group geographic regions of the United States according to their predominant political allegiance. The students would have to ascertain how to determine predominant political allegiance and classify the regions based on existing political parties, all of which would be known to the teacher. Some low-level decisions (complex thinking strategy) might be required for regions without a clear or decisive political leaning, but most of the cognition would consist of enabling skills and low-level classification behaviors. Neither content nor processes would be enriched.

A Type III approach might consist of asking students to identify characteristics of subregions of their county. On the basis of these characteristics, small groups could predict and support their prediction of conflict or harmony during the next 25 years. This task would require drawing conclusions, making generalizations, evaluating, thinking critically, and making decisions. Curriculum content and process would be enriched and accelerated in terms of grade level.

In a Type IV approach, students could be asked to determine differences among teacher-identified regions and project future areas of possible conflict based on the differences. In this approach the problem is defined (by the teacher), but a variety of methods and solutions are open to students. Additionally, more content objectives are likely to be met as students look for regional characteristics that may aid them in finding similarities. Their approach will be more open, and more content necessarily will be included. During the solution of this problem, students will be developing concepts related to regional differences (which may be either concrete or abstract), deriving principles about causes of conflict (an abstract concept), drawing conclusions about the effects of differences (abstract concept), and generalizing (higher level thinking) about differences, regions, and conflict. In solving this problem, students also will be required to transform and apply information and skills in order to evaluate, make decisions, engage in critical and creative thinking, and solve defined subproblems. The structure of this activity not only teaches the content objective (the concept) but incorporates meaningful experience with higher levels of thinking. Content and processes are enriched and accelerated in terms of level of abstractness for grade level.

Using a Type V format, in which the problem definition is unknown to the teacher and students, a teacher might direct students to explore regional points of view related to economics (two abstract concepts). Students first would need to define the problem (i.e., what is a region, which regions to focus on). This definition would require classification of regional characteristics and elements, derivation of the principles underlying regional delineations, generalizing about many regions from one or a few, drawing conclusions about specific regions, and making decisions as to the focal points for the investigation. The problem solutions require intricate interplay of the developmental processes and complex thinking strategies. The concept will have been taught at a high level of abstractness, and the cognition therefore will be at a correspondingly complex and abstract level. Curriculum content and process have been enriched and accelerated in terms of abstractness for grade level.

Curriculum Development

Each developmental process may be examined and taught through superimposing the concept of problem type on the skill in the context of content to be learned and then structuring or examining learning experiences accordingly. We are not suggesting that each skill should be taught as each of the four problem types; their purpose is to suggest a way to approach curriculum design. The reader should note that Type V problems necessarily move the thinker to the top of the spiral model, where undefined and real-life problems are found. When classification and Type V problems intersect, other developmental processes and complex thinking strategies are transformed and applied to the problem. In other words, Type V problems by definition entail the developmental processes and require complex thinking strategies. Classification or any other developmental process may be used or taught in a Type V format, but the skill will not be used in isolation. The inter-relatedness of complex cognitive operations is apparent in the above analysis of Type V situations; teaching a developmental process within a Type V format requires the use of complex thinking strategies.

Enrichment. Using the spiral model–problem-solving approach to planning curriculum enables teachers to examine the thinking processes being taught, practiced, and learned, and facilitates the enrichment of curriculum content. As increasing numbers of Types III, IV, and V problems are planned, thematic organization and more abstract and complex content may be included. By moving away from the clearly defined, rote-memory and comprehension-based activities and concept attainment, the progression naturally is toward bigger ideas that are more inclusive and more abstract. For example, if students were to learn about the values among people in different periods of time (Taba et al., 1971) through a variety of independent methods (Type IV), a natural progression would occur toward the causes and effects of these values in the various societies. This progression toward the abstract and complex is natural when the structure for curriculum design incorporates higher levels of thinking and problem solving within the context of the content to be taught and learned.

Acceleration. Acceleration of learning experiences for gifted students must occur in two ways. First, gifted students are developmentally advanced (Silverman, 1986), and the intellectually gifted can process more abstract ideas at an earlier age than other students (Clark, 1983). This means that a concept of difference designed to be taught to eighth-grade students, such as the differences in goals that result in conflict (Taba et al., 1971), probably is appropriate for sixth-grade gifted students.

Second, gifted students can move through, or process, information and ideas more quickly than other students. For example, intellectually gifted students may not only begin processing abstract concepts such as *conflict* at an earlier age than their age peers, but they also may move more quickly through developmental process activities and be able to apply the concept to undefined or real-life problems far sooner than their age-mates. An instructional unit that might require 6 weeks for most students to complete not only should be taught earlier and at a higher or more abstract level, but also may be completed by gifted students within 3 or 4 weeks.

Level of material and pace of instruction are dimensions of acceleration that mesh with the inclusion of enriched learning within a problem-solving approach to curriculum development. The spiral model of thinking may be used as an infrastructure for acceleration and enrichment of content, process, and product. When these factors are in place, the stage is set for the catastrophic event, the desired change, and the emergence of a qualitatively different curriculum.

Summary

Acceleration and *enrichment* are terms used to describe both curriculum and service-delivery models. The primary focus of this chapter has been on the curricular aspects of both, and their necessarily complementary nature. Components of curriculum, the content, instructional and learning processes, and expected student products, all must be enriched *and* accelerated. The resulting curriculum is not just enriched, nor is it just accelerated. Through a dynamic interaction of factors, it has become differentiated for gifted learners.

REFERENCES

Anderson, J. R. (1980). *Cognitive psychology and its implications.* San Francisco, Freeman.

Berliner, D. C. (1986). Catastrophes and interactions: Comments on "the mistaken metaphor." In C. J. Maker (Ed.), *Critical issues in gifted education: Defensible programs for the gifted* (pp. 31–38). Rockville, MD: Aspen.

Bloom, B. S., Englehart, M. D., Furst, E., Hill, W. H., & Krathwohl, D. R. (1956). *Taxonomy of educational objectives, handbook I: Cognitive domain.* New York: McKay.

Clark, B. (1983). *Growing up gifted* (2nd ed.). Columbus, OH: Merrill.

Davis, G. A., & Rimm, S. B. (1989). *Education of the gifted and talented* (2nd ed.). Englewood Cliffs, NJ: Prentice-Hall.

Feldhusen, J. F., & Wyman, A. R. (1980). Super Saturday: Design and implementation of Purdue's special program for gifted children. *Gifted Child Quarterly, 24,* 15–21.

Fox, L. H. (1979). Programs for the gifted and talented: An overview. In A. H. Passow (Ed.), *The gifted and the talented* (pp. 104–126). Chicago: National Society for the Study of Education.

Getzels, J. W. (1964). Creative thinking, problem solving, and instruction. In E. R. Hilgard (Ed.), *Theories of learning and instruction* (NSSE 66th Yearbook, pp. 240–267). Chicago: University of Chicago Press.

Getzels, J. W., & Csikszentmihalyi, M. (1967). Scientific creativity. *Science Journal, 3*(9), 80–84.

Guilford, J. P. (1967). *The nature of human intelligence.* New York: McGraw-Hill.

Howley, A., Howley, C. B., & Pendarvis, E. D. (1986). *Teaching gifted children.* Boston: Little, Brown.

Kaplan, S. N. (1974). *Providing programs for the gifted and talented.* Ventura, CA: Office of the Ventura County Superintendent of Schools.

Kaplan, S. N. (1979). *Inservice training manual: Activities for developing curriculum for the gifted/talented.* Ventura, CA: Office of the Ventura County Superintendent of Schools.

Maker, C. J. (1982a). *Curriculum development for the gifted.* Rockville, MD: Aspen.

Maker, C. J. (1982b). *Teaching models in education of the gifted.* Rockville, MD: Aspen.

Maker, C. J. (1986). *Frames of discovery: A process approach to identifying talent in special populations.* Unpublished paper available from author, Division of Special Education and Rehabilitation, University of Arizona, Tucson, AZ 85721.

Parnes, S. J. (1981). CPSI: The general system. In W. B. Barbe & J. S. Renzulli (Eds.), *Psychology and education of the gifted* (pp. 304–314). New York: Irvinton.

Renzulli, J. S. (1977). *The enrichment triad model: A guide for developing defensible programs for the gifted and talented.* Ventura, CA: Office of the Ventura County Superintendent of Schools.

Sato, I. S., & Johnson, B. (1978). Multifaceted training meets multidimensionally gifted. *Journal of Creative Behavior, 12,* 63–71.

Schiever, S. W. (1990). *A comprehensive approach to teaching thinking.* Needham Heights, MA: Allyn and Bacon.

Silverman, L. K. (1986). *Perfectionism.* Denver: Gifted Child Development Center.

Taba, H., Durkin, M. C., Fraenkel, J. R., & McNaughton, A. H. (1971). *A teacher's handbook to elementary social studies: An inductive approach.* Reading, MA: Addison-Wesley.

Van Tassel-Baska, J. (1981, December). *The great debates: For acceleration.* Speech presented at the CEC/TAG National Topical Conference on the Gifted and Talented Child, Orlando, FL.

Van Tassel-Baska, J. (1986). Acceleration. In C. J. Maker (Ed.), *Critical issues in gifted education: Defensible programs for the gifted* (pp. 179–196). Rockville, MD: Aspen.

Williams, F. E. (1972). *A total creativity program for individualizing and humanizing the learning process* (instructional materials). Englewood Cliffs, NJ: Educational Technology Publications.

9

The Schoolwide Enrichment Model: A Comprehensive Plan for the Development of Creative Productivity

JOSEPH S. RENZULLI and SALLY M. REIS   *University of Connecticut, Storrs*

*T*he schoolwide enrichment model (SEM) (Renzulli & Reis, 1985) is a combination of two earlier models that were developed to identify high-potential youth and to promote the development of gifted behaviors and creativity in young people. *The enrichment triad model* (Renzulli, 1977c) was the original formulation of the work that has evolved into the SEM. Several years of research and development on the triad model led to modifications in the procedures for identifying students for special services, and the result of this effort was an expanded identification and programming system entitled *the revolving door identification model* (Renzulli, Reis, & Smith, 1981). Widespread implementation of the combined triad–revolving door model provided opportunities for additional research designed to overcome a broad range of problems. The products of this research, coupled with a much wider acceptance of broadened conceptions of giftedness (see Chapter 4), have resulted in the development of the model described in this chapter.

A visual representation of the SEM is presented in Figure 9.1. The overall goals of the model are as follows:

1. To promote advanced-level learning and creative productivity in young people by providing various types and levels of enrichment to a broader spectrum of the school population than the 3 to 5% usually served in traditional programs for the gifted.
2. To integrate special program services with the regular curriculum and to develop a cooperative rather than competitive relationship between regular classroom teachers and personnel assigned to gifted programs.
3. To minimize concerns about elitism and the negative attitudes that are often expressed toward students participating in special programs for the gifted and talented.
4. To improve the extent and quality of enrichment for all students and to promote a *radiation of excellence* (Ward, 1965) throughout all aspects of the school environment.

Extensive research studies and field tests have shown that the model is easy and inexpensive to implement and that it is highly effective in achieving these four major goals. However, although these goals are a common focus of all schools using the model, we emphasize that there is no such thing as a "pure" SEM program. Each school must examine its own philosophy, resources, and administrative structure and then adopt or adapt those parts of the model that take into account the unique aspects of each local school or district. A flexible approach to both identification and programming is necessary for two important reasons. First, local conditions and resources always must be considered. Second, unless flexibility is encouraged a program model can easily inhibit local innovations and ownership that ultimately can result in better ways of identifying and serving high-ability youngsters (Reis, 1983).

The remainder of this chapter is divided into nine major sections. The first deals with theory and research underlying the SEM, mainly through reference to previously published works. The second describes specific steps in the identification procedures used within the SEM. The third section describes the organizational components and the service-delivery components of the model. The

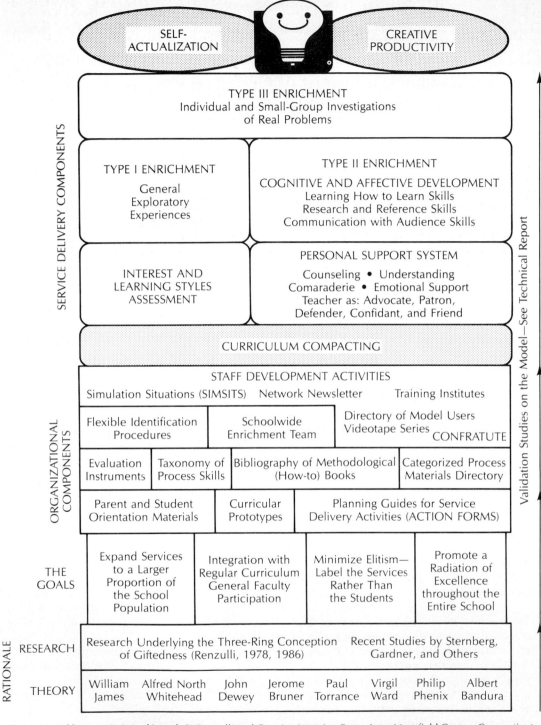

SELF-ACTUALIZATION

CREATIVE PRODUCTIVITY

SERVICE DELIVERY COMPONENTS

TYPE III ENRICHMENT
Individual and Small-Group Investigations
of Real Problems

TYPE I ENRICHMENT
General
Exploratory
Experiences

TYPE II ENRICHMENT
COGNITIVE AND AFFECTIVE DEVELOPMENT
Learning How to Learn Skills
Research and Reference Skills
Communication with Audience Skills

INTEREST AND LEARNING STYLES ASSESSMENT

PERSONAL SUPPORT SYSTEM
Counseling • Understanding
Comaraderie • Emotional Support
Teacher as: Advocate, Patron,
Defender, Confidant, and Friend

CURRICULUM COMPACTING

ORGANIZATIONAL COMPONENTS

STAFF DEVELOPMENT ACTIVITIES
Simulation Situations (SIMSITS)   Network Newsletter   Training Institutes

Flexible Identification
Procedures

Schoolwide
Enrichment Team

Directory of Model Users
Videotape Series
CONFRATUTE

Evaluation
Instruments

Taxonomy of
Process Skills

Bibliography of Methodological
(How-to) Books

Categorized Process
Materials Directory

Parent and Student
Orientation Materials

Curricular
Prototypes

Planning Guides for Service
Delivery Activities (ACTION FORMS)

THE GOALS

Expand Services
to a Larger
Proportion of
the School
Population

Integration with
Regular Curriculum
General Faculty
Participation

Minimize Elitism—
Label the Services
Rather Than
the Students

Promote a
Radiation of
Excellence
throughout the
Entire School

RATIONALE

RESEARCH

Research Underlying the Three-Ring Conception
of Giftedness (Renzulli, 1978, 1986)

Recent Studies by Sternberg,
Gardner, and Others

THEORY

| William James | Alfred North Whitehead | John Dewey | Jerome Bruner | Paul Torrance | Virgil Ward | Philip Phenix | Albert Bandura |

Validation Studies on the Model—See Technical Report

Source: Used by permission of Joseph S. Renzulli and Creative Learning Press, Inc., Mansfield Center, Connecticut.

Figure 9.1 Overview of the Schoolwide Enrichment Model.

next four sections elaborate on central organizational and service-delivery components: curriculum compacting, Type I enrichment (general exploratory experiences), Type II enrichment (group training activities), and Type III enrichment (individual and small-group investigations of real problems). The eighth section summarizes procedures for evaluating Type III enrichment projects. The ninth reviews research on the triad–revolving door model.

Theory and Research Underlying the Schoolwide Enrichment Model

The Three-Ring Conception of Giftedness

A major part of the rationale underlying the SEM can be found in a wide range of studies summarized in the original article on the three-ring conception of giftedness presented in Figure 9.2 (Renzulli, 1978), related articles that have been written in more recent years (Hoge, 1988; Reis & Renzulli, 1982; Renzulli, 1982; Renzulli & Reis, 1985; Treffinger & Renzulli, 1986), and recent work on the development of gifted behaviors by such persons as Bloom (1985), Gardner (1983), and Sternberg (1985). Additionally, several studies on both the three-ring conception of giftedness and the components of the SEM are summarized in a

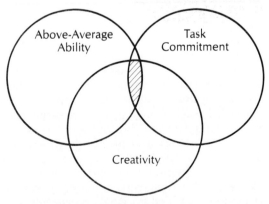

Source: Used by permission of Joseph S. Renzulli and Creative Learning Press, Inc., Mansfield Center, Connecticut.

Figure 9.2   What makes giftedness?

comprehensive technical report (Renzulli, 1988) that is available upon request from the authors.

Space does not permit a detailed presentation of this broad array of research. However, we urge readers to examine these references because taken collectively, this research represents the most powerful argument that can be put forth to support the type of programming model recommended in this chapter. This research clearly and unequivocally tells us that gifted behaviors can be developed in persons who are not necessarily those who earn the highest scores on standardized tests. Two major implications of this research for identification practices are equally clear. First, an effective identification system must consider other factors in addition to test scores, and these factors must be given equal weight in the selection process. We can no longer just give lip service to nontest criteria or believe that because tests yield numbers they are inherently more valid than other procedures.

A second research-based implication will undoubtedly be a major controversy in the field for many years, but it must be dealt with if we ever expect to defuse a major criticism of programs for the gifted. Simply stated, we must reexamine identification procedures that result in the total *pre*selection of certain students and the concomitant implication that these youngsters are and always will be "the gifted." This absolute approach (i.e., either you have it or you don't have it) coupled with the almost total reliance on various test scores is not only inconsistent with what the research tells us but arrogant in the assumption that we can use a one-hour segment of a young person's total existence to determine if he or she is gifted.

The alternative to such an absolutist view is that we may have to forego the tidy and comfortable tradition of deciding on the first day of school who is gifted and who is not. Rather, our orientation must be redirected toward developing gifted behaviors in certain students (not all students) at certain times (not all the time) and under certain circumstances. This trade-off for tidiness and administrative expediency will result in a much more flexible approach to both identification and programming and a system that not only shows respect for research on gifted and talented people but is both fairer and more acceptable to other educators and the general public.

Another part of the rationale underlying the SEM concerns the practical aspects of identification. It is very easy for gifted students to become victims of complicated and indefensible identification procedures that sometimes become so complex they overshadow the major purpose of providing high-quality services. Through careful field testing and modification based upon feedback, we have streamlined the identification procedures with a careful eye on what is reasonably practical within the context of any school setting.

Two additional points should be noted. First, it is not necessary for a student to possess all three characteristics—above-average ability, high task commitment, and high creativity—in order to be eligible for special services. Rather, our initial target audience consists of students who display or have the potential to display above-average ability in one or more academic areas, or in special aptitudes such as music, art, drama, leadership, or interpersonal skills. The other two rings are considered *developmental objectives* that we attempt to promote in the target population and bring together in an interactive fashion with one another and with above-average ability, thus yielding the shaded portion of Figure 9.2. The SEM can be viewed as providing the opportunities, resources, and encouragement (the concept of ORE) that are designed to create task commitment and creativity and promote dynamic interactions among the three rings in Figure 9.2.

Finally, a theoretical concept such as the three-ring conception of giftedness can only formulate the general conditions that are both necessary and sufficient to define the concept at hand—giftedness. The best way to discover what a theoretical concept *really* means is to examine how it is applied, how it affects decision making, and how it influences policy or practice. The three-ring conception is offered in a practical perspective because this is the purpose to which it will be applied. To a pragmatist, the ultimate value of any theoretical concept is its usefulness in translating research findings into defensible practices. Our concern is with the practical application of theory, and therefore the value of the three-ring conception of giftedness can best be determined by examining the identification procedures that are guided by the concept, as well as the research that led to the development of the concept in the first place.

Features Underlying the Model

One of the most important features underlying the SEM is that it was designed to create a variety of important roles and responsibilities for regular classroom teachers and other school personnel as well as those persons specifically assigned to programs for the gifted. This feature of our model is important for three major reasons. First, in the popular pullout or resource room approach, highly able students spend the vast proportion of their time in regular classrooms under the direction of regular classroom teachers. The advanced abilities that brought these students to our attention in the first place certainly justify some modifications in the regular curriculum and in activities that go on in regular classrooms.

Second, many of the enrichment experiences emphasized in special programs can benefit other students. Particularly, process-oriented activities, such as thinking skills exercises based on Bloom's (1956) *Taxonomy of Educational Objectives* and other process models (Schlichter, 1986; Taylor, 1986; Williams, 1986), are clearly appropriate for most students.[1] Process-oriented activities should be integrated with the regular curriculum whenever possible. Further, such activities may be used as performance-based criteria for identifying those students who should be provided with advanced opportunities, resources, and encouragement. The fact that process activities are not often included in regular curricular experiences is not a sufficient rationale for assuming that they are appropriate only for the gifted. Such integration is indeed one of the goals for general educational change that we are attempting to achieve in the SEM.

Third, an integrated rather than an exclusory model will help eliminate the *condition of separateness* that is almost universal in schools that provide special programs for the gifted. Distrust, competitiveness, suspicion, and even outright hostility may exist between members of the general faculty and special program personnel. These negative attitudes often lead to subversion, a loss of public confidence, and in many cases a reduction or even elimination of special services. A good deal of this condition of separateness is a direct result of the ways in which programs have been organized. The unintentional but nevertheless self-defeating exclusion of classroom teachers from what might be called enrichment teaching have limited opportunities for both student growth and the improvement of teaching skills. There are many ways that regular teachers and special program personnel can share and exchange individual interests and talents, teaching strengths, special training, enrichment materials, community resources, and time. Such an exchange will benefit all students who are potentially able to develop and display gifted behaviors. The SEM has been designed to provide an organizational plan for achieving these goals through the maximum utilization of both specialists and the general faculty.

The SEM Identification System

In this section we will outline the specific steps of an identification system that is designed to translate the three-ring conception into a set of practical procedures for selecting students for special programs. The focal point of this system is a talent pool of students that serves as the major (but not the only) target group for a wide variety of supplementary services. The goals of this identification system, as it relates to the three-ring conception of giftedness, are threefold:

1. To develop creativity and/or task commitment in talent pool students and other students who may come to our attention through alternative means of identification.
2. To promote learning experiences and support systems that promote the interaction of creativity, task commitment, and above-average ability (i.e., that bring the rings together).

3. To provide opportunities, resources, and encouragement for the development and application of gifted behaviors.

Talent pools will vary in size depending on the general nature and ability levels of the total student body. In schools with unusually large numbers of high-ability students, talent pools may extend beyond the 15% level that we ordinarily recommend in schools that reflect the achievement profiles of the general population. Even in schools where achievement levels are below national norms, there still are upper level students who need services beyond those provided for the large majority. Some of our most successful programs have been in inner-city schools that serve disadvantaged and bilingual youth. Even though these schools were below national norms they recognized the need to provide supplementary services to approximately 15% of their populations.

Talent pool size is also a function of the availability of resource persons and the extent to which the general faculty is willing to (1) make modifications in the regular curriculum and classroom for above-average-ability students, and (2) provide various kinds of enrichment and mentoring services.

Since teacher nomination plays an important role in the identification system, an important consideration is the extent of orientation and training that teachers have received regarding both the program and nomination procedures. We recommend the use of a training activity that is designed to orient teachers to the behavioral characteristics of superior students (Renzulli & Reis, 1985, pp. 203–210).

Also important is, of course, the type of program for which students are being identified. The identification system that follows is based on programs that include both enrichment and acceleration; it can be used for enrichment and acceleration services that are carried out in self-contained or pullout programs. Regardless of the type of organizational model used, it is also recommended that a strong component of *curriculum compacting* (Renzulli et al., 1981) be a part of the services offered to talent pool students.

For purposes of demonstration, the example that follows is based on the formation of a 15%

talent pool. Larger or smaller talent pools can be formed simply by adjusting the figures used in this example.

Step 1: Test Score Nominations

If we were using nothing but test scores to identify a 15% talent pool, the task would be ever so simple! Any child who scored above the 85th percentile (using local norms) would be a candidate. In this identification system,

however, we have made a commitment to leave some room in the talent pool for students whose potentials may not be reflected in standardized tests. Therefore, we begin by dividing our talent pool in half (see Figure 9.3), and we place all students who score at or above the 92nd percentile (again, using local norms) in the talent pool. This approach guarantees that traditionally bright youngsters will automatically be selected, and they will account for approximately 50% of our talent pool.

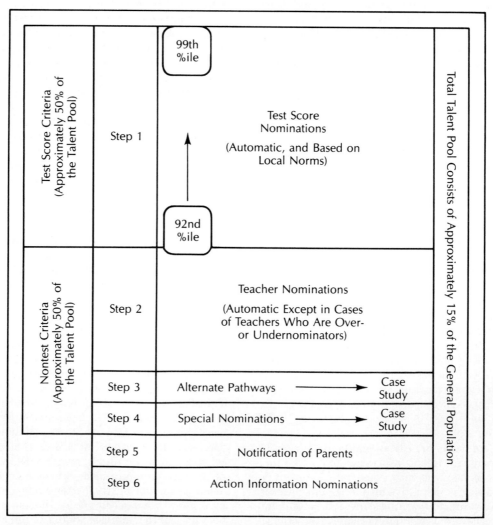

Figure 9.3   The Renzulli identification system.

Any regularly administered standardized test (e.g., intelligence, achievement, aptitude) can be used for this purpose. However, we recommend that admission to the talent pool be granted on the basis of any *single* test or subtest score. This approach enables students who are high in verbal *or* nonverbal ability (but not necessarily both) to gain admission, as well as students who may excel in one aptitude (e.g., spatial, mechanical). This process also guarantees admission to bright underachievers.

Programs that focus on special areas such as the arts, leadership, and athletics should use the nontest criteria described in the following steps as major indicators of above-average ability in a particular talent area. In a similar fashion, whenever test scores are not available, or we have some question as to their validity, the nontest criteria should be used. This approach (i.e., the elimination or minimization of Step 1) is especially important when considering primary-aged students, disadvantaged populations, or culturally different groups.

Step 2: Teacher Nominations

Teachers should be informed of all students who have gained entrance through test score nominations so that they will not have to do needless paperwork for students who have already been admitted. Step 2 allows teachers to nominate students who display characteristics that are not easily determined by standardized tests (e.g., high levels of creativity or task commitment; unusual interests or talents; or special areas of superior performance or potential). With the exception of nominations from teachers who are overnominators or undernominators, nominations from teachers are treated on an equal basis with test score nominations. That is, we do not refer to students nominated by test scores as the "truly" gifted, and the students nominated by teachers as the "moderately" or "borderline" gifted. Nor do we make any distinctions between the two groups in the opportunities, resources, or services provided other than the normal individualization that should be a part of any program that attempts to meet unique needs and potentials. Thus, for example, if a student gains entrance

on the basis of teacher nomination because he or she has shown advanced potential for creative writing, we would not expect this student to compete in an advanced math group on an equal basis with students who scored at or above the 92nd percentile on a math test. Nor should we arrange program experiences that would place the student with talents in creative writing in an advanced math cluster group. Special programs should first and foremost respect and reflect the individual characteristics that led to student placement in the talent pool.

A teacher nomination form and rating scales (Renzulli, Smith, Callahan, White, & Hartman, 1976) are used for this procedure. The rating scales are not used to eliminate students with lower ratings. Instead, the scales are used to provide a summary profile of each nominated student. In cases of teachers who are overnominators, a request is made that they rank-order their nominations for review by a schoolwide committee. Procedures for dealing with under or non-nominators will be described in Step 4.

Step 3: Alternative Pathways

All schools adopting this identification system make use of test score and teacher nominations. Alternative pathways are considered local options and are pursued in varying degrees by individual school districts. Decisions about which alternative pathways might be used should be made by a local planning committee, with consideration given to variations in grade level. For example, self-nomination is more appropriate for students who may be considering advanced classes at the secondary level.

Alternative pathways generally consist of parent nominations, peer nominations, tests of creativity, self-nominations, product evaluations, and virtually any other procedure that might lead to initial consideration by a screening committee. The major difference between alternative pathways and test score nomination is that in the former admission is *not* automatic. In other words, students nominated through one or more alternative pathways are reviewed by a screening committee, after which selection decisions are made. In most cases the screening committee carries out a case study that includes examination of all previous school records; interviews with students, teachers, and parents; and the administration of individual assessments that may be recommended by the committee. In some cases, students who are recommended on the basis of one or more alternative pathways are placed in the program on a trial basis.

Step 4: Special Nominations (Safety Valve No. 1)

Special nominations represent the first of two *safety valves* in this identification process. This procedure involves circulating a list of all students who have been nominated through one of the procedures in Steps 1 through 3 to all teachers within the school, and in previous schools if students have matriculated to another building. This procedure allows previous-year teachers to nominate additional students who have not been recommended by their present-year teacher. It also allows resource teachers to make recommendations based on their experience with students who have already been in the talent pool or students they may have encountered as part of enrichment experiences in regular classrooms. This step allows a final review of the total school population and is designed to circumvent the opinions of present-year teachers who may not appreciate the abilities, style, or even personality of a particular student. One last sweep through the population also helps to pick up students who may have turned off to school or developed patterns of underachievement as a result of personal or family problems. This step also helps to overcome the general biases of an undernominator or a non-nominator. As in the case of alternative pathways, special nominations are not automatic. Rather, a case study is carried out by and the final decision rests with the screening committee.

Step 5: Notification and Orientation of Parents

A letter of notification and a comprehensive description of the program is forwarded to the parents of all talent pool students indicating that their youngster has been placed in the talent pool for the year. The letter does *not* proclaim that their child has been certified as "gifted." Rather, it explains the nature of the program and extends an invitation to parents for an orientation meeting. At this meeting a description of the three-ring conception of giftedness is provided as well as a thorough explanation of program policies, procedures, and activities. Parents are informed about criteria for admission to the talent pool, that it is carried out on an annual basis, and that additions to talent pool membership might take place during the year as a result of evaluations of student participation and progress. Parents are invited to make individual appointments whenever they wish additional information about the program or their own child. A similar orientation session is provided for students, with emphasis once again placed on the program services and activities. Students are *not* told that they are "the gifted," but through a discussion of the three-ring conception and procedures for developing general and specific potentials, they come to understand that the development of gifted behaviors is a program goal as well as part of their own responsibility.

Step 6: Action Information Nominations (Safety Valve No. 2)

In spite of our best efforts, this system occasionally overlooks students who, for one reason or another, are not selected for talent pool membership. To help overcome this problem, orientation related to spotting students with high interest in regular curriculum topics is provided for all teachers. We also provide a wide variety of in-class enrichment experiences that might result in recommendations for special services. This process is facilitated through the use of a teacher training activity and an instrument called an *action information message*.

Action information can best be defined as the dynamic interactions that occur when a student becomes extremely interested in or excited about a particular topic, area of study, issue, idea, or event that takes place in or out of school. It is derived from the concept of performance-based assessment, and it serves as the second safety valve in this identification system. The transmission of an action information message does not mean that a student will automatically revolve into advanced-level services. However, it serves as the basis for a careful review to determine if such services are warranted. Action information messages are also used in talent pool settings (i.e., pullout groups, advanced classes, cluster groups) to make determinations about the pursuit of individual or small-group investigations (Type III enrichment in the triad model).

Discussion

In identification systems that follow the traditional screening-plus-selection approach, the "throwaways" have usually been those students who qualified for screening on the basis of nontest criteria. Thus, for example, in these systems a teacher nomination is used only as a ticket to take an individual or group ability test, but the test score typically is the deciding factor. The many and various good things that led to the nominations by teachers may be totally ignored when it comes to the final selection decision—and the multiple criteria game ends up being a smoke screen for the same old test-based approach.

The implementation of the identification system described above has helped to overcome this problem as well as a wide array of other problems associated with selecting students for special programs. Generally, students, parents, teachers, and administrators have expressed high degrees of satisfaction with this approach (Renzulli, 1988), and the reason for this satisfaction is plainly evident. By picking up that layer of students below the top few percentile levels and by leaving some room in the program for students to gain entrance on the basis of nontest criteria, we have eliminated the justifiable criticism that these students also need special opportunities, resources, and encouragement. The research underlying the three-ring conception of giftedness clearly tells us that such an approach is justified in terms of what we know about human potential. By eliminating the endless number of headaches traditionally associated with identification, we have gained an unprecedented amount of support from teachers and administrators, many of whom formerly resented the very existence of special programs.

Structure of the SEM: Organizational and Service-Delivery Components

Our experience has shown that successful programs are always based on plans that clearly delineate two major dimensions of a programming model. In the SEM we refer to these dimensions as *organizational components* and *service-delivery components*. By organizational components we mean those noninstructional activities that lead to putting the program in place. Examples of organizational components include the guided activities of planning teams; needs assessments; staff development; materials selection; and program evaluation. Service-delivery components are direct instructional activities and the many and varied things that teachers do with students in order to fulfill the major objectives of the overall programming model. Included in this domain are lessons designed to promote the development of thinking processes; procedures for modifying the regular curriculum; and the specific steps involved in guiding students through independent study activities.

Although the real payoff of any special program is the extent and quality of organizational and service delivery components that have a direct impact on students, there are a number of other background components that are necessary for organizing and implementing service-delivery activities. These planning and organizing components not only acknowledge the best theory and research underlying special programs, but they also provide a common vocabulary, a frame of reference, and a clarification of the roles and responsibilities of all persons involved in the special program. As such, these background organizational components introduce a remarkable element of efficiency into the overall process of program planning and implementation.

The Schoolwide Enrichment Team

One of the best ways to expand the full range of services that might be made available to advanced-level students is through the development of a schoolwide enrichment team. An enrichment team is neither a policy-making body nor an advisory committee, but rather a working group of faculty members and parents who have specific responsibilities for organizing the overall enrichment effort for an entire school.

There are two important reasons for establishing an enrichment team. The first of these addresses the question, Is enrichment only good for the gifted? An affirmative answer to this question would certainly relegate the regular school program to a meager diet of basic skills and routine learning experiences. There are few, if any, educators of bright students who would not insist that all youngsters should have opportunities for various types and levels of enrichment. Many of the general enrichment activities used in programs for the gifted can also be used with a broader segment of the school population.

The second reason deals with the essential role of faculty involvement in a schoolwide enrichment program. Too often, a sad but not uncommon by-product of traditional gifted programs, whether they are accelerated mathematics classes or resource rooms, is that classroom teachers falsely assume that all the needs of identified students are being met by the special programs. In many districts where a program is started, classroom teachers continue to routinely assign regular curriculum work to their brightest students. Quite often, resource teachers have little or no interaction with classroom teachers or with the regular curriculum, and so the two programs exist side by side as essentially separate entities. One way to avoid this is to organize a schoolwide enrichment team that will develop a sense of faculty and community ownership of the enrichment program. We have found that when classroom teachers are encouraged to become actively involved in the program, they eventually come to regard efforts to meet the needs of bright students as a joint venture to be shared by all faculty members.

Over the last several years many school districts have implemented outstanding enrichment programs based on the SEM. In almost every case, the first step was the organization of an in-service program to acquaint staff with the definition, identification, and program-ming aspects and to establish an enrichment team. This team is then able to work cooperatively to achieve the major objectives of Type I and Type II enrichment (described later), and to enrich the lives of all students by expanding the scope and experiences provided by the school. This gives teachers direction in making decisions about the kinds of process-oriented enrichment activities that should be organized for particular groups of students, and ways to stimulate new interests that might lead to intensive follow-up (Type III) activities by individuals or small groups.

The most effective way to organize an enrichment team is to recruit members from various segments of the school and community. The enrichment team should include parents, community resource persons, administrators, classroom teachers, (who represent primary, middle, and upper grades in the elementary school), art/music or physical education instructors, and the librarian or media specialist (if one exists). At the secondary level, the enrichment team can include representatives from each department (if the high school or middle school is small), or separate enrichment teams can be organized for each department. Representatives from each departmental team can then meet on a periodic basis with the schoolwide enrichment team. It can also be effective to include students on the enrichment team.

The key to successful functioning of the enrichment team is specificity of tasks and a division of labor among team members. The *action form concept* (see next section) can help provide task-specific direction to enrichment team activities. Since team members can devote only a relatively small portion of their time to this endeavor, it is essential that tasks be broken down into clearly targeted activities. If a designated resource teacher or enrichment specialist is not present in the school, we recommend the appointment of a chairperson who is organized and efficient and gets along well with other faculty members. We strongly advocate that this person have some release time in addition to his or her regularly scheduled planning time. One hour a week that an administrator can arrange for the chairperson of the enrichment team to use as planning time communicates a very important message to the chairperson and the entire faculty: We value what you are doing and we support your efforts.

Finally, no one should ever be forced to serve on the enrichment team. We strongly advocate the inclusion of a building principal, even if he or she only attends meetings on a periodic basis. But no one should serve on the team who truly does not want to be involved. We have found that once the benefits of the various types of enrichment experiences become obvious, more faculty members become interested in joining the team in subsequent years.

Other Organizational Features

Throughout several years of experience and research in triad–revolving door programs, we have identified certain major activities that are necessary for planning and implementation. Each of these activities relates to one or more of the specific objectives described in the following sections. In each case, we have developed a planning guide (action form) and/or a teacher training activity (simulated situation, or SIMSIT). We also developed strategies for evaluating each component of our model.

Action Forms

The purpose of action forms is to break down programming activities into their component parts in order to achieve a division of labor and time management objectives. In some ways, the action forms might be thought of as "gentle enforcers." That is, the forms themselves focus energy and activities on achieving the objectives set forth for various components of the model. Several action forms have been designed for each service in our model. Two sample action forms appear in Figures 9.4 and 9.5.

Each form is intended to accomplish two important objectives of overall program development. First and foremost, the forms may be used as guides or road maps for the accomplishment of particular tasks; the forms help give direction by providing a list of alternative resources or activities from which specific selections might be made. Second, the forms serve as documentation of the accomplishment of program activities. In this regard, information included on the forms provides ready-made data for program evaluation.

Teacher Training Activities (SIMSITs)

Each component of our model includes one or more SIMSITs. The SIMSITs were designed to fulfill an important function in the training of teachers. Although comprehensive knowledge about the content of any field is a major part of the overall training of professionals, the ability to *apply* one's knowledge in practical situations represents the real payoff so far as effective training is concerned.

Numerous SIMSITs were developed as a result of several years of experience. As triad and revolving door programs grew in popularity, we had the opportunity to study teacher training needs and the critical incidents in which certain kinds of highly specific implementation skills were required. These experiences helped us to learn what skills are necessary for teachers planning to implement particular components of the model. Some skills relate to direct work with students, while others concern program organization and development activities, public relations, and the management skills required by coordinators.

Program Evaluation

In addition to action forms and SIMSITs, our model includes procedures for evaluating the objectives set forth for each service-delivery component. After policy decisions have been made with regard to the adoption of the overall model and the objectives of the respective delivery components, the correlated evaluation instruments provide a package of ready-made instruments and procedures.

The evaluation forms should be thought of as a supermarket of software from which you can make selections according to the emphases within your own program. The evaluation instruments have been purposely developed to analyze the stated objectives on summary pages. As such they provide a ready-made and built-in evaluation system that can be presented whenever persons request information about the effectiveness of the respective service-delivery components.

Services to Talent Pool Students

Before the types of services (see Figure 9.1) that are regularly provided to talent pool students are described, it is important to point out a major function of these services beyond their obvious enrichment and/or acceleration purposes. The involvement of students in both regular and special program activities and their reactions to such involvement form the basis for the second level of identification in the SEM. In other words, these services provide the performance-based learning situations that help us identify which individuals should revolve into advanced-level experiences based on high interest in particular topics or problem areas.

Two types of general enrichment are provided for talent pool students on a regularly scheduled basis. Whenever possible, these enrichment experiences, or ones of similar design and purpose, are also made available to students in the general school population. Decisions regarding which students (in addition to talent pool members) will participate in general enrichment are based upon factors such as the difficulty level of the material, its relation to the regular curriculum, the size of the group that can be accommmodated, and the interests of students in the general population. In many cases general enrichment is offered on an invitational basis; it also is frequently planned in conjunction with regular curriculum topics. This approach helps to minimize concerns about elitism, integrate special program services with the regular curriculum, and achieve the radiation of excellence that is one of the overall goals of our model.

In addition to participating in general enrichment experiences, all talent pool students receive two additional services: (1) interest and learning style assessment and (2) curriculum compacting. In the following sections, we will describe each of these services.

Interest Assessment

Building educational experiences around student interests is probably one of the most recognizable ways in which schoolwide enrichment programs differ from the regular curriculum. In numerous evaluation studies when bright students were asked what they liked best about being in a special program, the first response almost always dealt with the greater freedom allowed for selecting topics of study. Conversely, when asked about their greatest objection to the regular curriculum, students frequently referred to the limited opportunities to pursue topics of their own choosing. Indeed, high-ability students' views of the regular curriculum, as far as freedom of choice is concerned, are extremely negative. As one youngster put it, "They tell us what book we have to use, what page, paragraph, and problem we should be on, and how long we should spend on that problem."

A planned strategy for helping students examine their present and potential interests is based on an instrument called the *Interest-A-Lyzer* (Renzulli, 1977a). This instrument is a 13-item questionnaire designed to assist students in exploring their areas of interest. The Interest-A-Lyzer has been used with students in Grades 4 to 9; it has also been adapted for use with younger children (McGreevey, 1982) and adults (Renzulli, 1977b). The items consist of a variety of real and hypothetical situations to which students are asked to respond in terms of the choices they would make (or have made) were they involved in these situations.

The Interest-A-Lyzer services to open up communication both within the student and between the student and his or her teacher. It also facilitates discussion between children with similar interests who are attempting to identify areas for advanced-level studies. The major interest-area patterns from the instrument are (1) fine arts and crafts, (2) scientific and technical, (3) creative writing and journalism, (4) legal, political, and judicial, (5) mathematics, (6) managerial, (7) historical, (8) athletic and outdoor-related activities, (9) performing arts, (10) business, and (11) consumer action and ecology-related activities.

It is important to keep in mind that the above topics represent general fields or families of interest, and that there are numerous ways in which an individual might pursue a topic in any particular field. Thus, general interests must be refined and focused so that eventually students will arrive at relatively specific problems within a general field or combination of fields.

Learning Style Evaluation

Although numerous definitions of *learning style* can be found in the educational and psychological literature (Smith, 1976), the definition we recommend for use in designing individualized educational programs is one that focuses on preferences for specific and identifiable learning activities: (1) projects, (2) drill and recitation, (3) peer teaching, (4) discussion, (5) teaching games, (6) independent study, (7) programmed instruction, (8) lecture, and (9) simulation.

The *Learning Styles Inventory* (Renzulli & Smith, 1978b) is a research-based instrument that was developed to guide teachers in planning learning experiences that take into account the learning style preferences of students. The instrument requires approximately 30 minutes to complete and provides descriptive information about student attitudes toward the above nine general modes of instruction. The inventory consists of a series of items that describe various classroom learning experiences, and students are asked to respond in terms of how pleasant they find participation in each one.

One of the innovative components of this instrument is the teacher form that accompanies each set of student materials. This form enables teachers to look at the range of instructional strategies used in their own classrooms. The items parallel those on the student form, but in this case teachers respond in terms of how frequently each activity occurs in the classroom. The profile of instructional styles resulting from this procedure can be compared with individual student preferences and thus can serve to facilitate a closer match between how teachers instruct and the styles to which students respond most favorably. Research has shown that this matching of styles not only enhances student learning but promotes a more positive attitude toward school.

This is not to say that instruction should be guided solely by learning style preferences. Rather, it indicates that teachers should be in a position to make informed decisions about the areas or units within which style differences can be incorporated. Indeed, unless at some point in the school day or week teachers are organizing activities that accommodate the varying learning style preferences of their students, it is not likely that a comprehensive individualization program is actually taking place.

Curriculum Compacting

Curriculum compacting is designed to adapt the regular curriculum to meet the needs of above-average students by either eliminating work that has been previously mastered or streamlining work that may be mastered at a pace commensurate with the student's ability. Curriculum compacting has three major objectives: (1) to create a more challenging learning environment, (2) to guarantee proficiency in the basic curriculum, and (3) to buy time for more appropriate enrichment and/or acceleration activities.

Rationale for Curriculum Compacting

One need only enter any classroom in the country and observe the above-average students to realize that the work being assigned is oftentimes too easy. In fact, textbooks have dropped two grade levels in difficulty over the past 10 to 15 years. As a result of this change in basic textbooks and because repetition is built into all curriculum programs to reinforce learning, many bright students spend most of their time in school doing things they already know. With curriculum compacting, we can remedy this situation by increasing the challenge level of the work while also providing enrichment experiences and opportunities for independent and small-group work that is commensurate with their abilities.

If we can clearly demonstrate that a bright student has mastered a great deal of the regular curriculum, then we can argue that this student is therefore eligible for a different curricular experience. Most of the elementary mathematics and language arts systems include a wide assortment of pretests, unit tests, level tests, and yearly assessments. These and teacher-designed assessments (especially at the secondary level) can be used to document the proficiency that will allow us to prove mastery of the basic skills for our brightest students, enabling them to become involved in more challenging work.

If curriculum compacting is utilized and explained to students, they will realize that demonstrating proficiency in the basic curriculum can earn them the opportunity to become involved in more interesting work. This process may also eliminate one of the major problems faced by students participating in resource programs: making up all the work that their peers completed while they were involved in the resource program. Curriculum compacting allows them to participate in the resource program during their *curricular strength times,* and therefore eliminates the problem of students being greeted at the door by their classroom teacher and handed the 15 worksheets that were completed by other students in their absence.

How to Use the Compacting System

Curriculum compacting is designed around an action form called *The Compactor* (Renzulli & Smith, 1978a). This form (see Figure 9.4) should be completed cooperatively by classroom teachers and resource teachers and should be maintained as part of the student's individual record. Every effort should be made to revise and update the form on a regular basis, and it should serve as a means for joint planning by the regular teacher and the resource teacher.

The Compactor is divided into three columns: "Curriculum Areas To Be Considered for Compacting," "Procedures for Compacting Basic Material," and "Acceleration and/or Enrichment Activities." It can be completed when a classroom teacher identifies the strength areas of an above-average student. The form details how the child has proved that the skills within the strength area have been mastered and then suggests the appropriate enrichment and possible acceleration activities that will provide advanced learning experiences.

Two essential requirements for successful compacting are (1) careful diagnosis and (2) a thorough knowledge of the content and objectives of a unit of instruction. Once these requirements have been met, the actual procedures for carrying out the process are quite simple.

Teachers must first identify the curricular strength areas of talent pool students and any other student who has demonstrated mastery of the basic curriculum. Column 1 of the Compactor ("Curriculum Areas To Be Considered for Compacting") is used to record general and specific indications of student strengths. Information included should answer the questions:

- What are the general indications of student strength in this area?
- What content and/or objectives of the specific unit to be taught have already been mastered?

General indications of strength can be found in student records, standardized tests, classwork, or teacher observations. They are used to identify the subject area(s) in which a student might be considered for compacting. One of the best ways to determine in what areas a student has strengths is to ask the teacher who had the student in his or her class the previous year. Additionally, teachers can train themselves to spot curricular strength areas and students in need of curriculum compacting. Teachers should watch students who finish tasks quickly and well, and also students who finish their reading assignments first. Teachers should also try to watch for students who appear bored during instruction time and who consistently daydream in class.

Once the general areas of strength have been selected, a specific diagnosis of the skills to be taught must be obtained. Diagnostic instruments in basic skills (reading, language,

INDIVIDUAL EDUCATIONAL PROGRAMMING GUIDE

The Compactor

Prepared by Joseph S. Renzulli
Linda H. Smith

NAME _____ AGE _____ TEACHER(S) _____ Individual Conference Dates and Persons Participating in Planning of IEP

SCHOOL _____ GRADE _____ PARENT(S) _____

CURRICULUM AREAS TO BE CONSIDERED FOR COMPACTING Provide a brief description of basic material to be covered during this marking period and the assessment information or evidence that suggests the need for compacting:	PROCEDURES FOR COMPACTING BASIC MATERIAL Describe activities that will be used to guarantee proficiency in basic curricular areas.	ACCELERATION AND/OR ENRICHMENT ACTIVITIES Describe activities that will be used to provide advanced level learning experiences in each area of the regular curriculum

☐ Check here if additional information is recorded on the reverse side.

Figure 9.4 The Compactor (actual size 11" × 17").

Source: Used by permission of Joseph S. Renzulli and Creative Learning Press, Inc., Mansfield Center, Connecticut.

125

and mathematics) are usually readily available in the form of pretests, end-of-unit tests, or summary exercises that contain a sampling of the major concepts presented in a designated unit of instruction. Such tests are usually keyed to specific pages and/or skills activities, allowing appropriate prescription of activities for needed skills. In subject areas without these tools, teachers must ask themselves:

- Why am I teaching this?
- What are my goals?
- Do any of my students already know this material?
- How will I evaluate whether my students have mastered this material?

In most cases, the evaluation planned for the end of an instructional unit can also be used as a preassessment to identify previously mastered content and skills.

Column 2 ("Procedures for Compacting Basic Material") is used to describe instructional activities that will be used to guarantee proficiency in basic curricular areas. In column 2, the classroom teacher should indicate any learning activities that will be eliminated because of the proficiencies documented in column 1. Some teachers simply make a photocopy of the pre- or post-test used to document proficiency and attach it to the Compactor. Other teachers use column 2 to indicate for a specific time period the manner in which previously mastered work will be eliminated. There are many different ways to document proficiency, but it is important to remember that column 2 should be used to document what students already know or are capable of learning at their own rapid pace.

The final step in curriculum compacting is to explore a wide variety of acceleration and/or enrichment alternatives. If teachers have been successful in helping gifted youngsters master the regular curriculum in a more economical and efficient manner, they will have provided some time for these students to pursue advanced-level studies. Teachers will also

have concrete evidence (test scores) that basic material has been mastered.

The third column of the Compactor can be used to expand the written record of individualization. The first step in completing this column is to make some basic decisions about the subject matter boundaries within which enrichment activities will fall. For example, if several mathematics curriculum units have been compacted, a teacher must decide whether or not the extra time available will be devoted to mathematics enrichment or acceleration. The philosophy of a program, the availability of resources, or practical considerations such as scheduling restrictions may influence this decision.

Although practical and organizational concerns may place restrictions or limits on enrichment alternatives, the crucial consideration in making decisions about advanced-level opportunities is the interest of the student. In the situation described above, there should be no question whatever about an advanced mathematics experience if the student is genuinely interested in math. However, a problem may arise if a student is taught advanced math when he or she would rather pursue some other topic or area of study.

One of the best ways to complete the Compactor's third column is to develop a separate resource list of all available enrichment and acceleration activities within a given school district. As resources and special services expand, the growing list can serve as an important part of the planning and program development process.

Students should be provided with an orientation to the compacting process to enable them to realize that doing their best work in school may earn them time to work on something in which they have a keen interest. For example, if a youngster can demonstrate proficiency in grammar, he or she may then earn the opportunity to select a novel to read, view filmstrips about famous authors, write original short stories, compose poetry, or select an area of interest in language arts. This self-selection of activities often encourages underachieving students to demonstrate mastery in order to earn time to pursue personal interests.

Type I Enrichment (General Exploratory Experiences)

Type I enrichment consists of exploratory experiences designed to expose students to new and exciting topics, ideas, and fields of knowledge not ordinarily covered in the regular curriculum. Both talent pool and other students should be exposed to Type I enrichment, which can enrich the lives of all students by expanding the scope of experiences provided by the school. Type I enrichment is carried out through a variety of procedures, such as visiting speakers, field trips, demonstrations, interest centers, and the use of audiovisual materials.

An enrichment team consisting of teachers, parents, and the building principal has the main responsibility for planning a wide variety of Type I activities. The teacher-coordinator of the enrichment program works with the team as a resource person and helps to arrange for and carry out activities planned by the team. This approach helps to accomplish a number of important objectives. First and foremost, *all* students are given at least some opportunity to participate in certain enrichment experiences as their interest dictates, and the school therefore becomes a more exciting and stimulating environment for everyone. Second, this approach avoids the always-difficult task of defending why certain general enrichment activities are available only to gifted students. Third, the enrichment team becomes a vehicle for more effective coordination between the regular curriculum and experiences that are offered as part of the enrichment program. Finally, expanding the scope of the general enrichment program to the total school population helps to minimze concerns about elitism by making at least some of the enrichment experiences available to larger number of students.

Type I enrichment serves a very special purpose for students in the talent pool. Because of their familiarity with the overall programming model, these students are aware that Type I enrichment represents an invitation to more advanced levels of involvement. Thus, talent pool students self-select those topics in which they may want to pursue an intensive research study, creative endeavor, or other investigative activity.

Planning and Implementing Type I Enrichment

We have built the Type I planning and implementation process around a series of action forms. The Type I planning guide (see Figure 9.5) can be completed for a given subject area, grade level, or combination of the two (i.e., fourth grade–social studies).

The vertical column on the left-hand side of this action form includes several ways in which Type I experiences can be provided for students in the talent pool as well as other students who might participate in various Type I activities. The blank spaces across the top of the Type I planning guide, which specify the particular activity or source, are completed by teachers (and sometimes students). Brainstorming sessions should be organized around a topic or subtopics, and activity suggestions should be directed toward the major features of Type I (topics, issues, etc.) not ordinarily covered in the regular curriculum.

The major responsibility for organizing the overall Type I effort in a school belongs to the enrichment team and the subgroup of this team that we call the Type I committee. Although this Committee plans and organizes meetings, the success of this endeavor rests with the specificity of topic–grade-level planning and the extent of involvement by teachers who will be affected by such planning.

The enrichment team should remember that identifying Type I sources is accomplished over a long period of time. Work should be begun on a modest scale and resources added continually. As the number of Type I sources increases over the years, procedures for disseminating this information should be formalized so that eventually a Type I source guide can be published and distributed on a regular updated basis throughout all schools in the district.

The Type I dimension can be a very exciting aspect of your program because it will bring into the schools an almost unlimited number

Check all that apply:
— General Matrix _____
— Grade Level _____
— Subject Area _____

Methods of Delivery																						
I. Resources Persons																						
Speakers																						
Mini-Courses																						
Demonstrations																						
Artistic Performances																						
Panel Discussion/Debate																						
Other _____																						
II. Media																						
Films																						
Filmstrips																						
Slides																						
Audio Tapes/Records																						
Videotapes																						
Television Programs																						
Newspaper/Magazine Articles																						
Other _____																						
III. Other Resources																						
Interest Development Centers																						
Displays																						
Field Trips																						
Museum Programs																						
Learning Centers																						
Other _____																						

Source: Used by permission of Joseph S. Renzulli and Creative Learning Press, Inc., Mansfield Center, Connecticut.

Figure 9.5 Type I planning guide.

and variety of experiences that are not ordinarily covered in the regular curriculum. This approach can increase the number of supporters and advocates of enrichment programming, and therefore its payoff can be in both good public relations and the many educational experiences that will be provided for students. In SEM (Renzulli & Reis, 1985) we listed numerous specific sources and activities for Types I, II, and III enrichment, procedures for organizing, recording, and evaluating these activities, and guidelines for the establishment of interest-development centers. Also included are sample forms, dissemination vehicles, recruitment letters, evaluation instruments, and teacher training activities.

Type II Enrichment (Group Training Activities)

Type II enrichment includes instructional methods and materials that are designed to promote thinking and feeling processes. Four major objectives included in Type II enrichment are to develop:

1. General skills in creative thinking and problem solving, critical thinking, and affective processes such as sensing, appreciating, and valuing
2. A variety of how-to-learn skills such as note taking, interviewing, classifying, analyzing data, drawing conclusions, etc.
3. Skills in the appropriate use of advanced-level reference materials such as reader's guides, directories, abstracts, etc.
4. Written, oral, and visual communication skills that maximize the impact of students' products upon appropriate audiences

Within each objective, the targeted skills exist along a continuum ranging from very basic manifestations of a given skill or ability to higher and more complex applications. We therefore developed a plan for Type II enrichment that is designed to develop all four objectives in both the general population and talent pool students. This approach offers many advantages. First, it avoids the totally unsupportable assertion that only the gifted should have an opportunity to develop their thinking and feeling processes. Second, we need not spend our time and energy trying to defend which activities are, and which are not, good for high-ability students. Since most process activities are open-ended and exist along a continuum of difficulty, they can be used with groups of various ability levels. Third, this approach represents a systematic and organized procedure for expanding the scope of the regular curriculum and enriching the learning experiences of all students.

There are three different dimensions of Type II enrichment used within the SEM. The first dimension is the type of planned, systematic enrichment that can be organized in advance for any given grade level, group, or regularly scheduled part of your special program. This section will concentrate mainly on this dimension.

The second dimension of Type II enrichment consists of process training skills that cannot be planned in advance. Experiences in this category usually result from student interests arising out of regular curricular experiences, planned Type I and Type II experiences, or nonschool interests. In many cases these unplanned training experiences may be the result of previous training, and we therefore must remain flexible in deciding whether to add Type II enrichment that may not have been included in our original formulation for a given year or group of students.

The third dimension of Type II enrichment training consists of processes that should be taught in connection with a Type III activity. A major focus of teacher guidance in Type III situations is providing advanced-level training in the methodological and process skills necessary for carrying out advanced investigative and creative activities. As students begin work on a Type III project, materials should be reviewed to identify appropriate process training skills. For example, if one or more students decide to pursue a Type III experience related to oral history, you can quickly identify process training activities related to interviewing and other oral history techniques by examining the titles of enrichment materials related to this skill.

Planning and Implementing Type II Enrichment

A major part of our effort to prepare a comprehensive plan for process development has been to organize a taxonomy of Type II enrichment processes. The taxonomy is organized around the four major objectives of Type II enrichment and 14 subcategories of process training:

Type II Taxonomy

I. Cognitive and affective training
   A. Creative thinking skills
   B. Creative problem solving and decision making
   C. Critical and logical thinking
   D. Affective skills
II. How-to-learn skills
   A. Listening, observing, and perceiving
   B. Reading, note taking, and outlining
   C. Interviewing and surveying
   D. Analyzing and organizing data
III. Advanced research skills and reference materials
   A. Preparation for Type III investigations
   B. Library skills
   C. Community resources
IV. Written, oral, and visual communication skills
   A. Visual communication
   B. Oral communication
   C. Written communication

Each of the 14 subcategories is further divided into specific skills that can serve as the basis for planning and for selecting and reviewing materials. The taxonomy can also be used for the construction of a process-oriented scope and sequence chart for any given group, grade level, subject area, or total program. Further, the items in the taxonomy have been used to construct needs assessment questionnaires and evaluation instruments. The total taxonomy contains more than 250 specific skills. Space does not permit a complete listing; however, one of the 14 subsections is presented as an example.

Specific Skills From Objective I: Cognitive and Affective Training

C. Critical and logical thinking

Conditional reasoning	Inferences
Ambiguity	Inductive reasoning
Fallacies	Deductive reasoning
Emotive words	Syllogisms
Definition of terms	Probability
Categorical propositions	Dilemmas
Classification	Paradoxes
Validity testing	Analysis of:
Reliability testing	Content
Translation	Elements
Interpretation	Trends and patterns
Extrapolation	Relationships
Patterning	Organizing principles
Sequencing	Propaganda and bias
Flow charting	Analogies
Computer programming	

The major purpose of the taxonomy is to serve as a guide in the review and selection of enrichment materials. Over the years, we have used this organizational plan to analyze and classify more than 700 sets of enrichment activities according to grade-level classification (primary, middle, secondary) as well as thinking process categories. New materials are reviewed and classified as they become available. The result of this overall effort has been the development of an extensive materials laboratory.

Several forms have been designed to aid school districts and enrichment teams in the development of a scope and sequence plan. (These forms may be found on pp. 314–317 and 349–356 in *The Schoolwide Enrichment Model* [Renzulli & Reis, 1985].) These forms are designed to facilitate cooperative planning by resource teachers and classroom teachers. They also provide an opportunity for input and suggestions from area subject matter coordinators or general curriculum coordinators in the school district. Although initial efforts to complete the scope and sequence forms might begin on a grade-level and building-by-building basis, the forms may also guide the development of a districtwide plan for Type II enrichment activities that will be recommended for various grade levels and in particular subject matter areas.

Type III Enrichment (Individual and Small-Group Investigations of Real Problems)

Type III enrichment is the highest level of experience offered in programs using the SEM. While interest and learning styles assessment, Types I and II enrichment, and curriculum compacting are guaranteed to students in the talent pool (See Figure 9.6), the ability to revolve into Type III enrichment depends on the students' interests, motivation, and desire. In other words, Type III enrichment is self-selected and optional. While students are encouraged to undertake Type III investigations, they are not forced to participate.

We define Type III enrichment as investigative activities and artistic productions in which the learner assumes the role of a first-hand inquirer—thinking, feeling, and acting like a practicing professional. The five major objectives of Type III enrichment are:

1. To provide opportunities in which students can apply their interests, knowledge, creative ideas, and task commitment to a self-selected problem or area of study
2. To acquire advanced-level understanding of the knowledge (content) and methodology (process) that are used within particular disciplines, artistic areas of expression, and interdisciplinary studies
3. To develop authentic products that are primarily directed toward bringing about a desired impact upon a specified audience
4. To develop self-directed learning skills in the areas of planning, organization, resource utilization, time management, decision making, and self-evaluation
5. To develop task commitment, self-confidence, feelings of creative accomplishment, and the ability to interact effectively with other students, teachers, and persons with advanced levels of interest and expertise in a common area of achievement

As mentioned earlier, the process of revolving into a Type III investigation begins with the transmission of an *action information message* (AIM), which is an anecdotal comment about the high level of interest of an individual or small group of students. The AIM can originate from a variety of sources and can be sent on a specially designed elementary or secondary form (see Renzulli & Reis, 1985, pp. 398–399), or by a verbal exchange or an informal note. An AIM should be directed to whoever is in charge of facilitating Type III investigations, either a resource teacher or other designated persons. In cases where there are no special program personnel, the AIM should be directed to the chairperson of the enrichment team or persons who have been preselected to receive AIMs in particular categories (e.g., primary science, middle-grade creative writing, etc.). In the discussion that follows, we assume the presence of a resource teacher but recognize that these duties will be shared by others if resource teachers are not a part of the program in a particular school.

When an AIM is sent or delivered to the resource teacher or whoever will facilitate the Type III study, certain steps should be immediately followed (see Figure 9.7). First, the resource teacher either contacts or is contacted by the classroom teacher. The resource teacher should gather as much information as possible about the individual student or group of students. The student's interest in the topic, commitment to completing tasks, and curricular strength areas should be analyzed by both teachers. If the individual student or group of students shows particular strengths in certain subject areas, the resource teacher may also want to discuss strategies for curriculum compacting at this time.

The next step involves an interview with the student or group of students. The resource teacher may want to invite the classroom teacher to a very brief and informal preinterview meeting in order to gain background information about the student(s). At this time, the two teachers can decide if the classroom teacher should be involved in the student interview. Such involvement should be encouraged because this participation will result in a

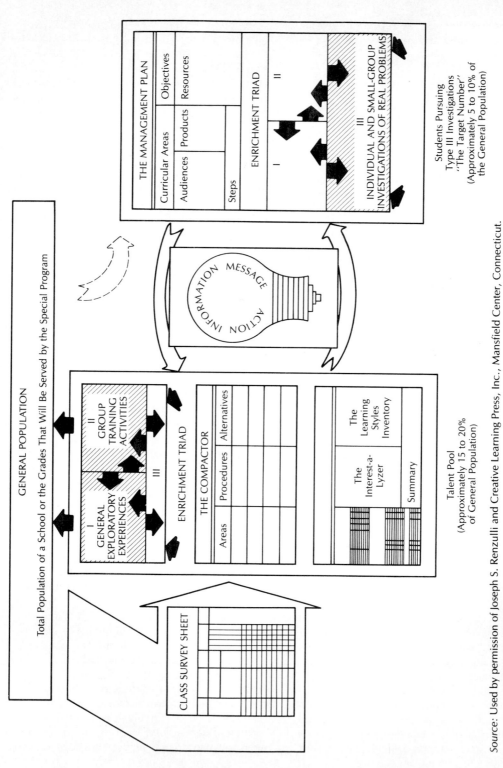

GENERAL POPULATION

Total Population of a School or the Grades That Will Be Served by the Special Program

THE MANAGEMENT PLAN

Curricular Areas	Products	Objectives
Audiences		Resources
Steps		

ENRICHMENT TRIAD

I   II   III

INDIVIDUAL AND SMALL-GROUP INVESTIGATIONS OF REAL PROBLEMS

Students Pursuing
Type III Investigations
"The Target Number"
(Approximately 5 to 10% of
the General Population)

INFORMATION MESSAGE ACTION

I
GENERAL
EXPLORATORY
EXPERIENCES

II
GROUP
TRAINING
ACTIVITIES

III

ENRICHMENT TRIAD

THE COMPACTOR

Areas	Procedures	Alternatives

The
Interest-a-
Lyzer

The
Learning
Styles
Inventory

Summary

Talent Pool
(Approximately 15 to 20%
of General Population)

CLASS SURVEY SHEET

Source: Used by permission of Joseph S. Renzulli and Creative Learning Press, Inc., Mansfield Center, Connecticut.

Figure 9.6   Relationship among the general population, talent pool, and students pursuing Type III investigations.

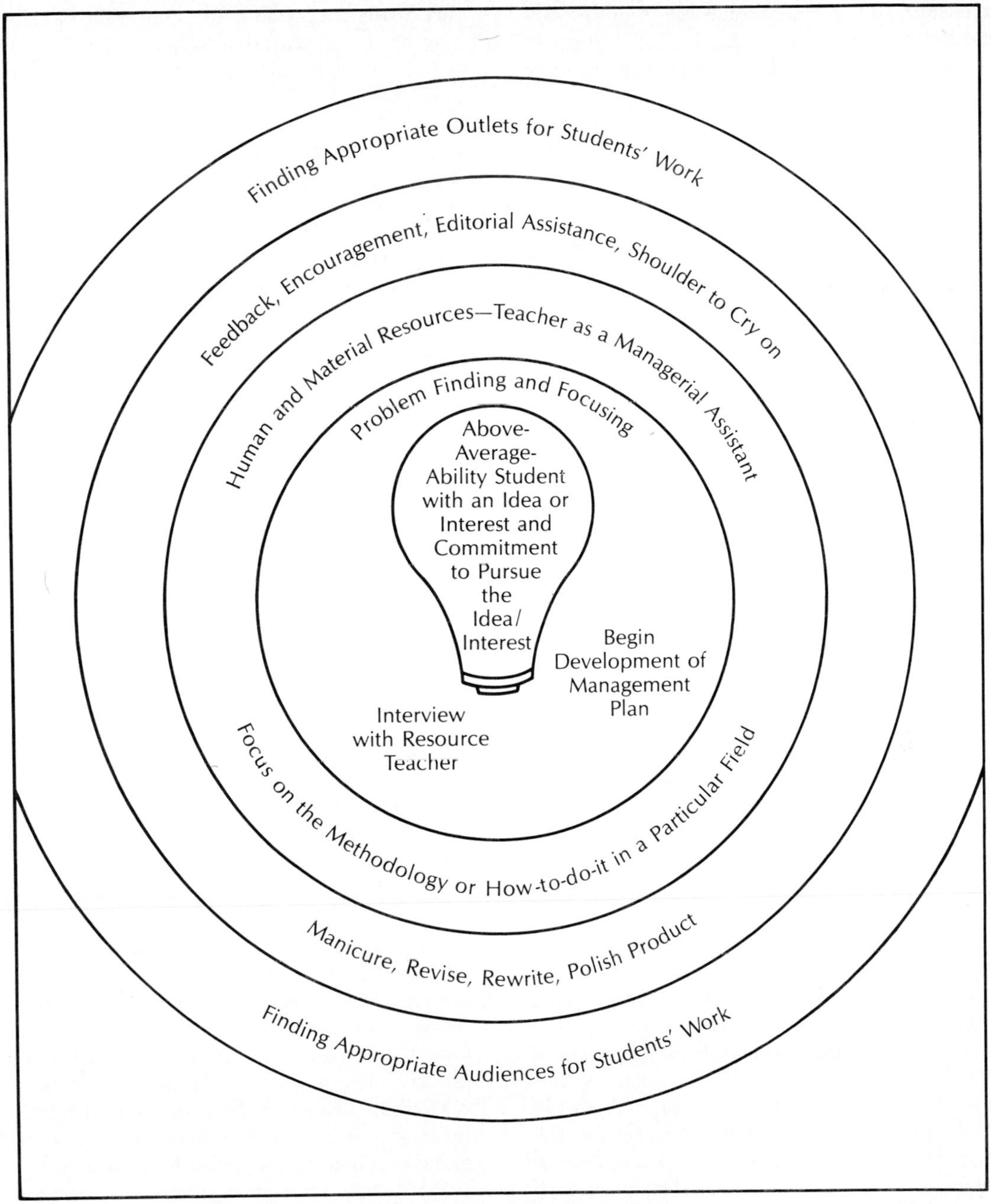

Finding Appropriate Outlets for Students' Work
Feedback, Encouragement, Editorial Assistance, Shoulder to Cry on
Human and Material Resources—Teacher as a Managerial Assistant
Problem Finding and Focusing
Above-Average-Ability Student with an Idea or Interest and Commitment to Pursue the Idea/Interest
Begin Development of Management Plan
Interview with Resource Teacher
Focus on the Methodology or How-to-do-it in a Particular Field
Manicure, Revise, Rewrite, Polish Product
Finding Appropriate Audiences for Students' Work

Source: Used by permission of Joseph S. Renzulli and Creative Learning Press, Inc., Mansfield Center, Connecticut.

Figure 9.7 Targeting on Type III.

greater interest and understanding in both students' projects and the overall nature of what is actually happening in the resource room.

Several important topics should be dealt with at the time of the student interview. Especially, the resource teacher should try to assess how much interest is really present for further pursuit of the topics. To further analyze the student's desire to complete the task, questions about procedures should also be asked at this time. For example, if a Type III idea for a monthly student newspaper is being discussed, the resource teacher should ask questions that will reveal whether or not the student has thought about the task commitment that will be required to complete the project or product. These questions might include: (1) How do you think you should get started? (2) How many hours do you think it will take you to organize completely a monthly school newspaper? (3) How many other students do you think you will need to involve? (4) How will you recruit reporters? (5) How can you reproduce your newspaper? (6) Do you have any ideas that might help you develop a newspaper that is somewhat different from others you have seen?

The point of this interview is not to frighten away individuals or small groups of students from beginning an investigation or product-oriented study. It is, rather, to reserve the time and energies of resource teachers for students who have a genuine interest in their subject and a sincere desire to work.

If the resource teacher and the classroom teacher agree that the student or group of students should begin working in the resource room, certain scheduling details must be followed. If a resource room and resource teacher do not exist in the school, the classroom teacher must reach his or her own decision about the student's project and should try to revolve the student into a particular place in the room or school where the student can begin work. If space exists in the resource room, schedules should be devised that allow the student or group of students, whenever possible, to be out of the classroom during a time when the teacher is covering work that the student or students have already mastered. At this time, procedures should be implemented to compact

each student's regular curriculum so that time may be made available to begin the Type III project. In addition, a contract or planning guide called the management plan (Renzulli & Smith, 1977) that documents the nature and scope of the student's proposed investigation should be completed. The management plan is another action form that helps students formulate their objectives, locate and organize appropriate resources, and identify relevant outlets and audiences for their creative work.

Problem Finding and Focusing

Once a student has revolved into a Type III experience, the first major responsibility of the teacher is to help the student identify the specific question(s) or idea(s) he or she is going to pursue. The process of problem finding and focusing should begin by first determining the students' general area(s) of interest. This determination can be made through the formal submission of an AIM, or it might result by simply observing the way in which a youngster responds to experiences in the regular curriculum, planned Type I and/or Type II enrichment activities, or informal out-of-school interests. It is absolutely essential for students to view the special program as a place where they can bring their interests and ideas and gain assistance in determining whether or not an idea might develop into a Type III project.

Most teachers have little difficulty recognizing general families of interest—scientific, historical, literary, mathematical, musical, or athletic. However, problems arise when they attempt to capitalize upon these general interests and use them as the starting point for (1) focusing on specific interests, and (2) structuring the specific interests into researchable problems. How teachers deal with interests, both general and specific, is crucial and if handled improperly will undoubtedly get students off on the wrong track.

One youngster, for example, expressed an unusual interest in sharks. The teacher appreciated the child's enthusiasm and reacted in what he thought was an appropriate fashion: "I'm glad that you have such a great interest in sharks—why don't you do a report about sharks?" Those awful words, "do a report" led to an inevitable end result—yet-another summary of facts and drawings based entirely on information copied from encyclopedias and "all-about" books. Some training in reporting is a necessary part of good education for all students. Indeed, the pursuit of new knowledge should always begin with a review of what is already known about a given topic. The end result of a Type III investigation, however, should be a cognitive contribution that goes beyond the already-existing information that is found in encyclopedias and similar sources.

How can teachers help students learn to focus problems and become involved in advanced types of creative and productive projects? The first step is to help students ask the kinds of questions raised by persons who do investigate research within particular fields of knowledge. However, we are faced with a practical problem. Because most teachers are not well-versed in asking the right questions about specific fields of study, we must assist students in obtaining the methodological books (or resource persons, if available) that routinely list these important questions. In other words, if we want to ask the right questions about problem-focusing in anthropology, then we must begin by looking at techniques used by anthropologists.

We can avoid the error of confusing traditional reporting with Type III investigations by keeping the concept of raw data in mind. Raw data can be thought of as relatively unorganized bits and pieces of information that can be gathered and analyzed in order to reach a conclusion, discover a principle, support an argument, or create a unique product or presentation. The ways in which researchers use data and the purposes toward which data are directed are important considerations in defining a Type III experience.

It is impossible for teachers to become experts in all the methodological techniques of the many fields of study in which their students might develop an interest. Our major responsibility in problem focusing and the other activities for facilitating Type III enrichment described below is to (1) know about the existence of methodological resource books in the various fields of knowledge, (2) know where such books are located and how we can obtain

them for students, (3) take the time and effort necessary to help them obtain these materials, which are frequently located in places other than our schools, and (4) provide or obtain the assistance that might be necessary for interpreting advanced-level material that might be difficult for younger students to understand.

Focusing on Methodology

The second major responsibility of teachers in facilitating Type III enrichment is to give students methodological and managerial assistance. Methodological assistance means helping students acquire and make appropriate use of the specific data-gathering tools and investigative techniques that are necessary for authentic research in particular fields of study. Every field of organized knowledge can be defined, in part, by its methodology. This methodology can be found in certain kinds of how-to guidebooks or manuals, which are the key to escalating studies beyond traditional report writing. The correct guidance by teachers during this phase of a study can almost guarantee that students will be first-hand investigators rather than reporters. This step involves shifting our emphasis from learning *about* topics to learning how one gathers, categorizes, analyzes, and evaluates information in particular fields.

Managerial assistance consists of helping students make arrangements for obtaining the types of data and resources necessary for Type III investigations. Setting up an interview with a public official, arranging for the distribution of a questionnaire to students or parents, and providing transportation to a place where data will be gathered are examples of managerial functions. Additional activities might include helping students gain access to laboratories or computer centers, arranging for the use of a college library, helping students gain access to a telephone or photocopying machine, or driving downtown to pick up photographic materials or electronic parts. The teacher's responsibilities resemble those of a combined research assistant, advocate, ombudsman, campaign strategist, and enthusiastic friend. At this stage of product development the student should be the leader and emerging expert, while the teacher assumes a supportive rather than authoritative posture. A teacher's typical comments should be: "What can I do to help you? Are you having any problems? Do you need to get a book from the university library? Would you like to bounce a few ideas off me? Are there some ways we might explore to raise the money you need for solar cells?"

The major purpose of the managerial role is to help the student stay on track and move toward each intermediate goal and accomplishment. A planned strategy for bringing the teacher up to date on progress between meetings creates a vehicle for fulfilling the managerial role. A log, notebook, or annotated time line are good examples of such vehicles. And of course, this procedure should involve a review of the management plan and the notation of appropriate information in the respective sections of the plan.

The Editorial and Feedback Process

Even the most experienced researchers, writers, and creative producers need feedback from persons who can reflect objectively upon a given piece of work. For young scholars, who are just beginning to experience the common frustration of first-hand inquiry, this feedback must be given in a firm but sensitive manner. The major theme underlying the feedback process is that almost everything can be improved upon in various degrees through revisions, rewriting, and attention to details, both large and small. This message must be conveyed to students without harsh criticism or discouraging comments. Each student must be made to feel that the teacher's most important concern is to help the aspiring artist or scholar reach the highest possible level of excellence. Just as a champion athlete or dancer knows that a rigorous coach has the performer's best interests at heart, so also must students learn that critical feedback is a major service that good teachers must offer.

There are several ways students can learn about the relationship between high quality and the feedback process. Authors such as Gottschalk (1969) describe the functions of succeeding drafts of historical manuscripts, with examples of first drafts and edited copies of the same manuscript. A similar strategy is to locate in the student's area of research well-written journal articles, or other products, that profoundly illustrate how a particular method was described or results were reported. Outstanding examples of work completed by other students of the same age will also provide prototypes as well as the motivation to pursue necessary revisions.

Finding Outlets and Audiences for Student Products

If the Type III dimension of our model is to have maximum value in the overall development of young scholars and creative producers, major attention must be given to helping them find appropriate outlets and audiences for their most creative efforts. This concern is once again modeled after the modus operandi of creative and productive individuals. If we could sum up in as few words as possible the raison d'être of highly creative artists and scholars, it would certainly be *impact upon audience.* Creativity is a source of personal satisfaction and self-expression, but much of the reward comes from bringing about desired changes in the human condition. The writer hopes to influence thoughts and emotions; the scientist carries out research to contribute to the knowledge of his or her field; and artists create products to enrich the lives of those who view their works. Teachers can help young people acquire this orientation by encouraging them to develop a *sense of audience* from the earliest stages of a Type III investigation.

The teacher's role is to help students consider how people typically communicate results within the given fields of art and science. Once again, we can look to the activities of practicing professionals and to the how-to books for guidance. In most cases, young artists and scholars will be restricted to local outlets and audiences, but there will be occasions when products of unusual excellence can be shared with larger audiences.

Although school and local audiences are an obvious starting point in the search for outlets, teachers should always help students look for more comprehensive outlet vehicles and audiences. Many organizations, for example, prepare newsletters and journals at the state and national levels, and they are usually receptive to high-quality contributions by young people. Similarly, state and national magazines often carry outstanding work by young people. Whenever student products achieve unusually high levels of excellence, encourage the students to contact publishing companies and magazines that specialize in or are receptive to the contributions of young writers, artists, and researchers. Just as gifted athletes extend their involvement into larger and larger fields of competition, so also should our most able young scholars and artists be encouraged to reach out beyond the local levels of success they have achieved. This process involves an element of risk taking. However, we have built in an element of success by beginning the process at the local or school level. Moreover, we have also built in the opportunity for a real-world experience by helping young people to learn about the rigors and challenges of the creative producer as he or she attempts to reach out to wider audiences.

Procedures for Evaluating Type III Enrichment

The Student Product Assessment Form

The student product assessment form (SPAF) was the result of a comprehensive research project (Reis, 1981) directed toward (1) establishing the reliability and validity of this instrument and (2) assessing the quality of products produced by students. The instrument is composed of 15 items designed to assess both individual aspects and overall excellence of products. Each item describes a single characteristic on which raters focus their attention. Items 1 through 8 are divided into three related parts:

1. *The key concept.* This concept is always presented first and is printed in large type. It focuses the rater's attention on the main idea or characteristic being evaluated.
2. *The item description.* Following the key concept are one or more descriptive statements

about how the main idea or characteristic might be reflected in the student's product.
3. *Examples.* In order to help clarify the meaning of the items, actual examples of students' work is provided. These examples are intended to elaborate upon the meaning of both the key concept and the item description. The examples are presented after each item description.

Item 9 contains seven different components that detail an overall assessment of the product. When completing these ratings, raters attempt to evaluate the product in terms of their own values and opinions regarding the quality, esthetics, utility, and function of the overall contribution.

The results of this product assessment should be summarized in the main body of an evaluation report. It is important to make the raters aware that the SPAFs, management plans, and actual products are available for their review. For a final report, it is not necessary to submit every product for a formal evaluation. A stratified random sample (by grade level and various areas of student interest) can be used to provide a fair picture of the types of work that are being pursued in the special program.

Research on the Triad–Revolving Door Model

Although the triad–revolving door model is a relatively new system for identification and programming, its effectiveness has been documented by a series of studies and field tests in schools with widely differing socioeconomic levels and program organizational patterns. Using a population of 1,162 students in Grades 1 through 6 in 11 school districts, Reis and Renzulli (1982) examined several variables related to the effectiveness of the triad–revolving door model. The talent pools in each district and at each grade level were divided into two groups. Group A consisted of students who scored in the top 5% on standardized tests of intelligence and achievement. Group B consisted of students who scored 10 to 15 percentile points below the top 5%. Both groups participated equally in all program activities.

The SPAF (Renzulli et al., 1981) was used to compare the quality of products from each group. A double-blind method of product coding was used so that judges did not know group membership (i.e., A or B) when evaluating individual products. An analysis of variance indicated no significant differences between Group A and Group B with respect to the quality of students' products. These findings verify the three-ring conception of giftedness underlying the triad–revolving door model and clearly support the effectiveness of the model in serving a group that is larger than the traditional top 5%.

Questionnaires and interviews were used to examine several other factors related to overall program effectiveness (Reis, 1981). The data indicated that feelings about the revolving door program—gathered from classroom teachers, administrators, students in the talent pools, and their parents—were generally positive. Many classroom teachers reported that their involvement in the program had favorably influenced their teaching practices. Parents whose children previously had been in traditional programs for the gifted did not differ in their opinions about the revolving door program from parents whose children had been identified as gifted under the expanded revolving door criteria. Resource teachers—many of whom had been involved previously in traditional programs for the gifted—overwhelmingly preferred the revolving door identification procedure to the traditional reliance on test scores alone.

Additional research (Delisle & Renzulli, 1982) examined academic self-concept and locus of control. This study established the importance of nonintellective factors in creative production and verified earlier research related to the three-ring conception of giftedness. Using a stepwise multiple regression technique to study the correlates of creative production, Gubbins (1982) found that above-average ability is a necessary but not sufficient condition for high-level productivity. The roles of task and time commitment and the importance of student interests were verified. A study of student, parent, and classroom teachers' attitudes toward the revolving door model (Delisle, Reis, & Gubbins, 1981) revealed support for this approach and a high degree of cooperation among all persons involved in the implementation of a revolving door program.

Cooper (1983) examined the attitudes of superintendents, principals, and special education–pupil personnel services directors in eight Connecticut school districts that had field-tested the SEM during the 1980–81 and 1981–82 school years. It was concluded that SEM's goals were attainable, although the gifted program had not been integrated into the total school curriculum as thoroughly as anticipated. More students were served, however, and elitism minimized. Schools with administrators actively involved in the program reported a *radiation of excellence* (Ward, 1965) throughout their buildings.

Starko (1986) examined the effects of the SEM on student creative productivity and self-efficacy regarding creative productivity. This research compared students who participated in SEM programs for at least 4 years with students who qualified for such programs but received no services. Questionnaires were used to determine the number of creative products produced by both groups, both within school programs and in independent activities outside school, as well as to gather information about attitudes and skills associated with creative productivity. Information on self-efficacy was collected using an original instrument based on Bandura's self-efficacy theory and the components of creative productivity presented in the SEM. Results indicated that students who became involved in independent study projects in the SEM more often initiated their own creative productivity outside school than did students in the control group. Starko also found that participation in this enrichment program had an increased positive effect on students' attitudes toward school when compared with attitudes of the control group.

Skaught (1987) examined the nature of the social acceptability of talent pool students at the elementary level in a school using the SEM. Past research indicated that identified gifted students perceive themselves as ostracized by their classmates (Torrance, 1963; Webb, Meckstroth, & Tolan, 1982), and some gifted children report encountering hostility and ridicule from fellow students who mock the advanced abilities of brighter children (Delisle, 1984; Feldhusen, 1985).

In this study, sociometric measures were taken to determine the social acceptability of talent pool students before and after receiving special services for high-ability students. Pretest and post-test scores on a peer relationship scale of a self-concept test were used to assess the talent pool students' perceptions of peer acceptance. Results indicated that students identified as above average in an SEM program were positively accepted by their peers. Skaught also found that a condition of "separateness" did not exist in schools where the SEM had been implemented.

Olenchak (1987) examined the effects of a yearlong application of the SEM, using experimental and control schools. Subjects consisted of 1,698 elementary-grade students, 236 teachers, 120 parents, and 10 principals. The study sought to determine if the SEM would result in measurable changes on selected variables. Quantitative data analysis revealed significant changes in student attitudes toward learning, but not in teacher attitudes toward teaching. Student creative products were numerous and exceeded the norm of typical student creative output. Most notable among qualitative data analysis were remarkably favorable changes in attitudes toward education of the gifted by classroom teachers and the general student population; large increases in student-centered enrichment activities and work on self-selected interests; greater cooperation among classroom teachers and gifted education specialists; and more favorable attitudes toward special programming on the part of parents.

Conclusion

We and our colleagues have spent several years conducting a variety of research studies on various components of the SEM. Eight dissertation-length studies have been completed, and research currently underway is examining long-term effects of participation in triad-based programs. The completed studies are summarized in a two-volume technical report (Renzulli, 1988) and numerous research articles in professional journals.

Because our model focuses on the development of complex kinds of creative productivity in young people, the effectiveness of our efforts must be examined through a combination of quantitative and qualitative research designs. Since we are attempting to promote more complex and applied types of growth in young people, our research, by necessity, could not routinely employ the types of designs traditionally used to evaluate the achievement of basic skills. For example, since one of the major goals of triad-based programs is to achieve integration with and impact upon the total school program, we have sought to answer research questions related to the attitudes of general faculty, parents, and administrators. These avenues of research are important for helping services for bright youngsters to become accepted as an important component of a school's overall educational effort.

If there is one aspect of our model in which we take the most pride, it is that we have taken the time to examine implementation in a variety of school settings and to introduce modifications growing out of the research data. We hope that in the years ahead additional research studies by both supporters and critics of the model will be conducted, and that additional refinements in the model will be introduced whenever there is solid evidence that such modifications are warranted. Although services to bright youngsters are obviously the major goal of this and any other programming model, we also believe that the goals of good science must be a primary concern of persons offering innovative practices to the education public.

NOTES

1. The rationale for this approach has been presented elsewhere (Renzulli, 1977c, pp. 1–13).

REFERENCES

Bloom, B. S. (1956). *Taxonomy of educational objectives, handbook I: Cognitive domain.* New York: McKay.

Bloom, B. S. (Ed.). (1985). *Developing talent in young people*. New York: Ballantine.

Cooper, C. (1983). *Administrator's attitudes toward gifted programs based on the enrichment triad/revolving door identification model: Case studies in decision-making*. Unpublished doctoral dissertation, University of Connecticut, Storrs.

Delisle, J. R. (1984). *Gifted children speak out*. New York: Walker & Company.

Delisle, J. R., Reis, S. M., & Gubbins, E. J. (1981). The revolving door identification and programming model. *Exceptional Children, 48,* 152–156.

Delisle, J. R., & Renzulli, J. S. (1982). The revolving door identification and programming model: Correlates of creative production. *Gifted Child Quarterly, 26,* 89–95.

Feldhusen, J. F. (Ed.). (1985). *Toward excellence in gifted education*. Denver: Love.

Gardner, H. (1983). *Frames of mind*. New York: Basic.

Gottschalk, L. (1969). *Understanding history: A primer of historical method* (2nd ed.). New York: Knopf.

Gubbins, E. J. (1982). *Revolving door identification model: Characteristics of talent pool students*. Unpublished doctoral dissertation, University of Connecticut, Storrs.

Hoge, R. D. (1988). Issues in the definition and measurement of the giftedness construct. *Educational Researcher, 17,* 12–17.

McGreevy, A. (1982). *My book of things and stuff: An interest questionnaire for young children*. Mansfield Center, CT: Creative Learning.

Olenchak, F. R. (1987). *The schoolwide enrichment model in elementary schools: A study of implementation stages and the effects on educational excellence*. Unpublished doctoral dissertation, University of Connecticut, Storrs.

Reis, S. M. (1981). *An analysis of the productivity of gifted students participating in programs using the revolving door identification model*. Unpublished doctoral dissertation, University of Connecticut, Storrs.

Reis, S. M. (1983). Creating ownership in gifted and talented programs. *Roeper Review, 5,* 20–23.

Reis, S. M., & Renzulli, J. S. (1982). A research report on the revolving door identification model: A case for the broadened conception of giftedness. *Phi Delta Kappan, 63,* 619–620.

Renzulli, J. S. (1977a). *The Interest-a-lyzer*. Mansfield Center, CT: Creative Learning.

Renzulli, J. S. (1977b). *The adult Interest-a-lyzer*. Storrs, CT: Bureau of Educational Research, University of Connecticut.

Renzulli, J. S. (1977c). *The enrichment triad model: A guide for developing defensible programs for the gifted*. Mansfield Center, CT: Creative Learning.

Renzulli, J. S. (1978). What makes giftedness? Reexamining a definition. *Phi Delta Kappan, 60,* 180–184, 261.

Renzulli, J. S. (1982). What makes a problem real? Stalking the illusive meaning of qualitative differences in gifted education. *Gifted Child Quarterly, 26,* 148–156.

Renzulli, J. S. (Ed.). (1988). *Technical report of research studies related to the revolving door identification model*. Storrs, CT: Bureau of Educational Research, University of Connecticut.

Renzulli, J. S., & Reis, S. M. (1985). *The schoolwide enrichment model: A comprehensive plan for educational excellence*. Mansfield Center, CT: Creative Learning.

Renzulli, J. S., Reis, S. M., & Smith, L. H. (1981). *The revolving door identification model*. Mansfield Center, CT: Creative Learning.

Renzulli, J. S., & Smith, L. H. (1977). *The management plan for individual and small group investigations of real problems*. Mansfield Center, CT: Creative Learning.

Renzulli, J. S., & Smith, L. H. (1978a). *The compactor*. Mansfield Center, CT: Creative Learning.

Renzulli, J. S., & Smith, L. H. (1978b). *The learning styles inventory: A measure of student preference for instructional techniques*. Mansfield Center, CT: Creative Learning.

Renzulli, J. S., Smith, L. H., Callahan, C., White, A., & Hartman, R. (1976). *Scales for rating the behavioral characteristics of superior students*. Mansfield Center, CT: Creative Learning.

Schlichter, C. (1986). Talents unlimited: Applying the multiple talent approach in mainstream and gifted programs. In J. S. Renzulli (Ed.), *Systems and models for developing programs for the gifted and talented* (pp. 352–390). Mansfield Center, CT: Creative Learning.

Skaught, B. J. (1987). *The social acceptability of talent pool students in an elementary school using the schoolwide enrichment model*. Unpublished doctoral dissertation. University of Connecticut, Storrs.

Smith, L. H. (1976). *Learning styles: Their measurement and educational significance*. Unpublished doctoral dissertation, University of Connecticut, Storrs.

Starko, A. J. (1986). *The effects of the revolving door identification model on creative productivity and self-efficacy*. Unpublished doctoral dissertation, University of Connecticut, Storrs.

Sternberg, R. J. (1985). A componential theory of intellectual giftedness. *Gifted Child Quarterly, 25,* 86–93.

Taylor, C. W. (1986). Cultivating simultaneous student growth in both multiple creative talents and knowledge. In J. S. Renzulli (Ed.), *Systems and models for developing programs for the gifted and talented* (pp. 306–351). Mansfield Center, CT: Creative Learning.

Torrance, E. P. (1963). *Education and the creative potential*. Minneapolis: University of Minnesota Press.

Treffinger, D. J., & Renzulli, J. S. (1986). Giftedness as potential for creative productivity: Transcending IQ scores. *Roeper Review, 8,* 150–154.

Ward, V. S. (1965). *Educating the gifted: An axiomatic approach*. Columbus, OH: Merrill.

Webb, J. T., Meckstroth, E. A., & Tolan, S. S. (1982). *Guiding the gifted*. Columbus: Ohio Psychology.

Williams, F. E. (1986). The cognitive-affective interaction model for enriching gifted programs. In J. S. Renzulli (Ed.), *Systems and models for developing programs for the gifted and talented* (pp. 461–484). Mansfield Center, CT: Creative Learning.

10

The Autonomous Learner Model for the Gifted and Talented

GEORGE T. BETTS   *University of Northern Colorado, Greeley*

■ The autonomous learner model (ALM) for the gifted and talented was first developed to meet the diversified cognitive, emotional, and social needs of the gifted and talented at the high school level. After 6 years of program development, implementation, and evaluation, the model was extended so that it now is used in schools and school districts throughout the United States and Canada on a K–12 basis.

The overall goal of the model is to provide students the many necessary opportunities and experiences to become independent, self-directed learners. In other words, by the time they graduate from high school, students need to be lifelong learners (Betts & Knapp, 1981). Emphasis in the model is placed on a structured but flexible approach to guiding students from dependence to independence and from conformity to individuality.

The concept of becoming an independent learner applies not only to the cognitive development of the students, but also to emotional and social development. Not only do we want the gifted to develop their gifts and pursue their passions, but we want them to be healthy, fully functioning people. Cognitive development alone is not enough.

Historical Background

In the early 1970s, administrators and teachers at Arvada West High School in Jefferson County, Colorado, felt that the diversified educational needs of students were not being met. As a result, many educational options were developed and implemented. Some ideas worked and continue to be used, while others were abandoned after 2 or 3 years.

During 1973 to 1974 student unrest was one of the major issues of the times. Some students were skipping classes, experimenting with drugs and alcohol, and dropping out of school. The principal at Arvada West High School wanted new and innovative programs that would address the problems faced by the staff. One major concept was developing a program for the gifted and talented. This was a unique idea at the time because programs for the gifted and talented in the state of Colorado existed only at the elementary and junior high school levels.

The philosophy was to develop a new program not *for* the gifted, but *with* the gifted. In other words, from the very beginning the plan was "Don't do it to them, but with them; they know what they need." A representative task force (including students) was developed and had the task of defining what it means to be gifted and talented, developing identification procedures, and developing an approach to meet their diversified cognitive, emotional, and social needs.

Where to begin? The Jefferson County public school system also was involved in the development of programs for the gifted and talented and began a districtwide approach to program implementation. Nineteen pilot schools were selected in 1976–1977 to develop programs, after receiving district support that included a complete staff development program led by Dr. Irving Sato of the National/State Leadership Training Institute for the Gifted and Talented. Teachers and administrators from the 19 schools participated in a series of 2- and 3-day workshops conducted by national leaders in the area of the gifted and talented. Much of the local leadership of the project came from Dr. Harry Morgan, the district coordinator for the gifted and talented. Each school was assigned a core team whose members were responsible for developing individual programs within their schools.

District personnel worked with Dr. Sato in the areas of awareness, definition, program planning, and program implementation. Dr. Sandra Kaplan presented material on the differentiation of curriculum for the gifted and on gifted students' characteristics and needs, both cognitive and social. She also contributed information on program prototypes, curriculum, and independent study. From Dr. Joseph Renzulli the group learned about the enrichment triad model and later, the revolving door model. Dr. Abraham Tannenbaum presented information on definitions and a comprehensive plan for the development of programs for the gifted and talented.

Basic Principles of the Autonomous Learner Model

As a result of the information obtained from consultation with nationally recognized leaders; a review of the literature; the background and educational training of the teachers, counselors, and administrators; and information received from students and parents, the school-wide task force outlined the following principles, which have continued to be refined over the past several years in the development of the ALM. Several of the current basic principles (Betts, 1985) also are presented here.

Integration of the Total Individual

While observing and evaluating programs for the gifted and talented, I became aware that the majority of programs placed their main emphasis on developing the cognitive domain of the individual, rather than taking an integrative or holistic approach. When working directly with gifted and talented students in a school setting, it becomes apparent that a broad range of experiences are necessary. Besides emphasizing the cognitive, it also is essential to include emotional and social development. A major goal of the ALM is to encourage individuals to become independent, self-directed learners who have abilities and positive attitudes in the cognitive, emotional, and social domains.

Self-Esteem

A key ingredient of happiness and success in life is the development of positive self-esteem. The manner in which a person perceives the self and the way feelings toward this self are interpreted by the individual will help predict the behavior and effectiveness of the person. The more positive I am toward myself, the more positive I will be toward my peers, teachers, parents, other adults, and the world in which I live. Self-esteem is the major factor in fostering positive growth and fulfillment.

Social Skills

How can some people with outstanding intelligence be unable to interact and communicate effectively with other people? What can educators and parents do to help our gifted and talented become more effective in their interactions? In the ALM appropriate social skills are discussed, demonstrated, role-played, reinforced, and evaluated by the individual and by the teacher-facilitator. A major factor of success in life depends on the ability to communicate effectively with other people. To be able to listen and to send appropriate messages therefore is an essential factor in the ALM.

Student-Based Content

The majority of content presented to students in today's schools falls in the area of *prescribed content*. People outside the school decide what should be taught and when. That information is given to people who develop textbooks and workbooks, which are sold to school districts that give them to teachers, who then teach the prescribed content. In many cases this might be appropriate, but those working in the area of education of the gifted are interested in the development of *student-based content*.

In discussions with E. Paul Torrance in Aspen, Colorado, in 1981, I learned an important concept that may become a central theme in the education of the gifted. Torrance developed the concept of *passions* in terms of student-based content (Torrance, 1988, in press). He stated that gifted and talented students do not have interests and hobbies, they have passions. They fall in love with things, topics, or ideas that become the central theme of what they want to know and pursue. True motivation comes from learning what you want to know, not what a teacher wants you to learn. Some gifted students have discovered their passions by the time they are 5, and will devote a lifetime to them, unless we educators and parents interfere with and destroy the passions. Other students have 5 to 10 passions in 2 weeks (which is why parents should rent, but not buy, the clarinet!).

Educators involved in the development of programs for the gifted and talented need to "protect the passions" of these students. During their day, their week, and their 13 years of public school education, their passions should be protected and facilitated. When looking at gifted adults who are fully functioning, one finds that they are following and living their passions.

Open-Ended Learning Experiences

Convergent learning and convergent daily lessons and units are developed to help children achieve a basic comprehension of the prescribed content, which has been been presented to them through lectures, readings, and worksheets. However, gifted and talented students need school experiences that are open-ended, that provide them with opportunities to have input into and ownership of their own learning. What is to be learned should not already have been decided by the adult educators. With this approach the students might begin by planning to go from A to B, but actually end up at C or M or Z. True learning becomes a process of exploring content and developing it into a new product that is created by the student, rather than prescribed by the teacher or the textbook.

Lifelong Learners

To begin this section, it is essential to review the *big bottle, little bottle theory of education.*

The concept is evident in elementary school but is seen more at the secondary level and is almost universal at the college and university level.

The "big bottle" in this theory is the teacher or the professor, while the "little bottles" are the students. The semester or quarter begins and the little bottles show up and sit in rows, sometimes with assigned seats. Each bottle is approximately 5 to 6 inches high. The bottles are a variety of shapes and are made with a variety of materials. Some are cheap glass, while others are plastic. In the bottom of each bottle is a few drops of a green liquid, which represents knowledge that has been accumulated from previous classes and from experiences outside the classroom and school. The liquid is beautiful, and the green color of the knowledge is very attractive.

After the little bottles have entered the room and are seated in their chairs in straight rows, the big bottle enters the room. The big bottle is not made of cheap glass or plastic. It is a beautiful cut-glass bottle. The big bottle is completely full of the green liquid, the knowledge. In fact, there is so much knowledge that in some instances the liquid is even spilling over.

The lectures begin, and the big bottle begins to pour into each of the little bottles. The students take notes and the liquid is gradually dispersed. By midterm, the little bottles are half-full and the big bottle is half-empty. The lectures continue until time for the final exam. If you look into the traditional classroom that has a big bottle, little bottle mode of operation, you will see that the little bottles are now totally full and the big bottle is nearly empty.

The final exam begins and students write answers to the basic knowledge and comprehension questions. The liquid is slowly transferred from the little bottles back to the big bottle. The result is that after the final exam has been completed and a few days have passed, the big bottle is once again full and the little bottles have acquired only a few extra drops of green liquid (knowledge). Both are waiting for the next semester or the next quarter, and once again the process of big bottle, little bottle education begins anew.

However, little bottles can also function as big bottles and can discover and develop learning on their own. A major goal of the ALM is to develop our children and youth not as little bottles, but as autonomous learners with the skills, concepts, and attitudes necessary for lifelong learning. In other words, they become responsible for themselves and learn to decide what they want to learn, how to learn it, what resources they will need, how the process will be followed, and finally, what will be developed as an outcome. They have become self-directed learners, and learning has become an adventure, in and out of the school, for the rest of their lives.

Teacher as Facilitator

Within the ALM, the role of the teacher changes to facilitate the students in becoming lifelong learners. Teachers develop skills to facilitate learning, rather than just dispensing knowledge. Emphasis is placed on the process of learning as well as the content. The teacher does not tell students what is to be learned and how to learn it but prepares them to learn how to become more and more independent and self-directed. As time progresses, the students gain more skills and become more responsible for their own learning. The seminar and in-depth study dimensions of the model provide students with the opportunity to be independent learners rather than students. They decide what to learn and how to learn it and then proceed to participate in their in-depth studies.

Time and Space Restrictions

If the ALM is implemented completely, modifications must be made in the school to allow students to break from traditional time and space restrictions. Once learners have moved to the seminar and in-depth study dimensions of the model, they must be able to spend hours or days out of school to pursue their appropriate activities, involved in the community in a mentor relationship, a university, or a business-related situation.

Basic Goals of the ALM

There are eight basic goals of the ALM for the gifted and talented (Betts, 1985).

Student-learners will:

1. Develop more positive self-concepts.
2. Comprehend their own giftedness in relationship to self and society.
3. Develop the skills appropriate to interact effectively with peers, siblings, parents, and other adults.
4. Increase their knowledge in a variety of subject areas.
5. Develop thinking, decision-making, and problem-solving skills.
6. Participate in activities selected to facilitate and integrate their cognitive, emotional, and social development.
7. Demonstrate responsibility for their own learning in and out of the school setting.
8. Ultimately become responsible, creative, and independent learners.

Profiles of the Gifted and Talented

We must do more than develop an approach for the education of the gifted and talented that identifies them as one group that can be described in one specific way. After 10 years of program development, observations, and the use of qualitative research techniques, Betts and Neihart (1988) developed an approach for giving specific consideration to different personality types of the gifted and talented. When children are young, they can be identified in many of these following types. However, after several years in school, students usually settle into one or two of the types described by Betts and Neihart.

Type I students, the *successful*, are usually the ones who are first identified for programs for the gifted and talented. They do well in the classroom, become "teacher pleasers," and are readily identified through the use of achievement and intelligence test scores and teacher nominations. According to Tannenbaum (1983), they have the potential for being gifted but have not developed all the abilities and attitudes necessary for being gifted.

When Type I students first begin school, they are very creative and autonomous in their attitudes and behavior, but they make the mistake of losing their autonomy and creativity. By the time they are in high school they have become more convergent and are conforming more to the demands of the adults around them. They are no longer independent but depend on the system.

The *challenging,* the Type II students, do not conform but do not lose their creativity and autonomy. They remain independent but bored and frustrated because the system does not work for them. They have not developed "appropriate behavior" and have not learned to work within the system. Many times they are not selected for gifted programs because of their inappropriate behavior.

Most school environments are not conducive to the growth and development of the gifted and talented. Many administrators and other school personnel do not necessarily comprehend the concept of the gifted child, nor do they know how to accommodate these children. As a result, some children conform and some act out, while others begin to hide their giftedness. These Type III children are labeled the *underground.* They do not feel confident enough to be spontaneous, and they begin to hide their abilities. Their belonging needs are extremely strong, and the children do whatever is necessary to ensure an opportunity to be like everyone else.

Additionally, there are other gifted children and youth whom we called the *dropouts,* the Type IV students. Although many educators understand that students drop out of school, they have not been able to develop approaches or programs that identify these children early in their school careers. Appropriate statistics are not available regarding the proportion of gifted students who drop out of school. It is a problem, but we do not know exactly how much of a problem it really is. These students drop out of school, and they often drop out of life; in other words, they commit educational and professional suicide. SENG, Supporting the Emotional Needs of the Gifted, is one organization that was developed by educators, psychologists, and parents of gifted children after the suicide of 16-year-old gifted computer whiz Dallas Egbert in 1980.

There is a need for a closer "marriage" between educators in special education and those in gifted education. Many students who are identified as visually impaired, emotionally disturbed, learning disabled, and so forth, may

also be gifted, although their gifts may never be identified. Those studied are Type Vs, the double-labeled. Goertzel and Goertzel (1962) presented many examples of handicapped people who became extremely successful in their lives and made profound impacts on society. These people typically would not have been identified for programs for the gifted because they had special needs.

What is it that gifted and talented children can become? What can we do? These are two of the most important questions that parents, teachers, and administrators can ponder. Basic goals must be developed to determine what our gifted can become. The author and other teachers, parents, and administrators believe that the gifted and talented have the potential of becoming learners rather than students. Tannenbaum (1983) also believes the gifted have the ability to go beyond the role of "consumers of knowledge" to become "producers of knowledge." The gifted and talented can become autonomous learners, Type VIs, with the necessary skills, concepts, and attitudes for lifelong learning.

Selection for Participation in the Autonomous Learner Model

Rather than identifying a small fixed group of gifted and talented children and youth, educators involved with the ALM have modified the identification procedure so that it is flexible and will select more students. Students may choose total involvement in the ALM and other opportunities, or they may be involved for one or two grading periods and then make a decision whether or not to continue.

The decision to be involved is made by students and parents when they receive invitations for different programming options. The word *identification* is not used in the process of selecting students for involvement in the ALM. *Selection* is the word of choice, as it is more acceptable to teachers, administrators, parents, and school board members. The following is an outline of the selection steps and procedures:

1. Definition of giftedness
2. Ongoing staff development

3. Classroom/school activities
4. Discussions of giftedness and the selection process
5. Nominations
6. Reflections and assessment
7. Interviews
8. Additional information
9. Selection and notification
10. Appeal and ongoing search/selection
11. Ongoing programming expansions

Definition

It is important that a definition of giftedness is selected that is consistent with the district's views of giftedness. If the intent is to serve the achieving, intellectually gifted, a definition that describes this population should be used.

Many districts endorse the multidimensional Marland (1972) definition for selection but then identify only the intellectually or academically gifted. There is an inconsistency in this approach. Definition must match selection and programming.

The definition that is usually used with the ALM is one that identifies three types of students who may become autonomous learners through participation in the ALM. These include the *intellectually gifted,* the *creatively gifted,* and the *talented.* Many districts have been successful in identifying the intellectually and creatively gifted but have been less successful in including the talented. Two reasons exist for this: Either the districts encounter difficulty in successfully defining *talented,* or the large number of students who would be selected presents an obstacle.

In addition to the three types listed above, there also is a need to include underachieving students. Some districts are beginning to specify that a certain percentage (10–20%) of selected students must be underachieving, instead of having programming that includes only those students who have already learned to be successful in school.

Ongoing Staff Development

Who are the gifted and talented? Which definition is our district using? What is the procedure for selection? What should we be doing specifically for them? What is my role? What is the ALM for the gifted and talented? These and many other questions should be covered in staff development. Educators need to learn, on an ongoing basis, about the gifted and talented, beginning with definitions, characteristics, selection procedures, and programming options. Often, for the first 2 or 3 years, districts have in-services on the basics of giftedness and then move on to other topics; knowledge of the field is limited to past in-services. This is known as the vaccination theory of staff development: Once administered, it is never needed again! It is essential to continue staff development until the skills and techniques needed for the gifted in special settings, as well as in the regular classroom, have been mastered and are being used by all school and involved community personnel.

Classroom/School Activities

If educators are to correctly select the gifted and talented, the search must go beyond test scores and teacher recommendations. Gardner (1983) explains that students can be selected through the use of specific activities in the regular classroom. This provides the opportunity to collect further information to be used for selection through performance. Creativity and higher level thinking skill activities are included, as well as activities that promote independence and self-directed learning in the regular classroom.

Discussions of Giftedness and the Selection Process

The process for selection of the gifted and talented begins at the beginning of the school year, and the final selections can be made by the end of the school year. After staff development meetings and classroom and school activities, it is time to discuss the selection process that is being used and the role of the staff in the selection of students. This brings closure and a deeper understanding of the process for educators.

Nominations

Nominations are now sought from all available sources, including teacher and parent nominations, results of test scores, community nominations, peer nominations, and self-nominations. Teacher nominations seem to be more accurate at this point because students have been given the opportunity to perform in specialty areas.

Reflections and Assessment

What do we now know about the students who have been nominated for selection? Do we have enough information or is more needed? The selection committee looks closely at the accumulated information and begins to make their first judgments. Additional information may be obtained through further assessment, which is not given in a traditional manner to all the students. If the committee needs more information concerning intellectual functioning, it is recommended that individual tests of intelligence be used instead of group tests. Also, measures of creative behaviors are given at this time.

Interviews

An important component that appears to be highly effective is the use of individual interviews (or small group interviews in the case of young children) to gain additional information about the students. Not every student will participate in an interview; it is used at the discretion of evaluators when additional information concerning their skills, concepts, and attitudes is needed for final selection.

Additional Information

Parent and community-member interviews are included, as well as meetings and discussions with teachers (both current and past) to gain additional information that may be helpful. Is there anything we have missed? Are the students underground, acting out, or resisting the process? Information discovered here will be used for final selection.

Selection and Notification

The selection committee now begins the process of carefully assessing the needs of the students and the programming options available for them. The committee then makes final selections. Rather than making decisions on the basis of static information, the committee makes decisions based on all information that it has accumulated. Again, it is important to look for all categories of the gifted and talented that have been included in the operational definition selected by the district. This might be broad enough to include the achieving and underachieving intellectually gifted, creatively gifted, and talented. The final notifications of decisions are shared with parents, teachers, school support personnel, and administrators.

Appeal and Ongoing Search/Selection

Are we totally accurate in our selection process? No, probably not. District personnel do overlook students and incorrectly select students. Any person not included in the final selection process is now given the opportunity to make a written appeal to the district for further evaluation and assessment.

In the classroom and throughout the school, the search continues through the development and use of new techniques and activities that will help in more effective selection.

Ongoing Programming Expansions

It is hoped that the day has passed when gifted students are identified by IQ and achievement test scores and then placed together in one structured environment. In other words, there are many different types of gifted and talented students and so there must be many different options for them within the school setting. Each year, more programming options are added to the ALM to meet the diversified needs of gifted and talented students. Annual meetings of school personnel and central school administrators are held to determine what modifications and additions can be made to provide still more options.

Program Search

The ALM approach begins by assuming that much is already being done for the gifted and talented; it is necessary to identify existing methods and then proceed to add new and unique experiences. A program search is used to ensure that existing activities, programs, and so forth, can be included in the final programming for the gifted and talented. Educators have the opportunity to include what they are already doing intuitively and systematically. After completion of the program search, discussions are held to determine what already exists, what is still needed, and how it all can be brought together to provide a systematic approach for meeting the diversified cognitive, academic, social, emotional, and physical needs of the gifted and talented.

The ALM synthesizes the options for the gifted and talented. It becomes a clearinghouse for services and tends to bring students and staff together since it offers flexibility and openness for the ongoing development of programming options.

Autonomous Learner Model Description

The basic ALM consists of five major dimensions (see Figure 10.1). These five dimensions are designed to provide gifted and talented students with the appropriate experiences that are necessary to facilitate their growth as autonomous learners. Each dimension outlines information, experiences, attitudes, skills, and concepts necessary for the growth of students, teachers, and, at times, parents.

Orientation Dimension

Orientation is the first dimension of the model. It is the foundation dimension for involvement in programming for the gifted and talented. Basic questions such as, What does it mean to be gifted? Why was I selected for this program? and, Will my life be different now that I am in a

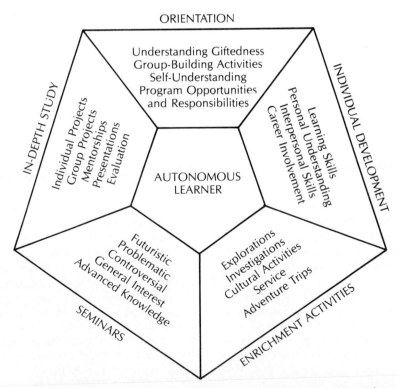

Source: Copyright © 1985 by Autonomous Learner Publications and Specialists, Greeley, Colorado. Used by permission of the author and publisher.

Figure 10.1 The autonomous learner model for the gifted and talented.

program for the gifted and talented? are discussed. Experiences are planned that help students understand why they are involved in the ALM, what it entails, and what they will be able to accomplish through involvement in the model. The orientation dimension of the ALM is divided into four areas, which are presented to the students at the same time:

Understanding giftedness
Group-building activities
Self-understanding
Program opportunities and responsibilities

Understanding Giftedness. This is the first area introduced to the students. Several activities are presented that focus on understanding giftedness through the use of biographies and autobiographies of eminent gifted people. Students conduct research on a person of their choice and try to understand the person as thoroughly as possible. If the person is alive, the student tries to communicate directly with him or her. The final activity with the biographies is called the Night of the Notables; at this event students actually assume the role of the person they have selected, complete with costumes. Guests, including parents, administrators, school board members, and teachers, are invited to visit with each eminent person and to view the learning centers that students have developed to portray the life and accomplishments of the eminent people.

This project has become one of the most popular activities used in the ALM. It is not the only activity in this area but seems to set the stage for future understanding of giftedness by the students. Another activity in this area involves asking the students to develop their own definitions of *giftedness* and present them in a creative manner.

Group-Building Activities. What does it mean to form a group? What different roles are assumed in a group? How do people learn to work effectively as a group? Is it necessary to work together as group members? These and many other questions are discussed in this area of the orientation dimension of the ALM.

Activities are presented that help students to become team members and to learn to work effectively together. For example, the final activity is a student retreat, which is usually held over a weekend away from school. The retreat is organized and implemented by the students themselves. They decide what the retreat will be like, what activities will be used, and what outcomes they hope to achieve.

Self-Understanding. When students are first selected for programming for the gifted, many are uncertain exactly why they were selected. Therefore, time is spent discussing information obtained from the identification procedures. What do we know about them from test scores, from parent and teacher recommendations, from interviews, and from the final selections? All this information is presented and reviewed with the students to help them gain a better understanding of self.

Program Opportunities and Responsibilities. It is important for both students and parents to understand the opportunities and responsibilities of the model. Emphasis is placed on developing an in-service on the model for parents so that students eventually will be able to communicate what they have completed and what they will be doing in the future.

Individual Development Dimension

The second dimension of the model is *individual development* (see Figure 10.2). Students are involved in activities designed by them and by teachers to develop skills, concepts, and attitudes necessary for lifelong learning. This dimension, especially, should not be done *to* the students, but *with* the students.

The entire dimension is explained to the students and then they are asked where involvement should begin. The decision of which skills, concepts, and attitudes to include is left to the students. After these decisions are made, the students and teachers select the curriculum to be developed for each of the selected skills, concepts, and attitudes.

Learning Skills. The ongoing development of cognitive skills, such as creativity, thinking skills, organizational skills, and research

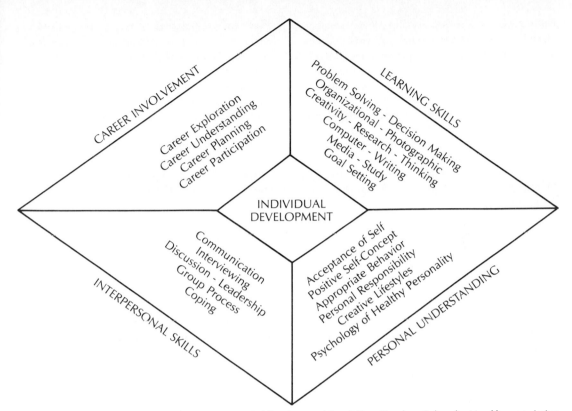

Source: Copyright © 1985 by Autonomous Learner Publications and Specialists, Greeley, Colorado. Used by permission of the author and publisher.

Figure 10.2   Individual development—Dimension 2.

skills, is essential for facilitating students' growth as autonomous learners.

Personal Understanding. While skills are being developed, positive attitudes toward self are being facilitated through activities relating to the acceptance of self and the development of a positive self-concept.

Interpersonal Skills. There are many identified gifted and talented students who are in need of developing interpersonal skills. These include the ability to communicate effectively with other students, teachers, parents, and other adults.

In addition, it is essential to develop discussion skills as well as group process skills. These are skills that will become increasingly valuable to gifted and talented students as they become self-directed, independent learners.

Career Involvement. Gifted and talented students are often concerned with their futures and what they can do with their abilities. The area of career involvement provides them with the opportunity to explore many different potential career choices and to learn what is required in order to develop abilities in the selected areas.

When students have been involved in many aspects of career development, they are given the opportunity to actually experience two or three careers of their choice, usually by working with mentors in those fields.

Enrichment Activities Dimension

Dimension 3 of the ALM is *enrichment activities,* which helps students learn more about what is out there in their community and the world at large. By the time students reach this third dimension, more responsibility is placed on them to decide what they want to learn. The concept of *student-based content* is presented to them. They are given the opportunity to decide what topics to study and how they want to study these selected topics.

The majority of content within most schools is prescribed by the school board, administrators, and teachers. For example, a second-grade student in a traditional classroom may want to be involved in an in-depth study of Native Americans. However, the teacher may discourage the student from such an in-depth pursuit, since the study of Native Americans may be part of the prescribed content to be presented to students in a later grade! The ALM gives students the opportunity to study what is meaningful to them.

Seminar Dimension

By the time students have reached *seminars,* the fourth dimension of the ALM, emphasis is placed on the *production* of ideas and topics. Students are now seen as independent *learners* instead of *students.* More responsibility is placed on the learners. In addition, more freedom and opportunities are available. At this point, some students thrive on the freedom to direct their learning, while others struggle and require additional guidance and understanding. Not all learners will respond in the same way to the opportunities and responsibilities of this dimension. Learners need to be encouraged but should not be pushed until they feel they have a good chance of being successful.

Topics are selected by small groups of three to five learners and are usually in their passion areas. The topics have been categorized in the following areas: futuristic, problematic, controversial, general interest, and advanced knowledge.

In-Depth Study

A main goal for each learner who participates in the model is the attainment of autonomous learning skills. *In-depth study,* the fifth dimension of the ALM, is designed to facilitate the learners' involvement in an in-depth study. Ei-

ther independently or in small groups of two or three, the learners develop an in-depth study contract that outlines a description of the study, objectives and activities, questions to be answered, a time-line, a list of human and material resources, and a plan for ongoing and final presentations.

It is highly recommended that the teachers also become involved in in-depth studies of their choice. This involvement gives them a deeper understanding of the process and shows the learners that their teachers are also independent lifelong learners who seek knowledge through in-depth studies.

In-depth study is the most demanding and challenging dimension of the ALM. Once learners have developed the contract, they are able to initiate their projects. At this time, it is a requirement that the learners find mentors who will be involved on a continual basis. The learners are also responsible for developing ongoing presentations and then a final presentation that must be given to an appropriate audience. The final evaluation plan is developed by the learner; the final completion of the in-depth study involves the learner, the mentor, and the teacher-facilitator. Most studies are completed in between 2 months and 2½ years. Learners are responsible for at least 90% of their learning in the in-depth studies, but support from mentors and teacher-facilitators is still required from time to time.

The End Result: The Autonomous Learner

Betts and Neihart (1988) describe autonomous learners as "students who have developed strong, positive self-concepts because their needs are being met; they are successful and they receive positive attention and support for their accomplishments from adults and peers, and they frequently serve in some leadership capacity within their school or community" (p. 252).

They are better prepared for the future because they have learned success. Autonomous learners have developed the skills, concepts, and attitudes necessary to take them into the unknown, the world of tomorrow.

REFERENCES

Betts, G. (1985). *Autonomous learner model for the gifted and talented.* Greeley, CO: Autonomous Learning Publications and Specialists.

Betts, G., & Knapp, J. (1981). Autonomous learning and the gifted: A secondary model. In A. Arnold (Ed.) *Secondary programs for the gifted* (pp. 29–36). Ventura, CA: Office of the Ventura Superintendent of Schools.

Betts, G., & Neihart, M. (1988). Profiles of the gifted. *Gifted Child Quarterly, 32,* 248–253.

Gardner, H. (1983). *Frames of mind.* New York: Basic.

Goertzel, V., & Goertzel, M. (1962). *Cradles of eminence.* Boston: Little, Brown.

Marland, S., Jr. (1972). *Education of the gifted and talented. Report to the Congress of the United States by the U.S. Commissioner of Education* (Vol. 1). Washington, DC: U.S. Government Printing Office.

Tannenbaum, A. (1983). *Gifted children: Psychological and educational perspective.* New York: Macmillan.

Torrance, E. P. (1988). The nature of creativity as manifest in its testing. In R. W. Sternberg (Ed.), *The nature of creativity* (pp. 43–75). New York: Cambridge University Press.

Torrance, E. P. (in press). *The blazing drive: The creative personality.* Buffalo, NY: Bearly.

11

Mathematically Talented Children: Can Acceleration Meet Their Educational Needs?

CAMILLA PERSSON BENBOW *Iowa State University, Ames*

My telephone rings. It is a conscientious teacher from one of the local schools. I am being contacted because of my history of working with mathematically talented children through my involvement in the Study of Mathematically Precocious Youth (SMPY) program. The teacher, Mrs. Wilson, has in her fifth-grade class a bright boy, Joey, who seems to be especially talented in mathematics. He has exhausted the fifth-grade mathematics curriculum and already knows all the material covered in sixth grade, even though she has been forbidden to teach it to him. Partly because of the inappropriateness of the mathematics available to Joey in the elementary school, his father has hired a tutor to work with him on algebra. Although this is challenging to Joey, it of course creates great difficulties for Mrs. Wilson when she is teaching mathematics. Joey is tuned out and bored. Moreover, Joey keeps getting further and further ahead of the class. What can she do with Joey? How can she keep him from getting bored? Should she give him enrichment worksheets even though he has already mastered the topics covered? In any case, she is running out of these sheets; and they do not seem to be of much interest to Joey. She suspects that for him this is just more of the same. Is it really challenging to have to do 20 rather than 10 problems on concepts he has already mastered? It seems to Mrs. Wilson that this approach is a punishment for knowing the mathematics: "Since you know it all, you can do 20 rather than 10 problems."

My response to her dilemma is that before we proceed further, I need to know Joey's ability level. Although Mrs. Wilson offers the information that he is in the 99th percentile in mathematics on the *Iowa Test of Basic Skills*, this is not sufficient for me. Is Joey a 99, a 99.9, or a 99.99 percentile student? The test is not of sufficient difficulty for Joey to determine if he is the top 1 in 100 in mathematics or the top 1 in 10,000. Mrs. Wilson's experiences with Joey cannot provide the necessary information either. We need further testing. Yet even though I have no suitable test scores available, I tell the teacher that I suspect that the best available option for Joey is to accelerate his grade placement in mathematics by a few years. Since Joey seems to be advanced in almost all areas, he also may need to skip a grade.

Why did I give this advice? What justification did I have for these suggestions, which are counter to what most school personnel and parents would judge to be beneficial? Because of social and emotional concerns, most parents and educators are wary of acceleration. Is there a sound basis for their belief? What about elitism? Is it elitist to provide special educational opportunities to students who are already doing so well? These are the issues to be addressed in this chapter. First, however, a historical introduction is required to set the stage.

Some Background

The SMPY was founded by Julian C. Stanley in 1971 at Johns Hopkins University (JHU) in order to identify mathematically precocious individuals with the intent of helping them educationally. Over a 12-year period, more than 10,000 preadolescent boys and girls were identified through participation in SMPY talent searches. Especially for those students who exhibited extremely high mathematical aptitude, SMPY intervened in their education.

Students were counseled regarding educational acceleration and were offered out-of-school educational opportunities that SMPY was field-testing for effectiveness.

Moreover, SMPY launched a longitudinal study to investigate the development of intellectually talented students and to assess the impact of educational interventions on their development. About 3,000 talented individuals are being tracked throughout their adult lives to discover what happens to such individuals. The SMPY longitudinal study is similar to the classic Terman studies, but it is much larger and studies the long-term effects of educational facilitation on talented individuals' development.

In 1986 SMPY split into two branches: one remained at JHU, and the other was established at Iowa State University (ISU). SMPY at JHU emphasizes educational facilitation for extremely precocious youth (i.e., top 1 in 10,000). SMPY at ISU conducts the longitudinal research program and provides educational facilitation to highly able students through the Iowa Talent Search and the Challenge for Youth—Talented and Gifted (CY-TAG) program. CY-TAG, which was cofounded by me in 1986, is a summer residential program for intellectually talented 12- to 15-year-olds. Participants study for 3 weeks one of several academically rigorous courses offered in various disciplines, such as mathematics or biotechnology. Courses are at the college level.

Why Use Tests for Identification?

In the preceding example (a true story), it becomes apparent that the staff of SMPY believes in the use of tests for identification of talent and for educational programming. SMPY from the start relied on standardized testing. Past research had shown that the most effective means of identifying gifted students is through the use of tests (Pegnato & Birch, 1959). Moreover, Stanley (1976) found that 5-year-old test scores were a better predictor of who would perform well in a high-level mathematics contest than were concurrent teacher recommendations. In the Terman study, more gifted students were identified through testing the youngest member of the class than through testing students recommended by teachers. Test scores are valid and reliable indicators of academic success, and they can be meaningfully interpreted.

The reader may now wonder why Joey's test score that the teacher reported was insufficient. It was insufficient because the test clearly was not difficult enough for Joey; when an individual scores at the 99th percentile, we do not know how well he or she, in this case Joey, could have scored on a more difficult test. Because the test did not have sufficient *ceiling,* we could not determine if Joey was just *able* or *extremely able.* Different courses of action need to be taken for very able versus extremely able students. Educational acceleration, for example, is appropriate only for the extremely able.

Finally, the test scores cited by the teacher were achievement rather than aptitude scores. Having surveyed the literature, Stanley concluded that an aptitude test, especially a reasoning test, would be a far better predictor of success in mathematics than items measuring learned concepts, learned algorithms, or computational speed and accuracy (Stanley, 1977; Stanley & Benbow, 1986). An aptitude test would also be far better at identifying students with high potential for later high achievement in mathematics irrespective of whether this potential had been given the opportunity to be developed.

Therefore, knowing that Joey scored in the 99th percentile on a standardized achievement test was insufficient because it did not tell us Joey's overall level of functioning and it did not tell us anything about his reasoning ability, except that presumably it was high. To provide this necessary information, SMPY began using the College Board Scholastic Aptitude Test (SAT) with 7th- rather than 12th-graders in talent searches.

Talent Searches

In order to identify large numbers of mathematically talented students, SMPY developed the concept of an annual talent search and conducted six separate searches in March 1972, January 1973 and 1974, December 1976, and

January 1978 and 1979. During those years 9,927 intellectually gifted junior high school students between 12 and 14 years of age were tested. Students in the mid-Atlantic region were eligible to participate in a SMPY talent search if they had scored in the upper 5% (1972), 2% (1973 and 1974), or 3% (1976, 1978, and 1979) in mathematical ability on the national norms of a standardized achievement test battery administered as part of their schools' regular testing program (i.e., the type of test scores Mrs. Wilson was citing for Joey).

In a talent search, students took the College Board SAT mathematics section (SAT-M) and, except in 1972 and 1974, also the verbal section (SAT-V). When given to these seventh- and eighth-graders, the test produced scores ranging from chance to the top score possible (i.e., 800). Moreover, mean scores were comparable to those earned by a national sample of high school students. Because with this gifted group the test produced a full range of scores, it was neither too difficult (*floor effect*) nor too easy (*ceiling effect*), and the test was appropriate from a psychometric viewpoint. Yet how well did the SAT fulfill our need for a test measuring high reasoning ability?

What Does the SAT Score of a Seventh-Grader Mean?

The SAT-M and SAT-V were designed to measure developed mathematical and verbal reasoning abilities, respectively, of above-average 12th-graders (Donlon & Angoff, 1971). Most of the students in the SMPY talent searches, however, were in the middle of the seventh grade and under age 13. In the case of the SAT-M, few had received formal opportunities to develop their abilities in algebra and beyond (Benbow & Stanley, 1982a, 1982b, 1983). Our rationale is that most of these students were demonstrably unfamiliar with mathematics from algebra onward, yet many of them were able to score high on a difficult test of mathematical reasoning. Presumably, this could occur only through extraordinary analytic ability. We concluded that the SAT-M must function far more at an analytic reasoning level for the SMPY students than it does for high school juniors and seniors, most of whom

have studied abstract mathematics for several years (Benbow & Stanley, 1981, 1983). Moreover, because the SAT is so difficult and many view the talent searches as competitions, our methodology also appears to screen for high motivation in a rather crude manner.

Therefore, SMPY's operational definition of talent is a high SAT score at an early age. That is, the staff of SMPY views giftedness to be synonymous with precocity. Though simplistic, this view seems justifiable. Jackson and Butterfield (1986) and Sternberg and Davidson (1985) concluded that gifted and talented students process information similar to the way older individuals do rather than using different strategies. They are precocious. Moreover, Keating (1975) found that gifted children enter Piaget's stage of formal operations earlier than average-ability children. We (Dark & Benbow, in press) found that our gifted students did indeed process information in a quantitatively but not qualitatively different manner. In addition, their memory processes were similar to those of older individuals (see Dark & Benbow, in press; Keating & Bobbitt, 1978). Our students were especially superior in short-term memory processes, consistent with the literature (e.g., Jackson & Butterfield, 1986; Keating & Bobbitt, 1978; McCauley, Kellas, Dugas, and DeVillis, 1976; Peck & Borkowski, 1983; Rabinowitz & Glaser, 1985; Sternberg & Davidson, 1985). Yet our students did show enhanced problem translation ability. In sum, there is support for equating giftedness with precocity.

Widespread Dissemination of the Talent Search Concept

By 1980 SMPY had demonstrated the effectiveness and usefulness of the limited regional talent search model and stopped conducting the searches temporarily. The talent search concept was ready for implementation on a nationwide basis. The staff at SMPY helped other organizations take over that responsibility. Through the Center for the Advancement of Academically Talented Youth (CTY) at JHU, Center for Talent Development at Northwestern University, Rocky Mountain Talent Search at the University of Denver, the Talent

Identification Program (TIP) at Duke University, and several smaller, local talent search programs, the talent search concept has now been implemented across the nation, and approximately 80,000 gifted students participate every year (see Chapter 12 by Sanford J. Cohn). SMPY did continue, however, to identify, as part of a national talent search, one special group of students, students who represent the top 1 in 10,000 in mathematical reasoning ability, showing SAT-M scores above 700. In 1989 SMPY at ISU launched the Iowa Talent Search.

Other Testing Alternatives

Although SMPY has traditionally used the SAT as its identification instrument, there are other tests that are consistent with our theoretical considerations described earlier and could be used. The Ravens Progressive Matrices is an excellent alternative. It is a test of nonverbal reasoning. Through SMPY's research program we have determined that it correlates highly with SAT-M scores and predicts extremely well performance in SMPY's mathematics programs (to be described). Moreover, the Ravens test has three different levels, which makes it an appropriate test to use with elementary through high school students.

Another alternative is to use the American College Testing Program (ACT) examinations. Although these tests are more achievement than aptitude oriented, scores are provided in four different areas (Mathematics, English, Reading, and Science Reasoning). Depending upon the student and the program alternatives available, this set of scores could be useful. We now use ACT scores in the Iowa Talent Search and as eligibility criteria for our CY-TAG program. Other talent search programs have also adopted the ACT as an identification instrument.

Why Acceleration?

In the example introducing this chapter, we mentioned to the teacher that acceleration was probably in order for her seemingly talented student, Joey. For the extremely precocious student, as Joey appeared to be, educational acceleration is probably the method of choice when adjusting the curriculum. Much research supports its use (e.g., Daurio, 1979; Kulik & Kulik, 1984; Robinson, 1983). Although most educators and parents are wary about acceleration, SMPY chose to emphasize educational acceleration rather than enrichment. There were both logical and empirical reasons for this (Benbow, in press).

Our rationale was that the pacing of educational programs must be responsive to the capacities and knowledge of individual children. As the late Halbert Robinson (1983) stated so well, this conclusion is based upon three basic principles derived from developmental psychology. The first is that learning is a sequential and developmental process. The second is that there are large differences in learning status among individuals at any given age. Although the acquisition of knowledge and the development of patterns of organization follow predictable sequences, children progress through these sequences at varying rates (Bayley, 1955, 1970; George, Cohn, & Stanley, 1979; Keating, 1975; Keating & Schaefer, 1975; Keating & Stanley, 1972; Robinson & Robinson, 1976). This produces precocity in the case of the gifted.

The final principle derived from research in developmental psychology that supports the use of educational acceleration is what Hunt (1961) referred to as "the problem of the match." Effective teaching involves assessing the student's status in the learning process and posing problems slightly exceeding the level already mastered. This conclusion is based on the premise that "learning occurs only when there is an appropriate match between the circumstances that a child encounters and the schemata that he/she has already assimilated into his/her repertoire" (Hunt, 1961; p. 268). Hunt notes that "the principle is only another statement of the educator's adage that teaching must start where the learner is" (p. 268). Work that is too easy causes boredom and results in no new learning; work that is too advanced or difficult cannot be comprehended.

These three principles, as delineated by Robinson (1983), form the guiding premise behind SMPY's work. Its implication for education, as interpreted by SMPY, is that the pace of educational programs must be adapted to the capacities and knowledge of individual children. Clearly, gifted students are not at the same levels academically as their average-ability classmates. Moreover, what is offered in the regular classroom for all children cannot possibly meet the requirement of a match. Acceleration, which involves the adaptation of existing curricula, rather than writing new curricula, is the most productive and practical alternative for meeting this need.

Providing a rationale for the use of acceleration can be approached from yet another theoretical perspective. This perspective is based on work in both developmental and cognitive psychology. Csikszentmihalyi and Robinson (1986) and Feldman (1986) have argued that domains of knowledge (e.g., knowledge in physics) have developmental characteristics that coincide with individual proclivities. That is, each domain or area has its own specific stages through which an individual must progress. In addition, it takes much time (and sustained effort [Wallach, 1985]) to create a great work (Gruber, 1986). This includes time for practice, to master domains of knowledge, for movement through the stages and levels of a domain (Bamberger, 1986; Feldman, 1986), for "crystallizing experiences" to occur (Walters & Gardner, 1986), and for integration and reorganization of cognitive structures (Mumford & Gustafson, 1988). It has been found that improving knowledge bases results in students' learning and adopting more efficient cognitive strategies (Rabinowitz & Glaser, 1985). Accelerative programs improve knowledge bases. Further, since mastery of a domain's knowledge base is necessary for creativity (Bradshaw, Langley, & Simon, 1983; Langley, Simon, Bradshaw, & Zytkow, 1986; Simonton, 1984; Snow, 1986), it is anticipated that educational acceleration could also enhance creative production.

In addition, early career development is necessary to give talented individuals a firm grasp of the field's existing understandings, as well as the ability to identify significant problems within its framework (Chi, Feltovich, & Glaser, 1981; Zuckerman, 1983). This takes time, too. Since giftedness can be viewed as precocity (functioning as an older individual),

SMPY began using the curriculum designed for older students with gifted younger students to give them more time and opportunity for the sustained effort needed to create great works.

The use of educational acceleration or curricular flexibility can be justified from a purely practical point of view. Curricular flexibility involves utilizing what you already have in place, already available educational programs, to meet the needs of talented students. Because acceleration is extremely flexible, teachers or administrators can choose and adapt the various options in ways to fit their schools' unique circumstances and their students' individual abilities, needs, and interests. Moreover, adapting existing curricula, rather than writing new curricula, avoids the common criticism of elitism levied against programs for the gifted and costs little for a school system to adopt. The use of educational acceleration may even result in cost savings. In sparsely populated environments, such as rural areas, where few gifted students are likely to be identified at any one grade level or even clusters of grades, acceleration may be the only practical alternative for meeting the needs of the gifted. From one perspective, acceleration takes us back to the one-room schoolhouse at the turn of the century.

Finally, acceleration is especially appropriate in the areas of mathematics and science. In these areas the knowledge required for high-level performance is sequential and can be determined fairly well. That is, the stages of the domain have been reasonably well described and established.

Why Did SMPY Focus on Mathematical Talent?

Many individuals have asked why Julian Stanley and his staff focused almost exclusively on mathematical talent. As Csikszentmihalyi and Robinson (1986) have argued, talent depends upon the social context. Different talents are valued by different societies and times. SMPY focused on mathematical talent because of its high utility in our society (Stanley, 1977). As Krutetskii (1976) stated: "The development of the sciences has been characterized recently by a tendency for them to become more mathematical. . . . Mathematical methods and mathematical style of thinking are penetrating everywhere" (p. 6). Moreover, Kuhn (1962) noted that an overwhelming majority of events can be ascribed to the work of mathematicians or mathematically brilliant men. The United States requires many well-trained individuals with mathematical talent, and we face a shortage (National Science Board, 1982; Office of Technology Assessment, 1988; Shakhashiri, 1988). SMPY's programs, which emphasize mathematical educational acceleration, directly address this need.

Educational Acceleration: The Options

Since 1972 the staff of SMPY has been experimenting with various alternatives to present to their students who express a desire for more rapid educational growth. Although they have been articulated in earlier publications (Benbow, 1986; Benbow & Stanley, 1983; Stanley & Benbow, 1982, 1983a, 1983b), they will be described below, especially those dealing with mathematics and science.

When one speaks of acceleration, the first alternative that comes to mind is skipping grades. For a student advanced in all subject areas, this may be the mechanism of choice, especially if that student is at a school transition point (e.g., entering the last year of elementary school). In this same class of accelerative options is beginning school 1 year early, which is an alternative especially suitable for girls because they generally mature at an earlier age than boys. Moreover, later on in school girls are less willing than boys to leave their social group and skip to a higher grade, regardless of how inappropriate the curriculum may be for them (Fox, 1974, 1976). Entering school or the first grade early allows precocious students to stay with their peer group throughout their schooling years. This makes it easier on the students socially, especially since gifted students usually prefer older playmates.

Another accelerative alternative is to condense grades 9 through 12 into 3 years, or to

have students enter college 1 or 2 years early with or without a high school diploma. Skipping the last year of high school, which many gifted students view as being a waste of time and even frustrating, has become popular and is no longer a rare decision for a gifted student to make. In fact, a number of institutions have set up specific programs and procedures for applicants who wish to enter college after the 11th grade. In addition, several states automatically award a high school diploma after the successful completion of 1 year of college. For the gifted student, the primary benefit of entering college early is that it allows him or her to reach more quickly the intellectually stimulating courses available at the college level. For the gifted student, development of knowledge bases, discussed above, occurs generally in college level course work.

Another option is to have the talented students take as many stimulating high school courses as possible while fulfilling high school graduation requirements. Then either on released time from high school, at night, or during summers the student enrolls in one or two college courses each semester. Accrued credits can be applied to high school or college graduation requirements, or preferably both.

Another possibility for providing work at the college level is through the Advanced Placement (AP) program. AP offers able and motivated students the opportunity to study at the college level while remaining in high school. Programs of study are offered in over 20 disciplines, such as biology, chemistry, English, mathematics, physics, and computer science. Depending upon examination results at the end of the program, successful students receive college credit, advanced standing, or both. For those small schools where there are insufficient students to fill AP classes, faculty-supervised independent study arrangements can be instituted, using AP syllabi. The various AP syllabi and detailed and informative guidelines for setting up and conducting AP classes can be obtained at a minimal cost by writing to College Board Publications Orders, Box 2815, Princeton, NJ 08541.

If an appropriate course is not available, a gifted student can be offered a mentoring arrangement or take correspondence courses

of Joey. A few months before their 11th birthday, one twin scored 720 on the SAT-M and 310 on the SAT-V. The other scored 690 on the SAT-M and 280 on the SAT-V. Again, these scores indicated that the boys were extremely precocious. Their abilities were at least in the top 1 in 10,000 range. Although young, they clearly demonstrated a need for fast-paced mathematics. There was no need to advise the parents about skipping the children one grade since that had already been done.

As for their mathematics, these boys had been learning prealgebra in school. The boys therefore were admitted into our fast-paced mathematics class offered in the summer. Because the boys had not taken Algebra I, we began our diagnostic testing at that level. Yet even though they had not enrolled in a formal course entitled Algebra I, they had already mastered the concepts taught in that course. A few misconceptions were evident, however, and these were cleared up in a matter of a few hours. We then tested their knowledge of Algebra II. In this case, substantial material had not been mastered, and instruction was targeted at that level. During the 3-week program, by studying only concepts not already mastered the twins managed to complete and become certified for having completed Algebra II.

That fall the boys entered middle school. Suitable arrangements could not be worked out for the boys to study geometry within their own school system. It was arranged that they come to ISU and complete geometry through the SMPY Math Clinic, the academic-year version of the summer fast-paced classes. The SMPY Math Clinic meets every other Saturday for 3 hours and incorporates a correspondence aspect into the fast-math class. During that academic year, one of the twins, the abler one, completed the entire precalculus sequence and became ready to study calculus as an eighth grader. The other twin almost finished the sequence. During the following summer while his slightly abler brother studied biotechnology at CY-TAG, he finished his precalculus. During the second session of CY-TAG, the two brothers studied computer programming (PASCAL) together. In the fall they returned to the SMPY Math Clinic to study AP calculus (BC).

Again the following school year arrangements could not be made for the boys to study math within their school system. Thus, although their school grants the boys credit, they are studying calculus with us. When they complete calculus, presumably they will enroll in an appropriate college mathematics course; it is important that students continue to take mathematics throughout high school. Because their verbal abilities are not in the truly exceptional range, further grade skipping is probably not necessary. In high school they are being advised to enroll in AP courses. Thus, by the time these two brothers enter college, they also should have accumulated many credits and some advanced standing. They too will be able to receive greater depth and breadth in their college training.

We became aware of one talented girl through publicity about our CY-TAG program. Because Anne had scored in the top 3% on the Iowa Test of Basic Skills in math, she became qualified to participate in a talent search, which for her was conducted by Duke University. Her school had informed her about the talent search and gave her an application form. As part of the talent search she took the SAT and scored 550 on the SAT-M and 380 on the SAT-V at age 13 years and 1 month. These scores qualified Anne for ISU's CY-TAG program in mathematics. She applied and was accepted. Although Anne's scores were excellent by any criteria, within that class she was among the lowest in ability. Yet she was highly motivated. During the 3 weeks she completed Algebra I at a high level. She was, therefore, ready to take either Algebra II or geometry as an eighth-grader.

Her middle school, however, did not offer either of those two courses. The principal offered Anne the option of a supervised correspondence course, for which the school paid. Because Anne had enjoyed so much the atmosphere of our fast-paced math class during the summer, even though she had felt "dumb" in comparison with the other members of the class, she also wanted to continue with our program during the academic year. As a result, Anne enrolled in our Math Clinic. We recommended that she study Algebra II with her school and geometry with us. Anne, however, wanted to pursue geometry only, which she did. Because Anne was such a hard and conscientious worker, she managed to complete geometry in just one semester. Because the drive to the Math Clinic was over 2 hours each way, Anne took the spring semester off but returned to CY-TAG the following summer to study mathematics. During the second summer Anne completed Algebra II.

Now that she is a high school student, the course offerings available to her finally are appropriate, for at least a couple of years. Probably when she is a junior, Anne will need to enroll in a college mathematics course on either released time or at night. A local community college may be the most practical option for her. Skipping grades or entering college early probably is not advisable for Anne as long as her need for advanced mathematics is met. In all areas except math, Anne should be challenged in high school, especially if AP courses are taken.

Conclusions

The foregoing case histories illustrate well how the various options devised by SMPY can be used together to provide an appropriate learning environment for the gifted child. More draconian measures are needed for the extremely precocious than for the very able. The elegance of the SMPY model of curricular flexibility is that through its use an individual program can be tailored to meet the needs of each intellectually talented student. The goal is to strive for a combination of options that reflect the best possible alternative for educating a specific gifted child. Curricular flexibility, a policy that is endorsed by the seminal Richardson study (Cox, Daniel, & Boston, 1985) will enable a precocious and motivated child to achieve at a high level (e.g., Brody & Benbow, 1987; Stanley & Benbow, 1983b). Further, it must be emphasized that no study to date has shown acceleration to be detrimental to social and emotional development (Brody & Benbow, 1987; Daurio, 1979; Pollins, 1983; Richardson & Benbow, in press; Robinson, 1983). Unfortunately, educators are often biased against acceleration, even though research has shown it to be one of the most viable

methods for providing an appropriate education for the gifted (Daurio, 1979; Gallagher, 1975; Pollins, 1983; Robinson, 1983). The concluding message from this chapter is that educators should allow and encourage curricular flexibility for gifted students. The reactions to the Richardson study indicate that indeed this is the direction to which schools are turning.

REFERENCES

Bamberger, J. (1986). Cognitive issues in the development of musically gifted children. In R. J. Sternberg & J. E. Davidson (Eds.), *Conceptions of giftedness* (pp. 388–413). New York: Cambridge University Press.

Bartkovich, K. G., & George, W. C. (1980). *Teaching the gifted and talented in the mathematics classroom*. Washington, DC: National Education Association.

Bartkovich, K. G., & Mezynski, K. (1981). Fast-paced precalculus mathematics for talented junior-high students: Two recent SMPY programs. *Gifted Child Quarterly, 25,* 73–80.

Bayley, N. (1955). On the growth of intelligence. *American Psychologist, 10,* 805–818.

Bayley, N. (1970). Development of mental abilities. In P. H. Mussen (Ed.), *Carmichael's manual of child psychology* (3rd ed., Vol. 1, pp. 1163–1209). New York: Wiley.

Benbow, C. P. (1986). SMPY's model for teaching mathematically precocious students. In J. S. Renzulli (Ed.), *Systems and models in programs for the gifted and talented* (pp. 1–25). Mansfield Center, CT: Creative Learning.

Benbow, C. P. (in press). Meeting the needs of gifted students through use of acceleration: A neglected resource. In M. C. Wang, M. C. Reynolds, & H. J. Walberg (Eds.), *Handbook of special education* (Vol. 2). New York: Pergamon.

Benbow, C. P., & Stanley, J. C. (1981). Mathematical ability: Is sex a factor? *Science, 212,* 118–119.

Benbow, C. P., & Stanley, J. C. (1982a). Consequences in high school and college of sex differences in mathematical reasoning ability: A longitudinal perspective. *American Educational Research Journal, 19,* 598–622.

Benbow, C. P., & Stanley, J. C. (1982b). Intellectually talented boys and girls: Educational profiles. *Gifted Child Quarterly, 26,* 82–88.

Benbow, C. P., & Stanley, J. C. (1983). Sex differences in mathematical reasoning ability: More facts. *Science, 222,* 1029–1031.

Bradshaw, G. F., Langley, P. W., & Simon, H. A.

(1983). Studying scientific discovery by computer simulation. *Science, 222,* 971–975.

Brody, L. E., & Benbow, C. P. (1987). Accelerative strategies: How effective are they for the gifted? *Gifted Child Quarterly, 31,* 105–110.

Chi, M. T. H., Feltovich, P., & Glaser, R. (1981). Categorization and representation of physics problems by experts and novices. *Cognitive Science, 5,* 121–152.

Cox, J., Daniel, N., & Boston, B. O. (1985). *Educating able learners: Programs and promising practices.* Austin: University of Texas Press.

Csikszentmihalyi, M., & Robinson, R. E. (1986). Culture, time, and the development of talent. In R. J. Sternberg & J. E. Davidson (Eds.), *Conceptions of giftedness* (pp. 264–284). New York: Cambridge University Press.

Dark, V. J., & Benbow, C. P. (in press). Enhanced problem translation and short-term memory: Components of mathematical talent. *Journal of Educational Psychology.*

Daurio, S. P. (1979). Educational enrichment versus acceleration: A review of the literature. In W. C. George, S. J. Cohn, & J. C. Stanley (Eds.), *Educating the gifted: Acceleration and enrichment* (pp. 13–63). Baltimore: Johns Hopkins University Press.

Donlon, T. F., & Angoff, W. H. (1971). The scholastic aptitude test. In W. Angoff (Ed.), *The College Board admissions testing program* (pp. 15–47). Princeton, NJ: College Entrance Examination Board.

Favazza, A. (1983). *The relationship of verbal ability to math.* Unpublished doctoral dissertation, Johns Hopkins University, Baltimore.

Feldman, D. H. (1986). Giftedness as a developmentalist sees it. In R. J. Sternberg & J. E. Davidson (Eds.), *Conceptions of giftedness* (pp. 285–305). New York: Cambridge University Press.

Fox, L. H. (1974). A mathematics program for fostering precocious achievement. In J. C. Stanley, D. P. Keating, & L. H. Fox (Eds.), *Mathematical talent: Discovery, description, and development* (pp. 101–125). Baltimore: Johns Hopkins University Press.

Fox, L. H. (1976). Sex differences in mathematical precocity: Bridging the gap. In D. P. Keating (Ed.), *Intellectual talent: Research and development* (pp. 183–214). Baltimore: Johns Hopkins University Press.

Gallagher, J. J. (1975). *Teaching the gifted child.* Boston: Allyn and Bacon.

George, W. C., Cohn, S. J., & Stanley, J. C. (1979). *Educating the gifted: Acceleration and enrich-ment.* Baltimore: Johns Hopkins University Press.

Gruber, H. E. (1986). The self-construction of the extraordinary. In R. J. Sternberg & J. E. Davidson (Eds.), *Conceptions of giftedness* (pp. 247–263). New York: Cambridge University Press.

Hunt, J. M. (1961). *Intelligence and experience.* New York: Ronald.

Jackson, N. E., & Butterfield, E. C. (1986). A conception of giftedness designed to promote research. In R. J. Sternberg & J. E. Davidson (Eds.), *Conceptions of giftedness* (pp. 151–181). New York: Cambridge University Press.

Keating, D. P. (1975). Precocious cognitive development at the level of formal operations. *Child Development, 46,* 276–280.

Keating, D. P., & Bobbit, B. L. (1978). Individual and developmental differences in cognitive processing components of mental ability. *Child Development, 49,* 155–167.

Keating, D. P., & Schaefer, R. A. (1975). Ability and sex differences in the acquisition of formal operations. *Developmental Psychology, 11,* 531–532.

Keating, D. P., & Stanley, J. C. (1972). Extreme measures for the exceptionally gifted in mathematics and science. *Educational Researcher, 1*(9), 3–7.

Krutetskii, V. A. (1976). *The psychology of mathematical abilities in school children.* Chicago: University of Chicago Press.

Kuhn, T. S. (1962). *The structure of scientific revolutions.* Chicago: University of Chicago Press.

Kulik, J. A., & Kulik, C. C. (1984). Effects of accelerated instruction on students. *Review of Educational Research, 54,* 409–425.

Langley, P. W., Simon, H. A., Bradshaw, G. F., & Zytkow, J. M. (1986). *Scientific discovery: Computational explorations of the creative process.* Cambridge, MA: MIT Press.

McCauley, C., Kellas, G., Dugas, J., & DeVillis, R. F. (1976). Effects of serial rehearsal training on memory search. *Journal of Educational Psychology, 68,* 474–481.

Mezynski, K., & Stanley, J. C. (1980). Advanced placement oriented calculus for high school students. *Journal for Research in Mathematics Education, 11,* 347–355.

Mumford, M. D., & Gustafson, S. B. (1988). Creativity syndrome: Integration, application, and innovation. *Psychological Bulletin, 103,* 27–43.

National Science Board. (1982). *Today's problems, tomorrow's crises.* Washington, DC: National Science Foundation.

Office of Technology Assessment. (1988). *Educating scientists and engineers: Grade school to grad school*. Washington, DC: U.S. Government Printing Office.

Peck, V. A., & Borkowski, J. G. (1983, April). *The emergence of strategic behavior in the gifted*. Paper presented at the biennial meeting of the Society for Research in Child Development, Detroit.

Pegnato, C. W., & Birch, J. W. (1959). Locating gifted children in junior high schools: A comparison of methods. *Exceptional Children, 25,* 300–304.

Pollins, L. M. (1983). The effects of acceleration on the social and emotional development of gifted students. In C. P. Benbow & J. C. Stanley (Eds.), *Academic precocity: Aspects of its development* (pp. 160–178). Baltimore: Johns Hopkins University Press.

Rabinowitz, M., & Glaser, R. (1985). Cognitive structures and process in highly competent performance. In F. D. Horowitz & M. O'Brien (Eds.), *The gifted and talented: Developmental perspectives* (pp. 75–98). Washington, DC: American Psychological Association.

Richardson, T. M. & Benbow, C. P. (in press). Long-term effects of acceleration on social and emotional adjustment of mathematically precocious youth. *Journal of Educational Psychology.*

Robinson, H. B. (1983). A case for radical acceleration: Programs of the Johns Hopkins University and the University of Washington. In C. P. Benbow & J. C. Stanley (Eds.), *Academic precocity: Aspects of its development* (pp. 139–159). Baltimore: Johns Hopkins University Press.

Robinson, N. M., & Robinson, H. B. (1976). *The mentally retarded child* (2nd ed.). New York: McGraw-Hill.

Shakhashiri, B. (1988, April). *Developing a national will to improve quality of science education in America*. Paper presented at UCSMP Second International Conference on Mathematics Education, Chicago.

Simonton, D. K. (1984). *Genius, creativity, and leadership*. Cambridge, MA: Harvard University Press.

Snow, R. E. (1986). Individual differences and the design of educational programs. *American Psychologist, 41,* 1029–1034.

Stanley, J. C. (1976). Test better finder of great math talent than teachers are. *American Psychologist, 31,* 313–314.

Stanley, J. C. (1977). Rationale of the Study of Mathematically Precocious Youth (SMPY) during its first five years of promoting educational acceler-

ation. In J. C. Stanley, W. C. George, & C. H. Solano (Eds.), *The gifted and the creative* (pp. 75–112). Baltimore: Johns Hopkins University Press.

Stanley, J. C. (1978). SMPY's DT-PI model: Diagnostic testing followed by prescriptive instruction. *Intellectually Talented Youth Bulletin, 4,* 7–8.

Stanley, J. C. (1979). How to use a fast-pacing math mentor. *Intellectually Talented Youth Bulletin, 6,* 1–2.

Stanley, J. C., & Benbow, C. P. (1982). Educating mathematically precocious youths: Twelve policy recommendations. *Educational Researcher, 11*(5), 4–9.

Stanley, J. C., & Benbow, C. P. (1983a). Extremely young college graduates: Evidence of their success. *College and University, 58,* 361–371.

Stanley, J. C., & Benbow, C. P. (1983b). Intellectually talented students: The key is curricular flexibility. In S. Paris, G. Olson, & A. Stevenson (Eds.), *Learning and motivation in the classroom* (pp. 259–281). Hillsdale, NJ: Erlbaum.

Stanley, J. C., & Benbow, C. P. (1986). Youths who reason exceptionally well mathematically. In R. J. Sternberg & J. E. Davidson (Eds.), *Conceptions of giftedness* (pp. 361–387). New York: Cambridge University Press.

Stanley, J. C., Keating, D. P., & Fox, L. H. (1974). *Mathematical talent: Discovery, description, and development*. Baltimore: Johns Hopkins University Press.

Sternberg, R. J., & Davidson, J. E. (1985). Cognitive development in the gifted and talented. In F. D. Horowitz & M. O'Brien (Eds.), *The gifted and talented: Developmental perspectives* (pp. 99–124). Washington, DC: American Psychological Association.

Wallach, M. A. (1985). Creativity testing and giftedness. In M. D. Horowitz & M. O'Brien (Eds.), *The gifted and talented: Developmental perspectives* (pp. 99–124). Washington, DC: American Psychological Association.

Walters, J., & Gardner, H. (1986). The crystallizing experience: Discovering an intellectual gift. In R. J. Sternberg & J. E. Davidson (Eds.), *Conceptions of giftedness* (pp. 306–331). New York: Cambridge University Press.

Zuckerman, H. (1983). The scientific elite: Nobel laureate's mutual influences. In R. S. Albert (Ed.), *Genius and eminence* (pp. 241–252). Elmsford, NY: Pergamon.

12

Talent Searches

SANFORD J. COHN   *Arizona State University, Tempe*

What Stanley gave us when he began to use the College Board's Scholastic Aptitude Test (SAT) in his talent searches was far more than just another way to identify gifted students (Stanley, 1977a, 1979, 1982; Stanley & Benbow, 1986). The SAT, administered to 12- and 13-year-olds, offers a realistic and practical guide to future educational planning by able youths (and their families) who are concerned about optimally developing their academic abilities (Fox, 1981; George, 1979). The SAT is widely recognized as a difficult measure of mathematical and verbal reasoning ability even for those for whom it was originally intended, college-bound high school juniors and seniors. Earning respectably high scores when only a seventh- or eighth-grader carries a clear message to teachers, counselors, and administrators: Somehow, the curriculum and pace must have a closer match to the student's assessed abilities (Cohn, 1986, 1988).

Administering the SAT out of level was not a lucky guess or some creative epiphany (Keating, 1975; Keating & Stanley, 1972; Solano, 1979; Stanley, 1951, 1954, 1959, 1973). It was the logical solution to a mental measurement problem: How does one assess the intellectual capacities of the extremely able? A test of reasoning power was sought such that scores would identify the highly able child who has not had the advantage of stimulating educational experiences (Stanley, 1977a). Typical achievement tests require far more prior knowledge and thereby fail to identify those who are powerful reasoners but who lack specific educational opportunities. The SAT, on the other hand, only requires prior knowledge at roughly the eighth- or ninth-grade level.

Stanley began the talent searches because he recognized that schools were failing to meet the educational needs of mathematically able students. Reports since the inception of the talent searches have only served to corroborate Stanley's foresight (Cohn, 1987). Because he knew that he would have to interact with teachers and administrators to articulate the unusual, advanced talent of his mathematical prodigies, he found the SAT an excellent bearer of news that a child was unexpectedly brilliant—even smarter than everyone thought him or her to be. After all, he or she performed well on tests known to be difficult for youths who are 4 or 5 years older.

To take part in the talent search requires a confident and robust state of mind. Ability is not the only characteristic that is being assessed in the talent search application process (Stanley, 1977a). Motivation to develop one's abilities is also being examined, particularly after the potential participant has read the SAT practice materials and has taken the sample examination offered by the Educational Testing Service (ETS). A gentle step is even taken to ensure that the youngsters have an earnest desire to take part by having them sign the application forms in addition to their parents.

The talent search process, then, has from the outset sought the "able and eager"—those youths who possess outstanding mathematical and/or verbal reasoning ability as well as the desire to see such abilities developed to their full power (George, 1979).

In the sections that follow, I will examine briefly the history of talent search, the talent search process, why the SAT was chosen as the instrument of the talent search, the nature and predictive value of the SAT, educational alternatives for talent search students, interpreting individuals' scores on the SAT, how to take part in one of the many annual talent searches, and how to start a talent search. I will also discuss how the measurement concept underlying the talent search, out-of-level administration of standardized ability tests, has been applied to the search for students who are even younger than those of typical talent search age.

A Brief History of the Origin of the Talent Search

"David" was 12 years old in the summer of 1968 when he took part in a special computer class at Johns Hopkins University (Stanley, 1973; Stanley, Keating, & Fox, 1974). His instructor noticed that David performed spectacularly on the computer, doing things that gave typical graduate students trouble. David's instructor suspected that he was a budding mathematical genius and that, in all likelihood, he was being seriously undereducated mathematically in his regular school.

David's instructor called Professor Julian C. Stanley, a world-renowned mental-measurements expert, also at Johns Hopkins, to inquire about possible assessment of David's apparent outstanding mental abilities. In January of 1969 Stanley administered David a battery of college-level tests of mathematical, mechanical, and verbal aptitude, including the College Entrance Examination Board (CEEB) SAT and several of the CEEB achievement tests.

David's performance at age 13 on these tests exceeded those of most freshman at Johns Hopkins. On the basis of his performance on this battery of extremely difficult tests, Stanley, David, and David's parents began a study of educational alternatives that led to David's entering Johns Hopkins at the age of 13½ earning his bachelor of arts degree at age 17, and his master of science degree in computer science 5 months later. Today David is a professor of computer science at a major American university.

Between 1968 and 1971, two other students came to Stanley's attention. In each case, he administered a battery of tests designed for highly able older students, including the SAT. Each student performed well enough to arouse Stanley's curiosity about other similar students. In the fall of 1971, with the help of a grant from the Spencer Foundation, Stanley systematized the concept of administering the SAT to students of junior high school age to identify excellent mathematical reasoners in his Study of Mathematically Precocious Youth (SMPY). In 1972 SMPY conducted its first talent search for mathematically precocious youths (Stanley et al., 1974).

In the 7 years that followed SMPY conducted five more talent searches, accumulating a total of nearly 10,000 talent search participants over the six cohorts of young SAT test takers (Benbow & Stanley, 1980, 1983; Fox & Cohn, 1980). By 1984 regional talent searches had been instituted at Arizona State University, Duke University, Johns Hopkins University, Northwestern University, and the University of Denver, and local talent searches had been undertaken at more than 20 other sites (Cohn, 1983).

By 1985 to 1986, over 83,000 12- and 13-year-olds had taken the SAT as participants in annual talent searches conducted that year by more than 30 institutions and universities throughout the United States (Burton, 1988). Presently, an estimated 90,000 to 100,000 youths are young SAT takers each year as participants in a variety of talent search efforts or on their own.

Goals of the Talent Search

The primary goal of the talent search effort is to identify brilliant mathematical and verbal reasoners, so that they and their families can plan appropriate educational experiences to help them develop their outstanding abilities as fully as possible (Cohn, 1988). Secondary goals of the talent search focus on recognizing the outstanding talents of the youths who score well on the SAT and providing them with honors, awards, and in some cases scholarships for advanced educational course work (Stanley, 1977a).

The Talent Search Process

Since its inception as a search for splendid mathematical reasoners, the talent search has expanded to include verbal talent as well as mathematical talent (Cohn, 1980, 1983; George, 1979). Students in the seventh grade, and eighth grade for some talent search efforts, who score in the top percentile ranks on standardized achievement tests related to mathematical and/or verbal reasoning ability (typically above the 95th or 97th percentiles, depending on the talent search institution) are informed via their school teachers, counselors, friends, or news releases about the opportunity to take the SAT as a participant in one or more talent search efforts.

Those who choose to take part typically complete an application with the talent search institution and register for the SAT directly with the admissions testing program of the ETS to take the SAT at a December or January national administration of the test. Before the student sits for the SAT, the talent search institution sends him or her information about the SAT and a sample test (*Taking the SAT*, published by ETS). Most students take this practice test to familiarize themselves with the item types that appear on the test.

About two-thirds of those who register to take part in the talent search with the talent search institutions actually take the SAT. The score distribution of these young students spans the full range of possible scores, from below chance (200) to near perfect (800). It is the capacity of this difficult instrument to differentiate individual differences in abilities among this highly able group that makes the talent search process so valuable.

Why the SAT?

The goal of the early talent searches was to find young people who could reason extremely well mathematically while knowing only simple mathematical facts. Stanley and his colleagues (Stanley, 1977a) did not want scores to depend on the participant's rote knowledge of algebra and higher mathematics concepts or on computational ability. Moreover, a mathematical *reasoning* test of sufficient difficulty was required so that the average participant in the talent search would score about halfway between a chance score and a perfect score.

It was necessary for schools to be able to understand the results of the testing and interpret them properly. Further, because of the likelihood that the talent search would reach far beyond its humble beginnings, the SMPY staff wanted, in addition to considerations of reasoning content and difficulty, a test that was prepared professionally, carefully standardized, and highly secure. The SAT offered the talent searchers all these properties. In addition, it was widely recognized by school teachers and administrators as a difficult measure of overall development in mathematical (and verbal) reasoning ability. Junior high school students who perform well on the SAT are perceived as demonstrating truly outstanding capacities to reason.

The Nature of the SAT

The SAT is composed of three sections: the mathematical reasoning section (SAT-M), the verbal reasoning section (SAT-V), and the Test of Standard Written English (TSWE) (see Cohn, 1985).

The SAT-M is primarily a test of mathematical reasoning ability. Formal courses in algebra and Euclidean geometry are not required to do well on the test. Rather, knowledge of basic arithmetic processes, introductory algebra, and geometry form the item content (Donlon, 1985). Two kinds of items are used in this section: regular mathematics items and quantitative comparisons. Mathematics reasoning of the type tested by the SAT-M helps students learn such subjects as arithmetic, algebra, geometry, trigonometry, calculus, statistics, probability theory, engineering, computer science, mathematical economics, mathematical psychology, mathematical sociology, and such physical sciences as physics, physical chemistry, and astronomy.

The SAT-V is a test of general verbal development, mainly verbal reasoning and reading comprehension. Scores on the SAT-V often reflect the various verbal opportunities one has had and has benefited from, in school and out, during one's lifetime. The SAT-V is intended to be a systematic sample of that development.

Four item types constitute the SAT-V: antonyms, analogies, sentence completions, and reading comprehension. Item content is drawn from a variety of substantive areas spanning the humanities and the sciences. Verbal ability of the kind tested by the SAT-V helps students achieve well in writing, English, reading and literature, history, geography, anthropology, linguistics, psychology, philosophy, foreign languages, and other verbal courses. Of course, it also helps students learn mathematics and the sciences.

The TSWE is not a reasoning test, but rather a test of developed skill in recognizing correct English usage. Two types of items are used in this test: usage and sentence correction. Usage items require the recognition of writing that does not follow the conventions of standard written English; sentence correction items require not only the recognition of unacceptable phrasing, but also a choice of the best way to rephrase the incorrect sentence component.

The SAT-M and SAT-V are scored on a standard score scale ranging from 200 to 800. According to recent national norms, the average high school junior or senior scores 372 on the SAT-V, whereas the average high school college-bound senior scores 430. The average high school junior or senior *male* scores 416 on the SAT-M, the *female* 390; whereas the average high school college-bound *male* scores 500 on the SAT-M, the *female* 450.

The TSWE is scored on a standard score scale ranging from 20 to 60 with the average college-bound senior scoring 42.

The Predictive Value of the SAT for Brilliant Seventh- and Eighth-Graders

There are four ways in which the predictive validity of the SAT for highly able seventh- and eighth-grade students has been demonstrated. First, underage students who do well on the SAT also do well in advanced-level course work, such as that provided by the Advanced Placement (AP) program, concurrent enrollment in college course work while still in high school or even junior high school, or special accelerated summer programs. These educational opportunities require faster-than-usual passage through more-difficult-than-usual material (Benbow & Stanley, 1983; Fox, 1979; Keating, 1976; Solano & George, 1976; Stanley, 1977b; Stanley & Benbow, 1981–1982; Stanley et al., 1974).

Second, the process of administering mathematical and verbal reasoning tests out of level removes the ceiling effect that plagues the evaluation of very high ability students. This procedure has been used successfully with students who are even younger than talent search age (Cohn, 1988). For example, students who are too young to take the SAT but perform well on other out-of-level ability tests, such as the School and College Ability Tests (SCAT), also perform well in advanced-level, fast-paced course work (Cohn, 1984).

Third, this method of identifying mathematical and verbal reasoners and subsequently providing them with relevant academic course work has been applied successfully in a number of school-based settings (Cohn, 1984). Specifically, schools that have adopted out-of-level testing to identify academically gifted students find that these students perform well in advanced-level, fast-paced courses of study.

Fourth, extensive follow-up studies have been conducted primarily by SMPY and spin-off organizations to determine what happens to talent search participants (Benbow & Stanley, 1983; Cohn, 1980). The evidence overwhelmingly supports the use of talent search to identify highly able reasoners who are eager to develop their abilities. Higher scoring participants tend to earn more honors and more advanced standing, enter college earlier, and complete college with greater success than those who score less well.

Unusual Educational Alternatives

Many students who take part in the talent searches enroll in summer programs designed to offer them educational experiences commensurate with their outstanding abilities. While most of these activities allow seventh- and eighth-grade students, as well as older students, to pursue areas of learning that are new to them, such as psychology or anthropology, topics in the sciences, and so forth, there remains a dedication to provide these youths the opportunity to study precalculus mathematics at an enriched level of content and at a faster-than-typical pace. It has not been unusual, for example, for students who are excellent mathematical reasoners, as evidenced by their high scores on the SAT, to complete 5½ years of precalculus mathematics course work in a single summer of intense study (Benbow & Stanley, 1983; Brody, 1984; Cohn, 1980; Mezynski & Stanley, 1980).

Some youths have demonstrated extraordinary ability in both mathematical and verbal reasoning and have developed their skills in subjects related to both areas. As a result, they have advanced far faster through the educational age-grade progression than their more typical age-mates. By a carefully planned use of strategic grade skipping, a few youths have entered college on a full-time basis as much as 6 years early. Moreover, they have engaged college course work and the challenge of collegiate life with great success (Nevin, 1977).

Still other highly able young people have arranged a schedule that combines high school and college course work. Many youths who take part in the talent searches find great value in the CEEB's AP courses and examinations and the International Baccalaureate program, both of which allow them to earn college credits while they are still in high school (Cox, Daniel, & Boston, 1986).

Clearly, the most directly immediate educational benefit of taking part in a talent search comes with the opportunity to participate in one of the many summer programs designed to facilitate the academic progress of these youths. While most of the offerings of these programs enrich the spectrum of subject areas available to bright and eager students, the most dramatic successes typically arise from the more accelerative options, such as fast-paced mathematics and science courses. These and other educationally accelerative options are discussed in greater detail in Chapter 11 by Benbow.

An important fact to remember is that the accomplishments of thousands of these academically able young people are dramatically large. They are accomplishments unheard of prior to the start of the talent searches. In research studies documenting the value of the SAT as a predictor of academic success the findings are not merely statistically significant. The programs are profound in their capacity to enable highly able and eager students to proceed educationally as fast and in as great a depth and breadth as they wish.

Out-of-Level Testing Applied to Younger Students

Programs created at the Center for Academic Precocity (CAP) at Arizona State University have applied the concept of out-of-level ability assessment to a broader age range of students than just seventh- and eighth-graders (Cohn, 1984). When SCAT is used as an analog to the SAT, children as young as age 7 have been identified for fast-paced arithmetic and other classes, such as advanced reading and discussion classes, and classes designed to provide science exploration.

Interpreting the SAT Score

In addition to the many educationally facilitative alternatives for youths who score well on the SAT, an important value of talent search remains learning more about oneself and one's profile of cognitive skills.

Norms

When a youth takes part in a talent search that uses the SAT, along with his or her score report is sent a set of norms against which the score can be compared. These norms, however, are based upon scores of college-bound high school juniors and seniors. Usually, the institution conducting the talent search also sends the participant, under separate cover, a set of norms for seventh- and eighth-graders who have taken the test. These out-of-level norms allow the talent search participant to compare his or her performance with other students of the same age who have taken this difficult test.

Norms for 12,606 seventh-graders and 10,849 eighth graders appear in Tables 12.1

and 12.2. These norms are based on partici-
pants over a 5-year period in Arizona State
University's Project for the Study of Academic
Precocity (PSAP) talent searches (in 1986
PSAP became CAP).

When these norms are used, a score of 500
on the SAT-V, for example, shows a seventh-
grade participant performing better than
96.2% of other highly able youths of the same
age, who compose the normative group for Table 12.1. Similarly, a score of 610 on the SAT-M
shows an eighth-grade female participant performing better than 98.5% of other highly able
girls the same age, who compose the normative
group for Table 12.2.

Educational Implications

Over years of working with youths who have
taken the SAT, researchers have learned that
performance at certain levels on the SAT-V or
SAT-M suggests success in various educational
alternatives, such as those mentioned previously in this chapter. The sections that follow
offer guidelines for the educational implications of performance on the SAT by seventh-
grade students. By adding 50 points to the following categories, the reader can apply these
guidelines to eighth-grade students.

Scores at or below Chance. A chance
score is one that would be earned on the basis of
probability. For example, if a test contains 100
items, each with 4 multiple-choice options, a
person who simply filled in the answer sheet
with random responses would earn a score
close to 25, the chance score.

Talent search participants who earn scores
of chance or below (roughly, 230 SAT-V, 270
SAT-M, depending on the form of the test) need
to remember that they are still performing in
the top 3 to 5% of their age group with respect
to mathematical and/or verbal reasoning ability. This is true because in most talent searches
students must qualify by scoring in the top 3rd
to 5th percentile relative to students their own
age on tests that relate to mathematical and/or
verbal reasoning ability.

Among the educational options appropriate
for youths who score at this level are:

- Honors-level course work in relevant subject
  matter
- Enrichment seminars, such as interdisciplinary studies
- Educational opportunities in the community, offered by institutes of science and industry, art museums, libraries (Hyman,
  1982), and so on
- Academic counseling

**Scores between Chance and 500
(SAT-M) or 430 (SAT-V).** A score of 500 on
the SAT-M is equivalent to the average score
earned by college-bound high school senior
males. Similarly, a score of 430 on the SAT-V is
equivalent to the average score earned by
college-bound high school seniors of either sex.
Educational options worth considering for
youths who have scored at this level include
those listed for the previous group and:

- Starting a course sequence in relevant subject matter early, but at a regular pace (for
  those scoring at the lower end of this score
  range)
- Compacting a course sequence in relevant
  subject matter (for example, completing 2
  years' worth of French in 1 year)
- University summer or academic-year classes
  for able and eager youths (some allow eligibility in this score range)

**Scores between 510 and 630 (SAT-M) or
440 and 590 (SAT-V).** Talent search participants who earn scores in this score range are
performing on the SAT well above the average
college-bound high school senior. In addition to
those options listed for previous score ranges,
the following options might be suitable:

- Individualized study at a fast pace and advanced level in relevant subject matter
- Concurrent enrollment in university course
  work while still in junior or senior high
  school
- Challenge examinations to earn credit for
  regular school work
- Early access to AP program classes in relevant subject matter
- Carefully planned grade skipping, depending on the student's interest in moving ahead
  rapidly academically

Table 12.1
Norms of 12,606 Seventh-Graders Who Took the SAT for the First Time as Participants in Talent Searches Conducted by Arizona State University's PSAP, Now the CAP

Score Scale	Mathematics		Verbal	TSWE	Score Scale
	Males	Females			
800	99.9	99.9	99.9		
790	99.9	99.9	99.9		
780	99.9	99.9	99.9		
770	99.9	99.9	99.9		
760	99.9	99.9	99.9		
750	99.9	99.9	99.9		
740	99.9	99.9	99.9		
730	99.9	99.9	99.9		
720	99.8	99.9	99.9		
710	99.7	99.9	99.9		
700	99.7	99.9	99.9		
690	99.6	99.9	99.9		
680	99.5	99.9	99.9		
670	99.4	99.9	99.9		
660	99.3	99.9	99.9		
650	99.1	99.9	99.9		
640	99.1	99.9	99.9		
630	98.8	99.8	99.8		
620	98.6	99.8	99.8		
610	98.3	99.7	99.7		
600	97.7	99.7	99.7	99.7	60
590	97.2	99.5	99.6	99.5	59
580	96.4	99.3	99.4	99.2	58
570	95.5	99.1	99.3	98.9	57
560	94.4	99.0	99.0	98.3	56
550	93.4	98.7	98.8	97.5	55
540	92.6	98.3	98.5	97.0	54
530	91.6	97.8	98.0	95.8	53
520	89.8	96.9	97.4	94.8	52
510	88.4	96.3	96.9	93.4	51
500	86.8	95.5	96.2	91.3	50
490	84.8	94.5	95.3	90.4	49
480	82.1	92.9	94.4	88.1	48
470	79.0	90.9	93.2	86.1	47
460	75.8	88.7	91.6	83.5	46
450	73.0	86.5	90.1	80.3	45
440	70.1	84.3	87.9	78.6	44
430	65.8	80.9	85.3	75.4	43
420	62.6	78.2	82.9	72.3	42
410	58.4	74.4	79.8	69.3	41
400	54.8	70.8	77.0	65.4	40
390	50.5	66.5	72.7	63.6	39
380	45.5	61.1	69.0	59.0	38
370	41.5	56.6	63.9	54.2	37
360	36.6	50.9	60.0	50.7	36
350	31.6	44.1	54.7	46.1	35
340	27.3	38.9	48.7	43.7	34
330	22.0	31.1	43.9	39.6	33

Score Scale	Mathematics		Verbal	TSWE	Score Scale
	Males	Females			
320	18.2	26.4	38.4	35.3	32
310	14.9	21.9	32.7	31.8	31
300	11.8	16.6	27.8	27.8	30
290	8.9	11.9	22.8	25.9	29
280	6.0	7.6	18.3	20.8	28
270	3.5	4.6	13.7	17.5	27
260	2.3	3.0	11.1	14.8	26
250	1.5	1.9	7.5	12.7	25
240	0.6	0.9	5.9	10.9	24
230	0.3	0.4	3.8	8.6	23
220	0.1	0.3	2.7	6.5	22
210	0.1	0.1	1.5	5.0	21
200	0.1	0.1	0.1	0.1	20
Mean	395.6	363.4	344.2	35.7	
SD	88.3	70.3	76.1	9.3	
N	6,111	6,494	12,606	12,606	

Note: Figures shown represent *percentage scoring below* the score indicated on the score scale. The score scale on the left-hand side of the page is for SAT-M and SAT-V; the score scale on the right-hand side of the page is for TSWE.

Table 12.2
Norms for 10,849 Eighth-Graders Who Took the SAT for the First Time as Participants in Talent Searches Conducted by Arizona State University's PSAP, Now the CAP

Score Scale	Mathematics		Verbal	TSWE	Score Scale
	Males	Females			
800	99.9	99.9	99.9		
790	99.9	99.9	99.9		
780	99.9	99.9	99.9		
770	99.9	99.9	99.9		
760	99.9	99.9	99.9		
750	99.9	99.9	99.9		
740	99.8	99.9	99.9		
730	99.7	99.9	99.9		
720	99.6	99.9	99.9		
710	99.4	99.9	99.9		
700	99.3	99.9	99.9		
690	98.9	99.8	99.9		
680	98.7	99.8	99.9		
670	98.4	99.7	99.8		
660	98.0	99.6	99.8		
650	97.4	99.5	99.6		
640	96.6	99.3	99.6		
630	95.9	99.1	99.5		
620	95.0	98.9	99.3		

(continued)

Table 12.2 continued

Score Scale	Mathematics		Verbal	TSWE	Score Scale
	Males	Females			
610	94.0	98.5	99.0		
600	92.9	97.9	98.7	98.9	60
590	91.5	97.2	98.4	98.5	59
580	89.8	96.4	98.1	97.5	58
570	87.6	95.3	97.6	96.8	57
560	85.1	94.2	96.9	95.0	56
550	82.9	93.0	96.1	93.1	55
540	80.4	91.7	95.1	91.8	54
530	77.8	90.2	94.0	89.5	53
520	73.8	87.6	92.9	87.6	52
510	70.7	85.6	91.5	85.1	51
500	67.9	83.7	89.6	81.2	50
490	64.7	80.9	87.6	79.2	49
480	61.0	77.6	85.4	75.5	48
470	56.9	73.8	82.4	72.5	47
460	52.4	68.8	79.1	68.7	46
450	48.6	65.2	76.4	64.4	45
440	45.2	61.3	72.5	61.9	44
430	40.8	56.3	68.5	57.8	43
420	37.2	52.1	64.6	53.9	42
410	32.0	46.9	60.1	50.3	41
400	29.1	42.7	56.1	45.7	40
390	25.7	38.3	50.7	43.5	39
380	22.2	33.3	46.7	39.2	38
370	19.5	28.9	40.9	34.5	37
360	15.9	24.6	36.8	30.8	36
350	13.2	20.0	31.4	26.7	35
340	11.0	16.3	26.2	24.5	34
330	8.2	12.3	22.2	21.4	33
320	6.9	10.0	18.0	18.0	32
310	5.7	8.0	14.5	15.5	31
300	4.1	5.6	11.5	12.8	30
290	2.7	3.9	8.6	11.7	29
280	1.8	2.6	6.7	9.0	28
270	1.1	1.6	4.6	7.1	27
260	0.8	1.1	3.6	5.7	26
250	0.4	0.6	2.1	4.6	25
240	0.2	0.3	1.6	3.7	24
230	0.1	0.1	1.1	2.8	23
220	0.1	0.1	0.7	2.1	22
210	0.1	0.1	0.3	1.5	21
200	0.1	0.1	0.1	0.1	20
Mean	452.2	416.1	389.4	40.4	
SD	94.8	81.7	81.5	9.2	
N	5,232	5,616	10,849	10,848	

Note: Figures shown represent *percentage scoring below* the score indicated on the score scale. The score scale on the left-hand side of the page is for SAT-M and SAT-V; the score scale on the right-hand side of the page is for TSWE.

Scores between 640 and 800 (SAT-M) or 600 and 800 (SAT-V). Talent search participants who score at this level are performing extremely well on difficult tests of verbal and mathematical reasoning ability. All the educational alternatives listed for the previous score ranges should be considered. Additionally, one might contemplate:

• Part-time early entrance to a college or university
• Full-time early entrance (possibly with advanced standing) to a college or university

The Talent Searchers

In 1972, 356 Baltimore, Maryland, area youths took part in Stanley's first mathematics talent search. By 1985 to 1986 the concept had spread such that over 83,000 seventh- and eighth-graders had taken the SAT as part of 32 different talent searches conducted throughout the United States (Burton, 1988).

The greatest number of participants took part in one of the large regional talent searches conducted by the Center for Academic Precocity (CAP) at Arizona State University (through 1986), the Center for the Advancement of Academically Talented Youth at Johns Hopkins University, the Midwest Talent Search at Northwestern University, the Rocky Mountain Talent Search at the University of Denver, and the Talent Identification Program at Duke University (Cohn, 1983).

Numerous other colleges and universities had initiated talent search efforts by the mid-1980s. Among them were the University of California at Berkeley, the California State University at Sacramento, and the University of Wisconsin at Eau Claire. Each of these institutions, as well as those mentioned above, received cooperation from the ETS in the form of a unique test report code that allowed score reports to be sent directly to the institutional talent searchers, as well as to the student participants.

Stanley's original SMPY at Johns Hopkins University and, more recently, at Iowa State University, continues to conduct a search for youths who score 700 or better on the SAT-M

prior to their 13th birthday. To become part of this elite group of extremely mathematically able youths, one has to register for the SAT, meet the requirement of scoring 700 or above on SAT-M before age 13, and have an official score report sent to SMPY. There are no additional costs, as there are with most of the other major talent search groups. The benefits include a virtual fountain of information about unusual educational opportunities and challenges.

Since 1985, an increasing number of institutions are conducting talent search efforts on a more local level. For example, by August, 1989, Iowa State University will begin its own talent search. The CAP at Arizona State University, much like the Talent Search Project at California State University at Sacramento, has focused its efforts on demonstrating the benefits of the talent search and associated educational programing on a statewide level. The advantages of this more local focus center on greater flexibility and include:

• An attitude of outreach to local community schools
• Serving a broader age range of the able population
• Lower costs
• Better articulation with local school districts
• Opportunities for personal educational counseling and interpretive materials that focus on local needs

For schools in rural communities that can encourage a sufficient number of students to take part in the talent search, for example, CAP staff will conduct a test administration at the local school. This capacity to be more flexible and serve community needs expands the potential for the talent search to become a meaningful resource to highly able young people throughout the nation.

Little is required for an institution to initiate a talent search of its own—except a willingness to undertake the effort. If the scheduled national administrations of the SAT are used, one need only get a score report identification number from the ETS. Qualifying institutions can also use the ETS Multiple Assessment Program to administer the SAT on dates other than the national administration dates and at other locations. One then needs only interpretive materials, such as normative information and guidelines for educational implications provided in previous sections of this chapter.

Epilogue

The effects that talent search and SMPY have had on the field of educating the gifted have been enormous. The Stanley studies (SMPY), with a population of nearly 10,000 mathematically precocious youths under longitudinal study, dwarf the monumental Terman studies of the early 20th century. Literally millions of mathematically and verbally gifted young people have been helped by the many talent search efforts spawned by SMPY's early and dramatic success. The use of educational alternatives, mainly accelerative in nature, that prior to 1972 were rarely considered, such as grade skipping, concurrent enrollment, and subject matter acceleration, has changed the nature of how gifted children are served in schools throughout the country. The field has broadened, and continues to broaden, its repertoire of services from which able youths, their families, and educators can choose.

The future holds many exciting prospects as the talent searches spread and become characterized by a more grass roots level of effort. Consider these probable trends:

- Schools will become more likely to practice continuous progress and use more flexible pacing and placement of able students in their classes.
- Articulation will likely improve between local schools and colleges and universities that offer special summer and academic-year classes for academically talented young people.
- Parents will have greater access to academically substantive services for their academically gifted children.
- Advances in assessment technology and the availability of models of rigorous academic curricula will likely result in increased availability of appropriately challenging educa-

tional experiences for the academically gifted (Resnick & Resnick, 1985).
- Able children will take more responsibility for their own educational planning as they learn more about themselves, their abilities and developed skills, and the many educational opportunities for their enhancement and growth.

REFERENCES

Benbow, C. P., & Stanley, J. C. (1980). Sex differences in mathematical reasoning ability: Fact or artifact? *Science, 210,* 4475.

Benbow, C. P., & Stanley, J. C. (Eds.). (1983). *Academic precocity.* Baltimore: Johns Hopkins University Press.

Brody, L. E. (1984). *The effects of an intensive summer program on the SAT scores of gifted seventh graders.* Unpublished doctoral dissertation, Johns Hopkins University, Baltimore.

Burton, N. W. (1988). *Survey II: Test-taking history for 1980–81 young SAT-takers.* New York: College Entrance Examination Board.

Cohn, S. J. (1980). *Two components of the Study of Mathematically Precocious Youth's intervention studies of educational acceleration: Chemistry-physics facilitation and longitudinal follow-up.* Unpublished doctoral dissertation, Johns Hopkins University, Baltimore.

Cohn, S. J. (1983). Talent Search: A national and international effort. *Chronicle of Academic and Artistic Precocity, 2*(1), 1–3.

Cohn, S. J. (1984). Project F.U.T.U.R.E.: A progress report after three prototype years of serving intellectually gifted students. *Journal for the Education of the Gifted, 7,* 103–119.

Cohn, S. J. (1985). Review of the College Board Scholastic Aptitude Test and Test of Standard Written English. In J. V. Mitchell (Ed.), *The ninth mental measurements yearbook* (pp. 622–624). Lincoln, NB: The Buros Institute of Mental Measurement.

Cohn, S. J. (1986). The optimal match strategy: An academic alternative for gifted students. In L. Kanevsky (Ed.), *Issues in gifted education* (pp. 44–68). San Diego: San Diego City Schools.

Cohn, S. J. (1987, April–May). The crisis in American education: Its implications for the academically able. *The Principal, 22*(4), 1–7.

Cohn, S. J. (1988). Assessment of the gifted child and adolescent. In C. J. Kestenbaum & D. T. Williams (Eds.), *Handbook of clinical assessment of children and adolescents* (Vol. 1, pp. 355–376). New York: New York University Press.

Cox, J., Daniel, N., & Boston, B. (1986). *Educating able learners: Programs and promising practices.* Austin: University of Texas Press.

Donlon, T. F. (1985). *The technical handbook for the College Board Scholastic Aptitude Test and Achievement Tests.* New York: College Entrance Examination Board.

Fox, L. H. (1979). Programs for the gifted and talented: An overview. In A. H. Passow (Ed.), *The gifted and talented: Their education and development.* (Seventy-eighth yearbook of the National Society for the Study of Education, pp. 104–126). Chicago: University of Chicago Press.

Fox, L. H. (1981). Identification of the academically gifted. *American Psychologist, 36,* 1103–1111.

Fox, L. H., & Cohn, S. J. (1980). Sex differences in the development of mathematical precocity. In L. H. Fox, L. Brody, & D. Tobin (Eds.), *Women and the mathematical mystique* (pp. 94–111). Baltimore: Johns Hopkins University Press.

George, W. C. (1979). The talent-search concept: An identification strategy for the intellectually gifted. *Journal of Special Education, 13,* 221–237.

Hyman, M. B. (1982). Science museums and gifted students. *Chronicle of Academic and Artistic Precocity, 1*(2), 1–3.

Keating, D. P. (1975). Testing those in the top percentiles. *Exceptional Children, 41,* 435–436.

Keating, D. P. (Ed.). (1976). *Intellectual talent: Research and development.* Baltimore: Johns Hopkins University Press.

Keating, D. P., & Stanley, J. C. (1972). Extreme measures for the exceptionally gifted in mathematics and science. *Educational Researcher, 1*(9), 3–7.

Mezynski, K., & Stanley, J. C. (1980). Advanced placement oriented calculus for high school students. *Journal for Research in Mathematics Education, 11,* 347–355.

Nevin, D. (1977). Young prodigies take off under special program. *Smithsonian, 8*(7), 76–82.

Resnick, D. P., & Resnick, L. B. (1985). Standards, curriculum, and performance: A historical and comparative perspective. *Educational Researcher, 14*(4), 5–20.

Solano, C. H. (1979). The first D: Discovery of talent, or needles in a haystack: Identifying the mathematically gifted child. In N. R. Colangelo & R. T. Zaffrann (Eds.), *New voices in counseling the gifted* (pp. 89–106). Dubuque: Kendall/Hunt.

Solano, C. H., & George, W. C. (1976). College courses and educational facilitation of the gifted. *Gifted Child Quarterly, 20,* 274–285.

Stanley, J. C. (1951). On the adequacy of standardized tests administered to extreme norm groups. *Peabody Journal of Education, 29,* 145–153.

Stanley, J. C. (1954). Identification of superior learners in grades ten through fourteen. *Supplementary Educational Monograph, 81,* 31–34.

Stanley, J. C. (1959). Test biases of prospective teachers for identifying gifted children. *School and Society, 87,* 175–177.

Stanley, J. C. (1973). Accelerating the educational progress of intellectually gifted youths. *Educational Psychologist, 10,* 133–146. (Reprinted in W. Dennis & M. W. Dennis [Eds.], *The intellectually gifted: An overview* [pp. 179–196] New York: Grune & Stratton.)

Stanley, J. C. (1977a). Rationale of the Study of Mathematically Precocious Youth (SMPY) during its first five years of promoting educational acceleration. In J. C. Stanley, W. C. George, & C. H. Solano (Eds.), *The gifted and the creative: A fifty-year perspective* (pp. 75–112). Baltimore: Johns Hopkins University Press.

Stanley, J. C. (1977b). The predictive value of the SAT for brilliant seventh and eighth graders. *College Board Review,* No. 106, 2–7. (Reprinted in *International Schools Journal* [1981], No. 2, 39–48.)

Stanley, J. C. (1979). The study and facilitation of talent for mathematics. In A. H. Passow (Ed.), *The gifted and talented: Their education and development* (Seventy-eighth yearbook of the National Society for the Study of Education, pp. 169–185). Chicago: University of Chicago Press.

Stanley, J. C. (1982). Identification of intellectual talent. In W. B. Schrader (Ed.), *Measurement, guidance, and program improvement* (New Directions for Testing and Measurement Series No. 13, pp. 97–109). San Francisco: Jossey-Bass.

Stanley, J. C. & Benbow, C. P. (1986). Youths who reason exceptionally well mathematically. In R. J. Sternberg & J. E. Davidson (Eds.), *Conceptions of giftedness* (pp. 361–387). New York: Cambridge University Press.

Stanley, J. C. & Benbow, C. P. (1981–1982). Using the SAT to find intellectually talented seventh graders. *College Board Review,* No. 122, 2–7, 26.

Stanley, J. C., Keating, D. P., & Fox, L. H. (Eds.). (1974). *Mathematical talent: Discovery, description, and development.* Baltimore: Johns Hopkins University Press.

13

Ability Grouping and Gifted Students

JAMES A. KULIK and CHEN-LIN C. KULIK   *University of Michigan, Ann Arbor*

bility grouping has long been a controversial practice in American education. Ever since the first ability-grouped classes were formed in American schools more than 100 years ago, educators have been debating their merits. Some have supported ability grouping, arguing that teachers cannot meet the needs of all children in mixed-ability classes. Others have denounced ability grouping as an undemocratic practice that stigmatizes children in lower tracks.

Educational researchers have been conducting research studies to help settle the controversy for nearly three-quarters of a century. In a typical study a researcher compares criterion-test performance of students who have been taught in homogeneous classrooms with the performance of students taught in mixed-ability classes. By 1936, when the National Society for the Study of Education published a yearbook on grouping of pupils, seven or eight comprehensive reviews of such research studies were available (Whipple, 1936). One of these reviews alone contained 140 references, including 108 reports of experimental studies (Billett, 1932). In the years since, researchers have continued to study grouping and reviewers have continued to try to make sense of their findings.

Until recently the central message from the reviewers has been that nothing is established with certainty. The evidence has seemed too unclear and contradictory for broad conclusions. In recent years, however, two major reviews have been published that report finding more consistency in the accumulated research findings (Oakes, 1985; Slavin, 1987). These reviews report that ability grouping is an educationally ineffective practice.

Oakes's reviews of grouping research appears in her book *Keeping Track* (Oakes, 1985). According to her, students in the top tracks gain nothing from grouping and other students suffer clear and consistent disadvantages, including loss of academic ground, self-esteem, and ambition. Just as important, Oakes argues that tracking is unfair since it denies all students exposure to a common curriculum. Grouping became popular, she believes, because it helped keep immigrants separate from other Americans, and it continues to hold a place in American education because it maintains the separation of majority and minority Americans. In Oakes's view, grouping is racist in root and stem.

Slavin's reviews of grouping research have also emphasized negative results. Comprehensive programs of grouping were Slavin's (1987) target in a review of findings from elementary schools. According to Slavin, the evidence unequivocally refuted the assertion that ability-grouped class assignment can increase student achievement. Slavin's 1988 review was directed toward a broader target: comprehensive grouping programs, separate classes for gifted students, and special education programs for students with learning problems. All such programs, Slavin argued, lack features that might make them educationally sound. The best evidence, he concluded, shows that comprehensive grouping, special education, and special programs for the gifted are not beneficial.

It would be easy to dismiss such conclusions as atypical and possibly biased. But it would also be a serious mistake. Oakes's and Slavin's conclusions are being taken seriously in American education today. School boards are reconsidering grouping practices and special programs for the gifted on the basis of such claims. Oakes and Slavin have formulated views that are attractive to an influential part of the public, and their conclusions are being used as justification for important changes in the education of the gifted today.

Our purpose here is to examine evaluation results of programs that group students for instruction by ability. The evaluation results come from controlled studies of grouping carried out over a period of more than 50 years by many different investigators. The method that we use in examining results is a formal statistical one, *meta-analysis*. The method contrasts sharply with the informal analytic approaches used by Oakes and Slavin in their reviews.

Meta-Analytic Methodology

The key problem for reviewers of grouping studies has been the variation in study results. Students from ability-grouped classes outperform students from mixed-ability classes in some studies; in other studies, there is no difference; and in still others, students in mixed-ability classes perform at a higher level. Applied educational research is not like research in the natural sciences, in which study conditions and study results can often be replicated exactly. In applied educational research, replications are never exact, and results of different studies are seldom identical.

To integrate findings from the many studies of grouping, reviewers have written two major types of reviews: narrative reviews and box scores. Narrative reviews simply present verbal descriptions of studies and study results. The reviewers rely on reasoning and insight to find a pattern in the accumulation of results, and they use narrative and rhetorical devices to convey this pattern to readers. Billett (1932), Borg (1966), Goldberg, Passow, and Justman (1966), and many others have written narrative reviews of grouping research. Box-score reviewers tally the votes for and against an educational treatment, and they then present their results in tabular and narrative form. Findley and Bryan (1971) and the research division of the National Education Association (1968) include box scores in their reviews of grouping research.

The main problem with both narrative and box-score reviews is their subjectivity. The biases of a narrative reviewer can influence the

studies selected for review, the description of the studies, and the conclusions drawn from them. Narrative reviewers do not have to stick to the data. When studies of an issue run into the hundreds and findings are complex, narrative reviewers usually can find what they want to find in the results. Reviewer bias also can affect box scores of review results. Box-score reviewers seldom explain how they select studies for their reviews or the basis on which they classify study results as positive, negative, or mixed. In addition, box-score reviewers oversimplify experimental results, reducing a wealth of experimental conditions and outcomes to a few numbers.

To overcome the shortcomings of narrative and box-score reviews, Glass (1976) developed the technique of meta-analysis. The term refers to a set of methods for statistically analyzing a large collection of results from individual studies for the purpose of integrating the findings (Glass, McGaw, & Smith, 1981). Reviewers who carry out meta-analyses first locate studies of an issue by clearly specified procedures. They then characterize the outcomes and features of these studies in quantitative or quasi-quantitative terms. Finally, meta-analysts use multivariate techniques to describe findings and relate characteristics of the studies to outcomes. Glass's meta-analytic techniques are far less subjective than the methods used in narrative reviews and far more powerful than those used in box-score reviews.

One of Glass's major innovations was his use of *effect-size* measures in research reviews. Glass measured effect sizes in several different ways but most often used standardized mean differences as his measure of size of effect. Sometimes called *Glass's effect size,* this index gives the number of standard-deviation units that separate outcome scores of experimental and control groups. It is calculated by subtracting the average score of the control group on the outcome measure from the average score of the experimental group and then dividing the remainder by the standard deviation of the measure. For example, if a coached experimental group obtains an average score of 550 on the Scholastic Aptitude Test (SAT) and an uncoached control group averages 500, the effect size for the coaching treatment is 0.5 since the standard deviation on the SAT is 100.

Cohen (1977) and others had demonstrated in numerous places that an index of effect size could be useful in designing research studies, but Glass was among the first to appreciate the contribution that this index could make to research reviews. Glass's introduction of the index made sophisticated statistical analysis of review results possible because it provided a way of expressing effects from a variety of studies on a common scale. Glass's effect sizes changed the nature of the reviewer's job.

Methodologists have written a number of books on meta-analytic methods in recent years (Glass et al., 1981; Hedges & Olkin, 1985; Hunter, Schmidt, & Jackson, 1982; Rosenthal, 1984), and reviewers have conducted numerous meta-analyses of research findings. In a recent monograph, for example, we described results from more than 100 reports on the application of meta-analytic methodology in education alone (J. A. Kulik & Kulik, 1989). In addition, meta-analytic methodology has also been used extensively in psychology and in the health sciences. Reviewers have used it to draw general conclusions on such diverse subjects as the effectiveness of psychotherapy and the effectiveness of coronary bypass surgery.

A number of recent meta-analytic reports are relevant to questions of ability grouping of students for special instruction. This chapter is based on findings from four of these (C.-L. C. Kulik & Kulik, 1982; C.-L. C. Kulik, 1985; J. A. Kulik & Kulik, 1984; J. A. Kulik & Kulik, 1987). The meta-analyses cover three major types of grouping programs: (1) ability grouping programs for all students, (2) separate instruction for talented students, and (3) accelerated instruction for talented students.

Ability Grouping for All Students

Many ability grouping programs assign students of a wide range of abilities to homogeneous groups according to their academic aptitude. Students in such programs are often separated into three levels of ability, and thus the programs have been called *XYZ grouping*. When the different ability groups are taught in separate classrooms, the grouping is referred to as *between-class* grouping. When the different groups are taught in a single classroom, the grouping is called *within-class* grouping.

Between-Class Grouping

We found a total of 49 controlled studies of between-class grouping (Table 13.1). Each of the studies compared the performance of students who had been taught in homogeneous classes with the performance of students taught in mixed-ability classes.

Achievement. In 28 of the 49 studies the level of achievement was higher for students taught in homogeneous classes, and in the remaining 21 studies the achievement level was higher in the mixed-ability classes. This box-score count provides insufficient evidence to reject the null hypothesis of no effect of comprehensive grouping plans on the overall achievement of students.

Effect sizes make things clearer. The average effect of grouping was to raise student performance by 0.06 standard deviations. This effect is statistically significant, $t(48) = 2.04, p < .05$, but it is by no means a large effect. Cohen (1977) describes effects of 0.8 standard deviations to be large, effects of 0.5 standard deviations to be moderate, and effects of 0.2 standard deviations to be small. By these standards, the average effect of between-class grouping is very small. It is equivalent to a gain on a grade-equivalent scale of about one-half month or a gain in percentile rank from the 50th to the 52nd percentile.

Of the 49 studies of between-class grouping, 40 reported results separately by ability level. Effects turned out to vary as a function of student aptitude. The average effect size was 0.12 for high-aptitude, 0.04 for middle-aptitude, and 0.00 for low-aptitude students. The average effect size of 0.12 for high-ability students was significantly higher than the average effect size of 0.00 for low-ability students, $t(38) = 2.45, p < .05$.

We undertook further analyses to determine whether results of the studies were related to study features. We examined 11 features of 4 different types: program characteristics, such as duration; characteristics of study methodology, such as the use of a control for teacher effects or historical effects; features of the study setting; and publication features. None of the 11 features, however, were significantly related to study results. Studies with different features seemed to produce similar results. For example, in the 20 studies in which grouping was restricted to a single subject area, student test scores rose by 0.09 standard deviations; in studies of comprehensive, full-day grouping, student scores rose by a similar amount, 0.03 standard deviations.

Self-Esteem. We found 15 studies of the effects of between-class grouping on student self-esteem (Table 13.2). In 6 of the 15 studies, self-concepts were more favorable overall in homogeneous classes; in the remaining 9 studies, self-concepts were more favorable in the heterogeneous classes. Only 1 of the 15 studies, however, found an average effect that was not trivial or small.

The average overall effect of grouping in the 15 studies was to decrease self-esteem scores by -0.06 standard deviations. This effect is both very small and statistically nonsignificant. Each of the 15 studies also reported results separately by ability level. The average effect size was -0.14 on high-aptitude students, -0.16 on middle-aptitude students, and 0.15 on low-aptitude students. The effects on high- and low-aptitude students were not significantly different.

Attitudes. A smaller number of studies investigated grouping effects on student attitudes toward the subject matter and toward school (Table 13.2). Four of the six studies of subject matter attitudes found trivial or small effects, one study found a moderate positive effect, and one found a strong positive effect. The average effect size in the six studies was 0.27. In each of the four studies of attitudes toward school, the effect size was trivial. The average effect size in the four studies was 0.04.

Other Programs for All Students

During the 1950s and 1960s, evaluators began examining effects of a special type of grouping program then in use in mathematics and reading education. In elementary schools, children were often assigned to ability groups within a class for their mathematics and reading work, and in some schools students from several different grades were put into homogenous classes for reading instruction without regard to grade level. The first type of program is called *within-class* grouping, as noted earlier; the second type became widely known during the 1960s as the *Joplin plan*.

Within-Class grouping. Nine of the 15 studies of within-class programs (Table 13.3, bottom section) reported a higher overall achievement level for students grouped within classes for instruction, and 6 studies reported a higher overall achievement level in classes taught without such grouping. In 5 of the 15 studies, differences in overall achievement level in the two types of classes were large enough to be statistically significant. In each of these 5 studies, the performance of students from the grouped class was higher. This box-score difference tends to favor within-class grouping over whole-class instruction, but the box-score count is not lopsided enough to be absolutely conclusive.

Analysis of size of effects makes the situation clearer. The average overall effect in the 15 studies was 0.17 standard deviations. This average effect was different from zero at a marginal level of significance, $t(14) = 2.10, p < .10$. Six of the studies of within-class grouping reported results separately by ability group. Effects were similar for students of high, middle, and low ability taught in grouped and ungrouped classrooms. The average effect size was 0.29 for the high-ability students, 0.17 for the middle-ability students, and 0.21 for the low-ability students. The difference in effect size for high- and low-aptitude students was not statistically significant.

Effects also varied in size in the 15 studies. The largest positive overall effect was 0.82 standard deviations; the largest negative effect was -0.22 standard deviations. Further analyses were carried out to determine whether such

Table 13.1

Major Features and Achievement Effect Sizes in 49 Studies of Between-Class Grouping

Study	Starting Grade	Course Content	Duration of Instruction	Overall	Effect Size	By Ability Group	
					High	Middle	Low
Adamson, 1972	7, 8	M	2 years	0.17	0.05	0.44	0.11
Atkinson & O'Connor, 1963							
Elementary level	6	C	1 year	0.52	0.38	0.52	0.66
Secondary level	7	M	2 years	0.26	0.55		-0.06
Bailey, 1968	10	M	1 year	-0.01	0.18	-0.19	
Barker Lunn, 1970							
Study I	2[a]	C	3 years	-0.01	-0.01	0.02	-0.03
Study II	3[a]	C	1 year	-0.27			
Barthelmess & Boyer, 1932	4	C	1 year	0.38	0.33	0.41	0.28
Barton, 1964	9	L	1 year	0.07	0.20		0.01
Berkun, Swanson, & Sawyer, 1966	3–5	L	1 year	0.32	0.44		0.21
Bicak, 1963	8	Sc	21 weeks	-0.02	-0.06		0.01
Billett, 1928	9	L	30 weeks	0.10	-0.04	0.02	0.33
Borg, 1964							
Elementary level	4, 6	C	1 year	0.30	0.52	0.38	0.02
Secondary level	7, 8	C	1 year	-0.21	-0.18	-0.25	-0.21
Breidenstine, 1937							
Elementary level	2–6	C	3 years	0.08	0.19	0.02	-0.17
Secondary level	7–9	C	2 years	-0.03	0.03	0.01	-0.08
Bremer, 1958	1	L	1 year	-0.12	-0.29	0.01	-0.07
Cochran, 1968	8	C	1 year	0.18[b]			
Daniels, 1961	1[a]	C	4 years	-0.27			
Drews, 1963	9	L	1 year	-0.05	-0.15	0.04	-0.04
Fick, 1963	7	C	1 year	0.20	0.40	-0.01	0.08
Flair, 1964	1	C	1 year	0.04	0.57	-0.16	0.01
Fogelman, Essen, & Tibbenham, 1978	7[a]	C	5 years	0.02			

Study	Grade	Subject	Duration				
Goldberg, Passow, & Justman, 1966	5	C	2 years	-0.13	-0.02	-0.20	-0.22
Hartill, 1936	5, 6	C	20 weeks	0.02	-0.15	0.06	0.26
Holy & Sutton, 1930	9	M	1 semester	0.28			
Johnston, 1973	1	C	1 year	-0.03			
Kline, 1964	9	C	4 years	-0.14	0.07	-0.14	-0.50
Koontz, 1961	4	C	1 year	-0.35	-0.23	-0.27	-0.42
Loomer, 1962	4–6	C	1 year	-0.02	0.01		-0.04
Lovell, 1960	10	L	1 year	0.25	0.30		0.05
Marascuilo & McSweeney, 1972	8	So	1 year	0.15	0.38	0.04	0.04
Martin, 1959	6–8	C	2 years	-0.07	0.19	-0.25	-0.16
Morgenstern, 1963	4	C	3 years	0.15	-0.17	0.12	0.59
Moses, 1966	4–6	L	1 semester	0.05	0.12	0.05	-0.01
Newbold, 1977	7–9[a]	C	1 year	0.08	0.13	-0.02	0.05
Peterson, 1967	7, 8	C	1 year	-0.09	0.12	-0.38	-0.01
Platz, 1965	9	Sc	1 semester	0.19	0.20	-0.08	0.44
Provus, 1960	4–6	M	1 semester	0.27	0.63	0.12	-0.08
Purdom, 1929	9	C	18 weeks	0.01	-0.02	-0.08	0.07
Rankin, Anderson, & Bergman, 1936	2–5	C	2 years	0.07	0.08	0.07	0.08
Svensson, 1962							
Elementary level	5	C	48 weeks	0.18	0.00	-0.11	-0.24
Secondary level	8	C	48 weeks	-0.09	-0.32	-0.29	-0.35
Thompson, 1974	11	So	1 year	-0.34	0.06	0.02	-0.10
Vakos, 1969	11	So	12 weeks	-0.01			
Wardrop, Cook, Quilling, Klausmeier, Espeseth, & Grout, 1967	3	M	1 semester	0.22	-0.01	1.20	
Wilcox, 1963	7	C	2 years	-0.07	0.11		-0.54
Willcutt, 1967	7	M	1 year	-0.05			-0.33
Worlton, 1928	4–7	C	3 years	0.39	0.47	0.33	0.40
Zweibelson, Bahmuller, & Lyman, 1965	9	So	1 year	0.11			

Note: C = combined; L = language arts; M = mathematics; Sc = science; So = social science.

[a] Grade level is approximate; it was estimated from the student ages reported in the study.

[b] ES is approximate; it was estimated from the direction and reported significance of the difference between treatment groups.

183

Table 13.2
Average Effect Sizes for Nonintellective Outcomes of Between-Class Grouping

Study	Self-Concept Overall	Self-Concept by Ability Group			Attitude toward Subject	Attitude toward School
		High	Middle	Low		
Adkison, 1968	0.06	−0.39		0.52		
Barker Lunn, 1970	−0.05	−0.07	−0.18	0.12		
Bicak, 1963					0.03	
Borg, 1964						
Elementary level	−0.28	−0.20	−0.36	−0.29		
Secondary level	−0.06	−0.01	−0.18	−0.03		
Deitrich, 1964	0.13	0.65	−0.18	−0.33		
Drews, 1963	−0.09	−0.98	0.16	0.56		
Dyson, 1967	0.13	−0.02		0.21		
Erickson, 1973	−0.60	−0.40		−0.81		
Fick, 1963	−0.04	0.00	−0.04	−0.08		
Goldberg, Passow, & Justman, 1966	−0.14	−0.31	−0.16	0.24		
Marascuilo & McSweeney, 1972	0.23	−0.24	−0.15	1.08	0.43	
Morgenstern, 1963	−0.15	0.32	−0.56	0.71		
Peterson, 1967						−0.02
Platz, 1965					0.05	
Sarthory, 1968	0.02	−0.01		0.04		
Tauber, 1963	0.20	0.01	0.08	0.48		
Wilcox, 1963	−0.29	−0.40		−0.13	−0.12	0.01
Willcutt, 1967					0.21	0.15
Zweibelson, Bahnmuller, & Lyman, 1965					1.00	0.03

differences in overall effects were related to study features. Two of the features showed a significant relationship to study outcome: (1) control for instructor effects, and (2) the use of flexible versus permanent ability groups in classes. Effects were significantly greater in studies without a control for instructor effects, that is, in studies in which different instructors taught in the grouped and ungrouped classes. Effects were also significantly greater in those studies with fixed rather than flexible assignment to ability groups. Because of the small number of studies involved, however, these findings should be considered tentative.

Joplin Plan. A total of 16 studies investigated effects of the Joplin plan for cross-grade grouping in one or two subjects (Table 13.3, top section). Of these studies, 12 found that students achieved more when taught under the Joplin plan, and 3 studies found that students achieved less; for 1 study the effect size was zero. Although suggestive, these box-score results do not provide conclusive evidence that the Joplin plan has positive effects on student achievement.

The average effect size in the 16 studies was 0.23. This effect was different from zero at a marginal level of significance, $t(15) = 2.03, p < .10$, but it was not significantly different from the average effect found in programs of between-class grouping. Like effects of other grouping programs, Joplin plan effects varied greatly, from an unfavorable effect of -0.95 to a highly positive effect of 0.89. Because of the small number of studies of the Joplin plan that were available to us, however, it was not possible to carry out further analyses of relations between study features and study outcomes.

The important point to note about grouping programs designed for all students is that they raise overall achievement levels by a very small amount on the average: about 0.05 standard deviations for between-class programs, 0.15 standard deviations for within-class programs in mathematics, and 0.25 standard deviations for Joplin plans in reading. The gains are not significantly different from one another, but they are large enough to be considered statistically different from a zero gain.

Effects of grouping also vary as a function of student ability level. Effects are clearest on higher aptitude students. They are smaller, but not negative, for middle- and low-aptitude students. It seems likely that teachers dealing with above-average groups introduce material that is more challenging into the classroom. Teachers apparently teach middle- and low-aptitude groups in much the same way that they teach mixed-ability ones.

Nor does ability grouping have devastating effects on student self-esteem. Overall, effects of grouping on self-esteem are near zero, and effects may be slightly positive for low-ability students and slightly negative for high-aptitude ones. Talented students may become slightly less satisfied with themselves when taught with their intellectual peers; slower students may gain slightly in self-confidence when they are taught with other slower learners.

Finally, it is impossible to say with statistical certainty why certain programs produce positive effects and others produce negative ones. Slavin (1987, 1988) has speculated that grouping has maximum positive effects on student achievement when (1) it is done for only one or two subjects, (2) students remain in mixed-ability classes most of the day, (3) grouping greatly reduces heterogeneity in a specific skill, (4) group assignments are frequently reassessed, and (5) teachers vary the level and pace of instruction according to students' needs. We investigated each of these factors in this meta-analysis, and we found no direct evidence that any of them were significantly related to grouping effects.

Separate Grouping of Gifted Students

Some grouping programs are designed especially to meet the needs of gifted and talented students. Such programs provide special instruction for such students in separate classrooms or in separate groups in otherwise conventional classrooms. Students in programs for the gifted and talented are typically a distinctive group. They are unusually high

Table 13.3
Major Features and Achievement Effect Sizes in Studies of the Joplin Plan and Within-Class Grouping

Study	Starting Grade	Course Content	Weeks of Instruction	Effect Size			
				Overall	By Ability Group		
					High	Middle	Low
Studies of the Joplin Plan							
Carson & Thompson, 1964	4–6	R	1 year	0.00			
Cartwright & McIntosh, 1972	1–2	C	2 years	−0.35			
Chismar, 1972	4–8	R	1 year	0.10			
DeGrow, 1964	4–6	R	1 year	0.03			
Green & Riley, 1963	4–6	R	1 year	0.36			
Halliwell, 1963	1–3	R & S	1 year	0.66			
Hart, 1959	4–5	R	1 year	0.89			
Ingram, 1960	1	R	3 years	0.64			
Jones, Moore, & Van Devender, 1967	1	R	3 years	0.33			
Kierstead, 1963	3–8	R	1 year	−0.01	−0.04	−0.01	0.08
Moorhouse, 1964	4	R	5 semesters	0.50	0.61	0.74	0.34
Morgan & Stucker, 1960	5–6	R	1 year	0.36	0.31		0.46
Nichols, 1969	1	R	2 years	−0.95			
Rothrock, 1961	4–5	R	1 year	0.48			
Russell, 1946	4–6	R	2 years	0.01			
Skapski, 1960	3	R	3 years	0.57	0.63	0.52	

Studies of Within-Class Grouping

Study	Grade	Subject	Duration				
Bierden, 1970	7	M	1 year	-0.16			
Campbell, 1965	7	M	1 year	-0.16	0.23	-0.37	-0.32
Cignetti, 1974	7, 8	O	9 weeks	0.09	0.27	0.22	-0.41
Dewar, 1963	6	M	23 weeks	0.36	0.29	0.29	0.43
Eddleman, 1971	5	M	9 weeks	-0.16			
Harrah, 1955	7, 8, 9	C	1 semester	-0.03			
Jones, 1948	4	C	1 year	0.29	0.24	0.27	0.37
Monroe, 1922	2, 5, 7	C	1 year	-0.08			
Mortlock, 1970	11	M	1 year	-0.22			
Putbrese, 1971	4	M	1 year	0.10			
Shields, 1927	7	L	6 weeks	0.82			
Slavin & Karweit, 1984	3-6	M	1 semester	0.43	0.41	0.38	0.50
Smith, 1960	2-5	M	1 semester	0.41	0.28	0.25	0.68
Spence, 1959	4-6	M	30 weeks	0.60			
Wallen & Vowles, 1960	6	M	1 semester	0.27			

Note: C = combined; L = language arts; M = mathematics; O = others; R = reading; S = spelling.

and unusually homogeneous in academic aptitude. Methods and materials used in programs for the gifted also are often distinctive. Those in charge of such programs usually believe that their students have special needs, and the teachers and program administrators often have strong commitments to meeting these needs. The result is typically a highly challenging educational program.

Separate Classes for the Gifted

Many of the programs provide instruction for the gifted in separate classrooms. We found reports on 25 controlled evaluations of programs that provided separate classes for gifted students (Table 13.4, top section).

Achievement. Of the 25 studies, 19 found that talented students achieved more when they were taught in homogenous classrooms. In the remaining 6 studies, performance of talented students was better when they were taught in mixed-ability classes. In 11 of the 25 studies, the difference in achievement of talented students taught in homogenous versus mixed-ability classes was great enough to be considered statistically significant. Each of these 11 studies favored homogeneous grouping of talented students.

The average effect size in the 25 studies was 0.33. This effect was significantly greater than the average effect of 0.06 standard deviations for between-class programs for representative populations, $t(73) = 4.43, p < .001$. The effect of 0.33 standard deviations was also significantly greater than an effect size of zero, $t(24) = 4.85$, $p < .001$. An effect size of 0.33 means that teaching talented students in homogeneous rather than mixed-ability classes raised their scores on achievement tests by 0.33 standard deviations. To interpret this effect more fully, it is useful to refer to areas of the standard normal curve. Approximately 63% of the area of this curve falls below a z-score of 0.33. We can conclude, therefore, that in the typical study, approximately 63% of the talented students in the special classes outperformed the typical talented student in the mixed-ability classes.

Although the effect of separate classes for the gifted was modest in the typical study in this group, effects varied in size from a low of −0.27 to a high of 1.25 standard deviations. The variation was great enough to lead us to suspect that factors other than grouping played a role in determining study outcome. However, we were unable to establish through further analyses that study features were significantly related to achievement outcomes. The small number of studies available for analysis might account in part for this failure to find significant relations.

Self-Esteem. Six of the 25 studies of separate classes for the gifted investigated effects on self-concept. In 4 (Table 13.4) of the 6 studies, self-concepts were more favorable when the talented students were taught in separate classes. In the remaining 2 studies, self-concepts were more positive when talented students were taught in heterogeneous classes. The size of the effect was small or trivial, however, in all but one of the studies. The average effect size in all 6 studies was 0.02.

Attitudes. Very few of the 25 studies examined attitudinal effects of separate classes for gifted students. One study (Mikkelson, 1963) examined effects on subject matter attitudes and found a trivial effect. Two studies (Enzmann, 1963; Tremaine, 1979) reported strong positive effects on student attitudes toward school.

Within-Class Programs for the Gifted

We also found reports on 4 within-class programs for the gifted (Table 13.4, bottom section.) In each of these studies, the students taught in the grouped class received the higher examination scores. In 3 of the 4 studies, the difference in examination scores of grouped and ungrouped classes was statistically significant. Thus, the set of 4 provides good evidence that gifted students who are given separate instruction within otherwise conventional classes benefit from this special treatment. The average effect size in the 4 studies was 0.62. It is statistically unlikely that an effect this large would be found by chance, $t(3) = 4.77, p < .05$.

Table 13.4
Major Features and Effect Sizes in 26 Studies of Grouping Programs Designed Especially for Talented Students

Study	Starting Grade	Course Content	Duration of Instruction	Effect Size Achievement	Effect Size Self-Concept
Separate Classes for the Gifted					
Alam, 1969	3	C	7 years	0.52	0.10
Becker, 1963	6	C	1 year	-0.18	0.01
Bell, 1959	5	C	1 year	0.68	
Bent, McDonald, Rothney, & Sowards, 1969	4	C	4 years	0.22	
Cluff, 1964	4	C	2 years	0.23	
Doolin, 1956	11	So	26 weeks	0.27	0.18
Enzmann, 1963	9	C	4 years	0.28	
Evans & Marken, 1982	6–8	C	2 years	-0.05	
Gray & Hollingworth, 1931	2–4[a]	C	3 years	0.17	
Hinze, 1957					
Elementary level	4–6	C	1 semester	-0.01	
Secondary level	7, 8	C	1 semester	-0.01	
Howell, 1962	9	C	1 year	1.25	
Karnes, McCoy, Zehrbach, Wollersheim, & Clarizio, 1963	2–5	C	2 1/2 years	0.52	
Kellogg, 1960	4	C	3 years	0.64	
Koukeyan, 1976	4–6	M	26 weeks	-0.13	
Luttrell, 1959	6	C	28 weeks	0.70	-0.09
Mahler, 1962	7–8	C	1 year	0.20	
McCall, 1928	2–6	C	2 years	0.60	
McCown, 1961	10	C	3 years	0.36	
Mikkelsoen, 1963	7	M	1 year	-0.27	-0.38
Rodgers, 1979	3–6	O	1 year	-0.38	
Schwartz, 1942					
Elementary level	1–6	C	1 semester	0.32	
Secondary level	7, 8	O	1 semester	0.37	
Simpson & Martinson, 1961					
Elementary level	5, 6	C	1 year	0.48	
Secondary level	8, 11, 12	C	1 year	0.44	
Tremaine, 1979	12	C	1 year	0.55	0.29
Within-Class Grouping					
Ivey, 1965	4	M	28 weeks	0.50	
Long, 1957	11	M	25 weeks	0.38	
Simpson & Martinson, 1961	1, 5, 6	C	1 year	1.00	
Ziehl, 1962	2, 3	C	4 years	0.62	

Note: C = combined; L = language arts; M = mathematics; So = social science; O = others.
[a] These are approximate grades, estimated from ages reported in the study.

189

Programs in which talented students are grouped together for instruction produce clearly positive results. The gifted students in such programs gain more academically than they do when taught in mixed-ability classes. Two characteristics of special programs for gifted students may account for their effectiveness. First, the students in such programs are highly selected. They are unusually high and unusually homogeneous in academic aptitude. None of the groups in XYZ programs are so distinct in aptitude. Because the intellectual level is so high and the variation so low in separate classes for the gifted, adaptation of instruction to special class needs is possible. Second, teachers in such classes usually have a strong commitment to meeting the needs of gifted students. The opportunity for adapting instruction exists, and teachers of classes for the gifted usually make use of this opportunity.

Accelerated Classes for the Gifted

Acceleration of the gifted can take a variety of forms. Programs encompass everything from radical acceleration of individual students to more modest programs of advancement via summer school work. We were able to find 26 studies of accelerated instruction in the literature. A detailed description of results from our analyses of these 26 programs has already been published (J. A. Kulik & Kulik, 1984), and so we present only a summary of our results here.

The 26 studies did not examine effects of radical acceleration but instead evaluated more modest forms of rapid advancement. These included grade skipping, compressing a curriculum for talented students (e.g., 4 years in 3), and extending the calendar to speed up the progress of such students (e.g., completing the work of 4 years in 3 school years with 5 summer sessions).

The 26 studies used two different study designs that reflected fundamentally different research purposes. For one group of studies, the researcher's purpose was to determine whether accelerated students learned more than initially comparable students who were not accel-erated. In these studies, students in the groups being compared were initially equivalent in age and aptitude, but because one group was accelerated and the other was not, the two groups differed in grade level when educational outcomes were measured. The second group of studies had a different purpose. Talented accelerated students often ended up in the same classrooms with talented nonaccelerates who were a year or more older. The purpose of this second group of studies was to determine whether the younger accelerates performed as well on tests as did the older non-accelerates. In studies of this type, the groups being compared were equivalent in grade level and intelligence quotient when outcomes were measured, but the groups differed in chronological age and in mental age.

These two types of studies produced distinctly different results. All of the 13 studies with same-age control groups showed greater achievement in the accelerated classes; the average effect size in these studies was 0.88. The average effect size in the 13 studies with older comparison groups was 0.05. Studies with older comparison groups were as likely to produce positive as negative differences between groups.

Only a small number of studies investigated other outcomes of acceleration, and findings were not entirely consistent from study to study. On the average, however, acceleration appeared to have little or no effect on attitude toward school or school subjects. Acceleration had a strong effect on vocational plans in 2 studies but trivial effects on student plans in 4 other studies. The effect on vocational plans apparently vaired as a function of program type. There was no evidence of consistent positive or negative effects from acceleration on popularity, adjustment, or student participation in school activities.

This meta-analysis showed that gifted students are able to handle the academic challenge that accelerated programs provide. Two major findings supported this conclusion. First, talented youngsters who were accelerated into higher grades performed as well as the talented older pupils already in those grades. Second, in the subjects in which they were accelerated, talented accelerates showed almost a year's advancement over talented same-age nonaccelerates.

Summary

The evidence is clear that high-aptitude and gifted students benefit academically from programs that provide separate instruction for them. Academic benefits are positive but small when the grouping is done as a part of a broader program for students of all abilities. Benefits are positive and moderate in size in programs that are specially designed for gifted students. Academic benefits are striking and large in programs of acceleration for gifted students.

Evidence is less clear about noncognitive outcomes of programs of separate instruction for high-aptitude and gifted students. Despite their importance, such outcomes are not studied frequently by educational researchers, and only tentative conclusions can be drawn. One of these conclusions is that ability-grouping programs have little or no consistent overall effect on student self-esteem. The programs certainly do not lead talented students to become smug, nor do they cause student self-esteem to plummet. The available literature also suggests some program-specific effects of grouping. For example, certain programs of accelerated instruction clearly have an effect on the vocational plans of youngsters; other programs do not. The design of specific programs undoubtedly plays a role.

Oakes (1985) and Slavin (1987, 1988) have reached conclusions different from ours about programs of separate instruction for high-aptitude and gifted students. Their conclusions, however, are based on subjective reviews and informal analyses of the literature on grouping. Oakes, for example, bases her conclusions on an idiosyncratic review of other reviews. Slavin's conclusion about factors that affect grouping effectiveness should also be regarded as speculative. Slavin offers no statistical tests of his hypotheses, and our statistical tests provide no support for his speculations.

Whereas Oakes and Slavin believe that programs of separate instruction for high-aptitude and gifted students are unnecessary, ineffective, and unfair, we conclude that the opposite is true. Programs of separate instruction for high-aptitude and gifted students are usually effective, they are fair to both gifted and talented students and to other students in our schools, and they are necessary if we wish to cultivate our nation's resources of intellectual talent.

REFERENCES

Adamson, D. P. (1972). Differentiated multi-track grouping vs. uni-track educational grouping in mathematics. *Dissertation Abstracts International, 32,* 3771A. (University Microfilms No. 72–2564)

Adkison, M. R. (1968). A comparative study of pupil attitudes under conditions of ability and heterogeneous grouping. *Dissertation Abstracts, 28,* 3869A. (University Microfilms No. 66-3322)

Alam, S. J. (1969). A comparative study of gifted students enrolled in separate and regular curriculums. *Dissertation Abstracts, 29,* 3354A. (University Microfilms No. 69-6057)

Atkinson, J. W., & O'Connor, P. (1963). *Effects of ability grouping in schools related to individual differences in achievement-related motivation* (final report). Ann Arbor: University of Michigan. (ERIC Document Reproduction Service Number ED 003 249)

Bailey, H. P. (1968). A study of the effectiveness of ability grouping on success in first year algebra. *Dissertation Abstracts, 28,* 3061A. (University Microfilms No. 68-1249)

Barker Lunn, J. C. (1970). *Streaming in the primary school.* Hove, Sussex, England: King, Thorne, & Stace.

Barthelmess, H. M., & Boyer, P. A. (1932). An evaluation of ability grouping. *Journal of Educational Research, 26,* 284–294.

Barton, D. P. (1964). An evaluation of ability grouping in ninth grade English. *Dissertation Abstracts, 25,* 1731. (University Microfilms No. 64-9939)

Becker, L. J. (1963). An analysis of the science and mathematics achievement of gifted sixth grade children enrolled in segregated, partially segregated and nonsegregated classes. *Dissertation Abstracts, 24,* 1446. (University Microfilms No. 63-6737)

Bell, M. E. (1959). A comparative study of mentally gifted children heterogeneously and homogeneously grouped. *Dissertation Abstracts, 19,* 2509. (University Microfilms No. 00-22,982)

Bent, L. G., McDonald, R., Rothney, J., & Sowards, W. (1969). *Grouping of the gifted: An experimental approach.* Peoria, IL: Bradley University. (ERIC Document Reproduction Service No. ED 040 519)

Berkun, M. M., Swanson, L. W., & Sawyer, D. M. (1966). An experiment on homogeneous grouping for reading in elementary classes. *Journal of Educational Research, 59,* 413–414.

Bicak, L. (1963). Achievement in eighth grade science by heterogeneous and homogeneous classes. *Dissertation Abstracts, 23,* 2367. (University Microfilms No. 63-1192)

Bierden, J. E. (1970). Behavioral objectives and flexible grouping in seventh grade mathematics. *Journal for Research in Mathematics Education, 1,* 207–217.

Billett, R. O. (1928). A controlled experiment to determine the advantages of homogeneous grouping. *Educational Research Bulletin, 7,* 190–196.

Billett, R. O. (1932). *The administration and supervision of homogeneous groupings.* Columbus: Ohio State University Press.

Borg, W. R. (1964). *An evaluation of ability grouping.* Logan: Utah State University. (ERIC Document Reproduction Service Number ED 001 177)

Borg, W. R. (1966). *Ability Grouping in the Public schools* (2nd ed.). Madison, WI: Dembar Educational Research.

Breidenstine, A. G. (1937). The educational achievement of pupils in differentiated and undifferentiated groups. *Journal of Experimental Education, 5,* 91–135.

Bremer, N. (1958). First grade achievement under different plans of grouping. *Elementary English, 35,* 324–326.

Campbell, A. L. (1965). A comparison of the effectiveness of two methods of class organization for the teaching of arithmetics in junior high school. *Dissertation Abstracts, 26,* 813–814. (University of Microfilms Order No. 65-06726)

Carson, R. M., & Thompson, J. M. (1964). The Joplin plan and traditional reading groups. *Elementary School Journal, 65,* 38–43.

Cartwright, G. P., & McIntosh, D. K. (1972). Three approaches to grouping procedures for the education of disadvantaged primary school children. *Journal of Educational Research, 65,* 425–429.

Chismar, M. H. (1972). A study of the effectiveness of cross-level grouping of middle school underachievers for reading instruction. *Dissertation Abstracts International, 32,* 5101A. (University Microfilms No. 72-9249)

Cignetti, M. J. (1974). A study of intraclass grouping and traditional groupings on students' terminal achievements during the last nine weeks in first semester typewriting. *Dissertation Abstracts International, 35,* 5765A. (University Microfilms No. 75-05121)

Cluff, J. E. (1964). The effect of experimentation and class reorganization on the scholastic achievement of selected gifted sixth grade pupils in Wichita, Kansas. *Dissertation Abstracts, 25,* 1676–1677. (University Microfilms No. 64-10,059)

Cochran, J. R. (1968). Grouping students in junior high school. *Educational Leadership, 18,* 414–419.

Cohen, J. (1977). *Statistical power analysis for the behavioral sciences* (revised ed.). New York: Academic.

Daniels, J. C. (1961). The effects of streaming in the primary school: Comparison of streamed and unstreamed schools. *British Journal of Educational Psychology, 31,* 119–126.

DeGrow, G. S. (1964). A study of the effects of the use of vertical reading ability groupings for reading classes as compared with heterogeneous groupings in grades four, five, and six in the Port Huron area schools of Michigan over a three-year period. *Dissertation Abstracts, 24,* 3166–3167. (University Microfilms No. 64-804)

Deitrich, F. R. (1964). Comparison of sociometric patterns of sixth-grade pupils in the school systems: Ability grouping compared with heterogeneous grouping. *Journal of Educational Research, 57,* 507–513.

Dewar, J. A. (1963). Grouping for arithmetic instruction in sixth grade. *Elementary School Journal, 63,* 266–269.

Doolin, R. B. (1956). An experiment with moderately gifted children in the public high schools of Cedar Rapids, Iowa. *Dissertation Abstracts, 16,* 111. (University Microfilms No. 56-2170)

Drews, E. M. (1963). *Student abilities grouping patterns and classroom interactions.* East Lansing: Office of Research and Publications, Michigan State University.

Dyson, E. (1967). A study of ability grouping and the self-concept. *Journal of Educational Research, 60,* 403–405.

Eddleman, V. K. (1971). A comparison of the effectiveness of two methods of class organization for arithmetic instruction in grade five. *Dissertation Abstracts International, 32,* 1744A. (University Microfilms No. 71-25035)

Enzmann, A. M. (1963). A comparison of academic achievement of gifted students enrolled in regular and in separate curriculums. *Gifted Child Quarterly, 7,* 176–179.

Erickson, G. R. (1973). A study of the self-esteem and academic self-concepts of ability- and randomly-grouped ninth graders. *Dissertation Abstracts International, 33,* 5550A. (University Microfilms No. 73-10548)

Evans, E. D., & Marken D. (1982). Multiple outcome assessment of special class placement for gifted students: A comparative study. *Gifted Child Quarterly, 26,* 126–132.

Fick, W. W. (1963). The effectiveness of ability grouping in seventh grade core classes. *Dissertation Abstracts, 23,* 2753. (University Microfilms No. 63-794)

Findley, W. G., & Bryan, M. M. (1971). *Ability grouping: 1970, status, impact and alternatives.* Athens: University of Georgia, Center for Educational Improvement. (ERIC Document Reproduction Service No. ED 060 595)

Flair, M. D. (1964). The effect of grouping on achievement and attitudes toward learning of first grade pupils. *Dissertation Abstracts, 25,* 6430. (University Microfilms No. 65-03,259)

Fogelman, K., Essen, J., & Tibbenham, A. (1978). Ability grouping in secondary schools and attainment. *Educational Studies, 4,* 201–212.

Glass, G. V. (1976). Primary, secondary, and meta-analysis of research. *Educational Researcher, 5,* 3–8.

Glass, G. V., McGaw, B., & Smith, M. L. (1981). *Meta-analysis in social research.* Beverly Hills: Sage.

Goldberg, M. L., Passow, A. H., & Justman, J. (1966). *The effects of ability grouping.* New York: Teacher's College.

Gray, H. A., & Hollingworth, L. S. (1931). The achievement of gifted children enrolled and not enrolled in special opportunity classes. *Journal of Educational Research, 24,* 255–261.

Green, D. R., & Riley, H. W. (1963). Interclass grouping for reading instruction in the middle grades. *Journal of Experimental Education, 31,* 273–278.

Halliwell, J. W. (1963). A comparison of pupil achievement in graded and nongraded primary classrooms. *Journal of Experimental Education, 32,* 59–64.

Harrah, D. D. (1955). A study of the effectiveness of five kinds of grouping in the classroom. *Dissertation Abstracts, 16,* 715. (University Microfilms No. 00-16039)

Hart, R. H. (1959). The effectiveness of an approach to the problem of varying abilities in teaching reading. *Journal of Educational Research, 52,* 228 231.

Hartill, R. W. (1936). *Homogeneous grouping.* New York: Bureau of Publications, Teacher's College, Columbia University.

Hedges, L. V., & Olkin, I. (1985). *Statistical methods for meta-analysis.* Orlando, FL: Academic Press.

Hinze R. H. (1957). Achievement of fast learners in a partially segregated elementary school program, with special reference to science instruction. *Dissertation Abstracts, 18,* 496. (University Microfilms No. 58-4203)

Holy, T. C., & Sutton, D. H. (1930). Ability grouping in the ninth grade. *Educational Research Bulletin, 9,* 419–422.

Howell, W. J. (1962). Grouping of talented students leads to better academic achievement in secondary school. *Bulletin of NASSP, 46,* 67–73.

Hunter, J. E., Schmidt, F. L., & Jackson, G. B. (1982). *Meta-analysis: Cumulating research findings across studies.* Beverly Hills, CA: Sage.

Ingram, V. (1960). Flint evaluates its primary cycle. *Elementary School Journal, 61,* 76–80.

Ivey, J. D. (1965). Computation skills: Results of acceleration. *The Arithmetic Teacher, 12,* 39–42.

Johnston, H. J. (1973). The effect of grouping patterns on first-grade children's academic achievement and personal and social development. *Dissertation Abstracts International, 34,* 2461A. (University Microfilms No. 73-25, 893)

Jones, D. M. (1948). An experiment in adaptation to individual differences. *Journal of Educational Psychology, 39,* 247–272.

Jones, J. C., Moore, J. W., & Van Devender, F. (1967). A comparison of pupil achievement after one and one-half and three years in a nongraded program. *Journal of Educational Research, 61,* 75–77.

Karnes, M. B., McCoy, G., Zehrbach, R. R., Wollersheim, J. P., & Clarizio, H. F. (1963). The efficacy of two organizational plans for underachieving intellectually gifted children. *Exceptional Children, 29,* 438–446.

Kellogg, R. M. (1960). An analysis of the achievement of segregated and non-segregated gifted pupils. *Dissertation Abstracts, 21,* 2630. (University Microfilms No. 60-5240)

Kierstead, R. (1963). A comparison and evaluation of two methods of organization of the teaching of reading. *Journal of Educational Research, 56,* 317–321.

Kline, R. E. (1964). A longitudinal study of the effectiveness of the track plan in the secondary schools of a metropolitan community. *Dissertation Abstracts, 25,* 324. (University Microfilms No. 64-4257)

Koontz, W. F. (1961). A study of achievement as a function of homogeneous grouping. *Journal of Experimental Education, 30,* 249–253.

Koukeyan, B. B. (1976). Evaluation of a vertical-horizontal enrichment program for the math-gifted students in fourth, fifth and sixth grades. *Dissertation Abstracts International, 37,* 5587A. (University Microfilms No. 77-04835)

Kulik, C.-L. C. (1985, August). *Effects of inter-class grouping on student achievement and self-esteem.* Paper presented at the annual meeting of the American Psychological Association, Los Angeles. (ERIC Document Reproduction Service No. ED 263 492)

Kulik, C.-L. C., & Kulik, J. A. (1982). Effects of ability grouping on secondary school students: A meta-analysis of evaluation findings. *American Educational Research Journal, 19,* 415–428.

Kulik, J. A., & Kulik, C.-L. C. (1984). Effects of accelerated instruction on students. *Review of Educational Research, 54,* 409–426.

Kulik, J. A., & Kulik, C.-L. C. (1987). Effects of ability grouping on student achievement. *Equity and Excellence, 23,* 22–30.

Kulik, J. A., & Kulik, C.-L. C. (1989). Meta-analysis in educational research [monograph]. *International Journal of Educational Research, 13,* 221–340.

Long, R. G. (1957). A comparative study of the effects of an enriched program for the talented in advanced algebra classes. *Dissertation Abstracts, 18,* 529. (University Microfilms No. 00-24831)

Loomer, B. M. (1962). Ability grouping and its effects upon individual achievement. *Dissertation Abstracts, 23,* 1581. (University Microfilms No. 62-4982)

Lovell, J. T. (1960). Bay High School experiment. *Educational Leadership, 17,* 383–387.

Luttrell, J. (1959). A comparative investigation of academic achievement and personality development of gifted sixth grade pupils in a special class and in regular classrooms in the public school of Greensboro, North Carolina. *Dissertation Abstracts, 19,* 2536. (University Microfilms No. 59-52)

Mahler, F. L. (1962). A study of achievement differences in selected junior high school gifted students heterogeneously or homogeneously grouped. *Dissertation Abstracts, 22,* 2267. (University Microfilms No. 61-5675)

Marascuilo, L. A., & McSweeney, M. (1972). Teaching and minority student attitudes and performance. *Urban Education, 6,* 303–319.

Martin, W. B. (1959). Effects of ability grouping on junior high school achievement. *Dissertation Abstracts, 19,* 2810. (University Microfilms No. 59-1108)

McCall, W. A. (1928). Comparison of the educational progress of bright pupils in accelerated and in regular classes. *Twenty-seventh yearbook of the National Society for the Study of Education, Part II.* Bloomington, IL: Public School Publishing Co.

McCown, G. W. (1961). A critical evaluation of the four track curriculum program of the District of Columbia Senior High School with recommendations for improvements. *Dissertation Abstracts, 21,* 2558. (University Microfilms No. 60-4928)

Mikkelson, J. (1963). An experimental study of selective grouping and acceleration in junior high school mathematics. *Dissertation Abstracts, 23,* 4226. (University Microfilms No. 63-2323)

Monroe, W. S. (1922). *Relation of sectioning a class to the effectiveness of instruction* (Bulletin No. 11). Urbana: Bureau of Educational Research, College of Education, University of Illinois.

Moorhouse, W. F. (1964). Interclass grouping for reading instruction. *Elementary School Journal, 64,* 280–286.

Morgan, E. F., Jr., & Stucker, G. R. (1960). The Joplin Plan of reading vs. a traditional method. *Journal of Educational Psychology, 51,* 69–73.

Morgenstern, A. (1963). A comparison of the effects of heterogeneous and homogeneous (ability) grouping on the academic achievement and personal-social adjustment of sixth-grade children. *Dissertation Abstracts, 24,* 1054. (University Microfilms No. 63-6560)

Mortlock, R. S. (1970). Provision for individual differences in eleventh grade mathematics using flexible grouping based on achievement of behavioral objectives: An exploratory study. *Dissertation Abstracts International, 30,* 3643A. (University Microfilms No. 70-04148)

Moses, P. J. (1966). A study of the effects of inter-class grouping on achievement in reading. *Dissertation Abstracts, 26,* 4342. (University Microfilms No. 66-741)

National Education Association. (1968). *Ability grouping* (Research Summary 1968-S3). Washington, DC: Research Division, National Education Association.

Newbold, D. (1977). *The Banbury group enquiry.* Oxford, England: NEER.

Nichols, N. (1969). Interclass grouping for reading instruction. *Educational Leadership Research Supplement, 26,* 588–592.

Oakes, J. (1985). *Keeping track.* New Haven: Yale University Press.

Peterson, R. L. (1967). An experimental study of the effects of ability grouping in grades seven and eight. *Dissertation Abstracts, 28,* 130A. (University Microfilms No. 67-7768)

Platz, E. F. (1965). The effectiveness of ability grouping in general science classes. *Dissertation*

Abstracts, 26, 1459–1460A. (University Microfilms No. 65-6914)

Provus, M. M. (1960). Ability grouping in mathematics. *Elementary School Journal, 60,* 391–398.

Purdom, T. L. (1929). *Value of homogeneous grouping.* Baltimore: Warwick & York.

Putbrese, L. M. (1971). An investigation into the effect of selected patterns of grouping upon arithmetic achievement. *Dissertation Abstracts International, 32,* 5113A. (University Microfilms No. 72-08388)

Rankin, P. T., Anderson, C. T., & Bergman, W. G. (1936). Ability grouping in the Detroit individualization experiment. In G. M. Whipple (Ed.), *The grouping of pupils. Thirty-fifth yearbook, Part I, National Society for the Study of Education* (pp. 277–288). Chicago: University of Chicago Press.

Rodgers, B. S. (1979). Effects of an enrichment program screening process of the self-concept and others-concept of gifted elementary children. *Dissertation Abstracts International, 40,* 3906A. (University Microfilms No. 80-02135)

Rosenthal, R. (1984). *Meta-analytic procedures for social research.* Beverly Hills, CA: Sage.

Rothrock, D. G. (1961). Heterogeneous, homogeneous or individualized approach to reading. *Elementary English, 38,* 233–235.

Russell, D. H. (1946). Inter-class grouping for reading instruction in the intermediate grades. *Journal of Educational Research, 39,* 462–470.

Sarthory, J. A. (1968). The effects of ability grouping in multi-cultural school situations. *Dissertation Abstracts, 29,* 457A. (University Microfilms No. 68-11664)

Schwartz, W. P. (1942). *Effects of homogeneous classification on the scholastic achievement and personality development of gifted pupils in the elementary and junior high school.* Unpublished doctoral dissertation, New York University, New York.

Shields, J. M. (1927). Teaching reading through ability-grouping. *Journal of Educational Methods, 7,* 7–9.

Simpson, R. E., & Martinson, R. A. (1961). *Educational programs for gifted pupils: A report to the California legislature prepared pursuant to Section 2 of Chapter 2385, Statutes of 1957.* Sacramento: California State Department of Education. (ERIC Document Reproduction Service Number ED 100 072)

Skapski, M. K. (1960). Ungraded primary reading program. *Elementary School Journal, 61,* 41–45.

Slavin, R. E. (1987). Ability grouping and student achievement in elementary schools: A best-evidence synthesis. *Review of Educational Research, 57,* 293–336.

Slavin, R. E. (1988). Synthesis of research on grouping in elementary and secondary schools. *Educational Leadership, 46*(1), 67–76.

Slavin, R. E., & Karweit, N. (1984, April). *Within-class ability grouping and student achievement.* Paper presented at the annual meeting of the American Educational Research Association, New Orleans.

Smith, W. M. (1960). The effect of intra-class ability grouping on arithmetic achievement in grades two through five. *Dissertation Abstracts, 21,* 563. (University Microfilms No. 60-02984)

Spence, E. S. (1959). Intra-class grouping of pupils for instruction in arithmetic in the intermediate grades of the elementary school. *Dissertation Abstracts, 19,* 1682. (University Microfilms No. 58-5635)

Svensson, N.-E. (1962). *Ability grouping and scholastic achievement.* Stockholm: Alqvist & Wiksell.

Tauber, M. C. (1963). An experimental study of the relationship between certain selected social and emotional factors and ability grouping of high school students. *Dissertation Abstracts International* 3263. (University Microfilms No. 63-1353)

Thompson, G. W. (1974). The effects of ability grouping upon achievement in eleventh grade American history. *Journal of Experimental Education, 42,* 76–79.

Tremaine, C. D. (1979). Do gifted programs make a difference? *Gifted Child Quarterly. 23,* 500–517.

Vakos, H. N. (1969). The effect of part-time grouping on achievement in social studies. *Dissertation Abstracts International, 30,* 2271A. (University Microfilms No. 69-20,066)

Wallen, N. E., & Vowles, R. O. (1960). The effect of intraclass grouping on arithmetic achievement in the sixth grade. *Journal of Educational Psychology, 51,* 159–163.

Wardrop, J. L., Cook, D. M., Quilling, M., Klausmeier, H. J., Espeseth, C., & Grout, C. (1967). *Research and development activities in R/I units of two elementary schools of Manitowoc, Wisconsin, 1966–1967.* Madison: University of Wisconsin Research and Development Center for Cognitive Learning. (ERIC Document Reproduction Service No. ED 019 796)

Whipple, G. M. (Ed.). (1936). *The grouping of pupils. Thirty-fifth Yearbook, Part I, National Society for the Study of Education, 35.* Chicago: University of Chicago Press.

Wilcox, J. (1963). A search for the multiple effects of grouping upon the growth and behavior of junior high school pupils. *Dissertation Abstracts, 24,* 205. (University Microfilms No. 63-4574)

Willcutt, R. E. (1967). Ability grouping by content subject areas in junior high school mathematics.

Dissertation Abstracts, 28, 2152A. (University Microfilms No. 67-16,440)

Worlton, J. T. (1928). The effect of homogeneous classification on the scholastic achievement of bright pupils. *Elementary School Journal, 28,* 336–345.

Ziehl, D. C. (1962). An evaluation of an elementary school enriched instructional program. *Dissertation Abstracts International, 24,* 2743. (University Microfilms No. 62-04644)

Zweibelson, I., Bahnmuller, M., & Lyman, L. (1965). Team teaching and flexible grouping in the junior high school social studies. *Journal of Experimental Education, 34,* 20–32.

14

Saturday and Summer Programs

JOHN F. FELDHUSEN   *Purdue University, Lafayette, Indiana*

Gifted and talented youth have special needs that are not typically addressed in regular school programs. Among these special needs are the following:

1. Challenging instructional activites to facilitate intellectual growth
2. Opportunities to learn new material at a faster pace than is typical in the regular classroom
3. Instruction at higher skill levels and at more abstract and complex conceptual levels
4. Clarification and confirmation of the levels and nature of their special talents, aptitudes, or abilities
5. Talented and knowledgeable teachers who can develop high-level expectations and goals
6. Interaction with challenging and supportive peers
7. Access to diverse topics, disciplines, and content that are not ordinarily taught in regular school programs
8. Opportunities for in-depth research, exploratory investigations, and creative synthesizing of ideas

Pullout/resource room programs typically address several of these needs. Full-time, self-contained classes for the gifted can accomodate most of these areas of need if the teachers are well trained in teaching the gifted and if they have a differentiated curriculum that specifically addresses these needs. But most gifted youth have only a limited pullout/resource room experience (Cox, Daniel, & Boston, 1985; Gallagher, Weiss, Oglesby, & Thomas, 1983). While the full-time, self-contained class may provide the ideal educational opportunity for gifted youth (Feldhusen & Treffinger, 1985), this form of service for the gifted probably will not be implemented in many schools in the United States. Thus, supplementary program services on Saturday and in the summer or after school are needed to fill in some of the missing educational experiences.

We have organized and conducted Saturday and summer classes and some after-school classes for gifted youth at Purdue University's Gifted Education Resource Institute since 1977 and have described and evaluated them in a series of publications (Feldhusen & Clinkenbeard, 1982; Feldhusen & Hansen, 1987; Feldhusen & Koopmans-Dayton, 1987; Feldhusen, Rebhorn, & Sayler, 1988; Feldhusen & Robinson-Wyman, 1980; Feldhusen & Ruckman, 1988; Feldhusen & Sokol, 1982; Follis & Feldhusen, 1983). These evaluations have led us to conclude that Saturday, summer, and after-school programs can be very beneficial to gifted youth in providing challenging instruction (Need 1), faster pace (Need 2), higher conceptual levels (Need 3), talented teachers who evoke high-level expectations (Need 5), interaction with challenging peers (Need 6), a wide variety of topics of study (Need 7), and in-depth research and investigation (Need 8). The need for clarification and confirmation of their gifts and talents (Need 4) may be indirectly addressed through experiences in classes, but it should also be directly addressed in school through counseling programs for the gifted.

The purpose of this chapter is to delineate the organization and operation of Saturday and summer programs. Secondarily, it also addresses the identification and evaluation process in such programs. Overall, Saturday and summer programs will be viewed as supplements to in-school programs. A major assumption is that gifted and talented youth need a variety of high-level, challenging experiences to facilitate their growth and development toward creative leadership careers in the

197

arts, professions, business, sciences, humanities, or government.

The major topics to be addressed are the following:

1. Identification-selection
2. Organization of classes
3. Curriculum development
4. Teacher selection and training
5. Supervision
6. Evaluation of student progress
7. Program evaluation

Identification-Selection

Giftedness or talent shows itself predominantly as precocity, or intellectual development beyond chronological age. Very young children show alertness or verbal behaviors that are harbingers of gifts or talents. Fluent discourse in a 2-year-old, recognition of words in print by a 3-year-old, or advanced reasoning skills in a 4-year-old are all possible signs of giftedness or special talent. Parents and teachers can observe the kindergartner who can already do simple addition and subtraction, the first-grader who draws with good perspective, or the second-grader who has unusual skill in pantomime. By third grade some potentially gifted youth are reading sixth- to eighth-grade-level books or carrying out research activities with moderate sophistication. Still other youth in Grades 4 and 5 are mechanical whizzes or have extraordinary vocabularies.

All these signs of giftedness or talent have appeared early or ahead of schedule. Parents see them in the family situation, and teachers whose classrooms are organized in ways to facilitate exploratory behavior can also see them. Both can be valuable sources of information for the identification process. However, the ultimate way to identify gifted and talented youth is to give them an opportunity to manifest their abilities in a high-powered, creative learning situation. Thus, an ideal identification-selection system looks for signs of giftedness and talent, avoids false negatives by being relatively generous in assessments, and seeks to give children a chance to demonstrate ability in a program.

The identification-selection process should also involve multiple measures as *alternative* ways of seeing gifts and talents. Unfortunately, schools often use multiple measures and expect children to show high ability on all of them in order to be selected for a program. The identification process often seems to be viewed as "gatekeeping" rather than as a search for talent.

Saturday Programs

The Super Saturday program at Purdue University serves children from age 2½ through high school. Approximately 40 enrichment and accelerated classes are offered each semester for 9 Saturdays, and similar classes are offered in summers in 2-week blocks on a daily attendance basis. These classes are for students who live within a 100-mile radius from Purdue University. Classes are offered in science, mathematics, computers, literature, composition, foreign languages, and special enrichment topics for preschoolers. College credit classes are also offered to high school students.

A variety of identification-screening devices are used, such as standardized achievement test scores, group and individual intelligence test results, and nominations by parents or school personnel. Generally, achievement test scores are expected to be at or above the 90th percentile, IQ scores are expected to be above 120, and parent or teacher nominations are expected to be indicative of strong talent or ability. Any one factor will do. No child is denied an opportunity to try a semester in the program if a parent or teacher argues the case for the child's talent. However, high school students who enroll for the college credit classes must rank in the top 10% in grade point average and be recommended by a school official.

Summer Programs

Summer residential programs serve youth from Grades 4 to 12. The summer programs are also designed to serve more highly gifted students. Five summer residential programs are offered at Purdue University; all are quite academic and accelerative. Each of the programs offers a number of elective classes in science, mathematics, literature, and composition, as well as specialty courses in philosophy. Comet is a 1-week program for children who have completed 4th or 5th grade; STAR is a 2-week program for students who have completed 6th, 7th, or 8th grade; PULSAR/PALS is a 2-week program for students who have completed 9th, 10th, or 11th grade; and PCCP/NOVA, the Purdue College Credit Program, is a 2- or 3-week program for students who have completed 9th, 10th, or 11th grade.

There is a unique and specialized identification plan for each of these programs. Students in the Comet, PULSAR/PALS, and PCCP/NOVA programs are expected to score in the top 10% in mathematics, science, language arts, or social studies on the appropriate section of a standardized achievement test in the area in which they plan to enroll in courses. Alternatively an IQ score of 125 or a grade-point average of 3.5 (based on A = 4.0) will be accepted. Recommendations from two teachers also are required. Students in the STAR program must have taken the Scholastic Aptitude Test (SAT) in 6th, 7th, or 8th grade and scored 500 in math, 430 in the verbal area, or 43 on the Test of Standard Written English (TSWE), depending on the area in which they wish to enroll for classes. For composition classes the TSWE score must be at the selection level; for mathematics, science, and computer classes a math score of 500 is required; and for literature, philosophy, history, and social studies a verbal score of 430 is required. Alternative scores will always be considered, but prospective students are urged to take the recommended tests and submit those scores.

Organization of Classes

Courses for the gifted in all Saturday and summer programs should be carefully organized to meet students' special needs. This means that the content should be several grade levels beyond their regular grade placement, presented at a faster pace, and focused on more abstract and complex concepts and problems. There should be a variety of readings and other resources and a regular assignment of homework or independent study. There should also be much opportunity to work together in small groups. It is also desirable to hold class sessions for at least 2 hours to facilitate in-depth discussions, research and other investigations, and project activity. Gifted students should be actively involved in the learning process, not passive receivers of information, and they should not be subjected to lengthy repetitive drill.

All summer residential programs offer morning and afternoon class sessions, each about 2 hours long. Late afternoons are devoted to physical recreation, and the period after the evening meal is time for free play. Early evenings (7:00 to 8:00 P.M.) are often used for career education speakers or seminars on special topics. The period from 8:00 to 10:00 P.M. is study time. The evening closes with free time for a late snack, visiting one another's rooms, or music and games in the recreation room.

Saturday program classes meet from 9:30 to 11:30 A.M. for 9 consecutive Saturdays. The Saturday college credit classes for high school students meet from 9:00 A.M. to 12:30 P.M. for 16 weeks. In the Super Summer program, classes meet from 9:30 to 11:30 A.M. or from 1 to 3 P.M. Monday through Friday for 2 weeks.

A nominal fee is charged for enrollment in all these programs. Extensive efforts are made to recruit minority students and students from poor families, and a variety of scholarships are offered on the basis of need and ability.

Curriculum

The curriculum of special programs for gifted youth should provide opportunities for challenging academic studies in areas that relate to their special talents, aptitudes, and interests. If a youngster has high-level ability in mathematics, he or she should be given opportunities for accelerated learning in mathematics. However, the same youngster may also be moderately talented verbally and interested in foreign language study. Thus, a good program should offer both opportunities: accelerated instruction in the major talent area and enriching experiences in other domains. All Purdue programs offer such opportunities.

The summer and Saturday programs at Purdue University offer classes in science, mathematics, computer science, literature, composition, art, social studies, and specialty topics. Table 14.1 shows the courses offered in a Super Saturday semester, and Table 14.2 shows the classes offered in the summer programs. The curriculum is developed each year through a survey of needs and interests of students enrolled in previous semesters. However, the curriculum is also open to new offerings proposed by instructors who perceive a need for a course in a particular area.

Curriculum development is guided by the training and orientation sesions held each semester for the instructors in the Super Saturday program and each spring for the instructors in the summer programs. Printed guides also spell out the expectations. Instructors are required to file a course plan that includes objectives, a content outline, resource materials, and a pretest and post-test. All courses are intended to operate at a challenge level at least 2 years higher than the age-grade level of the students enrolled. Guidance for curriculum planning and teaching strategies is also provided in the training sessions, which focus on such topics as (1) the *Taxonomy of Educational Objectives* by Bloom, Englehart, Furst, Hill, and Krathwohl (1956), (2) thinking skills, (3) small-group work, (4) problem solving, (5) project activity, and (6) principles for differentiating curriculum in gifted education. Implementation of the curriculum plan is checked by classroom observers who visit each teacher in the summer programs every 3rd or 4th day.

Curriculum development for the gifted should be guided by principles like those shown in Table 14.3. All these principles should be implemented with a recognition that the major general characteristic of the gifted is their precocity: Their intellectual or artistic abilities are advanced beyond what is typical for their age. Thus, they need higher-level and faster-paced instruction that deals more in abstractions and complex ideas and pursues topics in greater depth. Once planned, the curriculum must then be put into practice with gifted students by teachers who have an appropriate repertoire of strategies that are differentiated to fit the characteristics of gifted students.

Table 14.1
Super Saturday Courses

Science:
Experience in Science K–1
Young Astronauts 2–3
Dinosaurs 3–4
Nature Studies 4–6
Computer-Based Science Lab 6–8
Space 4–6
Aviation Tech 5–8
Engineering 6–8

Mathematics:
Math in Action K–1
Math Problem Solving 2–4
Statistics 4–6

Language Arts:
Drama 3–5
Creative Writing 3–5
Edgar Allen Poe 6–9

Foreign Language:
Japanese 2–4
Spanish 3–5

Preschool:
Creative Discovery Learning, age 2
Creative Thinking through Children's Literature, age 3–5

Visual Arts:
Drawing and Painting 1–6
Three-dimensional 7–12

Social Studies:
Inventions 1–2
Indians 2–4

Computers:
Introduction to Computer 1–2
Computer Graphics 3–4
BASIC 3–5
PASCAL 7–12

Other:
Models 4–6
Magic 5–7
Typing 5–7
Chess 5–8
SAT Prep 7–12

Teacher Selection and Training

Elsewhere I proposed that teachers of the gifted should have the following characteristics (Feldhusen, 1985):

1. They should be intelligent and knowledgeable in general.
2. They should have broad interests.
3. They should be hard working and achievement oriented.
4. They should be well organized.
5. They should be enthusiastic.
6. They should have a good sense of humor.
7. They should be flexible.
8. They should understand and accept gifted students.

Some of these may be characteristics that all teachers should have. Above all, teachers of the gifted should be highly knowledgeable or skilled in the subject matter they are teaching, verbally articulate, and enthusiastic and energetic in their presentations and interactions with students. They especially should be able to convey the joy of mastering a field and of being deeply knowledgeable in it so they can inspire gifted youth to pursue the discipline that the teachers represent.

Recent research on teaching the gifted also shows that there is a set of skills or competencies that can be learned and used to teach the gifted more effectively (Maker, 1975; Seeley, 1979; Sisk, 1975). Table 14.4 presents one such list of competencies. In essence, these competencies make it possible for teaching to be differentiated to fit the characteristics and needs of gifted students.

The Super Saturday and summer programs at Purdue University seek teachers who exhibit the characteristics listed above and provide training to develop the competencies needed to teach gifted students well. Teachers are recruited from the ranks of university professors and students and from public schools. Teachers for the summer programs are also recruited nationally to bring in a wider variety of points of view, interests, and talents. All recruited teachers receive 1 day of training each semester for Super Saturday and 1½ days each year for the summer programs.

The topics presented at training sessions were listed in the Curriculum section. They vary from semester to semester and from year to year according to needs perceived by the observers who visit all the classes in action. The topics are always selected to stress the

Table 14.2
Courses Offered in the Summer Residential Programs

COMET:
Social Studies
Science
Math
English

PCCP/NOVA:
Contemporary Economic Problems
Introduction to Psychology
Math Problem Solving with Computers
Social Problems
Advanced Freshman Composition
Issues of Justice
Debating Public Classes

STAR:
Algebra
Spanish
Experimental Geometry
Introduction to Electrical Engineering
Modern Literature
Probability and Statistics
Creative Writing
Critical Reasoning Thinking
Introduction to Computer Science
Neuropsychology
French
Chemistry
Biology and Human Anatomy
Etymology
Latin American Literature
Robotics

PALS/PULSAR
Organic Chemistry
Introduction to Research
Advanced Algebra and Trigonometry
Creative Writing
Introduction to Psychology
Physics of Vibration
Shakespeare and the Actor
Pentathlon
Introduction to Electrical Engineering
Statistics and Probability
Modern Fiction and Film
Leadership
American History
Microbiology

Table 14.3
Curriculum Principles

1. Focus on *major ideas,* issues, themes, problems, concepts, and principles.
2. Emphasize the need for a *large knowledge base.*
3. When possible use an *interdisciplinary* approach.
4. Emphasize in-depth *research* and *independent study* with original and high-level products or presentations.
5. Teach *research skills and thinking skills* as metacognitive processes.
6. *Incorporate higher level thinking skills in content* study—in discussions, independent study, research, and writing.
7. *Increase the level, complexity, and pace* of the curriculum to fit the precocity of the students.
8. Teach methods for *independence, self direction,* and self-evaluation in learning.

competencies needed to differentiate instruction to fit the special needs and characteristics of the gifted. All teachers are required to attend the training sessions, which are usually scheduled a week or two before the beginning of each new semester or summer. The training day always includes general sessions plus specialized meetings for teachers in each of the curriculum areas. A typical training day might follow this schedule:

Table 14.4
Competencies of Teachers of the Gifted

1. Knowledge of nature and needs of gifted
2. Skill in utilizing tests and test data
3. Skill in utilizing group dynamics
4. Skill in counseling and guidance
5. Skill in developing lessons in creative thinking
6. Skill in utilizing strategies such as simulation
7. Skill in providing learning opportunities at all levels of cognition
8. Skill in relating the cognitive and affective dimensions
9. Knowledge of new developments in education
10. Knowledge of current research in gifted
11. Skill in demonstrating lessons for gifted
12. Skill in conducting action research

Source: From "Teaching the Gifted and Talented Teachers: A Training Model" by Dorothy Sisk, 1975, *Gifted Child Quarterly, 19,* pp. 81–88. Copyright © 1982 by the National Association for Gifted Children. Reprinted by permission of the author and publisher.

1. Registration, coffee, and doughnuts
2. General session
3. Developing the pretest and post-test
4. Strategies for teaching thinking skills
5. Lunch
6. Breakout sessions
   a. Science
   b. Composition
   c. Math and computers
   d. Literature
   e. Art
   f. Special classes
7. Closing orientation session

Supervision

While considerable emphasis should be placed on training teachers to work with the gifted and to differentiate instruction to meet their needs and fit their special characteristics, there is also a great need for supervision and evaluation of teacher performance in the classroom to ensure that good principles of teaching are implemented. Some teachers grasp the principles well but have great difficulty putting them to use in the classroom.

Teachers in both the Saturday and summer programs are visited about every third or fourth day by a trained observer who spends approximately 30 to 50 minutes in the classroom. Observers' visits are not prescheduled. They sit in the back of the room and use the form shown in Figure 14.1 to evaluate the teacher and the pattern of activity. A

1. *Subject matter differentiation:*
   _____ A. Appropriateness of depth and breadth
   _____ B. Concept orientation
   _____ C. Teacher expertise

2. *Clarity of teaching:*
   _____ A. Verbal communication skills
   _____ B. Nonverbal communication skills
   _____ C. Clear and specific directions
   _____ D. All necessary points addressed
   _____ E. Sufficient illustrations and examples (e.g., use of analogies, similies, etc.)
   _____ F. Student comprehension as evidenced by responses and involvement

3. *Motivational techniques:*
   _____ A. Teacher energy and enthusiasm
   _____ B. Variety (warm-ups, brainteasers, etc.)
   _____ C. Student enthusiasm and persistence demonstrated

4. *Pace of instruction:*
   _____ A. Individualized needs accommodated
   _____ B. Appropriate for the group
   _____ C. Avoidance of unnecessary repetition, drill, use of examples

5. *Opportunity for self-determination of activities by student:*
   _____ A. Adequate choices offered
   _____ B. Student-directed activities
   _____ C. Individual interests accommodated

6. *Student involvement in a variety of experiences:*
   _____ A. Discussions, small-group activities, movies, field trips, learning centers, etc.
   _____ B. Purposeful use of movement
   _____ C. Creative thinking, problem solving, independent study processes
   _____ D. Learning style accommodation

7. *Interaction between teacher and student, student and peers, appropriate to course objectives:*
   _____ A. Activities that promote group feeling
   _____ B. Respect for individuals and their ideas
   _____ C. Appropriate use of humor
   _____ D. Sense of order promoting self-discipline

8. *Opportunity for student follow-through of activities outside class (homework):*
   _____ A. Open-endedness, allowing for creativity and individual interest and pace
   _____ B. Builds upon or prepares for classroom activities
   _____ C. Variety of assignments
   _____ D. Encouragement of and assistance in further study for interested students
   _____ E. Handouts and instructions are clearly printed and thorough

(continued)

Figure 14.1 Observers' evaluation form.

9. *Emphasis on higher level thinking skills:*
   _____ A. Bloom's taxonomy evidenced in teacher questioning, activities, teaching aids
   _____ B. Critical thinking activities (e.g., logic, simulations, scientific process, etc.)

10. *Emphasis on creativity:*
    _____ A. Creative thinking skills (fluency, flexibility, originality, elaboration)
    _____ B. Accepting atmosphere
    _____ C. Encouragement of risk-taking
    _____ D. Open-ended questioning
    _____ E. Models creative behavior

11. *Lesson plans designed to meet program, course, and daily objectives:*
    _____ A. Sense of planning with flexibility
    _____ B. Student-centered

12. *Use of teaching and learning aids:*
    _____ A. Inclusion of audiovisual materials, models, demonstrations, etc.
    _____ B. Clearly printed and grammatically correct
    _____ C. Appropriate/necessary
    _____ D. Variety of materials/aids used

Figure 14.1   continued

global rating of 5 (*outstanding*) to 1 (*not satisfactory*) is completed for each numbered item, and special areas of strength or weakness are noted by the subcategories for each item. Additional comments are also written concerning the teachers' strengths and areas needing improvement.

Following the visit a meeting is arranged between the observer and the teacher to discuss the evaluation and plan for improvement if needed. Feldhusen and Hansen (1987) and Feldhusen and Koopmans-Dayton (1987) reported empirical studies of the teaching and teacher evaluation in the Saturday program. They concluded that the system was effective in bringing about high-quality and properly differentiated instruction for gifted students. The system for observation and evaluation is chiefly a formative approach designed to help teachers implement abstract principles of teaching, not a summative evaluation to label them "good" or "bad." Through the meetings with observers most teachers are able to im-

prove their teaching and sustain high-quality performance. However, in a few cases the observers found teachers' performance so consistently bad that the teachers had to be replaced. Overall, however, the supervision system is producing excellent teaching of gifted youth.

Evaluation of Student Progress

Student progress should be evaluated regularly. However, achievement in programs for the gifted is more difficult to evaluate because the goals focus on thinking skills, problem solving, independent research, and project activity—all of which are less easily assessed than subject matter mastery. Nevertheless, measurement instruments and procedures are emerging for assessment in all these areas, and, of course, mastery of some relevant content remains a goal of most good programs for the gifted. Ennis (1985) reviewed 11 tests of critical thinking; Feldhusen and Treffinger

(1985) reviewed tests for the assessment of creative thinking; Hoover (1988) reviewed problem-solving tasks and the underlying processes or abilities; and Karnes and Collins (1981) presented a comprehensive inventory of instruments and procedures for assessing gifted and talented elementary and secondary school students. It appears that a wide variety of instruments is available to assess the higher level process skills emphasized in gifted programs. However, most of these tests are not as well standardized or well known as the widely used intelligence and achievement tests.

Assessment of learning among gifted students is often difficult to carry out reliably because of the *ceiling effect*. This means that many of these students get all or nearly all items correct on a test, and with all scores in the narrow range at the top of the scale there is little or no reliable differentiation among the levels of their performance. Put another way, they don't really have a chance to show the full extent of what they have learned. Still another problem is that when students score at the extreme ends (high or low) of a scale on a pretest, they are apt, due to the statistical artifact called regression toward the mean, to score lower on the post-test even though they may have made real learning gains.

In light of these problems, off-level testing can and should be used. For the gifted, this means taking a grade-level form of a test that is higher than their age or grade placement. For example, in one project gifted fourth-graders were pretested and post-tested with the junior high school form of the Stanford Achievement Test. This opened higher level challenges on the test and higher range norms. Similarly, the administration of the SAT to seventh- and eighth-graders in the regional talent searches is a radically off-level form of testing.

There is also much agreement that gifted students should have increasing experience with self assessment and not remain totally dependent on tests and teachers for evaluation of their achievement. Self-assessment can involve them in the evaluation of their projects and presentations, as well as the general grading of their work in mathematics, science, language arts, and social studies. Their self-evaluation can be compared with test and teacher assessments to help them grow in self-evaluation skills.

Several of the summer programs use off-level SAT test scores for selection, and other off-level standardized achievement testing is offered for admission to both the Saturday and summer programs at Purdue University. There is also a recognition that group intelligence test scores, submitted as admission criteria for the Saturday program, while often comfortably above the cutting level of 120 are nevertheless likely to be limited by ceiling effects. Thus, youngsters who score at the level of 140 on a pencil-and-paper test have been found scoring 165 on the Standford-Binet Form L-M.

Evaluation of student achievement in nearly all Saturday and summer programs involves pre- and post-testing. The development of a pretest gives the teacher a good understanding of the skills and concepts to be taught, and scores from the pretest show clearly the range of entry knowledge of the gifted students. For gifted students the pretest also often shows that some students know nearly all the information that is to be taught. Teachers must then quickly adjust the curriculum upward to fit those students.

Evaluation of student achievement should also involve subjective ratings by both teacher and students. Figure 14.2 shows an evaluation form used in several programs for the gifted. Note that the student rates himself or herself on these skills, and then the teacher does the ratings. If discrepancies are large, a student-teacher conference is held and the outcome is noted in the Comments section. The evaluation form then goes home to parents.

Evaluation is a continual process that should serve both formative and summative purposes in Saturday and summer programs. Formative evaluation is the daily and weekly assessments that are used to correct deficiencies and confirm strengths. Summative evaluation provides benchmark assessments of the level of achievements at the end of longer periods such as a semester or year. Both forms of evaluation should guide assessment in Saturday and summer programs for the gifted.

Student _____ School Year _____

O = outstanding   M = minimal
A = average (for this class)   N = needs improvement

Demonstration of	Student	Teacher
1. Originality and creativity	_____	_____
2. Organizational ability	_____	_____
3. Communication of ideas	_____	_____
4. Elaboration of ideas	_____	_____
5. Evaluating ability	_____	_____
6. Planning ability	_____	_____
7. Research ability	_____	_____
8. Problem-solving skills	_____	_____
9. Fluency and flexibility skills	_____	_____
10. Independent study skills	_____	_____

Degree of

	Student	Teacher
1. Cooperation	_____	_____
2. Self-motivation	_____	_____
3. Responsibility	_____	_____
4. Self-discipline	_____	_____
5. Leadership	_____	_____

Comments by student:
_____
_____

Comments by teacher:
_____
_____

Comments by parents:
_____
_____

Parent Signature _____

Figure 14.2 Evaluation of gifted student's performance.

Program Evaluation

Program evaluation should be a regularly occurring event in summer and Saturday programs. Is the program achieving its goals? Are the goals worthwhile? Is the identification process admitting youngsters who cannot profit from the program? Is it excluding children who should be in the program? Are the teachers differentiating for the gifted in their teaching strategies? Is the curriculum sound and appropriate for the gifted? Are the students making significant gains in the process skills? Is the program meeting the needs of highly gifted students?

These are all possible program evaluation questions. The answers to some will come from the analysis of test scores; others may be answered with student, parent, and teacher ratings; and still others may best be evaluated with ratings of student projects, performances, or presentations.

Program evaluations should be carefully planned, and it is often desirable to have the assistance of an outside evaluator. Finding ways to evaluate in relation to all the goals may involve carefully planned pre- and post-testing; observation of teachers and students in action in the classroom; and ratings by teachers, parents, students, and/or outside observers of the attainment of students in the program. Ratings can focus on student behavior in classes, their presentations or performances, or their projects' end products. Such procedures for individual student evaluation often yield valuable information for program evaluation.

Program evaluation is often narrowly conceived as giving a test or two or having an outside evaluator come in for a day or two to make judgments about the program. Good evaluation involves long-range planning, looking closely at program operations (formative), and assessing long-range effects of the program on gifted students (summative). In essence, the planners of program evaluation identify the questions they want to answer and the sources of information that will provide answers.

Evaluation of all Saturday and summer programs at Purdue University is carried out periodically precisely by identifying the questions to be answered and the sources of information appropriate to answer the questions. Student achievement is evaluated by compiling the results of pre- and post-testing in all courses (Feldhusen & Koopmans-Dayton, 1987; Thorkildsen, 1985). Student and parent perceptions of the strengths and weaknesses of courses are assessed with end-of-course rating forms and with long-range follow-up ratings. Teacher performance is evaluated by compiling the results of supervisor observations

and ratings of their performance (Feldhusen & Koopmans-Dayton, 1987). Long-range achievements of summer program students are evaluated with follow-up questionnaires sent to parents and students. An outside evaluation specialist also was used recently to conduct a goal-free evaluation of the Saturday program. One of his findings was that the most highly gifted youth were often not challenged properly in Super Saturday classes. As a result, new high-challenge classes have been added to the curriculum.

Saturday and summer programs should have carefully planned, ongoing program evaluation commitments. It is not unusual for program leaders to become totally absorbed in daily operations and to forget the need for evaluation. Some dedicated program leaders may also suffer from weak egos and be reluctant to face up to evaluation. However, the results of sound program evaluation can be used to make the good decisions that lead to growth and development toward excellent programs for gifted and talented youth.

Summary

Saturday and summer programs for the gifted enhance the educational experiences of these students by offering opportunities for truly accelerated and enriched learning experiences in their areas of special interest and talent. These programs make it possible for them to interact with and be stimulated by other gifted and talented youth. Such interaction serves to confirm their talents and supports the development of a positive self-concept concerning their gifts and talents.

A good program includes a reliable system for assessing the talents and abilities of students, well-organized classes in all areas of the curriculum, carefully planned curricula, properly selected and trained teachers, supervision of teaching and classes to ensure high-quality instruction, systematic evaluation of individual student progress, and comprehensive program evaluation. The overall payoff is sound learning and social experiences that help gifted and talented youth clarify and understand their own potentials, set high-level career goals, and experience the intellectual joy of academic and personal growth to the limits of their ability.

REFERENCES

Bloom, B. S., Englehart, M. D., Furst, E. J., Hill, W. H., & Krathwohl, D. H (1956). *Taxonomy of educational objectives, cognitive domain* (Handbook 1). New York: McKay.

Cox, J., Daniel, N., & Boston, B. O. (1985). *Educating able learners, programs and promising practices.* Austin: University of Texas Press.

Ennis, R. H. (1985). Tests that could be called critical thinking tests. In A. L. Costa (Ed.), *Developing minds* (pp. 303–304). Alexandria, VA: Association for Supervision and Curriculum Development.

Feldhusen, J. F. (1985). The teacher of gifted students. *Gifted Education International, 3,* 87–93.

Feldhusen, J. F., & Clinkenbeard, P. R. (1982). Summer programs for the gifted: Purdue's residential programs for higher achievers. *Journal for the Education of the Gifted, 5,* 178–184.

Feldhusen, J. F., & Hansen, J. B. (1987). Selecting and training teachers to work with the gifted in a Saturday program. *Gifted International, 4*(1), 82–93.

Feldhusen, J. F., & Koopmans-Dayton, J. D. (1987). Meeting special needs of the gifted through Saturday programs: An evaluation study. *Gifted International, 4*(2), 89–101.

Feldhusen, J. F., Rebhorn, L. S., & Sayler, M. F. (1988). Appropriate design for summer gifted programs. *Gifted Child Today, 11*(4), 2–5.

Feldhusen, J. F., & Robinson-Wyman, A. (1980). Super Saturday: Design and implementation of Purdue's special program for gifted children. *Gifted Child Quarterly, 24,* 15–20.

Feldhusen, J. F., & Ruckman, D. R. (1988). A guide to the development of Saturday programs for gifted and talented youths. *Gifted Child Today, 11*(5), 56–61.

Feldhusen, J. F., & Sokol, L. (1982). Extra school programming to meet the needs of gifted youth. *Gifted Child Quarterly, 26,* 51–56.

Feldhusen, J. F., & Treffinger, D. J. (1985). *Creative thinking and problem solving in gifted education.* Dubuque: Kendall/Hunt.

Follis, H., & Feldhusen, J. F. (1983). Design and evaluation of summer academic leadership program for the gifted. *Roeper Review, 6,* 92–94.

Gallagher, J. J., Weiss, P., Oglesby, K., & Thomas, T. (1983). *The status of gifted/talented education: United States survey of needs, practices and policies.* Los Angeles: Leadership Training Institute.

Hoover, S. M. (1988). *An exploratory study of the scientific problem finding ability of highly intelligent students.* Unpublished doctoral dissertation, Purdue University, West Lafayette, IN.

Karnes, F. A., & Collins, E. C. (1981). *Assessment in gifted education.* Springfield, IL: Thomas.

Maker, C. J. (1975). *Training teachers for the gifted and talented.* Reston, VA: Council for Exceptional Children.

Seeley, K. R. (1979). Competencies for teachers of gifted and talented children. *Journal for the Education of the Gifted, 3,* 7–13.

Sisk, D. (1975). Teaching the gifted and talented teachers: A training model. *Gifted Child Quarterly, 19,* 81–88.

Thorkildsen, T. A. (1985). *Identification of summer program participants: A look at predictive validity.* Unpublished doctoral dissertation, Purdue University, West Lafayette, IN.

15

Special Residential High Schools

PENNY BRITTON KOLLOFF   *Cranbrook Schools, Bloomfield, Michigan*

This chapter describes a growing national trend in the education of gifted students, the development of special residential high schools for young people of exceptional intellectual and academic ability. In the past decade, at least six states have established these schools and a number of other states are in various stages of planning similar schools. Stanley (1987) recommended that any state that has at least 300 National Merit semifinalists each year should explore the possibility of a residential high school.

To provide structure to the chapter, the present discussion will focus on residential high schools for the gifted that have been established and supported by state legislatures. These schools exhibit common characteristics that merit consideration regardless of their locations, curricula, students, and faculties. These are commonalities that must be addressed in any proposed residential high school. This chapter will elaborate on those elements.

Rationale

Since the early 1970s, programs for gifted students have proliferated across the United States as local schools have created various accommodations for their high-ability learners. Approaches for high school students have generally taken the form of advanced or honors courses, opportunities for acceleration to higher level classes, or, in some cases, enrollment in college classes while still in high school (Cox, Daniel, & Boston, 1985). Depending on the definition of *gifted*, programs of these types usually are directed at meeting the needs of up to 10% of the students in a school. However, if these students are considered a homogeneous group, then the most academically and intellectually advanced among them will still have unmet needs.

The typical high school is unable to offer the number of advanced courses or a sufficiently diverse curriculum to provide for the gifted learner who, for example, is capable of mastering all the mathematics courses the school has to offer within a year or two of entrance. At a time when many of the nation's secondary schools do not offer a physics course, some do not include a course in chemistry, and the majority of students do not have an opportunity to go beyond the second year of a foreign language, concerns must focus on making advanced courses accessible to the most intellectually capable students. If small, perhaps rural schools do not have large enough enrollments to offer the most advanced classes or are not be able to provide teachers for those courses, educators, parents, and students must seek alternatives. It is this most advanced group of students for whom special schools are being developed.

The student for whom a special residential school may be the most appropriate educational approach possesses certain characteristics. These highly gifted learners may be defined as individuals who are capable of mastering content in much shorter amounts of time than is required by other students and who are at the same time able to engage in complex processes at high levels of abstraction. In short, these are students who need a quite different curriculum from that offered by most schools.

The author wishes to acknowledge the assistance of Karen Hall Fuson, librarian, Burris Laboratory School, in locating information and publications from the existing residential high schools.

Instruction for these students requires faculty who are specialists in areas of advanced content and who are capable of delivering appropriately fast paced, high-level instruction. Again, most schools, necessarily addressing the needs of the majority of their students, do not have such faculty available.

There is yet another recognized need of gifted students, that of interaction with others of similar ability in a supportive climate. At best, schools provide these opportunities on a limited basis (several hours a week, perhaps in one or two classes in which students are grouped by ability). However, fears of elitism, strong feelings against tracking, and parent or teacher resistance, prevent schools from going further to group students for large portions of their time.

The above conditions, combined with the relatively recent goals of achieving academic excellence in our educational systems, developing the talented as a source of future economic and social leadership, and establishing highly visible efforts linking political, economic, and educational institutions, have led to the realization that special residential schools are an appropriate way of meeting the needs of many of the nation's most talented young people. Recognition of the importance of meeting these needs, and an acknowledgement that long-term benefits may accrue from an investment in the education of the exceptionally gifted, have resulted in new proposals to state legislatures to create and sustain residential high schools for highly gifted students selected from within the state.

Each state that establishes a school has the opportunity to create a program that (1) directly benefits its own students and (2) provides leadership in the state educational community. This leadership emerges as curricula are developed and tested with the residential students, as programs bring teachers from local schools to the campus to work with the students and faculty, and through activities that take the resources of the residential school to others schools in the state. A sense of commitment to the larger community, stemming from the need to return some of the investment by the state, keeps the residential school from becoming insular. Initiatives for educational reform innovation can begin in such a school and spread throughout the state.

An Early Example

In 1978, then Governor James B. Hunt, Jr., and the General Assembly of North Carolina, proposed the first residential high school for gifted students of that state. In the fall of 1980 the North Carolina School of Science and Mathematics, in Durham, accepted its first class of junior year students and began a program designed to meet the academic, social, and emotional needs of a cross-section of the brightest students in the state. In addition to the direct benefits to the students who attend the school, approaches are developed to disseminate the curricula and teaching methods to other schools throughout the state.

The North Carolina school, which has served as a model for similar schools throughout the country, currently serves a student body of juniors and seniors drawn from all geographic areas of the state. These classes represent a balance among race, socioeconomic level, and sex. The faculty is composed of individuals with content expertise, many of whom hold doctoral degrees and for whom there is no requirement that they be certified teachers. The curriculum itself offers opportunities for students to accelerate and enrich their academic programs; the overall program incorporates independent study, community service, and other extracurricular elements and seeks to provide a balanced experience for students.

This most successful school, one which has received a great deal of national attention, can also point to benefits to the state that invested in the plan. A large number of graduates elect to attend colleges and universities in North Carolina, and there is an expectation that many of them will choose to remain in the state to enter professional careers and raise their families. Many businesses and industries have chosen to locate in North Carolina in part because of the state's demonstrated commitment to excellence in education. These are persuasive arguments as other state legislatures consider similar plans.

Characteristics of Special Residential Schools

The Students

Most residential high schools admit students at Grade 11 for the beginning of a 2-year experience. Illinois, an exception, admits students who are beginning Grade 10. Because they are established through legislative action and supported by state funds, the schools are committed to enrolling a student body that profiles the population of the state. Consideration is given to balancing the various groups that make up the state. Sizes of the schools range from about 300, or about 150 per grade, up to about 800.

Identification and selection of students for participation in a special residential school is a complex process that starts well before the beginning of the academic year in which a student is admitted. Applicants take standardized tests such as the Scholastic Aptitude Test (SAT), the PSAT, or similar off-level tests. Additional assessments such as tests of critical thinking or written products may be required by the particular residential school, along with interviews for finalists. Subjective and objective assessments are combined to arrive at admissions decisions. Most of the existing schools use test scores, high school grades, recommendations, and interviews to assemble a profile of each applicant.

In addition to evidence of academic achievement and ability, residential schools look for students who show a potential to succeed in a program that requires independent work and who demonstrate the maturity to live away from home while attending a rigorous academic school.

The Faculty

Instructors for these exceptionally talented students come from high schools, colleges and universities, and the private sector. Most residential schools report that their faculties comprise individuals with advanced degrees, with about half having earned doctorates. There is a great deal of flexibility concerning the requirements for "certification" of teachers in these schools. Efforts are made to recruit teachers with outstanding academic credentials and the ability to work well with gifted students. Schools want individuals who can inspire young, gifted students outside the classroom, offer support for creative ideas, and become role models as productive adults.

Residential schools often have special visiting teacher/scholar programs that bring teachers from around the state to the residential site to work with the students. These individuals work with students, develop curricula, observe and implement teaching methods, and return home to adapt the techniques and materials for their high-ability students and share them with other teachers.

Facilities

Special residential schools require special facilities. Because of the nature of the schools, there must be a complex of buildings that accommodates both the instructional and the living components of the programs. Existing residential schools have addressed this need in several ways. The first of these special schools for gifted students, the North Carolina School of Science and Mathematics, is located in a former hospital complex that has been converted into dormitories, classrooms, laboratories, a library, and recreational areas. The Illinois Math and Science Academy moved into a high school building that had been vacated. Initially, some classrooms were turned into dormitory rooms while others remained classrooms or became laboratories or other needed spaces. Dormitories have since been constructed on the academy campus.

Several residential high schools are located on college or university campuses where the needed facilities already exist with little need for modification. The Louisiana School for Math, Science, and the Arts is located on the campus of Northwestern State University in Nachitoches. The Texas Academy of Mathematics and Science is a part of the University of North Texas, Denton. The Mississippi School for Math and Science is on the campus of the Mississippi University for Women in Columbus. The South Carolina Governor's School for Science and Mathematics is located at Coker

College in Hartsville. In most of these situations, while the residential high school and the college or university exist on the same campus, there are separate facilities for the two student bodies. Dormitories house only high school students, and restrictions apply to the interaction of high school with older students.

The Curriculum

At the heart of residential schools for gifted students are the curricula that are especially designed to meet their needs. With an emphasis on mathematics and science in most programs, students usually advance rapidly through high-level coursework in these and other areas. The curricular offerings in these schools may fit one of several different models. The College Board Advanced Placement (AP) program is the foundation of the curriculum for some. Students who spend 2 years in a residential high school may take many AP classes and/or exams, thus enabling them to begin college or university with 1 year or more of credit in several areas. Stanley (1987), in fact, urges that the curriculum for a school of this kind include courses that prepare students to take AP exams in calculus, physics, chemistry, computer science, and biology. At the Illinois Mathematics and Science Academy, the completion of the 3-year curriculum takes students through the beginning university curricula and prepares them to take a variety of AP exams in mathematics and sciences. Since the Illinois school is not located on a university campus, the courses are developed and offered within the residential school itself.

Residential schools located on college or university campuses virtually always incorporate university courses into the curriculum of the high school. Students may take courses (e.g., languages) not offered in the residential school curriculum or other specialized courses that can balance and supplement the curriculum of the high school. The curriculum of the Texas Academy of Mathematics and Science consists of university honors courses for which the students earn college credit in addition to completing the requirements for high school graduation. In their 2 years at the Texas Acad-

emy, students simultaneously complete the last 2 years of high school and the first 2 years of college.

Although the major emphasis of special residential high schools is typically science and mathematics, all these schools incorporate strong communications and arts programs into the curriculum. The Louisiana School for Math, Science, and the Arts goes a step further in offering students the opportunity to focus on math/science, humanities, or the creative and performing arts. A student may select one or more of these areas in which to concentrate.

Most of these special high schools also develop unique curricular offerings in addition to the AP courses and college or university courses. Humanities, English, and social studies courses may be organized in ways different from the traditional secondary curriculum. The nature of the learners and the faculty lend themselves to the development of courses that explore broad, interdisciplinary themes, epistemology, and the historical and philosophical foundations of disciplines.

Overall, the curriculum of special residential high schools is characterized by its appropriateness to the education of gifted students. These schools are able to offer a program of high-level courses, a curriculum with breadth and depth. Students can pursue a sequence of courses in mathematics and sciences that includes advanced courses typically unavailable in most high schools. Both advanced and nontraditional offerings in other areas may be available in residential schools.

Several additional curricular components are also a part of residential high schools. Mentorships, internships, and research and independent study opportunities are incorporated into the program to allow various degrees of individualization for the students. In many of the schools, students are encouraged to pursue original research projects. Residential schools located on university campuses may arrange for students to work on projects with faculty mentors. Schools located near high-tech centers, research and medical facilities, or other industries in the scientific field can place students in internships where they are able to experience involvement in the actual workings of these organizations.

Extracurricular Program

Beyond the school day, residential students may be involved in community service projects, recreational activities, faculty-student projects, clubs, competitions, and contests. The residential schools offer many of the same activities students would find in their local schools, including musical and theatrical performance groups; individual and team sports; foreign language, science, and math organizations; and service clubs. The campuses develop diverse extracurricular programs based on the interests and talents of the students. Students often have opportunities to attend seminars, lectures, symposia, and other events that take place at the schools themselves and on nearby college campuses.

Following the example set by the North Carolina school, other such institutions have established a requirement that students become involved in campus and community service. Projects may involve activities such as tutoring, volunteering in hospitals or similar institutions, or assisting local agencies and organizations.

Benefits of Special Residential Schools

A number of groups benefit from special residential schools for gifted students. Most important, of course, are the students themselves who attend and are challenged at their levels by an appropriately rigorous curriculum.

Recognizing that there is potential for wider benefits to education in the state, the majority of residential schools have outreach programs. These involve bringing teachers from schools around the state to the residential site as visiting scholars and instructors, or in some cases using satellite capabilities to transmit courses from the residential school to schools throughout the state where other students may take advantage of the curriculum. Further, classes developed and tested at residential schools can be adapted by interested teachers for use with gifted students elsewhere in the state. Workshops and institutes at the residential schools bring teachers together during the summer to learn about techniques and materials for educating the gifted.

Special Issues

The establishment of special residential high schools raises a number of issues that must be resolved before such a school can open. One of the first is a concern of communities that the residential schools will take their top students away from the local high schools in a kind of "brain drain." Generally, however, these residential schools enroll students from throughout the state and no one area sends a disproportionate number of students.

An important issue raised by legislators, parents, and local schools is that of young students leaving home 2 or 3 years before they ordinarily would leave to attend college. For the residential high schools located at colleges and universities, there are additional concerns to be addressed related to placing young people on campuses with older students. Existing residential high schools have limited the interactions among high school and college students by housing them separately and segregating the two groups for social and, in most cases, academic activities.

Another often repeated concern is that of elitism, a fear that placing the most talented students together in a school of this type will lead to feelings of superiority and special favor among the selected students. Schools address this concern by structuring for the students involvement in outside community volunteer activities and by requiring that they share in the responsibilities for maintaining their school. Most schools communicate to the students the expectation that the students will repay in these ways the investment in their education made by the state.

When considering state-supported residential high schools, questions are always raised about the composition of the student body. Schools are asked to ensure that the classes will be balanced in terms of geographic, racial, ethnic, sexual, and socioeconomic representation. This brings up the question—often unspoken—of quotas. How does a school balance the student body while homogeneously grouping the students in terms of academic and intellectual ability? Most of the schools specify in their written materials that they are committed to achieving a student body that is diversified and that geographic and other variables are considered by the admissions committee. Stanley (1987), however, in discussing residential high schools for mathematically talented youth, urges that minimum ability levels be established for selection and that these levels not be modified to accommodate outside pressures. According to Stanley, these minimum levels should be developed by each state and should use as a reference point the average SAT scores achieved by male college-bound seniors in that state. In accord with Stanley's view, the Texas Academy of Mathematics and Science has set a minimum acceptable score of 550 on the mathematics portion of the SAT with an overall minimum of 1000 on the combined verbal and mathematics parts of the test. The North Carolina School of Science and Mathematics, in contrast, has set no minimum scores, believing that admissions criteria must be flexible to allow for special situations, for example, a student who has recently emigrated to this country and is not yet fluent enough in English to achieve the minimum scores on the SAT (Eilber, 1987).

Another major consideration affecting the establishment of special residential schools is the provision of a total, rounded experience for the students who attend. This involves support services, such as academic and personal counseling, and a program of extracurricular opportunities including athletics, arts, clubs, and social activities. Since students are on campus 24 hours a day, 7 days a week, the planning must be comprehensive and must address the needs of the total student. Residential staff must be prepared to assist students as they adjust to living away from home for the first time, encountering an extremely demanding curriculum, and attempting to balance their academic and social interests and commitments in a new community.

Existing residential high schools for the gifted carefully and thoughtfully plan their calendars to include long weekends at home, as well as opportunities for students to become involved in outside interests at the school. Staff members are alert to signs of stress, depression, and homesickness. They also are attuned to student behaviors that reveal problems in adjusting to the new environment, such as missing classes, failing to complete assignments, excessive socializing, or withdrawal from interactions with others. While there may be relatively few instances of these types of difficulties, they represent the kinds of issues that set residential schools apart from other schools and must be addressed in planning for and staffing such a school.

Judging Success of Residential Schools

The impact of special residential schools is assessed in several ways. The North Carolina School of Science and Mathematics evaluated aspects of the program that originally were stated as potential benefits. For example, surveys taken after 10 years revealed that 67% of the graduates had enrolled at in-state colleges and universities for their freshman year; by their junior year 73% were registered at in-state colleges and universities (Johnston, 1988); and 82% were studying science or mathematics in college.

Additional benefits to the state's educational system were evidenced in the number and scope of the outreach programs. Academically talented students from throughout the state attend the North Carolina school in the summer for advanced instruction in math and science. Teachers from the state spend summer months on campus working with the school's faculty to learn techniques that can be used in their home schools. There is anecdotal evidence that the school has encouraged local schools throughout the state to provide more math and science to students (Johnston, 1988).

The graduating classes of the residential schools typically have produced very large numbers of National Merit Scholar semifinalists and finalists. For example, in the first Illinois Mathematics and Science Academy graduating class, 38% of the seniors were National Merit semifinalists.

Also, students graduating from residential high schools have attracted millions of dollars in scholarship offers. The Louisiana School for Math, Science, and the Arts reported that the first four graduating classes received scholarship offers amounting to over $12 million. Individual awards and recognition have included student-designed experiments for the NASA space shuttle program and membership on the International Physics Olympiad.

Conclusions

The establishment of state-supported residential schools for gifted students is a movement whose time has come. States are seeking ways to meet the educational needs of high-ability students, and they recognize that for the most gifted of their students, an appropriate and effective method for meeting those needs is to group them together in one location and offer them an educational program more advanced and more challenging than the programs available in the local schools.

Beginning slowly, with the North Carolina School of Science and Mathematics and the Louisiana School for Math, Science, and the Arts the only such schools for several years, the movement has picked up momentum, and at present nearly one-fifth of the states have either established or authorized the establishment of an academic-year residential high school for gifted students. The issue is being studied by many other states. As perceptions of the success and the "return on investment" increase, more states are certain to follow the examples of those which have assumed leadership in the development of special residential high schools. Particularly meaningful and convincing will be evidence that these schools benefit those who attend as well as education statewide, and that they provide incentives for the long-term economic growth of the states.

As a final comment, there is a growing recognition among educators and legislators of the need for different kinds of services and programs to correspond to different types and levels of giftedness. While many local schools will continue to address these needs through cluster groups, pullout programs, self-contained classrooms, and honors courses, state leaders will heed the recommendations of experts and the examples of states pioneering in the development of residential high schools and establish such schools for their most talented and, perhaps, most underserved population of gifted students.

REFERENCES

Cox, J., Daniel, N., & Boston, B. (1985). *Educating able learners.* Austin: University of Texas Press.

Eilber, C. R. (1987). The North Carolina School of Science and Mathematics. *Phi Delta Kappan, 68,* 773–777.

Johnston, F. (1988, March 14). School of science and math—10 years old and growing. *The Durham Morning Herald.*

Stanley, J. C. (1987). State residential high schools for mathematically talented youth. *Phi Delta Kappan, 68,* 770–772.

PART IV

Creativity and
Thinking Skills

16

The Assessment of Creativity

CAROLYN M. CALLAHAN *University of Virginia, Charlottesville*

Issues and problems involved in the assessment of creativity have received considerable attention both in the general areas of psychology and educational psychology and in the specific field of education of the gifted and talented. The concept of creativity is illusive and, therefore, its measurement is difficult. However, creativity, like beauty, truth, or justice, is a construct about which everyone has some ideas and beliefs. People seem to "know it when they see it," even if they can't define it.

Psychologists and psychometricians have been struggling for the past 30 years to define creativity and translate that definition into operational terms that will yield instruments that will satisfactorily measure the trait in children and adults. These efforts have yielded many definitions of creativity, a plethora of approaches and instruments, and a literature that is often contradictory and confusing about the usefulness of those instruments. This chapter will address the issues that affect the appropriate use of creativity assessment in identifying the gifted and in evaluating the effects of programs oriented toward the development of creativity and creative thinking skills.

Creativity and Giftedness

The notion that creativity is in some way a part of the definition of giftedness has been approached from a variety of perspectives. A brief review is in order here because the various approaches have had an influence on the ways we view creativity, and ultimately the ways in which we incorporate use of the currently available measures of creativity into programs for the gifted.

For some, the creatively gifted form a separate category of gifted students. This orientation is reflective of the widely cited and adopted U.S. Office of Education (USOE) definition of giftedness. If a school district or program adopts this view of giftedness, then the identification of gifted children must include a separate process for identifying children who are creative but are not necessarily of high intellectual ability, or gifted in specific academic areas, or talented in the fine and performing arts, or possessing leadership skills. Other individuals (notably Renzulli, 1978) have presented strong arguments that creativity is a fundamental component of all giftedness, or to be true to Renzulli—gifted behavior. That is, the creatively gifted should not exist as a category unto itself. Rather, we should identify children with ability or talents in particular disciplines or academic areas who also possess those characteristics that would lead us to conclude that they are also creative in that area. According to Renzulli (1978), these creative abilities as he conceives of them go beyond the divergent thinking skills assessed by many of the instruments to be discussed in this chapter.

Many programs for the gifted do not include creativity in their definitions of giftedness but include specific goals within the curriculum for gifted students that call for the development of creative thinking skills.

Uses of Creativity Assessment Tools in Gifted Education

The most widespread use of measures of creativity in gifted education is in the identification of students for special programs or special services. The second most frequent use is in the evaluation of the effectiveness of various intervention or instructional strategies in improving skills in creative thinking or problem solving. Recently, there has been an emphasis on using the results of creativity instruments as diagnostic tools to yield data for instructional planning. At least one research study has used the Torrance Tests of Creative Thinking as a diagnostic tool for helping teachers identify specific skill strengths and weakness of their students (Bogner, 1981; Jensen, 1978). Carlson (1974) reported using identified creative thinking strengths as a basis for working with learning-disabled children.

Validity and Reliability of Creativity Assessment

Before instruments designed to assess creativity are evaluated, it is important to review the meaning of terms used to assess the quality of any measurement tool and to discuss these terms relative to creativity instruments.

Reliability

The first characteristic of a test of creativity that must be evaluated is the reliability of the instrument. Different types of reliability evidence are required of different types of instruments. Any instrument that is subjectively scored (that is, when the scorer must make some judgment in the scoring) requires the establishment of *inter-rater reliability,* that is, assurance that two individuals scoring the same test would come up with the same results. This is particularly important in tests of creative production. It would be gravely unjust if individuals were identified as creative or not creative depending on who happened to score their tests.

Tests that are used to select students for a program or predict performance in a program should also exhibit stability, or *test–retest reliability.* That is, we expect that if we identify a child as highly creative today, he or she will also be identified as creative if tested a week or a month or a year later.

All tests with alternative forms should have *equivalent forms reliability* (also known as parallel forms reliability). Equivalent forms reliability is an index of the degree to which the same person would earn similar scores on the two forms of the test. Equivalent forms reliability (in conjunction with stability) is especially important if we wish to assess the effects

of a program by administering one form of the test in the fall and another form in the spring. We would not want any differences we find to occur because of differences in the test.

Reliability indices are usually correlation coefficients with a range from .00 (absolutely no reliability) to 1.00 (perfectly reliable). A test with perfect reliability would yield the same score for a given student regardless of when the test was taken, which form was administered, or who scored the exam (assuming, of course, that the student had not changed between two administrations of the test).

Validity

Many studies of creativity instruments present considerable data on the reliability of the instruments, and few experts quarrel with the reliability of most creativity tests. The issue of validity is quite another matter. The question of validity of creativity instruments is a question of whether these instruments truly measure creativity. In light of the wide variation in definitions of creativity, it is easy to see that, depending on the definition of creativity, a given test can be considered to be highly valid or not at all valid. Validity is also a question of whether a test serves the purpose it was designed to serve. For example, a test designed to *predict* creative behavior should actually be validated with evidence that individuals who score high on the test are more likely to produce creative products than those who score lower on that test.

Four types of validity are considered in the evaluation of creativity tests. In assessing *content validity,* we examine the test to see whether or not the items on the test reflect the definition of creativity we have accepted. *Predictive validity* is established by examining the relationship between scores on the creativity test and creative productivity or performance at a later time. *Concurrent validity* is demonstrated by correlating the scores on one creativity assessment with either scores on other creativity tests or current measures of creativity productivity. Finally, *construct validity* is established through a complex process of examining the way the instrument performs in a variety of tests of theory and in its relationship to other instruments. For example, we expect a test of creativity to correlate more highly with another test of creativity than with a test of intelligence.

Approaches to the Measurement of Creativity

The types of assessment tools that have been developed to assess creativity can be categorized along two dimensions (at least). First, the instruments may be categorized as performance and/or product oriented, or they may be categorized as oriented toward measuring personality characteristics of the individual, or they may rely on collecting biographical information. Second, creativity instruments may also be categorized according to whether the individual being assessed completes a series of tasks (generally considered a test), reports on his or her attitudes, values, or feelings (a self-report instrument), or is evaluated on a scale by others—teachers, parents, or peers. The instruments discussed in this chapter have been categorized on these two dimensions in Table 16.1.

Of course, these tests also vary along a subjectivity–objectivity dimension with some of the personality assessments being very subjectively scored (e.g., Thematic Apperception Test, Murray, 1943); some performance tests having very specific scoring guides but involving some subjective judgments (e.g., Thinking Creatively with Sounds and Words, Torrance, Khatena, & Cunnington, 1973); and some self-report instruments being objectively scored by counting the number of times a student

Table 16.1
Types of Selected Creativity Instruments

	Test	Self-Report	Peer Rating	Teacher Rating	Parent Rating	Expert Rating
Performance/product:						
Torrance Tests of Creative Thinking	X					
Judging Criteria Instrument		X	X			
Thinking Creatively in Action and Movement	X					
Thinking Creatively with Sounds and Words	X					
Remote Associates Test	X					
Detroit Public Schools Creativity Scale				X	X	
Personality/attitudes/values:						
Thematic Apperception Test	X					
Khatena-Torrance Creative Perception Inventory		X				
GIFT		X				
GIFFI		X				
Your Style of Learning and Thinking		X				
Creative Behavior Checklist				X		
Rorschach Inkblot Test	X					
Biographical inventories:						
Biographical Inventory—Creativity		X				
Alpha Biographical Inventory		X				
Other:						
Creativity Assessment Packet	X	X		X	X	
Creativity Process Inventory				X		

checks a particular item (e.g., Something about Myself, Khatena & Torrance, 1976).

Performance Instruments

The most common type of creativity assessment used in the identification of gifted and talented students is performance assessments, and the most common of these are the tests derived from the divergent production component of Guilford's structure of intellect model. These instruments present a series of open-ended tasks to the person taking the test and direct the testee to generate as many responses as possible. For example, the student might be asked to list the possible consequences of the disappearance of the color red. The tasks are scored for fluency (the number of responses), flexibility (the number of different categories into which the responses fall), originality (the statistical infrequency of such responses in a norm group), and, sometimes, elaboration (the amount of detail given in the response). The earliest of these assessments was developed by Guilford himself, but the most widely used instruments of this nature are the Torrance Tests of Creative Thinking—Verbal and Figural Forms (TTCT; Torrance, 1966a).

Although these tests are most often used as identification instruments, they are also used in some program evaluations and research studies for outcome measures. The problems associated with the use of these instruments in this fashion will be discussed in a later section of this chapter.

Other researchers have attempted to develop ratings of creative performance by developing scales with specific criteria for rating the products of creativity. For example, Eichenberger (1978) developed an instrument called the Judging Criteria Instrument for evaluating creativity in the physics classroom.

Personality Instruments

These instruments are based on the assumption that individuals who have those personality traits commonly identified in research on creative individuals have the potential for making creative contributions themselves.

The approaches to assessing the degree to which students possess those traits are through self-reports on such instruments as the What Kind of Person Are You? scale developed by Khatena and Torrance (1976) and through ratings by parents, teachers, or peers. The items on self-report scales most often include descriptive phrases or adjectives and ask the individuals to check all items that might describe them, or ask them to assess the degree to which they possess a characteristic by checking a point on a Likert rating scale. Ratings of personality by persons who know the student have a similar format.

Some personality instruments used as general assessment instruments have also been used to assess creativity (e.g., the Rorschach Inkblot Test, Rorschach, 1951; the Adjective Checklist, Domino, 1970).

Biographical Indices

Believing that past performance of creative activities is the best predictor of future creative behavior, several authors have constructed surveys that ask the respondent to report on past achievements, involvement in certain kinds of contests, extracurricular activities, and so forth, that correspond to those activities associated with creative behavior (Schaefer, 1969, 1970a, 1970b).

A Review of Commonly Used Instruments

There are literally hundreds of instruments that have been developed to assess creativity, creative problem-solving skills, and specific skills within each of those domains. This chapter, however, will focus only on a selection of those instruments readily available for use and applicable within a school setting. Further listings of creativity tests are available in the *Journal of Creative Behavior* (see particularly Davis, 1971; Kaltsounis, 1972; Kaltsounis & Honeywell, 1980). In addition, the *Mental Measurements Yearbooks* and *Test Critiques* present critical reviews of published instruments, and the *Dictionary of Unpublished Experimental Mental Measures* (Volumes 3 and 4) presents a brief overview of instruments reported in psychological and educational journals (Goldman & Busch, 1982; Goldman & Osborne, 1985).

A Review of Selected Performance Assessments

The Torrance Tests of Creative Thinking. The most extensively researched and widely used instruments for assessing creativity are the Torrance Tests of Creative Thinking (Torrance, 1966b). The verbal form of the tests, Thinking Creatively with Words, is made up of a series of tasks that elicit responses to questions such as "What are all the uses you can think of for a brown paper bag?" or "What would happen if there were no gravity?" All the items on the figural form of the test, Thinking Creatively with Pictures, require the examinee to complete a drawing based on an abstract stimulus and give a title to that drawing. Both the verbal and figural tests have two forms.

The scoring of the test is described in great detail in the administration and scoring manuals, but the tests may also be scored through a scoring service. Each subtest is scored for fluency, flexibility, and originality. The figural test items are also scored for elaboration. The student receives total fluency, flexibility, and originality scores. The test developer strictly cautions against combining those scores into a "total creativity" score.

Inter-rater reliability as assessed by correlating scores assigned to the same tests by different raters has been reported in the technical manual (Torrance, 1966b) and in subsequent studies as very high (usually greater than .90). However, Rosenthal, DeMars, Stilwell, and Graybeal (1983) found that even though the correlation between raters was high, there were significant mean differences across three self-trained raters. That is, even though the individual raters had given scores that ranked the students in approximately the same order, some raters gave scores that were, overall, higher than scores assigned by other raters. Thus, if a cutoff score is to be used in any selection process, it is important that the same rater rate all protocols or that ad-

justments be made for differences across raters. Similarly, if these tests are used to measure changes in students over time in a program, it is important that the same raters score both the pretests and the post-tests. In addition, the open-ended nature of these tests demands a considerable expenditure of time in scoring. Torrance has collaborated with Ball (Ball & Torrance, 1980) in the creation of a streamlined scoring method.

Predictive validity is of concern if this test is to be used for identification of creativity in gifted students. Torrance (1984) reported on two longitudinal studies in which scores on early versions of the instruments were correlated with accomplishments in adulthood with validity coefficients of .51 for males and .43 for females (over 12 years) and .63 (over 20 years). Although these coefficients do not predict perfectly, they are as high as predictive validity coefficients for intelligence or achievement test scores in predicting adult achievement (Torrance, 1981a; 1984). For example, in the study reported by Torrance, the predictive validity coefficients of intelligence tests ranged from −.02 to .34. In another longitudinal study by Torrance and Wu (1981), students identified as highly creative earned as many post–high school degrees, honors, and other academic achievements as their high-IQ counterparts; excelled over the high-IQ group on four criteria of adult achievement (number of publicly recognized creative achievements, quality of highest creative achievements, number of personal creative achievements, and quality of future career images); and equalled the achievements of those identified as highly creative and highly intelligent. Howieson's (1981, 1984) results were not as impressive (total scores on TTCT correlated .30 with ratings of creative achievement outside school in one study, and verbal scores failed to correlate significantly with adult achievement in the other).

Concerns about the use of the instrument also stem from studies that have demonstrated that performance on the TTCT can easily be affected by changing the testing conditions. Scores on divergent tests have been shown to be influenced by changing time limits (Torrance & Ball, 1978), whether or not children were interrupted from an interesting or an uninteresting classroom activity for testing (Elkind, Deblinger, & Adler, 1970; Kirkland, 1974; Kirkland, Kilpatrick, & Barker, 1976), whether tests were timed or untimed (Wallach & Kogan, 1965), whether students were tested in the same room in which intelligence tests had previously been administered (Boersma & O'Bryan, 1968), whether the tests were administered under gamelike or testlike conditions (Hattie, 1980), whether the tests were administered in an enriched or a barren environment (Friedman, Raymond, & Feldhusen, 1978), whether testing was preceded by brief warm-up activity (Carroll, 1980), and whether there were modest changes, seemingly innocuous differences, in directions during administration (Lissitz & Willhoft, 1985).

Reviews of the tests have varied from critical conclusions that the tests should be used for research and experimentation only (Chase, 1985) to recommendations that even though "no test can purport to represent a comprehensive assessment of the many forms and expressions of creativity, . . . [t]he TTCT offers useful insights into several relevant dimensions" and can be used effectively if used with other assessments and with "sensitivity and good judgment by qualified professionals" (Treffinger, 1985; p. 1634).

Thinking Creatively in Action and Movement. Another test by Torrance based on the measurement of ideational fluency, but using movement as the vehicle for expressing this characteristic, is Thinking Creatively in Action and Movement (TCAM; Torrance, 1981b). This instrument is designed for use with children as young as preschool age and yields fluency and originality scores on such tasks as generating ways of moving from one side of the room to the other, putting a cup in a wastebasket, or pretending to move like a tree or a snake. Children may give verbal or kinesthetic responses.

Short-term stability reported in the manual is very high (.84). Inter-rater reliability reported in the manual is .99 for fluency and .96 for originality. Inter-rater reliability reported in Tegano, Moran, and Godwin (1986) is .95 and in Cropley (1986) is between .93 and .99 across the subscores.

Concurrent validity of the TCAM was investigated by Tegano et al. (1986) by comparing scores on that instrument with scores on the Multidimensional Stimulus Fluency Measure (MSFM; Godwin & Moran, 1986), which is a verbal measure of fluency. Total fluency scores on the MSFM and TCAM were significantly correlated, as were total originality scores. The conclusion of these researchers was that "to varying degrees, the subtests of the instruments measured the same construct, thereby establishing construct validity" (p. 391). Construct validity evidence was also presented by Reisman, Floyd, and Torrance (1981), who found that scores on the TCAM correlated significantly with Piagetian tasks and a math inventory, both of which were described by the authors as divergent tasks. However, the Tegano et al. (1986) study found significant correlations between ideational fluency scores on these instruments and IQ, raising questions about the independence from intelligence of creativity as measured by this instrument. The TCAM scores in that study also correlated significantly with age, raising questions about the stability of test scores over a long period of time.

Reviews of this test have lamented the lack of more extensive validity evidence, particularly construct and predictive validity and have suggested that in its present form it cannot be recommended for educational decisions about individual students (Evans, 1986).

Thinking Creatively with Sounds and Words. Another instrument developed under the direction of Torrance, this test is actually two separate tests: Sounds and Images, and Onomatopoeia and Images (Torrance et al., 1973). The tests require students to describe the mental images they associate either with various familiar and abstract sound effects or with words. The technical data on this instrument are very similar to those of Thinking Creatively with Action and Movement, and the review by Houtz (1985) concluded that this test also needed further evidence of validity before using it to identify creatively gifted students.

The Remote Associates Test. Another performance assessment of creativity is the Remote Associates Test (RAT). The tasks presented in this test ask the individual to generate a word that can be associated with three stimulus words. For example, you might be presented with the words *birthday, surprise,* and *line*. The word *party* can be associated with all of the three stimulus words. The assumption that underlies this test is that creative individuals are able to make many associations to a given stimulus, thus allowing them to generate connections more easily than less creative persons.

Although validity studies of the RAT have shown moderate correlations with ratings of creative writing samples (Lynch & Kaufman, 1974) and with faculty ratings of creativity in architecture and psychology students, other studies have failed to find such correlations when studying physicists and engineers (Mednick, 1962; Wallach, 1970). The RAT's validity has been further criticized because it punishes imaginative responses (Davis, 1975), because studies of the processes used by persons taking the test fail to parallel the associative process described by the authors (Perkins, 1981), and because it is so highly correlated with intelligence scores (Davis & Belcher, 1971; Dice, 1976; Ward, 1975). The most recent review of this instrument in the *Mental Measurements Yearbook* pointed out the nonexistence of validity data for the high school form of the test, criticized it as a measure of convergent production, and recommended that it "be considered a research instrument and not be used for counseling or placement purposes at the present time" (Backman & Tuckman, 1978, p. 370).

Judging Criteria Instrument. The assessment of the outcomes of general instruction in techniques for improving creativity or in specific discipline-oriented instruction in creativity has been approached through the use of expert ratings and ratings by teachers and peers. One such instrument, the Judging Criteria Instrument (Eichenberger, 1978), was developed for use by self and peers in assessing creativity in a physics class using rating scales based on fluency, flexibility, originality, elaboration, worth to science, potential for working, social acceptance, and usefulness. This rating scale was validated by comparing ratings by

peers and self to scores students earned on the TTCT and judgments of physical science teachers. Peer ratings were shown to have greater concurrent validity than self-ratings.

Detroit Public Schools Creativity Scales. Parke and Byrnes (1984) reported another attempt to create rating scales for discipline-specific creativity, the Detroit Public Schools Creativity Scales, which include scales in art, music composition, music performance, drama, poetry, short story/novel writing, speech, and dance. These scales were derived from the examination of factors used by experts in evaluating performance in these domains and were proposed for use both in identification of talent and in evaluation of programs in these domains. At this time, very little evidence is available on the reliability or construct validity of these instruments.

Other Specific Discipline Scales. Kulp and Tarter (1986) developed a rating scale that is applied to art products generated from five basic geometric figures. Although only sixth-graders were used in the initial assessments of the reliability and concurrent validity of the instrument, the results looked promising. Hocevar (1979b) developed a series of scales to measure creative activity in fine arts, crafts, performing arts, math-science, literature, and music. Internal consistency reliabilities ranged from .63 to .90; however, validity evidence is not currently available.

A Review of Selected Personality Assessments

The Khatena-Torrance Creative Perception Inventory. These two self-rating scales, Something about Myself (SAM) and What Kind of Person Are You? (WKOPAY), were designed to identify creatively gifted adolescents and adults (Khatena & Torrance, 1976). Individuals are asked whether statements such as "When I think I have an interesting idea I like adding to it to make it more interesting" are like them or unlike them. Validity studies on this instrument have shown moderate but significant correlations of the

SAM with tests of verbal originality (Kaltsounis, 1975; Khatena, 1971), and with scores on the Onomatopoeia and Images subtest of Thinking Creatively with Sounds and Words ($r = .34$ $p < .01$; Khatena & Bellarosa, 1978). The WKOPAY and the SAM correlated significantly with a measure of readiness for self-directed study (Khatena & Bellarosa, 1978). Validity correlations of the WKOPAY scale with a Vividness of Imagery scale ranged only from .01 to .20. To date, there is no evidence of predictive validity.

Group Inventory for Finding Creative Talent. Designed to assess the creative potential of children in Grades 1 to 6, this self-report inventory (GIFT) actually has three forms: one for primary students in Grades 1 and 2, one for elementary students in Grades 3 and 4, and one for students in upper elementary Grades 5 and 6 (Rimm & Davis, 1976). Students are presented with a series of statements to which they answer yes or no, indicating their interests and attitudes on items tied to dimensions of creative thinking such as breadth of interests, imagination, independence, and so forth. For example, a yes response to "I ask a lot of questions" indicates imagination. The checklists also contain items of a biographical nature such as "Sometimes my mom and dad and I make things together." The studies of reliability and validity of these tests are reported in a series of articles by the tests' authors (Rimm & Davis, 1976, 1980, 1983). Reported split-half reliability estimates were .80, .86, and .88 for revised versions of the GIFT; however, stability estimates over 6 months were considerably lower (.56) and were considered "disquieting" for individual assessment by Dwinell (1985) in her review in the *Mental Measurements Yearbook*. Reliabilities for kindergarten students were considered unacceptably low by Rimm and Davis (1976).

Rimm and Davis (1976) contended that the content validity of the test was established by the selection of items that paralleled those of established instruments. Criterion-related validity was based on correlating GIFT scores with a composite score made up of teacher ratings of creativeness and experimenter rating of short stories and pictures (except for Grade 1).

Validity coefficients ranged from .20 to .54 (all statistically significant), but the validation research was criticized by Wright (1985) as limited in its selection of teacher ratings and judges' scoring as criteria. Wakefield (1985a) correlated GIFT scores with scores on measures of divergent production and concluded that GIFT and divergent test scores assessed only "marginally related aspects of creativity" (p. 351). Rimm and Davis (1976) also reported significantly higher scores for students nominated as creative by art teachers and a significant correlation (.21) with the Unusual Uses subtest of the TTCT.

Dwinell (1985) concluded that while "GIFT does not appear to be an especially strong instrument for identifying creativity, . . . when used with other identification procedures it can be considered useful and fairly valid for selecting students of varied backgrounds and cultures to participate in special programs which would encourage creative thinking" (p. 455). Wakefield (1985b) concluded that at Grades 4 to 6 GIFT appeared reliable and valid enough for use in identifying students who had personality characteristics like those of creative persons, but he was less positive about the use of this instrument for grades K–3.

Group Inventory for Finding Interests (I and II). These inventories represent an extension of GIFT to the junior and senior high school level (Davis & Rimm, 1980, 1982). The reported internal consistency reliabilities were above .90, and the average validity coefficient (correlations of scores with writing and teacher ratings) was .45 (Davis, 1989).

The instrument has been criticized for a seeming cultural/class bias in several of the items (e.g., "I attend concerts," and "I own painting and drawing supplies"). The requirement that it be scored by a scoring service not only is expensive but also precludes examination of the underlying assumptions in the scoring and the low criterion-related validity coefficients (Weeks, 1985).

Creative Attitude Survey. This instrument by Schaefer (1970a, 1970b, 1971) has been used to evaluate training programs in creativity through the assessment of confidence in one's ideas, appreciation of fantasy, theoretical and aesthetic orientation, openness to impulse expression, and use of novelty. Reliability studies on fourth- and fifth-grade students yielded Spearman-Brown reliability coefficients of .81 and .75 and stability indices over 5 weeks of .61. Two of these studies, which investigated changes in scores after training in creativity programs, showed significantly higher scores for students receiving such training. McKee (1985) concluded in her review of the instrument that although this instrument had not been widely used, it "could be included in the evaluation of programs to foster creativity in elementary age children" (p. 207).

Your Style of Thinking and Learning. One currently popular area of study within the field of creativity is the left brain/right brain dominance issue and its applicability to the study of creativity. Not surprisingly, there have been attempts to assess creativity through assessment of brain dominance. One of the most widely cited of these instruments is Your Style of Thinking and Learning (Torrance, Reynolds, Ball, & Riegel, 1978; Torrance, Reynolds, Riegel & Ball, 1977). Unfortunately, this instrument is fraught with problems in its theoretical concepts (it seems contrary to existing brain research on several dimensions), its scoring procedures, and its technical qualities. Fitzgerald and Hattie (1983) reviewed the theoretical properties and found them to be lacking in a sound basis. Their investigation of its psychometric properties yielded low reliabilities and a lack of concurrent validity.

Creative Behavior Checklist for Disadvantaged Children. On this instrument, teachers are asked to check for the presence or absence of a set of characteristics presumed to be characteristic of creative individuals. Validity is very questionable. In reported studies, this instrument correlates more strongly with reading and arithmetic subtests of the Stanford Achievement Test ($r = .59$) than with TTCT ($r = .08$) (Goldman & Osborne, 1985).

Other Personality Instruments. Although considerable work has been done on the use of free response, projective measures such as the Thematic Apperception Test (Murray, 1943) and the Rorschach Inkblot Test to assess creativity (Baker, 1978; Wakefield, 1986), they are not discussed here because the ethical use of such instruments requires considerable training in psychological assessment and clinical licensure. Use of these measures and other free response and perceptual processing measures has been considered valid in the research on scientific creativity (Gough, 1985) and creativity in general (Smith & Carlsson, 1987). However, they have not received very much attention as tools to assess creative potential or achievement in the school setting, because of the expense of administration and the complexity of scoring, as well as the nature of the assessment. Use of objective personality instruments has also not been a widely accepted practice because of the extremely sensitive nature of the other constructs measured, the time required for administration, and the expense associated with assessment.

Review of Selected Biographical Inventories

Biographical Inventory—Creativity. The 165 items on this test yield (1) creative art scores for females, (2) creative writing scores for females, (3) creative math and science scores for males, and (4) art-writing scores for males (Schaefer, 1970a). Hocevar (1979b) pointed out in his review of the issues surrounding the measurement of creativity that the best predictor of future behavior is past behavior and used that argument to support the use of such instruments. Studies of the predictive power of past creative behavior have been carried out by Holland and Nichols (1964) and Richards, Holland, and Lutz (1967a, 1967b). Particular studies supporting the validity of the Biographical Inventory have been carried out by Anastasi and Schaefer (1969), Schaefer (1969), and Schaefer and Anastasi (1968).

Alpha Biographical Inventory. The Alpha Biographical Inventory evolved from extensive studies of scientists and engineers at

NASA by the Institute for Behavioral Research in Creativity (1968). The test produces prediction scores for academic success and creativity. Its 300 items sample hobbies, interests, experiences, childhood experiences, and so forth. Validation studies are largely limited to studies on adult scientists.

Combination Instruments

The Creativity Assessment Packet. The Creativity Assessment Packet (CAP) comprises two tests plus an observational-rating scale completed by parents or teachers (Williams, 1980). One of the tests is similar to other measures of figural divergent production and is similarly scored. The second test is a list of personality characteristics on which the students rate themselves using a 3-point scale ranging from *mostly true about me* to *mostly untrue about me*. The final scale consists of 48 items (8 related to each of six modes of creative thinking defined by Williams in his model of creativity) on which the child is rated by a parent or a teacher. The test has been severely criticized for poor norming samples, reliance on intuition for interpretation of the completed profile, and unclear and inadequate reliability and validity evidence (Fekken, 1985).

The Creative Process Inventory. Most rating scales for use by teachers in rating creativity of students have been greatly criticized. However, a recently developed scale (Kirschenbaum, 1986) based on assessing *contact* (amount and accuracy of reported details and attraction to diverse aspects of the environment), *consciousness* (amount and relevance of ideas and questions, ideational fluency, and nonconformity of judgment), *interest* (amount of time and effort spent on independent projects, task commitment), and *fantasy* (amount of impact of images expressed verbally or pictorially) has promise for reliable and valid use of teacher input. Initial assessments of internal reliability and validity reported by Kirschenbaum (1986) suggested that this instrument may evolve into a useful technique of collecting data for selection to programs.

Underlying Issues in the Assessment of Creativity

The above descriptions and reviews have already suggested that there is still considerable disagreement in the field about the degree to which we have constructed instruments that validly measure the construct of creativity. On one hand, some reviewers have concluded that "existing measures of creativity give us useful information about thought processes that are involved in creative talent" (Treffinger, 1980, p. 24) and "at present, there seems little question that tests measuring creative abilities, creative personality, and biographical traits, or else evaluating the creativeness of products, work reasonably well. Reliabilities are high and validities are good" (Davis, 1989, p. 271). On the other hand, many reviewers have concurred with Sternberg's (1986) opinion:

> The measures of creativity currently available to us measure creativity in a less meaningful (some might say—trivial) way than would correspond to people's implicit theories of creativity. Thinking of unusual uses for a paper clip, for example, and similar tasks, would seem to draw relatively little upon the lack of unconventionality, integration and intellectuality, aesthetic taste and imagination, decision skills and flexibility, perspicacity, and drive for accomplishment and recognition that are seen as essential aspects of creativity. (p. 189)

The Use of Measures of Divergent Production and Current Scoring

One of the major issues that still plagues the assessment of creativity is the degree to which tests of divergent production are valid assessments of the elusive construct of creativity. This issue is a long-standing one and is based on the diversity of theoretical approaches to defining creativity itself and studies that have failed to correlate judgments of classroom creativity with scores on divergent production tasks (e.g., Roweton, Farles, Donham, Wleklinski & Spencer, 1975). This issue was raised by Treffinger, Renzulli, and Feldhusen (1981) and continues to make our judgments about the validity of the tests conflicting and confusing. Torrance and his colleagues, in response to criticisms of the limitations of the dimensions of fluency, flexibility, and originality, have explored alternative scoring approaches to the TTCT (Torrance & Hall, 1980), but no validation studies have warranted the use of these alternatives.

The degree to which the fluency, flexibility, and originality measures obtained from scoring such divergent production instruments as the TTCT or the divergent tasks of Wallach and Kogan (1965) are interrelated or independent measures, whether they can be combined to yield a single index of creativity, and the degree to which fluency has been a contaminating factor in the measurement of originality have all been investigated in the literature (Hocevar, 1979a; Runco & Albert, 1985). Further, according to Hocevar (1979a), when subjective and objective scores on an originality dimension of a divergent production test are compared, while controlling for fluency factors, "Responses designated as 'original' by the criterion of statistical rarity are not necessarily subjectively judged as original" (p. 298).

Fluency as a Contaminating Factor. There is general agreement that fluency is a *contaminating factor* in the assessment of originality. That is, the more responses a student gives, the higher the originality score is (Clark & Mirels, 1970; Dixon, 1979; Seddon, 1983). Likewise, the higher the fluency score, the higher the flexibility score (Torrance, 1966b). Obviously, the more responses a student gives, the more likely it is that there will be many categories of responses and more original responses. Hocevar (1979a) concluded from his studies of the relationship between fluency and originality scores that the fluency contamination in current instruments resulted in failure to truly assess these conceptually distinguished factors. Several authors (Clark & Mirels, 1970; Seddon, 1983) have tried to develop schemes for combining scores and for controlling for the influence of the fluency factor, but none have been widely tested or become accepted practice. The research of Runco and Albert (1985) also indicated that only the figural tests of divergent production were reliable measures of originality in the general population after fluency was controlled. Runco (1986), in a study of gifted students only, found that fluency, flexibility, and originality were not independent traits and concluded that fluency alone was a sufficient indicator of divergent production as one aspect of creative thinking. Developers of the tests of divergent production argue that the subscores may not be combined into a single index; however, little guidance is provided as to how the individual subscores are to be interpreted in the identification of creative abilities, and there has been no resolution of the question of the independence of the factors.

Intelligence and Creativity

One of the most severe criticisms leveled against tests of creativity is the charge that they often correlate more highly with tests of intelligence than they do with each other, especially when administered under traditional testlike conditions. Katz (1983), for example, found significant correlations between the Quick Test of Intelligence and the verbal forms of the TTCT. However, research studies have been contradictory on this issue, with much debate over the influence of timed versus untimed conditions (Wallach & Kogan, 1965), the population studied (Yamamoto, 1974), the instruments (intelligence and creativity) used in the study (Richards, 1976), and even the kinds of statistical analyses used (Hattie & Rogers, 1986). Hattie (1980), for example, reported higher correlations among creativity variables than correlations between intelligence and creativity under both testlike and gamelike conditions; and Runco and Albert (1985) reported higher correlations among scores on several creativity assessments than between creativity scores and measures of achievement in gifted students.

General Versus Specific Assessment

A further issue is whether a general process of divergent production should be assessed or whether there should be specific tests that best assess creativity in specific disciplines. This issue relates to the debate of whether creativity in science is different from creativity in music or whether the creativity of artists is different from the creativity of writers. Zegas (1976) investigated the concurrent validity of tests of divergent productivity of advanced students in art, music, and writing and found that students in art scored higher on tests of figural productivity than did the general population, students of music scored higher on scores of symbolic production, and advanced writing students scored higher on semantic production. Only the English majors scored significantly higher than the general population when total scores were compared, suggesting that specific tests may be more valid than a generalized assessment. It should be noted, however, that Zegas (1976) emphasized that even these data are limited in that they are not longitudinal or predictive and that creativity is a "constellation of many traits and abilities. Therefore, it cannot be assumed that divergent productions is the only factor allied with successful creative performance" (p. 176).

Cultural, Racial, and Socioeconomic Bias

The influence of cultural, racial, and socioeconomic bias is central to the evaluation of any assessment tool. Too often school personnel assume that creativity tests are culture free or nonbiased by their very nature. Such assumptions are unwarranted. Torrance (1976), for example, while concluding that "[o]verall, there were no racial or socioeconomic differences" between scores of groups of children, conceded that in some studies using certain of the tasks from the TTCT, "black children excelled white children on certain tasks and white children excelled blacks on others" (p. 139). Argulewicz and Kush (1984) found that scores of Anglo-American children were significantly greater than scores of Mexican-American children on two of the three TTCT verbal scores (fluency and originality) and approached significance on the third (flexibility). However, they found no differences on the figural scores or on the creativity subscale of the Scales for Rating Behavioral Characteristics of Superior Students (Renzulli, Hartman & Callahan, 1975). Earlier discussions of personality and biographical instruments have pointed to other examples of potential bias.

Using Creativity Instruments for Student or Program Evaluation

Although most instruments discussed in this chapter are used primarily for identification of gifted and talented students, program administrators and teachers sometimes search for instruments to measure the impact of instruction on students in gifted programs. Often, tests such as the TTCT are used for this purpose without consideration of some inherent problems in doing so. First, any instrument that is designed to measure a stable, consistent personality trait is not likely to be sensitive to changes in individuals (Amabile, 1982). Second, an instrument used for identification cannot be used for assessing change as the students are likely to exhibit regression-toward-the-mean effects (getting lower scores simply because of a statistical phenomenon). Finally, very often the very things we teach as part of the process of creative thinking may mitigate against high performance. For example, if one teaches evaluation as part of solving problems, will the students self-monitor their performance on a task of divergent thinking and use criteria other than those of the scoring guide?

Amabile (1982, 1983) proposed that new methodologies and assessments need to evolve through the use of judges to subjectively rate specific products in a global fashion. This methodology has yielded reliable results and, in several studies, has successfully differentiated influences of environmental factors on creativity.

What Does It All Mean?

At this point the reader may feel very confused about the usefulness of the instruments that have been developed to assess creativity in the gifted. Should they be used? Under what conditions? What kind of information will be obtained? A few summary points may help to address these issues.

1. No one of the available instruments by itself seems to be a satisfactory measure of the elusive construct we call creativity, but individual instruments seem to measure some of the skills involved in creative thinking, to assess a number of characteristics associated with creative behavior, or to be reasonable means of assessing creative products.

2. Any instrument considered for the assessment of creativity either for identification purposes or evaluation of programs should be carefully examined to ensure a match between the definition of creativity espoused by the author and the definition of creativity accepted by the program.

3. Multiple measures of creativity using a variety of types of assessment are most likely to yield a valid assessment of creativity. A thorough screening and identification process should collect some performance data, some personality data (self-report and adult ratings), and some evidence of creative productivity.

4. If instruments such as the Torrance Tests of Creative Thinking are to be used, the test administrators should exercise considerable care to ensure that all students are given the test under the same standardized conditions—particularly if students' scores will be compared. Further, if pre–post-test comparisons are to be made, it is very important that test administration conditions remain constant across time.

5. Any instrument considered should be weighed in terms of its validity for the intended use of the instrument.

6. Individuals' subtest scores and scores from multiple instruments should not be summed into a unitary "creativity score." The evidence should be considered as individual pieces of data.

7. Avoid "homemade" instruments—tests or rating scales. As Treffinger (1980) pointed out, it is highly unlikely that inexperienced test makers will be able to accomplish what years of development and research by experts in the field have not been able to accomplish.

8. Build a data base on the predictability of creativity instruments for identifying students in your school (Treffinger, 1980). The individual nature of schools, definitions of giftedness

and creativity, and student populations as well as the limitations of the tests as discussed above may affect the reliability or validity of an instrument in a particular setting.

9. All instruments should be carefully studied for any indication of cultural, racial, gender, or socioeconomic bias. Not only should school officials consider the instrument on its face, but studies that have evaluated such differences should be examined.

10. Do not abandon the commitment to identify the trait of creativity simply because of the difficulties involved. Rather, look for consistent patterns and indicators from many sources, both at and outside school. While making every attempt to use valid and reliable information, do not ignore the subjective judgments of reliable and knowledgeable sources.

REFERENCES

Amabile, T. M. (1982). Social psychology of creativity: A consensual assessment technique. *Journal of Personality and Social Psychology, 43,* 997–1013.

Amabile, T. M. (1983). *The social psychology of creativity*. New York: Springer-Verlag.

Anastasi, A., & Schaefer, C. E. (1969). Biographical correlates of artistic and literary creativity in adolescent girls. *Journal of Applied Psychology, 53,* 267–273.

Argulewicz, E. N., & Kush, J. C. (1984). Concurrent validity of the SRBCSS Creativity Scale for Anglo-American and Mexican-American gifted students. *Educational and Psychological Research, 4,* 81–89.

Backman, M. E., & Tuckman, B. W. (1978). [Review of *Remote Associates Form: High School Form*]. In O. Buros (Ed.), *The eighth mental measurements yearbook* (Vol. 1, p. 370). Highland Park, NJ: Gryphon.

Baker, M. (1978). The Torrance Tests of Creative Thinking and The Rorschach Inkblot Test: Relationships between two measures of creativity. *Perceptual and Motor Skills, 46,* 539–547.

Ball, O. E., & Torrance, E. P. (1980). Effectiveness of new materials developed for training the streamlined scoring of the TTCT, Figural A and B forms. *Journal of Creative Behavior, 14,* 199–203.

Boersma, F. J., & O'Bryan, K. (1968). An investigation of the relationship between creativity and intelligence under two conditions of testing. *Journal of Personality, 36,* 341–348.

Bogner, D. (1981). Creative individual education programs (IEPS) from creativity tests. *Creative Child and Adult Quarterly, 6,* 160–162.

Carlson, N. A. (1974). *Using the creative strengths of a learning disabled child to increase evaluative effort and academic achievement.* Unpublished doctoral dissertation, Michigan State University, East Lansing.

Carroll, J. (1980). The effect of warm-up experiences on creativity scores. *Journal of Creative Behavior, 14,* 214–222.

Chase, C. I. (1985). [Review of *Torrance Tests of Creative Thinking*]. In J. Mitchell, Jr., *The ninth mental measurements yearbook* (Vol. 2, pp. 1630–1634). Lincoln, NE: Buros Institute of Mental Measurement.

Clark, P. M., & Mirels, H. L. (1970). Fluency as a pervasive element in the measurement of creativity. *Journal of Educational Measurement, 7,* 83–86.

Cropley, C. (1986). *Divergent thinking in young handicapped children.* Unpublished doctoral dissertation, University of Washington, Seattle.

Davis, G. A. (1971). Instruments useful in studying creative behavior and creative talents: Part 2. *Journal of Creative Behavior, 5,* 162–165.

Davis, G. A. (1975). In frumious pursuit of the creative person. *Journal of Creative Behavior, 9,* 75–87.

Davis, G. A. (1989). Testing for creative potential. *Contemporary Educational Psychology, 14,* 257–274.

Davis, G. A., & Belcher, T. L. (1971). How shall creativity tests be measured? Torrance Tests, RAT, Alpha Biographical, IQ. *Journal of Creative Behavior, 5,* 153–161.

Davis, G. A., & Rimm, S. (1980). *Group inventory for finding interests.* Watertown, WI: Educational Assessment Service.

Davis, G. A., & Rimm, S. (1982). Group Inventory for Finding Interests (GIFFI) I and II: Instruments for identifying creative potential in the junior and senior high school. *Journal of Creative Behavior, 16,* 50–57.

Dice, M. (1976). In search of creativity: Some current literature. *Gifted Child Quarterly, 20,* 196–204.

Dixon, J. (1979). Quality versus quantity: The need to control for the fluency factor in originality scores from the Torrance tests. *Journal for the Education of the Gifted, 2,* 70–79.

Domino, G. (1970). Identification of potentially creative persons from the Adjective Check List. *Journal of Consulting and Clinical Psychology, 35,* 48–51.

Dwinell, P. L. (1985). [Review of *Group Inventory for Finding Interests*]. In J. Mitchell (Ed.), *The ninth mental measurements yearbook* (Vol. 1, pp. 362–363). Lincoln, NE: Buros Institute of Mental Measurement.

Eichenberger, R. J. (1978). Creativity measurement through use of judgment criteria in physics. *Educational and Psychological Measurement, 38,* 221–227.

Elkind, D., Deblinger, J., & Adler, D. (1970). Motivation and creativity: The context effect. *American Educational Research Journal, 7,* 351–357.

Evans, E. D. (1986). [Review of *Thinking Creatively in Action and Movement*]. In D. Keyser & R. Sweetland (Eds.), *Test critiques* (Vol. 5, pp. 505–512). Kansas City: Testing Corporation of America.

Fekken, G. C. (1985). [Review of *Creativity Assessment Packet*]. In D. Keyser & R. Sweetland, (Eds.), *Test critiques* (Vol. 2, pp. 211–215). Kansas City: Testing Corporation of America.

Fitzgerald, D., & Hattie, J. A. (1983). An evaluation of the Your Style of Learning and Thinking inventory. *British Journal of Educational Psychology, 53,* 336–346.

Friedman, F., Raymond, B. A., & Feldhusen, J. F. (1978). The effects of environmental scanning on creativity. *Gifted Child Quarterly, 22,* 248–251.

Godwin, L. G., & Moran, J. D. (1986). *Reliability and validity of an instrument for measuring creativity in preschool children.* Manuscript submitted for publication.

Goldman, B. A., & Busch, J. C. (1982). *Directory of unpublished experimental mental mesurements* (Vol. 3, pp. 162–164). New York: Human Sciences.

Goldman, B. A., & Osborne, W. L. (1985). *Directory of unpublished experimental mental measurements* (Vol. IV, pp. 157–163). New York: Human Sciences.

Gough, H. G. (1985). Free response measures and their relationship to scientific creativity. *Journal of Creative Behavior, 19,* 229–240.

Hattie, J. (1980). Should creativity tests be administered under testlike conditions? An empirical study of three alternative conditions. *Journal of Educational Psychology, 72,* 87–98.

Hattie, J., & Rogers, H. J. (1986). Factor models for assessing the relation between creativity and intelligence. *Journal of Educational Psychology, 78,* 482–485.

Hocevar, D. (1979a). Ideational fluency as a confounding factor in the measurement of originality. *Journal of Educational Psychology, 7,* 191–196.

Hocevar, D. (1979b, April). *Measurement of creativity: Review and critique.* Paper presented at the annual meeting of the Rocky Mountain Psychological Association, Denver, CO.

Holland, J. L., & Nichols, R. (1964). Prediction of academic and extra-curricular achievement in college. *Journal of Educational Psychology, 55,* 55–65.

Houtz, J. C. (1985). [Review of *Thinking Creatively with Sounds and Words*]. In D. Keyser & R. Sweetland (Eds.), *Test Critiques* (Vol. 4, pp. 666–672). Kansas City: Test Corporation of America.

Howieson, N. (1981). A longitudinal study of creativity: 1965–1975. *Journal of Creative Behavior, 15,* 117–135.

Howieson, N. (1984). *The prediction of creative achievement from childhood measures: A longitudinal study in Australia, 1960–1983.* Unpublished doctoral dissertation, University of Georgia, Athens.

Institute for Behavioral Research in Creativity. (1968). *Manual for the Alpha Biographical Inventory.* Greensboro, NC: Prediction Press.

Jensen, L. R. (1978). Diagnosis and evaluation of creativity, research and thinking skills of academically talented elementary students. *Gifted Child Quarterly, 5,* 98–110.

Kaltsounis, B. (1972). Instruments useful in studying creative behavior and creative talents: Part 3. *Journal of Creative Behavior, 6,* 268–274.

Kaltsounis, B. (1975). Further validity on Something about Myself. *Perceptual Motor Skills, 40,* 94.

Kaltsounis, B., & Honeywell, L. (1980). Additional instruments useful in studying creative behavior and creative talent. *Journal of Creative Behavior, 14,* 56–67.

Katz, A. N. (1983). Relationship of the Ammon's Quick Test of Intelligence to verbal and nonverbal tests of creativity. *Psychological Reports, 52,* 747–750.

Khatena, J. (1971). Children's version of Onomatopoeia and Images: A preliminary validity study of verbal originality. *Perceptual and Motor Skills, 33,* 26.

Khatena, J., & Bellarosa, A. (1978). Further validity evidence of Something about Myself. *Perceptual and Motor Skills, 47,* 906.

Khatena, J., & Torrance, E. P. (1976). *Manual for Khatena-Torrance Creative Perceptions Inventory.* Chicago: Stoelting.

Kirkland, J. (1974). On boosting divergent thinking scores. *California Journal of Educational Research, 25,* 69–72.

Kirkland, J., Kilpatrick, A., & Barker, W. (1976). Sex difference in boosting divergent thinking

scores by the context effect. *Psychological Reports, 38,* 430.

Kirschenbaum, R. J. (1986). Assessing creative power in the identification of gifted and talented students. *Roeper Review, 9,* 54–62.

Kulp, M., & Tarter, B. J. (1986). The creative processes rating scale. *The Creative Child and Adult Quarterly, 11,* 173–176.

Lissitz, R. W., & Willhoft, J. L. (1985). A methodological study of the Torrance Tests of Creativity. *Journal of Educational Measurement, 22,* 1–11.

Lynch, M. D., & Kaufman, M. (1974). Creativeness: Its meaning and measurement. *Journal of Reading Behavior, 4,* 375–394.

McKee, M. G. (1985). [Review of *Creativity Attitude Survey*]. In D. Keyser & R. Sweetland (Eds.), *Test Critiques* (Vol. 3, pp. 206–208). Kansas City: Test Corporation of America.

Mednick, S. A. (1962). The associative basis of the creative process. *Psychologocial Review, 69,* 222–232.

Murray, H. A. (1943). *Thematic Apperception Test manual.* Cambridge, MA: Harvard University Press.

Parke, B. N., & Byrnes, P. (1984). Toward objectifying the measurement of creativity. *Roeper Review, 6,* 216–218.

Perkins, D. N. (1981). *The mind's best work.* Cambridge, MA: Harvard University Press.

Reisman, F. K., Floyd, B., & Torrance, E. P. (1981). Performance on Torrance's Thinking Creativity in Action and Movement as a predictor of cognitive development of young children. *Creative Child and Adult Quarterly, 6,* 205–210.

Renzulli, J. S. (1978). What makes giftedness: Re-examining a definition. *Phi Delta Kappan, 60,* 180–184.

Renzulli, J. S., Hartman, R. K., & Callahan, C. M. (1975). Scale for rating the behavioral characteristics of superior students. In W. B. Barbe & J. S. Renzulli (Eds.), *Psychology and education of the gifted* (pp. 264–273). New York: Wiley.

Richards, R. L. (1976). A comparison of selected Guilford and Wallach-Kogan Creative Thinking tests in conjunction with measures of intelligence. *Journal of Creative Behavior, 10,* 151–164.

Richards, J. M., Holland, J. L., & Lutz, S. W. (1967a). Assessment of student accomplishment in college. *Journal of Educational Psychology, 8,* 343–355.

Richards, J. M., Holland, J. L., & Lutz, S. W. (1967b). Assessment of student accomplishment in college. *The Journal of College Student Personnel, 8,* 360–365.

Rimm, S., & Davis, G. A. (1976). GIFT: An instrument for the identification of creativity. *Journal of Creative Behavior, 10,* 178–182.

Rimm, S., & Davis, G. A. (1980). Five years of international research with GIFT: An instrument for the identification of creativity. *Journal of Creative Behavior, 14,* 35–46.

Rimm, S., & Davis, G. A. (1983, September–October). Identifying creativity. *G/C/T, 29,* 19–23.

Rorschach, H. (1951). *Psychodiagnostics: A diagnostic test based on perception* (P. Lemkaw & B. Kronenberg, Trans.) New York: Grune & Stratton.

Rosenthal, A., DeMars, S. T., Stilwell, W., & Graybeal, S. (1983). Comparison of interrater reliability on the Torrance Tests of Creative Thinking for gifted and nongifted children. *Psychology in the Schools, 20,* 35–40.

Roweton, W. E., Farles, J. E., Donham, R., Wleklinski, D. J., & Spencer, H. L. (1975). Indices of classroom creativity. *Child Study Journal, 5*(3), 151–161.

Runco, M. (1986). The discriminant validity of gifted children's divergent thinking test scores. *Gifted Child Quarterly, 30,* 78–82.

Runco, M. A., & Albert, R. S. (1985). The reliability and validity of ideational originality in the divergent thinking of academically gifted and nongifted children. *Educational and Psychological Measurement, 45,* 483–501.

Schaefer, C. (1969). The prediction of creative achievement from a biographical inventory. *Educational and Psychological Measurement, 29,* 431–437.

Schaefer, C. E. (1970a). *Biographical Inventory Creativity.* San Diego: Educational and Industrial Testing Service.

Schaefer, C. E. (1970b). *Manual for Biographical Inventory Creativity (BIC).* San Diego: Educational and Industrial Testing Service.

Schaefer, C. E. (1971). *Creativity Attitude Survey.* Jacksonville, IL: Psychologists and Educators.

Schaefer, C. E., & Anastasi, A. (1968). A biographical inventory for identifying creativity in adolescent boys. *Journal of Applied Psychology, 52,* 42–48.

Seddon, G. M. (1983). The measurement and properties of divergent thinking ability as a single compound entity. *Journal of Educational Measurement, 20,* 393–402.

Smith, G. J. W., & Carlsson, I. (1987). A new creativity test. *Journal of Creative Behavior, 21,* 7–14.

Sternberg, R. (1986). Intelligence, wisdom, and creativity: Three is better than one. *Educational Psychologist, 21,* 175–190.

Tegano, D. W., Moran, J. D., III, & Godwin, L. J. (1986). Cross-validation of two creativity tests designed for preschool children. *Early Childhood Research Quarterly, 1,* 387–396.

Torrance, E. P. (1966a). *Torrance Test of Creative Thinking: Directions manual and scoring guide, Verbal Test B.* Princeton, NJ: Personnel.

Torrance, E. P. (1966b). *Torrance Tests of Creative Thinking: Norms-technical manual.* Princeton, NJ: Personnel.

Torrance, E. P. (1976). Creativity testing in education. *Creative Child and Adult Quarterly, 1,* 136–148.

Torrance, E. P. (1981a). Empirical validation of criterion-referenced indicators of creative ability through a longitudinal study. *Creative Child and Adult Quarterly, 6,* 136–140.

Torrance, E. P. (1981b). *Thinking creatively in action and movement.* Bensenville, IL: Scholastic Testing.

Torrance, E. P. (1984). Some products of 25 years of creativity research. *Educational Perspectives, 22*(3), 3–8.

Torrance, E. P., & Ball, O. (1978). Effects of increasing the time limits of the Just Suppose Test. *Journal of Creative Behavior, 12,* 281.

Torrance, E. P., & Hall, L. K. (1980). Assessing the further reaches of creative potential. *Journal of Creative Behavior, 14,* 1–19.

Torrance, E. P., Khatena, J., & Cunnington, B. F. (1973). *Thinking creatively with sounds and words: Directions manual and scoring guide.* Bensenville, IL: Scholastic Testing.

Torrance, E. P., Reynolds, C. R., Ball, O., & Riegel, T. (1978). *Revised norms—Technical manual for Your Style of Learning and Thinking.* Athens: Department of Educational Psychology, University of Georgia.

Torrance, E. P., Reynolds, C. R., Riegel, T., & Ball, O. E. (1977). Your Style of Learning and Thinking forms A and B: Preliminary norms, abbreviated technical notes, scoring keys, and selected references. *Gifted Child Quarterly, 21,* 563–573.

Torrance, E. P., & Wu, T. H. (1981). A comparative longitudinal study of the adult creative achievements of elementary school children identified as highly intelligent and as highly creative. *Creative Child and Adult Quarterly, 6,* 71–76.

Treffinger, D. J. (1980). The progress and peril of identifying creative talent among gifted and talented students. *Journal of Creative Behavior, 14,* 20–34.

Treffinger, D. J. (1985). [Review of *Torrance Tests of Creative Thinking*]. In J. Mitchell (Ed.), *The ninth mental measurements yearbook* (Vol. 2, pp. 1632–1684). Lincoln, NE: Buros Institute of Mental Measurement.

Treffinger, D. J., Renzulli, J. S., & Feldhusen, J. F.

(1981). Problems in the assessment of creative thinking. In W. Barbe & J. S. Renzulli (Eds.), *Psychology and education of the gifted* (pp. 58–62). New York: Irvington.

Wakefield, J. F. (1985a, March). *Towards creativity: Problem finding in a divergent-thinking exercise.* Paper presented at the meeting of the Southeastern Psychological Association, Atlanta, GA.

Wakefield, J. F. (1985b). [Review of *Group Inventory for Finding Creative Talent*]. In D. Keyser & R. Sweetland (Eds.), *Test critiques* (Vol. 2, pp. 332–336). Kansas City: Test Corporation of America.

Wakefield, J. F. (1986). Creativity and the TAT blank card. *Journal of Creative Behavior, 20,* 127–133.

Wallach, M. A. (1970). Creativity. In P. Mussen (Ed.), *Carmichael's manual of child psychology* (3rd ed., Vol. 2, pp. 1211–1272). New York: Wiley.

Wallach, M. A., & Kogan, N. (1965). *Modes of thinking in young children.* New York: Holt, Rinehart & Winston.

Ward, W. C. (1975). Convergent and divergent measurement of creativity in children. *Educational and Psychological Measurement, 35,* 87–95.

Weeks, M. (1985). [Review of *Group Inventory for Finding Interests*]. In J. Mitchell, Jr. (Ed.), *The ninth mental measurements yearbook* (Vol. 1, pp. 362–363). Lincoln, NE: Buros Institute of Mental Measurement.

Williams, F. E. (1980). *Creativity assessment packet.* East Aurora, NY: DOK.

Wright, D. (1985). [Review of *Group Inventory for Finding Creative Talent*]. In J. Mitchell (Ed.), *The ninth mental measurements yearbook* (Vol. 1, p. 363). Lincoln, NE: Buros Institute of Mental Measurement.

Yamamoto, K. (1974). Threshold of intelligence in academic achievement of highly creative students. *Journal of Experimental Education, 32,* 401–405.

Zegas, J. (1976). A validation study of tests from the divergent production plane of the Guilford structure of the intellect model. *Journal of Creative Behavior, 10,* 170–178, 188.

17

Teaching Creative Thinking

GARY A. DAVIS   *University of Wisconsin, Madison*

A core goal of programs for the gifted and talented is teaching thinking skills, and the premier thinking skill is creativity. It is not surprising that every program planner and teacher of the gifted is preoccupied with ways to challenge students' creativity and to strengthen their creative thinking skills and abilities.

The main purpose of this chapter is to reflect on the goals of creativity training, and strategies for achieving them. First, however, let us look at some issues and considerations that relate to teaching creative thinking: individual differences in creativity, responsiveness to creativity training, and motivation to create; the creative climate; and whether creativity training must be embedded in a content area.

Individual Differences in Creativity

One of the most common questions I am asked is , "Can creativity be taught, or are you born with it?" Sometimes the issue is raised in a more negative form—"I don't think you can teach creativity, you either have it or you don't!" Of course, just as there is wide variation in every other mental and physical characteristic, there are also tremendous individual differences in affective dispositions toward creativity and innate creative abilities. Realistically, no amount of the most carefully orchestrated creativity training can mold an average person into a Leonardo Da Vinci, Marie Curie, Thomas Edison, William Shakespeare, Pablo Picasso, or Orson Welles. *At the same time, however, it also is absolutely true that every individual can raise his or her creative skill, creative productivity, and creative living to a higher level*. A seemingly irrefutable argument for the trainability of creativity is simply that with interest and effort, all of us can make better use of the creative abilities we were born with.

Individual Differences in Responsiveness to Creativity Training

There also are individual differences in receptiveness to creativity training. Some children and adults respond quickly and positively to such training. They learn that, yes indeed, they can imagine, visualize, create, and solve problems better than they expected. The capability was there all along; they just never attempted to use it. Others seem impervious to creativity training, due perhaps to disinterest, rigidity, conformity pressures, insecurity, or other creativity-stifling habits.

I teach graduate and undergraduate courses in creative thinking that have two purposes. First is the academic goal of transmitting a body of knowledge about issues, theories, characteristics, processes, tests, and techniques of creativity, along with strategies for teaching for creative growth. The second purpose, of course, is to help students become more creatively productive by raising their creativity consciousness, explaining how others use creativity techniques, and motivating them to use their creative abilities. One of our studies showed that, *on average,* students who completed the course improved in their affective creative traits—creative attitudes and predispositions and self-ratings of creativity—significantly more than students who had registered for but had not yet taken the course (Davis & Bull, 1978).

However, based on my own observations, there are always substantial differences in the degree to which students' creative potential is affected by the course. Some register for the course and meet the requirements but appear to remain relatively untouched by the potentially valuable principles and concepts. Other students experience changes in their self-perceptions of creativeness and their actual creative output; they discover capabilities they did not know they had. As three examples, one person wrote her first and potentially publishable children's book as a direct result of the class, another invented an educational game that was sold to Fisher Price Toys, and another began writing poetry, and lots of it, for the very first time. One memorable testimony was, "Now I do weird things!"

There are wide differences then, not only in creative predispositions and innate creative abilities, but in responsiveness to creativity training. Teachers should be prepared for these differences and perhaps ready to work a little harder with the low-receptivity students.

Individual Differences in Motivation to Create

There are also large differences in motivation for creativity. A high energy level, which may take the form of total involvement in and commitment to a project, is a common characteristic of creatively productive people. Related traits are high levels of adventurousness, spontaneity, creative risk taking, curiosity, and wide interests.

Some motivation theorists, most notably Berlyne (1960) and Farley (1986), assume that the high level of energy and arousal seeking that is so common among creative people is regulated by the reticular activating system (RAS) in the brainstem. According to the theory, creative and adventurous activities are sought in order to raise an uncomfortably low RAS arousal level to a more optimal state. There is not much we can do about the RAS. However, the RAS hypothesis does not prevent a teacher from stimulating an interest in creative thinking, exercising creative skills and abilities, or engaging students in challenging and satisfying artistic and scientific work.

Creative Atmosphere

We do not need a long discussion of the focal importance of a receptive and reinforcing creative atmosphere. Rogers (1962) called it *psychological safety;* in brainstorming it is known as *deferred judgment*. The creative personality includes a *creativity consciousness*—a readiness to think creatively and a receptiveness to the zany ideas of others. If creative ideas are not reinforced—or worse, if they are criticized or squelched—normal children and adults simply will not produce creative ideas in those unreceptive circumstances.

Must Creativity Be Taught in a Subject Matter?

In Chapter 8 Schiever and Maker argued that thinking skills must be taught within a subject matter. The argument was simply that students must have something to think *about*. Others scholars, for example, Keating (1980), also have argued that creativity must be taught within a subject area. I disagree. Effective creativity training may be content free, or it may be embedded in a specific content or subject.

The issue will be clearer if examined in the context of one of my favorite creativity concepts: Maslow's (1954) distinction between *self-actualized creativity* and *special talent creativity*. While it includes much more (see Davis, 1990), self-actualized creativity primarily is the mentally healthy tendency to approach all aspects of one's life—personal, professional, avocational—in a creative fashion. On the other hand, special talent creativity, as the name suggests, refers to people who possess an obviously outstanding creative talent or gift in art, literature, music, theater, science, business, or other areas. They may or may not be self-actualized in the mentally healthy sense.

Self-actualized creativity is a general creativeness that is content free. Many successful creativity courses, programs, workshops, and educational workbooks try to strengthen creative attitudes and awareness, creativity techniques, underlying creative abilities, and perhaps the Osborn-Parnes creative problem-solving model (Parnes, 1981; described later). These efforts seek to help the learner understand creativity and approach personal, academic, and professional problems in a more creative fashion. The approach is sensible, common, and effective (e.g., Davis &

Bull, 1978; Edwards, 1968; Parnes, 1978; Smith, 1985; Stanish, 1977, 1981; Torrance, 1979; Torrance & Myers, 1970; Von Oech, 1983), and it does not tie the training to a particular subject or content.

On the other hand, the goal of a program for the gifted and talented might well be to strengthen creative thinking and problem-solving skills as they relate directly to a specific subject such as creative writing, photography, theater, botany, architecture, astronomy, or dinosaurs. Students are given (or find) a project or problem and proceed to clarify it, consider various approaches, find a main solution or resolution, and then create or prepare the project or problem for presentation. Throughout, students identify and resolve numerous subproblems, evaluate their methods and results, and acquire knowledge and develop technical skills in the content area. This strategy clearly fits Maslow's special talent type of creativeness. In view of the popularity and soundness of Renzulli's enrichment triad and revolving door models, both of which highlight independent projects in content areas, this approach also is appropriate and effective (see e.g., Chapter 9 by Renzulli and Reis).

Of course, components of special talent creativity appear while teaching general (self-actualized) creativeness. For example, within a "content-free" creativity session students may do exercises in content areas. For example, they might brainstorm a science-, history- or math-related problem, or they might do creative writing or art activities. Conversely, creative projects in a subject area (special talent creativity) help develop creative attitudes and abilities that generalize beyond the specific topic at hand.

We turn now to an examination of affective and cognitive goals of teaching for creative growth, and some strategies and activities for reaching those goals.

Goals of Creativity Training

The Variety of Approaches to Teaching Creativity

In view of the mystery and complexity of creativity, it is not surprising that efforts to "teach creativity" include an endless variety of strategies, methods, and activities. For example, as noted in the previous section, many teachers involve their gifted students in independent projects in some art or science area. They reasonably assume that these projects foster such general creative problem-solving attitudes, skills, and abilities as independence, problem defining, information gathering, idea generating, evaluating, decision making, and communication, plus specific technical skills related to the topic area. There also may be growth in interpersonal cooperation, leadership, and followership. We already noted that independent projects are reasonable and defensible.

Another common creativity-teaching strategy, which is more in the self-actualized creativity category, is engaging students in divergent thinking problems, for example, listing unusual uses for Ping-Pong balls or unicorn horns, listing improvements for bathtubs or Cracker Jacks, designing a dog-walking machine or garbage-collection system, or speculating on "What would happen if" we had an eye in the back of our heads, there were no football, or Los Angeles suddenly became the South Pole. Sometimes these thinking problems are presented as exercises in brainstorming, complete with an explanation of the brainstorming principles (rules) of deferring judgment, listing lots of ideas, and encouraging wild ideas. The assumption is that practice in divergent thinking strengthens creative skills and abilities and may cultivate an interest in creative thinking. We will return to the strategy of exercising creative thinking skills and abilities in a later section.

Some teachers explain the lifestyles, attitudes, and thinking habits of eminent creative persons. As described in Chapter 10 by Betts, students themselves can research the life of a creative person and perhaps design and create a learning center that explains the person's personality, thinking style, and accomplishments. The hope is that students will come to better understand creativity and creative people and perhaps even pursue the exploratory attitudes and technical talents of these people.

A few teachers may even try creative dramatics, with its implicit requirement of on-the-spot improvisation of ideas, movement, and emotions and its heightened sensory awareness. Children can do *warm-up* exercises, perhaps stretching themselves into the biggest thing they can, or scrunching themselves into the smallest thing they can be. They can do *movement* exercises, perhaps creating circles with their bodies ("This is a two-armed circle," "This is a chicken circle"), while the rest of the group copies the same circle. There also are people machines, with small groups assembling themselves into a cuckoo clock, a pinball machine, or a bureaucratic machine, which does nothing. Students can do sensory awareness exercises, such as the popular blind (trust) walk, with one student leading the "blind" partner down stairs, to the water fountain, or to meet the school secretary. There also are *pantomime* and *play making,* with students creating simple environments (e.g., a bowling alley, the dentist's office, a fishing scene) or more complex plots (e.g., Goldilocks, building a space station on the moon) (see, e.g., Davis, 1990, Davis & Rimm, 1989, or Way, 1967, for creative dramatics exercises and ideas).

Perhaps we can better define this shapeless concept of creativity training if we itemize some main goals and objectives of the previous and other sorts of creativity-training activities. The objectives are not complicated, and the list is short. We will look at:

- Fostering creativity consciousness and creative attitudes
- Improving students' metacognitive understanding of creativity and creative people
- Exercising creative abilities
- Teaching creative thinking techniques
- Involving students in creative activities

Fostering Creativity Consciousness and Creative Attitudes

In teaching for creative development, we want students to become more *creativity conscious* and acquire attitudes conducive to creative thinking and creative behavior. Ironically, creativity consciousness is both the most important aspect of becoming a more creatively productive person and also the easiest to teach. Creativity consciousness is a natural outgrowth of virtually any type of classroom creativity exercises and activities.

However, creativity consciousness is not aided if exercises are so disguised that students are unaware they are "doing creativity." For example, in an ancient history lesson a teacher might ask students to think of all the uses cave people might find for birds' nests. The development of creativity consciousness and creative attitudes would be better served by clearly introducing the problem as a *creativity exercise* and by overtly encouraging novel and unconventional thinking: "Now let's use our imaginations and practice our creativity. Let's imagine we are cave people. We're all dressed in our animal skins and we live in our smoky cave. Uglug just walked in with a dozen big birds' nests, and we need to think of different ways we might use them. Let's think of as many different and unusual kinds of ideas as we can." That evening, when Mom or Dad asks "What did you do in school today?" the child can say, "We practiced creative thinking. We imagined we were cave people and we tried to think of creative uses for birds' nests. I thought they would make good pillows, if we smoked out the bugs. Joey wanted to use them as bait for a hawk trap. Jenny wanted to set 'em on fire and roast Dino-Dogs!"

By creative attitudes—which creatively productive people must have—I mean that students must value creative ideas and innovations; they must be receptive to the unusual and perhaps far-fetched ideas of others; and they must be consciously disposed to think creatively, play with ideas, and become involved in creative activities. An awareness of barriers to creativity—habits, traditions, rules, policies, and particularly conformity pressures—may also help students dare to be different. Every college course in creativity and every professional workshop stresses creativity consciousness, appropriate creative attitudes, and common barriers to creative thinking and behavior.

Creativity consciousness may be helped if students understand the importance of creativity in the history of civilization, which may be seen as a history of creative innovations in every field. Older and brighter students may also grasp the importance of creativity for one's personal development. Rogers (1962) and, as mentioned before, Maslow (1954), after many thoughtful years of incubating the matter, decided that creativity and self-actualization—developing your potential, becoming what you are capable of becoming, being an independent, forward-growing, fully functioning, democratic-minded, and mentally healthy individual—are intimately related. Nothing can be more important to life satisfaction—*your* life satisfaction—than becoming self-actualized, which must include developing creative attitudes and a cultivating a more creative lifestyle.

All the remaining creativity training goals and related activities contribute to creativity consciousness and to the development of creative attitudes and predispositions.

Improving Students' Metacognitive Understanding of Creativity

Some of the most effective and impressive programs for teaching thinking skills, for example, de Bono's (1973, 1983) CoRT (Cognitive Research Trust) strategies and Lipman's philosophy for children (Lipman, Sharp, & Oscanyan, 1980), deliberately foster students' metacognitive understanding of the thinking skills. Students learn what each skill means and why, when, and how it should be used. I believe it is also important to help students metacognitively understand the topic of *creativity* itself. An increased understanding of creativity helps raise creativity consciousness, demystify creativity, and convince students that given their present abilities they are perfectly capable—with interest and effort—of hatching creative ideas and producing creative things. For example, students can be helped to understand:

- The nature of creative ideas as modifications of existing ideas, new combinations of ideas, and products of analogical thinking
- Attitudes and personality traits that contribute to one's creative imagination and creative productivity, for example, creativity consciousness, confidence, risk taking, adventurousness, humor, open-mindedness, curiosity, wide interests, and needs for alone time
- How creative people use deliberate techniques to extend their intuition and spontaneous imagination

- What is measured by tests of creativity, such as the Torrance Tests of Creative Thinking (Torrance, 1966).
- The nature of the creative process, as represented in the Wallas (1926) *preparation, incubation, illumination,* and *verification* stages or the far more useful steps in the creative problem-solving model (Isaksen & Treffinger, 1985; Parnes, 1981). The creative process also can be viewed as a *change in perception,* or a mental transformation. Visual puzzles, optical illusions, and *Far Side* cartoons can be used to illustrate this sudden "seeing" of new meanings, new combinations, or new modifications. Further, creativity techniques, described in the next section, illustrate conscious creative (idea finding) processes.

Depending on their ages and abilities, students also can learn about definitions and theories of creativity; abilities that underlie creative expression; habits and social pressures that block or squelch creativity; and the importance of creativity to themselves and society.

Exercising Creative Abilities

There is no logical reason that creative skills and abilities, whatever they may be, cannot be strengthened through practice and exercise—the same way we strengthen other skills and abilities (e.g., typing, arithmetic, chemistry problem solving, and baseball). The four best known cognitive creative abilities are the Guilford-Torrance *fluency, flexibility, originality,* and *elaboration* (Guilford, 1967; Torrance, 1966). These logically may be exercised with open-ended, divergent thinking problems—for example, thinking of product improvement, listing unusual uses for objects, listing outcomes for What would happen if . . . problems, or finding solutions for an unlimited number of other divergent thinking and brainstorming problems, as in workbooks and texts by Stanish (1979), Myers and Torrance (1965), Torrance (1979), and Torrance and Myers (1970).

A longer list of creative abilities that can be exercised would include *analogical thinking,* as in workbooks by Gordon (1974a; Gordon & Poze, 1972) and Stanish (1977); *visualization* and *imagination* (e.g., Bagley & Hess, 1984; DeMille, 1955; Eberle, 1971); *sensitivity to problems,* perhaps strengthened by having students ask questions about a phenomenon ("What don't we know about clouds, the moon, eggs, *Tyrannosaurus rex?"*); *predicting outcomes of problem solutions;* and *evaluating,* perhaps using an evaluation matrix in which each idea is rated according to a half-dozen or so criteria, as in Stanish (1981) and future problem solving (discussed in a future section). There are many more abilities underlying creativity for which exercises could be identified, for example, Bloom's taxonomic categories of *analysis* and *synthesis* (Bloom, Englehart, Furst, Hill, & Krathwohl, 1956), and also *logical reasoning, planning, prioritizing, recognizing relevancy, making inferences, critical thinking,* and any of dozens of other thinking skills (for a review, see Davis & Rimm, 1989).

Teaching Creative Thinking Techniques

It is not easy for adults or children to adopt quickly an unfamiliar thinking method or problem-solving technique. Nonetheless, creative people do use creativity techniques, consciously or unconsciously, and the techniques work. Personally, I have found ideas for comical (more-or-less) dialogues by creating checklists of well-known children's stories or movies (e.g., *Alice in Wonderland, Cinderella, Snow White*), famous people and comedians (e.g., Woody Allen, Sigmund Freud, Barbara Walters), and myths (e.g., Frankenstein), and using these as analogical sources of inspiration (Davis, 1983, 1985). I also have used the morphological synthesis method, a matrix technique, to generate approximately 900 exercises that use creativity procedures such as brainstorming, analogical thinking, "What would happen if . . . ?" and visualization to teach values and moral thinking (Davis, in press).

Perhaps the most common and widely used idea-finding technique is deliberate analogical thinking. Every issue of every newspaper includes creative political cartoons and/or cartoon strips analogically derived from such sources as popular movies, TV commercials, historical events, or current news events. As a recent example, a diapered baby with a toy mallet poised above a fat spider used Clint Eastwood's famous line, "Go ahead, make my day!" In recent years a Rambo-like caricature of Ronald Reagan was entitled "Ronbo"; a Japanese warlord (shogun) caricature of Jimmy Carter was entitled "Shonuff!" Numerous classical compositions are analogically based on previous melodies: All 15 of Liszt's *Hungarian Rhapsodies* were taken from Gypsy folk tunes, and the *Star Spangled Banner* came from an English drinking song. Every one of Shakespeare's plays is rooted in historical events or other plays or literature. Many inventions and scientific discoveries, such as the cockleburr-inspired Velcro, the cotton gin, and Darwin's natural selection, also came from analogical thinking (see Gordon, 1974b, or Davis, 1990, for more examples of analogical thinking in art, invention, and discovery).

A brief description of the best-known idea-finding techniques would run as follows. Osborn's (1963) famous *brainstorming,* as the reader undoubtedly knows, evolves around deferring judgment and looking for unusual, even wild ideas. As Osborn noted, you cannot be critical and creative at the same time. Brainstorming produces a creative atmosphere, encourages imagination, teaches creative attitudes such as receptiveness to wild ideas, and teaches students to consider many ideas before settling on a solution.

Attribute listing (Crawford, 1978) includes two substrategies, *attribute transferring* and *attribute modifying*. The first technique, transferring attributes from one situation to another, is basically analogical thinking, as described above. The second attribute-listing strategy involves listing and then modifying important attributes of a product or process. For example, plots for short stories can be created by listing ideas for characters, important story objects (e.g., a magic cat or secret formula), settings, goals, and obstacles (Davis, 1985; Shallcross, 1981). Any consumer product can be modified by thinking of ideas for such conspicuous attributes as size, shape, color, material, function, intended market, product name, and others.

Morphological synthesis, a matrix procedure, is an extension of attribute modifying. Ideas for one attribute are listed along one axis of a matrix, ideas for another attribute are listed along another axis, and dozens of new idea combinations can be found in the cells of the matrix.

The *checklist* technique involves using entries on an idea checklist for inspiration. The best known checklist, designed expressly for creative thinking and problem solving, is Osborn's "73 idea-spurring questions"—adapt, modify, magnify, minify, substitute, reverse, and so forth. Other idea checklists are reproduced in Davis (1973, 1985).

Finally, three idea-finding techniques based in Gordon's (1960, 1978) analogy-based *synectics* methods are *direct analogy,* looking for analogically related problems and solutions in nature; *personal analogy,* imagining oneself to be a problem object; and *fantasy analogy,* imagining how in one's wildest imagination one would like the problem to be solved.

More extensive descriptions of these and other creativity techniques may be found in Davis (1990) and Feldhusen and Treffinger (1980). It is important to note that all these techniques originated as a personal idea-finding technique used by some creatively productive person. The strategies were made conscious, knowable, and teachable. Some engaging workbooks that teach one or more of these techniques are *Imagination Express* (Davis & DiPego, 1973), *Sunflowering* (Stanish, 1977), *Hippogriff Feathers* (Stanish, 1981), *The Hearthstone Traveler* (Stanish, 1988), *Making It Strange* (Gordon, 1974a), and *Teaching is Listening* (Gordon & Poze, 1972).

Involving Students in Creative Activities

The most logically sound answer to the question How can we teach creativity? is this: Involve students in activities that intrinsically require creative thinking and problem solving. It is virtually assured that creative attitudes, abilities, and skills will be strengthened in the course of actual creative involvement.

I already mentioned Renzulli's Type III enrichment and his revolving door model, both of which focus on individual or small-group projects and investigations of real problems. There is no limit to the variety of possible projects. Renzulli (1977) and Reis and Burns (1987) itemized several hundred possibilities (partly reproduced in Davis and Rimm, 1989) in the categories of visual arts and performing arts; math, science, and computers; literature, writing, and communication; social sciences, culture, and language; business and economics; and miscellaneous (e.g., bridge, chess, horses, karate, magic, and sailing).

In addition to involving students in projects, there are many other excellent ways to engage students in beneficial creative activities. Particularly, the future problem-solving (FPS) program teaches students to use an effective five-step creativity model: They gather information related to a general futuristic problem (e.g., related to garbage disposal, underwater colonization, or changing family structures); identify problems within the larger problem; generate ideas for the main problem; itemize meaningful criteria and evaluate the ideas; and prepare their best solution for presentation. According to Crabbe (1982), FPS raises students' awareness of the future and teaches communication skills, teamwork skills, research skills, and how to use an effective creative problem-solving model.

Another excellent program specifically designed to involve students in creative activities and creative thinking is Odyssey of the Mind, formerly Olympics of the Mind. Each team works for months on such long-term projects as designing and building aircraft that perform certain tasks; creating balsa structures that support frankly astonishing amounts of weight; or creating theatrical scenes based on specified literature. At each weekly meeting students also practice solving short-term, on-the-spot problems, such as listing different types of rocks or giants, or reacting to a Ping-Pong ball. Students know they get more points for creative answers, and so they make a strong effort to stretch their imaginations ("Rock Hudson," "Flintstones," "Rock and roll," "IBM is the giant of the computer business," "It's an egg from a plastic bird!").

The very effective Osborn-Parnes creative problem-solving (CPS) model (Isaksen & Treffinger, 1985; Parnes, 1981) engages students in divergent and convergent thinking at each of five steps of fact finding, problem finding, idea finding, solution finding (idea evaluation), and acceptance finding (idea implementation). While designed as a structured adult problem-solving method, it may be used to involve secondary students in solving real problems and also elementary children, as described in *CPS for Kids* (Eberle & Stanish, 1985).

Comment

The purpose of this chapter has been to clarify goals and objectives of some useful approaches to strengthening creative attitudes, skills, and abilities. One naturally is tempted to ponder efficiency and cost-effectiveness questions. That is, for a fixed amount of teacher–student contact time, a fixed student working time, and a fixed dollar budget, which activity or combination of activities will produce the greatest increment in creative potential? Unfortunately, the complexities of the matter, for example, the age, abilities, interests, and needs of the particular students, along with a virtual absence of relevant research, make it impossible to specify an all-around ideal recipe.

My best recommendation is that *all* the activities and approaches described in this chapter be included in a comprehensive creativity training effort. There also is a recommended sequence, which by a wild coincidence matches the order in which the topics were presented. First, cultivating an awareness of creativity and molding creative attitudes, dispositions, and motivations are the logical beginning places. This affective dimension of creativity can be addressed as a special introductory topic; creativity consciousness and creative attitudes will also be fostered throughout all forms of creativity exercises and activities. Students should learn that they have the ability to think of creative ideas and produce creative products, if they use that ability.

Second, improving students' metacognitive understanding of creativity—creative people, ideas, processes, definitions, techniques, tests, and so forth—is a sensible next step that can be integrated with the first.

Third, divergent thinking exercises, including brainstorming sessions, are intended to strengthen creative abilities and will further strengthen creative attitudes and awarenesses.

Fourth, teaching and practicing creative thinking techniques may or may not make students facile users of these strategies, but such activities at least will increase their understanding of where ideas come from. They also might internalize the virtues of considering lots of ideas, thinking of unusual (perhaps even far-fetched) ideas, and deferring judgment, as in the brainstorming ground rules. Many may come to realize that they can extend their intuitions by using techniques to modify and combine ideas, and that they can think analogically to solve problems and create just as highly creative people do.

Finally, involvement in creative activities and creative problem solving will capitalize on the creative attitudes, strengthened skills and abilities, and general understanding of creativity and creativity techniques to further develop students' creative thinking and problem solving in concrete content areas.

REFERENCES

Bagley, M. T., & Hess, K. K. (1984). *200 ways on using imagery in the classroom.* New York: Trillium.

Berlyne, D. E. (1960). *Conflict, arousal, and curiosity.* New York: McGraw-Hill.

Bloom, B. S., Englehart, M. D., Furst, E. J., Hill, W. H., & Krathwohl, D. R. (Eds.). (1956). *Taxonomy of educational objectives. Handbook I: Cognitive domain.* New York: McKay.

Crabbe, A. (1982). Creating a brighter future: An update on the future problem solving program. *Journal for the Education of the Gifted, 4,* 2–9.

Crawford, R. P. (1978). The techniques of creative thinking. In G. A. Davis & J. A. Scott (Eds.), *Training creative thinking* (pp. 52–57). Melbourne, FL: Krieger.

Davis, G. A. (1973). *Psychology of problem solving: Theory and practice.* New York: Basic.

Davis, G. A. (1983). *Student study guide to accompany Educational Psychology: Theory and Practice.* New York: Random House.

Davis, G. A. (1985). *Creative thinking and problem solving* (computer disk and manual). Buffalo, NY: Bearly.

Davis, G. A. (1990). *Creativity is forever* (3rd ed). Dubuque: Kendall/Hunt.

Davis, G. A. (in press). *Creative teaching of values and moral thinking*. East Aurora, NY: DOK.

Davis, G. A., & Bull, K. S. (1978). Strengthening affective components of creativity in a college course. *Journal of Educational Psychology, 70,* 833–836.

Davis, G. A., & DiPego, G. (1973). *Imagination express: Saturday subway ride*. East Aurora, NY: DOK.

Davis, G. A., & Rimm, S. B. (1989). *Education of the gifted and talented* (2nd ed.). Englewood Cliffs, NJ: Prentice-Hall.

de Bono, E. (1973). *CoRT thinking*. Elmsford, NY: Pergamon.

de Bono, E. (1983). The direct teaching of thinking as a skill. *Phi Delta Kappan, 64,* 703–708.

DeMille, R. (1955). *Put your mother on the ceiling*. New York: Viking/Compass.

Eberle, B. (1971). *Scamper*. East Aurora, NY: DOK.

Eberle, B., & Stanish, B. (1985). *CPS for kids*. Carthage, IL: Good Apple.

Edwards, M. O. (1968). A survey of problem-solving courses. *Journal of Creative Behavior, 2,* 33–51.

Farley, F. H. (1986, May). *The big T in personality. Psychology Today*, pp,. 47–52.

Feldhusen, J. F., & Treffinger, D. J. (1980). *Creative thinking and problem solving in gifted education*. Dubuque: Kendall/Hunt.

Gordon, W. J. J. (1960). *Synectics*. New York: Harper & Row.

Gordon, W. J. J. (1974a). *Making it strange* (Books 1–4). New York: Harper & Row.

Gordon, W. J. J. (1974b). Some source material in discovery by analogy. *Journal of Creative Behavior, 8,* 239–257.

Gordon, W. J. J. (1978). Synectics. In G. A. Davis & J. A. Scott (Eds.), *Training creative thinking* (pp. 14–29). Melbourne, FL: Krieger.

Gordon, W. J. J., & Poze, T. (1972). *Teaching is listening*. Cambridge, MA: SES Associates.

Guilford, J. P. (1967). *The nature of human intelligence*. New York: McGraw-Hill.

Isaksen, S. G., & Treffinger, D. J. (1985). *Creative problem solving: The basic course*. Buffalo, NY: Bearly.

Keating, D. P. (1980). Four faces of creativity: The continuing plight of the intellectually underserved. *Gifted Child Quarterly, 24,* 56–61.

Lipman, M., Sharp, A. M., & Oscanyan, F. S. (1980). *Philosophy in the classroom* (2nd ed.). Philadelphia: Temple University Press.

Maslow, A. H. (1954). *Motivation and personality*. New York: Harper & Row.

Myers, R. E., & Torrance, E. P. (1965). *For those who wonder*. Boston: Ginn.

Osborn, A. F. (1963). *Applied imagination* (2nd ed.). New York: Scribner's.

Parnes, S. J. (1978). Can creativity be increased? In G. A. Davis & J. A. Scott (Eds.), *Training creative thinking* (pp. 270–275). Melbourne, FL: Krieger.

Parnes, S. J. (1981). *The magic of your mind*. Buffalo, NY: Creative Education Foundation.

Reis, S. M., & Burns, D. R. (1987). A schoolwide enrichment team invites you to read about methods for promoting community and faculty involvement in a gifted education program. *Gifted Child Today, 49*(2), 27–32.

Renzulli, J. S. (1977). *Enrichment triad model: A guide for developing defensible programs for the gifted and talented*. Mansfield Center, CT: Creative Learning.

Rogers, C. R. (1962). Toward a theory of creativity. In S. J. Parnes & H. F. Harding (Eds.). *A source book for creative thinking* (pp. 63–72). New York: Scribner's.

Shallcross, D. J. (1981). *Teaching creative behavior*. Englewood Cliffs, NJ: Prentice-Hall.

Smith, E. (1985, September 30). Are you creative? *Business Week*, pp. 80–84.

Stanish, B. (1977). *Sunflowering*. Carthage, IL: Good Apple.

Stanish, B. (1979). *I believe in unicorns*. Carthage, IL: Good Apple.

Stanish, B. (1981). *Hippogriff feathers*. Carthage, IL: Good Apple.

Stanish, B. (1988). *The hearthstone traveler*. Carthage, IL: Good Apple.

Torrance, E. P. (1966). *Torrance Tests of Creative Thinking*. Bensenville, IL: Scholastic Testing Service.

Torrance, E. P. (1979). *The search for satori and creativity*. Buffalo: Creative Education Foundation.

Torrance, E. P., & Myers, R. E. (1970). *Creative learning and teaching*. New York: Dodd, Mead.

Von Oech, R. (1983). *A whack on the side of the head*. New York: Warner.

Wallas, G. (1926). *The art of thought*. New York: Harcourt, Brace & World.

Way, B. (1967). *Development through drama*. London: Longman.

18

Developing Talent, Creativity, and Eminence

HERBERT J. WALBERG   *University of Illinois at Chicago*
MANFRED P. HERBIG   *Ruhr University of Bochum, Bochum, West Germany*

Syntheses of research studies show that the quantity and quality of instruction have strong effects on learning. So does constructive stimulation in classrooms, homes, peer groups, and mass media (Walberg, 1984; Walberg & Herbig, in press). This research has implications for developing creativity, talent, and eminence since both general knowledge and a disciplined mastery of special fields are required for exceptional performance. Efficient mastery, moreover, results in additional time for the development of higher accomplishments. During the last two decades educational psychologists have analyzed and compiled about 8,000 studies on how general learning can be intensified. This work together with research on talent development of gifted children is the subject of this chapter.

According to Havighurst (1958), "A talented or gifted child is one who shows consistently remarkable performance in any worthwhile line of endeavor" (p. 19). Yet practice perfects talent, and persistence can overcome initial deficits, handicaps, and inabilities. Sosniak (1988a, 1988b, 1988c, 1988d), for example, found, "The concert pianists invested an average of 17 years studying, practicing, and performing before they reached the exceptionally high level of learning" (Sosniak, 1988c, p. 409). Gruber and Davis (1988, p. 265) highlight the reliable finding that "creative work takes a long time," months, years, and decades. What we call creative is often difficult, astonishing, and extremely effective. A feeling of need for the eminent performance and the creative product also seems to be indispensable.

Eminence may be characterized by rare rather than unique accomplishments. So it may be useful to think of it as being on one end of a continuum of performance or learning that is attainable by nearly anyone with sufficient instruction and perseverance (Bloom, 1976). Learning Japanese may appear daunting, but Japanese children are able to use their language creatively. Learning a language, though one of the most difficult human tasks, is completed by children learning their native language the world over. Even though vocabulary constitutes the most common test of intelligence, children's native abilities in their native language dwarf those of adults unexposed to it. Linguistic and other environments, especially if they are enduring and powerful, strongly shape accomplishments. People, moreover, are able to choose, influence, or determine their environments.

Contrary to the notion of instant creativity that was popular in the 1960s, distinguished accomplishment seems partly a matter of continual and concentrated effort over a decade or more. When Sir Isaac Newton was asked how he managed to surpass the discoveries of his predecessors in both quality and quantity, he replied, "By always thinking about them." Karl Friedrich Gauss said, "If others would but reflect on mathematical truths as deeply and continuously as I have, they would make my discoveries." Discovery may occur in an instant, but it usually require decades of preparation in the special field. Though intense perseverance seems to be necessary, it is not sufficient. Getzels and Csikszentmihalyi (1976), for example, found in longitudinal studies that those who turned out to be eminent visual artists could find appropriate problems on which to work. So problem finding, aesthetic ability, and originality seems to support later success more than mere craftsmanship and mastery of basics. Psychological studies of the lives of eminent painters, writers, musicians, philosophers, religious leaders, and scientists of previous centuries, as well as prize-winning adolescents today, reveal early, intense concentration on previous work in their fields (Bloom, 1985b).

The same fundamental thought processes, moreover, appear to be required in both elementary learning and advanced discovery, as Simon (1981), Sternberg (1988), and others have shown. The acquisition of knowledge and problem solving of beginners differ in degree rather than in kind from the mental activities of experts. The scarce resources are opportunity and concentration rather than the amount of information available or the processing capacity of the mind, both of which, for practical purposes, are unlimited.

The major constraints on the acquisition and processing of knowledge, according to Simon (1981), are the few items of information, perhaps two to seven, that can be held in immediate, conscious memory, and the time required, 5 to 10 seconds, to store an item in long-term memory. Experts differ from novices in science, chess, and other fields that have been studied not only in having more information in permanent memory but also, and more significantly, in being able to process it efficiently. Among experts, for example, items of information are more thoroughly indexed and thus can be rapidly brought to conscious memory. The items, moreover, are elaborately associated or linked with one another. Two consequences of these associations are called into play in problem solving from the most elementary to the most advanced endeavors. One is the ability to recover information by alternative links, even when parts of the direct indexing are lost, and the other is the capacity for extensive means–ends, or trial-and-error, searches.

Bloom (1985a) concluded from his studies on eminent people in music, art, athletics, mathematics, and science that always "there is a long and intensive process of encouragement, nurturance, education, and training, which brings people to their specific excellence. So these results question earlier views of eminence as conditioned on "special gifts and innate aptitudes" (p. 3). This accords with Bloom's perspective on "human conditions and [school] learning" (Bloom, 1976). Bloom sees "potential equality of all human beings" (Bloom, 1985a, p.5); their

abilities can be developed to a mastery level by suitable teaching and learning strategies. His analysis of the rearing of talented children may give teachers and parents a perspective on their common task—to foster the enormous pool of potential talent.

Based on Campbell's blind-variation and selective-retention model of creative thought (Campbell, 1960), Simonton (1988) presented a *chance-configuration theory* that predicts the creative productivity at time t dependent on the age of the person. The differential equation uses the *initial creative potential,* the *ideation rate,* and the *elaboration rate.* Although the initial creative potential is mainly an individually confirmed parameter, the ideation and the elaboration rates differ among the research fields. The theory shows the importance of early start and early stimuli, which are dependent on the home environment. Firstborn and single children, for example, may have an advantage in creative potential since they may get more attention at the outset (Simonton, 1988).

Bloom (1985b) gives concrete results about the role of home environment and early learning for the development of talent. Parents serve as models of the work ethic in demonstrating that, for instance, work comes before play and that achievement, success, and doing one's best are important. Parents of eminent prize winners from different fields have been willing to devote their time, their resources, and their energy to their children's development. The family routines are structured to give the children appropriate responsibilities and a chance to practice self-discipline. After the child has shown interest in a talent field, parents and other adults work to deepen interest. To excel, to do one's best, to work hard, and to spend time constructively are expected of the child. The parents' interest can serve as a model. They act as "good teachers" and even shape the environment according to the child's interest.

Talent and Expertise

Creative talent is the rich, complex association of cognitive elements, perhaps also involving affective and psychomotor connections.

Achievement is the acquisition of such elements from the environment and their recall to conscious memory or recognition in the environment. Creativity (including problem finding and solving) is the trial-and-error search for novel and useful solutions by combinations of stored and externally found elements. As Sternberg and Davidson (1985) concluded, "Precocious children form connections at a much more rapid rate than do ordinary children, and exceptional adults have formed exceptionally large numbers of variegated stimulus-response connections" (p. 44).

Following Aristotle and Simon (1981), this parsimonious account calls attention to time for the acquisition and association of elements; the importance of the richness of the environment; and the natural continuity and linkage of creativity with achievement. The account can help explain why creativity has appeared mysterious: If creative problem solving consumes time and exhausts mental resources, it leaves no capacity to observe and understand the detailed mechanisms and processes of creativity itself. But such subconscious thinking may be necessary to result in greater efficiencies in memory and thought, and in teaching and learning. Ericsson, Chase, and Faloon (1980), for example, showed that an undergraduate of average intelligence, given 230 hours of instruction and practice based on such notions, raised his memory for numbers from 7 to 79 digits. This amount is nine times larger than that taken by psychologists as indicative of superior intelligence and as large as that of stage mnemonicists. Of course it could be difficult to produce such results for higher cognitive processes like analysis, synthesis, and evaluation (Bloom, Englehart, Furst, Hill & Krathwohl, 1956) and to apply their implications in educational practice. For this reason, time and concentration are likely to remain essential for learning and creativity in the future.

The greatest advantage of the expert and difficulty for the novice is *chunking,* the representation of abstract groups of items as linked clusters that can be efficiently processed. Such chunks may underlie mental processes ranging from childhood learning to scientific discoveries. Simon (1981) estimates that 50,000

chunks, about the same magnitude as the recognition vocabulary of college-educated readers, may be required for expert mastery of a special field. The highest achievements in various disciplines, however, may require a memory store of 1 million chunks, which may take even the most accomplished persons about 70 hours of concentrated effort per week for a decade to acquire. Mozart and Bobbie Fisher are rare exceptions.

The prospect of such prodigious and sustained concentration should impress but not defeat the novice. Yet only a small fraction of the total is required for basic mastery. An extra hour or two per day, perhaps taken from the usual 4 to 5 hours that American schoolchildren typically watch television, may enable them to attain levels of achievement and creativity far beyond the ordinary in many fields.

Matthew Effects and Consequences

Current learning and behavior are strongly determined by the past; a good start enhances later opportunities and environments. Important evidence in communication, early childhood development, cognitive psychology, and education shows that early advantages confer future advantages (Walberg & Tsai, 1984). This corroborates Merton's (1968) theory of *Matthew effects* (the rich getting richer; from the Gospel of Matthew). Concerning scientific creativity, Merton argued that initial advantages of university study, work with eminent scientists, early publication, job placement, and citation and other recognition combine multiplicatively over time to confer tastes, skills, habits, rewards, and further opportunities that cumulate to produce highly skewed productivity in scientific work. Similarly, outstanding science departments attract distinguished or potentially distinguished faculty and students, grants, facilities, intellectual contacts, and other factors over time that lead to probable continuing distinction.

The effects are dynamic in that they affect one another over time periods. The theory, however, is parsimonious and highly generalizable in another sense: It may be said that environments affect growth and growth affects later environments. The specifics of development and creativity in science are merely instances of the general and pervasive phenomenon.

What such Matthew effects accomplish in essence may even be simpler: sustained and concentrated effort necessary for distinction. Such effort is well explained in Simon's (1954) Berlitz model of learning a foreign language, which is a relatively difficult adult task requiring perhaps as much effort as the lower levels of creativity. Simon assumes that an individual can choose the amount of practice, that practice makes the language activity easier, that ease increases the pleasantness of the activity, and that pleasantness increases practice. He hypothesizes that excessive difficulty slows practice because it is unpleasant; but if practice persists through temporary difficulty, practice will become pleasant and will persist through mastery.

For creativity, something more than mere mastery, it can be imagined that early encouragement, specific goals, clear attainments, continued effort, and appropriately high standards are required. Such things lead to further effort, attract the attention of outstanding teachers and coaches, and result in the usual positive-skew distribution of achievement and performance, creativity and eminence. It seems parsimonious and useful to view the acquisition of knowledge and skill as similar to, and continuous with, the attainment of creativity and eminence. The differences are not of kind but of degree with respect to natural and contrived social environments, stimulation and encouragement, concentration and effort.

Families, schools, and universities are the chief agencies for the acquisition of knowledge, and they can also foster creativity. To the extent that they are efficient, they can accomplish more of both; and they can foster more creativity not merely in elites but in masses of students. In the first two decades of life, moreover, greater efficiency can result in greater creativity in individuals and society. A rapid acquisition of basic cultural literacy and a general education, leaves more time for the acquisition of advanced knowledge and for creativity.

Generally, the scarce resources are educational expertise and human time. This means the amount of time invested by parents, educators, coaches, and learners or creators themselves. Since we now have a reasonably good understanding of educational productivity, the problem of increasing acquisition and creativity is in large part putting efficient procedures into place.

Enhancing Academic and Talent Productivity

A compilation of quantitative effects in nearly 3,000 studies of learning in homes and schools shows that education can be made far more productive, which can allow more time for the development of talent and eminence. Three groups of nine factors require optimization to increase learning (Walberg, 1984):

A. Aptitude
   1. Ability or prior achievement, as measured on the usual standardized tests
   2. Development, as indexed by age or stage of development
   3. Motivation or self-concept, as indexed by personality tests or willingness to persevere on learning tasks
B. Instruction
   4. The amount of time students engage in classroom learning
   5. The quality of the instructional experience including both its psychological and its curricular aspects
C. Psychological environment
   6. The curriculum or academic environment of the home
   7. The social climate of the classroom group
   8. The peer group outside school
   9. Exposure to mass media, notably television

Generally, stimulation and encouragement are what make a difference in the home and school. The curriculum of the home, for example, refers to informed parent–child conversations about school and everyday events; encouragement and discussion of leisure reading; monitoring and joint critical analysis of television and peer activities; deferral of immediate gratifications to accomplish long-term human-capital goals; expressions of affection and interest in the child's academic and other progress as a person; and, perhaps, among such serious efforts, humor and happiness, smiles, laughter, caprice, and serenity.

What Works (Bennett, 1987) shows the results of research on teaching and learning that should be applied when educating a child in school and at home. Good relationships between parents and teachers are required. Basic cultural skills like speaking, reading, and writing; counting and estimating; awareness and cooperation promote learning. These basics aid the acquisition of more complex cognitive and creative procedures in the domains of language, numbers, and behavior. Teachers and parents are able to influence the environment of the learning child. As Bloom (1985a, 1985b) showed, eminent people have often been reared in extremely efficient environments that enable them to develop the basics early and their talents and interests quickly.

Particular methods of teaching and certain new programs in schools are much more effective than others. These include mastery learning, cooperative learning, and adaptive education. These and other methods and their comparative effects on learning are described elsewhere (Walberg, 1984). Most of these methods are well researched insofar as acquisition is concerned. Open education is seemingly useful in fostering creativity, though it is a perhaps rather forgotten method and has been dismissed by many educators. Some characteristics of open programs are multiage grouping, open space, and team teaching. From the start, open educators tried to encourage educational outcomes that reflected such rarely measured goals as cooperation, critical thinking, self-reliance, constructive attitudes, and lifelong learning. Raven's (1981) summary of surveys in western countries, including England and the United States, shows that when given a choice, educators, parents, and students rank these goals as more important than standardized test scores and school marks.

Although open education, like its precursors, faded from view, it was massively researched by dozens of investigators whose work has been little noted. Perhaps the synthesis of this research may be useful to educators who want to base practice on research rather than on fads, or to those who will evaluate future descendants of open education. For example, Hedges, Giaconia, and Gage (1981) synthesized 153 studies of open education, including 90 dissertations. They found a moderate positive effect upon adjustment, attitudes toward schools and teachers, curiosity, and general mental ability, and a slight positive effect on cooperativeness, creativity, and independence. Students in open classes thus did no worse in standardized achievement and slightly to moderately better on several outcomes that educators, parents, and students hold to be of great value. In a further step Giaconia and Hedges (1982) identified from their prior synthesis the studies with the largest positive and negative effects on several outcomes in order to differentiate more and less effective program features. Those programs that were more effective in producing the nonachievement outcomes—constructive attitudes, creativity, and good self-concepts—showed reduced academic achievement on standardized tests. Perhaps children in such programs had little experience with such tests. At any rate, it appears from the two most comprehensive syntheses that open classes on average enhance creativity, independence, and other nonstandard outcomes without detracting from academic achievement, unless such classes are extreme.

What is the creativity-enhancing teacher like? Chambers (1973) asked several hundred creative psychologists and chemists to describe the teachers who had the greatest facilitating and inhibiting influences on their creative development. The most facilitative had the following characteristics (in order of importance): They treated students as individuals; encouraged students to be independent; served as models; spent considerable time with students outside class; indicated that excellence was expected and could be achieved; were enthusiastic; accepted students as equals; directly rewarded students' creative behavior or work;

were interesting, dynamic lecturers; and were excellent on a one-to-one basis. Inhibiting teachers, on the other hand, had the following characteristics: They discouraged students' ideas and creativity; were insecure; were hypercritical; were sarcastic; were unenthusiastic; emphasized rote learning; were dogmatic and rigid; did not keep up with field; were generally incompetent; had narrow interests; and were unavailable outside the classroom.

Bloom (1985b) showed that teachers of the early years need not excel in their fields. The initial teachers in swimming and music were chosen mainly because of proximity and availability. Rarely were they outstanding in talent. They were encouraging and liked children; they rarely criticized. They were able to shape the beginnings of learning like a continuous game. They cooperated with parents by informing them about goals and possibilities and by asking for help in monitoring the child's talent-oriented activities (Bloom, 1985b).

In the field of mathematics the school teachers seemed to be of extraordinary influence: The initiation was mainly by those teachers

> assigned to particular high school (or junior high school) classes. Some of these were good teachers of initial mathematics. The most successful ones (in the eyes of our mathematicians) were the ones who helped them grasp the larger patterns in the subject and who encouraged them to discover the underlying ideas. Such teachers would allow the students to find and use alternative procedures for solving particular mathematics problems. (Bloom, 1985b)

During the middle and the later years the role of teachers is different; they must provoke outstanding performance.

But the results are not general and depend on the field of eminence (Kitano & Kirby, 1986). Social giftedness, for example, may be more self-induced or discovered. Lech Walesa, one of the most impressive social leaders of the eighties, has been characterized as a

> tremendously dynamic speaker. . . . His gift is to express the mood of the crowd at any given moment. Confusion before clearness in the crowd

confuses him, and then, suddenly, he is crystal clear, and leading them. Walesa is a shipyard worker. How did he develop these exceptional abilities? As he said to admiring children, "Learn from yourselves! Like me. I went to vocational school and ended up a Nobel. Don't wait for others to tell you what to do. I'm getting old. I will fall. You will have to carry on." (Weschler, 1988, p. 60)

Childhoods of Highly Eminent Adults

We turn now to our own research, starting with a study of more than 200 highly eminent men from artistic, scientific, and political domains born between the 14th and 20th centuries (Walberg, 1982). This research exposed their common psychological traits as well as family, educational, and cultural conditions. Ratings of their childhood characteristics and environments made from respected biographies showed their distinctive intellectual competence and motivation, social and communication skills, general psychological wholesomeness, and both versatility and concentrated perseverance during childhood. Most were stimulated by the availability of cultural stimuli and materials related to their field of eminence and by teachers, parents, and other adults. Although most had clear parental expectations for their conduct, they also had the opportunity for exploration on their own (see also Bloom, 1985a, 1985b; Cox, 1926; McCurdy, 1957; Simonton, 1987).

The sample of persons for the research traces back to the work of James McKean Cattell, founder of the biographical volumes *American Men of Science* (now called *American Men and Women of Science*). In 1903, Cattell listed in rank order of imputed eminence the 1,000 most eminent people, based on the number of words that had been written about each in American, English, French, and German biographical dictionaries (Cattell, 1903).

Soon after Cattell's publication, Catherine Cox and Lewis Terman (the developer of the Stanford-Binet intelligence test) began a fascinating psychological study of part of Cattell's sample (Cox, 1926). They eliminated the least eminent half of the sample, persons who had apparently been included only because of aristocratic or noble birth, and those born before 1450. Cox and several associates combed more than 3,000 sources including encyclopedias, biographies, and collections of letters in the Stanford and Harvard university libraries for information on the mental development of each of the remaining 282 persons (which included 3 women). From this information, Cox and two associates each independently estimated the IQ of each person. Cox's analysis and our own reanalysis of Cox's data showed that the reliability of these careful estimates compares reasonably well with that of group IQ tests now given to children in school classes.

For additional estimates of eminence and comparisons with Cattell's 1903 list, we counted the number of words in the primary biographical articles on each of the 282 persons in the 1935 *New International Encyclopedia* and the 1974 *Encyclopedia Britannica*. Although the indices of eminence were in substantial agreement from one period to the next, there were some interesting changes. For example, philosophers lost and musicians and artists gained in estimated eminence from 1903 to 1974. Individuals also shifted in estimated eminence: For example, starting with the most eminent, the top 10 on the 1903 estimates were Napoleon, Voltaire, Bacon, Goethe, Luther, Burke, Newton, Milton, Pitt, and Washington. Based on the number of words written about each in 1974, the top 10 in order were Samuel Johnson, Luther, Rembrandt, da Vinci, Napoleon, Washington, Lincoln, Goethe, Beethoven, and Dickens. Based on the numbers of times they were cross-referenced in 1974, the top 10 were Descartes, Napoleon, Newton, Leibniz, Luther, Hegel, Kant, Darwin, Galileo, and da Vinci.

Confirming Cox's analysis, we found that persons with the highest average of the four indices of eminence had slightly higher estimated IQs (the correlation is .33) than others in the sample. There is no doubt that IQ and eminence are linked. But the linkage is not very tight, and the very brightest, by estimated IQ, are not necessarily "the best." Research on recent samples of writers, scientists, and adolescents who have won awards and prizes suggests that outstanding performance in various fields requires only moderately above average levels of intelligence. Higher levels of intelligence seem less important than other psychological traits and conditions (Walberg, 1969b, 1971).

On the other hand, moderate levels of intelligence seem indispensable. The most distinctive of all the childhood traits was rated intelligence; 97% of the sample were rated intelligent, which confirms the Cox-Terman IQ estimates. Other more wide ranging cognitive traits are also highly characteristic of the sample. The group as a whole exhibited convergent and divergent ability ranging from concentration and perseverance to versatility and fluidity.

The majority of the eminent persons also showed a large number of distinctive affective traits that collectively suggest psychological wholesomeness: The majority were rated ethical, sensitive, solid, magnetic, optimistic, and popular. Large percentages of the sample were exposed to stimulating family, educational, and cultural conditions during childhood. Slightly more than half were encouraged by parents, while a solid majority were encouraged by teachers and other adults and were exposed to many adults at an early age. Significantly more than half, 60%, were exposed to eminent persons during childhood.

About 80% were successful in school, the majority liked it, and fewer than a quarter had school problems. Seventy percent had clear parental expectations for their conduct; but nearly 90% were permitted to explore their environments on their own. So autonomy is a delicate and important principle in child rearing and teaching.

This research on childhood traits of highly eminent people confirms that early accomplishments often forecast later eminence. Alterable environments provided by teachers, parents, and peers seem to enhance the probabilities of distinguished accomplishments. Moreover, the findings accord with our studies of contemporary youth discussed next.

Artists and Scientists

Walberg (1969b) identified three groups from a national sample of 771 high school students:

those winning competitive awards in science, those winning awards in the arts, and their classmates who had won no recognition in these areas. These groups were compared on 300 biographical items in a long self-administered questionnaire. In social relations both creative groups tended more often than others to describe themselves as friendly, outgoing, self-confident, and finding books more interesting than people. Both groups had earlier and stronger interests in mechanical and scientific objects as well as the arts, they more often enjoyed professional-technical books, they more often visited libraries for nonschool reading, and they had greater numbers of books at home. Both creative groups were more interested in work with fine detail, more persistent in carrying things through, and had less time to relax. They liked school and applied themselves to their studies. They also did their work faster than their classmates.

The two groups of award winners felt more creative, imaginative, curious, and expressive, and tended to make more original suggestions to childhood playmates and to feel that it is important to be creative. In contrast to some previous formulations and empirical work, they had no greater propensity to suggest wild ideas, although they did find satisfaction in expressing ideas in new and original ways. They indicated that they were brighter than their friends and quicker to understand. Larger proportions of the two awarded groups expected to reach graduate degrees and to earn higher salaries after graduation. They also attached greater importance than other students did to money and saw responsibility as a relatively desirable job attribute. However, in choosing the best characteristic to develop in life, the award winners selected *creativity* more often and *wealth and power* less often. In short, creative artists and scientists were more friendly, outgoing, curious, and attentive to detail; they appeared more interested in and self-confident in their own creativity and intelligence; and they were more ambitious regarding their own education, salary, and, most important, creativity.

In contrast to the artists, the scientists indicated that people had more difficulty in talking to them about personal problems and that they had more difficulty making friends after changing schools. The scientists more often did not date or dated different girls rather than dating one at a time. They were less bothered by humiliating experiences and took less interest in other people's ideas. They read biography but were generally more bookish and interested than the artists, as one would expect, in books about science and mechanics rather than the arts, music, and writing. The scientists were also more interested in finely detailed work and were more apt to bring work to completion in spite of difficulty and distraction. Also in contrast to artists, they were less involved in organized school activities and more inclined academically, as expected, toward mathematics and science rather than music and the arts. There were significant tendencies for the scientists to more highly value and express confidence in their own intelligence, while the artists felt this way about their creativity. The scientists had higher educational aspirations, were more definitely decided about their future occupation, and tended to make carefully detailed plans rather than let fate take its course. In contrast to the artists, the scientists tended to favor *security* as the best characteristic of a job.

In summary, contrasted with responses of those winning no awards, both artists' and scientists' responses were wholesome and indicative of high aspirations for social status. The scientists seemed preoccupied with things and ideas rather than people and feelings, avoided intense emotional closeness to others, persisted in the face of difficulty, were attracted to academic work and detail, and were actively task oriented. Of course, mastery is crucial in the arts, and subconscious feelings play an important role in science. But the differences found imply that communicated inner feeling is the essential preoccupation of the artist (Beauty) while the single-minded, conceptual grappling with external realities is the sine qua non of science (Truth).

Varieties of Adolescent Creativity

It was possible to follow up this original survey with another national sample of nearly 3,000 high school physics students, many of whom had taken an IQ test. In no case was measured intelligence correlated with membership in prize-winning creative groups. This lack of relationship confirms prior studies of creativity and intelligence that have shown weak associations.

Chambers (1969), after reviewing research in this area, hypothesized that a minimal level of intellectual ability is essential for creative productivity, but that beyond a given floor, which varies in different fields, there is no relationship between measured intelligence and creativity. A fairly typical result is that of MacKinnon (1961). He found that a sample of creative architects scored higher on intelligence tests than did undergraduate students. However, when the architects were ordered according to their peer-rated creativity, the correlation between intelligence and creativity was found to be nonsignificant ($-.08$).

Based on his own research on creative writers and the work of others, Barron (1961) concluded that there were correlations around .40 between the two variables over the total range of intelligence, but that beyond an IQ level of 120, intelligence was a negligible factor in creativity. The mean IQs for boys and girls in our sample (Walberg, 1969b) were, respectively, 117 and 119. The group that elected to take physics in high school was generally higher in measured intelligence than the rest of the high school population. Moreover, the criteria for creativity employed in the study were not as stringent as those used by Barron and McKinnon for creative architects and writers, all of whom had earned national recognition. Nevertheless, a large part of the total sample of our high school study may have been beyond the minimal levels of mental ability required for winning awards and prizes in adolescent competition—which may explain the lack of relationship between intelligence and creativity.

Creative boys were different from boys who did not achieve distinction. In contrast to other students, the creative groups more often reported themselves as more creative and imaginative and as having more creative opportunities. They more often liked school, got high marks, and questioned their teachers. Also,

they more often thought it was important to be intelligent, had at least two cases of books in the home, studied and read outside school, and talked to adults about future occupations. Lastly, they more often followed through on their work despite difficulties and distractions.

These relationships confirm several findings from prior research and suggest that the creative groups in different fields resemble one another more than they resemble students who have not won distinction. The data from this research and two prior studies (Schaefer & Anastasi, 1968; Walberg, 1969a) and several hypotheses from a multidimensional theory of creativity (Chambers, 1969) converge on several general factors associated with creativity in adolescence. As identified by teacher nominations, creativity test scores, and self-reports, creativity is associated with (1) stimulation at home, (2) a wide and high level of involvement in both school and outside activities, (3) persistence and single-mindedness in following through with activities despite difficulties, and (4) strong intellectual motivation, although not necessarily extremely high levels of measured intelligence.

However, several differences among creative groups are worth noting. In our previous studies of historically eminent adults, artists characteristically had more diversified, less concentrated interests and opportunities than scientists. Performers and musicians in the high school sample tended to do more studying outside school, to have more creative opportunities, to think less of the importance of intelligence, and to be less persistent. Creative leaders and scientists, however, seemed to concentrate their energies more in school. They were more likely to question teachers, to be persistent, and to think it important to be intelligent. Thus, while all creative groups shared a high degree of involvement in all activities compared with other students, after these differences are considered, scientists and leaders tended to be more involved in academic life than were our performers and musicians. It would be interesting to investigate special schools for the performing arts to see if their students are intensively involved in their schoolwork.

Conclusion

Nine productivity factors of aptitude, instruction, and psychological environments affect academic learning. They also affect creativity, talent development, and later eminence as revealed in exceptional accomplishments. Acquiring a general education and the basics of special fields quickly and well enables students to develop higher talents and allows more time for such talents to result in distinguished contributions. Parents, teachers, peers, and students themselves can choose, influence, or determine the amount and quality of instruction and the nature of their extramural environments. It seems that all students in all talent groups might do much better by systematic application of general principles of educational psychology that indicate how learning, talent, and eminence can be enhanced.

REFERENCES

Barron, F. (1961). Creative vision and expression in writing and painting. In D. W. McKinnon (Ed.), *The creative person* (pp. 231–247). Berkeley: Institute of Personality Assessment Research, University of California.

Bennett, W. J. (1987). *What works: Research about teaching and learning* (2nd ed.). Washington, D.C.: U.S. Department of Education.

Bloom, B. S., Englehart, M. D., Furst, E. J., Hill, W. H., & Krathwohl, D. J. (1956). *Taxonomy of educational objectives, handbook 1: Cognitive domain.* New York: McKay.

Bloom, B. S. (1976). *Human characteristics and school learning.* New York: McGraw-Hill.

Bloom, B. S. (1985a). The nature of the study and why it was done. In B. S. Bloom (Ed.), *Developing talent in young people* (pp. 3–18). New York: Ballantine.

Bloom, B. S. (1985b). Generalizations about talent development. In B. S. Bloom (Ed.), *Developing talent in young people* (pp. 507–547). New York: Ballantine.

Campbell, D. T. (1960). Blind variation and selective retention in creative thought as in other knowledge processes. *Psychological Review, 67,* 380–400.

Cattell, J. M. (1903, February). A statistical study of eminent men. *Popular Science Monthly,* pp. 359–377.

Chambers, J. (1969). A multidimensional theory of creativity. *Psychological Reports, 25,* 779–799.

Chambers, J. A. (1973). College teachers: Their effect on creativity of students. *Journal of Educational Psychology, 65,* 326–334.

Cox, C. M. (1926). *The early mental traits of three hundred geniuses.* Stanford, CA: Stanford University Press.

Ericsson, K. A., Chase, W. G., & Faloon, S. (1980). Acquisition of a memory skill. *Science, 208,* 1181–1182.

Getzels, J. W., & Csikszentmihalyi, M. (1976). *The creative vision.* New York: Wiley.

Giaconia, R. M., & Hedges, L. V. (1982). *Identifying features of open education.* Stanford, CA: Stanford Center for Educational Research.

Gruber, H.E., & Davis, S. N. (1988). Inching our way on Mount Olympus: The evolving-systems approach to creative thinking. In R. J. Sternberg (Ed.), *The nature of creativity* (pp. 243–270). New York: Cambridge University Press.

Havighurst, R. J. (1958). The importance of education for the gifted. In N. B. Henry (Ed.), *Fifty-seventh yearbook of the National Society for the Study of Education* (pp. 5–21). Chicago: University of Chicago Press.

Hedges, L. V., Giaconia, R. M., & Gage, N. L. (1981). *Meta-analysis of the effects of open and traditional instruction.* Stanford, CA: Stanford University Program on Teaching Effectiveness.

Kitano, M. K., & Kirby, D. F. (1986). *Gifted education.* Boston: Little, Brown.

MacKinnon, D. W. (1961). Creativity in architects. In D. W. McKinnon (Ed.), The creative person (pp. 98–113). Berkeley: Institute of Personality Assessment Research, University of California.

McCurdy, H. G. (1957). The childhood pattern of genius. *Journal of Elisha Mitchell Science Society, 73,* 448–462.

Merton, R. K. (1968). The Matthew effect in science. *Science, 159,* 56–63.

Raven, J. (1981). The most important problem in education is to come to terms with values. *Oxford Review of Education, 7,* 253–272.

Schaefer, C. E., & Anastasi, A. (1968). A biographical inventory for identifying creativity in adolescent boys. *Journal of Applied Psychology, 52,* 42–48.

Simon, H. A. (1954). Some strategic considerations in the construction of social science models. In P. Lazarsfeld (Ed.), *Mathematical thinking in the social sciences* (pp. 142–161). Glencoe, IL: Free Press.

Simon, H. A. (1981). *Sciences of the artificial.* Cambridge, MA: MIT Press.

Simonton, D. K. (1987). Developmental antecedents of achieved eminence. *Annals of Child Development, 5,* 131–169.

Simonton, D. K. (1988). Creativity, leadership, and chance. In R. J. Sternberg (Ed.), *The nature of creativity* (pp. 38–426). New York: Cambridge University Press.

Sosniak, L. A. (1988a). Learning to be a concert pianist. In B. S. Bloom (Ed.), *Developing talent in young people* (pp. 19–67). New York: Ballantine.

Sosniak, L. A. (1988b). One concert pianist. In B. S. Bloom (Ed.), *Developing talent in young people* (pp. 68–89). New York: Ballantine.

Sosniak, L. A. (1988c). Phases of learning. In B. S. Bloom (Ed.), *Developing talent in young people* (pp. 409–438). New York: Ballantine.

Sosniak, L. A. (1988d). A long-term commitment to learning. In B. S. Bloom (Ed.), *Developing talent in young people* (pp. 477–506). New York: Ballantine.

Sternberg, R. J. (1988). A three-facet model of creativity. In R. J. Sternberg (Ed.), *The nature of creativity* (pp. 125–147). New York: Cambridge University Press.

Sternberg, R. J., & Davidson, J. E. (1985). Cognitive development in gifted and talented. In F. D. Horo-

witz & M. O'Brien (Eds.), *The gifted and talented* (pp. 37–74). Washington, DC: American Psychological Association.

Walberg, H. J. (1969a). Physics, femininity, and creativity. *Developmental Psychology, 1,* 45–54.

Walberg, H. J. (1969b). A portrait of the artist and scientist as young men. *Exceptional Children, 36,* 5–11.

Walberg, H. J. (1971). Varieties of creativity and the high school environment. *Exceptional Children, 38,* 111–116.

Walberg, H. J. (1982). Childhood traits and environmental conditions of highly eminent adults. *Gifted Child Quarterly, 25,* 103–107.

Walberg, H. J. (1984, May). Improving the productivity of America's schools. *Educational Leadership, 41,* 19–27.

Walberg, H. J., & Herbig, M. P. (in press). Educational productivity and second chance. In D. Inbar (Ed.), *Second chance in education.* Jerusalem, Israel.

Walberg, H. J., & Tsai, S.-L. (1984). Matthew effects in education. *American Educational Research Journal, 20,* 359–374.

Weschler, L. (1988, August 29). A reporter at large skirmish. *The New Yorker,* pp. 48–67.

19

Creating Our Own Pathways: Teaching Students to Think and Become Self-Directed

JOHN BARELL   *Montclair State College, Upper Montclair, New Jersey*

Toward a Definition

Michelangelo was the greatest artist of all time.

My friend, we have a real problem on our hands.

I wonder how I can improve my tennis game.

Do these statements involve thinking?

The answer to this question is yes! In general, the concept of thinking I am comfortable with suggests that thinking is a search for *meaning* that involves our being *adventurous* in the pursuit of alternatives, being *reasonable* in our evaluation of these alternatives, and, along the way, being *reflective* about our thought processes. This "quest for meaning," as Arendt (1977) describes it, is not, however, an entirely cognitive endeavor. Our search is always accompanied by dispositions or attitudes—for example, confidence in ourselves and openness to the ideas and feelings of others. The word *thoughtfulness* conveys this union of cognition and affect, thinking and feeling, a union that suggests how we create meaning from experience. Designing environments that invite students to behave more thoughtfully requires a more thorough understanding of the search for meaning.

Johnson (1975) defined meaningfulness as the extensiveness of "the network of referential associations." This means that we create meaning when we relate one idea to another or one fact to a concept. Mayer (1975) demonstrated that when students engage in relating ideas to a broad spectrum of experiences, those beyond the limits of the subject being studied, they are empowered to solve problems of greater novelty and complexity.

This is what thinking does, in part: It "always generalizes, squeezes out of many particulars . . . whatever meaning may inhere" (Arendt, 1977). This is the activity of poets and scientists alike—finding what Bronowski (1956) termed those *hidden likenesses* among objects, events, and ideas that seem so disparate. This requires intense thinking and can be seen as a problem to solve.

My focus in this chapter is on that kind of searching for meaning known as *problem solving,* but it is problem solving that encompasses figuring out the meaning of a poem, how to find our way through travelers' detours, and determining how to respond to someone's claim that "The nation should have a woman as President." Problem solving is not, therefore, narrowly defined as relating only to science and math, where some see very well structured problems with "right answers" generated by clearly defined algorithms (Marzano, 1988, p. 46). As will become evident, problem solving is broadly defined as figuring our way out of any situation or responding to any observation that involves "doubt, uncertainty or difficulty" (*Random House Dictionary,* 1967, definition of a problem).

Let me give you two examples to illustrate the specific definition of *to think* that I am using in this chapter.

Major portions of this chapter are adapted from *Pathways to Thoughtfulness: Enhancing Students' Thinking* by John Barell, New York: Longman, in press.

A Roadblock

Recently a colleague of mine and I were driving toward a nearby town to conduct a workshop. We had a road map and had been there twice before, so it appeared to be a relatively routine operation. As we neared the town line we noticed a roadblock just before a bridge over a major highway. A sign said DETOUR and I stopped the car. Here is a reconstruction of my mental processes:

> *All right, now what do we do? The detour sign says take a right and get onto Route 17 heading south. But we are in a hurry, and if we get lost we'll be late. What should we do to ensure that we don't waste any time?*

There was a trooper parked a few feet away and I got out and asked him where the detour led. He told me to follow the sign and soon I'd see another sign for a left turn and it would be very simple, really.

Is anything really simple? I asked myself and proceeded to follow his directions, which turned out to be inaccurate, and we *were* late!

A Computer Malfunction

Even more recently I got a very strange message on the computer I used to write this chapter. I was attempting to change one word in the text and thought I hit the wrong keys because embedded in the original text was a message that said something like, "No NMI . . . chip no. 07B5: 7536 . . . Reboot, etc." The odd thing about this message was that I couldn't extricate myself from it, because all the keys had become inoperative. I tried everything I could with all the keys in a variety of combinations, and nothing had any effect. What to do? Eventually, I called the manufacturer, who kept me on hold long-distance for 10 minutes, and all during that time I kept thinking, perhaps I should hang up and just turn off the machine and see what happens. What kept me from doing that was the fact that this very strange message had never before appeared on the screen and it was a unique situation not to have any of the keys do anything to the screen. So I hung on, and eventually the factory representative told me what the difficulty was: chip no. 07B5 : 7536 was about to fail—lose its memory—and I should consider doing something about it.

Now, let's analyze these two situations. What do they have in common? In the first place *both created within me some kind of uneasy feeling* of not knowing what to do. Something bothered me, and I was aware of an *uneasiness or perplexity* (Greene, 1973). I had encountered a situation characterized by some *doubt,* and I was *uncertain* about my course of action. In terms of Arendt's definition of thinking as a search for meaning, I found myself in situations fraught with *ambiguity* because there was little certainty about direction. In these instances what was ambiguous was a means of extricating myself from confusion.

Second, *I had hit a roadblock:* There were obstacles in my pathway.

A. The detour sign put an obstacle in my pathway, and I had to figure out what to do. My normal pathway was blocked.

B. The strange almost-from-outer-space message on my monitor prevented my changing the word in the text and made me stop and think: I don't know what to do in this unusual situation.

Both situations represented an interruption of the normal course of events, in which expectations were upset, resulting in patterns becoming "out of joint," as Hamlet noted.

Third, *I had to become actively involved in a mental process* if I wanted a successful resolution of the difficulty. I couldn't just sit back, relax, and follow the anticipated, predetermined pathway to the workshop or to correcting the textual error. I had to act, decide upon an approach or two or three, make decisions based upon prior experience, related knowledge and evidence, and put some plan into effect. Such action would probably remove the ambiguity and create a new situation I could successfully deal with. In order to understand the situation and make it meaningful, I had to become mentally and emotionally involved.

Fourth, I had encountered a situation in which *multiple options were present*. I could do a number of different things enroute to the workshop: follow the detour, ask questions, or turn around and find another way. With the computer I had to get help from a reliable resource. Before the situation was resolved, I had attempted a number of different approaches: consulting the repair facility where I had bought the machine, consulting a hacker recommended to me by a friend, and trying to learn from my two years' experience with this computer that has had a very limited number of difficulties.

Fifth, *each situation invited me to come to a conclusion or resolution* in the form of a course of action. As the result of my uneasy feeling of encountering an obstacle and deciding that I had to act and disclose all the options, I ultimately had to make a choice and carry out a plan. This plan would restore the situation to one in which actions and reactions fit into a recognizable pattern of events—one more meaningful to me.

Sixth, as a result of such action I could then *reflect upon my choices* and the relationship between feeling and thinking and evaluate this experience in order to learn from it. It is this reflection, to see causes and effects, that Dewey (1963) mentioned in *Education and Experience* as the essence of having *an experience*. Having an experience meant to Dewey in this instance making a series of events meaningful to ourselves. Without the reflection the danger is that these actions and responses become an undifferentiated mass of information without significant relationships established among them. Finding these relationships is one way of creating and disclosing to ourselves and others the meaning of experiences.

The foregoing characterize *some* of our activities and experiences with thinking. Thinking in these two instances was stimulated when I encountered some kind of doubt or perplexity; Dewey (1933) likened it to coming to a fork in the road: "Reflective thinking . . . involves (1) a state of doubt, hesitation, perplexity, mental difficulty, in which thinking originates, and (2) an act of searching, hunting, inquiring, to find material that will resolve the doubt, settle and dispose of the perplexity" (p. 12).

Dewey continues to expand this definition to include the nature of a problem as anything— "no matter how slight and commonplace in character—[that] perplexes and challenges the mind so that it makes belief at all uncertain. . . ." (p. 13). *This is the definition of problem that I am using here: "Problem" is not limited to well-structured situations found in mathematics and science. Rather "problem" refers to any "doubt, uncertainty, or difficulty" that we encounter in any human endeavor or subject of inquiry.* Thinking begins when we start attempting to resolve these uncertainties no matter how or where or when or why they occur.

Thinking begins for Dewey (1933) in that forked-road situation, "a situation that is ambiguous, that presents a dilemma, that proposes alternatives" (p. 14). Something "that disturbs [our] equilibrium" is what initiates thinking, or the search to resolve the dilemma.

How does the foregoing relate to Arendt's notion of thinking as a search for meaning? Let us consider those aspects of the roadblock and computer problems that do exemplify the search for meaning.

First, a discrepancy between givens and goals suggests the breaking of a pattern—the way things usually operate. Fixing them or figuring out a solution can be seen as setting things straight—recreating the stable pattern that may have existed before the ambiguities arose. Closing the gap between givens (being lost) and goals (trying to find a clear pathway) may result in creating a situation absent of ambiguity because of the effects of our solutions. As Greene (1973) noted, when the problem is resolved the tension it created (its uneasiness) would be allayed:

> . . . at least to the extent that the diverse feelings, perceptions, and ideas involved were balanced in relation to one another. When that balance occurred, a moment of equilibrium would ensue—until, once again, wondering began. (p. 108)

Second, creating our own pathways (philosopher Gilbert Ryle's 1979 definition of thinking) can be seen as establishing our own meaningful course of action. Our pathway is, to a large extent, conditioned by how we interpret and represent the problem (see Figure 19.1).

Search for meaning and understanding:
  What kind of problem is this and what can help us solve it?
    Recognize: What feelings do we have about the situation?
    Research: What information do we need to solve this?
    Relate: How is this related to other problems? What ideas or concepts do we recall from other problem types? What patterns are evident in these situations/problems?
    Represent: Can we draw a picture, graph, diagram of this problem?
    Reduce: Can we reduce the problem to several parts? Can we identify reasons that this problem exists?
    Reflect: What assumptions/biases/definitions should we question? Have we identified all significant information?
    Resources: Are there persons and things that can help?
  What do we want to do? (Help student set/define a specific objective: "How to ---" close gap between givens and our goals.
Be adventurous in our thinking: Think of different approaches and strategies. (Solve a smaller problem?)
  Generate alternative solutions: Brainstorm alternatives. Go beyond the boundaries. Be sure to challenge unstated assumptions and definitions.
Search for reasonableness: Anticipate results: If we do this, what will happen? Compare and contrast solutions using important characteristics. Select alternative based on criteria and good evidence.
Be reflective: Take action and monitor: How well are we doing? Do we need to revise our goals or strategies? Redefine the problem in new ways?"
  Evaluate our ways of solving this problem: How well did we do? Why? What would we do differently next time? Why?

Figure 19.1   Problem-solving processes.

Our internal representation determines our strategy (Hayes, 1981), and this act of representing reflects the meaning we give the problem or dilemma. So when students say, "I don't understand this problem," they are letting us know that they haven't figured out how to make it meaningful and, therefore, cannot represent it to themselves in words, pictures, or other symbols.

Understanding what a problem means suggests several other practical and philosophical considerations, from engaging students' *anticipatory set,* or web of prior experiences in the subject, to challenging them to reflect upon their personal (perhaps emotional) encounters with themes, ideas, and concepts. Greene (1973) speaks of exploring, in this way, both the "inner and outer horizons of the problem, making connections within the field of [the student's] consciousness. . . ." (p. 166).

Third, in order to figure out what to do, very often we try to *relate* one situation to another, thereby making it more meaningful (Figure 19.1) It is in the act of relating one idea, concept, or form of problem to others that we establish patterns of meaningfulness. In the roadblock situation, I asked the trooper for additional directions because after seeing the detour I immediately recalled several similar situations in which I had gotten lost just by attempting to follow the posted directions. Thus, I understood the potential for getting lost better because I related one situation to others. My action, therefore, was the result of better understanding of this particular roadblock situation. Thinking about the dilemma made it more meaningful and made my subsequent actions more appropriate as I sought a solution.

We may also ask varieties of questions to

conduct *research* or to *reflect* by challenging assumptions, thereby making the situation more meaningful: What do I know and what do I want to find out? What assumptions am I making and are they warranted? Even as we break a problem/dilemma/confusion into several parts (*reducing* it), we make it more manageable and, therefore, more comprehensible and solvable.

Thus, there would appear to be many ways in which thinking, and in particular problem solving, can be seen as an attempt to make situations and experiences more meaningful.

Thoughts But Not Thinking

Now I can hear some of you asking questions like these:

Am I thinking when I daydream and just have images floating around in my mind?

Is it thinking if I am driving down the road and see a lovely sunset and say, "Isn't that beautiful!"

Is thinking involved when I just see myself in a new job with more challenging responsibilities?

The answer to these questions may be no. These actions, by themselves, might not constitute thinking as defined above. These examples seem more like random thoughts, that is, concepts, images, ideas, anticipations, and so forth. We can be driving along immersed in creating a host of such conceptions, which might appear as single slides on a screen. However, when we take one, for example, noticing that the sunset is *beautiful* and ask, Why is it so beautiful? This might be the wonderment, the puzzle, or the uncertainty that would result in a chain of inquiry to find an answer, to find the reasons and evidence that support this conclusion.

The words *persistent* and *deliberate* and *purpose* can be used to differentiate what is idle and random from the real nature of thinking as defined in this chapter: picking any one of the random thoughts and trying to figure something out constitutes thinking. Real thinking would result in something akin to a longer slide show consisting (not necessarily in logical

sequence) of a number of different steps (or slides) that reflect our attempting to achieve a specific purpose (to reach a conclusion, solution, meaning, etc.). And why do we wish to do this? Probably some question or matter interests us at the moment. Perhaps we wonder about the perplexity that we have uncovered and through thinking we pursue a deliberate course of mental action to arrive at a conclusion.

Causes of Thinking

Let me summarize, briefly. Thinking as defined here is caused by encountering some sort of conflict, doubt, or perplexity, something that brings uncertainty about what to do. Natalia, a first-grader, summed this up with her definition of a problem: "If you don't know something and you have to find it out." We can encounter the doubt passively (against our will) as in the roadblock situation, or we can decide to engage such problematic situations actively, for example by choosing to write a book or improve our tennis game.

When we come upon or generate such situations, what do we do? The first thing, of course, is to *recognize* that we have some kind of difficulty, conflict, or problem of interest worth spending some time with. This is not always easy. When I asked ninth-graders how they knew if and when they had a problem, they spoke of not getting what they wanted, of something bothering them, or of not feeling good about some matter.

Some may be bothered by the notion that all thinking begins with a doubt, uncertainty, or difficulty—in other words, a problem. Please remember that I am using the word *problem* in its broadest sense to mean any matter that puzzles us. It certainly does not suggest a deep psychological problem, or only some situation involving numbers (math) or laws of physics. No, a problem is a concern we wish to focus upon. Our concern may be raised by a single slide up on the screen: my role in tomorrow's meeting. Then we ask, What role do I wish to play? and How can I best ensure that I play that role? This requires extended, persistent, and deliberate thinking and results in a number of slides being projected upon the screen. This succession of slides constitutes the *pathway* of our thinking.

The Process of Thinking

Once we recognize that we are in the midst of a situation characterized by doubt, uncertainty, or difficulty, most of the time we attempt to remove the sources of such doubt, and so forth. Gilbert Ryle (1979) described this process as creating a pathway, not following in someone else's footsteps: "Thinking is trying to better one's instructions; it is trying out promising tracks which will exist, if they ever do exist, only after one has stumbled exploringly over ground where they are not" (p. 78).

Thinking, therefore, is a process involving exploration and experimentation with no guarantee of success. When we think, we are taking a calculated risk that might end up successfully or might not. We are attempting to "better" [our] instructions"; that is, we begin to think when there is an absence of knowing exactly what to do. We must begin to figure things out for ourselves, even, as Ryle suggests, if it is attempting to spell the word *cat*.

> Pathfinding is not and cannot be path following. Pondering is precisely *not* knowing what steps to take but taking tentative steps all the same in order to learn something from their fate. (p. 92)

Thinking involves being tentative—like setting up many, many little hypotheses and testing them out in the form of taking steps to resolve a dilemma—as Edison did with attempting to create the light bulb.

> Thinking, then, can be saying things tentatively to oneself with the specific heuristic intention of trying, by saying them, to open one's own eyes, to consolidate one's own grasp, or to get oneself out of a rut. . . . (p. 92)

Thinking involves what we will later refer to as *self-talk,* a process of proceeding through the underbrush of the problem in order to find a solution or resolution. Self-talk is saying things to ourselves such as, What is my problem? How will I get out of it? What can I try?

What or who can help me? Where have I seen a situation like this before? I can solve this problem if I really persist at it. All these statements will eventually become internalized and part of a metacognitive repertoire for becoming aware of and controlling our approach to life's difficult situations.

Upon leaving Rosemarie Liebmann's high school class at semester's end, one student, Tom, said, "Thank you for helping me figure out what to do when I didn't know what to do." How, she asked, had this been accomplished? "It never occurred to me," he said, "to ask questions when I'm lost." This is the kind of self-talk that we all can engage in to begin the process of real thinking. Tom witnessed sufficient modeling of self-questioning and was asked enough times to write down his own questions in his thinking journal that by the end of the semester he realized that his teacher had helped him learn to think (Barell, Liebmann, & Sigel, 1988). These self-instructions can be thought of as the series of steps we take to find the pathway, and the series of slides we throw up on the screen that reflect our tentative steps.

Lauren Resnick (1987) has also given us a framework within which to ponder the nature of thinking. She describes the nature of thinking as:

Nonalgorithmic: The path of action is not fully specified in advance.

Complex: The total path is not "visible" (mentally speaking) from any single vantage point

Involving *nuanced judgment* and interpretations

Involving the application of *multiple criteria,* which sometimes conflict with one another

Involving *uncertainty*. Not everything is known that bears on the task at hand.

Self-regulation of the thinking process. We do not recognize higher order thinking in an individual when someone else "calls the plays" at every step.

Involving *imposing meaning,* finding structure in apparent disorder

Resnick's formulation is much like Ryle's even though she approaches thinking not from the philosophical point of view but from that of cognitive psychology. They use similar terms, following a path that is frought with uncertainty and involving multiple possible interpretations and solutions. One of the key phrases Resnick uses is *imposing meaning*. *Thinking is, indeed, very much a process of making something meaningful on our own and not one involving rote memory and routine operations at someone else's direction.* One high school student, Emily, when asked to define a problematic situation in her life focused upon the nature of schooling itself. Her reflections, written in her *thinking journal*, exemplify this definition of thinking as creating meaning:

> Sometimes I worry that I'm not equipped to achieve what I want, that I'm just a tape recorder repeating back what I've heard . . . . School is kind of unrealistic that way. Kids who do well often just repeat what the teacher has said . . . . I worry that once I'm out of school and people don't keep handing me information with questions and Scantron sheets I'll be lost. (Barell, in press)

Not being a tape recorder is precisely what thinking is all about: What do we do when the "problems" of life are not labeled and scored mechanically? Emily knows she is going to do what Natalia realized in first grade: "You have to figure it out."

Thus, we have definitions from different professions: philosophy, cognitive psychology, and science. All of them refer, in part at least, to this characteristic, as Resnick noted, of attempting to impose or create meaning by applying or creating structures from and for experience. *Thinking as a search for meaning is quite possibly one of the defining characteristics of being human.*

As Greene (1973) noted, this search for meaning is liberating: "To make sense is to liberate [oneself] . . ." (p. 163). By this she referred to calling all of life into question and, by this act, reflecting upon its very nature, purpose, and consequences. When we think, as Heidegger (1972) noted, we very likely cause some things to be *unthought*. To unthink something means to uncover and disclose preconceptions, assumptions, and myths that may no longer hold true. Arendt (1977) noted that thinking *unfreezes* what language has frozen

into consciousness. "The word 'house' is something like a frozen thought that thinking must unfreeze to get at the original meaning of the notion" (p. 78).

In these ways thinking can be liberating and, simultaneously, disturbing to both the thinker and those with whom she or he interacts. There are adults who have considerable difficulty with this kind of thinking when practiced by students who raise hands to question the adults' conclusions and/or patterns of behavior in class. But this is one theme of this chapter: *Thinking is liberating and empowering, and this is threatening to those who insist upon maintaining a status quo without question.*

Thinking, More Specifically

Let me now move from a definition and consideration of causal factors to try to specify in more detail some of the processes we usually associate with thoughtfulness: searching for meaning, being adventurous, being reasonable, and being reflective.

Searching for Meaning

If thinking involves creating a pathway, what does this look like when we encounter a dilemma or difficulty? In the instances cited above it means asking many of the following kinds of questions of ourselves:

Do I have a problem?

What kind of problem is it?

Do I *recognize* any feelings associated with this situation?

Do I need to conduct *research* and find out more information?

How can I *relate* it to my prior experience/ knowledge?

How can I *represent* the situation visually/ graphically?

Can I *reduce* this dilemma to several important elements or parts?

How can I *reflect* upon unstated assumptions, beliefs, biases?

What do I want to do? What is my objective?

What can help me? What kinds of *resources* do I need?

What will my overall *strategy* be?

What *alternatives* can I think of? (Be adventurous.)

Which ones are best and why? What evidence supports one alternative over another? Is there counterevidence to suggest a different approach? (Be reasonable.)

What action will I take and why?

How well am I doing? (Be reflective.)

How will I know if I succeeded?

How well did I do? What might I do differently next time? Why?

These processes are organized more explicitly in Figure 19.1, but this organization of steps is not intended to convey the notion that we follow them in a lock-step sequential way. As you can see, these questions involve trying to make sense out of the dilemma and then being adventurous, reasonable, and reflective. Let me take specific episodes to illustrate the search for meaning:

I realized I had a problem when a strange message arose on my computer and my expectations were violated. I *recognized* and eventually overcame feelings of frustration; I *researched* the problem quite thoroughly; and I tried to *relate* this situation to others. I *reflected* upon the assumption that computer experts knew what they were talking about. These processes helped me figure out what kind of problem I had and paved the way for figuring out what to do. Notice that recognizing and dealing with feelings are part of the creation of meaning.

In the roadblock situation, the way I *represented* the situation was most important. Once I had encountered the roadblock, was I able to envision a clear pathway to my destination, or, as it it turned out, did I see further complications? In planning to write a poem or a book, can I formulate a clear picture of the final product? As Hayes (1981) notes, the way we represent a problem determines the strategies we will use. Thus, in interpreting texts and in searching for the meaning in a math problem, the kinds of visual organizers (maps) or representations we create will be most important for clear thinking.

The reason searching for meaning is so important is that thoughtful people spend considerable time figuring out what a conflict or dilemma is all about before they jump in to generate solutions or plug numbers into a formula (Sternberg, 1985). Let us now turn to being adventurous in our thinking.

Being Adventurous

In many complex, problematic situations, we want to be adventurous and generate alternative solutions, interpretations, or perspectives. We can do this with a situation like finding a way to stop industrial pollution as well as with something like interpreting a poem by Yeats. Here are some processes that I have found helpful in attempting, as Ryle noted, "to open one's own eyes" to newer possibilities.

Problem Finding. In the problem with the computer, my initial definition of the problem was as follows: How to get the computer fixed (and lose the least amount of time). If I spend a little more time with the *problem-finding process,* I might rethink my definition of the situation in a number of different ways:

"How can I figure out if it is really malfunctioning?"(I almost automatically assumed there was permanent memory damage, even after the diagnostic tests proved satisfactory.)

"How can I get someone to remedy the situation without cost to me?"

"How can I get the computer to rectify itself?" (This seems impossible, but perhaps not!)

These are ways of redefining or relocating the problem. David Perkins (1981) observed that creativity may begin with how and where we locate the problem. Divergent and unusual solutions flow from a problem definition that looks at the situation from an unusual perspective. Getting the computer to rectify itself may be just such a creative approach. It's like the problem Perkins often discusses from the National Aeronautics and Space Administration (NASA). In engineering the Apollo space capsule, people formulated the problem this way: How to keep heat away from the capsule. One creative engineer saw it differently: How to find a substance that might deflect heat from the capsule. The result was the ablative heat shield that burned up as Apollo reentered the atmosphere. Perkins stresses that thinking about options *before* acting is characteristic of creative and productive thinkers.

Koestler (1964) calls such shifting of perspectives the "bisociation of matrices" and Marzano (1988) speaks of this creative phenomenon as shifting from one frame of reference or schema to another: "This process continues until the person has viewed the problem from many different perspectives" (p. 26).

Brainstorming. We all know that brainstorming involves generating many, varied possibilities without evaluation. But many of us are not that familiar with the actual processes we use to generate alternatives. Here are some that I have recognized in my own and others' thinking.

Using:
    My own experience
    Others' experiences
And:
    Adapting and combining different solutions
    Reflecting on unstated assumptions
    Relating this problem to others
    Recognizing my own feelings
    Representing the problem clearly

These processes may help us to be generative without being constrained by thoughts of practicality, feasibility, or effectiveness.

Playing with Variables. One good example is Einstein's *combinatory play* with elements of a problem, often invoked by asking "What if . . . ?" questions that might resemble his famous *Gedanken,* or thought experiment: "What if I were to ride along a ray of light, what would I see looking back?" (Barell, 1980).

Bronowski (1978) discussed the act of imagination as "the opening of the system so that it shows new connections. . . . All those who imagine take parts of the universe which have not been connected hitherto and enlarge the total connectivity of the universe by showing them to be connected." Thus, playing with variables involves what we often do during

problem solving: find new and significant relationships between examples, data, experiences, and the like. Bronowski described this act of the scientist as "finding hidden likenesses." So we see that part of imaginative activity is akin to critical inquiry in that it involves the basis of analogical reasoning: finding and making comparisons. Newton's relating the moon and a falling apple and Bohr's analogizing the atom to the solar system were creative insights that gave us new connections and new ways of viewing complex phenomena. Shakespeare's comparing life to a "walking shadow" involved the same kind of comparative or metaphoric activity.

Metaphoric Thinking. This is creating metaphors that aptly describe complex phenomena and help bridge the gap between the known and the relatively unknown (Barell, 1980). For example, if our nation is no longer a true melting pot, is it, then, more an enriched stew or a Darwinian class war among the fit and the not-so-fit? As another example, one high school student described finding a theme in literature as "getting to the heart of an artichoke."

Visualization. Representing a problem often leads to a productive solution. Einstein thought in "more-or-less clear images" as he speculated on riding along a ray of light (Ghiselin, 1955). These visual experiments (or *representations*) were the way he constructed meaning, as they were for Kepler, Bohr, and other scientists (Ferris, 1988).

Personal Projection. Joshua Lederberg, Nobel laureate in biology, noted that he had to begin imagining himself "*inside* of a biological or other situation" in order to be productive (Judson, 1980). Students are often not very good at this kind of reasoning (National Assessment of Educational Progress, 1986); if we expect them to become more empathic, we shall have to provide practice in this most important process.

Being adventurous or creative thus involves several different skills, but more important, it involves a frame of mind that searches for creative solutions (Perkins, 1985). Creativity involves seeing in other ways, seeing *as if* the atom were a solar system or the Wild West of the pioneers were "the very Eden which earth might still afford" (Kolodny, 1984).

Being Reasonable

Einstein engaged in playing with images before he would search for the reasonableness of those images. Being reasonable involves, as Resnick (1987) noted, "nuanced judgment." To make a judgment we collect evidence, challenge assumptions, define terms, identify biases, and examine counterexamples and evidence contrary to preferred solutions. In a word, part of finding our pathway through the brambles of a problematic situation is a process of analyzing and evaluating our options in accordance with the most accurate and reliable information available. We might use such information to project the consequences of our options or to weigh the pros and cons of each (Swartz & Perkins, 1989). In many instances we are making judgments in accordance with criteria (Lipman, 1988).

Critical thinking consists of analytic processes that help us resolve problems. In the roadblock and computer problems mentioned earlier, I had to pay particular attention to the following:

Identifying reliable, accurate evidence (road signs, computer chip information) in order to select the most reasonable option

Disclosing underlying assumptions (that state troopers are right; that computer technicians know what they are talking about) in order to identify the problem accurately

Reasoning causally and projecting consequences (searching for supporting evidence to confirm or disconfirm one or more hypotheses or options)

Reasoning analogically (how was either problem like any other?)

Using relevant criteria (a "good" solution to the computer problem would be feasible, practical, and as inexpensive as possible)

These skills are used by students when they analyze and evaluate claims such as "The Greeks developed the most advanced civilization in history." Evidence from recent studies (National Assessment of Educational Progress, 1986) suggests that when our students respond to such claims they are not very good at two critical thinking tasks: providing evidence for their conclusions and making good comparisons and contrasts.

There are other aspects of critical thinking. Paul's (1985) dialectical reasoning is one. Another is critical thinking in the strong sense, which involves examining complex issues from a variety of perspectives. These terms suggest that analyzing claims about the quality of a civilization as well as life's dilemmas is, as Resnick (1987) noted, complex and multilogical—it involves thinking from many different perspectives and thinking across disciplinary lines. Problems such as homelessness, the federal deficit, threats to this country's natural wildernesses, and abortion are complex life situations that lend themselves to being approached from diverse perspectives.

Cathy Skowron (1987) challenged her first-graders to have what McPeck (1981) called a "healthy skepticism" by presenting the story of Chicken Little. This teacher helped her students realize that had the animals looked up and not just immediately believed Chicken Little, they might have known that an acorn could have fallen instead of the sky. "It was the way she said it—like it was really true," said Jennifer. "Maybe if the first one didn't go, then the second one wouldn't go," added William. These students are beginning to question the credibility of sources and look for evidence on their own.

Being Reflective

While solving the problems of the detour and the computer, I was engaging in what Resnick calls "self-regulation." I was continually asking myself, "What am I doing now? Is this the best course of action? Am I pleased with what is happening? Am I reaching my objective?" and, at the end, "How well did I do in this case?" This is the kind of "self-talk" Tom learned to engage himself in when he said he was learning how to ask himself questions.

By engaging in this kind of self-talk, we are practicing *metacognition,* or reflecting on our own thinking. Sternberg (1985) refers to these metacognitive processes as executive skills because they surround our problem in much the way an executive oversees his or her plans and responsibilities (Figure 19.2) *Better thinkers, problem solvers, and readers are in control of their own thinking and make strategic decisions about what they know and don't know, where they are going, what they expect to find when they get there, and why* (Pressley, Goodchild, Fleet, Zajchowski, & Evans, 1987). Better thinkers, therefore, acquire and use knowledge about themselves, the tasks they are to perform, and the strategies that will benefit them in each case.

Metacognition can easily be related to our concept of thoughtfulness if we think in these strategic terms: *Planning, Monitoring,* and *Evaluating.*

Planning generally involves posing such questions as these: What is my problem? How do I feel about it? How will I approach it? What strategies and alternatives might I use? What do I expect to find when I finish this problem? Note that in the initial planning stages we are recognizing our feelings of confidence that we can solve the problem if we persist.

Monitoring generally involves keeping track of our progress—watching our mental script as it unfolds: How well am I doing now? What have I accomplished so far? Do I want to revise my goals, my plans?

Evaluating involves these concerns: Have I completed what I set out to do? How well have I succeeded? What criteria am I using here? What have I learned? How can I use what I now know in other places? Were I to do it all over again, what might I do differently and why?

These processes of self-regulation result from what Ryle (1979) called "saying things tentatively to oneself" with the intent of "open[ing] one's own eyes" to new ways of seeing so we can extricate ourselves from a dilemma. This "saying things tentatively to oneself" is the essence of metacognitive awareness. Our self-questioning is what makes us more aware and, eventually, gives us greater control of our own thinking: "Training in metacognition has been shown to result in improved study of text . . . particularly enhanced reading comprehension and recall . . . problem solving . . . and oral comprehension" (Baird & White, 1984).

They:
   Have confidence they can solve most problems.
   Persist.
   Control impulsivity.
   Listen to other people.
   Are open to others' ideas.
   Cooperate with others in solving problems.
   Are empathic.
   Are open to ambiguity and complexity.
   Approach problems from a variety of perspectives.
   Relate prior experience to current problems.
   Research problems thoroughly.
   Are open to many different possible solutions and evidence that may contradict favored points
      of view.
   Pose "WHAT IF" questions challenging assumptions and playing with variables.
   Are metacognitive: Plan, monitor, and evaluate their thinking.
   Are curious and wonder about the world around them. They ask "good questions."

Figure 19.2 Characteristics of thoughtful persons.

The result of such metacognitive aware- ness, we hope, will be more competent thinking (Pressley et al., 1987), and it may look like reflections of Tejal, a 10th-grader writing in her thinking journal: "I should learn to ask the kinds of questions my Dad asks me when I try to solve a problem. Maybe if I keep doing this with him I can learn to do it by myself" (Resnick, 1987).

Three specific ways of eliciting students' thinking processes that have met with consid- erable success are the following:

1. Ask process questions much more often, for example: "How did you arrive at that an- swer (or question)?" This strategy reveals the richness of students' idiosyncratic ways of ap- proaching and resolving problems (Costa, 1984; Peterson, Fennema, & Carpenter, 1988). Process questions following problem solving are designed to elicit students' problem-solving strategies, as ill-defined as these may be at first.

2. Have students like Tejal maintain thinking journals in which they record re- sponses to such questions as, What was the problem? How did I solve it? Did I solve it well? What would I do differently next time? Where in my life do I use such problem solving strategies? Students in Rosemarie Liebmann's high school classes kept these journals and rec- orded their emotional distress at confronting certain kinds of problems ("This problem scared me at first") as well as their ability to help friends use effective strategies, such as breaking problems down (reducing them) to smaller, more manageable parts (Barell, Liebmann, & Sigel, 1988).

3. Occasionally, ask students, "What are you learning about your own thinking?" First- graders can be quite candid about their own thinking. After a series of problem-solving ses- sions in a class, John, Evan, and Bob made these comments about their own progress: "Whenever we do this, other people come up with solutions and I can add on or make com- ments."

"My thinking was not too good because I was sort of copying other people's ideas." "I think my thinking was good. I had lots of ideas because I understand the problem." When asked how they go about solving problems, these same students generated their own rules: "Take the parts out of the problem you don't really need—get to the main problem." "Make the problem littler and littler." "Look at the problem from a different angle." "Believe in yourself!" (Barell, in press).

These strategies afford students opportuni- ties that are often overlooked by our focus on the products of other people's thinking. We sel- dom are concerned with the reasoning processes our students use to figure something out, because we are much more interested in their attaining an easily verifiable status of correctness.

Meaning, Adventurousness, Reasonableness, and Reflection in the Curriculum

What do we do with problem solving in the curriculum? The first thing to do is model these thinking processes by thinking aloud in front of our students, sharing with them how we approach complex situations. We then invite out students to engage in solving problems that do not require a great deal of background knowledge, such as "Your friend hit a ball through the neighbor's window. How would you respond to such a situation?" These content-free difficulties afford us an opportu- nity to see how students think through every- day dilemmas: What kinds of strategies do they use? What questions do they pose about such situations? Then we can move into our content areas and find the problematic within, for example, the humanities, where people have faced dilemmas and had to figure out what to do (e.g., If you were Macbeth, what would you do upon hearing the forecasts of the three weird sisters?; Barell, in press). In math and science we continually face problems, but what we do not do is help students focus on the strategies they use to solve these problems. Emphasizing strategic thinking involves *metacognitive awareness,* or understanding and taking more control of our thinking. This should be one of education's primary goals: achieving more self-direction of our own thinking and learning.

Dispositions and Instructional Processes

Now that we have sketched out some notions about what stimulates thinking, we can identify more specifically those dispositions that contribute to thoughtful behavior and can also mention instructional processes that foster and enhance its growth within our classrooms.

In order for me to deal with the roadblock problem, or another one I choose to engage in, I must possess certain attitudes or dispositions. Without the following it would be most difficult even to proceed:

Confidence that I can solve the problem by thinking about it

Persistence in the face of obstacles

Openness to alternatives; a *tentativeness* about premature closure

Willingness to cooperate with others

Ability to listen

Empathy with others' situations

Tolerance for ambiguity

Sense of objectivity and fairness about evidence and others' points of view

Sense that I am in control of this process and that the solution will not come about as the result of sheer luck or happenstance (internal locus of control)

Willingness to search for evidence that contradicts favored possibilities/solutions/perspectives

These are some of the dispositions that contribute to thoughtfulness. They are ones that we can model for students as we structure the environment with the goal of empowering them to take more responsibility for their own success. We can develop these dispositions by the ways in which we create the environment for thinking within our classrooms. Some of the significant strategies we employ toward this end include the following:

Modeling the thinking processes and dispositions

Setting high cognitive expectations

Engaging students in setting their own goals

Continually posing problems

Allowing quiet or wait time for responses

Quality responding to students' answers, questions, ideas, etc.

Fostering peer interaction

Working toward transfer of knowledge and thinking processes to situations beyond classroom walls

Becoming more metacognitive in our thinking, more aware of how we control our outcomes by planning, monitoring, and evaluating

Making adult, peer, and self-evaluations

These processes are a most significant aspect of any discussion of thoughtfulness, because the ways in which we model each one communicates messages about the attributes of thinkers we wish to emphasize (see Figure 19.2). The ways in which we communicate high expectations, pose problems, respond to students' feelings, and evaluate our progress send strong signals to students about, for example, our openness to alternative solutions, kinds of evidence, and ways of defining situations. These pedagogical moves are some of the tools we use to foster the search for meaning.

Conclusion

If we want students to become persons who are good at identifying and resolving meaningful dilemmas or conflicts, then we must daily provide for this within the classroom. We accomplish this task by designing environments that will foster certain attitudes—for example, a feeling that "I have control over my own successes." Our instructional program must be *problem centered,* that is, we must present our students with dilemmas, conflicts, discrepancies, and problems to investigate and resolve. We need to find within our subject areas those problematic situations that will stimulate creative inquiry and pathfinding.

Our curricular subjects are not mountains of factual data to cover. Quite the contrary, they are histories and displays of how humankind has attempted to make the myriad complexities of life meaningful. The disciplines we teach are more productively considered records of how we as a human race have solved problems we posed for ourselves and those posed by nature for us. One of our tasks as educators, as David Hawkins (cited in Duckworth, 1987) reminded us, is to uncover these mysteries or to disclose them to ourselves and our students. As we disclose these perplexities, we can model how they were solved and how they can or might be resolved so that our students begin to think of themselves not as vessels to be filled full of information but as explorers on the very edge of the realm of knowledge (Bruner, 1960).

We are aiming for more students to take those tentative steps toward thoughtfulness. As we empower children to take more control of their own thinking and learning, they will understand the comment of one of their peers: "I've realized I can solve most of my own problems." Such personal empowerment is one of our long-term educational goals.

REFERENCES

Arendt, H. (1977, November 28). Thinking—II. *The New Yorker,* p. 114.

Baird, J., & White, R. (1984, April). *Improving learning through enhanced metacognition: A classroom study.* Paper presented at the annual meeting of the American Educational Research Association, New Orleans.

Barell, J. (1980). *Playgrounds of our minds.* New York: Teachers College Press.

Barell, J. (in press). *Pathways to thoughtfulness: Enhancing students' thinking.* New York: Longman.

Barell, J., Liebmann, R., & Sigel, I. (1988). Fostering self-direction in students. *Educational Leadership, 45,* 14–17.

Bronowski, J. (1956). *Science and human values.* New York: Perennial Library.

Bronowski, J. (1978). *The origins of knowledge and imagination.* New Haven: Yale University Press.

Bruner, J. (1960). *The process of education.* New York: Vintage.

Costa, A. (1984). Mediating the metacognitive. *Educational Leadership, 42,* 57–62.

Dewey, J. (1933). *How we think.* Boston: Heath.

Dewey, J. (1963). *Education and experience.* New York: Collier.

Duckworth, E. (1987). *"The having of wonderful ideas" and other essays on teaching and learning.* New York: Teachers College Press.

Ferris, T. (1988). *Coming of age in the milky way.* New York: Morrow.

Ghiselin, B. (1955). *The creative process.* New York: New American Library.

Greene, M. (1973). *Teacher as stranger.* Belmont, CA: Wadsworth.

Hayes, J. (1981). *The complete problem solver.* Philadelphia: Franklin Institute Press.

Heidegger, M. (1972). *What is called thinking?* New York: Harper Torchbooks.

Johnson, R. (1975). Meaning in complex learning. *Review of Educational Research, 45,* 425–459.

Judson, H. F. (1980). *The search for solutions.* New York: Holt, Rinehart and Winston.

Koestler, A. (1964). *The act of creation.* New York: Dell.

Kolodny, A. (1984). *The land before her: Fantasy and experience of the American frontiers, 1630–1860.* Chapel Hill: University of North Carolina Press.

Lipman, M. (1988). Critical thinking—what it can be. *COGITARE, 3,* 1.

Marzano, R. (1988). *Dimensions of thinking.* Alexandria, VA: Association for Supervision and Curriculum Development.

Mayer, R. (1975). Information processing variables in learning to solve problems. *Review of Educational Research, 45,* 525–541.

McPeck, J. (1981). *Critical thinking and education.* Oxford: Martin Robertson.

National Assessment of Educational Progress. (1986). *The writing report card.* Princeton, NJ: Educational Testing Service.

Paul, R. (1985). Dialectical Reasoning. In A. Costa (Ed.), *Developing minds* (pp. 152–161). Alexandria, VA: Association for Supervision and Curriculum Development.

Perkins, D. (1981). *The mind's best work.* Cambridge, MA: Harvard University Press.

Perkins, D. (1985). What creative thinking is. In A. Costa (Ed.), *Developing minds* (pp. 58–62). Alexandria, VA: Association for Supervision and Curriculum Development.

Peterson, P., Fennema, E., & Carpenter, T. (1988). Using knowledge of how students think about mathematics. *Educational Leadership, 46,* 42–46.

Pressley, M., Goodchild, F., Fleet, J., Zajchowski, R., & Evans, E. (1987, April). *What is good strategy use and why is it hard to teach?: An optimistic appraisal of the challenges associated with strategy instruction.* Paper presented at the annual meeting of the American Educational Research Association, Washington, DC.

Random House Dictionary. (1967). New York: Random House.

Resnick, L. (1987). *Education and learning to think.* Washington, DC: National Academy Press.

Ryle, G. (1979). *On thinking*. Totowa, NJ: Rowan & Littlefield.

Skowron, C. (1987). Chicken Little. *COGITARE, 2*, 1.

Sternberg, R. (1985). *Beyond IQ*. New York: Cambridge University Press.

Swartz, R., & Perkins, D. (1989). *Teaching thinking: Issues and approaches*. Pacific Grove, CA: Midwest Publications.

PART V

Psychological and Counseling Services

20

Counseling Gifted Students

NICHOLAS COLANGELO   *University of Iowa, Iowa City*

◼ **T**he focus of educating the gifted has centered mostly on meeting their learning needs. Counseling needs, while long recognized, are a relatively recent emphasis. The focus of this chapter is on the counseling needs of gifted students: defining what these needs are and how they can be addressed. Teachers also are "counselors" to students, and when speaking of counseling needs I am addressing the role of teachers. However, this chapter focuses on the role of school counselors, and most comments are directed to them.

It may be helpful to provide a brief historical overview of counseling with gifted students as a means of setting present-day context. The gifted-child movement in the United States can be most clearly traced back to Lewis M. Terman. His pioneering longitudinal study of 1,528 gifted children formed the project titled Genetic Studies of Genius (Burks, Jensen, & Terman, 1930; Terman, 1925; Terman & Oden 1947, 1959). The Terman studies grounded the study of giftedness in an empirical and psychometric tradition. Also, the work dispelled negative myths and traditions regarding the gifted. For example, Terman and his colleagues showed that gifted children were physically superior and psychologically and socially more stable than their intellectually average peers. The studies indicated that giftedness was a "positive" and derailed any initial momentum in concerns of a psychological nature. I say "derailed" because the findings seemed to provide evidence that concern for social/psychological needs was not well founded. I also say "derailed" because the Terman sample has been shown to be nonrepresentative of giftedness and of the population of gifted youngsters.

Terman's sample was identified by use of the Stanford-Binet intelligence test, and his sample was nearly exclusively white and middle-class youngsters. (The original group recommended for the Stanford-Binet testing was picked by teachers; thus some teacher biases probably entered before the standardized testing.) Further, while Terman erased a number of myths, he created others, most notably the myth that gifted children are well adjusted and therefore do not need counseling services. Thus counselors and those in related professions were not an integral part of gifted education during its early development (Kerr, 1986; Webb, Meckstroth, & Tolan, 1982).

Leta Hollingworth (1926, 1942) was the first to contribute evidence indicating that gifted children do have social/emotional needs meriting attention. It was Hollingworth who brought to light the concern that the regular school environment did not meet the educational needs of the gifted. Rather, she wrote that the school environment was more likely to lead to apathy with these youngsters. She anticipated some of the difficulties in peer relations that receive attention today. Especially, she noted that there is often a gap between a gifted student's intellectual and emotional development, stating, "To have the intellect of an adult and the emotions of a child combined in a childish body is to encounter certain difficulties" (Hollingworth, 1942, p. 282).

The 1950s witnessed some major attention to counseling gifted students and the establishment of labs and guidance programs. John Rothney, a counselor educator, founded the Wisconsin guidance Laboratory for Superior Students (University of Wisconsin–Madison), which was headed by Rothney and later by Marshall Sanborn. The guidance laboratory was later renamed the Guidance Institute for Talented Students (GIFTS), which was headed by Charles Pulvino, Nicholas Colangelo, and then Philip Perrone (Colangelo & Zaffrann, 1979).

John Curtis Gowan was a major force in the 1950s to 1970s in promoting counseling services for the gifted. The 1960s and 1970s also witnessed increased sensitivity to issues dealing with gifted women, minorities, and disadvantaged, including counseling needs.

The 1980s saw the establishment of the Supporting the Emotional Needs of Gifted (SENG) program by James T. Webb at Wright State University after the suicide of Dallas Egbert, a highly gifted 17-year-old. SENG has continued its focus on addressing the counseling and psychological needs of gifted students. James Delisle at Kent State University expanded upon the concepts of depression and suicide among the gifted.

In 1982 Barbara Kerr established the Guidance Laboratory for Gifted and Talented at the University of Nebraska–Lincoln, to extend the work of both GIFTS and SENG (Myers & Pace, 1986). Linda Silverman, a psychologist, established the Gifted Child Development Center at Denver, Colorado. In 1988, the University of Iowa established the comprehensive Connie Belin National Center for Gifted Education with Nicholas Colangelo as director and Barbara Kerr as associate director. The Belin National Center has a strong focus on personal counseling, career guidance, and family counseling.

While the attention to counseling can be traced back to Hollingworth (1926), in reality counseling issues have not had a major influence on gifted education. It was only the 1980s that brought serious attention to counseling. At present, it is anticipated that as attention to gifted students continues to grow, counseling and psychological issues will become one of the distinguishing features of the growing movement in gifted education.

Counseling Issues

Self-Concept

One of the significant areas of research on counseling gifted students has been a focus on *self-concept*. Self-concept can be viewed as a "powerful system of cognitive structures that is quite likely to mediate interpretation of and response to events and behaviors directed at or involving the individual" (Nurius, 1986, p. 435). The definition of self-concept has evolved from a "collection of self-views" (e.g., Rogers, 1951; Snygg & Combs, 1949) to general good and bad feelings about oneself (McGuire, 1984) to recent theory and research on operationally defining the structure and contents of the self-concept (Nurius, 1986). Self-concept includes both self-perceptions and self-evaluation.

Self-concepts of gifted youngsters is a topic that has received considerable attention this past decade (Colangelo, Kelly, & Schrepfer, 1987; Karamessinis, 1980; Loeb & Jay, 1987; Ross & Parker, 1980). Most of the work has focused on either academic or social self-concepts. Although gifted students have appropriately high self-concepts regarding their academic abilities (Colangelo & Pfleger, 1978; Kelly & Colangelo, 1984; Tidwell, 1980), there have been inconsistent results on measures of nonacademic self-concepts. Some studies have suggested that in nonacademic areas gifted students have poorer self-concepts than their nongifted peers (Ross & Parker, 1980; Winne, Woodlands, & Wong, 1982). Results of other studies have indicated that social self-concepts of gifted students are higher than those of nongifted peers (Karamessinis, 1980; Kelly & Colangelo, 1984). Counselors must realize that there are a number of gifted students who have either negative or confused self-evaluations and that guidance is needed.

Closely related to self-concept is the attitude that gifted students have toward their own giftedness. Three books, *On Being Gifted* (American Association for Gifted Children, 1978), *Gifted Children Speak Out* (Delisle, 1984), and *Gifted Kids Speak Out* (Delisle, 1987) present testimonials from gifted children describing the impact of giftedness on their lives. The conclusion that can be drawn from these testimonials is that these children are ambivalent about their giftedness. Research has provided some confirmation of this ambivalence. Colangelo and Kelly (1983) found that while gifted youngsters were positive about being labeled gifted, they perceived nongifted peers and teachers as having negative views of them. A study by Kerr, Colangelo, and Gaeth (1988) indicated that the attitude of gifted adolescents toward their own giftedness was multifaceted. Adolescents reported that being gifted was a positive in terms of their own personal growth and in terms of academics. However, they reported it to be a negative in terms of social/peer relations.

The Kerr et al. finding is very relevant for school counselors since the issue focuses on human interaction. In individual counseling sessions counselors can discuss issues such as, What does it mean to be gifted? What do I like about being gifted? What do I not like about being gifted? If I were not gifted, what would be better for me? If I were not gifted, what would be worse for me?

Group counseling also has strong potential for dealing with interpersonal concerns. In a group counseling setting, gifted students can explore their perceptions of how they feel about being gifted, and, perhaps more important, how they think others perceive them. I have found group counseling to be the single most effective avenue for communication among gifted youngsters. In a group setting they share experiences and articulate their perceptions. Either their views are validated or other perspectives are offered. I have found gifted students to be extremely receptive to feedback from other gifted students, especially during adolescence.

Counseling with Parents

Issues, both overt and subtle, arise when counselors work with parents. Parents are not always well informed and are anxious about the developmental needs of their gifted child (Colangelo & Dettmann, 1982, 1985b). A. O. Ross (1964) noted that parents' child-rearing practices usually are derived from the model of a "normal" child. When the child does not conform to the expectation of normal, parents may have difficulty in coping. For example, parents may feel that because the child is different he or she may become socially maladjusted (Bridges, 1979). Also, parents can feel inadequate because of the child's precocity (Packer, Ross, & Deutsch, 1980). The inadequacy usually takes two forms. Parents may feel they

cannot provide the emotional support a "different" child needs or that they cannot provide the intellectual stimulation or educational experiences needed.

The Effects of the Gifted Label on Families

Hobbs (1975) articulated the central dilemma associated with the labeling of children. He observed that the classficiation of students with school learning difficulties, whether based on cognitive or emotional factors, is a practical necessity in order to provide appropriate special programs for youngsters who cannot learn in regular classrooms. The problem with labeling is that a student becomes identified with the learning difficulty. Stereotypic attitudes and beliefs associated with the label can be falsely attributed to each labeled student. This, in turn, shapes the way others interact with the student and influences that student's self-perceptions. The adverse effects of labels on special education students have been widely acknowledged (Jones, 1972; Rist & Harrell, 1982).

The effects of labeling a youngster *gifted* also are problematic. Here we have youngsters who are labeled because they deviate from the norm in a positive direction. Nonetheless, their positive qualities do not ensure acceptance or appreciation (Robinson, 1986). American society in general and schools in particular are ambivalent toward the gifted. They are admired and envied, yet mistrusted (Colangelo & Dettmann, 1985b; Weiss & Gallagher, 1980).

Unfortunately, the effects of the gifted label on family dynamics has generated little empirical evidence. Peterson (1977) found that presence of a gifted child in the family was associated with increased sibling jealousy and competition in the family. Albert (1980) showed that the gifted child received a special position in the family and that family attention and resources were channeled to this youngster in greater proportion and intensity than to other siblings.

Cornell (1983) discovered that parents did not always agree on the accuracy of the label. When both parents agreed that the child was gifted, they had a positive reaction to the label. When one parent disagreed with the label, the reaction toward the child was mixed and typically more negative. When both parents disagreed with the label, the label typically was not perceived in a positive light. Cornell (1983) also found that siblings of gifted children were significantly less well adjusted emotionally and socially than siblings of nongifted children.

Colangelo and Brower (1987a, 1987b) extended the work of Cornell and found that indeed parents often did disagree with the label and that the disagreement centered on their conceptualization (or definition) of *gifted*. They also found that there were sibling difficulties in a family with a gifted child, that these difficulties were most intense when the child was first labeled, and that within 5 years there was no noticeable negative impact on siblings.

School counselors should anticipate difficulties in families when a child is first labeled gifted. It is at this time that the family needs assistance. First, counselors need to be certain that parents clearly understand why their child has been labeled gifted. Many school counselors hold parent discussion groups to clarify these issues. Second, counselors should help families anticipate changes as the families attempt to readjust to the label. For siblings the issue becomes their role and importance in the family. Siblings need to be validated for their own strengths and worth as family members. The good news is that the family will become accustomed to the label and positive adjustments are likely over the next few years. Counselors can effectively ease the initial strain and disruption by helping the family openly communicate at this juncture. Also, families simply alerted to likely changes seem better able to take some strain and disruption in stride and thus appear to adjust even more quickly.

Parent–School Interactions

One of the most important issues confronting counselors is the parent–school relationship (Colangelo & Dettman 1983, 1985b; Dettmann & Colangelo, 1980). The underlying issue regarding this relationship concerns the role the school should take in providing special educational opportunities for gifted students.

Colangelo and Dettmann (1982) developed a counseling model (see Figure 20.1) conceptualizing four types of parent–school interactions involving gifted students.

Type I (cooperation) is an interaction based on the attitude by both parents and schools that the school should be active in gifted education. The tendency here is for open sharing of information about the child and cooperation between parents and schools. Typically, the gifted are identified and given special educational opportunities commensurate with their needs. The underlying assumption by both parents and schools is that the most effective way to develop exceptional ability is through overt special educational considerations (e.g., honors classes, advanced classes, resource rooms, independent projects, ability groupings, and grade skipping).

Type II (conflict) is an interaction based on conflicting attitudes by (active) parents and the (passive) school regarding the role of the school. Parents believe that their gifted child needs special programming by the school in order to develop his or her abilities. However, the school believes that the typical school curriculum is adequate to meet the needs of all youngsters, including the gifted. Also, it is typical for the school to believe that special programs should be a priority for students with handicaps and learning disabilities. The school in this situation feels that parents are pushy and demand unnecessary attention for gifted youngsters. The parents feel they must be aggressive or pushy, otherwise the school will simply ignore the needs of their child.

Type II interactions often are the most difficult for parents and school. Schools tend to view gifted education as an albatross. Parents tend not to support the school and often blame the school for problems of boredom and lack of motivation and achievement in their child. The child is sometimes encouraged by parents to reject the school's evaluations and requirements (e.g., report card grades, classwork) as accurate assessments of his or her abilities.

I have found that parents usually take one of three approaches in this Type II conflict. One is that they continually fight the school. They may either demand meetings for further discussion or join forces with other parents to as-

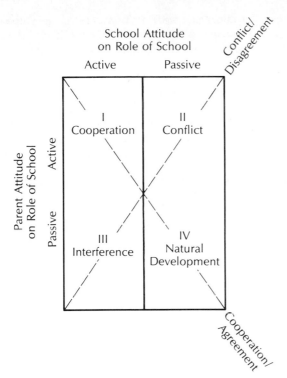

School Attitude
on Role of School

Active   Passive

Conflict/
Disagreement

	I Cooperation	II Conflict

Parent Attitude
on Role of School

Active

Passive

	III Interference	IV Natural Development

Cooperation/
Agreement

Figure 20.1 Interaction model depicting attitudes of parents and schools regarding the role of the school in gifted education.

Source: Reprinted by permission of the authors and publisher from N. Colangelo and D. F. Dettmann (1982), "A Conceptual Model of Four Types of Parent–School Interactions" *Journal for the Education of the Gifted, 5,* pp. 120–126, Figure 1.

sert their position. In the second approach parents take it upon themselves to provide the special programs needed by a child. This may include summer enrichment activities, museum trips, college courses, tutors, mentors, and sometimes even private schools. Obviously, this approach is limited by the educational background and financial resources of the parents. The third approach occurs when parents feel hopeless. They believe that they can have no real effect and all they can do is complain. For many parents the end result is a withdrawal from direct communication with the school.

Type III (interference) interactions are also based on conflict but with a reversal of the dynamics found in Type II. In Type III the school wants to provide actively for the gifted child but the parents do not agree. Parents are unsure if special programs for gifted are helpful or necessary. They are concerned about what effect identification and labeling may

have on their (gifted) child as well as on siblings who may not be identified. Furthermore, parents may be concerned that special recognition will damage their child's peer relationships. These parents may view identification and special programs as an interference in the normal educational development of their child. Meanwhile, the school believes that the child does need special considerations and is willing to provide such programs. However, the school is often frustrated by parents' refusing to let their child participate in these special programs.

Type IV (natural development) interactions are based on agreement by both parents and schools that the role of the school should be passive. This belief is founded on the premise that high ability will take care of itself ("cream rises to the top") and that very little can be done meaningfully to nourish extraordinary ability. Essentially, both parents and schools view the typical school curriculum and extracurricular activities as providing enough challenge and variety to stimulate the development of high potential and ability. In Type IV interactions, parents and schools recognize and support the youngster's efforts but believe that the natural development of talent will take its course if it is truly there.

I have indicated in Figure 20.1 that the four types of interactions can be grouped along two dimensions: cooperation/agreement and conflict/disagreement. These dimensions are shown in Figure 20.1 as dotted lines along the diagonals. The cooperation/agreement diagonal includes Type I and Type IV interactions. While the reasons for cooperation and agreement differ in Types I and IV interactions, both parents and schools are congruent in their view of the role of the school. The conflict/disagreement diagonal includes Type II and Type III interactions. These interactions have in common the theme of conflict or disagreement regarding the school's role in gifted education.

Implications of Parent–School Interactions

It is important to note that the model (see Figure 20.1) accounts for both process and outcome. The process relates to the nature of the interactions, that is, cooperative or conflictual. The outcome relates to the four possible types of content and results of the interactions when parents and school communicate about the school's role in gifted education.

The model can be used as a diagnostic instrument for helping both parents and school staff understand their interactions. The model also provides counselors with a framework for understanding their interactions with parents and other school staff—thus insight into *how* they will deal with issues regarding programming for gifted children. Counselors can use this model not only to determine the type of interaction the school *has* with parents but also to assess that type of interaction that would be *preferred*.

Underachievement

Perhaps the most intense counseling focus has been on the underachieving gifted student. The issue of the underachieving gifted is confusing because of disagreement in definition and inconsistent results from interventions (Dowdall & Colangelo, 1982; Whitmore, 1980). (For a more comprehensive treatment of underachievement see Chapter 24 by Rimm.)

Underachievement is seen as a discrepancy between an assessment of potential and actual performance (Dowdall & Colangelo, 1982). The discrepancy is between:

a. two standardized measures (e.g., IQ and achievement test)
b. a standardized measure and performance (e.g., IQ and grade point)
c. two nonstandardized measures (e.g., teacher expectation and performance on daily assignments)

To a school counselor, the discrepancy between scores is not as critical as the interpersonal dynamics involved in underachievement. Rather than looking at it as a psychometric event, I look at it as a relationship between the gifted student and teacher, parent(s), and sometimes peers.

I have found that for *some* gifted students underachievement is a way to express either a need for attention or a need for control over a situation. Underachieving brings considerable attention from both teachers and parents, in extreme cases almost doting behavior. Adults are so preoccupied that the gifted youngster will not make good use of his or her gifts that they give a great deal of energy and time to him or her. Counselors can usually break the attention-getting cycle by having parents and teachers not overly respond to (or even ignore) the underachieving behavior. They can give attention when the child is achieving well and minimize attention when the child is not achieving. The equation is rather simple. If the child wants your attention, he or she will soon learn that the attention is forthcoming only when certain achieving behaviors (and attitudes) are present. The child will want to do more of these kinds of behaviors because the reward is the valued attention.

A gifted youngster who uses underachievement as a means to gain control of a situation is more difficult to work with. For such youngsters poor achievement is a way to show teachers and parents that they (gifted students) can do what they want. A typical reaction by teachers and parents to this kind of defiance is to attempt to force the student to do the task and do it at levels comparable to expectations. This situation can become a vicious and nonproductive cycle.

The counselor can work with teachers and parents to help them quit the fight. It is more likely the student will diminish the fight relationship if there is no one to fight. Minimizing the power struggle will allow more opportunity for the student to perform because he or she is more free to do so.

Again, I am a strong proponent of group counseling to help gifted students better understand their behaviors and motives and learn new patterns of interactions. It is in the rich atmosphere of a group of peers with a trained leader (school counselor) that a gifted youngster can explore motives and consequences of underachieving behavior.

Career Counseling

What do gifted students aspire to after their formal education? What unique career counseling needs do gifted students manifest?

In a comprehensive analysis of the top 5% of the 1986 American College Testing (ACT) program, Kerr and Colangelo (1988) found that these students "were much more likely to desire help with occupational and educational goals than help with personal concerns" (Kerr & Colangelo, 1988, p. 46).

Gifted students often have a problem with *multipotentiality,* that is, the ability to succeed in a number of different fields. The "excess" of possibilities becomes frustrating for young people trying to make a choice. In essence, they need to say no to an array of legitimate possibilities. Gifted students tend to have varied and strong interests, and a single career goal seems too limiting. Also, gifted students experience some unique pressures regarding what careers are "appropriate" for their abilities. Kerr and Colangelo (1988) found that the top-scoring ACT students were relatively narrow in their choices. Engineering, medicine, and to some extent law were the overwhelming

choices. Liberal arts and education were very low priorities.[1] While it is difficult to interpret these patterns, it seems that gifted students are encouraged to pursue the typical high-status professions. These students chose engineering even when their outstanding strengths were in English and social studies (Kerr & Colangelo, 1988).

Most gifted students intend to continue their formal education well beyond the undergraduate years. Thus they need to understand that extended formal education may mean a delay in attaining economic independence and perhaps starting families. This issue is particularly on the minds of gifted girls who try to project family issues six to eight years beyond high school (Kerr, 1981).

Finally, there can be high expectations by family and school personnel for a top student to choose a high-status university and career. These students may not feel free to "follow their hearts" because they will have to justify such decisions to a public that "can't believe you would waste your talent in *that* field!"

Gifted young people, by definition a small number of students at a school, may have few opportunities to discuss career and life plans with peers (Kerr, 1986). The combination of multipotentiality, extended formal instruction, expectations of others, and a limited opportunity for true peer discussions can easily justify special attention by a counselor. Despite special career counseling needs of gifted students, many of these individuals receive little attention from counselors who believe the gifted do not need it or who do not know how to counsel them (Kerr, 1981). Research indicates that gifted students would welcome individual and group counseling focusing on career planning. Counselors who plan a career counseling program with this population of students will be met with enthusiasm.

Moral Development

An area that has received minimal attention is that of giftedness and moral development. The dominant approach to the study of moral reasoning and moral development has been the theory and research of Lawrence Kohlberg.

Kohlberg (1958, 1976) showed that moral judgment progressed through qualitatively different stages in a sequence that was universal and invariant. Kohlberg based his theory on clinical interviews with participants who were presented with hypothetical moral dilemmas followed by a series of open-ended, probing questions.

Kohlberg's procedures have been criticized in several areas, including reliability and validity of his assessment measures (Kurtines & Greif, 1974), sex bias (Gilligan, 1977, 1982), dilemmas—irrelevant to everyday experience (Colangelo, 1977; Leming, 1973; Straughan, 1975)—and the inadequacy of the dilemmas to sample the diverse moral problems perceived by people (Colangelo, 1982; Yussen, 1977).

Yussen (1977) and Colangelo (1982) conducted studies in response to some of these criticisms and to the use of hypothetical moral dilemmas in general. Yussen asked students in Grades 7, 9, and 12 to formulate their own moral dilemmas. Colangelo asked the same of students in Grades 9 to 12 who had been identified as intellectually gifted. Both Yussen and Colangelo found that their students generated stories quite different from Kohlberg's hypothetical dilemmas. Also, both Yussen and Colangelo found that the age and sex of the individuals influenced some of the characteristics of their written dilemmas.

Colangelo (1982) conducted a study on how gifted adolescents formulate and resolve moral dilemmas. The 125 gifted students (Grades 9–12) who participated in the study were asked to both formulate a moral problem and then indicate how it should be resolved. Colangelo (1982) and Colangelo and Dettmann (1985a) developed a system for analyzing and rating the content of the problems and solutions.

The following is a summary of the most important findings from Colangelo (1982):

1. All the major characters in the Kohlberg dilemmas were male. Content analysis for my study revealed that gifted boys virtually always wrote about male protagonists and gifted girls more often wrote about female protagonists.

2. Kohlberg used adults as the main characters in his dilemmas. In my study gifted students wrote about dilemmas in which the characters were of their own age group (84% of protagonists were adolescent age).

3. Kohlberg's dilemmas involved family and authority relationships. Gifted students wrote about friendships and love relationships as the primary areas of moral conflict (combined, these constituted 53% of the dilemmas). Only 12% of the stories involved family relationships and even fewer (6%) involved authority relationships.

4. Kohlberg's dilemmas focused essentially on two types of issues: public welfare, and life and death. A rather amazing finding was that our raters were able to identify 36 different moral issues in the stories written by gifted adolescents. These issues included family relationships, peer relationships, sexual relationships, alcohol, drugs, self-concept, cheating, stealing, life and death issues, and reporting infractions.

Examples

One of the richest aspects of the study was the actual stories and solutions written by the gifted adolescents. The stories indicate sensitivity, wit, imagination, humor, and reflection. Below are a few examples taken directly from the writing of the students. Examples 1 to 3 and solutions are quoted from Colangelo (1982), pp. 228–230, with permission of the publisher.

Example 1: 10th-Grade Boy

Problem

Some people have no direction in life. They just float through never trying anything that might challenge the first beliefs they encountered. They are lazy. They don't care. They assume a state of apathy. They try to out-nothing each other. They drift. They don't try to discover why they exist. They just try to survive and take one breath after another. They have no foresight. They live and don't know why they are living or try to find out why. They never look at things in depth. They just skim off what they need and leave the rest. They don't care for anything but themselves. They go to church because it is the socially correct thing to do. They take little personal interest in anything. They don't raise questions. They don't make a fuss, they just accept. That is what I think is basically wrong today.

Solution

To remedy this I think schools could play a greater role in getting people to learn how to think, question, and express themselves peacefully. We should be conditioned to ask about things we don't understand. We should be taught to gather information and draw our own acceptable conclusion.

Example 2: 11th-Grade Boy

Problem

Steve and Mike were two good friends. One Friday night after a football game Steve bought some beer for him and Mike to drink. Steve was sure that Mike would go along with this and drink the beer with him. This was not so! Mike told Steve that he didn't believe in drinking alcoholic beverages. Steve got terribly mad and tried talking Mike into drinking with him. Mike listened to Steve's arguments, but still said no. Finally, Steve told Mike that he didn't ever want to go any place with him again. This was it for Mike. He said he would try just one to keep Steve happy. One led to another until Mike went home drunk.

Solution

If Mike wanted to get out of drinking just this one time, he could have made up an excuse. This isn't the solution, though. If Mike and Steve want to stay friends as they have been before this happened, Mike should explain to Steve why he doesn't drink. Then tell him this is what he is going to stick to if they want to stay friends.

Example 3: 9th-Grade Girl

Problem

Nancy is a bright 9th grader at a small junior high school. She relates well to people and is active in many organizations. Nancy is also fairly new to the school; she has been there for only a little over a year.

Nancy's friends include both boys and girls from all three grades. One friend Nancy has become close to is Dave. Although Dave is only a 7th grader, Nancy enjoys his company and shares many of his athletic interests. Unfortunately, Dave is also the only black student attending the small school. He, too, is very popular with all the students. Still, the students in the school begin to talk about Nancy and Dave. Several of the students say that Nancy is merely trying to prove a point; she is demonstrating her lack of prejudice.

Eventually, of course, this gets back to Nancy, and she is faced with a difficult problem. Nancy can try to ignore these stories and the peer pressure, or she can stop spending time with Dave. The first choice seems impossible, but Nancy knows the second one is unfair. What can she do?

Solution

I feel that the most important strength that a person can have is moral courage. If you know what is right and wrong—if you have defined this in your own mind—there is no choice. I wouldn't like the pressure, but I would continue to enjoy Dave's company. In the long run, being true to your convictions will make you a stronger, more confident person. I try not to respond unfairly to pressure from the outside, which is unfair in itself.

Implications for Counselors

The preferred way to get youngsters to reflect on moral issues is to provide an atmosphere of open discussion in which their thinking is challenged and in which they can explore strengths and inconsistencies in their own moral thinking. This is opposed to an indoctrination approach in which "right and wrong" or a preferred perspective is "taught" to the student by an adult or authority.

So what do the results of my study offer to counselors and teachers who may conduct discussions relating to moral dilemmas with gifted students? First, gifted adolescents are highly sensitive to moral aspects in a number of daily-life situations. They do not relegate morality to a small compartmentalized part of their lives. Second, discussions of hypotheticals need to be sensitive to the sex of the protagonist. Gifted boys are most responsive to stories involving a male, about their age, in a conflict. For gifted girls, the same is true of stories with a female protagonist. In a group of both boys and girls, it is important to provide a balance of hypotheticals with regard to the sex of the protagonist.

One of the issues that did arise as a moral dilemma was self-concept (10% of issues were rated as self-concept issues). As mentioned earlier, the self-concept issue includes a search for identity, purpose, and self-evaluation. Such a search for identity may be considered a moral issue in the sense of clarifying one's own moral values and moral self-concept.

My approach to studying moral reasoning with gifted adolescents does not provide any useful fix on "how moral" they are. Also, my research offers inconsequential direction in terms of how these adolescents might act in a given real-life situation. What this line of research does offer are guidelines for counselors as they begin to explore with gifted adolescents what these students see as the domains of morality and how they think about these domains. Gifted youngsters have strong yet varied moral sensitivities, but they need opportunities to explore and share their own moral thinking. I would encourage school counselors (especially) and teachers to create opportunities for gifted youngsters, in small groups, to generate what they believe to be moral issues and to clarify their own thinking as they struggle for resolutions.

Developing a School Counseling Program for Gifted Students

There are two ways to envision a school counseling program for gifted students: as *remedial* or as *developmental*. In a remedial approach the counselor is on call for difficulties as they arise. It is the primary function of the counselor to have the expertise to intervene in problem situations and either help solve the problem or minimize the difficulty. This approach is largely therapeutic.

In the developmental approach the counselor does some therapy and is on call, but these are minor matters in terms of time and energy. The primary work of the developmentally oriented counselor is to establish an environment in school that is conducive to the educational growth of gifted students. Such an approach is predicated on knowledge of both the affective and cognitive needs of gifted youngsters. This approach also includes ongoing work with parents of the gifted, not because there is a problem per se, but because of the recognition that gifted children pose unique challenges to parents.

I strongly advocate a developmental approach to counseling with gifted students. I believe giftedness is not a problem to be solved but a unique challenge to be nourished as a recognition of differences among youngsters. Also, a developmental approach is not dependent on research evidence that gifted youngsters are at risk. In a therapy model such evidence would be necessary in order to justify having a counselor with expertise in working with the gifted.

A developmental counseling program needs the following components:

1. An articulated and coherent rationale
2. A program of activities that are based on the affective and cognitive needs of youngsters
3. A trained counselor(s) who is well grounded not only in counseling but also in knowledge about giftedness
4. A minimum of attention on rehabilitative (therapy) services but a strong component of individual, family, and teacher consultations
5. Input and participation from teachers, administrators, parents, and the youngsters who are served
6. A component for the continued professional development of the counselor so that he or she may keep pace with the latest research and practices on the counseling needs of gifted youngsters

Summary

While concern for the counseling needs of gifted youngsters can be traced back to Leta Hollingworth's work over 60 years ago, the emergence of counseling as a major force in the education of the gifted and talented is a phenomenon of the last decade. Counseling is predicated on the belief that gifted youngsters do have some unique social and emotional needs compared with their age-mates and that these unique needs demonstrate themselves not only within the gifted youngsters but in family and peer interactions, and daily school life.

These unique needs exist, and counseling is a necessary component in the development of talent. Gifted youngsters live in a context of ambiguity about themselves and about the perceptions of others. A developmental counseling program in a school will help minimize such ambiguity and will help gifted students liberate their strengths.

NOTE

1. See Chapter 23 by Perrone for further information on career selection by gifted students.

REFERENCES

Albert, R. S. (1980). Family positions and the attainment of eminence: A study of special family positions and special family experiences. *Gifted Child Quarterly, 24,* 87–95.

American Association for Gifted Children. (1978). *On being gifted.* New York: Walker & Company.

Bridges, S. (1979). The gifted child in its family. In J. J. Gallagher (Ed.), *Gifted children: Reaching their potential* (pp. 333–346). Jerusalem: Kollek.

Burks, B. S., Jensen, D. W., & Terman, L. M. (1930). The promise of youth. In L. M. Terman (Ed.), *Genetic studies of genius* (Vol. 3). Stanford, CA: Stanford University Press.

Colangelo, N. (1977). *Identifying moral judgment in interviews.* Unpublished doctoral dissertation, University of Wisconsin–Madison.

Colangelo, N. (1982). Characteristics of moral problems as formulated by gifted adolescents. *Journal of Moral Education, 11,* 219–232.

Colangelo, N., & Brower, P. (1987a). Gifted youngsters and their siblings: Long-term impact of labeling on their academic and social self-concepts. *Roeper Review, 10,* 101–103.

Colangelo, N., & Brower, P. (1987b). Labeling gifted youngsters: Long-term impact on families. *Gifted Child Quarterly, 31,* 75–78.

Colangelo, N., & Dettmann, D. F. (1982). A conceptual model of four types of parent–school interactions. *Journal for the Education of the Gifted, 5,* 120–126.

Colangelo, N., & Dettmann, D. F. (1983). A review of research on parents and families of gifted children. *Exceptional Children, 50,* 20–27.

Colangelo, N., & Dettmann, D. F. (1985a). Characteristics of moral problems and solutions formed by students in Grade 3–8. *Elementary School Guidance and Counseling, 19,* 260–271.

Colangelo, N., & Dettmann, D. F. (1985b). Families of gifted children. In S. Ehly, J. Conoly & D. M. Rosenthal (Eds.), *Working with parents of exceptional children* (pp. 233–255). St. Louis: Mosby.

Colangelo, N., & Kelly, K. R. (1983). A study of student, parent, and teacher attitude towards gifted programs and gifted students. *Gifted Child Quarterly, 27,* 107–110.

Colangelo, N., Kelly, K. R., & Schrepfer, R. M. (1987). A comparison of gifted, general, and special learning needs students on academic and social self-concept. *Journal of Counseling and Development, 66,* 73–77.

Colangelo, N., & Pfleger, L. R. (1978). Academic self-concept of gifted high school students. *Roeper Review, 1,* 10–11.

Colangelo, N., & Zaffrann, R. T. (Eds.). (1979). *New voices in counseling the gifted.* Dubuque: Kendall/Hunt.

Cornell, D. G. (1983). Gifted children: The impact of positive labeling on the family system. *American Journal of Orthopsychiatry, 53,* 322–335.

Delisle, J. R. (1984). *Gifted children speak out.* New York: Walker & Company.

Delisle, J. R. (1987). *Gifted kids speak out.* Minneapolis: Free Spirit.

Dettman, D. F., & Colangelo, N. (1980). A functional model for counseling parents of gifted students. *Gifted Child Quarterly, 24,* 139–147.

Dowdall, C. B., & Colangelo, N. (1982). Underachieving gifted students: Review and implications. *Gifted Child Quarterly, 26,* 179–184.

Gilligan, C. (1977). In a different voice: Women's conceptions of self and morality. *Harvard Educational Review, 47,* 481–517.

Gilligan, C. (1982). *In a different voice: Psychological theory and women's development.* Cambridge: Harvard University Press.

Hobbs, N. (Ed.). (1975). *The future of children: Categories, labels, and their consequences.* San Francisco: Jossey-Bass.

Hollingworth, L. S. (1926). *Gifted children: Their nature and nurture.* New York: Macmillan.

Hollingworth, L. S. (1942). *Children above 180 IQ.* New York: World Book.

Jones, R. (1972). Labels and stigma in special education. *Exceptional Children, 38,* 553–564.

Karamessinis, N. P. (1980, May/June). Personality and perceptions of the gifted. *G/C/T,* 11–13.

Kelly, K. R., & Colangelo, N. (1984). Academic and social self-concepts of gifted, general, and special students. *Exceptional Children, 50,* 551–554.

Kerr, B. A. (1981). *Career education for gifted and talented.* Columbus, OH: ERIC Clearinghouse on Adult Vocational and Career Information.

Kerr, B. A. (1986). Career counseling for the gifted: Assessments and interventions. *Journal of Counseling and Development, 64,* 602–604.

Kerr, B. A., & Colangelo, N. (1988). The college plans of academically talented students. *Journal of Counseling and Development, 67,* 42–48.

Kerr B., Colangelo, N., & Gaeth, J. (1988). Gifted adolescents' attitudes toward their giftedness. *Gifted Child Quarterly, 32,* 245–247.

Kohlberg, L. (1958). *The development of modes of moral thinking and choice in years ten to sixteen.* Unpublished doctoral dissertation, University of Chicago.

Kohlberg, L. (1976). Moral stages and moralization: the cognitive developmental approach. In T. Lickona (Ed.), *Moral development and behavior* (pp. 31–53). New York: Holt, Rinehart and Winston.

Kurtines, W., & Greif, E. F. (1974). The development of moral thought: Review and evaluation of Kohlberg's approach. *Psychological Bulletin, 81,* 453–470.

Leming, J. S. (1973). *Adolescent moral judgment and deliberation on classical and practical moral dilemmas.* Unpublished doctoral dissertation, University of Wisconsin–Madison.

Loeb, R. C., & Jay, G. (1987). Self-concept in gifted children: Differential impact in boys and girls. *Gifted Child Quarterly, 31,* 9–14.

McGuire, W. J. (1984). Search for self: Going beyond self-esteem and reactive self. In R. A. Zucher, J. Arnoff, & A. I. Rubin (Eds.), *Personality and the prediction of behavior* (pp. 73–120). New York: Academic.

Myers, R. S., & Pace, T. M. (1986). Counseling gifted and talented students: Historical perspectives and contemporary issues. *Journal of Counseling and Development, 64,* 548–551.

Nurius, P. S. (1986). Reappraisal of the self-concept and implications for counseling. *Journal of Counseling Psychology, 33,* 429–438.

Parker, M., Ross, A., & Deutsch, R. (1980). Parenting the gifted adolescent. *Roeper Review, 2,* 40–42.

Peterson, D. (1977). The heterogeneously gifted child. *Gifted Child Quarterly, 21,* 396–408.

Rist, R., & Harrell, J. (1982). Labeling the learning disabled child: The social ecology of eductional practice. *American Journal of Orthopsychiatry, 52,* 146–160.

Robinson, A. (1986). Brave new directions: Needed research on the labeling of gifted children. *Gifted Child Quarterly, 30,* 11–14.

Rogers, C. (1951). *Client-centered therapy: Its current practice, implications, and theory.* Boston: Houghton Mifflin.

Ross, A. O. (1964). *The exceptional child in the family.* New York: Grune & Stratton.

Ross, A., & Parker, M. (1980). Academic and social self-concepts of the academically gifted. *Exceptional Children, 47,* 6–10.

Snygg, D., & Combs, A. W. (1949). *Individual behavior: A perceptual approach to behavior* (rev. ed.). New York: Harper.

Straughan, R. R. (1975). Hypothetical moral situations. *Journal of Moral Education, 4,* 183–189.

Terman, L. M. (1925). Mental and physical traits of a thousand gifted children. In L. M. Terman (Ed.), *Genetic studies of genius* (Vol. 1). Stanford, CA: Stanford University Press.

Terman, L. M., & Oden, M. H. (1947). *The gifted child grows up.* In L. M. Terman (Ed.), *Genetic studies of genius* (Vol. 4). Stanford, CA: Stanford University Press.

Terman, L. M., & Oden, M. H. (1959). *The gifted group at mid-life.* In L. M. Terman (Ed.), *Genetic studies of genius* (Vol. 5). Stanford, CA: Stanford University Press.

Tidwell, R. (1980). A psycho-educational profile of 5,593 gifted high school students. *Gifted Child Quarterly, 24,* 63–68.

Webb, J. T., Meckstroth, E. A., & Tolan, S. S. (1982). *Guiding the gifted child.* Columbus: Ohio Psychology.

Weiss, P., & Gallagher, J. J. (1980). The effects of personal experience on attitudes toward gifted children. *Journal for the Education of the Gifted, 3,* 194–206.

Whitmore, J. (1980). *Giftedness, conflict, and underachievement.* Boston: Allyn and Bacon.

Winne, P., Woodlands, M., & Wong, B. (1982). Comparability of self-concept among learning disabled, normal, and gifted students. *Journal of Learning Disabilities, 15,* 470–475.

Yussen, S. R. (1977). Characteristics of moral dilemmas written by adolescents. *Developmental Psychology, 13,* 162–163.

21

Emotional Development and Emotional Giftedness

MICHAEL M. PIECHOWSKI   *Northland College, Ashland, Wisconsin*

Searching for a Model of Emotional Development

Different Senses of Emotional Development

This chapter addresses the characteristics of emotional development of gifted children and also gifted adults. Emotional development does not stop in adulthood; on the contrary, it can be all the more intense. It might be helpful, therefore, for the parents and the teachers of the gifted to find case examples and theoretical models with which to compare their own experiences.

What constitutes the domain of emotional development is far from clearly defined. How do emotions develop? How does the understanding of emotions come about? What is the role of socialization in shaping emotions? How does early emotional experience influence later life? These are some of the questions that address different aspects of emotional development. The list that follows identifies representative approaches to emotional development. However, what is most applicable to our understanding of emotional growth of gifted and talented children *and* adults will take us beyond this list. Approaches include emotional development as:

1. *The development of emotions:* This approach is the most basic. Its task is to follow the emergence of different emotions in the child's expressive repertoire as well as the emergence of the ability to recognize emotions in others (Hesse & Cicchetti, 1982).

2. *A step-by-step parallel to Piaget's stages of cognitive development:* Piaget (1967) and other authors (Harter, 1977; Hesse & Cicchetti, 1982) have made attempts to show how children's understanding of emotions in one-

self and in others, as well as their ability to deal with complex and mixed emotions, follows the stages of cognitive development.

3. *A function of socialization:* Here emotional development is conceived in terms of skills and tasks of self-management, self-reward, interpersonal competence, and the development of self-concept. This is the standard approach in textbooks on child development.

4. *Psychosexual development:* In the classic psychoanalytic approach, emotions are the function of the sexual and the aggressive drives. They are governed by the pleasure principle: the desire to reduce or eliminate unpleasurable affect (Sandler & Sandler, 1978).

5. *A series of psychosocial challenges:* These are deciding milestones when facing life's developmental demands, for example, whether to trust or to mistrust, whether to be industrious or feel inferior and avoid challenging tasks, whether to partake of intimacy or lapse into isolation. This is Erikson's theory of how each individual's sense of self develops in meeting a succession of critical social and personal tasks (Erikson, 1963). The self develops in terms of a sense of mastery and competence, intimate relations with others, and personal identity. All are emotionally significant areas.

6. *Extension of attachment theory* (Bowlby, 1969, 1973): The initial bond between the baby and its caregiver is the foundation of emotional life that subsequently grows out of the original attachment pattern (Sroufe, 1979). Attachment as a framework for emotional development lays emphasis on the reciprocal interactions between the child and its caregivers. This is where one's sense of significance and worth is formed and maintained. The theory explains particularly well the long-term effects of loss of attachment figures, the devastating effects of loneliness, and difficulties in relationships with others as a consequence of injury in the development of early attachments (Bowlby, 1980; Parkes & Stevenson-Hinde, 1982).

7. *Self-actualization:* Maslow's (1970) theory of self-actualization is a speculative scheme of a hierarchy of human needs. The lower needs are for physical survival, safety, love and belonging, and self-esteem, and the higher needs are for self-actualization. Maslow thought originally that satisfaction of lower needs prepares the realization of higher needs. Self-actualization would then appear within easy reach of anyone fulfilled in terms of self-esteem and all the other lower needs. Maslow realized later that there is nothing automatic about self-actualization.

If there is one feature that knowers of giftedness agree on, it is the tremendous range of individual differences in children and adults of exceptional ability. No standardization and no norms are valid here. The approaches listed present generalized models of emotional development. They apply to the gifted as they do to all children. There is, of course, room for adapting general models, such as Piaget's or Erikson's, to the gifted. In this manner Clark (1983) adapted Maslow's hierarchy of needs to the specific developmental needs of gifted children. However, the general models and their adaptations do not directly address the outstanding features that are characteristic of the emotional development of the gifted.

There is one model that does address characteristics of the gifted: Dabrowski's theory of emotional development. Dabrowski's concept of developmental potential addresses a core of personal characteristics that distinguish the gifted in a most pronounced way. His idea of levels of development provides a broad framework for understanding the making of emotional giftedness and self-actualization.

Before introducing the theory let us first address the emotional intensity and sensitivity of the gifted and Dabrowski's concept of developmental potential. We shall then consider emotional giftedness as a phenomenon for which Dabrowski's theory provides a proper place. Self-actualization is another phenomenon that sits well in the framework of Dabrowski's theory. The question of the relationship between emotional giftedness and self-actualization then follows.

For understanding the emotional development of the gifted and talented, the significance of the theory can be put this way:

1. Dabrowski's theory helps to make sense of the individual experience of turmoil, self-doubt, self-loathing, desperate search for meaning, feeling different, and feeling weak, unbalanced, irrational, self-critical, and too sensitive and too intense at the same time.
2. The theory identifies methods of coping with the troubled cauldron of overexcitabilities (to be explained) and presses to resolve conflicts arising from positive maladjustment (to be explained), from self-judgment, or from the search for a deeper meaning of one's life.
3. The theory shows the connection between emotional giftedness and self-actualization and restores the latter to its original meaning.
4. The theory provides a set of concepts that are helpful in understanding and guiding multilevel development (to be explained).
5. The theory has generated research on personal growth, self-actualization, and giftedness.

The Concept of Developmental Potential

Emotional sensitivity and emotional intensity are often cited as distinguishing most gifted children, and the highly gifted especially (Barbe, quoted in Clark, 1983, p. 104; Silverman, 1983; Webb, Meckstroth, & Tolan, 1982; Whitmore, 1980). These characteristics account for their vulnerabilities in childhood (Roedell, 1984) and get them into trouble at school (Richert, Alvino, & McDonnel, 1982). Seeing themselves so different from others, they begin to doubt themselves. They ask themselves, What is wrong with me? (Tolan, 1987) and look in the catalog of mental disorders for the appropriate label to apply to themselves.

Dabrowski (1967, 1972) studied the mental

health of intellectually and artistically gifted youths. He took the intensity of their emotions, their sensitivity and proneness to riding a roller coaster of emotional extremes, as part and parcel of their psychophysical makeup. Creative individuals as a rule live at a level of intensity unknown to the rest. Rather than view this as neurotic imbalance or the brink of insanity, he saw it as a positive potential for further growth.

Dabrowski's concept of developmental potential includes talents, special abilities, and intelligence, plus five primary components: psychomotor, sensual, intellectual, imaginational, and emotional (Table 21.1). Conceived broadly as five dimensions of psychic life, these components have many possible expressions: *psychomotor*—an augmented capacity for being active and energetic—expressed as movement, restlessness, drivenness; *sensual*—an enhanced differentiation and aliveness of sensual experience; *intellectual*—avidity for knowledge and the search for truth—expressed as discovery, questioning, and love of ideas and theoretical analysis; *imaginational*—the power of thought creation—expressed through vividness of imagery, richness of association, liking for the unusual, and a facility for dreams, fantasies, and inventions; and *emotional*—the heart—recognized in the great depth and intensity of emotional life expressed through a wide range of feelings, attachments, compassion, heightened sense of responsibility, and scrupulous self-examination. These five dimensions to a varying degree give talent its power (Piechowski, 1979, 1986). They may be thought of as modes of experiencing or as channels of information flow that can be wide open, narrow, or barely present. Dabrowski called them *forms of psychic overexcitability* to underline the enhancement and intensification of mental activity much beyond the ordinary. Overexcitabilities contribute to the individual's psychological development, and thus their strength can be taken as a measure of developmental potential. Our interest here lies chiefly in the emotional dimension.

When gifted people, and those who live and work with them, are introduced to these concepts there is often an instant recognition and a sense of relief. It helps to find out that there is a theoretical model that makes sense out of a manner of feeling and acting that is so often at odds with normal behavior and expectations of happy—or grim, as the case may be—adjustment. It helps for once to feel legitimate in one's "abnormal" reactions and what one cannot help experiencing and wanting to express.

When I was a teenager and read about manic-depressive disorder, I announced that finally I knew what was wrong with me. Of course, I was told that all teenagers are manic-depressive to a modest extent, but I knew I was connecting with something more than that—and it has followed me ever since—both the pain and the joy of the world are often too much to handle. A good therapist finally pointed out to me that I wouldn't give up being able to write my novels so I should quit trying to drive out of myself the very qualities that made me able to write them. "Easy for her to say," I thought. She didn't have to live with being crazy. Imagine my joy at having this craziness referred to as "channels of information flow" and "modes of experiencing"! (Tolan, personal communication)

The stronger these overexcitabilities are, the less welcome they are among peers and teachers (unless they, too, are gifted). Children characterized by strong overexcitabilities are often made to feel different, apart from others, embarrassed, and guilty for being different. Criticized and teased for what they cannot help, they begin to believe there is something wrong with them. Sometimes they learn to disguise it, sometimes they seek refuge in fantastic worlds of their own creation, and sometimes they try to "normalize" it and suffer in consequence the agonies of those who deny their own potential (Maslow, 1971).

Giftedness in the Affective Domain

Intensity and Emotional Sensitivity

The intensity of emotional reactions, especially in children, may sometimes be difficult to understand, especially when they strike seemingly out of the blue and the child is strongly upset over "nothing." It requires considerable patience and knowledge of the child

Table 21.1
Forms and Expressions of Psychic Overexcitability

Psychomotor

Surplus of energy:
Rapid speech; marked enthusiasm; fast games and sports; pressure for action; delinquent behavior
Psychomotor expression of emotional tension:
Compulsive talking and chattering; impulsive actions; delinquent behavior; workaholism; nervous habits (tics, nail biting)

Sensual

Sensory pleasures:
Seeing, smelling, tasting, touching, hearing
Sensual expression of emotional tension:
Overeating, masturbation, sexual intercourse, buying sprees

Intellectual

Probing questions
Problem solving
Learning:
Curiosity; concentration; capacity for sustained intellectual effort; extensive reading
Theoretical thinking:
Thinking about thinking; introspection; preoccupation with certain problems; moral thinking and development of a hierarchy of values; conceptual and intuitive integration

Imaginational

Free play of the imagination:
Illusions; animistic and magical thinking; image and metaphor; inventions and fantasy; poetic and dramatic perception
Spontaneous imagery as an expression of emotional tension:
Animistic imagery; mixing of truth and fiction; dreams; visual recall; visualization of events; fears of the unknown

Emotional

Somatic expressions:
Tense stomach, sinking heart, flushing
Intensity of feeling:
Positive feelings; negative feelings; extremes of feeling; complex feelings; identification with others' feelings
Inhibition (timidity, shyness)
Affective memory
Concern with death
Fear and anxiety
Feelings of guilt
Depressive and suicidal moods
Relationship feelings:
Need for protection; attachment to animals, significant others; perceptions of relationships; emotional ties and attachments; difficulty of adjustment to new environments; loneliness; concern for others (empathy); conflict with others
Feelings toward self:
Self-evaluation and self-judgment, feelings of inadequacy and inferiority

Source: Reprinted by permission of the authors and publisher from "Developmental Potential" by M. M. Piechowski, in *New Voices in Counseling the Gifted,* edited by N. Colangelo and R. T. Zaffrann, p. 31, copyright © 1979 by Kendall/Hunt, Dubuque, Iowa.

to see that this "overreaction" comes from the child's sensitivity and need for his or her own order of things to be preserved. That children need order and predictable routines is common knowledge. To a sensitive and intense child who may be disequilibrated often by his or her own emotions, departure from something routinely expected, for example, the way a story is told, may be extremely upsetting simply because the need for support is all the greater. The strongest support, without doubt, is the parent's loving patience and acceptance.

To illustrate how emotional intensity and sensitivity are experienced, a few examples will be given. These expressions form part of an *Inventory of Emotional Style* (Piechowski, unpublished). The items of the inventory were constructed, without much change, from written responses of subjects who answered the overexcitability questionnaire (Lysy & Piechowski, 1983; Piechowski & Colangelo, 1984; Piechowski & Cunningham, 1985; Piechowski, Silverman, & Falk, 1985).

Positive feelings take the form of being "flooded by unexpected waves of joy" or feeling "incredibly alive—every cell, muscle, etc., feels stimulated. I have incredible energy then and hardly need any rest," or, "Sometimes I can be so happy that I want to laugh and cry or be silent and shout, all at the same time." Beautiful music or beauty of nature can move a person to tears. Barron (1968) found this to be a particularly frequent occurrence for creative people. Occasions that others miss or find merely pleasing are to these people intense unforgettable experiences. For some exceptional individuals even pain has another dimension. Again to quote one of the subjects: "Even the greatest pain that I have felt has been ecstatic and full of life." Religious and spiritual experience can overtake such persons completely just as they are capable of communion with nature or merging with a painting or a piece of music. It makes one wonder if what the world really needs today is but a good dose of emotional overexcitability or intensity.

Emotional intensity has been studied by Larsen, Diener, and Emmons (1986), who developed an affective intensity measure. (This measure could probably serve well as a measure of emotional overexcitability.) Intense individuals experience their emotions quite strongly. They are emotionally reactive, and often their emotions soar high and dip down into the dark depths. Individuals lacking in intensity experience their emotions mildly and with only minor fluctuations. The degree of intensity of emotional response is a stable individual characteristic and quite independent of what actually evoked the emotion. Emotional intensity, or its lack in unemotional people, is a characteristic of temperament that can be observed early in life (Larsen & Diener, 1987). According to Larsen and Diener, individuals characterized by high intensity of emotions lead more complex and more interesting lives.

Emotional sensitivity is another matter. Emotionally intense individuals can also be very sensitive—sensitive to the feelings of others, sensitive to others' being hurt, sensitive to injustice, but also sensitive to criticism and pain. There are children and adults for whom to see, in reality or on the screen, someone being physically hurt is more painful than if they were injured themselves. Grant (1988) reports the case of a man who could not bear to watch the Three Stooges because of the hitting and hurting.

So far we have no systematic studies of emotional sensitivity, but there is an accumulated wealth of clinical material. If an emotional child grows up with too much criticism and ridicule, the child then begins to protect himself or herself by emotional withdrawal. A more enduring protection is to form an inner shield, but the price is high. The result is loss of emotional vitality, lack of enjoyment of one's successes and achievements, and lack of a sense of who one is.

When a child responds to a psychological instrument that asks about his or her feelings of joy, sadness, or anger and how strong they are, we do not know if the answer, "I am never particularly happy or unhappy" is an expression of a temperamentally unemotional child or of a child who has suffered an emotional trauma that led to walling off of feeling. It is a matter that urgently calls for attention and further study.

Alice Miller (1981) describes in her book *Prisoners of Childhood* (republished as *The Drama of the Gifted Child*) how she traced in her psychoanalytic clients the process of emotional self-denial. She found that the emotional sensitivity and intelligence of gifted children make them well attuned to the feelings and desires of their parents. As they naturally want to please them and be of help to them, they may muffle the call of their own potential and instead become what their parents want them to be. In the extreme case the roles end up being reversed. The child becomes the emotional caretaker of the parent because the parent still demands to be mothered or fathered. The younger the child, the heavier the burden and the more serious the consequences developmentally. Gifted children caught in this process lock away their own feelings and desires. In adulthood they begin to feel a curious emotional void, a loss of sense of self that was never their own but an acquired one to suit someone else. (A case of a gifted boy who won much recognition in school for his academic and athletic achievements but at the age of 30 found himself adrift is described by Piechowski [1987].)

Miller's book has been an eye-opener to a great many gifted adults who have found in it their own life story. Reading it has led some to seek therapy, and with good results. It has to be made clear that coming upon these insights helps to identify the problems but does not remove them. Emotional problems of this nature, developed in the course of a long relationship that distorted the emotional design of secure attachment and trust in one's parents, cannot be successfully corrected by oneself alone. It is necessary to relive the significant moments that precipitated the emotional blocking and come into ownership of one's feelings and one's self. A task of this magnitude and intensity can be carried out only in the security of the therapeutic alliance with a psychotherapist who has the requisite knowledge and experience in this particular process.

The Case for Emotional Giftedness

Annemarie Roeper (1982, p. 24) raised the question of emotional giftedness as an innate capacity:

Can a person be emotionally gifted?

I believe there are people who have such a gift. They are the people who have the capacity to integrate their emotions, intellect, and creativity against enormous odds. They are people who deal realistically with life and move normally through their developmental phases. I have observed children who are particularly sensitive toward their own and to other people's feelings and who dare to act upon this awareness.

Some gifted children show enormous empathy with others, surpassing at times the compassion of adults who are more limited by society's expectations. As a result, adults may not understand a child's reaction. For example, during a chess tournament, John, the obvious winner, began to make careless mistakes and lost the game. When asked what happened, he replied, *I noticed my opponent had tears in his eyes. I could not concentrate and lost my desire to win.* John's empathy was greater than his ambition. Many adults, especially those who supported John, were disappointed. Yet, one could argue that his reaction was a more mature one than theirs for his self esteem did not depend on winning the competition [emphasis in the original].

Such examples of empathy, unselfishness, and consideration for others are readily found among gifted children if one looks for them. Seymour (1987) describes two brothers of whom the older at age 7 was accelerated from second to fourth grade. Everyone was impressed by this boy's exceptional intelligence and verbal facility. His brother, a year younger and also highly gifted, was by contrast considered "average." The older boy's imagination and sensitivity to others were less spectacular than his intelligence. He had a violent temper and often hit his brother who, though younger, was the larger of the two. The younger brother did not strike back but would rather walk away; despite his anger and obvious pain he controlled himself, and he was only 7 years old. On a school trip to the zoo this very young boy, unlike his classmates, showed a concentrated interest in every animal. And he very much wanted to feed the goat. A couple leaving the zoo asked him if he would like to have a bag of corn they were carrying. Seymour says that she expected him to take the corn and head for the goat display. Instead, he came up to his classmates and offered everyone corn, and when the bag was almost empty he went to see the goat. Seymour found this attention to others to be a consistent trait in this boy. From responses to her parent questionnaire, Silverman (1983) collected numerous observations of emotional sensitivity and compassion in highly gifted children as young as 2½ and 3.

Considerateness, compassion, and understanding of others are characteristics of what Gardner (1983) called *personal intelligence*. Actually Gardner made a strong case for two personal intelligences: intra- and interpersonal. Among the eight criteria for according a domain the status of separate intelligence, one is the evidence of exceptional talent and achievement. In the case of personal intelligences, the evidence is an outstanding degree of self-knowledge, moral leadership, and inspiration to others. The core capacity of *interpersonal* intelligence is "the ability to notice and to make distinctions among other individuals and, in particular, among their moods, temperaments, motivations, and interactions" (p. 239). The core capacity of *intrapersonal* intelligence is "access to one's own feeling life—one's range of affects and emotions: the capacity instantly to effect discriminations among these feelings, and eventually, to label them . . . to draw upon them as a means of understanding and guiding one's own behavior" (p. 239). Clearly, it is easier to observe someone act with compassion and sensitivity to others' feelings than to see a person's self-knowledge. Developmentally, we would expect empathy and concern for others to come first. Empathetic acts—responses to another's distress and a desire to soothe—have been observed in infants (Borke, 1971; Hoffman, 1979). The capacity for empathy and unselfish acts is common in preschoolers (Radke-Yarrow, Zahn-Waxler, & Chapman, 1983).

The fruition of intrapersonal intelligence is a highly developed sense of self that does not depend on winning recognition, winning over others, or other such external boosters. Neither does it depend, as in Roeper's example, on being loyal to one's supporters. Gardner (1983) mentions Socrates, Jesus Christ, Mahatma Gandhi, and Eleanor Roosevelt as those exceptional individuals "who appear to have understood much about themselves and about their societies and to have come to terms successfully with the frailties of the human condition, while at the same time inspiring others around them to lead more productive lives" (p. 252). Guided by humility, compassion, and understanding, their conscience is a reliable guide. But it is one thing to point to such luminaries and quite another to describe how they got to be who they became. What is their talent and how did it develop? How was it trained? If we are to look for what makes for "outstanding talent and achievement" in the area of self-knowledge, considerateness, and compassion, we must, as in other talent areas, look for the trainers, teachers, and guides. Our interest here is in the inner realm, the knowledge of self and of one's feeling life.

In the case of Socrates and Jesus Christ, the teachers and guides are unknown. We have to allow for self-instruction, for the person being his own teacher, or having an internal teacher such as the inner voice, compassion, or the love of God. Brennan (1987) and Grant (1988) each have in their studies a detailed case of a person who was taught, as it were, by an inner voice.

In the case of Gandhi we find a powerful mix of Hindu tradition, the strong influence of his mother, personal distaste for dishonesty and untruthfulness, and the guidance of individuals whom Gandhi himself chose for their wisdom and purity of intentions. His goal was to live a life of truth so that he could find God. Practicing nonviolence (*ahimsa*) with utmost conviction and consistency was his method. He chose to be a lawyer, but he found it difficult at first to practice law, partly because of his paralyzing shyness, and partly because of the pressure to enter litigation and push to win a case. Later it became clear to him that what he must strive for was to bring the parties in conflict to a harmonious agreement in which each side could see its advantage (Gandhi, 1948/1983, p. 117):

> I felt that my duty was to befriend both parties and bring them together. I strained every nerve to bring a compromise. . . . But both were happy over the result, and both rose in public estimation. My joy was boundless. I had learnt the true

practice of law. I had learnt to find out the better side of human nature and to enter men's hearts. I realized that true function of a lawyer was to unite parties riven asunder.

Gandhi as a child and as a man was a being of intense emotions and sensuality, great sensitivity, rich imagination, and relentless intellectual and spiritual inquiry. His emotional giftedness lay in his ardent concern to have no blemish on his character (punishment for an infraction caused him the greatest pain by the very fact that he deserved it), his ability to befriend people, his joy in serving others (he tells how he developed a passion for nursing the sick), and his dedication to abolish any kind of discrimination based on color, caste, religion, nationality, social position, or wealth. Other than his belief in the power of prayer, his devotion to truth as his guiding principle, and his sensitive conscience, we do not gain much insight into his inner growth. True, he struggled to overcome his crippling shyness and at times would spend a sleepless night to be able to come to the right decision, but his inner voice developed early, and as he wrote, he had taught himself to follow the inner voice: "I delighted in submitting to it. To act against it would have been difficult and painful to me" (p. 118). Still one gets the impression, and probably for lack of documentation a wrong one, that his "experiments with Truth" were the result of an early mold of character given to steadfast practice of chosen principles. Doubt, hesitation, inner conflict, all those things that appeal to our neurotic psychological tradition, are not in good supply in Gandhi's case. Nevertheless, he makes an eminent case for emotional giftedness.

By contrast, Eleanor Roosevelt's life brings us closer to discovering some of the methods she applied in her inner growth. Through her we get a close look at the inner workings of emotional giftedness. As a child and as a woman she was a being of intense emotions, great sensitivity, rich imagination, and thirst for learning. Her development, however, was not embedded in the rich soil of closely knit family affections as Gandhi's was. As a child she felt that only her father loved her, but she lost him early. Out of a serious, sensitive child

beset with numerous fears, feeling unattractive and out of place, she became a woman of energy and ability who impressed everyone by her serenity and poise. What were the mainsprings of this transformation? A diary entry when she was 14 gives some indication of young Eleanor's striving to become a better person. After expressing her dismay at not being able to live up to an ideal, she wrote: "I can feel it in me sometimes that I can do much more than I am doing and I mean to try till I succeed" (Lash, 1971, p. 112).

The driving forces of Eleanor's life were a sense of duty, a desire for love and belonging, a willingness to be of service, and a determination to develop her individual identity on an equal basis with her husband. Above all, she was propelled by compassion toward those in need, whether material or emotional or to fulfill a personal goal. Because she made sense of the sorrows of her own childhood, she had a thorough understanding of the emotional needs of children and adolescents (VanderVen, 1984). In her last book, *You Learn by Living* (1960), she offers a surprising amount of insight into the tasks and methods of developing knowledge of oneself. These methods will be described in the section on Level IV and self-actualization.

Self-knowledge, whe wrote, requires courage and discipline. She pointed out, too, our natural inclination toward self-deception ("protective veiling"):

> You must try to understand truthfully what makes you do things or feel things. Until you have been able to face the truth about yourself you cannot be really understanding in regard to what happens to other people. But it takes courage to face yourself and to acknowledge what motivates you in the things you do.
>
> This self-knowledge develops slowly. You cannot attain it all at once simply by stopping to take stock of your personal assets and liabilities. In a way one is checked by all that protective veiling one hangs over the real motives so that it is difficult to get at the truth. But if you keep trying honestly and courageously, even when the knowledge makes you wince, even when it shocks you and you rebel against it, it is apt to come in flashes of sudden insight. (Roosevelt, 1960, pp. 63–64).

Self-knowledge, she emphasized, also means knowing one's strengths, especially one's inner strength needed in times of difficulty. She stressed the necessity of taking responsibility for one's life: "In the long run, we shape our lives and we shape ourselves. The process never ends until we die. And the choices we make are ultimately our own responsibility" (Roosevelt, 1960, p. xii).

Dabrowski's Theory

Positive Disintegration

Working toward self-knowledge is a way of forging an inner transformation. This is the core of Dabrowski's theory of *positive disintegration* (Dabrowski, 1964, 1967; Dabrowski & Piechowski, 1977). By this paradoxical name he wanted to emphasize the dismantling and tearing down that occurs in one's inner being. What is experienced as lower is gradually removed and replaced by what is experienced as higher. This split between higher and lower in oneself takes many forms but is distinctly and spontaneously experienced by emotionally gifted people.

Earlier we discussed Dabrowski's concept of developmental potential. It addresses the outstanding feature of the gifted, their greatly intensified manner of experiencing in one or more of the five dimensions: psychomotor, sensual, intellectual, imaginational, and emotional. We discussed emotional giftedness as growing out of emotional overexcitability combined with a will to change oneself and to help others, including those who find roadblocks in the realization of their potential. The examples of Mohandas Gandhi and Eleanor Roosevelt underscore the link between a strong emotionality and finding one's mission in life in serving others. Not everyone finds it as readily as Mohandas and Eleanor did.

Dabrowski's theory is very much about this quest. It comes from a deep longing for something emotionally more satisfying: an ideal of love, an ideal of brotherhood, an ideal of beauty, an ideal of justice, an ideal of honesty, an ideal of caring, an ideal of responsibility, an ideal of humility, an ideal of truth, or all such

ideals. To be faithful to the call of an ideal demands self-sacrifice.

Gifted children feel this call early, but they find themselves as strangers in a strange land where schools do not value learning, where the ignorant hold power over sages, where the insensitive denounce feeling as a trouble factor, where victims are blamed for their misfortune, where authority gains its power from the blindness of the governed, where those who care always seem alone, and where reality means only the tangible, visible, measurable, and for sale. Clark (1983, p. 126) makes the point that an intense sense of justice and unwavering idealism appear early in the emotional growth of gifted children and that it is hard for them to understand why the adults are not doing anything to correct what is so blatantly wrong and unfair in the world. The gifted have trouble adjusting to a world where everything appears to stand on its head. In his youth Dabrowski struggled with these antinomies, and not finding resolution in the theories of his day, he eventually forged a new one.

Levels I and II

Dabrowski outlined a hierarchy, or typology if you will, of emotional development (see Table 21.2). Level I is represented by self-serving motivations, manipulativeness, self-protectiveness, exploitation, and wheeling and dealing, where others are seen only as similar to oneself or, if they are not materialistic, greedy, ambitious, power hungry, or striving for status, regarded as weak and naive. Level II is represented by submission to mainstream values and conventions. In this case the self derives its definition from fulfilling the expectations that others hold for one. Elkind's (1984) term *the patchwork self* applies here. In this type of growth a person perceives an underlying sameness in people revealed in expressions like "Do your own thing" or "Everyone is entitled to his opinion." No one's values are perceived to be better than anyone else's (again a criterion of sameness but in value currency). Absolute values are rejected: "There is no absolute truth; everything is relative." What one subscribes to is the continuous flux of change

Table 21.2
Levels of Emotional Development

V   Life inspired by a powerful ideal, such as equal rights, world peace, universal love and compassion, sovereignty of all nations
A magnetic field in the soul—Dag Hammarskjøld

IV   Self-actualization; ideals and actions agree: "What ought to be, will be"; strong sense of responsibility
Behind tranquility lies conquered unhappiness—Eleanor Roosevelt

III   Sense of the ideal but not reaching it; moral concerns: higher versus lower in oneself
Video meliora proboque deteriora sequor—Marcus Tullius Cicero

II   Lack of inner direction; inner fragmentation—many selves; submission to the values of the group; relativism of values and beliefs
A reed in the wind

I   Dominant concern with self-protection and survival; self-serving egocentrism; instrumental view of others
Dog-eat-dog mentality

without much direction. In more sensitive individuals there may be further sense of inner fragmentation ("I feel split into a thousand pieces"). Personal growth in Level II is typically the struggle toward the emancipation of an individual sense of self, a struggle that can be quite heroic. To give up believing what one has always been told and accepted as truth is a radical step in an arduous process of reconstruction. Belenky, Clinchy, Goldberger, and Tarule (1986) in their study of women's development identify a number of distinct steps in such a process.

Level III: The Fight for One's Principles

Dabrowski developed his theory as a protest against a world upside down. If Freud explored the impersonal conflict between blind desires of the individual and prohibitions of society, Dabrowski explored the conflict in which the individual stands in judgment of himself or herself. The prelude to this process is surprise and astonishment with the world and with oneself. It is an awakening. When the idealism of youth gives way to compromise and assimilation to being like other people, as in Level II, something essential is lost. In *Resurrection* Tolstoy (1961) tells the story of Dimitri Nekhludov, a young prince who underwent

this unappealing change when he left home and, as was customary, joined the Imperial Guards.

Then he was an honest unselfish youth with a heart open to every good suggestion; now he was a depraved, accomplished egotist, who cared for nothing but his own pleasure. . . . Then he regarded his spiritual self as real; now the real was his healthy, vigorous, animal self. . . . And all this terrible change came about only because he had ceased to believe himself and placed all his confidence in others. . . . If a man believes himself he often has to give judgment against his lower self, which seeks easy joys, but when he puts his trust in others, there is nothing to decide; everything has already been decided against the spiritual self, and in favor of the animal self. Moreover when he trusted in his own judgment he was always blamed, whereas now, trusting others, he received nothing but the approval of those about him. . . . He had at first made a fight for his principles; it was a hard struggle, because everything that seemed right to him seemed wrong to other people; and vice versa, all that he regarded as evil was applauded by his world. The struggle ended in his surrender; he gave up his own ideals and adopted those of other people. (pp. 51–52)

Nekhludov ceased to be true to himself.

Tolstoy illustrates here the vulnerability of

the young self in the face of the power of peer pressure in the largest sense. Young persons find peers not only in those who share their pursuit of "easy joys" but also in those with whom they compete, with whom they make deals and arrive at mutually profitable understandings and convenient arrangements. Thus one set of values overpowers another: one stronger merely by the number of people subscribing to it, one weaker because of germinating alone. And yet what is it about those "weaker" values and principles that they manage to come back? Or perhaps we should ask: What is it about these people who develop a strong reaction to having given up their ideals?

In Tolstoy's story, Nekhludov gradually recovers his earlier idealism and in the end firmly opposes the corrupt values of his society. Eleanor Roosevelt underwent a similar awakening when in her young adulthood she stopped, as she said, absorbing the tastes and personalities of those about her and affirmed her own values and beliefs: "They all in their sureness and absolute judgment on people and affairs going on in the world make me want to squirm and turn bolshevik" (Lash, 1971, p. 245). The phenomenon of an awakened self, or of an awakened conscience, is the phenomenon of conversion. But we must qualify that this kind of conversion comes from the inner being of the person. Dabrowski in his theory attempted to give systematic account of this process. First, there may be a reaction of surprise, or even of shock, when one takes a step back and looks at oneself, or, as Eleanor Roosevelt put it, "even when it shocks you and you rebel against it, it [self-knowledge] is apt to come in flashes of insight." Or, the process may be moved along by a gradual but ever deeper probing, self-examination, and self-evaluation, as illustrated in the life of Lieutenant Louis Font.

In 1970 a radio program, "Frontiers of Faith," carried an interview by Dr. Paul Deats, Jr., with Lieutenant Louis Paul Font of the U.S. Army. Lieutenant Font was then 23, a distinguished graduate of West Point (in the top 5% of his class). He came from a Kansas family steeped in strong traditions of "God and country." In 1967 to 1968, his last year as a cadet, he began having "twinges of conscience"

about the war in Vietnam. The words of the prayer that every cadet memorized and recited struck him "as life itself": "Give us sympathy for those who sorrow and suffer, suffer not our hatred of hypocrisy and pretense ever to diminish, guard us against flippancy and irreverence in the sacred things in life." He found himself in "the divisive situation of being in army uniform and objecting to the war my army was waging."

After graduation he was recommended for graduate study in the Kennedy School of Government at Harvard, where one of his professors was Henry Kissinger. The war in Vietnam struck Lieutenant Font as immoral and unjust, but no one around him saw it this way. His classmates were mostly government officials and some military men, all older than he. Yet four months before getting his master's degree, he filed for the status of conscientious objector (CO). He sacrificed his lifelong dream of a military career and gave up earning his graduate degree. He felt that he had to file for CO status as soon as he realized that this was what he had to do because "it would have been insincere to wait. I would not even think of waiting." This was emotionally so compelling to him because it was congruent with everything he most strongly believed. It did not happen all at once. Prior to graduate school he did not have the time to do the intensive self-searching that this required.

Dabrowski called this process *positive maladjustment,* because such persons are in direct conflict with the values around them, which they are expected to adopt—this is maladjustment—but they come into congruence with their own deeply felt values, which is its positive aspect. Being true to oneself is a positive step in personal growth. Filing for CO status was Lieutenant Font's "decision for self," a decisive action taken on the path toward self-actualization" (Brennan, 1987).

Lieutenant Font's conflict was between his values and the actions of the government he served. However, one can be in conflict with oneself over one's own behaviors and proclivities. This is then an inner conflict, as Cicero expressed so well: *"Video meliora proboque, deteriora sequor"* ("I see what is better and approve it, yet I follow what is worse"). The dynamics of inner conflict are expressed in dissatisfaction with oneself, even to the point of self-loathing for failing one's ideals, falling short of one's potential, perceiving oneself lacking in compassion, helpfulness, and so forth. Dabrowski called all such feelings engaged in judging oneself "multilevel," because a person feels a split between higher and lower in oneself. The pull of one's inner ideal is the higher element. This is not the customary striving after a *self-ideal,* which can be anything one desires in terms of attributes and achievements, but the universal ideal of becoming a better human being in the sense of Gandhi's truth, Eleanor Roosevelt's compassion in action, or Lieutenant Font's ideal of being to true to oneself.

Here then is the crucial difference between Levels II and III. While much attention may be given in Level II to self-improvement, inner growth is not conceived in multilevel terms of higher versus lower, the ideal versus the actual. The position of some dialectical developmentalists seems to focus exclusively on the Level II type of experience. In their view, the struggle between competing motivations does not lead to assimilation and integration at a higher level; rather the person cycles back and forth, responding first to one need and then another (Wrightsman, 1988, p. 130). No truly integrated individual sense of self can grow out of chronic wavering, hesitation, ambivalence, and recycling of the same issues.

Awakening from that ushers in multilevel inner growth. Moral questions and issues of personal responsibility become important and are intensely felt. But not infrequently the isolation in which this leaves a youngster or adult makes him or her prey to doubt. A meaningful dialogue is possible only with those who have traveled a similar path. This is why it is often difficult for an adolescent or adult to find a counselor or psychotherapist who understands multilevel inner growth (Level III). Being surrounded by people who accepted the atrocities of Vietnam brought doubt to Lieutenant Font in his searching process: "I was wavering. Am I a conscientious objector? Am I not? What is my duty to my country? What does it mean that I am a military officer? Am I other things first before I am a military officer, such as a U.S. citizen, such as a human being?"

Such questions asked of oneself make one aware of the singular individuality of every human being, because the answers must come from within the person. They have to be felt; they cannot be provided by someone else, because if they were we would be back in another mainstream version of ready-made values and conventions. There is a strong and logical connection between the process of personal growth and the realization that others truly are individuals, because there is nothing more individual than the development of a single organism. The set of genes is unique. When it is not we have clones, and clones, being exact copies, have no individuality.

One fundamental process of inner growth is standing back and examining one's inner self. The more one does this, the more one tries to lift the "protective veiling," the more one becomes aware of the disparity between the call of the ideal and the way one is. The ideal is what makes one begin to feel more and more deeply what one ought to be. This process of self-examination and self-judgment Dabrowski called "subject-object in oneself," a term he borrowed from Kierkegaard. It results in a more empathic understanding of other people and an even stronger realization that they, too, have their own and very individual life and development to follow.

Level IV: Self-Actualization

This stance of judging and correcting oneself, but of empathy and individual understanding toward others, is, for the most part, absent in Level II. This is why the growth process in Level II is a struggle to attain one's individual sense of self, while in Level III it is a struggle to live up to one's inner ideal. In Level IV it is no longer a struggle, because one lives more closely to one's ideal self and draws strength from it. Therein lies the connection with Level V, in which the inner ideal becomes a radiant and powerful field of spiritual force.

Eleanor Roosevelt's ideal was Christ: "If we believe in Democracy and that it is based on the possibility of a Christ-like way of life, then everybody must force himself to think through his own basic philosophy, his own willingness to live up to it and to help carry it out in everyday life" (Roosevelt, 1940, p. 76). It is worth pausing to examine this remarkable statement. She says, in effect, that there is no shortcut to true democracy but that all must examine their lives and start to implement every day and with everyone the ideal of cooperation, good will, and brotherhood that Christ set for us. Such a program has the hallmark of a level of inspiration higher than self-actualization. Few knew how closely to this ideal she actually lived: "She was a woman with a deep sense of spiritual mission. . . . Christ's story was a drama that re-enacted itself repeatedly in her thoughts and feelings. Amid the worldliness, the pomp, and the power of Washington she managed to hold vivid and intimate communion with Christ with a child's innocence and simplicity" (Lash, 1971, p. 391).

Inner transformation in this kind of inner growth is carried out by means of definite methods. One can identify several of these in the way she coped with inner conflict and the emotional pain that love often brings. One such method was quiet contemplation, another was hard work, and yet another was self-discipline (concentration, the practice of inner calm, and good organization of daily activities). She wrote that among the most difficult things to accept are those limitations in ourselves that make us unable to meet the need of someone we love, be it spouse, child, or friend. She then went on to say that our further emotional growth and maturity depend on this choice: that either we learn to meet that need or we allow someone else to meet it, "without bitterness or envy" (Roosevelt, 1960, p. 67). If I cannot marry the person I love, I can still let him or her marry someone else, and keep on loving and keeping that deep bond alive and growing. Deep bonds do not require that people eat breakfast together every day, or that they must have a physical hold on each other.

To survive the unbearable heartbreak of her husband's unfaithfulness—an event in which her private happy world collapsed, and in which she was all alone—she discovered the power of quiet contemplation. She started making trips to a cemetery that contained a statue, a tall bronze figure with a striking expression on her face, created by Saint-Gaudens. To Eleanor Roosevelt that face expressed a peace "beyond pain and beyond joy." She later told a friend that she went there to "sit and look at that woman. And I always came away somehow feeling better. And stronger. I've been here many, many times" (Hickok, 1962, pp. 91–92). This contemplative practice was her very own psychotherapy, which later enabled her to say, "Behind tranquility lies conquered unhappiness."

With the pain of loss she coped by burying herself in work. She did this when her brother died and again when F.D.R.'s death created a void in her life: "As time went on, the fact that I kept myself occupied made my loneliness less acute. . . . My philosophy has been that if you have work to do and do it to the best of your ability you will not have so much time to think about yourself" (Roosevelt, 1958, p. 7).

Her emotional gifts and victories were supported by mature self-discipline. She trained herself to maintain inner calm and to work with concentration amidst noise and commotion. As remarkable as this seems, to her it was just common sense, and to say "I don't have enough time" was in her judgment a poor excuse for defective planning and lack of organization:

> We have all the time there is. The problem is: How shall we make the best use of it? There are three ways in which I have been able to solve that problem: first, by achieving an inner calm so that I can work undisturbed by what goes on around me; second, by concentrating on the thing in hand; third, by arranging a routine pattern for my days . . . remaining flexible enough to allow for the unexpected. There is a fourth point which, perhaps, plays a considerable part in the use of my time. I try to maintain a general pattern of good health so that I have the best use of my energy whenever I need it.
>
> I learned that the ability to attain this inner calm, regardless of outside turmoil, is a kind of inner strength. It saves an immense amount of wear and tear on the nervous system. (Roosevelt, 1960, pp. 25–26, 27)

Eleanor Roosevelt's life is an example of self-actualization (Piechowski & Tyska, 1982; see Table 21.3) and no doubt of even more

Table 21.3
Traits of Self-Actualization

Autonomy:
  More efficient perception of reality
  Acceptance
  Quality of detachment
  Autonomy
  Resistance to enculturation
Problem-centeredness:
  Problem centering
  Discrimination between means and ends
Spontaneity:
  Spontaneity, simplicity, naturalness
  Continued freshness of appreciation
  Creativeness
  Peak experiences
Feeling of fellowship with others:
  Gemeinschaftsgefühl
  Democratic character structure
  Unhostile sense of humor
Interpersonal relations
Imperfections

than that. Maslow's composite picture of self-actualizing individuals fits exactly Dabrowski's construct of persons in Level IV, a conception of the kind of people who have developed a strong sense of universal values and whose extraordinary sense of responsibility leads them to take up tasks for the sake of others (Piechowski, 1978). Maslow (1970) pointed out that these people are strongly focused on problems outside themselves. They focus on problems rather than on the protection or enhancement of their own ego. They perceive tasks to fulfill because they respond to the need and urgency of the times.

With Level IV comes the genuine realization that each individual human being one encounters has within him or within her a store of unrealized potential. Coming upon the face of a beautiful child amidst people unshaped by heavy labor, Saint-Exupéry exclaimed, "Protected, cultivated, what could not this child become? It is the sight, a little bit in all these men, of Mozart murdered" (Smith, 1959, p. 100). This kind of vision might as well characterize Level V, a vision of every human being in its unrealized potential of immortal spirit. This level of development brings with it the incomprehensible freedom found in total selflessness, in love truly unconditional, expecting nothing in return, love that accurately perceives the divine spark even in the most darkened soul.

Dabrowski's theory is complex. Each level, and especially levels III, IV, and V, is characterized by a number of developmental dynamisms. A few of these have been mentioned: in Level III, astonishment with oneself, positive maladjustment, dissatisfaction with oneself, subject-object in oneself; in Level IV, self-therapy (illustrated by Eleanor Roosevelt's quiet contemplation), inner psychic transformation, and personality ideal. A more detailed exposition of the theory must be sought in a number of available and unavailable sources (Brennan, 1987; Dabrowski, 1964, 1967; Dabrowski & Piechowski, 1977; Hague, 1988; Lysy & Piechowski, 1983; Miller & Silverman, 1987; Nelson, 1989; Piechowski, 1975, 1978; Weckowicz, 1988). As with any conceptually rich theory, we must remind ourselves that a mere skeletal outline will not bring forth for us the understanding that only closer study and application can give.

One conceptual bridge of the theory needs to be clarified. Dabrowski was well aware of the importance of the environment in either promoting or inhibiting a person's growth, but he did not elaborate on it. His basic idea was that developmental potential (the overexcitabilities, talents, special abilities, and intelligence) comes in different magnitudes and strengths. In a totally depriving environment even the strongest developmental potential will not succeed, just as a musical gift will not develop in a tone-deaf environment, empty of musical instruments. If the environment is partially negative, then a strong developmental potential can overcome it, although not totally. Eleanor Roosevelt's story is a good example of this. There were some positive influences—privileged social status, availability of excellent education, and her father's love for her—and some negative ones—the lack of love from her mother, the unsteadiness and unreliability of her father, the early loss of him, the severity of her grandmother who then raised her. These left her with emotional scars and a vulnerability that stayed with her to the end (Lash,

1984). Yet it is quite clear that she kept making positive and growthful choices all her life just as she set down in *You Learn by Living* (Roosevelt, 1960). It is striking how often she employs the language of personal growth. To make the point, higher levels of development depend on the presence of strong developmental potential in a favorable environment. We find this potential among the gifted. Strong developmental potential and giftedness go together. However, not every kind of giftedness is associated with a strong developmental potential.

Self-Actualization and Emotional Giftedness

The correspondence between the two constructs, Maslow's self-actualization and Dabrowski's Level IV, enabled Brennan (1987) to conduct a search for the seemingly rare highly developed individual. Using nominations and the instrument for assessing levels of development, he cast a net that caught several self-actualizing fish. Individuals assessed to be developmentally representative of Level IV were found to meet the criteria of self-actualization. They also showed evidence of giftedness in their childhood.

It is not hard to see that while the world of academic psychology accepts the notion of self-actualization as Maslow's legacy, at the same time it either doubts the existence of self-actualizing people or, worse yet, confuses self-actualization with self-absorbed individualism (e.g., Geller, 1982; Smith, 1973; for a review of this issue see Waterman, 1984). Surely part of this doubt comes from the fact that no studies of self-actualizing people have been made in the years following Maslow's untimely death. The only two case studies were of historical figures, but they were recent, and so no more than a drop in the academic bucket (Piechowski, 1978; Piechowski & Tyska, 1982). Brennan's study is of great significance. He found self-actualizing people who are not famous and who are living now, in our times. He showed that looking for self-actualizing people among the gifted is a sure way of finding them.

He studied their developmental histories and found that they all have been emotionally wounded in different ways and had to make the significant *decision for self* in order to live a life true to themselves. Did he find them to be emotionally gifted? Of the three cases, one excels in this. This is a woman, a social worker, with an unusual degree of inborn intuition and sensitivity to others. It enables her to find common ground and establish rapport with anyone. She has been praised for her facility to work with psychiatric patients. However, it has its thorns: "I am in pain because they are in pain. . . . I feel that pain so much that I'll do anything to make them feel better" (Brennan, 1987, p. 208).

From this all too brief review we can conclude that giftedness in general—in the sense of intellectual potential, breadth of interests, and emotional intensity—is a necessary condition for self-actualization. However, self-actualization is not synonymous with emotional giftedness. Perhaps this ought to be clarified a little. A person may be emotionally gifted, in the sense of caring, understanding, nurturing, forming strong attachments, empowering others, being nonjudgmental and accepting of others, yet blind to his or her own gifts, self-critical, even self-punitive. For such a person the struggle for self-acceptance is yet to be won. Self-actualizing people are self-accepting and with a sense of humor about it. They have a mission in life, and if that mission is to serve others directly out of compassion and concern for their individual dignity, as Gandhi and Eleanor Roosevelt did, then self-actualization and emotional giftedness blend into one. However, if the mission is to help humankind indirectly, through research, reform, art, poetry, music, or probing the mysteries of life and the universe, then emotional giftedness might not be as strongly manifest.

By what signs, then, can we recognize the potential for self-actualization and the potential for emotional giftedness in young people? Some signs have been mentioned: emotional overexcitability expressed in the intensity and sensitivity to feelings in others and in oneself, empathy and understanding of others, early emergence of ethical concerns about being fair to others, worrying about subtle issues in how others are affected by one's actions, or anything that we can recognize as proper to the domain of personal intelligences.

Emotional life is difficult to observe from the outside. For this reason, clinical investigations and subjects who are willing to disclose the movement of their inner life are the only means of gaining some insight. Grant's (1988) recent study of the diverse types of moral development is an excellent example of the richness of insight into the emotional life of individuals that opens up to a skilled investigator. Comparing written responses to the items of the overexcitability questionnaire with responses obtained in a interview revealed that the protected privacy of writing led to more emotional self-disclosures than did the interview. This was found with gifted youngsters 9 to 13 years old (Piechowski, unpublished). An exploratory investigation of emotional growth has been carried out with gifted adolescents (Piechowski, 1989). Here only the principal findings are presented.

Emotional Growth of Gifted Children and Adolescents

In a 2-year follow-up study conducted in collaboration with Nicholas Colangelo, self-reports were obtained from gifted youngsters. At the beginning of the project they were 12 to 17 years old (Piechowski, Colangelo, Grant, & Walker, 1983). The purpose of the study was to find individual patterns of emotional development. The subjects were recruited from gifted programs in several high schools. The youngsters were given an open-ended questionnaire to tell what evoked in them strong positive feelings, what stimulated their minds, what was their conception of self, and the like. The items were designed to tap the five dimensions of developmental potential described at the beginning of this chapter. The results are given in more detail elsewhere (Piechowski, 1989).

This study revealed two constrasting types of development in gifted adolescents. In one type the orientation was pragmatic with definite and not too distant goals and not much inner exploration. This type of growth was called *rational-altruistic* because it closely fit with the type of character development described by Peck and Havighurst (1960). The other type was characterized by an awareness of inner life quite unlike that of the typical self-conscious adolescent. This type was called *introspective-emotional*. It is in this type that we see the potential for emotional growth as described by Dabrowski's theory. Several characteristics emerged. They are listed in Table 21.4.

Unlike many adolescents who live for the moment, are very peer-conscious, or are worried about their future, we have found in a number of gifted children an early awareness of their personal growth and its numerous possibilities, an eager anticipation and making ready for what is to come. One girl expressed it similarly at age 12, "I dream of being an adult," and at age 14, "I dream about how my life will be when I grow up. I dream lots and lots of ways I could be."

In response to the question about what attracted his attention in books, a boy of 17 expressed an intense inner push for emotional growth: "I want to be moved, changed somehow. I seek change, metamorphosis. I want to grow (not just in relation to books, either)."

Awareness of feelings and emotions gains importance. In reply to the question about who they are, several youngsters described themselves in distinctly emotional terms:

> [I am] A person who needs attention and a person that needs to be accepted. He can't be turned away because he gets hurt easily. (male, age 16)

Table 21.4
Characteristics of Emotional Growth of Introspective Gifted Adolescents

1. Awareness of growing and changing— awareness of many possible developmental paths
2. Awareness of feelings and conscious attention to them
3. Feelings of unreality
4. Inner dialogue and self-judgment
5. Searching, questioning, asking existential questions (problem finding)
6. Awareness of one's real self

I am a very misunderstood person. . . . People think that my life is easy because I am talented, but I have a lot of problems of my own just because of these talents. I often even get cut down for something good that I do. This is very hard to cope with. I am a very sensitive and emotional person. I get angered or saddened very easily. I can also get happy easily. I think I like this part of me. All these emotions somehow make me feel good about myself. . . . I am not a very confident person, though people think I am. (male, age 16)

I am a person who has feelings. . . . I have friends. I love life . . . . NOTE: I HAVE FEEL-INGS. (female, age 12)

The note of insistence on feelings shows at once their frustration when their feelings were ignored by others and how important they were to these gifted children's self-definition.

Empathy and understanding of others can be quite conscious, as for the girl just quoted (at age 14): "I can see myself in other people, I can see things I've done in what other people do. I *really* understand people's thoughts and actions because I think of times I was in their place." Expressions of understanding and caring for others were frequent in the responses of these youngsters.

Although adolescence is developmentally a time when interest in one's own and others' feelings comes to focus, the articulateness and insight of these gifted youngsters was rather exceptional. The emotional maturity and sensitivity that some youngsters achieve in late adolescence appears in the gifted—those engaged in emotional growth—in early adolescence. They show the signs of emotional giftedness.

Periods of intense emotional growth can bring on such sudden inner shifts as to produce moments of disequilibrium and estrangement. One feels at odds with the surroundings, as if suddenly alien to what was familiar before. Such feelings of unreality are not necessarily a cause for concern. What calls for concern is the fact that great emotional intensity and sensitivity combined with high intelligence make a youngster acutely aware of the precariousness of human existence and the precarious condition of our world. Because of

this, and because others understand it so little, gifted children can be extremely vulnerable and at risk (Leroux, 1986; Roedell, 1984).

Feelings of unreality are the inevitable product of great emotional intensity and feeling "different," while experiencing rapid shifts in perspective. For example, "Sometimes I think I am going insane and I wish I had someone intelligent to talk to" (female, age 16). In the next excerpt the feeling of unreality is combined with emotional experimentation, thinking of the parents as strangers, which can be interpreted as a step toward individual autonomy: "When I ask myself who I am, sometimes I wonder if I'm *really* here. Or, I'll look at mom and dad and ask myself, who are these people, and I try to picture them as total strangers" (female, age 15).

Inner dialogue and self-judgment are an essential part of moral growth. Although in his cognitive theory of moral development Kohlberg (1981) minimized the importance of emotions, the penetrating genius of William James (1902) saw a definite and necessary link between the strength of one's emotions and moral character. If beliefs and actions are to be congruent, a person must feel the issues with passion. For James, moral questions were real only to those who felt them so strongly that they felt called by them to an active response. Therefore, one had to begin with oneself. Self-judgment, then, is an evaluation of one's own self, the arduous way toward self-knowledge. Being self-critical is common among the gifted. To some it spells the danger of developing a negative self-image. One must, however, try to distinguish in each case if the self-criticism, which can appear very negative, is a spur toward growth or an obstacle in the person's growth.

Here are some examples of how these youngsters monitored themselves. Their sensitive consciences were fitted with a spur to self-correction—the opposite of most adolescents, who, paradoxically, can be very critical of everything and everyone and yet be lacking in self-judgment (Elkind, 1984). The following inner dialogue was a response to the question, "Do you ever think about your own thinking? Describe."

When I take a stand on something, I later wonder why I did that. I think about how I came to that conclusion. I think about if I was right, according to the norms of society. I think about my friends and other people I know and wonder if I really feel the way I let on, and if I am fooling myself by thinking things I really feel. (male, age 17)

The issues of right and wrong figure prominently here; this is in itself not unusual, but the process of sorting the issues out was already strongly autonomous. The writer examined the origin of his convictions and asked himself whether they were genuine or perhaps just self-deceptions. For contrast, here is a response to the question, "In what manner do you observe and analyze others?" from another 17-year old male.

Critically. I have an unusual ability for finding people's faults and discovering their vulnerabilities. I use this knowledge, too—sometimes even unconsciously. . . .

I am a manipulator, and it sometimes bothers me. I know how to handle friends, family, teachers, etc., which makes things comfortable for me but does sometimes bother my conscience. (Fleetingly, though.)

One might be inclined to wonder whether the future development of this boy would lead him to continue to muffle his conscience and become an even more skillful puppeteer pulling the strings in others to his own advantage. In his case this did not seem likely because in answer to the question about what most attracted his attention in a book, he wrote that the characters were important and that he wanted "to be able to understand them and relate to them—to sympathize with them. I want to be moved, changed somehow." A person to whom such feelings are important is not likely to ignore them in others or the impact on others of his actions. Colangelo and Brower (1987), for example, reported that their gifted subjects worried about the reactions and feelings of their siblings who were not included in the gifted program.

Searching, inquiring, and problem finding are those special abilities (Getzels & Csikszentmihalyi, 1975) enabling one to dis-

cover things that need discovering, questions that need to be asked, and problems that have yet to be conceived. Questioning, self-scrutiny, and the search for truth go together. Gifted youngsters often ask basic, philosophical, and existential questions. Somehow they develop a sense not only of objective truth but of inner truth as well.

Lots of times I wish I wouldn't think so much. It makes me very confused about a lot of stuff in the world. And I always wish I could think up answers instead of just questions. . . . My parents and all my adult friends don't understand. I wish I could talk to somebody who would have the same questions I do, *and* the answers to them. Maybe instead of somebody intelligent, I need somebody insane. (female, age 16)

In Delisle's (1984) extensive collection of responses from younger children, one can find similar responses about arguing with teachers or persistently asking questions. But moral concerns and evaluations, and issues of personal responsibility, are more typical of adolescents.

I think about my morals and what I really think is right and wrong. I often find that how I feel is a contradiction of what society thinks. This makes me wonder if there is something wrong with me. I concentrate on why and how I became this way and if I will always be this way. (male, age 17)

I live day to day like everyone else but I am continually frustrated with the shallowness of how we live and relate to one another.

Sometimes I hate myself because I am lazy and I feel unable to change. (female, age 16)

We see in these concepts keen questioning and self-scrutiny. We can recognize the Dabrowskian dynamisms of astonishment (first excerpt), dissatisfaction with oneself (second excerpt), and positive maladjustment (both excerpts). These youngsters are gifted not only in terms of their talents and abilities but in terms of character growth—they sincerely want to become better persons. Their self-knowledge is impressive for this age. It shows emotional giftedness in the making. It fits

Gardner's (1983) concept of intrapersonal intelligence.

Awareness of one's real self appears early in those engaged in intense emotional growth. Gifted youngsters quickly realize that their self-knowledge, the way they know and understand themselves, differs from the way others see and know them. They thus realize that their real self is hidden from others, and they can even be aware of keeping it that way.

> I'm somebody no one else knows. Some people see one part of me, others see other parts, it's like I'm acting. The real me is the one inside me. My real feelings, that I understand but can't explain. (female, age 14)

The development of self-awareness and self-understanding of these gifted youngsters traces the general direction described for adolescents by Broughton (1980), Selman (1980), and others. What is distinctive in the gifted is an acceleration of development and a greater intensity of existential questioning. And, importantly, they value their emotional side. It is not just awareness of having moods, feelings, and emotions but the realization that these are a distinct and essential part of one's self and for this the emotions are to be cherished.

Conclusions

The outstanding feature of the emotional development of the gifted is their emotional sensitivity and intensity. Sometimes it is hidden; sometimes it is prominent. In an exploratory study of emotional growth of gifted adolescents, we found that only a small number followed a type of growth oriented more toward outward achievement and recognition than toward introspection and emotional awareness. The introspective type of emotional growth was rather free of the self-consciousness and egocentrism characteristic of early adolescence. Instead it displayed an awareness of one's real self, an understanding of feelings and emotions, an empathic approach to others, and much focus on inner growth through

searching, questioning, carrying on an inner dialogue, and exercising self-corrective judgment. We associate these characteristics with emotional giftedness because it is in self-scrutiny and self-judgment that we find ourselves wanting; this leads us to develop a more accepting and compassionate understanding of others. Out of emotional sensitivity grows the desire to be of help to others, and the ideal of service is its fulfillment.

These features of emotional development of the gifted are built into Dabrowski's theory, which was developed on the basis of extensive clinical experience with gifted and talented youngsters and adults. The type of growth in which moral issues, concern for others, and probing existential questions arise with a degree of intensity that troubles an adult's or a youngster's mind because it is so different from the usual interests and preoccupations of one's peer group is described in detail by Dabrowski and placed in a large framework of levels of development. This framework makes sense to gifted people and gives them comfort. The comfort comes from realizing that the inner turmoil, the overwhelming feeling of being pushed to the wall, and the despair are part of the difficult process of changing and growing; it also comes from realizing that experiencing intensely the issues of right and wrong; or the emotional questions of rights, possessiveness, and freedom that arise in intimate relationships; or the struggles to free oneself from the negative messages and influences of one's past is inevitable in the striving for wholeness, balance, and inner harmony that is nourished by deeply felt ideals. Such struggles pave the way for self-actualization. By a peculiar coincidence, the construct of self-actualization fits into Dabrowski's theory so well that one could say that Maslow described what self-actualizing people are like and how they act, while Dabrowski mapped out the more abstract inner dynamics of their psychology.

Research quoted in the body of the chapter and clinical examples show that emotional giftedness and self-actualization can be recognized and distinguished, for they are not one and the same. Our present state of understanding is that all self-actualizing people so far studied in detail are gifted. On the other hand, not all emotionally gifted people are self-actualizing, because the kind of empathy and willingness to help and be of service that some people readily extend toward others they deny themselves. Lack of self-acceptance often combined with some self-defeating behaviors is an obstacle toward self-actualization. Yet this is not an obstacle toward compassion and caring. After all, giving others what one needs for oneself is a more constructive solution, and a more ennobling one, to one's existential crisis than anger, greed, or excessive self-indulgence.

Not all self-actualizing people appear to be emotionally gifted. But in some outstanding individuals the two qualities combine, as illustrated in the lives of Mahatma Gandhi and Eleanor Roosevelt as well as in cases of people now living who have been studied with proper tools. These examples and these studies are only a beginning of the effort needed to gain a more thorough knowledge of emotional giftedness and self-actualization. And let us not overlook the fact that self-actualization is a much distorted and misinterpreted term and we must restore its original meaning. We will never know what self-actualization really means if we rely on paper-and-pencil measures. It can be truly understood and known only through the lives of self-actualizing people.

Dabrowski's concept of developmental potential provides the means toward identifying potential for higher levels of development. The higher levels in his developmental hierarchy describe types of emotional development that we encounter in the gifted, and with the aid of his theory we can make better sense of it for them and for ourselves. What Dabrowski develops particularly well is the fight for one's principles that precedes self-actualization. Attempts to live by high ideals, to be true to oneself, meet with social opposition that is hard to escape. The character of Nekhludov in Tolstoy's *Resurrection* illustrates the process of becoming true to oneself. The case of Lieutenant Louis Paul Font turned conscientious objector illustrates in our times the sacrifice that it may demand. This drama is repeated in the lives of gifted children everywhere.

REFERENCES

Barron, F. (1968). *Creativity and personal freedom.* Princeton: New Jersey: Van Nostrand.

Belenky, M. F., Clinchy, B. McV., Goldberger, N. R., & Tarule, J. M. (1986). *Women's ways of knowing.* New York: Basic.

Borke, H. (1971). Interpersonal perception of young children: Egocentrism or empathy? *Developmental Psychology, 5,* 263–269.

Bowlby, J. (1969). *Attachment.* New York: Basic.

Bowlby, J. (1973). *Separation.* New York: Basic.

Bowlby, J. (1980). *Loss.* New York: Basic.

Brennan, T. P. (1987). *Case studies of multilevel development.* Unpublished doctoral dissertation, Northwestern University, Evanston, IL.

Broughton, J. (1980). The divided self in adolescence. *Human Development, 24,* 13–32.

Clark, B. (1983). *Growing up gifted* (2nd ed.), Columbus, OH: Merrill.

Colangelo, N., & Brower, P. (1987). Gifted youngsters and their siblings: Long-term impact of labeling on their academic and personal self-concepts. *Roeper Review, 10,* 101–103.

Dabrowski, K. (1964). *Positive disintegration.* Boston: Little, Brown.

Dabrowski, K. (1967). *Personality-shaping through positive disintegration.* Boston: Little, Brown.

Dabrowski, K. (1972). *Psychoneurosis is not an illness.* London: Gryf.

Dabrowski, K., & Piechowski, M. M. (1977). *Theory of levels of emotional development* (2 vols.). Oceanside, NY: Dabor.

Delisle, J. R. (1984). *Gifted children speak out.* New York: Walker & Company.

Elkind, D. (1984). *All grown up and no place to go.* Reading, MA: Addison-Wesley.

Erikson, E. (1963). *Childhood and society* (2nd ed.). New York: Norton.

Frontiers of Faith (1970). Series: "One Nation—Indivisible?" Part II. NBC-TV in Association with the National Council of Churches. New York.

Gandhi, M. K. (1948/1983). *Autobiography.* New York: Dover.

Gardner, H. (1983). *Frames of mind.* New York: Basic.

Geller, L. (1982). The failure of self-actualization theory: A critique of Carl Rogers and Abraham Maslow. *Journal of Humanistic Psychology, 22,* 56–73.

Getzels, J. W., & Csikszentmihalyi, M. (1975). From problem-solving to problem-finding. In I. A. Taylor & J. W. Getzels (Eds.), *Perspectives in creativity* (pp. 90–116). Chicago: Aldine.

Grant, B. A. (1988). *Four voices: Life history studies of moral development.* Unpublished doctoral dissertation, Northwestern University, Evanston, Illinois.

Hague, W. (1988). Toward a holistic psychology of valuing. *Counseling and Values, 33,* 32–46.

Harter, S. (1977). A cognitive-developmental approach to children's expression of conflicting feelings and a technique to facilitate such expressions in play therapy. *Journal of Consulting and Clinical Psychology, 45,* 417–432.

Hesse, P., & Cicchetti, D. (1982). Perspectives on an integrated theory of emotional development. In D. Cicchetti & P. Hesse (Eds.), *New directions for child development, No. 16: Emotional development* (pp. 3–48). San Francisco: Jossey-Bass.

Hickok, L. (1962). *Reluctant First Lady.* New York: Dodd, Mead.

Hoffman, L. (1979). Maternal employment. *American Psychologist, 34,* 859–865.

James, W. (1902). *The varieties of religious experience.* New York: Modern Library.

Kohlberg, L. (1981). *The philosophy of moral development.* New York: Harper & Row.

Larsen, R. J., & Diener, E. (1987). Affective intensity as an individual difference characteristic: A review. *Journal of Research in Personality, 21,* 1–39.

Larsen, R. J., Diener, E., & Emmons, R. A. (1986). Affect intensity and reactions to daily life events. *Journal of Personality and Social Psychology, 51,* 803–814.

Lash, J. P. (1971). *Eleanor and Franklin.* New York: Norton.

Lash, J. P. (1984). *Eleanor and her friends.* New York: Doubleday.

Leroux, J. A. (1986). Suicidal behavior in gifted adolescents. *Roeper Review, 9,* 77–79.

Lysy, K. Z., & Piechowski, M. M. (1983). Personal growth: An empirical study using Jungian and Dabrowskian measures. *Genetic Psychology Monographs, 108,* 267–320.

Maslow, A. H. (1970). *Motivation and personality* (2nd ed.). New York: Harper & Row.

Maslow, A. H. (1971). *The farther reaches of human nature.* New York: Viking.

Miller, A. (1981). *Prisoners of childhood.* New York: Basic.

Miller, N. B., & Silverman, L. K. (1987). Levels of personality development. *Roeper Review, 9,* 221–225.

Nelson, K. C. (1989). Dabrowski's theory of positive disintegration. *Advanced Development, 1,* 1–14.

Parkes, C. M., & Stevenson-Hinde, J. (Eds.). (1982). *The place of attachment in human behavior.* New York: Basic.

Peck, R. F., & Havighurst, R. J. (1960). *The psychology of character development.* New York: Wiley.

Piaget, J. (1967). *Six psychological studies.* New York: Random House.

Piechowski, M. M. (1975). A theoretical and empirical approach to the study of development. *Genetic Psychology Monographs, 92,* 231–297.

Piechowski, M. M. (1978). Self-actualization as a developmental structure: A profile of Antoine de Saint-Exupéry. *Genetic Psychology Monographs, 97,* 181–242.

Piechowski, M. M. (1979). Developmental potential. In N. Colangelo & R. T. Zaffrann (Eds.), *New voices in counseling the gifted* (pp. 25–57). Dubuque: Kendall/Hunt.

Piechowski, M. M. (1986). The concept of developmental potential. *Roeper Review, 8,* 190–197.

Piechowski, M. M. (1987). Family qualities and the emotional development of older gifted students. In T. Buescher (Ed.), *Understanding gifted and talented adolescents* (pp. 17–23). Evanston, IL: Center for Talent Development, Northwestern University.

Piechowski, M. M. (1989). Developmental potential and the growth of self. In J. VanTassel-Baska & P. Olszewski-Kubilius (Eds.), *Patterns of influence: The home, the self, and the school* (pp. 87–101). New York: Teachers College Press.

Piechowski, M. M. *OE by OEQ and OEI.* Unpublished manuscript.

Piechowski, M. M., & Colangelo, N. (1984). Developmental potential of the gifted. *Gifted Child Quarterly, 28,* 80–88.

Piechowski, M. M., Colangelo, N., Grant, B. A., & Walker, L. (1983, November). *Developmental potential of gifted adolescents.* Paper presented at the National Association for Gifted Children annual convention, Philadelphia.

Piechowski, M. M., & Cunningham, K. (1985). Patterns of overexcitability in a group of artists. *Journal of Creative Behavior, 19,* 153–174.

Piechowski, M. M., Silverman, L. K., & Falk, R. F. (1985). Comparison of intellectually and artistically gifted on five dimensions of mental functioning. *Perceptual and Motor Skills, 60,* 539–549.

Piechowski, M. M., & Tyska, C. A. (1982). Self-actualization profile of Eleanor Roosevelt, a presumed nontranscender. *Genetic Psychology Monographs, 105,* 95–153.

Radke-Yarrow, M., Zahn-Waxler, C., & Chapman, M. (1983). Children's prosocial dispositions and behavior. In P. Mussen (Ed.), *Carmichael's manual of child psychology* (Vol. 4, 4th ed., pp. 469–545). New York: Wiley.

Richert, S. E., Alvino, J. J., & McDonnel, R. C. (1982). *National report on identification.* Sewell, NJ: Educational Improvement Center–South.

Roedell, W. C. (1984). Vulnerabilities of highly gifted children. *Roeper Review, 6,* 127–130.

Roeper, A. (1982). How the gifted cope with their emotions. *Roeper Review, 5,* 21–24.

Roosevelt, E. (1940). *The moral basis of democracy.* New York: Howell, Soskin.

Roosevelt, E. (1958). *On my own.* New York: Harper.

Roosevelt, E. (1960). *You learn by living.* New York: Harper. (Reprinted by Westminster Press, Philadelphia, PA.)

Sandler, J., & Sandler, A-M. (1978). On the development of object relations and affects. *International Journal of Psychoanalysis, 59,* 285–293.

Selman, R. L. (1980). *The growth of interpersonal understanding.* New York: Academic.

Seymour, D. (1987). *A case study of two young gifted brothers.* Unpublished manuscript.

Silverman, L. K. (1983). Personality development: The pursuit of excellence. *Journal for the Education of the Gifted, 6,* 5–19.

Smith, M. A. (1959). *Knight of the air.* London: Cassell.

Smith, M. B. (1973). On self-actualization: A transambivalent examination of a focal theme in Maslow's psychology. *Journal of Humanistic Psychology, 13,* 17–33.

Sroufe, L. A. (1979). The coherence of individual development. *American Psychologist, 34,* 834–841.

Tolan, S. S. (1987). Parents and profesionals, a question of priorities. *Roeper Review, 9,* 184–187.

Tolstoy, L. (1961). *Resurrection.* New York: Signet.

VanderVen, K. (1984, October). *The development of Eleanor Roosevelt and her relationships with children and youth.* Paper presented at the Eleanor Roosevelt Centennial Conference, Vassar College Poughkeepsie, New York.

Waterman, A. S. (1984). *The psychology of individualism.* New York: Praeger.

Webb, J. T., Meckstroth, E. A., & Tolan, S. S. (1982). *Guiding the gifted child.* Columbus: Ohio Psychology.

Weckowicz, T. E. (1988). Kazimierz Dabrowski's theory of positive disintegration and the American humanistic psychology. *Counseling and Values, 32,* 124–134.

Whitmore, J. R. (1980). *Giftedness, conflict, and underachievement.* Boston: Allyn and Bacon.

Wrightsman, L. S. (1988). *Personality development in adulthood.* Newbury Park, CA: Sage.

22

Family Counseling

LINDA KREGER SILVERMAN   *Gifted Child Development Center, Denver, Colorado*

Having a gifted child is a mixed blessing, and many parents feel battered in the bargain. From birth on, these children present an unusual set of challenges. They tend to begin life as active babies, sleeping less than their parents, responding intensely to their environment, often colicky. They exhaust their primary caretakers with their constant need for stimulation. Two gifted children in a family may be highly competitive (Ballering & Koch, 1984). More than two and the parents are outnumbered. But this is only the beginning.

Gifted children show advanced development in intellectual skills but may be average or even slow in the development of motor skills (Page, 1983; Rogers, 1986; Sebring, 1983). The unevenness of their development leads to frustration—for themselves and for their parents. It is not easy having an 8-year-old mind in a 5-year-old body. Decisions that are quite simple for other families—such as, Where should we send our child to school?—are often agonizingly difficult for parents of advanced children. Grade placement is another problem. Should the child be accelerated, kept at grade level, or held back? Peer relations can be a source of strain. Gifted children often enjoy playing with children older than themselves, mothering children younger than themselves, and relating to adults. They often have difficulty, however, playing with average children their own age.

Perhaps the greatest source of stress in the lives of parents of gifted children is the degree to which they are discounted. There are great emotional risks in going to the principal and saying, "I believe my child is gifted and has special needs." Too often parents hear the patronizing reply, "Yes, Mrs. Smith, all our parents think their children are gifted." No group has a more difficult time being taken seriously

than parents of gifted children. They need counselors who are knowledgeable about the gifted who can give them guidance in dealing with the educational system and with their complex home lives.

The Uniqueness of Rearing a Gifted Child

It is no easier to be a parent of a gifted child than it is to be a gifted child (Nathan, 1979). Dirks's (1979) research indicated that it may be even harder to be a parent. In counseling parents of the gifted for the past 25 years, I have found that a dozen unique concerns provoke them to seek psychological services:

- Observing that their child is "different"
- Desiring assessment of the child's abilities
- Feeling inadequately prepared to raise an exceptional child
- Determining appropriate school placement
- Needing assistance with school personnel
- Determining appropriate home stimulation and development of special talents
- Desiring information about available resources (such as enrichment programs)
- Coping with underachievement and lack of motivation
- Dealing with the child's intensity, perfectionism, heightened sensitivity, introversion, or depression
- Helping the child develop better peer relations
- Experiencing increased tension in the family as a result of the special needs of their gifted child(ren)
- Understanding their own giftedness

They also engage in counseling for reasons similar to those of other parents: poor family dynamics, stress-related disorders, conflicting perceptions of parents, divorce, sibling rivalry, depression or suicidal ideation in an adolescent, and so on.

Observing Differentness

When parents observe the advanced intellectual development of their child compared with their neighbors' children, they often begin to worry that he or she will be out of step with playmates or with the school curriculum. They may recognize on their own that their child is "different," or these developmental differences may be pointed out by others. Unfortunately, the advice they are likely to receive from friends, family, educators, pediatricians, or writers of popular articles tends to be counterproductive. The models of "good child rearing" that these well-meaning individuals espouse are derived from the development of average children (Ross, 1964; Sebring, 1983) and are frequently no more applicable to rearing gifted children than to rearing retarded ones. However, because gifted children look "normal," compared with many retarded children, it is more difficult for the adults in their lives—including their parents—to be aware of their unique needs.

Even extreme signs of precocious development do not automatically alert parents to the fact that they have a gifted child. Parents tend to distrust their own perceptions of their children's advanced abilities because of the pervasive myth that all parents think their children are special. More tend to overlook the signs of giftedness in their children than to overstate the case (Ginsberg & Harrison, 1977; Rogers, 1986). In Dickinson's (1970) study, just half of the children who tested in the gifted range had parents who recognized their children's high abilities. Dembinski and Mauser (1978) found that only 35% of the parents recognized their children as gifted before school age. Most of the rest were identified by the schools. Given the critical role played by the family in the first 6 years, it is unfortunate that information about early signs of giftedness is so difficult to obtain. We have found that parents of young children are more likely to seek the help of professionals

when they see a list of characteristics of gifted children (Silverman, Chitwood, & Waters, 1986).

Gaining Assessment

Gaining a meaningful assessment of a gifted child's abilities poses yet another set of roadblocks. Giftedness is usually defined as being selected for a gifted program. Many public schools do not assess giftedness until third grade and then use gross screening devices—group achievement tests, grades, teacher recommendation, and group intelligence tests—to determine placement in gifted programs. The criteria are achievement oriented, and the number of children identified is purely arbitrary—totally dependent on budgetary considerations. The inadequacy of this pervasive model is made clear when one looks at methods used to identify retarded children. The gifted and retarded are two ends of the same continuum, and the extent of developmental advancement is just as significant as the extent of developmental delay. Therefore, methods used to place the label *gifted* on a child should be as thorough, extensive, and well thought through as processes used for identifying the retarded.

As with other exceptionalities, the earlier gifted children are identified, the more favorable their development (Hollingworth, 1942; Witty, 1958). Researchers have consistently found parenting to be the most potent factor in the development of giftedness, creativity, and eminence (Albert, 1978; Bloom, 1985; Cox, Daniel, & Boston, 1985; Goertzel, Goertzel, & Goertzel, 1978; Sanborn, 1979). Therefore, if our objective is the optimum development of gifted children, we should encourage parent involvement and provide parents with the information they need to play an active role in identifying their children's abilities early in life and providing necessary support.

When parents do seek assessment of their children, they are usually fearful that they will be perceived as pushy or that their child will not qualify as gifted. Acquainting them with the characteristics of gifted children helps reassure them that diagnostic assessment is appropriate. After the testing, the counselor's job begins in earnest. Parents need help in interpreting the test scores, understanding discrepancies between scores obtained on different instruments, dealing with the implications of various ranges of giftedness, locating appropriate resources, sorting through the options, and coming to terms with the meaning of the child's giftedness in their lives. Although children seem to react favorably to the testing, it may take several months or even years for parents to adjust to the results of the assessment (Dirks, 1979).

Interpreting test scores for gifted children is actually quite complex and requires some expertise, because discrepancies in scores obtained on various instruments are much greater for the gifted than for any other population (Silverman, 1988a). The problem is particularly acute for highly gifted children, who may have differences as great as 50 points from one test to another (Silverman & Kearney, 1989). None of the modern tests were designed with the highly gifted child in mind, so these children rapidly reach the ceilings of the tests. If a child scores at or within 1 point of the ceiling on two or three subtests on any instrument, additional testing is recommended. The Stanford-Binet, Form L-M, is the best available supplement for children in the highly gifted range (Silverman, 1989a).

Feeling Inadequately Prepared

Several researchers have found that parents often feel inadequately prepared to meet the needs of a gifted child (Bridges, 1973; Dettmann & Colangelo, 1980; Dirks, 1979; Ross, 1964). This is a common reaction of parents of other types of exceptionalities, but the problems for parents of the gifted are compounded by other factors: myths and misinformation about the gifted (Dettmann & Colangelo, 1980); blatant or covert hostility toward the intellectually advanced (Marland, 1972); lack of societal support for the identification and nurturing of its gifted members (Hollingworth, 1940); lack of information about available resources (Dirks, 1979); limited financial resources of parents (Bloom,

1985); uneven development of the child (Ross, 1964); unclear or conflicting expectations of the child by the parents (Colangelo & Dettmann, 1983; Fine, 1977); and confusion about the child's role in the family (Dirks, 1979; Fine, 1977).

Certain behaviors and personality traits of gifted children also may be cause for concern. Whitmore (1979) listed nine behaviors that adults may find problematic in gifted or creative youngsters: not listening, dominating, tuning out, argumentativeness, refusal to comply with instructions, teasing or ridiculing, excessive competitiveness, desire to control others, and messiness with personal things and work. Many gifted children question authority (Ellenhorn, 1988; Silverman & Waters, 1988). Sebring (1983) suggested that "the nature and frequency of the gifted child's queries may not only vex the parents, but also lead them to construe such questioning as challenges to parental authority" (p. 97). He suggested that conflicts can be avoided if the parents understand that gifted children are independent thinkers and are really analyzing a demand when they argue.

Parents need information about giftedness to assist them in differentiating behavior that is normal for gifted children from dysfunctional behavior. Whitmore (1979) pointed out that the child may not perceive a behavior (e.g., argumentativeness) as a problem, and that it may be more of a problem for the parents. In this case, parents may need the counseling more than the child.

Gifted youngsters appear to respond well to democratic approaches in which they have a voice in decision making, and poorly to authoritarian parenting styles (Parker, Ross, & Deutsch, 1980). Although some children seem to thrive in authoritarian homes (Baumrind, 1971), the gifted have a keen sense of justice and tend to react against authoritarianism. Most people in our culture take "ageism" for granted—the belief that adults have more power, and therefore more rights and privileges, than children. Gifted children do not share this assumption.

Montemayor (1987) has found that conflicts with adolescents are resolved by accepting children as peers and sharing the power. I have found this to be true with younger gifted children as well. These children tend to behave manipulatively or disrespectfully in situations in which they feel powerless or not respected. The antidote is to help parents create a family system with a balance in power, in which all members feel supported.

One method of establishing a balance of power is by establishing a family council—usually a regularly scheduled meeting of the entire family. A family council provides direct experience in democratic decision making. Everyone is given an opportunity to air grievances, request changes in rules, learn negotiation skills, and practice effective communication techniques on a routine basis. Family council meetings can also be a vehicle for building self-esteem and family solidarity. A time for compliments can be included as well as a time for complaints. Gifted children can participate competently in family council meetings at about 7 or 8 years old.

Determining Appropriate School Placement

The counselor needs to be aware of the philosophies of giftedness in local schools and the availability of various types of special programs. Part of the guidance parents desire is information about options. If public school offerings are limited and the child qualifies for acceptance in a private school for the gifted, this alternative should be explored. The counselor can assist the parents in developing evaluation criteria for examining several preschools or private schools. With appropriate diagnostic information, schools can be selected that provide a good match with the child's learning style and range of abilities.

At the Gifted Child Development Center, we recommend that parents visit several potential schools and determine which ones are affordable, are responsive to giftedness, are within a reasonable distance, and appear congruent with their own philosophy. After they have narrowed the choice to a few alternatives, we suggest that they take their child to spend a morning or afternoon in the environment and help select his or her own school. We have

found that even 4-year-old gifted children can make effective choices of their school environment (Waters & Silverman, 1986). They often notice characteristics of the school that parents miss (e.g., how the children act on the playground).

Within the public schools, several choices may also be available (e.g., a pullout program, a magnet school across town, cluster grouping within the regular classroom). Parents may need to determine which of several alternatives is best for their child. A recurring question is the impact on social development of transporting children to a magnet or private school away from the neighborhood school. Since gifted children often have different sets of peers for different types of activities (Lewis, Young, Brooks, & Michalson, 1975; Roedell, 1985), they usually develop two sets of friends: school friends and neighborhood friends.

In schools with no gifted programs, or in the case of highly gifted children, the question of acceleration should be addressed. This is often a loaded topic, but the familiar biases are not supported by research (Daurio, 1979; Janos et al., 1988; Stanley, 1988; see Chapters 11 and 13). Strong opposition to acceleration may be countered by sharing information from the existing studies. Although many children have benefited from acceleration (Hultgren, 1989; Kearney, 1988), it remains unpopular with educators. Ironically, parents today are pressured to move in the opposite direction: to hold children back instead of accelerating them.

Gifted boys are sometimes held back at the kindergarten level on the assumption that it will enhance their social relationships. A 5-year-old boy with an 8-year-old mind can play chess, Scrabble, and board games with rules, but he has a very difficult time relating to 5-year-old boys with 5-year-old minds who do not yet understand the meaning of rules. He is likely to refuse to play the "baby" games of his age-mates. The solution to this problem is not retaining the child—so that next year he can be a 6-year-old with a 9-year-old mind still trying to adjust to 5-year-olds. A more appropriate solution to social adjustment difficulties is finding the boy true peers—age-mates of similar ability with whom he can be socially comfortable (Roedell, 1985; Silverman, 1989a).

Roedell (1988) wrote:

> When parents and teachers understand the implications of the differentness inherent in being gifted, they can create conditions that will support the child's positive social and emotional growth. The first step is to realize the inextricable link between social and cognitive development. . . . If the child also makes the discovery that communication with classmates is difficult, and that others do not share his/her vocabulary, skills or interests, peer interactions may prove limited and unsatisfactory. *We cannot ignore the gifted child's need for intellectual stimulation and expect social development to flourish.* (pp. 10–11, emphasis in original)

Assistance with School Personnel

A school counselor can help select the most effective teachers for the child and assist teachers in adapting their methods to meet the student's needs. At times, the counselor is also called upon to act as an advocate for the child. If a student is particularly unhappy and the teacher is unresponsive to the parents' attempts to ameliorate the situation, the counselor may have to intervene. A typical situation is when the parents feel that the child would be happier in first grade and the kindergarten teacher feels that the child is not ready. The counselor can observe the child in both kindergarten and first grade, request a staffing to discuss the placement, provide insights about the child, and mediate the situation.

Another typical scenario is the case of the junior or senior high school boy whose grades are *D*s and *F*s. At midterm his parents place him in counseling, but he does not see the point of trying to reverse the pattern. Even if he turned in all his assignments for the rest of the semester, his final grade would reflect the months of noncompliance, so why bother? The counselor can intervene on the student's behalf, approach each teacher, explain that the youth is now in counseling, and ask the teacher to allow him to have a fresh start. This will enhance the potential effectiveness of the therapeutic intervention.

Home Stimulation

Many parents are confused as to how much and what type of home stimulation is appropriate (Colangelo & Dettmann, 1983). They receive conflicting messages about the value of early home enrichment (Clark, 1988) and the perils of "hurrying" their children (Elkind, 1981). It is widely recognized that parents are their children's first teachers and that the first 5 years are the most critical learning period (Bloom, 1964). Yet, parents—particularly parents who are also teachers—often say anxiously, "I didn't teach my child to read—honestly. She just picked it up on her own." The fear that they will be seen as pushy prevents many parents from exercising their rightful role as educators.

A major study of individuals who achieved world-class recognition by the age of 30 (Bloom, 1985) highlights the important role parents play in the development of talent.

> We believe, as do the parents, that the parents' participation in the child's learning contributed significantly to his or her achievement in the field. We find it difficult to imagine how these children could have gotten good teachers, learned to practice regularly and thoroughly, and developed a value of and commitment to achievement in the talent field without a great deal of parental guidance and support. (p. 476)

Further confirmation of the role of the family comes from a study of the MacArthur Fellows, all of whom received substantial awards for their outstanding creativity (Cox, Daniel, & Boston, 1985).

> *Almost without exception the MacArthur Fellows pay tribute to their parents.* While the educational level of the parents varied, and the level of financial backing as well, virtually all the parents let their children know the value of learning by personal example. The parents supported without pushing. Their homes had books, journals, newspapers. They took the children to the library. The parents themselves read, and they read to their children. Most important, they respected their children's ideas. (p. 24, emphasis in original)

Additional research indicates that parents assist the development of their gifted young by encouraging autonomy (Dewing & Taft, 1973; Weisberg & Springer, 1961); providing a high degree of adult attention (Robinson, Roedell, & Jackson, 1979); strong family values and clear standards of conduct (MacKinnon, 1962); mutual trust and approval (Piechowski, 1987); holding high expectations for their children (Albert, 1978; Bloom & Sosniak, 1981); providing good role models (MacKinnon, 1962; Simonton, 1978); supporting their children's interests (Bloom & Sosniak, 1981); avid reading and reading frequently to children (Csikszentmihalyi & Beattie, 1979); and helping their children to believe in their dreams (Darnell, personal communication, November 15, 1988).

Parents should be encouraged to provide a stimulating home environment—including instruction—if the child is eager, interested, and enjoying the activities. If the experience is *fun* for both the parent and the child, it is not harmful. On the other hand, parents should be discouraged from pushing unwanted enrichment on their child to give him or her the "edge" in the competition of life. Felder (1986) provided some suggestions for home stimulation and guidelines for parents:

> These activities should be offered, not pushed, and they should be presented as games, not required exercises. If there is no interest, they should be dropped from the picture, and perhaps brought up again after a year or two.
>
> The object is . . . to allow the children to experience the joy that comes from allowing their interests, abilities, and gifts to develop naturally, not according to someone's arbitrary schedule of when learning is supposed to occur. (p. 176)

Locating Available Resources

It is important for the counselor to be prepared to answer questions about after-school enrichment programs, early college entrance, simultaneous enrollment in high school and college, internships, mentorships, and scholarships. In addition, parents need information about local, regional, and national support groups and conferences; newsletters, magazines, and journals; books for parents of the gifted; and books and software for gifted children. If the family is unhappy with the neighborhood school, the counselor can investigate open-enrollment policies within the district, enrollment in other districts, and private schools. If the student needs assistance in certain skill areas, the counselor should have on hand the names of competent tutors.

At the Gifted Child Development Center, we have found it necessary to make frequent referrals of gifted children to allergists, developmental optometrists, audiologists, occupational therapists, and play therapists. Many of the children who come to us for testing for giftedness also exhibit signs of learning disability (Silverman, 1989b). Gifted–learning-disabled children are a hidden population because the disability depresses the IQ score and the giftedness masks the disability. The net result is a child who appears "average."

Underachievement

Concern with a child's underachievement is the most frequent reason that parents of adolescents have consulted the Gifted Child Development Center. There are many possible causes of underachievement. We routinely administer a diagnostic battery to determine if there is a hidden learning disability involved in the student's lack of motivation or lack of success. We have found remarkable consistency in the test profiles of underachievers: high scores in vocabulary, abstract reasoning, spatial relations, and mathematical analysis, coupled with low scores in tasks requiring sequencing (repeating digits, repeating sentences, coding, arithmetic, and spelling) (Silverman, 1989b).

This pattern is indicative of a spatial learning style and also may suggest auditory sequential processing deficits (Silverman, 1989b). We go over the test results with the students and help them to understand that they are neither "dumb" nor "lazy." The testing itself has had an ameliorative effect on self-concepts of these young people. Through counseling and educational therapy, we help them understand their learning style and their strengths. We teach them (as well as their parents and teachers) methods of compensating for their deficiencies.

Parent counseling is an important part of this process. We have found that in the majority of cases the child's learning style and behavior echo the patterns established in childhood by one of the parents. Very frequently, that parent is the one who "gets on the child's case" the most. The child mirrors those qualities the adult most dislikes in him- or herself. I have had success turning around parents' attitudes toward their children by helping them recognize their own hidden learning disabilities. These parents are often "late bloomers." Since they have managed to compensate for their weaknesses, they are in the best position to understand the learning processes of their children and can become their children's greatest allies. A deeper bonding often ensues between parents and children through these discussions.

Perhaps the most comprehensive intervention model for underachievers was created by Whitmore (1980). The Cupertino Program for Highly Gifted Underachievers was an intensive approach employing the following strategies: early identification; self-contained classes made up solely of underachievers; extended day; smaller classes (16–21 students); in-depth diagnoses and continual assessment; student-centered curriculum, rich in creativity, problem-solving, and higher level thinking skills; individualized instruction; opportunities for self-directed learning and active inquiry; small-group interaction; extensive parent involvement; regular individual and group counseling within the context of the classroom; and teachers specifically trained in *counseling* as well as teaching strategies with underachieving gifted students.

Primary-grade students needed the program for 1 full year and intermediate-grade students for 2 years. Whitmore (1980) reported that the project produced "definite evidence that the later the intervention occurs, the longer the child will be in need of the special intensive program" (p. 206). The Cupertino project reminds us that most of the unsuccessful strategies attempted in the 1960s for reversing underachievement in high school

students were too little, too late (Dowdall & Colangelo, 1982; Tannenbaum, 1983). Today the picture is more hopeful.

Some success has been reported in the use of small-group counseling of underachievers and parent involvement in the counseling process (Jackson, Cleveland, & Merenda, 1975; Mink, 1964; Perkins & Wicas, 1971; Zilli, 1971). Shaw and McCuen (1960) described an intriguing group technique for counseling families of underachievers. They had a small group of underachieving students listen to the difficulties expressed by a group of parents for 45 minutes and then had the parents listen to the students for another 45 minutes. A unique aspect of the format was that in the first two sessions the students were matched with parents of other underachieving youth. At the end of four sessions, students felt that they were able to communicate more freely with their parents. Parents were able to gain insights into their own family dynamics by observing the dynamics of other families.

The major strategies for dealing with underachievement include early identification; obtaining individual diagnoses; interviewing parents to determine if the problem is school related or a pervasive part of the child's functioning at home as well; interviewing the student to determine interests, aspirations, and his or her assessment of causes and solutions; determining a plan of action with parents, teachers, and student and monitoring its implementation (Fine & Pitts, 1980); negotiating a fresh start with the teachers; adapting the curriculum to the student's learning style; teaching the student compensation techniques; obtaining a tutor to help the student learn skills; and family counseling.

Personality Variables

The complexity of the thought processes that mark individuals as gifted is mirrored in the intricacy of their emotional development. *Intensity, perfectionism,* and *heightened sensitivity* are three emotional tributaries of the gifted personality that appear most often in the counseling population with whom I have worked—

both children and adults (Silverman & Kearney, 1989). Intensity is the hallmark of passion, an important variable in the achievement of excellence (Feldman, 1979). Perfectionism is the driving force behind the pursuit of excellence (Silverman, 1987b). And heightened sensitivity is the basis of compassion. These three qualities combine to create a unique personality structure governed by a vision of the ideal. They also indicate a capacity to bring one's ideals to fruition.

Dabrowski and Piechowski (1977) have provided a theoretical framework for understanding the rich inner experience of the gifted. Studying gifted, creative, and eminent individuals, Dabrowski (1972) constructed a theory of emotional development that explains the unusual strivings and dedication of society's most gifted and evolved members. Piechowski (1979, 1986, 1987; Piechowski & Colangelo, 1984; see Chapter 21 by Piechowski) has shown that the gifted have greater potential for reaching higher levels of development—levels at which life is imbued with universal values, extraordinary responsibility, compassion, and dedication to service. This developmental potential grows out of the synthesis of emotional depth and intellectual awareness. "There is among gifted individuals a greater intensity of feeling, greater awareness of feeling, and greater capacity to be concerned" (Piechowski, 1987, p. 22).

Intense experience can lead to depression, and much of the depression stems from the individual's inability to reconcile his or her emotional experience with expected norms. Gifted adolescents and adults often feel that they should not have conflicts or negative feelings. They have been labeled "too sensitive," "too intense," "too perfectionistic" by so many people in their lives that they internalize the message that there is really something wrong with them. The counselor's first task is clearing up the misconception that strong feelings are inappropriate. The young person's family also needs this information.

Counselors inadvertently may attempt to cure the very qualities of the gifted that constitute their potential for higher development. In contrast, Ogburn-Colangelo (1979)

provided an example of how the application of Dabrowski's theory in a counseling context can *enhance* a gifted adolescent's potential. She helped her counselee see that her inner turmoil was positive, since her two conflicting desires (her need to develop her abilities and her attachment to family members who did not support these talents) were both positive. The counselor helped the student acknowledge her strengths: her sense of responsibility to her family, her awareness of her own talents, and her willingness to determine her own future. The counselor listened, helped the student sort out the problem by herself, and gave her confidence in her strengths and ability to cope with the situation. The counselee's developmental strengths became apparent within the framework of Dabrowski's theory.

I often introduce Dabrowski's theory to families of the gifted. The theory helps family members view their intense inner experiences as positive signs of development rather than as indicators of emotional disturbance. This frees energy being used in self-doubt and self-deprecation, making it available for the development of successful coping mechanisms (Silverman, 1987a). As each member of the family gains self-understanding, there is more awareness of the emotional experience of others in the family. Compassion and problem solving grow out of this enhanced awareness.

Another personality trait that I have found correlated with giftedness is introversion, which seems to increase with IQ (Silverman, 1986a). Introversion is not well understood in our society, so I spend a great deal of time explaining this personality type to parents. They are quite relieved to learn that the naturally reticent behaviors of their child, their spouse, or themselves are healthy rather than abnormal. My colleagues and I administer the Myers-Briggs Type Indicator (Myers, 1962) to families that come to our center for counseling and then interpret the results in terms of family dynamics. Families are usually surprised that their interactions can be depicted so accurately through a test. The result is that family members come to appreciate each other's differences to a greater extent and stop trying to mold each other into their own likenesses.

Peer Relations

Controversy exists in the field as to whether gifted children experience greater adjustment difficulties than children of lesser capabilities (Grossberg & Cornell, 1988; Janos & Robinson, 1985). Some of the obstacles to resolving this question are the lack of instrumentation suited to this population, the extent to which gifted children mask their problems, and the lack of differentiation in most studies between mildly, moderately, and highly gifted.

Using Harter's (1979) Perceived Competence Scale for Children, we found major discrepancies between children's cognitive and social self-concept at the moderately gifted range (132 IQ Stanford-Binet, Form L-M) (Silverman, Chitwood, & Waters, 1986). There were no differences between these scores for the nongifted in our sample, and insignificant differences for children in the mildly gifted range (120–131 IQ). As children increased in measured intelligence, so did the gap between their confidence in their intellectual abilities and their confidence in their social skills. Other researchers have had similar results. Katz (1981) also found increased discrepancies between cognitive and social self-concept scores on the Harter scale as a function of IQ. Ross and Parker (1980) found that gifted students had lower expectations for success in their social endeavors than in their academic ones, and Freeman (1979) reported that moderately gifted children (mean IQ 134) had fewer friends than "average" children (mean IQ 119).

Hollingworth (1942) contended that highly gifted children (above 145 IQ) were more prone to develop social adjustment problems than were mildly gifted children. Terman and Oden (1935) supported her conclusions. Grossberg and Cornell (1988) failed to find adjustment problems among children enrolled in gifted programs; however, this does not refute previous research. All the studies previously reported were of children *not* enrolled in gifted programs. When the highly gifted children we assessed were placed in a school for the gifted and then retested on the Harter scale, their cognitive and social self-concept scores were much closer together. Programs for the gifted

tend to have a beneficial effect on social relations (Higham & Buescher, 1987; Hultgren & Strop, 1985).

> In an environment where all students are gifted and where intelligence and ability are highly valued, social relationships flourish. For many, this is the first time that they feel "average" or "normal," which for adolescents, can be a great relief. (Higham & Buescher, 1987, p. 30)

The solution to peer problems for the gifted is usually the location of gifted peers (Roedell, 1985, 1988). I recommend that parents enroll their children in self-contained classes for the gifted (public or private), pullout programs, enrichment classes, or summer opportunities for the gifted in order to locate potential friends for them. Parents should also join support groups for parents of the gifted so that they can meet others with children close to their child's age. In rural areas, pen pals or computer buddies can reduce the feeling of isolation.

Contrary to superstitions about associations with other gifted students preventing these children from adjusting to the real world, their ability to relate to heterogenous groups increases from finding others like themselves. Higham and Buescher (1987) reported a carryover effect from the positive social experiences of adolescents in summer enrichment programs to their regular school experiences: The students felt more comfortable and socially adept. Once they had found friends who truly appreciated them, laughed at their jokes, and enjoyed their company, their self-confidence increased in other situations. They demanded less from average peers because they knew that somewhere someone liked them just the way they were.

Increased Tension

Although there are reports in the literature of increased tension in families caused by labeling a child gifted (Cornell, 1984; Dirks, 1979; Fine, 1977), I have seen little evidence of this in my practice. One reason my experience differs is that I rarely label one child in the family as the gifted one. My research indicates that when one child in the family is gifted, the rest are not far behind (Silverman, 1986a). In one study, we reviewed the IQ scores of 148 sets of siblings and found that 35.8% were within 5 points of each other, and 61.5% were within 10 points of each other (Silverman, 1988b). When discrepancies were much larger, one of the siblings usually had a learning disability or a history of chronic otitis media (inflammation of the middle ear), or else there was a substantial age difference between the siblings at the time of testing.

Several writers have indicated that there is an increase in friction in families in which there are gifted and "nongifted" siblings (Ballering & Koch, 1984; Cornell, 1984; Hackney, 1981; Pfouts, 1980; Sunderlin, 1981). Jealousy and competitiveness among siblings is quite common in this situation, and itself is usually "the bad guy" (see Chapter 20 by Colangelo for more on labeling). One variable that has not been studied is the effect on children of being perceived as nongifted when they are just as bright as the family "star."

Increased tensions do exist, however, when the family focuses on the *achievements* of one child over those of other children. Achievements and abilities are not synonymous. Sloane (1985) reported that parents who have devoted their lives to the tennis champion, concert pianist, or Olympic swimmer in their families have experienced occasional twinges at the neglect of other siblings. The tensions between parents reported by Cornell (1983) can also be explained as a focus on achievement, rather than ability. Fathers tend to perceive giftedness as achievement, whereas mothers perceive giftedness as developmental advancement (Silverman, 1986b). When these discrepant points of view are discussed in counseling, much of the tension is put to rest.

Gifted Children, Gifted Parents

Gifted children usually have gifted parents (Silveman & Kearney, 1989). Other studies have also shown that giftedness runs in families (Albert, 1978, 1980a, 1980b; Burks, Jen-

sen & Terman, 1930; Hollingworth, 1926; MacKinnon, 1962). I see giftedness as a quality of the family, rather than as a quality of one child that differentiates that child from the rest of the family. This lends a different cast to family counseling than an approach that assumes that gifted and nongifted children are randomly distributed in families.

It is painful for parents to acknowledge their own giftedness. Unfortunately, this aspect of parenting the gifted has received little attention in the literature. When we have known one parent's IQ, we have been able to predict the child's abilities within 10 points. Therefore, when a child is identified as gifted, the parents are probably gifted too. Testing their child means dealing with the implications for themselves.

It is not fashionable to speak of the hereditary component of giftedness. But the assumption that gifted children are randomly assigned to nongifted parents does a disservice to families of the gifted. Learning about their own giftedness has had a profound impact on many of the parents who have come to our Gifted Child Development Center. After having their child tested, parents have gone back to school, applied for scholarships, or changed career aspirations as a result of radically altered self-perceptions.

The reaction of the mothers has been particularly revealing. Most of the mothers with whom I have worked have flatly denied any possibility of their own giftedness: "He gets it from his father." These mothers may have gifted parents, spouses, siblings, and children and still see themselves as not gifted—as if the phenomenon could just skip over them. They suffer under the notion that giftedness equals achievement, so they have no basis for recognizing themselves as gifted. When they identify with the characteristics of giftedness in children, this perception slowly begins to change.

I remind mothers that they are their daughters' major role models and suggest that the greatest gift they can give their daughters is the acknowledgment of their own abilities. Otherwise, these girls come to believe, "If mommies can't be gifted, how can I be gifted?"

Counseling groups have been effective in helping women come to terms with their giftedness (Noble, 1989).

Conclusion

Giftedness is a family affair. There are far-reaching implications of this phenomenon for every member of the family. Whether gifted children are recognized or not, labeled or not, encouraged or not, there is no escape from the impact of giftedness on the family system: The characteristics and needs will still be there. Parents of the gifted have not been taken seriously, and this has compounded the problems. Too many of the normal attributes of giftedness are misjudged, and too much misinformation continues to be propagated. Few counselors are aware of the unique concerns of gifted families or prepared to give them appropriate guidance. Without this knowledge base, counselors may prove more harmful than helpful to these families. Counselors are needed who have special training in the area of giftedness and who understand the powerful emotional lives of their gifted clients.

REFERENCES

Albert, R. S. (1978). Observations and suggestions regarding giftedness, familial influence, and the achievement of eminence. *Gifted Child Quarterly, 22*, 201–211.

Albert, R. S. (1980a). Exceptionally gifted boys and their parents. *Gifted Child Quarterly, 24*, 174–179.

Albert, R. S. (1980b). Family positions and the attainment of eminence: A study of special family positions and special family experiences. *Gifted Child Quarterly, 24*, 87–95.

Ballering, L. D., & Koch, A. (1984). Family relations when a child is gifted. *Gifted Child Quarterly, 28*, 140–143.

Baumrind, D. (1971). Current patterns of parental authority. *Developmental Psychology Monograph, 4*(1, Pt. 2), 1–103.

Bloom, B. S. (1964). *Stability and change in human characteristics*. New York: Wiley.

Bloom, B. S. (Ed.). (1985). *Developing talent in young people*. New York: Ballantine.

Bloom, B. S., & Sosniak, L. A. (1981). Talent development vs. schooling. *Educational Leadership, 39*(2), 86–94.

Bridges, S. (1973). *Problems of the gifted child IQ-150*. New York: Crane, Russak.

Burks, B. S., Jensen, D. W., & Terman, L. M. (1930). *Genetic studies of genius: Vol. 3. The promise of youth: Follow-up of 1000 gifted children*. Stanford, CA: Stanford University Press.

Clark, B. (1988). *Growing up gifted* (3rd ed.). Columbus, OH: Merrill.

Colangelo, N., & Dettmann, D. F. (1983). A review of research on parents and families of gifted children. *Exceptional Children, 50*, 20–27.

Cornell, D. G. (1983). Gifted children: The impact of positive labeling on the family system. *American Journal of Orthopsychiatry, 53*, 322–336.

Cornell, D. G. (1984). *Families of gifted children*. Ann Arbor: UMI Research Press.

Cox, J., Daniel, N., & Boston, B. O. (1985). *Educating able learners: Programs and promising practices*. Austin: University of Texas Press.

Csikszentmihalyi, M., & Beattie, O. V. (1979). Life themes: A theoretical and empirical exploration of their origins and effects. *Journal of Humanistic Psychology, 19*(1), 45–63.

Dabrowski, K. (1972). *Psychoneurosis is not an illness*. London: Gryf.

Dabrowski, K., & Piechowski, M. M. (1977). *Theory of levels of emotional development* (Vols. I & II). Oceanside, NY: Dabor Science.

Daurio, S. P. (1979). Educational enrichment versus acceleration: A review of the literature. In W. C. George, S. J. Cohn, & J. C. Stanley (Eds.), *Educating the gifted: Acceleration and enrichment* (pp. 13–63). Baltimore, MD: Johns Hopkins University Press.

Dembinski, R. J., & Mauser, A. J. (1978). Parents of the gifted: Perceptions of psychologists and teachers. *Journal for the Education of the Gifted, 1*, 5–14.

Dettmann, D. F., & Colangelo, N. (1980). A functional model for counseling parents of gifted students. *Gifted Child Quarterly, 24*, 158–161.

Dewing, K., & Taft, R. (1973). Some characteristics of the parents of creative twelve-year-olds. *Journal of Personality, 41*, 71–85.

Dickinson, R. M. (1970). *Caring for the gifted*. North Quincy, MA: Christopher.

Dirks, J. (1979). Parent's reactions to identification of the gifted. *Roeper Review, 2*(2), 9–10.

Dowdall, C. B., & Colangelo, N. (1982). Underachieving gifted students: Review and implications. *Gifted Child Quarterly, 26*, 179–184.

Elkind, D. (1981). *The hurried child: Growing up too fast too soon*. Reading, MA: Addison-Wesley.

Ellenhorn, J. H. (1988). Rules, roles, and responsibilities. *Understanding Our Gifted, 1*(2), 1, 12–13.

Felder, R. M. (1986). Identifying and dealing with exceptionally gifted children: The half-blind leading the sighted. *Roeper Review, 8*, 174–177.

Feldman, D. (1979). The mysterious case of extreme giftedness. In A. H. Passow (Ed.), *The gifted and talented: Their education and development* (The 78th yearbook of the National Society for the Study of Education, Part I, pp. 335–351). Chicago: The University of Chicago Press.

Fine, M. J. (1977). Facilitating parent–child relationships for creativity. *Gifted Child Quarterly, 21*, 487–500.

Fine, M. J., & Pitts, R. (1980). Intervention with underachieving gifted children: Rationale and strategies. *Gifted Child Quarterly, 24*, 51–55.

Freeman, J. (1979). *Gifted children*. Baltimore, MD: University Park Press.

Ginsberg, G., & Harrison, C. H. (1977). *How to help your gifted child*. New York: Monarch.

Goertzel, M. G., Goertzel, V., & Goertzel, T. G. (1978). *Three hundred eminent personalities*. San Francisco: Jossey-Bass.

Grossberg, I. N., & Cornell, D. G. (1988). Relationship between personality adjustment and high intelligence: Terman versus Hollingworth. *Exceptional Children, 55*, 266–272.

Hackney, H. (1981). The gifted child, the family, and the school. *Gifted Child Quarterly, 25*, 51–54.

Harter, S. (1979). *Perceived competence scale for children*. Denver: University of Denver, Department of Psychology.

Higham, S. J., & Buescher, T. M. (1987). What young gifted adolescents understand about feeling different. In T. M. Buescher (Ed.), *Understanding gifted and talented adolescents: A resource guide for counselors, educators, and parents* (pp. 26–30). Evanston, IL: The Center for Talent Development, Northwestern University.

Hollingworth, L. S. (1926). *Gifted children: Their nature and nurture*. New York: Macmillan.

Hollingworth, L. S. (1940). The positive aspect of hereditary strength. In L. S. Hollingworth, *Public addresses* (pp. 98–103). Lancaster, PA: Science Press Printing.

Hollingworth, L. S. (1942). *Children above 180 IQ Stanford-Binet: Origin and development*. Yonkers-on-Hudson, NY: World Book.

Hultgren, H. (1989). A case for acceleration. *Understanding Our Gifted, 1*(3), 1, 8–10.

Hultgren, H., & Strop, J. (1985, April). *A profile of the characteristics, needs and counseling preferences of Talent Search Summer Institute partici-* *pants*. Paper presented at the annual meeting, American Educational Research Association, Chicago.

Jackson, R. M., Cleveland, J. C., & Merenda, P. F. (1975). Longitudinal effects of early identification and counseling of underachievers. *Journal of School Psychology, 13*, 119–128.

Janos, P. M., & Robinson, N. M. (1985). Psychosocial development in intellectually gifted children. In F. D. Horowitz, & M. O'Brien (Eds.), *The gifted and talented: Developmental perspectives* (pp. 149–195). Washington, DC: American Psychological Association.

Janos, P. M., et al. (1988). A cross-sectional developmental study of the social relations of students who enter college early. *Gifted Child Quarterly, 32*, 210–215.

Katz, E. L. (1981). *Perceived competence in elementary level gifted children*. Unpublished doctoral dissertation, University of Denver, Denver, CO.

Kearney, K. (1988). The highly gifted: School placement. *Understanding Our Gifted, 1*(2), 14–15.

Lewis, M., Young, G., Brooks, J., & Michalson, L. (1975). The beginning of friendship. In M. Lewis & L. A. Rosenblum (Eds.), *Friendship and peer relations* (pp. 27–66). New York: Wiley.

MacKinnon, D. W. (1962). The nature and nurture of creative talent. *American Psychologist, 17*, 484–495.

Marland, S. J. (1972). *Education of the gifted and talented* (Report to the Congress of the United States by the U.S. Commissioner of Education). Washington, DC: U.S. Government Printing Office.

Mink, O. G. (1964). Multiple counseling with underachieving junior high school pupils of bright-normal and higher ability. *Journal of Educational Research, 58*, 31–34.

Montemayor, R. (1987). Parents and adolescents: Understanding the cycles of conflict and affection in relationships. In T. M. Buescher (Ed.), *Understanding gifted and talented adolescents: A resource guide for counselors, educators, and parents* (pp. 24–25). Evanston, IL: The Center for Talent Development, Northwestern University.

Myers, I. B. (1962). Manual for the *The Myers-Briggs type indicator*. Palo Alto, CA: Consulting Psychologists.

Nathan, C. (1979). Parental involvement. In A. H. Passow (Ed.), *The gifted and talented: Their education and development* (The 78th yearbook of the National Society for the Study of Education, Part I, pp. 255–271). Chicago: University of Chicago Press.

Noble, K. (1989). Living out the promise of high

potential: Perceptions of 100 gifted women. *Advanced Development, 1,* 57–75.

Ogburn-Colangelo, M. K. (1979). Giftedness as multilevel potential: A clinical example. In N. Colangelo & R. T. Zaffrann (Eds.), *New voices in counseling the gifted* (pp. 165–187). Dubuque, IA: Kendall/Hunt.

Page, B. A. (1983). A parents' guide to understanding the behavior of gifted children. *Roeper Review, 5*(4), 39–42.

Parker, M., Ross, A., & Duetsch, R. (1980). Parenting the gifted adolescent. *Roeper Review, 2*(4), 40–42.

Perkins, J. A., & Wicas, E. A. (1971). Group counseling of bright underachievers and their mothers. *Journal of Counseling Psychology, 18,* 273–278.

Pfouts, J. H. (1980). Birth order, age spacing, I.Q. differences and family relations. *Journal of Marriage and the Family, 42,* 517–531.

Piechowski, M. M. (1979). Developmental potential. In N. Colangelo & R. T. Zaffrann (Eds.), *New voices in counseling the gifted* (pp. 25–57). Dubuque, IA: Kendall/Hunt.

Piechowski, M. M. (1986). The concept of developmental potential. *Roeper Review, 8,* 190–197.

Piechowski, M. M. (1987). Family qualities and the emotional development of older gifted students. In T. M. Buescher (Ed.), *Understanding gifted and talented adolescents* (pp. 17–23). Evanston, IL: The Center for Talent Development, Northwestern University.

Piechowski, M. M., & Colangelo, N. (1984). Developmental potential of the gifted. *Gifted Child Quarterly, 28,* 80–88.

Robinson, H. B., Roedell, W. C., & Jackson, N. E. (1979). Early identification and intervention. In A. H. Passow (Ed.), *The gifted and talented: Their education and development* (The 78th yearbook of the National Society for the Study of Education, Part I, pp. 138–154). Chicago: University of Chicago Press.

Roedell, W. C. (1985). Developing social competence in gifted preschool children. *Remedial and Special Education, 6,* 6–11.

Roedell, W. C. (1988). I just want my child to be happy: Social development and young gifted children. *Understanding Our Gifted, 1,* 1, 7, 10–11.

Rogers, M. T. (1986). *A comparative study of developmental traits of gifted and average youngsters.* Unpublished doctoral dissertation, University of Denver.

Ross, A. O. (1964). *The exceptional child in the family.* New York: Grune & Stratton.

Ross, A., & Parker, M. (1980). Academic and social self concepts of the academically gifted. *Exceptional Children, 47,* 6–10.

Sanborn, M. P. (1979). Counseling and guidance needs of the gifted and talented. In A. H. Passow (Ed.), *The gifted and talented: Their education and development* (The 78th yearbook of the National Society for the Study of Education, Part I, pp. 424–438). Chicago: University of Chicago Press.

Sebring, A. D. (1983). Parental factors in the social and emotional adjustment of the gifted. *Roeper Review, 6,* 97–99.

Shaw, M. C., & McCuen, J. T. (1960). The onset of academic underachievement in bright children. *Journal of Educational Psychology, 51,* 103–108.

Silverman, L. K. (1986a). Parenting young gifted children. *Journal of Children in Contemporary Society, 18*(3), 73–87.

Silverman, L. K. (1986b). What happens to the gifted girl? In C. J. Maker (Ed.), *Critical issues in gifted education: Vol. 1. Defensible programs for the gifted* (pp. 43–89). Rockville, MD: Aspen.

Silverman, L. K. (1987a). Applying knowledge about social development to the counseling process with gifted adolescents. In T. M. Buescher (Ed.), *Understanding gifted and talented adolescents* (pp. 117–130). Evanston, IL: The Center for Talent Development, Northwestern University.

Silverman, L. K. (1987b, June). *The crucible of perfectionism.* Paper presented at the Fourth International Conference on the Theory of Positive Disintegration, Warsaw, Poland.

Silverman, L. K. (1988a, September/October). Problems in assessing the gifted. *The Kaleidoscope,* pp. 3–5.

Silverman, L. K. (1988b, October). The second child syndrome. *Mensa Bulletin, No. 320,* pp. 18–20.

Silverman, L. K. (1989a). The highly gifted. In J. F. Feldhusen, J. VanTassel-Baska & K. R. Seeley Eds.), *Excellence in educating the gifted* (pp. 71–83). Denver: Love.

Silverman, L. K. (1989b). Invisible gifts, invisible handicaps. *Roeper Review, 12,* 37–42.

Silverman, L. K. Chitwood, D. G., & Waters, J. L. (1986). Young gifted children: Can parents identify giftedness? *Topics in Early Childhood Special Education, 6,* 23–38.

Silverman, L. K., & Kearney, K. (1989). Parents of the extraordinarily gifted. *Advanced Development, 1,* 41–56.

Silverman, L. K., & Waters, J. L. (1988, November). *The Silverman/Waters Checklist: A new culture-fair identification instrument.* Paper presented at the 35th annual convention of the National Association for Gifted Children, Orlando, FL.

Simonton, D. K. (1978). The eminent genius in history: The critical role of creative development. *The Gifted Child Quarterly, 22,* 187–195.

Sloane, K. D. (1985). Home influences on talent development. In B. S. Bloom (Ed.), *Developing talent in young people* (pp. 439–476). New York: Ballantine.

Stanley, J. (1988). Some characteristics of SMPY's "700–800 on SAT-M before age 13 group:" Youths who reason *extremely* well mathematically. *Gifted Child Quarterly, 32,* 205–209.

Sunderlin, A. (1981). Gifted children and their siblings. In B. S. Miller & M. Puce (Eds.), *The gifted child, the family, and the community,* (pp. 100–106). New York: Walker & Co.

Tannenbaum, A. J. (1983). *Gifted children: Psychological and educational perspectives.* New York: Macmillan.

Terman, L. M., & Oden, M. H. (1935). *Genetic studies of genius: Vol. 5. The promise of youth.* Stanford, CA: Stanford University Press.

Waters, J. L., & Silverman, L. K. (1986). *Educational alternatives for gifted children in the Denver metropolitan area.* Denver: Gifted Child Development Center.

Weisberg, P. S., & Springer, K. J. (1961). Environmental factors in creative function. *Archives of General Psychiatry, 5,* 554–564.

Whitmore, J. R. (1979). Discipline and the gifted child. *Roeper Review, 2,* 42–46.

Whitmore, J. R. (1980). *Giftedness, conflict, and underachievement.* Boston: Allyn and Bacon.

Witty, P. A. (1958). Who are the gifted? In N. B. Henry (Ed.), *Education for the gifted* (The 57th yearbook of the National Society for the Study of Education, Part II, pp. 42–63). Chicago: University of Chicago Press.

Zilli, M. J. (1971). Reasons why the gifted adolescent underachieves and some of the implications of guidance and counseling to this problem. *Gifted Child Quarterly, 15,* 279–292.

23

Career Development

PHILIP A. PERRONE   *University of Wisconsin, Madison*

My goals in writing this chapter are threefold. First, I want to explain briefly why counseling psychologists place such great importance on understanding career development of gifted students. Second, I want to introduce the reader to the writings of two career theorists. Gottfredson (1981) offers a structure that enables us to better understand gifted persons' career development because her theory is based on cognitive development. Holland's (1962, 1973) model helps in understanding the direction career development takes. Third, I will identify unique factors in career development of the gifted in order to highlight how their career development deviates from career development of other students.

Counseling Psychology and Career Development

Herr and Cramer (1988) succinctly define career development as "understanding the factors underlying free and informed choice, the evolution of personal identity in regard to work, and the transition, induction, and adjustment to work" (p. 98). Their definition suggests that successful career development is fundamental to achieving the promises of a democracy, namely, making free and informed choices. Their definition also suggests that free and informed career choices are the basis of adult mental health.

Gottfredson's Theory of Occupational Aspirations

Gottfredson (1981) has presented a theory of how occupational aspirations develop from early childhood through the college years, basing her theory on the writings of Van den

Daele's (1968) description of cognitive development and the formation of children's ego-ideals (see Table 23.1). She clearly took some liberty in compacting his 10 levels into 5 stages. Also, Gottfredson did not develop her theory in regard to Van den Daele's 9th and 10th levels of conceptual development. That is, she failed to elaborate on a 5th stage because only a tiny fraction of adolescents were seen as exhibiting behavior at this high level of career development. Because, according to Van den Daele, intelligence largely determines the rate at which children and adolescents move through these stages, gifted adolescents may very well make career plans and decisions from the referent point that characterizes this stage.

Gottfredson's theory rests on the assumption that individuals seek jobs compatible with their images of themselves. Gottfredson concurred with Van den Daele that social class, intelligence, and gender are the important determinants of self-concept and of career aspirations. In turn, the compromises made in career planning and career decisions revolve around *expectations,* which are products of social class; job *accessibility,* which is largely dependent upon having the aptitude and opportunity to meet entry requirements; and one's self-definition relative to sex roles.

Overview of Gottfredson's Theory

Gottfredson described four stages of conceptual development and hypothesized that conceptual development and career development leapfrog one another. These stages were identified as (1) an orientation to size and power (ages 3 to 5 years), (2) an orientation to sex roles (ages 6 to 8 years), (3) an orientation to social valuation (ages 9 to 13 years), and (4) an orientation to the internal, unique self (beginning around age 14). I will attempt to be consistent with

Table 23.1
Gottfredson's Stages of Occupational Aspirations

Van den Daele's Stages of Cognitive Development	Gottfredson's Stages
1. "I" distinct from others	1. Orientation to size and power (3 to 5 years)
2. Dichotomous organization of thought (pleasing others)	
3. Distinction of before and after (conflict avoidant)	2. Orientation to sex roles (6 to 8 years)
4. Generalization of common characteristics (little man or woman)	
5. Orientation to general sex role expectations (one of the group)	3. Orientation to social valuation (9 to 13 years)
6. Cues in on others' feelings, intentions (social conformist)	
7. Orientation to internalized principles (values) (social agent)	4. Orientation to the internal, unique self (beginning about 14 years)
8. Self-style valued more highly (personal goal orientation) (independent agent)	
9. Integration from among apparent diversity (creative) (striving for personal social good)	5. Integrated world view (late adolescence, young adulthood)[a]
10. Striving for transcendent good (self-actualization)	

[a] Prepared by the present author.

Gottfredson's perspective when making a 5th career development stage of Van den Daele's 9th and 10th levels, which Gottfredson only briefly described as an integrated world view evidenced through reflective consideration of the human situation.

To maintain the appropriate perspective throughout this chapter, it should be noted that children and adolescents, probably even most adults, do not focus on job activities in career decision making, but rather focus on both the lifestyle that corresponds to the occupation and the personalities of individuals they know who are engaged in the occupation. They know little about what people do on the job and even less about the pathways to entering various occupations.

The Five Stages

1. *An orientation to size and power (ages 3 to 5):* This is when the child first has an inkling of what *adult* means and what it means to be an adult. Career aspirations at this stage involve fantasy and immediate gratification with little

future time consideration. The adult is perceived as controlling all the resources relative to both activity and gratification, and thus adulthood is valued because of the control over desired resources exhibited by adults.

2. *An orientation to sex roles (ages 6 to 8):* Gender self-concept is thought to be consolidated in this stage of development. Children are oriented to differences in size between themselves and adults and between males and females. They equate size with power, and while the desire to "grow up" emerges, the child has little or no concept of how long the maturation process takes. Occupational preferences are sex-typed more along a *power-size* dimension than according to sex roles per se at this stage. Kohlberg (1966) noted that children are able to consistently differentiate between sex roles at this age regardless of parental role behavior. Gottfredson suggested that the developmental pattern regarding sex roles appears associated with cognitive development. The bottom line for Gottfredson was that children's occupational preferences in this stage reflect a concern with doing what is sex-appropriate.

3. *An orientation to social valuation (ages 9 to 13):* During this period such abstract and subtle factors as social class and ability become determinants of behavior and expectations. Differences in the prestige associated with various jobs are recognized, and social class and intellectual differences in behavior and attitude become more apparent to young adolescents. Also, peer influence on both behavior and aspirations is considerable. The emerging adolescent is able to cue into social class and intellectual differences in speech as well as in dress. In effect, the development of social class stereotypes and occupational stereotypes parallel one another, with preferences for higher occupational levels corresponding with higher levels of intelligence. Gottfredson noted that, "More able students aspire to higher level jobs, and within all ability groups the higher social class youngsters have the higher aspirations" (1981, p. 563). The combination of higher intelligence and higher social class free the individual to aspire to a wide range of high-level occupations because most occupations are seen as accessible. For most gifted individuals, going to college is a foregone conclusion. The only choice may be where to go and, in many instances, that too may not be an issue.

4. *An orientation to the internal, unique self (beginning around age 14):* As Gottfredson noted, this age frequently is referred to as the beginning of the adolescent identity crisis. During this stage additional criteria are used to assess the compatibility of the self with various occupations. Gottfredson noted that, typically, occupations that are perceived as inappropriate for one's sex are discarded first, followed by occupations that are outside one's *social class comfort range,* either being too low or too high. The amount of effort required to attain different occupational levels within different fields of occupational endeavor is also assessed, with individuals discarding any that appear to demand excessive effort—a thought that may not enter the minds of many gifted students. Holland's (1962) schema for differentiating between occupational fields will be introduced later in this chapter because it helps

to explain the particular direction that gifted students' career aspirations can take.

5. *Integrated world view evidenced through reflective consideration of the human situation (beginning in late adolescence or young adulthood):* Van den Daele noted that the transition into his highest two levels of conceptual development (Gottfredson's 5th stage) are not explained in terms of changes in cognitive processes. He implied that rich and diverse life experiences are the necessary precursors to attaining the conceptual level that constitutes this 5th stage. Van den Daele further discussed finding a striking difference in the career motivation of males and females, with *achievement* being more congruent with a masculine identity and *morality* more congruent with a feminine identity. One can only speculate whether child-rearing practices and adult role models of both sexes have changed sufficiently to bring his 1960 view into question.

What characterizes 5th-stage thought processes and behaviors? Van den Daele's descriptors include the following: Self–society relationships are being attended to from both an immediate and a historical perspective; intuition is trusted and valued; conflicts with society are recognized, accepted, and even welcomed; a world view is superordinate to self-interest; emphasis is on becoming; means are construed as coequal with ends; and the individual engages in poetic, dialectical thinking (Van den Daele, 1968).

A linear, rational, self–occupation congruence model of career planning and decision making is not applicable to a person's functioning at this value-based stage of conceptual wisdom. Probably, this 5th stage also is best reflected in the second series of career decisions that follow the completion of a college degree and possibly working for a few years.

In Gottfredson's view, the typical pattern of compromise is to sacrifice one's primary vocational interests first, job level second, and sex type last. Her rationale is that the individual first compromises those attributes that are least central to his or her self-concept and social identity. She also noted that as new criteria for judging self–occupation compatibility are applied, preferences become more complex and also narrower.

Holland's Theory

Gottfredson's writings provided an explanation of how career aspirations evolve. Holland (1962, 1973) provided a model that explains the particular occupational direction that gifted individuals' career aspirations take. I have included Holland's model for several reasons. First, Holland (1962) developed his model by analyzing responses from National Merit finalists, which suggests the model should be relevant in helping to explain the career path or direction that a gifted person pursues. Second, the model is an integral part of the Strong-Campbell Vocational Inventory, which is often administered and interpreted to college students when they are formulating their career plans. Third, a colleague and I (Post-Kammer & Perrone, 1983) successfully used Holland's model for studying the career pathways of 648 adults who had participated in a guidance program for gifted students at the University of Wisconsin–Madison during their high school years.

Holland's theory is based on the assumption that most people can be categorized into one of six personality types and that there are six corresponding kinds of environments. People are assumed to search for compatible environments that will let them exercise their skills and abilities and express their attitudes and values (Holland, 1973). Briefly, Holland's six personality types are:

1. *Investigative (I):* This type prefers activities in which he or she can observe, communicate using symbols, and be creative. The phenomena under investigation may be physical, biological, or social-cultural.

2. *Artistic (A):* The artistic person prefers freedom to manipulate one or more of the different modes of human expression to create art forms.

3. *Social (S):* This personality type prefers training, supporting, and teaching others while avoiding explicit, systematic activities.

4. *Enterprising (E):* The enterprising person prefers manipulating others to achieve his or her own goals or the goals of the organization while avoiding explicit, systematic procedures.

5. *Conventional (C):* The conventional type prefers explicit, ordered manipulation of data and has a low tolerance for ambiguous, unsystematic activities.

6. *Realistic (R):* This type prefers explicit, ordered manipulation of tools, machines, or animals and has a low tolerance for ambiguity.

Individuals seldom fall exclusively into one of these types, and so a system was devised to indicate primary and secondary types. Individuals are encouraged to explore various occupations listed under both the primary and the secondary personality types. In essence, Holland hypothesized a *goodness of fit* model of career development wherein individuals match their self-stereotypes with their stereotypes of primary work personalities.

Post-Kammer and I (Post-Kammer & Perrone, 1983) conducted a follow-up study in 1982 of 300 gifted males and 348 gifted females who graduated from 44 different Wisconsin high schools between 1962 and 1975. Respondents ranged in age from 24 to 35. We inquired about perceptions of their career development since graduating from high school and asked several questions regarding their current work activities and future plans. Interestingly, the age of the respondents was not a differentiating factor when analyzing responses, but there were gender differences in some areas.

Both females (73%) and males (57%) indicated that marriage or a close relationship with a significant other was their most important source of satisfaction. Work was listed as the most important satisfier by 37% of the males and 35% of the females. This finding would suggest that theories of career development should pay attention to the "coupling" tendency of most individuals and the importance of a close interpersonal relationship in overall life satisfaction.

When asked whether they had lived up to their full educational and vocational capabilities, few said yes, but most said they had done reasonably well vocationally (males 66% and females 61%) and educationally (males 56% and females 55%). In terms of work itself, males placed more importance on their income while females emphasized the importance of good relationships with co-workers and supervisors. This finding could be viewed as consistent with Van den Daele's findings (noted earlier) that males are more achievement oriented and females are more morality oriented.

A further analysis of these data (not reported in the original article) showed that after their present occupational status was categorized using Holland's six stages, none of the respondents were engaged in realistic occupations. No males and only a few females were engaged in conventional occupations. Very few females or males were engaged in artistic occupations, and those who were in artistic occupations had been fully involved with some art form while in high school. The majority of the males were engaged in investigative and enterprising occupations, and the majority of the females were engaged in investigative and social occupations such as teaching and social work. Some females entered social occupations because of others' expectations.

Within the investigative occupations there were discernible differences among those engaged in the physical, natural, and social sciences. These differences were at least partly predictable based on students' patterns of high school grades, their extracurricular activities, and their performance on standardized achievement test scores.

Necessary Environmental Conditions

Bloom and Sosniak (1981) detailed the learning conditions experienced by persons achieving excellence in three areas: artistic (concert pianists and sculptors), psychomotor (Olympic swimmers and tennis players), and cognitive (research mathematicians and research neurologists). A retrospective interview was used to obtain data from the most capable Americans they could locate in these three areas who had achieved an international level of accomplishment. Their main findings related to career development were as follows:

1. The majority had become highly involved in their particular field before age 12, and their parent(s) or a relative had a strong interest in the talent area. This significant person supported and encouraged development in the specific talent field.

2. The curriculum of the home consisted of language, resources needed to develop the special talent area, and high expectations for the child.

3. Most instruction was one-to-one.

4. Parents made adjustments in their lives in order for the child to acquire her or his talent.

5. Emphasis was more on mastery than competition.

6. By adolescence the parents' instructor role was transferred to an outside teacher.

7. Recitals, contests, or concerts served to heighten the level of learning and emotions prior to as well as during the performance. Effective teachers used the opportunity afforded by these performances to relate current skills to long-term goals.

8. Once the child embarked on learning his or her talent, from age 10 or so, other activities became subordinate.

9. During adolescence, 15 to 25 hours a week were spent practicing. During this same period their aspirations (career goals) ruled much of their lives.

The factors considered essential in the development of their talent provide convincing evidence that talent does not develop on its own and that aspirations are a major component in the career development of exceptionally gifted individuals.

Unique Aspects of Gifted Persons' Career Development

Thirty years of studying gifted persons' career development has led me to believe there are three sets of factors uniquely contributing to their career development: *psychological, psychocreative,* and *social.* By noting what I believe is unique in their career development I am attempting to define *giftedness* from a career development perspective.

Psychological Factors

1. Traditional sex-role stereotypes are less a factor in the self-identity of gifted persons compared with others.
2. There is a greater likelihood of gifted persons working at one job for life.
3. Work is central to the identity of gifted persons (high ego involvement).
4. They have a strong need to achieve mastery.
5. They have a strong desire, seemingly an innate need, to make an *impact* on society.
6. The gifted individual frequently feels exhilirated, rather than exhausted, when pursuing a goal; thus both means and ends are highly satisfying.

Psychocreative Factors

7. There is constant testing of personal and environmental limits, a challenge of the status quo, continual questioning of self and others, and less need for closure.
8. Gifted individuals are highly capable of creating their own futures.
9. They are risk takers.
10. They actually create, and even seek to maintain, dissonance in their lives as proof to themselves that they are fully engaged in life.

Social Factors

11. The gifted have greater future awareness (more emphasis on becoming than being).
12. They have a more worldly view.
13. They have a greater sense of social responsibility.

Conclusions

My conclusions regarding gifted children's and adolescents' career development are as follows:

1. Their conceptual and career development seem interdependent. If the two do leap-frog, fostering career development is essential to furthering conceptual development, and vice versa.

2. They are more likely to operate in the 5th stage of development (value-based) at critical career-decision-making points, such as high school and college graduation. Therefore, typical deductive career-decision-making strategies are inappropriate. Rather, creative and intuitive approaches to decision making are needed.

3. Because aptitudes are high, they are not likely to be limiting factors in making choices. The floor of acceptable occupations is high and the ceiling unlimited ("You can be whatever you want"). Therefore, gifted persons' career compromises, when necessary, are radically different from the norm. So much freedom of career choice can border on ambiguity, and ambiguity can be frightening and even destructive without structure and support from others.

4. Career pathways are oriented primarily toward Holland's investigative and enterprising occupations, suggesting the need to provide more precise information regarding the activities and lifestyles of individuals engaged in these two occupational areas.

5. Conflicting feelings may arise from having to engage in lengthy preparation periods. Such a commitment prolongs dependency, while gifted students feel a strong need for independence.

6. Gifted women receive conflicting and confusing signals from society relative to both the level of career aspiration that is deemed appropriate and the particular fields of study that are considered gender appropriate.

7. Gifted children from economically disadvantaged backgrounds require early intervention to reduce the limiting effects of a lower social class background and to raise their typically lower levels of career expectations.

REFERENCES

Bloom, B. S., & Sosniak, L. A. (1981). Talent development vs. schooling. *Educational Leadership, 39*(2), 86–94.

Gottfredson, L. S. (1981). Circumspection and compromise: A developmental theory of occupational aspirations. *Journal of Counseling Psychology Monograph, 28,* 545–579.

Herr, E. L., & Cramer, S. H. (1988). *Career guidance and counseling through the life span.* Glenview, IL: Scott, Foresman.

Holland, J. L. (1962). Some explorations of a theory of vocational choice: One- and two-year longitudinal studies. *Psychological Monographs, 76*(26, Whole No. 545).

Holland, J. L. (1973). *Making vocational choices: A theory of careers.* Englewood Cliffs, NJ: Prentice-Hall.

Kohlberg, L. A. (1966). A cognitive-developmental analysis of children's sex-role concepts and attitudes. In E. Maccoby (Ed.), *The development of sex differences* (pp. 82–173). Palo Alto, CA: Stanford University Press.

Post-Kammer, P., & Perrone, P. A. (1983). Career perceptions of talented individuals: A follow-up study. *Vocational Guidance Quarterly, 31,* 203–211.

Van den Daele, L. (1968). A developmental study of the ego-ideal. *Genetic Psychology Monographs, 78,* 191–256.

24

Underachievement and Superachievement: Flip Sides of the Same Psychological Coin

SYLVIA B. RIMM   *Family Achievement Clinic, Oconomowoc, Wisconsin*

∎ Half of the gifted children in the United States do not perform up to their tested abilities (National Commission on Excellence in Education, 1984). Although some of these students may reverse their underachievement patterns because of educational interventions or increasing maturity, some will underachieve for life. Giftedness itself does not ensure educational or creative success or productivity. There are risks and pressures (Rimm, 1987a) that accompany high intelligence and that detour potentially high achieving children toward defensive and avoidance patterns. The determinants of whether gifted children move toward superachievement—a level of success commensurate with their high potential—or toward underachievement appear to be related to their home, school, and/or peer environments (Rimm, 1986a).

The Pressures

The main pressures that some gifted children seem to feel include (1) the need to be extraordinarily intelligent and/or perfect; (2) the wish to be extremely creative and unusual, which they may translate as nonconforming; and (3) the concern with being admired by peers for appearance and popularity.

Although parents are often accused of pressuring their gifted children, typically these pressures arise by reason of the children's giftedness. They have internalized a sense of stress because adults in their environments have admired them for their academic accomplishment, their unusual ideas, and/or their appearance. The profuse praise that they receive reinforces their motivation but, when too extreme or frequent, may also cause them to feel too determined to accomplish the goals that are so admired or valued by others. They not only may feel pressured to achieve, but also may acquire a dependence on attention that can be an addiction. Thus, they find it difficult to function without continual praise and reinforcement. Their intrinsic reinforcement is diminished by their dependence on extrinsic reinforcement (Hom, Gaskill, & Hutchins, 1988).

If school and home environments foster successful relationships between effort and outcomes, it is more likely that children will manage the internalized pressures and will incorporate them as motivations toward achievement. Figure 24.1 illustrates four potential relationships between effort and outcomes (Rimm, 1987b).

Quadrant 1 represents achievement, or the appropriate relationship between effort and outcomes. These children may have internalized pressures to be bright, creative, and approved by others, but their goals represent realistic possibilities. These children enjoy and value attention but are not *attention addicted* or dependent on continual approval. Intelligence, creative production, and positive peer adjustment are appropriate and realistic goals for them because the goals are not set at perfectionistic extremes. These children may pressure themselves toward high grades, toward unique idea production, and toward approval by adults and friends, but they also feel a sense of intrinsic satisfaction with their accomplishments. They continue to set goals higher, but those goals represent potentially attainable achievements. They also demonstrate appropriate efforts. They have learned to work hard. They understand perseverance. They have the appropriate skills, including strategies for thinking, study, and creative

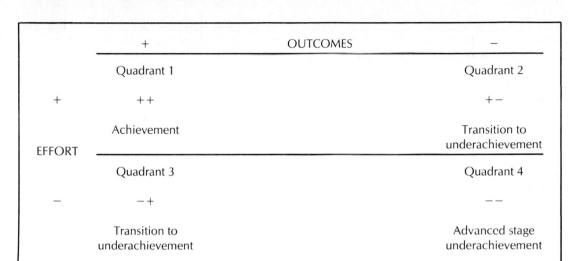

Figure 24.1 Relationship between effort and outcomes.

production. Their basic skills, including reading, math, and writing, are not deficient, although some may be stronger than others. Perseverance and an intrinsic enjoyment of challenge are already part of the process, and easy tasks are accomplished quickly in order that they may pursue more challenging activities. They will usually continue to achieve if they see the relationship between the learning process and its outcomes (Rimm, 1986a).

Quadrants 2 and 3 represent relationships between effort and outcomes that are transitional stages to underachievement. If the mismatch between effort and outcomes continues, children are likely to lose their sense of personal control over outcomes. This is likely to result in serious underachievement (Quadrant 4).

High-Risk School Environments

School environments that foster Quadrant 2 (positive effort, negative outcomes), a transitional stage of underachievement, are those that do not value high-achievement outcomes. In these situations, children may make appropriate efforts, but they do not gain satisfaction from their successful efforts. Some school environments that do not value or reward excellent school achievement include the following:

1. An anti-intellectual school atmosphere that sets high priorities for athletics or social status, but not for intellectual attainment or preparation for higher level education.
2. An antigifted atmosphere that considers gifted programming to be elitist and emphasizes the importance of all students being well adjusted and "fitting into a mold."
3. A rigid classroom environment that encourages all children to study identical materials at similar speeds or in similar styles.
4. Teachers who rigidly do not see the quality of children's work either because of different values, personal power struggles, or cultural or racial prejudice. They may cause children to feel unable to accomplish high-quality outcomes despite their efforts (Davis & Rimm, 1989; Rimm, 1980).

School environments that cause the Quadrant 3 (negative effort, positive outcomes) transitional stage of underachievement are those that value the children's accomplishments but do not provide them with tasks that encourage challenge or sustained efforts. In effect, the work is too easy. These schools value good grades and performance and, initially, grades reflect excellent performance. Children tend to feel positive about school, but they are not sufficiently challenged. Teacher bias against accelerated curriculum often prevents schools from challenging these students. Children learn that achievement is easy, that success is readily attainable, and that study and learning require little effort. Occasionally, they may comment about boredom or the lack of challenge, but as long as grades continue to be high they exhibit no problem behaviors.

When the curriculum becomes more complex or when students enter higher grades, where their peer population is more intellectually competitive, they feel they are not as intelligent as they believed they were earlier. Some learn more appropriate study habits. Others hide from their threatening feelings. They worry that they are not as smart as they would like to be, and they invent or discover a whole group of rituals and excuses that prevent them from making further effort.

One college student asked me if I thought her "brain cells might be dissolving," and many bright high school students have told me that "if you're smart, schoolwork should be easy." Peer messages about being "casual" or "cool" also reinforce a model of not making "too much" school effort. A fifth-grade boy's conclusion that he would like "to get all As without carrying a book" makes the point well.

Procrastination, incomplete assignments, disorganization, and careless work become the typical symptoms that initiate an underachievement syndrome for these students (Rimm, 1986a). They will change only when gradually persuaded to take the risk of making a higher school effort; and they will then find out that they are, indeed, highly capable. Perhaps even with appropriate effort, they will be required to set more realistic goals. Their school environments have simply not taught them the challenging *process* of achievement.

Quadrant 4 represents the advanced stage of underachievement syndrome (negative effort, negative outcomes). It results after children described in Quadrants 2 or 3 have not functioned as achievers for a period of time. Quadrant 4 underachievement takes place when children's habits, efforts, and skills cause them to lose their sense of control over their school outcomes. Teachers are less likely to identify these children as gifted because their intelligence or creativity may no longer be evi-

dent in the classroom. Even parents begin to doubt their children's abilities. They may recall that their children were "smart" at some point in the past, but now they may be willing to settle for their gifted children's very average and sometimes below-average achievement.

Quadrant 4 underachievement is difficult but not impossible to cure. When these children or adolescents are asked if they consider themselves intelligent, they usually acknowledge that they believe they are. However, the confidence they lack is related to their sense of being unable to accomplish or function in a way that will represent themselves as capable and productive. They have not internalized the process of achievement. Their goals may remain extremely high, but they expect some kind of magical deliverance or at least a lucky break instead of making directed efforts. They avoid challenges and automatically search for an easy way out.

High-Risk Home Environments

The family characteristics of underachievers have been described in several studies (Frazier, Passow, & Goldberg, 1958; French, 1959; Whitmore, 1980; Zilli, 1971). Rimm and Lowe (1988) targeted some critical differences between the families of 22 gifted underachievers (17 males, 5 females) and studies of the families of persons of high achievement and eminence. The main differences are highlighted and the findings summarized in Tables 24.1, 24.2, and 24.3.

Although both groups of parents showed concern about the achievement of their children, in the families of underachieving gifted, the modeling of intrinsic and independent learning, positive commitment to career, and respect for school were remarkably, although unintentionally, absent. The enrichment and fun of early childhood were often replaced by a plethora of activities and lessons that were so time consuming that they left little energy for continued home learning, independent projects, or family game playing. Management by parents of students' homework resulted in dependent patterns and parent–child arguments.

Table 24.1
A Comparison of Family Structural Characteristics of Eminent Gifted Versus Underachieving Gifted

Characteristics	Eminent Gifted[a]	Underachieving Gifted[b]	Comparison
Size of family	Small	2.59 children	Similar
Birth order	More than half oldest	59% oldest	Similar
Only children	Percentage varied	27%	Similar to some, different from some
Adopted children in family	Not reported	23%	Not reported, probably different
Male/female	More males	More males	Similar
Specialness	Earned specialness	Specialness displaced for 81%; 18% never earned specialness	Different
Age of parents at marriage	Older parents fairly typical	Mother, 30; father, 32	Similar
Education of parents	Higher education fairly typical	Mother, 15.7 years; father, 17.9 years	Similar
Parent loss	Low parent divorce, some parent loss	Low parent divorce, some parent loss	Similar

[a] Tables 24.1, 24.2, and 24.3 are based on research and writing by Bloom (1985); Goertzel and Goertzel (1962); Olszewski, Kulieke, and Buescher (1987); Walberg, Tsai, Weinstein, Gabriel, Rasher, and Rosencrans (1981); and Rimm and Lowe (1988).

[b] Based on a study by Rimm and Lowe (1988) of 22 families of 17 male and 5 female gifted underachievers.

Table 24.2
Family Climate

Characteristics	Eminent Gifted	Underachieving Gifted	Comparison
Child centeredness	Child-centered, high adult personal interest	Child-centered early, low adult personal interest	Similarities and differences
Discord and trauma versus secure supportive families	Mixed findings: Artists, authors more traumatic; scientists, mathematicians more secure	Considerable discord	Different
Parenting style	Mixed, but nonauthoritarian and consistent	Early liberal, then changed to 95% inconsistent "ogre" rituals	Different
Family relationships:			
Father–mother	Usually very good	68% good, 32% bad	Some differences
Child–mother	Usually good	59% poor	Different
Child–father	Usually good	63% poor	Different
Child–siblings	Usually good	45% poor	Different
Structure and organization	Consistent and predictable	Inconsistent; 95% indicated manipulating one or both parents	Different

Table 24.3
Values Espoused and Modeled by Parents

Characteristics	Eminent Gifted	Underachieving Gifted	Comparison
Achievement orientation	Valued work and achievement	Valued work and achievement	Similar
Grade expectations	Reasonable and unpressured	Reasonable and unpressured Mother's expectation: 3.2 GPA Father's expectation: 3.3 GPA	Similar
Early enrichment and activities	Provided	Provided	Similar
Social adjustment of children	Mixed	73% not well accepted by peers	Some differences
High energy of parents	Dramatically consistent	Mainly true	Some differences
Father's career	Mainly committed, positive and sharing interests	Considerable frustration with career; or if positive, not sharing interests	Different
Mother's career	Mainly homemakers, volunteers, busy and happy	Mainly homemakers, volunteers, busy but not satisfied	Different
Identification with same-sexed parent	Mixed results on identification; mainly, boys and girls identified with fathers	4 males identified with father; 1 female identified with mother	Different
School–home relationship	Mainly good and supportive; reasonable school adjustments	90% were oppositional, problem school environments	Different
Homework independence	Independence plus additional independent learning projects; some parent monitoring	59% depended on parents to help with homework; absence of independent learning projects; oppositional monitoring	Different
Intrinsic learning	Frequently modeled by parents	Rarely modeled by parents	Different

Many parents openly opposed teachers and school policies. Parents were involved in opposition to schools in 90% of the families. They rarely shared their own career interests with their children. Most fathers felt quite negative about their own work even though they had often invested many years in preparation for their high-level careers. Well-educated mothers who centered their lives on their children and volunteer activities often voiced frustration at their "nonprofessional" role. Although by societal standards these parents were successful achievers, from their children's perspectives they did not seem happy with their achievements. Green, Fine, and Tollefson (1988) also found that parents' attitudes toward their careers were related to their children's underachievement.

Unlike the theme of family organization and consistent and predictable expectations for conduct that ran through studies of giftedness and eminence (Bloom, 1985; MacKinnon, 1965; Walberg, Tsai, Weinstein, Gabriel, Rasher & Rosencrans, 1981), this theme was noticeably absent in the homes of the underachieving children studied by Rimm and Lowe. Differences between parents in standards, limits, and expectations provided unclear guidelines. In their study, 95% of the students (all but 1) indicated that they could manipulate one or both parents much of the time, and the parents of these children confirmed their children's observations. The absence of consistent leadership among these parents was remarkable.

Although most underachieving children spent their early childhood with parents who considered their parenting to be quite liberal, only one couple maintained that parenting philosophy. By school age, extreme differences in parenting styles emerged. In 95% of the families, one parent played the role of the parent who challenges and disciplines, and the other took the role of protector. There was increasing opposition between parents as the challenger became more authoritarian and the rescuer became increasingly protective. In 54% of the families, the father took on the role of disciplinarian; in 41%, the mother played the authoritarian role. These authoritarian–rescuer rituals are described by Rimm (1986a) as "ogre" games.

According to their parents, 18 of the 22 gifted underachievers were considered by their families to be "special." This sense of specialness was either attached to the parents' early discovery of their child's gifted abilities or based on a long-awaited birth or other unusual circumstance. Later, that specialness was withdrawn and the *special* attribution was given to another family member.

Sometimes the sense of specialness was lost as part of school adjustment. Clinical interviews indicated that all of our sample were given a great deal of early attention. More than half (12) had that attention withdrawn dramatically by a second sibling, who then received the *special* designation, or by a parent's remarriage. In 6 of the cases, only children adjusted poorly to sharing attention at school. In 4 of the cases, children never established a sense of specialness because another sibling was already designated as having that role.

Specific cases provide insights into the trauma felt by children whose specialness is displaced, for example:

Maureen, a gifted ninth-grader, had been adopted. She was showered with extreme quantities of adult attention for the first 6 years of her life. Her younger sister was an unexpected birth child to her parents. Maureen was not only an underachiever throughout school, but shared with the therapist that she could remember always resenting her younger sister, although she could not explain any reasons for her feelings.

Sandy was born to a single mother who felt guilt about her out-of-wedlock pregnancy. Sandy's mother centered almost every waking moment on her child. When her mother married, Sandy felt "disempowered" and angry at her stepfather, with whom she was determined not to share her mother's attention.

In most cases, when the "special" designation was withdrawn, the early dependence on extreme amounts of attention had the effect of causing the children to feel "attention neglected." The search for a way to recover the special attention involved behaviors that parents and teachers often labeled as "spoiled" or "arrogant." Efforts by teachers and parents to "put these children in their places" only increased the children's feelings of neglect and their defiant or nonproductive behaviors.

Characteristics and Directions of Underachievement

The characteristic found most frequently and consistently among underachieving children is low self-esteem (Davis & Rimm, 1989; Fine & Pitts, 1980; Whitmore, 1980). Although they acknowledge that they are intelligent, they do not believe themselves capable of accomplishing what their family or teachers expect of them. They may mask their low self-esteem with displays of bravado or rebellion, or with highly protective defense mechanisms (Covington & Beery, 1976; Fine & Pitts, 1980; Rimm, 1986a). For example, they may openly criticize the quality of the school or the talents of individual teachers, or else claim that they "don't care" or "didn't really try" in regard to a mediocre test score or class grade.

Related to their low self-esteem is their sense of low personal control over their own lives (Rimm, 1986a). If they fail at a task, they blame their lack of ability; if they succeed, they may attribute their success to luck. Thus, they may accept responsibility for failure, but not for success (Felton & Biggs, 1977). This attribution process in educational achievement has been related to the original theory of *learned helplessness* advanced by Seligman (1975). A child who does not see a relationship between his or her effort and the outcomes is likely to exhibit characteristics of learned helplessness and will no longer make an effort to achieve (see Figure 24.1). Weiner (1974, 1980) also emphasized that attributing success to *effort* leads to further effort, whereas attributing success to *task ease* or *luck* does not.

Low self-esteem leads the underachiever to nonproductive avoidance behaviors both at school and at home. For example, underachievers may avoid making a productive effort by asserting that school is irrelevant and that they see no reason to study material for which there is no use. Students may further assert that when they are really interested in learning, they can do very well. These kinds of avoidance behaviors protect underachievers from admitting their feared lack of productive ability. If they studied, they would risk *confirming* their possible shortcomings to themselves and to important others. If they do not study, they can use the nonstudying as a rationale for the failure, thus protecting their precarious feelings of self-worth (Covington & Beery, 1976).

Extreme rebellion against authority, particularly school authority, provides another route to protect the underachiever. The student may be eager to tell teachers, the principal, the superintendent, and even the board of education exactly how they ought to run the school. Faulting the school helps the underachiever avoid the responsibility for achieving by blaming the system.

Expectations of low grades and perfectionism—though apparent opposites—also serve as defense mechanisms for the underachieving child with low self-esteem. If the underachiever expects low grades, he or she lowers the risk of failure. Note that low goals are consistent with a poor self-image and low self-confidence. Reaching for goals that are impossibly high also provides safety for under-

achievers. They can use the "too high" goals as an excuse for not making a good effort. By contrast, achieving children set realistic goals that are reachable, and failures are constructively used to indicate weaknesses needing attention.

Two main directions of responses have been described by Rimm (1986a). She found underachievers to exhibit their defenses by *dependency* or *dominance*. Figure 24.2 shows these two directions. *Confirming* underachievers differ from those in the *nonconforming* category by their visibility. That is, conforming dependent and dominant students have characteristics that may lead to greater underachievement problems, but their underachievement is not as apparent. Nonconforming dependent and dominant underachievers already are exhibiting serious problems. The prototypical names used in Figure 24.2, *Passive Paul, Rebellious Rebecca,* and so forth, are used to emphasize the main characteristics of these underachievers, but any one child typically exhibits a group of these symptoms. Rimm also pointed out that some underachievers exhibit both dependent and dominant qualities.

Reversal of Underachievement

The underachieving gifted child continues to underachieve because the home, school, and/or peer group unintentionally supports that underachievement. The student is no longer motivated to achieve, and there may be deficiencies in skills necessary for achievement. Working below one's ability affects both immediate educational success and eventual career achievement. It is an important problem requiring attention.

While it may seem like a tall order to reverse a long-standing pattern of underachievement, Rimm's trifocal model has proved successful in case after case (Rimm, 1986a). She has found that the treatment of underachievement involves the collaboration of school and family in the implementation of six steps (see Figure 24.3).

1. Assessment
2. Communication

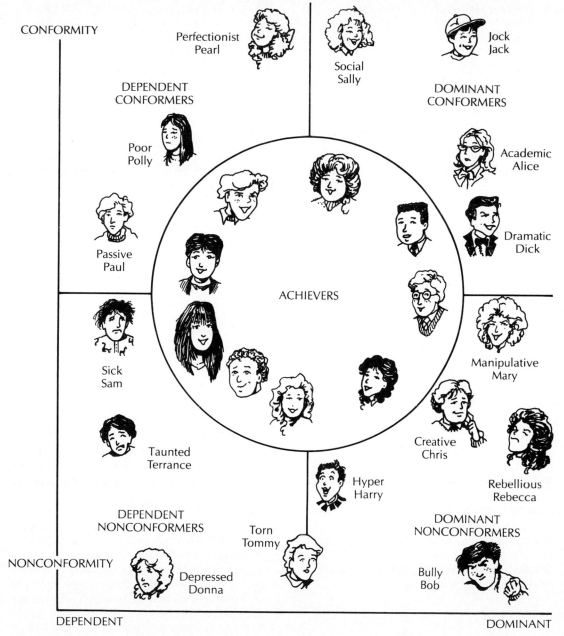

Figure 24.2 The inner circle of achievers.

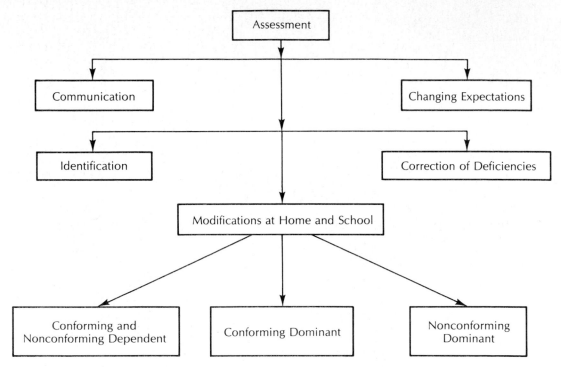

Source: Reprinted by permission from *Underachievement Syndrome: Causes and Cures,* by Sylvia B. Rimm, p. 131, copyright © 1986 by Apple Publishing Company, Watertown, Wisconsin.

Figure 24.3   Trifocal model for curing underachievement syndrome.

3. Changing expectations
4. Role model identification
5. Correction of deficiencies
6. Modifications of reinforcements

In addition to the use of the trifocal model, parents and teachers should have "patience, dedication and support" (Hoffman, Wasson, & Christianson, 1985).

Step 1: Assessment of Skills, Abilities, and Types of Underachievement

The first step in the underachievement reversal process is an assessment that involves the cooperation of the school psychologist, a teacher of the gifted, a counselor, and parents. Ideally, these persons should (1) have some background in measurement, (2) be sensitive to various learning and motivational styles

and problems, (3) be knowledgeable in behavioral learning theory, and (4) be aware of the special characteristics of gifted and creative children.

An *individual* intelligence test is a highly recommended first assessment instrument. That venerable IQ number has the potential to communicate important expectations related to the child's abilities. Since these children have not been motivated, it is likely that *group* intelligence test scores have underestimated their intellectual potential. It is possible that the underachievement may also depress scores obtained by individual testing. The WISC-R or the Stanford-Binet must be individually administered by a psychologist. The Slosson Individual Intelligence Test could be administered by a teacher or counselor. There also are other individual intelligence tests that can be administered by a psychologist to evaluate the learning potential of culturally deprived, non-verbal, non-English-speaking, blind, or deaf gifted children who also may need to be individually assessed. Examples of such instruments include the Nebraska Test of Learning Aptitude (Hiskey, 1966), used with deaf and hearing-impaired children; the *Arthur Adaptation of the Leiter International Performance Scale* (Arthur, 1950), for the deaf, the hearing-impaired, and children with speech or language difficulties; the Blind Learning Aptitude Test (Newland, 1969); and The Pictorial Test of Intelligence (French, 1964), for children with motoric handicaps. Some of these instruments are questionable in terms of their equivalence to the most conventionally accepted tests, namely, the Wechsler and Stanford-Binet scales, but all provide a reasonably acceptable predictor of the child's school-related capability.

During testing the examiner must be especially aware of particular task-relevant characteristics of the child: symptoms of tension, attention to the task, perseverance at the task, responses to frustration, problem-solving approaches, defensiveness, and responses to personal encouragement by the examiner. These reflect, in miniature, approaches to educational tasks that the child very likely uses in the classroom and home environments.

Intelligence testing should be followed by individual achievement tests to clearly assess strengths and deficits in basic skills, particularly reading and math.

A creativity test or inventory, which can be administered by the teacher or a psychologist, also should be part of the assessment. These produce not only a norm-referenced creativity score, but also descriptions of abilities, characteristics, and interests that are relevant to understanding the child's personality, creative potential, and learning style. The Group Inventory for Finding Creative Talent (GIFT; Rimm, 1976) and Group Inventory for Finding Interests (GIFFI; Davis & Rimm, 1982) tests include dimension scores such as Independence, Self-confidence, Imagination, Interests, and Challenge-Inventiveness that provide important insights for understanding the student.

Achievement Identification Measure (AIM;

Rimm, 1986b), Group Achievement Identification Measure (GAIM; Rimm, 1987a) and Achievement Identification Measure—Teacher Observation (AIM-TO; Rimm, 1988) are inventories developed for the identification of children's characteristics related to achievement or underachievement. GAIM can be used with students from Grades 5 through 12. AIM is completed by parents, and AIM-TO is a teacher observation instrument. The latter two instruments can be completed for any school-age student. The scores provide a description of the extent and type of the child's underachievement. Dimension scores reveal whether the student is mainly dependent or dominant or combines a mixture of both. Scores also permit insights into parent consistency in messages about achievement. A description of the dimension scores is provided in Table 24.4.

Finally, a parent interview also can be very helpful identifying underachieving patterns unintentionally maintained at home and school. Ideally, both parents should be at the interview. If only one appears, it is important to ask about the other parent's relationship to the child. Overall, the assessment of student abilities and home and school reinforcement contingencies is critical to the second step of the underachievement modification program.

Step 2: Communication

Communication between parents and teachers is an important component of the cure for underachievers. Either a parent or the teacher may initiate the first conference. The initiator should assure the other person of support rather than placing blame. If it appears to a teacher that the parents are not interested in or capable of working with him or her, the teacher should select another adult child advocate in the school with whom to work. Reversing the pattern without parent assistance is not as efficient but is nevertheless possible. A counselor, gifted coordinator, or resource teacher is often an excellent advocate.

The content of the communication between parents and teachers should include a discussion of assessed abilities and achievements as well as formal and informal evaluations of the

Table 24.4
Underachievement Inventories: Dimension Scores for AIM, GAIM, and AIM-TO

Competition

High scorers enjoy competition whether they win or lose. They are good sports and handle victories graciously. They do not give up easily.

Responsibility

High scorers are responsible in their home and schoolwork. They tend to be well organized and bring activities to closure. They have good study habits and understand that their efforts are related to their grades.

Achievement Communication

Children who score high are receiving clear and consistent messages from parents about the importance of learning and good grades. Their parents have communicated positive feelings about their own school experiences, and there is consistency between mother and father regarding messages of achievement.

Independence and Dependence

High scorers are independent and understand the relationship between effort and outcomes. They are able to share attention at home and in the classroom.

Respect and Dominance

High scorers are respectful toward their parents and teachers. They are reasonably well behaved at home and school. They value education. They are not deliberately manipulative.

child's expressions of dependence or dominance. Teachers should be careful to communicate in clear English. There is a tendency for educators to employ jargon that mystifies all intelligent adults who are not educators. Clear communication is especially important in order that adults at home and at school do not fall into the trap of continuing to reinforce the problem patterns (Rimm, 1985).

Step 3: Changing the Expectations of Important Others

Parent, teacher, peer, and sibling expectations are difficult to change. As noted above, IQ scores, if higher than anticipated, are very effective in modifying expectations. Anecdotal information also can provide convincing evidence of the child's abilities. For example, a teacher trying to convince an adolescent or his or her parents of the child's mathematical talent can explain that the child solves problems in an unusually clever way or seems to learn math concepts more quickly than anyone else in the class. A psychologist trying to convince a teacher that a child has unusual talent can describe the unusual vocabulary or problem-solving skills that the child revealed during testing. Specific descriptions of special strengths are good evidence of giftedness.

It is very important to underachieving children that parents and teachers be able to say honestly to them that they believe in their ability to achieve. The expectations of these important others are basic to the personal change in self-expectations that is necessary to reverse from underachievement to high achievement. Jackson, Cleveland, and Merenda (1975) showed in their longitudinal research with bright fourth-, fifth-, and sixth-grade underachievers that positive expectations by parents and teachers had a significant long-range effect on achievement in high school. Bloom's (1985) studies of talent development found that parents of research neurologists and mathematicians always expected their children to be very good students.

An interesting true story that emphasizes the role of teacher expectations for achievement follows:

It was the first teacher conference of the new year, a time when teachers may not yet know all the parents of their students. Ms. Dunn, a fourth-grade teacher, had two Janets in her class. One was an excellent student, positive and well-adjusted; the other had multiple problems and was very negative. When the second Janet's parents came for conference, Ms. Dunn mistook them for the first Janet's parents. She welcomed them with an enthusiastic description of their daughter's positive attitude only to be greeted by their shocked expression. She immediately realized her mistake, but rather than embarrass herself and the parents she continued her discussion about a "few areas" where Janet needed improvement.

The parents left the conference more positive about their daughter than ever before and conveyed this excitement to their child. The next day, to Ms. Dunn's surprise, Janet entered school with a big smile and a positive attitude. Her self-confidence and her school efforts were completely transformed. She ended the school year with Bs instead of the usual Ds that had been typical of earlier report cards. A chance faux pas had led to a dramatic change for Janet.

Yes, this really is a true story!

Because sibling competition frequently is a causal component of underachievement syndrome, changing the expectations of siblings is important. In the sibling rivalry that often exists, an achieving child may have assigned to a brother or sister the role of "loser," and the anticipated change of that role may feel threatening to the "winner." An individual and personal communication to the winner about the expected change is helpful. Parents should provide the assurance that the sibling's changed status will not displace the achiever's role. Genetically and environmentally a "whole smart family" is not only possible, but likely. This explanation may deter the achiever from subtly trying to sabotage the underachiever's improved status.

Step 4: Model Identification

A critical turning point for the underachieving child is the discovery of a model for identification. All other treatments for underachievement dim in importance compared with strong identification with an achieving model. Bloom's (1985; Bloom & Sosniak, 1981) biographical research with highly talented students showed that parents modeled the values and the lifestyles of successful achievers in the talent area. Radin (1976) argued that the best family environment for a gifted boy is provided "when a father is perceived as competent and strong, is pleased with his job, and permits his son to master tasks independently." Since this ideal situation is rarely provided for the gifted underachiever, parents and teachers need to manipulate the environment,

using information that we know encourages identification to help the student find a good model for that identification.

Research on parent identification (e.g., Mussen & Rutherford, 1963) indicates that the selected parent identification figure is nurturant and powerful, and shares common characteristics with the child. These same characteristics can be used to locate an appropriate achieving model for the underachieving gifted child. As a warning, however, an underachieving adolescent sometimes selects a powerful, nurturant model who shares the underachieving characteristics of the adolescent. This person may then become a strong model for underachievement.

Underachieving children should be matched with achieving persons to serve as models for them. Persons selected can serve in model capacities for more than one child. The model's actual role may be tutor, mentor, companion, teacher, parent, sibling, counselor, psychologist, minister, scout leader, doctor, and so on. One teacher may serve as a role model for many students. Persons who serve as appropriate role models may be invited to school to talk to students about their careers. Videotaping these talks may provide a continuing role model for other students. The model should have as many of the following characteristics as possible:

1. *Nurturance:* The model must care about the child assigned. Many adults are pleased to encourage youth with whom they can identify.
2. *Same sex:* Although identification with an opposite-sex model is possible, the similarity in sex facilitates identification.
3. *Similarities to child:* These may include religion, race, interests, talents, physical disabilities, physical characteristics, socioeconomic backgrounds, specific problem experiences, or any other characteristics that create the necessary easy rapport. When the child realizes that the model can be truly understanding, empathic, and sympathetic, because the model has experienced similar problems, rapport is more easily established and the process of identification is facilitated.

4. *Openness:* A model's willingness to share his or her own real problems in establishing him- or herself as an achiever is important for encouraging communication and identification, and for motivating the underachieving child.
5. *Willingness to give time:* Achieving adults frequently have shortages of this most precious commodity. However, it is impossible to be an effective, positive model without providing time. It can be work time, playtime, or talk time. Models who work on tasks with their child or play with their child can be the most effective. It becomes possible for the child to see firsthand their role models responding to challenge, winning and losing in competition, using different reasoning styles, leading, communicating, relating to others, and experiencing success and failures.
6. *Sense of positive accomplishment:* Although the model's life need not be perfect, the model must exhibit to the child the sense that his or her achievements have been personally fulfilling. Achievement involves sacrifice and postponed gratifications. The underachiever must recognize that these costs and postponements are worthwhile.

Step 5: Correcting Skill Deficiencies

The underachieving gifted child almost always has skill deficiencies as a result of inattention in class and poor work and study habits. However, because he or she is gifted, the skill deficiencies can be overcome reasonably fast. This is less of a problem for the very young child because the deficiencies are less likely to be extensive. Tutoring should be goal-directed, with movement to a higher reading or math group or acceptance into an accelerated class as the anticipated outcome. It should be of specified duration, for example, weekly for two months until the child takes a proficiency test, rather than ongoing. Ideally, the tutor should be an experienced and objective adult who recognizes the child's underachievement and giftedness. Parents or siblings are not appropriate since the personal relationships are likely to cause the child additional pressure and dependency. Children have described the assistance

given by an older sibling as "helpful," but as having a secondary effect of "making me feel dumb." The correction of skill deficiencies must be conducted carefully so that (1) the independent work of the underachieving child is reinforced by the tutor, (2) manipulation of the tutor by the child is avoided, and (3) the child senses the relationship between effort and the achievement outcomes. Charting progress during tutoring helps visually confirm the rapid progress to both child and tutor.

Sometimes underachieving gifted students actually have learning disabilities. Other times their dependent patterns merely look like learning disabilities. Table 24.5 compares dependencies to disabilities and can provide teachers with a diagnostic guide for detecting actual learning disabilities.

Step 6: Modification of Reinforcements at Home and School

Parent and teacher discussions will certainly identify some of the characteristics and manipulative rituals discussed in this chapter. These behaviors need to be modified by setting important long-term goals and some short-term objectives that can ensure immediate small successes for the child both at home and at school. These successful experiences should be reinforced by extrinsic rewards.

There are several considerations in determining the rewards to be used. First, they must be meaningful to the child. Money may be unimportant to a 6-year-old, while stars are not particularly motivating to the adolescent. They must also be within the value system and range of possibility for the givers of the rewards. Schools usually do not use money as a reward, and parents may not want to pay (bribe) their children to learn. There are, however, effective rewards within the value system of parents and within the capabilities of teachers to administer, for example, free time. The rewards should not be too large. In fact, they should be as small as possible yet effective enough to motivate behavior. They can be increased in value as necessary, but if one has already used large rewards, small rewards will no longer be effective. It is important always to supply the rewards agreed on, and to pay them

Table 24.5
Ways to Discriminate between Dependence and Disability

Dependence	*Disability*
1. Child asks for explanations regularly despite differences in subject matter.	Child asks for explanations in particular subjects which are difficult.
2. Child asks for explanation of instructions regardless of style used, either auditory or visual.	Child asks for explanations of instructions only when given in one instruction style, either auditory or visual, but not both.
3. Child's questions are not specific to material but appear to be mainly to gain adult attention.	Child's questions are specific to material, and once process is explained child works efficiently.
4. Child is disorganized or slow in assignments but becomes much more efficient when a meaningful reward is presented as motivation.	Child's disorganization or slow pace continues despite motivating rewards.
5. Child works only when an adult is nearby at school and/or at home.	Child works independently once process is clearly explained.
6. Individually administered measures of ability indicate that the child is capable of learning the material. Individual tests improve with tester encouragement and support. Group measures may not indicate good abilities or skills.	Both individual and group measures indicate lack of specific abilities of skills. Tester encouragement has not significant effect on scores.
7. Child exhibits "poor me" body language (tears, helplessness, pouting, copying) regularly when new work is presented. Teacher or adult attention serves to ease the symptoms.	Child exhibits "poor me" body language only with instructions or assignments in specific disability areas and accepts challenges in areas of strength.
8. Parents report whining, complaining, attention getting, temper tantrums and poor sportsmanship at home.	Although parents may find similar symptoms at home, they tend to be more sporadic than regular, particularly the whining and complaining.
9. Child's "poor me" behavior appears only with one parent and not with the other; only with some teachers and not with others. With some teachers or with the other parent the child functions fairly well independently.	Although the child's "poor me" behaviors may only appear with one parent or with solicitous teachers, performance is not adequate even when behavior is acceptable.
10. Child learns only when given one-to-one instruction but will not learn in groups even when instructional mode is varied.	Although child may learn more quickly in a one-to-one setting he/she will also learn efficiently in a group setting provided the child's disability is taken into consideration when instructions are given.

It is critical to realize that some children who are truly disabled have also become dependent. The key to distinguishing between disability and dependence is the child's response to adult support. If the child performs only with adult support when new material is presented he/she is too dependent, whether or not there is also a disability.

Source: Reprinted by permission from *Underachievement Syndrome: Causes and Cures* by Sylvia B. Rimm, p. 219, copyright © 1986 by Apple Publishing Company, Watertown, Wisconsin.

on a regular basis immediately after the activity is successfully completed. Rewards may be based on activities completed, or based on the quality of the activity. Rewards should never be paid for incomplete work or when the work is not attempted. Although stickers and money have been found to be effective, one-to-one attention by an adult is probably the most effective. Eventually, the student should find that the satisfaction of accomplishment is sufficiently reinforcing. Thus the extrinsic reinforcers used during the underachievement cure are only temporary, and intrinsic reinforcement becomes the only effective long-term motivator.

Modifying reinforcements for homework and study are an important component of reversing an underachievement syndrome. However, this modification by itself will not be sufficient. Dozens of other recommendations for home and school changes are described by Rimm (1986a) in her book specifically written on the underachievement syndrome.

Implications for Parenting

General recommendations for parenting gifted children emerge from the comparison of gifted underachievers with superachievers.

The preschool years: Child-centered environments are typical for gifted children. However, conferring adult status on intelligent children carries the risk of later disempowerment. Further, too much praise and admiration and the use of frequent superlatives confer a sense of specialness that can rarely be adjusted to in school. Dependence on too much external positive reinforcement may reduce intrinsically motivating behaviors, such as studying and learning.

Parenting styles: Styles of parenting seem to be much less important than consistency in parenting. Dissimilarities between parents, for example, with one expecting too much and the other protecting too much, are a main source of problems for children.

Homework and learning: Gifted children do not need regular help with homework. Positive monitoring of homework and study habits is effective. Encouraging intrinsically interesting learning experiences and independence is important.

Modeling: Parent valuing of personal careers and work provides an important model for children's achievement, depending on what they see and hear.

Organization: Reasonable standards of organization provide a model for organization and aid the development of family interests and independence.

Clinical experiences with underachievers indicate that school, home, and peer environments should be modified to cure underachievement syndrome in gifted children. Although the reversal is difficult, the satisfaction felt by the child and family and the achievement of potential contributions to society make effort worthwhile.

REFERENCES

Arthur, G. (1950). *The Arthur adaptation of the Leiter International Performance Scale.* Chicago: Stoelting.

Bloom B. S. (Ed.). (1985). *Developing talent in young people.* New York: Ballantine.

Bloom, B. S., & Sosniak, L. A. (1981). Talent development vs. schooling. *Educational Leadership. 39,* 86–94.

Covington, M. V., & Beery, R. G. (1976). *Self-worth and school learning.* New York: Holt.

Davis, G. A., & Rimm, S. B. (1982). Group inventory for finding interests (GIFFI) I and II: Instruments for identifying creative potential in the junior and senior high school. *Journal of Creative Behavior, 16,* 50–57.

Davis, G. A., & Rimm, S. B. (1989). *Education of the gifted and talented* (2nd ed.). Englewood Cliffs, NJ: Prentice-Hall.

Felton, G. S., & Biggs, B. E. (1977). *Up from underachievement.* Springfield, IL: Thomas.

Fine, M. J., & Pitts, R. (1980). Intervention with underachieving gifted children: Rationale and strategies. *Gifted Child Quarterly, 14,* 51–55.

Frazier, A., Passow, A. H., & Goldberg, M. L. (1958). Curriculum research: Study of underachieving gifted. *Educational Leadership, 16,* 121–125.

French, J. I. (1964). *Pictorial test of intelligence.* Boston: Houghton Mifflin.

French, J. L. (1959). *Educating the gifted: A book of readings.* New York: Holt.

Goertzel, V., & Goertzel, M. G. (1962). *Cradles of eminence.* Boston: Little, Brown.

Green, K., Fine, M. J., & Tollefson, N. (1988). Family systems characteristics and underachieving gifted adolescent males. *Gifted Child Quarterly, 32,* 267–272.

Hiskey, M. (1966). *Hiskey-Nebraska test of learning aptitude.* Lincoln, NE: Union College Press.

Hoffman, J. L., Wasson, F. R., & Christianson, B. P. (1985, May/June). Personal development for the gifted underachiever. *G/C/T,* pp. 12–14.

Hom, H. L., Jr., Gaskill, B., & Hutchins, M. (1988, April). Motivational orientation of the gifted student, thread of evaluation and its impact on performance. Presented at the annual meeting of the American Educational Research Association, New Orleans.

Jackson, R. M., Cleveland, J. C., & Merenda, P. R. (1975). The longitudinal effects of early identification and counseling of underachievers. *Journal of School Psychology, 13,* 119–128.

MacKinnon, D. (1965). Personality and the realization of creative potential. *American Psychologist, 20,* 273–281.

Mussen, P. H., & Rutherford, E. (1963). Parent-child relations and parental personality in relation to young children's sex-role preferences. *Child Development, 34,* 589–607.

National Commission on Excellence in Education. (1984). *A nation at risk: The imperative for educational reform.* Washington, DC: U.S. Government Printing Office.

Newland, T. E. (1969). *Manual for the blind learning aptitude test: Experimental edition.* Urbana, IL: Newland.

Olszewski, P., Kulieke, M., & Buescher, T. (1987). The influence of the family environment on the development of talent: A literature review. *Journal of the Education of the Gifted, 2,* 6–28.

Radin, N. (1976). The role of the father in cognitive, academic and intellectual development. In M. E. Lamb (Ed.), *The role of the father in child development* (pp. 237–276). New York: Wiley.

Rimm, S. B. (1976). GIFT: *Group inventory for finding creative talent.* Watertown, WI: Educational Assessment Service.

Rimm, S. B. (1980, September/October). Congratulations Miss Smithersteen, you have proved that Amy isn't gifted. *G/C/T,* 23–24.

Rimm, S. B. (1985, November/December). Identifying underachievement: The characteristics approach. *G/C/T,* 2–5.

Rimm, S. B. (1986a). *Underachievement syndrome: Causes and cures.* Watertown, WI: Apple.

Rimm, S. B. (1986b). *AIM: Achievement Identification Measure.* Watertown, WI: Educational Assessment Service.

Rimm, S. B. (1987a). Why do bright children underachieve? The pressures they feel. *Gifted Child Today, 10*(6), 30–36.

Rimm, S. B. (1987b). *GAIM: Group achievement identification measure.* Watertown, WI: Educational Assessment Service.

Rimm, S. B. (1988). *AIM-TO: Achievement identification measure teacher observation.* Watertown, WI: Educational Assessment Service.

Rimm, S. B., & Lowe, B. (1988). Family environments of underachieving gifted students. *Gifted Child Quarterly, 32,* 353–359.

Seligman, M. E. (1975). *Helplessness: On depression, development and death.* San Francisco: Freeman.

Walberg, H., Tsai, S. L., Weinstein, T., Gabriel, C. L., Rasher, S. P., & Rosencrans, T. (1981). Childhood traits and environmental conditions of highly eminent adults. *Gifted Child Quarterly, 25,* 103–107.

Weiner, B. (1974). *Achievement motivation and attribution theory.* Morristown, NJ: General Learning.

Weiner, B. (1980). *Human motivation.* New York: Holt.

Whitmore, J. R. (1980). *Giftedness, conflict, and underachievement.* Boston: Allyn and Bacon.

Zilli, M. J. (1971). Reasons why the gifted adolescent underachieves and some of the implications of guidance and counseling of this problem. *Gifted Child Quarterly, 15,* 279–292.

PART VI

Special Topics

25

Extreme Precocity

MARTHA J. MORELOCK and DAVID H. FELDMAN   *Tufts University*

In this chapter, types of extremely precocious children, as recorded in the research literature, are described, compared, and contrasted, incorporating discussion of educational programming. A taxonomy of manifestations of extreme precocity is presented, and implications for research are explored.

The Extremely Precocious Child

Human beings have long been fascinated by extreme precocity in childhood. The Biblical story of the child Jesus, who, at the age of 12, astonished the rabbis with his understanding, is perhaps the first recorded allusion to an extremely precocious child.[1] It was not until the 1700s, however, that more detailed narrative accounts of childhood precociousness began to appear in what was to become a developing literature of child psychology (Hollingworth, 1942). The earliest of these, written in 1726, described the child Christian Heinrich Heinecken. Barlow (1952) provides a synopsis of the life of Heinecken:

> Christian Friedrich Heinecken, a German, who was known as the "Infant of Lubeck," from the place where he was born in 1721, is said to have talked within a few hours after his birth. Besides his remarkable faculty for numbers, he is said to have known, at the age of one year, all the principal events related in the Pentateuch; at two was well acquainted with the historical events of the Bible, and at three had a knowledge of universal history and geography, Latin and French. People came from all parts to see him, and the King of Denmark had him brought to Copenhagen in 1724, in order to assure himself of the truth of what he had heard regarding him. But shortly after this, little Heinecken was taken ill and predicted his own death, which took place in

1725, at the tender age of four. (Barlow, 1952, pp. 135–136)

Christian Heinecken was, indeed, according to this account, extraordinarily precocious when it came to the ability to absorb abstract knowledge and to verbalize that knowledge. Childhood precocity, however, comes in numerous guises and raises a multitude of questions. There are, for example, child prodigies whose extraordinary performance in particular fields rivals that of adult professionals. Such a prodigy was the child musician and composer Wolfgang Amadeus Mozart (1756–1791), who, at the age of 6, toured Europe with his father, Leopold, and sister, Maria Anna, exhibiting the children's musicianship—particularly young Wolfgang's mastery of the violin, piano, and organ (Barlow, 1952).

Then, of course, there are astonishing cases like George and Charles—identical twin calendar calculators (Hamblin, 1966). George at the age of 6 and Charles at the age of 9 could answer spontaneously questions such as, "On what day of the week was your third birthday?" "The year is 31275; on what day of the week will June 6th fall?" Given a date, these twins could give the day of the week over a span of 80,000 years—40,000 backward or 40,000 forward. Such feats are the more astounding because the twins' tested IQs were between 40 and 50. Incredibly, although they could not count to 30, they swapped 20-digit prime numbers for amusement. They could easily factor the number 111 and remember 30 digits, but could not add.

Heinecken, Mozart, and George and Charles reflect the three major types of extremely precocious children found in the literature. Although young Heinecken lived prior to the development of IQ tests, his academic precocity was like that characteristic of the gifted child of extraordinarily high IQ. Mozart was a supreme example of the child prodigy, while George and Charles are classified as *idiot savants*. We will examine each of these variations of extreme precocity, noting the similarities and differences between them. We begin with the child of extraordinarily high IQ.

The Child of Extraordinarily High IQ

To understand the child of extraordinary IQ, it is necessary to understand something about the instrument that first defined and selected such children. Lewis M. Terman's Stanford-Binet Intelligence Scale, which first appeared in 1916 (Seagoe, 1975), was an extension and revision of the 1908 Binet-Simon Scale, which had been devised by the French psychologist Alfred Binet and T. Simon, his physician-collaborator. The Binet-Simon scale was a practical screening device for identifying children who, unable to succeed in the public schools of Paris, were in need of special programs. Terman's scale, however, incorporated a new theoretical premise—a definition of human intelligence. Terman defined intelligence as the ability to acquire and manipulate concepts—the shorthand symbols necessary for abstract thinking (Terman, 1975).

In extending the standardized instrument so that it reached higher levels of ability in late childhood, Terman and his associates paved the way for studies of the gifted (Seagoe, 1975). Terman himself began the first broad-scale study of gifted children (Terman, 1925–1959). A mammoth longitudinal project, it followed over 1,500 children with IQs of at least 140 into adulthood, middle age, and beyond.

It remained for Terman's contemporary Leta S. Hollingworth (Hollingworth, 1942) to conduct the first, and to date the only, systematic in-depth study devoted solely to children of extraordinarily high IQ. Hollingworth's observations concerning the special psychological, social, and educational needs of children above 180 IQ remain valuable today. In the following section, we discuss some of her findings.

Leta Hollingworth and Children above 180 IQ

Leta Hollingworth (1942) conducted case studies of 12 children (8 boys and 4 girls) testing above 180 IQ on the Stanford-Binet Intelligence Scale. She found that, although no one characteristic could be singled out as identifying accelerated development, early talking and reading most clearly differentiated these children from the average. Although this is an interesting finding, it is not a surprising one. The capacity for abstract, symbolic thought that Terman aimed at identifying through the Stanford-Binet was chiefly language-based conceptual facility. Consequently, children most adept at encoding and communicating logical thought through language were destined to be designated "the highly gifted." Early talking and reading are likely manifestations of such verbal-conceptual ability. On the other hand, the fact that these children were so different that no single characteristic other than language facility could apply to them all suggests that their individual profiles of abilities were not adequately captured by the IQ score.

Hollingworth observed that early recognition and provision of opportunities for their abilities consistently proved to foster the optimal development of such children. Although all her subjects showed superior learning ability, their actual accomplishments and the quality of their personal and social adjustment depended heavily on the way they were treated by those responsible for them.

Hollingworth discerned three major adjustment problems risked by children of above-180 IQ (Witty, 1951). First, they frequently failed to develop desirable work habits in a school setting geared to the capacities of average children. In such a setting, they generally spent considerable time in idleness and daydreaming. Consequently, they learned to dislike school.

To remedy this, Hollingworth (1942) proposed a combination of acceleration through the normal elementary curriculum plus enrichment experiences aimed at providing knowledge about cultural evolution as manifested through the development of common things such as clothing, lighting, trains, etiquette, and so forth. She believed that by understanding how things have developed in the past, these children would be encouraged to become innovative thinkers themselves.

A second problem noted by Hollingworth was difficulty in finding satisfying companionship. Consequently, these children risk becoming socially isolated. Children of extraordinarily high IQ, she observed, typically strive to play with others. Their efforts commonly fail, however, since age-mates do not share their interests, vocabulary, or desire for more complex activities. While older children may satisfy the extraordinarily gifted child's need for intellectual rapport, physically the younger child is at a disadvantage.

Because of this problem, Hollingworth believed that children of extraordinarily high IQ need to be educated for leisure. She especially espoused games like chess or checkers, which could be enjoyed by people of all ages and potentially could assist these children in bridging social gaps.

Hollingworth's research suggested that children of extraordinarily high IQ are unlikely to be accepted as leaders by age-mates. Leaders, Hollingworth (1926) concluded, are likely to be "more intelligent, but not too much more intelligent, than the average of the group led" (Hollingworth, 1926, p. 131). Consequently, she believed that beyond IQ 160, children have little chance of being popular leaders in a regular school setting. To develop leadership skills, asserted Hollingworth, such children need to be placed in special classes with others like themselves.

A third problem cited by Hollingworth was a certain vulnerability because of these children's intellectual capacity to understand and grapple with major philosophical and ethical issues before they are emotionally ready to deal with them. Hollingworth wrote, for example, of a 6-year-old boy of IQ 187 who "wept bitterly after reading how the North taxed the South after the Civil War" (Hollingworth, 1942, p. 281).

Hollingworth cautioned that such vulnerabilities must be understood and dealt with patiently by adults so as to avoid engendering lifelong emotional problems. She concluded, "To have the intelligence of an adult and the emotions of a child combined in a childish body is to encounter certain difficulties" (Hollingworth, 1942, p. 282).

In addition to issues of personality and social development, Hollingworth was interested in the level of achievement eventually displayed by children of extraordinarily high IQ. As of their early twenties, her own subjects boasted an impressive list of accomplishments. She notes that "before the age of 22 in all cases, one had pursued research in history, one in mathematics, one in chess, and two had become established in learned professions. One stood high in the national ranking for chess. A long list of medals and prizes had been won by them. All but one of those graduated from college had been elected to Phi Beta Kappa" (Hollingworth, 1942, pp. 248–249).

On the basis of her observations, Hollingworth concluded that children testing above 180 IQ constituted the "top" among graduates—the ones who predictably would win honors and prizes for intellectual work. While Hollingworth believed that the term *genius* should be reserved for those making original contributions of outstanding and lasting merit, she believed those testing 180 IQ and above in childhood could be regarded as "potential geniuses" (Witty, 1951). As shown in the following sections, a more recent study of adults testing above 180 IQ in childhood suggests Hollingworth's cautious stance is well warranted.

Extraordinarily High IQ and Achievement

A study (Feldman, 1984) using Terman's (Terman, 1925–1959) original research files, compared the lives of the 26 subjects scoring 180 or above on the Stanford-Binet with 26 of their counterparts of lesser IQ randomly selected from the original sample of over 1,500. A difference of 35 IQ points differentiated the average IQs of the groups in question (150 vs. 185). Although there was some evidence that the above-180-IQ subjects were more successful in their careers than the 150-IQ group, the difference was slight. A small number of distinguished *men* emerged from the above-180-

IQ group (i.e., an academic psychologist of international repute, a celebrated landscape architect, a judge, and a promising pollster who committed suicide at age 28), while a comparable group failed to emerge from either the 150-IQ women, the 150-IQ men, or the 180-IQ women. Even so, the degree of distinction of these 180-IQ men could not be considered to be on a par with genius.

What factors caused these extraordinarily endowed individuals to fail to fufill their / promise?

Explaining the Reluctance of Genius to Emerge

Research suggests several possible answers to the question raised in the previous section. A first potential explanation is suggested by Hollingworth's research pointing out the social and psychological risks plaguing those of extraordinarily high IQ. Intellectual ability of this type may well lay the groundwork for future eminence—especially in fields requiring academic excellence. It may be, however, that the higher the IQ, the more the benefits are counterbalanced by social adjustment problems imposed by such capacity.

In the case of females, additional barriers are raised by societal stereotypes of acceptable female roles and behavior. Terman (1975) and many others have noted the extent to which domestic and child-rearing responsibilities have historically interfered with expression of female abilities in the arts and sciences. More recently, researchers have pinpointed a number of psychological spin-off effects of societal attitudes that may impede career development among women, such as a "fear of success" (Horner, 1972) due to associated expectations of social rejection or, among successful women, a persistent belief that they are, in reality, unintelligent imposters simply fooling those believing otherwise (Clance & Imes, 1978).

All of the above notwithstanding, it may be that in predicting genius-level achievement, we need to consider more than individual capability or even motivation. Simonton (1984) proposed that works of genius are the result of a fortuitous melding of historical, social, and individual ingredients. The *Zeitgeist,* or spirit of the times, he pointed out, influences achievement by generating an economic, political, and philosophical backdrop that determines the sociocultural receptiveness to an individual with a particular set of abilities. At the same time, characteristics such as intelligence, morality, leadership qualities, productivity, aggressiveness, age, and belief determine how and to what extent a particular individual can utilize sociocultural opportunities. Genius, according to Simonton, is a matter of being the right person at the right place at the right time.

In searching for explanations for the nonemergence of genius, we have gone from the individual to the sociocultural and historical. There is one area, however, that remains to be examined—the IQ test itself. The IQ test, as conceived by Lewis Terman and derived from the original work of Alfred Binet, is a means of gauging an individual's capability of succeeding in school as it exists in our culture. Consequently, it mainly assesses an individual's proficiency with logical, linear, verbal-conceptual abstract thought. To assume that such a test can select out the potential for works of creative genius—in the multiplicity of fields in which such works might be done—is requiring more than it was ever equipped or could logically be expected to do.

A related question to be considered is that of the relevance of the concepts of genius and achievement in the first place. Some (Borland, 1986; Silverman, 1988) assert that questions of potential achievement—or even genius—are not the ones on which we should focus. The focus instead belongs on the children and how we can best design educational programming to meet their needs.

This change in focus is not, of course, a total shift. Hollingworth welcomed the Stanford-Binet because she believed it provided a means of selecting these children so that questions of how best to educate them could be answered. Today, however, some question whether we may soon lose the capability of psychometrically identifying the extraordinarily high IQ child. We address this issue next.

The Extraordinarily High IQ Child—An Endangered Species[2]

The identification of highly academically able children so that their needs can be met is not always easy in the classroom. Such children may fail to exhibit the interest and enthusiasm others expect of gifted children (Whitmore, 1980). Gifted programs requiring that children demonstrate task commitment or evidence of creativity in order to qualify may miss children functioning academically so far above their age-mates that classroom activities fail to spark creative behavior (Brown, 1984; Silverman, 1989). Psychometric data may prove especially helpful in identifying quick minds not obvious to the eye.

From the Stanford-Binet's first appearance in 1916 through its 1973 Terman-Merrill revision (Stanford-Binet, Form L-M), Terman's instrument remained the instrument of choice for identifying academically able children (Hagen, 1980; Martinson, 1974; Robinson & Janos, 1987). However, the Stanford-Binet: Fourth Edition (Thorndike, Hagen & Sattler, 1986), issued in 1986, is an instrument based on a construct of intelligence fundamentally different from that formulated by Terman. Consequently, some (Silverman & Kearney, 1989) argue that if older versions of the scale focusing more strongly on verbal-conceptual facility cease to be available, we may lose the ability to psychometrically identify the types of children studied by Hollingworth.

While psychometric data should always be used in conjunction with other sources of information (e.g., parent and teacher observations) (Morelock & Feldman, in press), to be left without an instrument of proven value for identifying extraordinarily academically able children would be unfortunate. We still know comparatively little about these rapid assimilators of abstract knowledge—and the cognitive processes lying beneath the superficial identification achievable through the IQ index.

Educating the Extraordinarily High IQ Child

Literature on educating "highly gifted children" generally incorporates a range extending from IQ 145 through IQ 180 and over (Sil-

verman, 1989). Some writers choose to subdivide this span into the "exceptionally gifted" (IQ 150 and over) and the "profoundly gifted" (IQ 180 and over) (Webb, Meckstroth, & Tolan, 1982). From the time of Hollingworth (1942), however, it has generally been implicitly assumed that the differences in educational needs among these subgroups is more a matter of degree than kind. Consequently, literature aimed at the "highly gifted" includes these more extreme categories.

Generally, an individualized program is essential in educating the highly gifted (Silverman, 1989). Two children with comparable measured IQs are likely to have quite different profiles of specific academic (Stanley, Keating, & Fox, 1974) and nonacademic strengths and weaknesses. Additionally, it is common for these children's profiles of abilities, on the Wechsler Intelligence Scale for Children—Revised, for example (Wechsler, 1974), to show peaks and valleys very similar to those seen with learning-disabled children (D. Wertlieb, personal communication, March 8, 1989).[3] A 7-year-old child with some abilities equal to those of a 14-year old and others that are at the normal level for his or her chronological age cannot be regarded as learning disabled since none of the measured abilities fall below the norm. Functionally, however, the child is dealing with the same kinds of wide discrepancies of ability plaguing a learning-disabled child. Like learning-disabled children, highly gifted children need support in dealing with the frustration inherent in such a situation. Also like learning-disabled children, highly gifted children need individualized educational programs addressing their various levels of ability.

Silverman notes that with these children's increased ability to deal with complexity, abstraction, and advanced concepts, "the need for repetition dramatically decreases, and the pace of instruction increases accordingly" (Silverman, 1989, p. 78). For optimal learning, Silverman recommends full-day programs conducted by specially trained teachers using a specially tailored curriculum. The menu of possible provisions includes the following (Silverman, 1989, p. 78).

Individualized education programs (IEPs)
Fast-paced, challenging courses
Self-contained classes
Acceleration
University-based programs
Mentors or tutors
Special schools or programs
Community enrichment opportunities
Home teaching
Counseling

There is, of course, one more extremely important factor to consider—the teacher. As Hollingworth somewhat brashly noted, "The foolish teacher who hates to be corrected by a child is unsuited to these children" (Hollingworth, 1942, p. 300). The best teacher for these children is one who (1) is knowledgeable about their emotional and educational needs and (2) conceives of himself or herself as a facilitator and collaborator in the learning experience. This means that the teacher should not invest a great deal in being an all-knowing authority figure. Simple admissions of "I don't know the answer to that, but let's think about how *we* can find out" frequently may be the most productive response.

Although peaks and valleys are commonly reflected in the ability profiles of extraordinarily high IQ children, they are most dramatic in the two other major categories of extreme precocity we will discuss—the prodigy and the idiot savant. We turn now to the prodigy.

The Prodigy

A *prodigy* is a child who, before the age of 10, performs at the level of an adult professional in some cognitively demanding field (Feldman, 1986). As a uniquely defined category of extreme precocity, the prodigy came into being only about a decade ago (Feldman, 1979). This is in spite of the fact that "prodigy" has been used loosely to refer to extraordinary youngsters for many years. The term historically meant any unnatural occurrence portending impending change (Feldman, 1986). Thus, it referred to an entire range of phenomena extending across the advent of happenings nota-

ble as uncanny or extraordinary and the existence of humans or animals regarded as "freak."

Eventually, as the term began to be used to refer more narrowly to extreme human precocity, the "sign" or "portent" aspect of its meaning was dropped, while the essential connotation of "unnatural" or "inexplicable" remained. Within this narrowed context, *prodigy* continued to be used indefinitely to refer to a broad range of manifestations of precocity (for example, see Barlow, 1952).

With the advent of IQ and its general acceptance as the measure of giftedness, the child prodigy became subsumed under the IQ umbrella (Feldman, 1979). Children who could compose sonatas at the age of 6 were assumed—implicitly, at least—to be high IQ children with penchants for given fields.

While the notion of IQ was beginning to dominate American concepts of giftedness, there appeared in the European literature two systematic research studies of child prodigies failing to support the congruence of prodigiousness and extraordinarily high IQ (Baumgarten, 1930; Revesz, 1925). Indeed, these were, up until 1980 (Feldman, 1980), the only scientific studies of child prodigies in the world literature.[4] We turn now to examine the only three prodigy studies existing in the research literature.

The Prodigy as Reflected in Research Literature

Revesz and Erwin Nyiregyhazi. Revesz (1925) conducted an in-depth case study of the 7-year-old Hungarian musical prodigy Erwin Nyiregyhazi, using a combination of interviews; observations of Erwin in and out of performing situations; anecdotes from family, teachers, and acquaintances; and formal assessments employing the available techniques of the day (e.g., the 1908 Binet-Simon Scale).

By parental accounts, Erwin was remarkable from a very early age. By the age of 2 he could reproduce correctly tunes sung to him, and by the end of his third year he demonstrated perfect pitch by reproducing on the mouth organ any melody sung to him. At 4, he began to play the piano and compose melodies. In his fifth year, the family began providing Erwin with formal music lessons. From age 6 to 12 Erwin became a celebrated performer, playing before the British royal family and other audiences in Budapest and Vienna.

Revesz provided a detailed analysis of Erwin's musical abilities, favorably comparing them with those of other legendary prodigies and great musicians of the day.

Additionally, Revesz used the Binet-Simon scale to assess Erwin's general mental capacity. Erwin scored a mental age 3 years beyond his chronological age of 7, or by modern reckoning slightly above 140 IQ.

Revesz, however, asserted that the test inadequately revealed Erwin's brilliant intellect, noting that the child "analyzed his own inner life in the manner of a trained psychologist" and "expressed himself with great caution and in remarkably pregnant phraseology" (Revesz, 1925, p. 42).

In spite of Erwin's remarkable musical talents and exhibited brilliance, Revesz asserted that the prodigy was indeed, in every aspect other than his music, a child: "Erwin was a child in the full sense of the word; a clever, gay, friendly, charming boy. . . . He played as children play, was fond of boyish exploits, and enjoyed them very much" (Revesz, 1925, pp. 57–58). The intriguing mixture of child and adult found by Revesz was noted again by Baumgarten, to whose work we next turn.

Baumgarten's Nine Prodigies. Baumgarten (1930) studied nine child prodigies including two pianists, two violinists, one orchestra conductor, one artist, one geographer, and one chess prodigy. Focusing specifically on the children as whole personalities rather than on their extraordinary achievements alone, she also examined patterns of different abilities manifested by them. Like Revesz, she wrote of the intriguing mixture of adult and child and the frequently noticeable display of childlike naïveté demonstrated by her subjects. Additionally, they appeared ambitious, pragmatic, wary of those who might harm their careers, passionately devoted to their fields, unafraid of public performance, and desirous of using their gifts to benefit their families.

On a battery of standardized intelligence tests, the children performed well as a whole—but not with the degree of extraordinariness conveyed by their special talents. Translated into contemporary IQ terms, the scores ranged from 120 to at least 160. Baumgarten concluded that her subjects' overall intellectual competence, as reflected in the test results, could not explain their outstanding performances in particular fields.

Baumgarten found surprising contrasts between various abilities within subjects. For example, violinists and pianists demonstrated poor hand coordination in bending wire, drawing, and folding and cutting—though one girl violinist had a talent for drawing. Additionally, a 6-year-old boy showing difficulty in making a circle out of two or three sections or a pentagon from two sections was, at the same time, extraordinarily good at map drawing.

Baumgarten concluded that it was necessary to go beyond the testing of intellectual abilities to explain the remarkable achievements of child prodigies. She felt that factors of inheritance, temperament, family, education, environment, and culture must be examined.

Child Prodigies and Human Potential

A study of six prodigies begun in 1975 (Feldman, 1980, 1986) included two chess players, a young mathematician, a musician-composer, a writer, and an "omnibus prodigy" who showed prodigious achievement in a number of areas, but who eventually began to focus on music composition and performance.[5] What eventually developed into an open-ended effort to observe, understand, and explain the prodigy phenomenon began as a straightforward psychological experiment designed to refute an esoteric point in cognitive-developmental psychology. The point in question was the Piagetian assertion that, universally, children's cognitive development proceeds in major predictable sequential stages grossly encompassing all of a child's thinking capacities at any given point in time. Accordingly, to account for a prodigy's adult level performance in a specific field, one would have to assume that the child's overall cognitive development was generally advanced beyond his or her years.

To test this assertion, four cognitive-developmental measures were administered to the two 8-year-old chess players and the 10-year-old musician-composer (Bensusan, 1976).[6] The results of the testing showed that these child prodigies in chess and music composition performed age-appropriately in logic, role-taking, spatial reasoning, and moral judgment. The traditional Piagetian conceptualization of cognitive development was thus seriously challenged.

These findings, like those of Revesz and Baumgarten, suggest that giftedness, rather than being a generalized endowment, is domain-specific.[7]

It is worth noting, in this discussion of formal assessment, that although IQ-type measures were not administered as a part of the larger study, one of the children—the omnibus prodigy—had been tested psychometrically before becoming a subject. With an IQ exceeding the measurement capabilities of available instrumentation, this child presented a case of prodigious achievement coexisting with equally extraordinary IQ.

Association with these six prodigies and their families has extended beyond a decade and has resulted in a theoretical framework, the *co-incidence theory,* seeking to explain not only prodigious development, but also all human achievement.

Co-Incidence Theory

Co-incidence has been defined as "the melding of the many sets of forces that interact in the development and expression of human potential" (Feldman, 1986, p. 11). These include intraindividual (e.g., biological and psychological), environmental (e.g., familial, societal, or cultural), and historical forces. We can think of them as comprising at least four different time frames bearing on the prodigy's appearance and development: the individual's life span, the developmental history of the field or domain, historical and cultural trends bearing on individuals and fields, and evolutionary time. Each of these will be discussed briefly.

Lifespan of the Individual. Aspects of this time frame include, first of all, biological

propensities predisposing an individual towards giftedness in certain fields. An example might be Gardner's (1983) concept of multiple brain-based intelligences (i.e., linguistic, musical, logical-mathematical, spatial, bodily-kinesthetic, interpersonal, and intrapersonal intelligences), each of which holds more or less potential for development within a particular individual (see Chapter 5 by Ramos-Ford and Gardner). Conceivably, a child "at promise" for prodigious achievement in music is equipped at birth with the intellectual, physical, and acoustic facilities necessary for extraordinary musical sensibility and performance.

Another factor included in this time frame is the point in the child's physical, social, and emotional developmental history when he or she is introduced to a domain. Playing the violin, for example, requires a certain degree of dexterity. Some children may develop the required dexterity earlier than others. The time of introduction to the instrument may thus be an important factor in whether violin playing becomes a source of pleasure or a source of frustration. Additionally, Csikszentmihalyi and Robinson (1986) noted that children's levels of social and emotional development may play important roles in determining their receptivity to domains. An adolescent grappling with age-appropriate issues of peer acceptance and popularity may opt out of long hours of piano practice and choose, instead, to spend the time socializing with peers. In the case of one chess prodigy, for example (Feldman, 1986), the attractions of the peer group proved powerful enough to jeopardize an intense commitment to the study of chess.

Another factor encompassed by the individual time frame is how likely the child's family is to nurture talent in a particular field. Mozart's musician-father, for example, fortuitously possessed the musical ability enabling him to instruct his son. He also must have valued the domain and been interested in it enough to spend many hours tutoring his children and accompanying them on their concert rounds—aside from any opportunistic motives he also may have had.

Degree of forthcoming parental support may also be affected by the child's gender. Goldsmith (1987) noted that historically, general cultural undervaluing of feminine achievement has resulted in (1) less likelihood that parents would provide necessary support for a female would-be prodigy to realize her potential and (2) a scarcity of documentation about existing girl prodigies.

Whether or not parents encourage domain-specific talents may be influenced by values or child-rearing patterns passed down from prior generations. Such "transgenerational influences" (Feldman & Goldsmith, 1986; Morelock, 1988) were apparently at work, for example, in the family of child-prodigy violinist Yehudi Menuhin. Menuhin's family had for centuries prior to his birth been shaped by a Hasidic Jewish tradition emphasizing not only the transcendent and communicative power of music, but also the development of boy prodigies groomed to assume religious leadership as rabbis. The fervor with which the Menuhin family encouraged Yehudi's musical talent may have had its roots in this centuries-old tradition.

Developmental History of the Field. Bodies of knowledge, like human beings, develop and change over time.[8] Consequently, the performance requirements and opportunities in various fields change as well. The life span of a would-be prodigy coincides with some portion of a domain's developmental history, the joint existence of the two allowing for a particular expression of the child's potential.

Prodigious achievement can only occur within domains accessible to children. This means that the domains must require little prerequisite knowledge and be both meaningful and attractive to children. Equally important is the adaptability of the domain's media and techniques to children (e.g., child-size violins are necessary for child prodigy violinists). Given these prerequisites, music performance and chess seem especially amenable to budding prodigies—as is substantiated by the fact that the largest proportion of child prodigies in recent decades emerge from these fields. Other fields produce comparatively few prodigies. There have been occasional writing prodigies, child prodigy visual artists (Goldsmith & Feldman, 1989), and on rare occasion a child prodigy in mathematics.

Historical and Cultural Time Frame. This time frame reflects historical and cultural trends affecting opportunities for learning. Prodigious achievement is necessarily influenced by the cultural importance attached to various domains. The revived interest in science and math during the 1950s because of the Soviet satellite initiatives is one example. Another is the fact that today, a potential chess prodigy in the Soviet Union is more likely to find institutionalized support and interest than would the same child in the United States.

Evolutionary Time Frame. Cultural and biological evolution provide the context within which all the other factors in prodigy development interact. Through biological variation and natural selection, human capabilities come into being and either flourish or cease to exist. Parallel evolutionary forces operate on cultures and their artifacts. This qualitative flux in the essence of humanity, and the products of humankind necessarily influence options for the expression of potential.

Co-Incidence and Prodigious Achievement

The child prodigy is the manifestation of a fortuitous concordance of the various forces of co-incidence in such a way as to maximize the expression of human potential. In each of the cases of prodigiousness contained in the research literature, there was, first of all, a child of unquestionably extraordinary native ability. This child was born into a family that recognized, valued, and fostered that ability when the child's introduction to the culturally available domain revealed its presence. The child was invariably exposed to the instruction of master teachers possessing superior knowledge of the domain and its history and imparting that knowledge in a way most likely to engage the interest and sustain the commitment of the child. For the child's part, there was generally exhibited a combination of inner-directedness and a remarkably passionate commitment to the field of extraordinary achievement. Such commitment holds social and emotional repercussions for the life of the prodigy, as we will see in the following sections.

Social and Emotional Concomitants of Prodigiousness

The prodigy shares with the extraordinarily high IQ child difficulties in establishing satisfactory peer relationships. The inner drive to master the domain of interest typically demands long hours of exacting effort. It is effort gladly devoted by the child pushed by the passion for mastery. Nevertheless, this extensive commitment leaves little time for more childlike pursuits and the forging of bonds with age-mates. If the child's domain-specific prodigiousness is accompanied by academic precocity (i.e., high IQ giftedness), he or she may experience as well all the difficulties pointed out by Hollingworth (1942).

Because of the inability of other children to keep up with the prodigy in his or her area of interest, the burden of finding some common ground for a friendship often falls to the prodigy. Consequently, friendships may become restricted to a very small group of others sharing interest in the area of prodigious specialization.

Also shared with the extraordinarily high IQ child is susceptibility to frustration from possessing widely disparate domain-specific abilities (Feldman, 1986). Prodigies, because of the ease with which they progress in their domain of expertise, may come to expect equal success in other areas. Unprepared for dealing with failure, they may find it hard to persevere and advance.

Family Relationships

The family is the catalyst for the co-incidence process (Feldman, 1986). It is the prodigy's parents who must locate necessary teachers and resources and facilitate the child's access to them. At times, this entails commuting to other cities or even uprooting the family unit permanently to resettle closer to a desired mentor. Because a prodigy progresses so rapidly, frequent changes may be required as the child outgrows a succession of mentors.

Such close parental involvement results in a longer and more intense period of dependence for prodigies than is the case in families with more typical children. As is often the case in families of handicapped children, especially close family ties may be engendered through common efforts to protect a "special" child from a potentially insensitive outside world. Though not usually the case, this protectiveness can sometimes be taken to an extreme. This is what apparently happened with piano prodigy Erwin Nyiregyhazi, who at the age of 18 was still apparently unable to tie his shoes, dress or feed himself, or make any of his career decisions (Feldman, 1986).

The strong commitment to talent development shared by prodigies and their families generally means some sacrifice by other family members. While many prodigies are only children, some do have siblings. Limited family resources may dictate that sibling talent goes unsupported. On the other hand, the prodigy's presence may influence the channeling of sibling potential. When Hepzibah Menuhin, the younger sister of child prodigy violinist Yehudi, asked to learn to play the violin like her older brother, her parents encouraged her to play the piano instead—since Yehudi needed an accompanist. When Yalta, the youngest sibling, later showed interest in the piano, she was often told to make herself useful around the house instead because the family didn't need another musician. Yet many believed Hepzibah and Yalta to be equally as talented as Yehudi (Rolfe, 1978). Neither Hepzibah nor Yalta showed signs of resentment. As is generally the case in families of prodigies (Feldman, 1986), they, like their parents, recognized the specialness of the prodigy child and seemed content to assume supporting roles. On the other hand, it is generally the case that—as in the Menuhin family—parents do acknowledge sibling talent and provide at least some degree of encouragement.

Having caught a glimpse of the dramatic showcasing of domain-specific talent characterizing the prodigy, we now turn to the last form of extreme precocity we will discuss—the idiot savant.

The Idiot Savant

The phenomenon of the "idiot savant," like that of the high IQ child and the child prodigy, has its own unique history. The term was coined in 1887 by Dr. J. Langdon Down of London (Down, 1887) to refer to severely mentally handicapped persons displaying advanced levels of learning in narrowly circumscribed areas.

Although intriguing in its own right, the term *idiot savant* fails to describe the individuals it labels, since they are generally neither "idiots" nor "savants." In Down's time, *idiot* referred to individuals operating at the lowest level of retarded intellectual functioning, as classified by practitioners on the basis of evaluation of speech and language capabilities (Scheerenberger, 1983). With the advent of IQ tests, idiocy was translated as encompassing the lowest portion of the IQ scale, spanning an IQ range of 0 to 20 (Craft, 1979).[9] In reality, however, the IQs of all known tested idiot savants have been above 20—usually in the range of 40 to 70 (Treffert, 1989).

The *savant* part of the term is a straightforward adaptation from the French word "to know" or "man of learning," which, although perhaps slightly more appropriate, is nevertheless a misnomer as well.[10]

Given the inappropriateness of the term as a whole and the pejorative connotation of the first part of it, a number of researchers (Charness, Clifton, & MacDonald, 1988; Rimland & Hill, 1983; Treffert, 1989) have suggested alternatives. Most recently, Treffert (1989) proposed *savant syndrome*—or just *savant*—as a more desirable name for the phenomenon. Based on a thorough review of the research literature on the savant appearing over the last century, Treffert described the phenomenon and proposed more precise classification terminology as well as a theoretical explanatory framework. His thoughts provide a valuable base as we continue to explore the savant.

Savant Syndrome—Definition and Description

Treffert defined savant syndrome as follows:

> Savant Syndrome is an exceedingly rare condition in which persons with serious mental handicaps, either from developmental disability (mental retardation) or major mental illness (early infantile autism or schizophrenia), have spectacular islands of ability or brilliance which stand in stark, markedly incongruous contrast to the handicap. In some, savant skills are remarkable simply in contrast to the handicap (talented savants or savant I). In others, with a much rarer form of the condition, the ability or brilliance is not only spectacular in contrast to the handicap, but would be spectacular even if viewed in a normal person (prodigious savants or savant II). (Treffert, 1989, p. xxv)

Treffert noted that the condition can be either congenital or acquired by a normal person after injury or disease of the central nervous system. It occurs six times as often in males as in females. Intriguingly, the skills can appear—and disappear—in an unexplained and sudden manner (Selfe, 1977; Treffert, 1989). Savant brilliance occurs only within very few areas: calendar calculating (as the twins George and Charles were able to do, described earlier in the chapter); music, chiefly limited to the piano; lightning calculating (the ability to do extraordinarily rapid mathematical calculations); art (painting, drawing, or sculpting); mechanical ability; prodigious memory (mnemonism); or, on rare occasion, unusual sensory discrimination (smell or touch) or extrasensory perception. Prodigious savants, however, occur primarily within the areas of music, mathematics (lightning and calendar calculating), and memory.

Research reveals a number of characteristics generally true of all savants. We discuss these next.

Characteristics of Savant Functioning

Generally, savants display minimal abstract reasoning ability combined with almost exclusive reliance on concrete patterns of expression and thought (Scheerer, Rothmann & Goldstein, 1945; Treffert, 1989). One savant (Scheerer, Rothmann, & Goldstein, 1945), for example, could memorize and sing operas in several languages, yet he had no comprehension of the abstract conceptual and symbolic meaning of words. In addition, there is a general incapacity for metacognition, or reflection upon one's internal thinking processes (LaFontaine, 1974; Scheerer, Rothmann, & Goldstein, 1945; Treffert, 1989). Calendar calculators, for example, commonly respond correctly to queries (e.g., "On what day of the week did September 1, 1744, fall?) without being able to explain how they arrived at the correct response. Those able to articulate rule-based strategies tend to have higher IQs than do their counterparts (Hermelin & O'Connor, 1986).

Another characteristic of savants is an immediate—seemingly intuitive—access to the underlying structural rules and regularities of their particular domain, be it music (Treffert, 1989), mathematical calculation (Hermelin & O'Connor, 1986; O'Connor & Hermelin, 1984) or art (O'Connor & Hermelin, 1987). Furthermore, the domain-specific rules intuitively "known" by savants are the same rules applied by those of normal or high reasoning ability who are skilled in the same area. Savants, however, bound by the structural rules of their domain, are incapable of being creative in the sense of producing totally original work. Thus, while a musical savant may imitate, improvise, or embellish based on preestablished constraining musical rules, he or she is generally incapable of composing (Treffert, 1989).

A further frequently noted aspect of the savant is a restricted range of emotion that precludes the experience of heightened passion, excitement, or sentiment (Treffert, 1989). This takes the form of generally flattened affect and—in the case of the performance of musical savants—shallow, imitative expressiveness lacking subtlety or innuendo.

While the talent of the mnemonist savant lies solely in his or her impressive memory for miscellaneous or mundane happenings, all savants claim incredibly powerful memories narrowly limited to their domains of achievement.

Treffert (1989), the first researcher to differentiate between *talented* and *prodigious* savants, reported that there have been only about 100 known prodigious savants in the world literature—12 to 15 of whom are currently living. Leslie Lemke is one who was

portrayed in depth by Treffert. In the following section we provide a synopsis of his portrayal of Lemke, followed by a discussion of what the prodigious savant adds to our understanding of extreme precocity.

Leslie Lemke

Leslie Lemke was born prematurely and given up for adoption at birth. Within the first few months of life, he developed retrolental fibroplasia—a condition common to premature babies in which the retina proliferates uncontrollably and that sometimes, as in Leslie's case, results in glaucoma with associated blindness. Consequently, Leslie had to have both eyes surgically removed.

At 6 months of age, Leslie, who was then blind, palsied, and mentally handicapped, was placed in a foster home under the care of 52-year-old May Lemke. May was an experienced nurse and governess who was well known for her skill as well as the love and devotion she showed in caring for children. When Leslie first arrived at the Lemke household, he was hardly able to cry, move, or swallow. May, however, refused to lose hope for Leslie, and, with her constant attention, Leslie was indeed able to develop.

By age 5½, Leslie was able to walk in spite of his spasticity. He also could repeat verbatim a whole day's conversation while impersonating each speaker's voice. Leslie's speech, however, was mainly repetitious, rather than social, with Leslie responding to questions by repeating them. About this age also, Leslie was discovered under a bed rhythmically strumming the bedsprings as if playing an instrument.

When Leslie was between the ages of 7 and 8, a piano was added to the Lemke household, and May, who played by ear, introduced Leslie to it by playing and singing for him and running his fingers up and down the keyboard. Leslie, too, began to play by ear. By age 8, under May's loving tutelage, Leslie also played the bongo drums, the ukelele, the concertina, the xylophone, and the accordian. By age 9, although he still required help in dressing and feeding himself, he could play the chord organ.

One incident marked in May's mind the fruition of the "miracle" of Leslie. One evening, when Leslie was 14 years old, the family watched a movie on television, after which May and her husband, Joe, retired for the evening. They were awakened at about 3:00 A.M. by strains of Tchaikovsky's Piano Concerto No. 1, the theme song to the movie they had seen earlier. Thinking that the television had been left on, May went into the living room to check and discovered Leslie at the piano playing the piece vigorously and flawlessly after having heard it only once.

Today, Leslie performs for concert audiences around the world. They are amazed by his prodigious memory. After once hearing a 45-minute opera tape, Leslie can transpose the music to the piano and sing the score back in its original foreign language. In addition, his songs are stored indefinitely, with Leslie recalling them and performing them without error after several years of intervening time. His repertoire includes thousands of pieces.

Leslie's IQ measures 58.

Explaining the Prodigious Savant

Treffert (1989) proposed an intriguing explanation for the phenomenon of the prodigious savant. Drawing upon the research of Geschwind and Galaburda (1987), he suggested that pre- or postnatal injury to the left hemisphere of the brain results in compensatory growth in the right hemisphere. This is manifested by the impairment of language and analytic thought (functions dominated by the left hemisphere) and a heightened capacity for right-brain-dominated functions (e.g., musical and spatial abilities).

Savant memory, proposes Treffert, is the manifestation of altered (compensatory) brain circuitry. Injury to the cerebral cortex, which normally manages conscious, cognitive-associative memory, causes memory functions to be shifted to a more primitive area of the brain (the *corticostriatal system*). Memory becomes nonassociative, habitual, emotionless, and nonvolitional. It becomes, in essence, a conditioned response.

Treffert affirmed, however, that even such extreme alterations in brain function and cir-cuitry fail to explain the prodigious savant's extensive access to the structural rules of domains. Such access, suggested Treffert, may be based on some inherited ancestral memory transmitted across generations.[11] This domain-specific memory, he continued, is inherited separately from general intelligence. Treffert concluded that once the groundwork is laid for savant skills, intense concentration, obsessive repetition, reinforcement from others for display of the special ability, and an unstoppable drive to exercise the ability produce the prodigious savant.

It has been suggested (Borkowski & Day, 1987; Spitz, 1982) that by contrasting groups of children representing the extremes of human talent—both the exceptionally able and the exceptionally disabled—we may come to more fully understand human intellectual capability as a whole.

Juxtaposing the Extremes—What We Learn from the Child of Extraordinary IQ, the Prodigy, and the Savant

We have examined a broad range of manifestations of human precocity. Each type, however, can be characterized in terms of (1) degree of generalized abstract reasoning ability and (2) extent and nature of domain-specific capabilities. Table 25.1 presents a breakdown of the various gradations and combinations of these reflected by the cases mentioned in this chapter. A number of interesting contrasts and similarities emerge from the research on these various forms of precocity.

Speculations on Abstract Reasoning, Emotion, and Precocity

All the types of precocious children mentioned in the research literature are described as highly attracted to and motivated by their respective areas of achievement. We suspect that this attraction derives at least partly from brain functioning particularly compatible with the cognitive demands of the area of activity. Descriptive terminology characterizing this attraction, however, ranges from *drive* to *passion,* depending on the type of precocity under discussion.

Table 25.1
A Taxonomy of Extreme Precocity

Type of Child	Characteristics
Extraordinarily high IQ– omnibus prodigy	Extraordinarily high abstract reasoning capability[a] plus extraordinarily advanced domain-specific skills in multiplicity of domains. Performs at adult professional level in multiple domains. Displays passionate involvement with numerous domains of prodigious achievement. Voracious appetite for academic knowledge.
Prodigy	Displays anywhere from above-average to extraordinarily high generalized abstract reasoning capability plus extraordinarily advanced domain-specific skill in a single domain. Performs at adult professional level in a single domain. Displays passionate involvement with domain of prodigious achievement. May demonstrate voracious appetite for academic knowledge.
Extraordinarily high IQ child	Extraordinarily high generalized abstract reasoning capability and may have notable domain-specific skills in one or more areas. May be intensely drawn to a number of different areas. May have a problem committing to a single area of interest. Voracious appetite for academic knowledge.
Prodigious savant	Minimal generalized abstract reasoning capability and islands of extraordinarily advanced domain-specific skill in one or more areas. Appears driven to exercise domain-specific capabilities. Concrete thinker.

Note: These classifications reflect the types of extreme precocity found in the research literature to date. Certain groups, such as mental calculators and mnemonists, are anomalous in that they display anywhere from minimal to extraordinarily high generalized abstract reasoning ability along with their islands of advanced skill. When minimal generalized abstract reasoning capability exists, such persons are classified as prodigious savants. According to the definition here, however, they cannot be classified as prodigies—even at higher levels of abstract reasoning ability—since standards for adult professional level performance do not exist in their areas of achievement.

[a] The generalized abstract reasoning capability referred to in this table is logical, verbal-conceptual facility.

Passion has been used to describe prodigies—those with sufficient generalized abstract reasoning abilities and concomitant conscious associative memory to come to love their domain of expertise. *Drive,* on the other hand, denotes the bare-bones motivation of the idiot savant. It is the motivation, according to Treffert, of those whose "habit" memory and lack of cognitive associations prevent a more interpretive and emotional type of mastery. We speculate that the intensity with which the savant and the prodigy conduct their pursuits is equally strong. Only the capacity for interpretation of that intensity differs.

An example of this interpretive difference is found in the way savant mental calculators and nonsavant mental calculators are reported as referring to their calculating ability. Nonsavant calculators are, first of all, generally conscious of the mental process by which they, over time, have explored the relationships among various numbers (Smith, 1983).

Furthermore, nonsavant calculators speak of numbers having become their "friends" in childhood. The Dutch mental calculator, Wim Klein, states, "Numbers are friends for me, more or less. It doesn't mean the same for you, does it, 3,844? For you it's just a three and an eight and a four and a four. But I say 'Hi, 62 squared.'" Similarly, Hans Eberstark, in recalling his lifetime experience with mental calculation, said he had different emotional reactions to various numbers, calling 36 arrogant, smug, and self-satisfied; whereas, he habored a personal affection for "the ingenious, adventurous 26, the magic, versatile 7, the helpful 37, the fatherly, reliable (if somewhat stodgy) 76" (Smith, 1983, p. xiii).

In contrast, the savant calculating twins, George and Charles, apparently never had any awareness of their methods. When asked how they did what they did, the twins simply replied "It's in my head and I do it" (Hamblin, 1966, p. 107). Their straightforward, concrete response—unembellished with associated nuances—is typical of the savant.

The concrete thought and flattened affect of the savant is in striking opposition to the thought and affect of the extraordinarily high IQ child. Silverman (1989) notes that extraordinarily high IQ children "manipulate abstract symbol systems with ease and become animated when dealing with complex relations involving many variables"—yet they may have difficulty with more concrete material, such as the rote memorization of facts (Silverman, 1989, p. 75). Equally intriguing is the fact that a tendency toward emotional intensity is cited as one of the hallmarks of this form of giftedness (Piechowski, 1979; Webb, Meckstroth, & Tolan, 1982).

Nature of the Domain

Something about the extraordinary domain-specific abilities of prodigies and savants may be revealed through studying the characteristics and structuring of the relevant domains (Goldsmith & Feldman, 1988, 1989; Treffert, 1989). It is, for example, especially intriguing that music may well be the domain in which most prodigies and most savants are found. From prodigy studies (Feldman, 1980, 1986) we learn that the self-contained and child-accessible nature of the domain provides a partial explanation. From savant studies (Treffert, 1989), however, we emerge with questions: What makes domains differentially assimilable into the human psyche? Why are the underlying structural rules of music (and math) so easily—even unconsciously—assimilated by the savant? Furthermore, to

what extent do prodigies as well, perhaps unconsciously, access the underlying structure of domains, thereby circumventing the more laborious conscious learning processes necessary for the rest of us?

The Catalytic Family

Research concerning high IQ children (Fowler, 1981), prodigies (Feldman, 1986; Feldman & Goldsmith, 1986), and prodigious savants (Treffert, 1989) confirms the critical importance of the family in coordinating and encouraging the development of extraordinary giftedness. Frequently, this is not even a conscious effort, but merely the unconscious establishment of a family milieu favoring particular activities or ways of looking at the world (Feldman & Goldsmith, 1986; Fowler, 1981). The fit of child to family may be a key issue here. Had Leslie Lemke or Wolfgang Amadeus Mozart grown up in a nonmusical family, it is questionable whether either would have developed the astonishing talent each eventually displayed.

Conclusion

It appears that there is much to be gained from additional comparative research in this area. Through it, perhaps we can begin to assemble the mysterious jigsaw puzzle before us. It is, after all, remarkable that the manifestations of extreme precocity fit together as they do, each highlighting the uniqueness of the others. Placed in careful juxtaposition, they begin to reveal the marvelous complexity and beauty residing in the spectrum of human potential.

NOTES

1. This story may be found in the Bible, King James Version, Luke 2:46–47.

2. The suggestive term *endangered species* is taken from Linda Silverman's May 1988 presentation at the Second National Conference on the Exceptionally Gifted, The Hollingworth Center for Highly Gifted Children, Auburn, ME. Dr. Silverman's presentation was entitled "The Extraordinarily Gifted: An Endangered Species?"

3. Dr. Donald Wertlieb is associate professor and chairman of the Eliot-Pearson Department of Child Study, Tufts University. He also maintains a private practice as a clinical-developmental psychologist.

4. Although these are the only systematic scientific studies of child prodigies on record, a number of biographical or psychohistorical accounts have been published providing interesting insights into the life of the prodigy. See, for example, Kathleen Montour's (1977) "William James Sidis: The broken twig" Norbert Wiener's 1953 autobiography, *Ex-Prodigy: My Childhood and Youth;* Amy Wallace's 1986 book (also about William James Sidis) *The Prodigy;* and Fred Waitzkin's 1984 book, *Searching for Bobby Fischer: The World of Chess, Observed by the Father of a Child Prodigy.*

5. At the age of 3½, when Adam, the omnibus prodigy, first entered the study, he was reported to read, write, speak several languages, study mathematics, and compose for the guitar (Feldman, 1980).

6. The four measures given were: (1) Inhelder and Piaget's (1958) five chemicals task, a test of the level of acquisition of various concrete and formal logical operations; (2) a role-taking task devised by John Flavell (1968) and his associates at the University of Minnesota, the aim of which is to test social-cognitive development by assessing the level of ability to take another's point of view; (3) a map-drawing exercise, an adaptation of Piaget and Inhelder's (1948) layout diagram task (Snyder, Feldman, & La Rossa, 1976), which gives a general estimate of the level of the coordination of spatial-logical reasoning; and (4) a psychometric measure of level of moral judgment and reasoning prepared by James Rest (1974) based on Kohlberg's stages of moral development (Feldman, 1980, p. 141).

7. Csikszentmihalyi and Robinson (1986, p. 278) define a *domain* as a "culturally structured pattern of opportunities for action, requiring a distinctive set of sensorimotor and cognitive skills—in short, a symbolic system such as music, mathematics, or athletics." A domain-specific skill, therefore, is one of the set of distinctive skills required by a particular domain. The term *field*, on the other hand, refers to the social organization of a domain—all the statuses pertinent to a domain and the patterns of behavior—or roles—expected from persons occupying the various statuses (Csikszentmihalyi & Robinson, 1986, p. 279).

8. We choose to define *genius* in terms of developmental changes in bodies of knowledge. That is, a creative contribution meriting the designation of genius is one that transforms an entire domain of human knowledge. One of such caliber, for example, was Albert Einstein's theory of relativity, which did, indeed, transform the domain of physics (Feldman, 1982).

9. The term *idiot* was used from 1910 to 1968 to refer to this portion of the IQ scale. In 1968, the World Health Organization adopted the term *profoundly retarded* to refer to this same range (Craft, 1979).

10. Bernard Rimland (1978) claims that the *idiot* in *idiot savant* is from the French *idiot,* meaning "ill-informed or untutored." This interpretation captures the paradoxical nature of the phenomenon (i.e., "untutored man of learning") without confusing the issue with IQ-associated connotations.

11. Treffert is not the first to suggest the possibility of genetically transmitted qualities of intellect. The idea has had a fair amount of support since, at least, Francis Galton's (1891) book *Hereditary Genius*. Also, Brill (1940) proposed inherited transmission of domain-specific gifts as a factor in lightning calculator abilities.

REFERENCES

Barlow, F. (1952). *Mental prodigies*. New York: Philosophical Library.

Baumgarten, F. (1930). *Wunderkinder psychologische Untersuchungen*. Leipzig: Johann Ambrosius Barth.

Bensusan, R. (1976). *Early prodigious achievement: A study of cognitive development*. Unpublished master's thesis, Tufts University, Medford, Massachusetts.

Borkowski, J. G., & Day, J. D. (1987). Research with special children: Issues, definitions, and methodologies. In J. G. Borkowski & J. D. Day (Eds.), *Cognition in special children: Comparative approaches to retardation, learning disabilities, and giftedness* (pp. 1–14). Norwood, NJ: Ablex.

Borland, J. H. (1986). IQ tests: Throwing out the bathwater, saving the baby. *Roeper Review, 6,* 163–167.

Brill, A. A. (1940). Some peculiar manifestations of memory with special reference to lightning calculators. *Journal of Nervous and Mental Disease, 90,* 709–726.

Brown, M. M. (1984). The needs and potential of the highly gifted: Toward a model of responsiveness. *Roeper Review, 6,* 123–127.

Charness, N., Clifton, J., & MacDonald, L. (1988). A case study of a musical mono-savant: A cognitive psychological focus. In L. K. Obler & D. A. Fein (Eds.), *The exceptional brain: Neuropsychology of talent and special abilities* (pp. 277–293). New York: Guilford.

Clance, P. R., & Imes, S. A. (1978). The imposter phenomenon in high achieving women: Dynamics and therapeutic intervention. *Psycho-*

therapy: Theory, Research, and Practice, 15, 241–245.

Craft, M. (Ed.). (1979). *Tredgold's mental retardation* (12th ed.). London: Bailliere Tindall.

Csikszentmihalyi, M., & Robinson, R. (1986). Culture, time, and the development of talent. In R. J. Sternberg & J. E. Davidson (Eds.), *Conceptions of giftedness* (pp. 264–284). New York: Cambridge University Press.

Down, J. L. (1887). *On some of the mental affections of childhood and youth.* London: Churchill.

Feldman, D. H. (1979). The mysterious case of extreme giftedness. In A. H. Passow (Ed.), *The gifted and the talented* (The 78th yearbook of the National Society for the Study of Education, pp. 335–351). Chicago: University of Chicago Press.

Feldman, D. H. (1980). *Beyond universals in cognitive development.* Norwood, NJ: Ablex.

Feldman, D. H. (1982). A developmental framework for research with gifted children. In D. H. Feldman (Ed.), *Developmental approaches to giftedness and creativity: New directions for child development* (pp. 31–45). San Francisco: Jossey-Bass.

Feldman, D. H. (1984). A follow-up of subjects scoring above 180 IQ in Terman's "Genetic studies of genius." *Exceptional Children, 50,* 518–523.

Feldman, D. H. (1986). *Nature's gambit: Child prodigies and the development of human potential.* New York: Basic.

Feldman, D. H., & Goldsmith, L. T. (1986). Transgenerational influences on the development of early prodigious behavior: A case study approach. In W. Fowler (Ed.), *Early experience and the development of competence: New directions for child development* (pp. 67–85). San Francisco: Jossey-Bass.

Flavell, J. H. (1968). *The development of role-taking and communication skills in children.* New York: Wiley.

Fowler, W. (1981). Case studies of cognitive precocity: The role of exogenous and endogenous stimulation in early mental development. *Journal of Applied Developmental Psychology, 2,* 319–367.

Galton, F. (1891). *Hereditary genius: An inquiry into its laws and consequences* (2nd ed.). New York: D. Appleton.

Gardner, H. (1983). *Frames of mind: The theory of multiple intelligences.* New York: Basic.

Geschwind, N., & Galaburda, A. M. (1987). *Cerebral lateralization: Biological mechanisms, associations, and pathology.* Cambridge, MA: MIT Press.

Goldsmith, L. T. (1987). Girl prodigies. Some evidence and some speculations. *Roeper Review, 10,* 74–82.

Goldsmith, L. T., & Feldman, D. H. (1988). Idiots savants—thinking about remembering: A response to White. *New Ideas in Psychology, 6*(1), 15–23.

Goldsmith, L. T., & Feldman, D. H. (1989). Wang Yani: Gifts well given. In W.-C. Ho (Ed.), *Yani: The brush of innocence* (pp. 50–62). New York: Hudson-Hills.

Hagen, E. (1980). *Identification of the gifted.* New York: Teachers College Press.

Hamblin, D. J. (1966, March 18). They are idiot savants—wizards of the calendar. *Life,* pp. 106–108.

Hermelin, B., & O'Connor, N. (1986). Idiot savant calendrical calculators: Rules and regularities. *Psychological Medicine, 16,* 1–9.

Hollingworth, L. (1926). *Gifted children: Their nature and nurture.* New York: Macmillan.

Hollingworth, L. (1942). *Children above 180 IQ: Stanford-Binet—origin and development.* Yonkers-on-Hudson, NY: World Book.

Horner, M. S. (1972). Toward an understanding of achievement related conflicts in women. *Journal of Social Issues, 28,* 157–175.

Inhelder, B., & Piaget, J. (1958). *The growth of logical thinking from childhood to adolescence.* New York: Basic.

LaFontaine, L. (1974). *Divergent abilities in the idiot savant.* Unpublished Ed.D. dissertation, Boston University School of Education.

Martinson, R. A. (1974). *The identification of the gifted and talented.* Ventura, CA: Office of the Ventura County Superintendent of Schools.

Montour, K. (1977). William James Sidis: The broken twig. *American Psychologist, 32,* 267–279.

Morelock, M. J. (1988). *Transgenerational influences on the development of children's talents, gifts, and interests.* Unpublished master's thesis, Tufts University, Medford, Massachusetts.

Morelock, M. J., & Feldman, D. H. (in press). The assessment of giftedness in preschool children. In E. Vazquez Nuttall, I. Romero, & J. Kalesnik (Eds.), *Assessing and screening preschoolers: Psychological, social, and educational dimensions.* Newton, MA: Allyn and Bacon.

O'Connor, N., & Hermelin, B. (1984). Idiot savant calendrical calculators: Math or memory? *Psychological Medicine, 14,* 801–806.

O'Connor, N., & Hermelin, B. (1987). Visual and graphic abilities of the idiot savant artist. *Psychological Medicine, 17,* 79–80.

Piaget, J. & Inhelder, B. (1948). *The child's conception of space.* London: Routledge and Kegan Paul.

Piechowski, M. M. (1979). Developmental potential. In N. Colangelo & R. T. Zaffrann (Eds.), *New voices in counseling the gifted* (pp. 25–57). Dubuque: Kendall/Hunt.

Rest, J. (1974). *Manual for defining issue test: An*

objective test of moral judgment development. Minneapolis: University of Minnesota.

Revesz, G. (1925). *The psychology of a music prodigy.* New York: Harcourt, Brace.

Rimland, B. (1978, August). Inside the mind of the autistic savant. *Psychology Today,* pp. 68–80.

Rimland, B., & Hill, A. L. (1983). Idiot savants. In J. Wortis (Ed.), *Mental retardation and developmental disabilities.* New York: Plenum.

Robinson, N. M., & Janos, P. M. (1987). The contribution of intelligence tests to the understanding of special children. In J. D. Day & J. G. Borkowski (Eds.), *Intelligence and exceptionality: New directions for theory, assessment, and instructional practices* (pp. 21–55). Norwood, NJ: Ablex.

Rolfe, L. (1978). *The Menuhins: A family odyssey.* San Francisco: Panjandrum/Aris.

Scheerenberger, R. C. (1983). *A history of mental retardation.* Baltimore: Brookes.

Scheerer, M., Rothmann, E., & Goldstein, K. (1945). A case of "idiot savant": An experimental study of personality organization. *Psychology Monograph, 58,* 1–63.

Seagoe, M. B. (1975). *Terman and the gifted.* Los Altos, CA: Kaufmann.

Selfe, L. (1977). *Nadia: A case of extraordinary drawing ability in an autistic child.* New York: Academic.

Silverman, L. K. (1988, May). *The extraordinarily gifted: An endangered species?* Paper presented at the Second National Conference on the Exceptionally Gifted, Hollingworth Center for Highly Gifted Children, Auburn, ME.

Silverman, L. K. (1988). From the editor. *Understanding Our Gifted, 1,* 2.

Silverman, L. K. (1989). The highly gifted. In J. Feldhusen, J. Van-Tassel-Baska, & K. R. Seeley (Eds.), *Excellence in educating the gifted* (pp. 71–82). Denver: Love.

Silverman, L. K., & Kearney, K. (1989). Parents of the extraordinarily gifted. *Advanced Development, 1,* 41–56.

Simonton, D. K. (1984). *Genius, creativity, and leadership.* Cambridge, MA: Harvard University Press.

Smith, S. B. (1983). The great mental calculators: *The psychology, methods, and lives of calculating prodigies, past and present.* New York: Columbia University Press.

Snyder, S., Feldman, D. H., & La Rossa, C. (1976). *A manual for the administration and scoring of a Piaget-based map drawing task.* Tufts University, Medford, Massachusetts. Summarized in O. Johnson (Ed.), (1976). *Tests and measurements in child development: A handbook II.* San Francisco: Jossey-Bass.

Spitz, H. H. (1982). Intellectual extremes, mental age, and the nature of human intelligence. *Merrill-Palmer Quarterly, 28,* 167–192.

Stanley, J. C., Keating, D. P., & Fox, L. H. (1974). *Mathematical talent: Discovery, description, and development.* Baltimore: Johns Hopkins University Press.

Terman, L. M. (Ed.) (1925–1959). *Genetic studies of genius* (Vols. 1–5). Stanford, CA: Stanford University Press.

Terman, L. M. (1975). Human intelligence and achievement. In M. V. Seagoe, *Terman and the gifted* (pp. 216–228). Los Altos, CA: Kaufmann.

Terman, L., & Merrill, M. (1973). *The Stanford-Binet Intelligence Scale* (3rd rev.). Boston: Houghton Mifflin.

Thorndike, R., Hagen, E., & Sattler, J. (1986). Technical manual, *Stanford-Binet Intelligence Scale: Fourth edition.* Chicago: Riverside.

Treffert, D. A. (1989). *Extraordinary people: Understanding "idiot savants."* New York: Harper & Row.

Waitzkin, F. (1984). *Searching for Bobby Fischer: The world of chess, observed by the father of a child prodigy.* New York: Random House.

Wallace, A. (1986). *The prodigy.* New York: Dutton.

Webb, J. T., Meckstroth, E. A., & Tolan, S. S. (1982). *Guiding the gifted child: A practical source for parents and teachers.* Columbus: Ohio Psychology.

Wechsler, D. (1974). *Wechsler Intelligence Scale for Children—Revised.* New York: Psychological Corporation.

Whitmore, J. (1980). *Giftedness, conflict, and underachievement.* Boston: Allyn and Bacon.

Wiener, N. (1953). *Ex-prodigy: My childhood and youth.* Cambridge, MA: MIT Press.

Witty, P. (1951). *The gifted child.* Boston: Heath.

26

Young Gifted Children

MICHAEL LEWIS and BARBARA LOUIS *Robert Wood Johnson Medical School,*
New Brunswick, New Jersey

Giftedness in young children can be approached from several perspectives. For example, we can ask what constitutes giftedness in young children. This is a definitional issue and one that has been discussed often in the literature regarding older children and adults. We can ask how a young child becomes gifted. This is a process-oriented question that involves genetic as well as environmental influences. Finally, we can ask if gifted preschoolers maintain their position and become gifted school children or even adults. The question of stability is, perhaps, the most complex question as it involves environmental as well as measurement issues. We will address each of these questions in turn. As assessments of intelligence across the first 2 years of life are known for their lack of predictability to later IQ (Lewis, 1983), this chapter will focus mainly on giftedness in the preschool period, that is, from 2 to 6 years of age.

Constituents of Giftedness in Young Children

Measurement of Giftedness

What is giftedness and how is it identified in very young children? Traditionally, giftedness has been determined by a given score on a standardized test of overall intelligence, usually the 98th percentile or above. This criterion bases giftedness on a *g* theory of intelligence, which states that intelligence consists of a single underlying factor, referred to as *g*, or general intelligence (Spearman, 1904). Intelligence is seen as an innate, general cognitive ability that is believed to be easily measurable by measuring a subset of *g* via any valid IQ test. As an innate characteristic, intelligence is not subject to qualitative change over the course of development. Thus, within a *g* theory, intelligence is viewed as a general, innate, and therefore stable ability that is generalizable across all aspects of intelligent functioning.

A general IQ measure is an average of many diverse abilities. As such, it is insensitive to specific areas of outstanding ability. Based on an overall IQ score, a child who possesses extremely high verbal skills and average to below average spatial skills will be determined to be of average intelligence. An alternative approach to giftedness has gained recent acceptance. Rather than a *g*-theory approach to the measurement of intelligence, a specific skills approach is recognized as a more valid assessment of a child's abilities.

Specific skills theories of intelligence have ranged from postulating anywhere from 3 (Thorndike, 1931) to 120 (Guilford, 1967) main types of intelligence. Despite their diversity, skills theories have one common postulate: A single, unitary *g* is not a sufficient model of the structure of intelligence. Intelligence is hypothesized to be a composite of underlying mental abilities (Thurstone, 1938). These abilities are considered to be independently measurable and are assumed to demonstrate no generalizability from one factor to another. The belief that intellect is composed of a "multitude of functions" (Thorndike, 1931) implies that giftedness requires a comprehensive range of measures. This produces a profile of skills for each child, thus eliminating the need for an average overall score. It then becomes possible to view a child's strengths within the context of a particular skill area. If a child exhibits extreme strength in a particular skill area (e.g., 98th percentile or above), he or she can be considered gifted in that area. It is then possible to individually tailor enrichment to each child's particular strengths, thus nurturing those abilities in which the child has exhibited precociousness.

Specific Skills and Giftedness in Young Children

Which skill areas have been found to distinguish young gifted children? Table 26.1 presents, by study, a set of specific skills that have been considered in discussing giftedness in young children. This set includes intellectual, affective, and social skills. We will consider each of these classes of skills separately.

Intellectual Skills. Before age 2½, children tend to have relatively limited verbal skills. Intelligence in preverbal children tends to be highly complex and not readily assessed by traditional IQ tests (Lewis & Michalson, 1985). In fact, early measures of attention and memory have been found to be better predictors of subsequent intellectual functioning than early performance on standardized IQ tests (Fagan & McGrath, 1981; Lewis, 1975). According to Lewis and Brooks-Gunn (1981), higher scores on IQ tests at age 2 were found for children who became more quickly disinterested in redundant stimuli at 3 months of age. Cognition, believed to be a particularly critical factor for gifted development in infants, has been postulated to comprise, at this early age, curiosity, attention, and superior memory (Lewis & Michalson, 1985).

Curiosity, concentration, memory, and sense of humor are seen as areas of differentiation between gifted and nongifted preschoolers (Freeman, 1985). Verbal intelligence, or advanced language development, also appears as an important indicator of giftedness at this age. Freeman (1985) found gifted children to be verbally precocious in three skill areas: talking, reading, and writing. This high verbal ability was found to be present as early as 3 years of age. According to Lewis and Michalson (1985), children later identified as gifted tend to utter sounds, first words, and speech earlier than average children. Educators have also cited a number of linguistic abilities as indices

of giftedness in young children: (1) advanced vocabulary, (2) use of language in a meaningful way, (3) richness of expression, elaboration, and fluency, and (4) a high frequency of questions (Lewis & Michalson, 1985). Lewis and Michalson also cited advanced memory skills as an indicator of giftedness in preschoolers. They said, however, that language ability is perhaps the primary determinant in identifying giftedness at this age.

B. White (1985) cited evidence from the Harvard Preschool Project for several intellectual abilities, in addition to an "obviously advanced capacity for language," that differentiate gifted from nongifted preschool children. In intellectual areas he cited: (1) an unusually well developed capacity to sense discrepancies or differences, including perceptual differences, discrepancies in temporally organized sequences, and errors in logic; (2) an ability to anticipate future events; (3) a more advanced ability to deal with abstractions; (4) an ability to take on the perspective of others, to utilize a less egocentric style of thinking; (5) a tendency to make interesting, often original associations; (6) a capacity to plan and carry out complicated activities; (7) a capacity to use resources effectively; and (8) an interesting perceptual style, including an ability to concentrate closely while still monitoring the surrounding environment and an ability to cope with more information per unit of time than most age-mates.

Affective Skills. Cognitive-intellectual development is not independent of affective factors (Lewis & Michalson, 1985). In attempting to differentiate gifted from nongifted infants, the quality of infants' affective responses to tests, as well as their test performance, needs to be considered. Affective factors such as pleasure in learning, and motivation, are believed to be important factors in intellectual development. In fact, pleasure in test taking has been shown, in some instances, to reflect infants' later ability better than actual test scores (Birns & Golden, 1972).

Good socioemotional adjustment seems to be characteristic of gifted preschoolers (Lewis & Michalson, 1985). Gifted children generally have been found to score higher than nongifted

Table 26.1
Indicators of Giftedness in Infants and Preschoolers

Lewis (1975).	Lewis and Brooks-Gunn (1981)	Guilford et al. (1981)	Fagan and McGrath (1981)	B. White (1985)	Lewis and Michalson (1985)	Freeman (1985)		
✓			✓		✓		Attention	INFANTS
	✓				✓		Memory	
					✓		Curiosity	
					✓		Pleasure in learning	
					✓		Motivation	
						✓	Curiosity	PRESCHOOLERS
						✓	Concentration	
		✓			✓	✓	Memory	
						✓	Sense of humor	
				✓	✓	✓	Advanced language development	
		✓			✓		High frequency of questions	
				✓			Sensitivity to discrepancies	
				✓			Anticipation of future events	
				✓			Abstract thinking	
				✓			Perspective taking	
				✓			Original thinking	
				✓			Complex planning and execution	
				✓			Effective use of resources	
				✓			Concentration, information capacity	
					✓		Self-concept	
					✓		Socioemotional adjustment	
					✓		Motivation	
					✓		Persistence	
					✓		Task orientation	
					✓		Social knowledge	
				✓	✓		Interact with older children/adults	
				✓			Ability to express affection/annoyance	
				✓			Ability to express pride in accomplishments	
				✓			Ability to role-play and make-believe	
				✓			Ability to follow and lead comfortably	
				✓			Capacity and desire to compete	

children on measures of self-concept. Also important during the preschool period are motivation, persistence, and task orientation. Their relation to rate of learning makes them important contributors to gifted achievement.

Social Skills. A number of advanced social skills have been found to be indicators of giftedness in young children. According to Lewis and Michalson (1985), gifted preschoolers develop social knowledge earlier than nongifted children. They also tend to interact more often with older children and with adults than with peers. B. White (1985) found a difference between gifted and nongifted preschoolers in their approach to social interchange. He found young gifted children especially able to: (1) get and hold the attention of adults in socially acceptable ways, (2) use adults as resources after first determining that they could not do something for themselves, (3) express affection or mild annoyance to adults and peers quite spontaneously, and (4) remark spontaneously about their pride in their accomplishments. White also found an increased tendency in gifted children to engage in role-playing and make-believe behaviors, with the roles they adopted tending more to point to the future. They could both follow and lead others comfortably, unlike average children, who tend to be comfortable only in one role or the other. He also found in gifted children an increased capacity and desire to compete.

Creativity

One pervasive problem in the identification of giftedness is the assessment of creativity. Standardized tests of intelligence, whether based on *g* or specific skills theory, do not provide a means of detecting high levels of creativity. Adherents to Guilford's (1967) structure-of-intellect model of intelligence assume that divergent thinking is the most obvious indication of creativity. Convergent thinking involves "zeroing in" on an answer that is specifically implied by the information given. Divergent thinking, on the other hand, involves searching for material that is only loosely related to what is already known so

that one's search model has a more broad-gauged template. Tests of divergent thinking (e.g., listing unusual uses for a common object) do not require a unique answer. The Guilford (1967) divergent thinking tests can be scored for eight subprocesses: (1) word fluency, the ability to rapidly generate words that fulfill particular structural requirements; (2) associational fluency, the ability to rapidly generate words that meet particular semantic requirements; (3) ideational fluency, the ability to generate, within a limited time, ideas that fulfill particular requirements; (4) expressional fluency, the ability to put rapidly into juxtaposition words that meet particular requirements of sentence structure; (5) spontaneous fluency, the ability to vary one's ideas over a wide range, even though this is not specifically called for on the test; (6) adaptive flexibility, the ability to vary one's ideas widely when the test requires that such variety be displayed; (7) redefinition, the ability to relinquish old ways of construing familiar objects in order to make use of them for a new purpose; and (8) originality, the making of responses that are statistically unique or unusual. Although tests of divergent thinking tend to measure something other than what is measured by IQ tests, they still have been found to play only a small role, if any, in actual creativity. No correlation has been found between divergent thinking scores and gifted professional accomplishment later in life.

Parental Beliefs Concerning Giftedness in Young Children

Parents also have beliefs about giftedness in their preschoolers (Louis & Lewis, 1989). These early judgments may stem from a belief that it is the parents' responsibility, as early as possible, to detect a child's ability in order to alter the environment to maximize potential (Fischer & Fischer, 1963). These implicit beliefs are of import because of the effect they may exert on the parent–child interaction (Bacon & Ashmore, 1986) and on the child's ultimate development (McGillicuddy-DeLisi, 1985).

Parents' beliefs about giftedness, like those of scientists, can follow a general or a specific skills theory of intelligence. Recently, we (Louis & Lewis, 1989) conducted a study involving 276 parents who believed their preschool children to be gifted. The parents responded to the open-ended question "Describe the kinds of things your child can do that you think are indicative of giftedness. Please be as specific as possible." The responses indicated that parents adhere to a specific skills theory of giftedness in young children.

Parental responses to the questionnaire were grouped into 26 categories. Table 26.2 presents the percentage of parental responses within each category, along with its respective rank order. Since parents could give more than one response, the cumulative percentage exceeds 100%.

What are the specific skills mentioned by parents and are they related to specific skills theories of intelligence as articulated in the scientific literature? Across this sample of parents, the abilities most frequently mentioned as reflecting giftedness were expressive language, exceptional memory, abstract thinking, development ahead of peers', curiosity, receptive language, and superior motor ability.

It is interesting to note that parents separate expression from comprehension in language. It would appear that it is easier for parents to attend to early production rather than comprehension because production is more obvious, while comprehension is a more subtle ability. All standardized tests of intelligence have both a production and a comprehension scale, or set of items, to assess language ability.

Table 26.2
Percentage of Parental Responses in Each of 26 Categories

Rank	Category	Percentage
1	Language: expressive-productive	60.5
2	Memory	55.1
3	Abstract thinking	29.3
4	Ahead of peers	26.4
5	Curiosity	25.4
6	Language: receptive-comprehensive	23.2
7	Motor ability	20.7
8	Nominations	17.8
9.5	Awareness of environment	16.7
9.5	Special knowledge	16.7
11	Early interest in books and reading	15.9
12	Word and symbol recognition	15.2
13	Learns quickly	14.1
14	Alphabet	13.4
15.5	Creativity-imagination	13.0
15.5	Socialization	13.0
17	Numbers	12.7
18.5	Attention span	12.3
18.5	Music	12.3
20	Spatial ability	9.1
21	Independence	4.7
22.5	Sleeping habits	3.6
22.5	Energy level	3.6
24	Art	2.5
25	Body parts	2.2
26	Leadership	0.4

The pervasive use of these items reflects the central importance given to language ability as a measure of intelligence (see, for example, the Stanford-Binet Intelligence Scale [Terman & Merrill, 1973], the McCarthy Scales of Children's Abilities [McCarthy, 1972], and the Wechsler Preschool and Primary Scale of Intelligence [WPPSI] [Wechsler, 1967]). Early language ability has been used by many as a marker of giftedness (e.g., Freeman, 1985; Lewis & Michalson, 1985; B. White, 1985).

In general, however, there has not been a strong relationship between the age at which the first word is spoken and subsequent language ability. This has led some to believe that early language usage may *not* be a good marker of giftedness. Why should this be? It simply may be that early language is not highly related to later giftedness; other factors may play a dominant role, for example, the social-emotional life of the child. Alternatively, it may be that our observation of the relationship has been flawed. For example, when we consider the overall correlation between early language acquisition and subsequent giftedness, we may forget that a lack of early speech may be related to low motivation or retardation; however, the presence of early speech is likely to reflect giftedness. The total sample is made up of two groups of subjects: children who do speak early and those who do not. Those who do speak early, are usually gifted. The group of those who do not speak early includes both gifted and slower developing children. Therefore, the overall relationship between early speech and subsequent ability is obscured.

Memory is the second most frequently mentioned ability. Memory is necessary for most complex cognitive abilities; thus superior memory, or early memory abilities, should reflect giftedness. Superior memory is measured by many tests of intelligence (e.g., the McCarthy scale, the Stanford-Binet scale, the WPPSI) and is seen as important in its influence on other abilities, such as language skills. For example, the McCarthy scale employs a number of verbal items in the construction of its memory scale.

Abstract thinking is also thought to be a basic component of general mental ability. For example, Renzulli (1986) stated that general ability consists of information processing capacities, the integration of experiences in such a manner as to adaptively generalize to novel situations, and the capacity for abstract thinking. Standardized tests commonly include abstract thinking as an integral element of intelligence. This ability is incorporated into such items as opposite analogies, similarities and differences, picture arrangement, definitions of abstract words, and others. Abstract thinking subsumes the ability to reason. Reasoning takes many different forms. Opposite analogies require not only a language ability but the ability to "reason out" the opposites of the items presented. The same reasoning ability applies to similarities and differences. The type of reasoning ability required for picture arrangement is causal-logical in its application. While "abstract thinking" is considered to be an important ability, it is clear that there are multiple skills involved.

Two skills that parents mention, and that are not usually found in intelligence tests, are curiosity and motor ability. Curiosity is a broad category, including inquisitiveness and exploration, and is seen by some as an integral aspect of creativity (Renzulli, 1986). Curiosity has been mentioned as an important aspect of intelligence both from a cognitive (Hunt, 1961) and from a motivational point of view (R. W. White, 1959). While many investigators feel that curiosity is an important feature of intelligence (Hunt, 1961; McCall, Eichorn, & Hogarty, 1977), it generally does not appear on standardized tests of mental ability in the form of either curiosity or creativity. However, curiosity may be an important aspect of knowledge acquisition (Lewis & Michalson, 1985). That is, curiosity may be an underlying factor, not directly measurable, involved in many aspects of intelligent functioning, arising from motivation and influencing the acquisition of knowledge. Parents in our study seemed to recognize curiosity as an important aspect of intelligence.

Motor ability is easily observed. Parents usually know developmental milestones and are aware of the normative ages of acquisition. Early attainment of common milestones signals advanced development to a parent, whereas late attainment may signal retardation. Generally, there is no relationship between motor ability and intelligence. However, pediatricians tend to use it as an indicator of mental development because children's motor development and intelligence *are* related at the extreme low end of the distribution (Honzik, 1983).

Although motor ability is used in some tests of infant intelligence (e.g., the Bayley Scales of Infant Development [Bayley, 1969]), it is recognized *not* to be a measure of cognitive ability. For example, Lewis, Jaskir, and Enright (1986) found a heavy component of manipulation (a motor ability) in young children that was not related to subsequent intellectual ability as measured by the Stanford-Binet Intelligence Scale. While motor ability is not a measure of intellectual development, advanced motor ability is used by parents as an indicator of giftedness. Why is this so? Probably because of its ease of observation and common, though inaccurate, stereotype.

Parental beliefs about giftedness tend to follow a specific skills structure that is consistent with the conclusions of researchers, with a few exceptions. While studies of giftedness mention general language ability, we have found that expressive language is more salient for parents than comprehension, a detail worth noting. Moreover, parents include precocious motor ability as an indicator, perhaps because of the attention some professionals (i.e., pediatricians) give to it or because of its ease of observation. Here, then, is a parental belief that is not consistent with those of experts.

Overall, there seems to be fair agreement on the constituents of giftedness in young children, among both scientific theories and parental implicit theories. The next issue to be addressed is the question of process. That is, what are the mechanisms by which a young child becomes gifted?

Mechanisms of Giftedness in Young Children

Genetic and Environmental Influences

Development in general, and cognitive development in particular, is the result of interacting forces both internal and external to the developing organism. Internal, or endogenous, influences involve such factors as biological maturation, temperamental variables, and various genetic predispositions that may impose constraints on the level of developmental attainment. External, or exogenous, influences are environmental forces that exert pressure on the individual and influence the course of development. The development of intelligence is a result of an interaction between genetic predispositions and environmental influences. A newborn can be seen as an organism constrained by its genetic blueprint within a range of potential intellectual attainment. Environmental influences will determine where within this range the individual's intellectual development will culminate. If the environment is optimal, development is expected to progress along the upper end of the child's genetic potential. Conversely, if the environment is extremely adverse, the child's development will be constrained toward the lower end of the range. Because nothing can be done at present to modify the genetic material with which an individual is endowed, it is the environmental influences on the development of intelligence that will be discussed.

The development of intelligence is believed to be a social process dependent upon the quality and organization of the human environment in which it evolves (Eisenberg, 1969). Sensory stimulation, both perceptual and social, is held to play an important role. It is the quality and meaningfulness of active experience, especially conversational interchange, that appear to be crucial. Environmental effects on cognitive development are believed to exert their influence through the quality of early learning experiences both within and outside the home (Rutter, 1979). High-quality learning experiences are expected to lead to optimal development; environmental deprivation results in cognitive deficits.

The home environment typically is the target for investigation into environmental influences on early cognitive development. Instruments such as the Home Observation for Measurement of the Environment (HOME) Inventory have been utilized as a measure of the quality of the home environment (Bradley & Caldwell, 1984). Moderate to strong correlations between the quality of the home environment and measures of cognitive development throughout the preschool years have been found using these instruments. Intensity of stimulation (Hayes, 1977), appropriate play materials, maternal involvement, organization of the environment, avoidance of restriction and punishment (Bradley & Caldwell, 1976; Elardo, Bradley, & Caldwell, 1975), variety in daily stimulation (Bradley & Caldwell, 1976; Elardo et al., 1975; Wachs, Uzgiris, & Hunt, 1971), and exposure to spoken language (Wachs et al., 1971) are environmental factors significantly correlated with infants' cognitive development. Interpersonal interactions, including care-giver sensitivity and responsivity, also appear to strongly influence early cognitive development (Bradley & Caldwell, 1976; Coates & Lewis, 1984; Elardo et al., 1975; Lewis, 1978).

Some early-deprivation effects have been found to be reversible. For example, Dennis (1973) demonstrated improvements in cognitive functioning when young children were removed from poor institutional environments and placed in better institutions or in adoptive homes. Studies of children rescued from extreme deprivation in middle or late childhood illustrate the possibility of at least partial cognitive recovery even during this later age period (Curtiss, 1977; Davis, 1947; Dennis, 1973; Kagan, 1976; Koluchova, 1972). The observation that later-adopted children tend to have lower IQs than children adopted in infancy (Dennis, 1973) has been taken as evidence that environmental influences exert a stronger effect on intellectual development during the preschool years than during later childhood (Clarke, 1984; Clarke & Clarke, 1976; Rutter, 1981a).

The concept of *canalization* (Scarr-Salapatek, 1976; Waddington, 1957) has been applied to early mental development in an effort to explain the differential effect of the environment on the development of intelligence across the early years (McCall, 1983). Canalization has as its basic principle a *creod,* or species-specific path along which all normal development progresses in the presence of appropriate environments. When perturbation in the environment occurs, atypical developmental patterns may result. Intrinsic to the notion of canalization is a *self-righting tendency.* When a behavior is highly canalized, the tendency is to return to the normal path of development following a deflection as a result of environmental influences. As behavior becomes less canalized, the tendency is to deviate further from the proscribed path in response to environmental anomalies and to remain in the new position. It is believed that mental development during the first 2 years of life is highly canalized. Between the ages of approximately 2 and 6 years it becomes less canalized and the environment begins to exert more lasting effects. As a consequence of these stronger and more enduring environmental effects, individual differences become more pronounced and, as a function of the stability of the environment, potentially more stable after this time. This approach suggests discontinuous and unpredictable development caused by the buffeting forces of the environment. It also implies that if the environment were to remain stable (or "appropriate") during this early period, so too would mental development.

Environmental Deprivation and Early Giftedness

Preliminary data from a study of giftedness in inner city preschool children conducted by the Institute for the Study of Child Development (Lewis, Louis, & Feiring, 1989) suggest that environmental deprivation may not exert its strongest influence on the development of giftedness until after the preschool period. Preschool children, ages 2 to 5, from the inner city of Newark, New Jersey, an economically depressed city consisting of a 77% minority population, have been tested on a variety of cognitive measures. These measures include standardized tests of intelligence that yield overall IQ scores as well as ability profiles (McCarthy Scales of Children's Abilities, Stanford-Binet Intelligence Scale, WPPSI).

Standardized tests of intelligence have been criticized as being culturally biased against minority populations. A 15-point disparity in scores on various standardized IQ tests has been the general finding when comparing the performance of blacks and whites in this country (MacKenzie, 1984). A mean of 100 is consistently found for the white population, compared with a mean of 85 for the black population. This disparity begins to be detectable as early as 3 to 4 years of age (Loehlin, Lindzey, & Spuhler, 1975). However, in our population of 271 minority preschool children tested to date, the mean IQ across all tests has been 102. Using a specific skills approach, which sets the criterion for giftedness as performance at or above the 98th percentile in any one of four skill areas, we identified 4% of our 2- to 5-year-old minority sample as gifted.[1]

These results suggest that the environment may begin to exert a more powerful effect on intellectual development as children reach school age. This is in keeping with an age-related differential-magnitude-of-effect model of environmental influences on giftedness. It also illustrates the importance of early enrichment programs for young gifted children, especially those from deprived backgrounds. If giftedness is not nurtured at an early age, it is vulnerable to extinction. This brings us to the question of the stability of giftedness.

Stability of Giftedness in Young Children

A central question in any discussion of giftedness in preschool children is that of stability: Do gifted preschoolers become gifted children and adults or do they eventually "level off"? The young gifted child certainly has a head start compared with his or her same-aged peers, and there is no reason to believe that this advantage is necessarily temporary. Given the proper nurturance, the possibility exists for the optimal development of any talent. The popular notion that giftedness in young children is transitory arises from common misconceptions regarding the stability of intelligence.

Before 3 to 4 years of age, the cross-age predictive ability of standardized IQ tests is modest at best and of little clinical value (Lewis & McGurk, 1972; McCall, Hogarty, & Hurlburt, 1972). Predictive ability increases rapidly from age 3 until after age 6, when cross-age correlations of IQ scores reach .80 and above (Bayley, 1949). The inception of this stability can be detected by around 2 to 3 years of age

(McCall, 1983). What mechanisms are responsible for the relative lack of stability found within the first 6 years of life?

Within the infancy period the problem of stability appears to lie within the measurement instruments themselves. The inability of infant intelligence measures to predict later levels of intellectual ability is well documented. Standardized measures such as the Bayley and Gessell, and nonstandardized tests constructed out of a Piagetian framework of sensorimotor development, have evidenced relatively little reliability as predictive measures of intelligence both within infancy and from infancy to later childhood (Lewis, 1973). Measures of attentional processes have shown much greater cross-age predictability than have traditional IQ scores (Honzik, 1983; Lewis, 1969; Lewis & Brooks-Gunn, 1981). Until the internal validity of infant measures is established, it is a fruitless effort to look elsewhere for possible causes of instability within the first 2 years of life. However, stability of IQ scores between the ages of 2 and 6 may be shown to be affected by environmental factors as well as measurement issues.

Environmental Factors in the Stability of Giftedness

Many features in the environment may influence the course of giftedness. These include ongoing deprivation as well as major stress events in the lives of children. If environmental influences exert stronger pressure on the course of development as children advance in age, the effects of chronic environmental deprivation will only begin to be visible after the infancy stage. This implies that although we may be finding gifted preschoolers in an extremely deprived environment (Lewis et al., 1989), these children may be at risk for losing their giftedness with continued exposure at their present level of deprivation.

Major stress events in the lives of young children also may contribute to a change in cognitive status across time, leading to lack of stability (Louis, 1989). There is a paucity of information regarding the effects of acute stress events on the development or the stability of intelligence within the first 6 years of life. What little does exist, however, suggests that there is an effect of major stress events upon early cognitive development. The experience of stress has been related to depressed performance levels on standardized tests of intelligence, at least in older children (Lefkowitz & Tesiny, 1985). An intermittent depressed performance may be one mechanism for the lack of stability of intelligence across the early years.

The most salient stress events for young children appear to center around issues of separation and loss. Included in this category are such stressors as the death of a parent, prolonged separation due to hospitalization of the child, and separation due to divorce.

Death of a close family member is believed to be the most potent stressor that can occur in a person's life (Elliott & Eisendorfer, 1982; Hamburg, Elliott, & Parron, 1982; Holmes & Rahe, 1967; Rabkin & Streuning, 1976). The experience of maternal death before the child is 5 is believed by some to be a factor in severe adult depression (Brown, 1982). Behavioral responses of young children to the death of a parent have been found to include eating and sleep disturbances, withdrawal, restlessness, dependency, regression, and concentration and learning difficulties (Krupnick & Solomon, 1988). Repeatedly, poor school performance has been found to be a behavioral consequence of childhood bereavement (Bedell, 1973; Binger, 1973; VanEerdewegh, Bieri, Parrilla, & Clayton, 1982). VanEerdewegh et al. (1982), in a study of 2- to 17-year-olds, found school performance to decline over time following the death of a parent. Between 1 and 13 months following the death, an increase in the number of children showing continued disinterest in school was found, despite an increased interest in general nonacademic activities. Intellectual impairment has been found in bereaved children as a result of parental death following prolonged illness (Douglas, Ross, & Simpson, 1968). Death of a sibling also affects the child. Guilt, even 5 years after the death, depressive withdrawal, self-punitive and accident-prone behaviors, and an excessive fear of death (Cain, Fast, & Erickson, 1964), as well as enuresis, somatic complaints, poor school performance, and school refusal (Binger, 1973), are

seen as consequences of sibling death. According to Cain et al. (1964), disturbances of cognitive functioning are found among some children. These children appear to use ignorance as a defense against the painful realities of loss.

Hospital admission is especially stressful for children between the ages of 6 months and 4 years (Illingworth & Holt, 1955; Prugh, Staub, Sands, Kirschbaum, & Lenihan, 1953; Schaffer & Callender, 1959). Two reasons have been cited for the enhanced effect of hospitalization during this early age period (Rutter, 1981b). First, stress among this group appears to be related to separation from the attachment figure. This is a time when selective attachments are being formed; however, young children are not yet skilled at maintaining an attachment relationship over a prolonged separation. Stress due to hospitalization is found to be greatly reduced by daily visitation or the presence of a parent or sibling. The second source of distress among hospitalized children centers around hospital procedures themselves and parental anxiety. Although older children may find a hospital stay unpleasant, psychiatric disorder is rarely a result of hospitalization in school-age children (Rutter, 1981a). Preschoolers, on the other hand, show an increased frequency of acute distress reaction, sometimes persisting for months after the experience (Rutter, 1981b). These symptoms include the typical separation reactions referred to by Bowlby (1973), including ambivalence toward the attachment figure upon reunion followed by a prolonged period of clinging behavior and separation anxiety. Distress related to a single hospital admission of 1 week or less appears to be transitory. However, the experience of two hospital admissions within the preschool years is associated with marked risk for long-term psychiatric disorder (Douglas, 1975; Quinton & Rutter, 1976).

Parental divorce has been the subject of much research in recent years. Investigators consistently have found a relationship between divorce and school-related outcome in children. Disruption in concentration and the ability to learn as well as difficulties in school achievement and social relationships have been consistent findings (Brown, 1980; Hetherington,

1989; Kelly & Wallerstein, 1976; Wallerstein, 1983). An inhibition of play has been found for preschool as well as elementary school–aged children (Wallerstein, 1977a, 1977b, 1983; Wallerstein & Kelly, 1975). School-aged children report an absorption in thinking about the divorce to the exclusion of other activities (Wallerstein, 1983). Preschool children tend to exhibit all the classic separation symptoms: behavioral regression, acute separation anxiety and concern about being abandoned by both parents, sleep disturbances, more tearful, irritable, aggressive behavior, and an inhibition of play (Wallerstein, 1977a, 1977b; Wallerstein & Kelly, 1975).

Major stressors have been viewed as capable of diverting development from an optimum to a suboptimum pathway, especially when affecting an immature individual (Bowlby, 1973). Withdrawal, a classic reaction of young children to separation (Bowlby, 1973, 1980), appears to provide a possible mechanism for perturbations in cognitive development.

Environmental effects on the development of intelligence exert their influence through their effect on the sensory system of the child. That is, the child is exposed to certain qualities in the world around him or her and processes them through the senses. Further assimilation of this novel information is dependent upon predetermined forces within the child, including genetic predispositions and previous developmental attainment. A child from a chronically deprived environment is virtually never exposed to potentially growth-inducing stimuli and, therefore, cannot benefit from such influences. A child who is withdrawn, on the other hand, may be exposed to a rich array of growth-inducing stimuli from which, under normal circumstances, he or she would optimally benefit. The state of withdrawal, however, prevents these stimuli from intruding upon the sensory system, thus effectively blocking their potential for developmental advancement.

A child's level of cognitive achievement at the time of separation also will determine the adverse effect upon the child's future cognitive development. A young infant, although visibly affected by the sudden absence of his or her primary care giver, shows greater evidence of disorientation or temporary behavioral disorganization than emotional disturbance (Raphael, 1983). Not yet cognitively capable of representational thought, that is, carrying with him or her a mental image of the absent mother, a very young infant only requires an adequate surrogate to fill the care-giving role, allowing resumption of the developmental process. For an older child or adult, the capacity for representational thought in combination with the capacity for abstract reasoning may serve as a buffer against total devastation in the face of a major loss. Preschool children, however, while possessing the capacity for representational thought, lack the ability to reason on an abstract level. The result of this interaction is an intense longing for the lost person in the absence of an understanding of death and an inability to realistically plan for the future. Children in this age group tend to withdraw (Raphael, 1983) and consequently may be vulnerable to a temporary arrest in development.

The result of an arrest in cognitive development is a decline in cognitive performance relative to one's peers. A child may recover from this temporary lag over time or, depending upon the duration and severity of reaction to the loss and the available environmental resources, may stabilize at the lower level. Either outcome will attenuate stability findings for children of this age range as a whole.

When studying the stability of intelligence over the first 6 years of life, it clearly is important to take into account major stress events in the lives of children. It is possible that those children who manifest the greatest degree of fluctuation across time are those who have experienced major stress events between measurement occasions during the early years of life. It is these children who may be attenuating overall findings of stability.

Research on the effects of acute stress has shown that single acute stressors early in life seldom lead to long-term deficits. Multiple acute stressors, however, are likely to lead to developmental perturbations. Children exposed to multiple acute stressors in combination with a chronically deprived environment are at greatest risk for long-term developmental damage (Rutter, 1979).

Invulnerability and Stability of Intelligence

Some children fail to exhibit any adverse effects of acute stress, even when multiple stressors are encountered over the early years of life. In fact, there exist children who in the face of events typically associated with a high probability of maladaptive outcome, manifest instead a high level of behavioral adaptation and competence (Garmezy, 1983). These are children referred to by Anthony (1978) as *invulnerables*.

We have found that gifted preschool children manifest many of the characteristics found to apply to invulnerable children. They are more competent, confident, humorous, flexible in their approach, and confident of the accessibility of adults in their environment (Freeman, 1985; B. White, 1985) than nongifted preschool children are. Invulnerable children also are found to manifest higher levels of intelligence than more highly susceptible children (Hetherington, 1989). Evidence of the relationship of invulnerability and intelligence level suggests that children in the gifted range of intellectual ability may be more invulnerable to major stress events than children of average or below-average ability. If this is the case, it is possible that stability is more strongly affected by major stress events in the lives of children in the lower ability groups than in the lives of the exceptionally able children.

Measurement Issues in the Stability of Giftedness

A core issue in any discussion of the stability of giftedness is measurement. The lack of predictability of early infant measures has been discussed. Two remaining issues that have potential impact on the stability of giftedness across the preschool years involve definitional and statistical issues in the measurement of stability.

Definitional Issues in the Measurement of Stability. The issue of *g* versus skills theory in the measurement of giftedness may influence the stability question. Indices of overall intelligence, IQ scores, have evidenced considerable instability across early childhood.

Greater stability may be found within specific skill domains. Recall that any measure of intelligence using an overall IQ score is merely an average of abilities in several different skill areas. As such, areas of particular strength or weakness are obscured. It perhaps is at these extreme ends of ability that stability is more likely to be found.

Lewis et al. (1986), using the Bayley Scales of Infant Development, identified across-age correlations that suggested a set of separable but related factors over the first 3 years of life. The strongest and most continuous of these factors seemed to be a verbal path that can be traced from 3 months (auditory production) through 24 months (verbal-symbolic and lexical) to 36-month Stanford-Binet scores. A nonverbal path also emerged: 12-month imitation and means–end thinking correlated positively with each other and with 24-month imitation and spatial factors. Both these 24-month factors correlated positively with 36-month Stanford-Binet scores. The 12-month means–end scores correlated strongly with 36-month Stanford-Binet scores. Thus, distinct verbal, spatial, and nonverbal paths of mental development emerged from the Lewis et al. data.

It is possible that stability will be found within the specific skill domains that represent a child's particular strengths and weaknesses, rather than within an average of all skills (i.e., overall IQ). If this is the case, increased stability of giftedness across the early years may be found within a specific skills paradigm.

Group Differences in Stability. Correlations are created from samples that are made up of a large proportion of children evidencing high stability of scores and a small proportion of children manifesting extremely low stability. What happens, however, if individual subgroups are identified and within-group comparisons are made? Perhaps the correlation between test ages is being reduced by one or two groups of children manifesting extremely unstable performance.

It seems that this is the case. In a group of data analyzed by McCall, Appelbaum, and Hogarty (1973), 36% of the subjects were found to exhibit considerable lack of stability of general intelligence between ages 2½ and 17.

However, 64% of the sample exhibited relative stability across time. These subjects were found within the high-average and gifted ranges of intelligence. Gifted children, while manifesting some variability, remained within the gifted range of ability (see Louis, 1989a). Greater stability also is found at the low end of the IQ distribution (Honzik, 1983; McCall, 1979, 1983).

Thus statistics using different groups may obscure the data to the point where they lose their meaning. We may need to isolate the extremes, that is, the children scoring in the gifted range, just as children at the low end of the continuum have been isolated for statistical purposes. These children may not develop along the same course as more normative children.

Fluctuating Range and Its Effect on Stability. Finally, we will discuss the possible effect of fluctuations in the distribution of scores about the mean obtained at different age levels of assessment. If a greater range of scores is expected at one age than another, lack of cross-age stability would be inevitable. For example, a 2-year-old with a "true" score of 100 can score anywhere from 89 to 111 on any given test occasion. A 6-year-old would range from 92 to 108 around his or her "true" score of 100. A 14-year-old would score between 92.5 and 107.5. It can be seen from a comparison of these figures that greater stability of intelligence can be expected between ages 6 and 14 than between ages 2 and 6 (Louis, 1989).

The greatest stability also is expected to be found within the lowest scoring group of children, based on evidence of the least amount of variability of scores. This is consistent with past research findings (e.g., McCall, 1979, 1983; Honzik, 1983).

Reviewing the age-by-ability confidence interval data provided by Sattler (1982) and the McCall et al. (1973) data, it is apparent that if stability is to be found within the 2- to 6-year age range, it will be within the low-average to high-average ranges of ability. It is perhaps necessary to remove the entire group of children scoring superior or above and involve them in separate analyses.

Conclusion

Several issues warrant attention in the discussion of young gifted children. Knowledge of the constituents of giftedness in preschoolers is important to their identification. Early verbal ability, strong memory skills, and abstract reasoning ability are seen by both researchers and parents as important indicators of giftedness. Researchers, as well as parents, adhere to a specific skills rather than a g theory of intelligence in the identification of giftedness in preschool children.

Giftedness is the result of genetic and environmental influences on the lives of young children. A child's level of developmental attainment is constrained by genetic predispositions. The course of development, however, is determined by environmental forces. These forces may exert a differential magnitude of effect across age, leading to an effect on the stability of giftedness.

The stability of giftedness may be affected by statistical as well as environmental issues. It is environmental factors, however, that fall more readily under our immediate sphere of influence. A differential magnitude of environmental effects explanation of the lack of stability of individual differences in the opening years of life, as delineated in this chapter, provides us with one rationale for the low predictability of giftedness from very young ages. This type of approach suggests discontinuous and unpredictable development caused by the buffeting forces of the environment. It implies that if the environment were to remain optimal during the preschool period and beyond, gifted status would remain stable. This is the most influential argument for early enrichment programs for young gifted children. Without nurturance and encouragement across these early years, giftedness is at the mercy of a fickle environment and may disappear. This is an important consideration in the study and education of young gifted children and one that should not be overlooked.

NOTE

1. One difficulty with using a specific skills criterion is that we do not know the expected percentage

for the population. Four separate skills are assessed (verbal, perceptual, quantitative, and memory). If 2% of the population scores at the gifted level on each skill, the maximum percentage across skills would be 8%, assuming no overlap in children across skill areas. The case of totally independent scores is unlikely due to correlation of performance across skills. The actual expected percentage is unclear but must lie between 2 and 8%.

REFERENCES

Anthony, E. J. (1978). A new scientific region to explore. In E. J. Anthony, C. Koupernik, & C. Chiland (Eds.), *The child in his family: Vulnerable children* (International yearbook, Vol. 4). New York: Wiley.

Bacon, M. K., & Ashmore R. D. (1986). A consideration of the cognitive activities of parents and their role in the socialization process. In D. M. Brodzinsky & R. D. Ashmore (Eds.), *Thinking about the family* (pp. 3–33). Hillsdale, NJ: Erlbaum.

Bayley, N. (1949). Consistency and variability in the growth of intelligence from birth to eighteen years. *Journal of Genetic Psychology, 75,* 165–196.

Bayley, N. (1969). *Bayley scales of infant development: Birth to two years.* New York: Psychological Corporation.

Bedell, J. (1973, November). *The maternal orphan: Paternal perception of mother loss.* Paper presented at the annual meeting of the Foundation of Thanatology, New York.

Binger, C. M. (1973). Childhood leukemia. Emotional impact on siblings. In E. J. Anthony & C. Koupernik (Eds.), *The child in his family: The impact of disease and death* (Vol. 2, p. 171–188). New York: Wiley.

Birns, B., & Golden, M. (1972). Prediction of intellectual performance at 3 years from infant tests and personality measures. *Merrill-Palmer Quarterly, 18,* 53–58.

Bowlby, J. (1973). *Attachment and loss: II: Separation, anxiety and anger.* London: Hogarth.

Bowlby, J. (1980). *Attachment and loss: III: Loss, sadness and depression.* New York: Basic.

Bradley, R., & Caldwell, B. (1976). Early home environment and changes in mental test performance from 6 to 16 months. *Developmental Psychology, 12,* 93–97.

Bradley, R. H. & Caldwell, B. M. (1984). Children: A study of the relationship between home environment and cognitive development during the first

5 years. In A. W. Gottfried (Ed.), *Home environment and early cognitive development: Longitudinal research* (pp. 5–56). New York: Academic.

Brown, B. F. (1980). A study of the school needs of children in one-parent families. *The Phi Delta Kappan, 61,* 537–540.

Brown, G. W. (1982). Early loss and depression. In C. M. Parkes & R. S. Hinde (Eds.), *The place of attachment in human behavior.* New York: Basic.

Cain, A. C., Fast, I., & Erickson, M. E. (1964). Children's disturbed reactions to death of a sibling. *American Journal of Orthopsychiatry, 34,* 741–752.

Clarke, A. M. (1984). Early experience and cognitive development. *Review of Research in Education, 11,* 125–160.

Clarke, A. M. & Clarke, A. D. B. (1976). *Early experience: Myth and evidence.* London: Open Books.

Coates, D. L. & Lewis, M. (1984). Infant interaction and infant cognitive status as predictors of school performance and cognitive behavior in six-year-olds. *Child Development, 55,* 1219–1230.

Curtiss, S. (1977). *Genie: A psycholinguistic study of a modern-day "wild child."* New York: Academic.

Davis, K. (1947). Final note on a case of extreme isolation. *American Journal of Sociology, 52,* 432–437.

Dennis, W. (1973). *Children of the creche.* New York: Appleton-Century-Crofts.

Douglas, J. W. B. (1975). Early hospital admissions and later disturbances of behaviour and learning. *Developmental Medicine and Child Neurology, 17,* 456–480.

Douglas, J. W. B., Ross, J. M., & Simpson, H. R. (1968). *All our future: A longitudinal study of secondary education,* London: Davies.

Eisenberg, L. (1969). The social development of intelligence. In H. Freeman (Ed.), *Progess in mental health* (pp. 167–177). New York: Grune & Stratton.

Elardo, R., Bradley, R., & Caldwell, B. (1975). The relation of infants' home environment to mental test performance from six to thirty-six months: A longitudinal analysis. *Child Development, 46,* 71–76.

Elliott, G. R., & Eisendorfer, C. (Eds.). (1982). *Stress and human health: A study by the Institute of Medicine, National Academy of Sciences.* New York: Springer.

Fagan, J. F., & McGrath, S. K. (1981). Infant recognition memory and later intelligence. *Intelligence, 5*(2), 121–130.

Fischer, J. L., & Fischer, A. (1963). The New Englanders of Orchardtown. In B. B. Whiting (Ed.), *Six cultures: Studies of child rearing.* New York: Wiley.

Freeman, J. (Ed.). (1985). *The psychology of gifted children: Perspectives on development and education*. New York: Wiley.

Garmezy, N. (1983). Stressors of childhood. In N. Garmezy & M. Rutter (Eds.), *Stress, coping, and development in children* (pp. 43–84). New York: McGraw-Hill.

Guilford, J. P. (1967). *The nature of human intelligence*. New York: McGraw-Hill.

Guilford, A. M., Scheuerle, J., & Schonburn, S. (1981). Aspects of language development in the gifted. *Gifted Child Quarterly, 25,* 159–163.

Hamburg, D., Elliott, G. R., & Parron, D. (1982). *Health and behavior: Frontiers of research in the biobehavioral sciences—A report of the Institute of Medicine*. Washington, DC: National Academy Press.

Hayes, J. (1977). *Premature infant development: An investigation of the relationship of neonatal stimulation, birth condition and home environment to development at age three years*. Unpublished doctoral dissertation. Purdue University, Lafayette, Indiana.

Hetherington, E. M. (1989). Coping with family transitions: Winners, losers, and survivors. *Child Development, 60,* 1–14.

Holmes, T. H., & Rahe, R. H. (1967). The social readjustment rating scale. *Journal of Psychosomatic Research, 11,* 213–218.

Honzik, M. P. (1983). Measuring mental abilities in infancy: The value and limitations. In M. Lewis (Ed.), *Origins of intelligence: Infancy and early childhood* (2nd ed., pp. 67–105). New York: Plenum.

Hunt, J. McV. (1961). *Intelligence and experience*. New York: Ronald.

Illingworth, R. S., & Holt, K. S. (1955). Children in hospital: Some observations on their reactions with special reference to daily visiting. *Lancet, 2,* 1257–1262.

Kagan, J. (1976). Resilience and continuity in psychological development. In A. M. Clarke & A. D. B. Clarke (Eds.), *Early experience: Myth and evidence* (pp. 97–121). London: Open.

Kelly, J., & Wallerstein, J. (1976). The effects of parental divorce: Experiences of the child in early latency. *American Journal of Orthopsychiatry, 46,* 20–32.

Koluchova, J. (1972). Severe deprivation in twins: A case study. *Journal of Child Psychology and Psychiatry, 13,* 107–114.

Krupnick, J. L., & Solomon, F. (1988). Death of a parent or sibling during childhood. In J. Bloom-Feshbach & S. Bloom-Feshbach (Eds.), *The psychology of separation and loss: Perspectives on development, life transitions, and clinical practice* (pp. 345–371). San Francisco: Jossey-Bass.

Lefkowitz, M. M., & Tesiny, E. P. (1985). Depression in children: Prevalence and correlates. *Journal of Consulting and Clinical Psychology, 53,* 647–656.

Lewis, M. (1969). A developmental study of learning within the first three years of life: Response decrement to a redundant signal. *Monographs of the Society for Research in Child Development, 34*(9, Whole No. 133). Chicago: University of Chicago Press.

Lewis, M. (1973). Infant intelligence tests: Their use and misuse. *Human Development, 16,* 108–118.

Lewis, M. (1975). The development of attention and perception in the infant and young child. In W. M. Cruickshank & D. P. Hallahan (Eds.), *Perception and learning disabilities in children* (Vol. 2, pp. 137–162). New York: Syracuse University Press.

Lewis, M. (1978). The infant and its caregiver: The role of contingency. *Allied Health and Behavioral Sciences, 1*(4), 469–492.

Lewis, M. (Ed.). (1983). *Origins of intelligence: Infancy and early childhood* (2nd ed.). New York: Plenum.

Lewis, M., & Brooks-Gunn, J. (1981). Visual attention at three months as a predictor of cognitive functioning at two years of age. *Intelligence, 5*(2), 131–140.

Lewis, M., Jaskir, J., & Enright, M. K. (1986). The development of mental abilities in infancy. *Intelligence, 10,* 331–354.

Lewis, M., Louis, B., & Feiring, C. (1989). *Inner City Gifted Project: Technical report, March*. Unpublished manuscript.

Lewis, M., & McGurk, H. (1972). Evaluation of infant intelligence: Infant intelligence scores—true or false? *Science, 178*(4066), 1174–1177.

Lewis, M., & Michalson, L. (1985). The gifted infant. In J. Freeman (Ed.), *The psychology of gifted children: Perspectives on development and education* (pp. 35–57). New York: Wiley.

Loehlin, J. C., Lindzey, G., & Spuhler, J. N. (1975). *Race differences in intelligence*. San Francisco: Freeman.

Louis, B. (1989). *Stress as a mediating factor in the stability of intelligence within the first six years of life*. Paper submitted in partial fulfillment of doctor of philosophy degree requirements, Rutgers University, New Brunswick.

Louis, B., & Lewis, M. (1989). *Giftedness in young children: Parental beliefs*. Unpublished manuscript, University of Medicine and Dentistry of New Jersey, New Brunswick, New Jersey.

MacKenzie, B. (1984). Explaining race differences in IQ: The logic, the methodology, and the evidence. *American Psychologist, 39,* 1214–1233.

McCall, R. B. (1979). The development of intellectual functioning in infancy and the prediction of later IQ. In J.D. Osofsky (Ed.), *Handbook of infant development* (1st ed., pp. 707–741). New York: Wiley.

McCall, R. B. (1983). A conceptual approach to early mental development. In M. Lewis (Ed.), *Origins of intelligence: Infancy and early childhood* (2nd ed., pp. 107–133). New York: Wiley.

McCall, R. B. Appelbaum, M. I., & Hogarty, P. S. (1973). Developmental changes in mental performance. *Monographs of the Society for Research in Child Development, 38*(3, Whole No. 150). Chicago: University of Chicago Press.

McCall, R. B., Eichorn, D. H., & Hogarty, P. S. (1977). Transitions in early mental development. *Monographs of the Society for Research in Child Development, 42*(3, Whole No. 171). Chicago: University of Chicago Press.

McCall, R. B., Hogarty, P. S., & Hurlburt, N. (1972). Transitions in infant sensorimotor development and the prediction of childhood IQ. *American Psychologist, 27,* 728–748.

McCarthy, D. (1972). *Manual for the McCarthy scales of children's abilities.* New York: Psychological Corporation.

McGillicuddy-DeLisi, A. V. (1985). The relationship between parental beliefs and children's cognitive level. In I. E. Siegel (Ed.), *Parental belief systems: The psychological consequences for children* (pp. 7–24). Hillsdale, NJ: Erlbaum.

Prugh, D. G., Staub, E. M., Sands, H. H., Kirschbaum, R. M., & Lenihan, E. A. (1953). A study of the emotional reactions of children and families to hospitalization and illness. *American Journal of Orthopsychiatry, 23,* 70–106.

Quinton, D., & Rutter, M. (1976). Early hospital admissions and later disturbances of behavior: An attempted replication of Douglas' findings. *Developmental Medicine & Child Neurology, 18,* 447–459.

Rabkin, J. G. & Streuning, E. L. (1976). Life events, stress, and illness. *Science, 194,* 1013–1020.

Raphael, B. (1983). *The anatomy of bereavement.* New York: Basic.

Renzulli, J. S. (1986). The three ring conception of giftedness. A developmental model for creative productivity. In R. J. Sternberg & J. E. Davidson (Eds.), *Conceptions of giftedness* (pp. 53–92). New York: Cambridge University Press.

Rutter, M. (1979). Maternal deprivation, 1972–1978: New findings, new concepts, new approaches. *Child Development, 50,* 283–305.

Rutter, M. (1981a). Maternal deprivation reassessed (2nd ed.). Harmondsworth: Penguin.

Rutter, M. (1981b). Stress, coping and development: Some issues and some questions. *Journal of Child Psychology and Psychiatry, 22,* 323–356.

Sattler, J. M. (1982). *Assessment of children's intelligence and special abilities* (2nd ed.). Boston: Allyn and Bacon.

Scarr-Salapatek, S. (1976). An evolutionary perspective on infant intelligence: Species patterns and individual variations. In M. Lewis (Ed.), *Origins of intelligence* (1st ed., pp. 165–197). New York: Plenum.

Schaffer, H. R., & Callender, W. M. (1959). Psychological effects of hospitalization in infancy. *Pediatrics, 24,* 528–539.

Spearman, C. (1904). General intelligence objectively determined and measured. *American Journal of Psychology, 15,* 201–293.

Terman, L. M., & Merrill, M. A. (1973). *Stanford-Binet intelligence scale: Manual for the third revision, form L-M.* Chicago: Riverside.

Thorndike, E. L. (1931). *Human learning.* New York: Appleton-Century-Crofts.

Thurstone, L. L. (1938). *Primary mental abilities.* (Psychometric Monographs No. 1). Chicago: University of Chicago Press.

VanEerdewegh, M. M., Bieri, M. D., Parrilla, R. H., & Clayton, P. J. (1982). The bereaved child. *British Journal of Psychiatry, 140,* 23–29.

Wachs, T. D., Uzgiris, I. C., & Hunt, J. McV. (1971). Cognitive development in infants of different age levels and from different environmental backgrounds. *Merrill-Palmer Quarterly, 17,* 283–317.

Waddington, C. H. (1957). *The strategy of the genes.* London: Allen & Son.

Wallerstein, J. (1977a). Responses of the pre-school girl to divorce: Those who cope. In M. F. MacMillan & S. Henao (Eds.), *Child psychiatry: Treatment and research* (pp. 269–292). New York: Brunner, Mazel.

Wallerstein, J. (1977b). Some observations regarding the effects of divorce on the psychological development of the pre-school girl. In J. Oremland & E. Oremland (Eds.), *Sexual and gender development of young children* (pp. 117–129). Cambridge, MA: Ballinger.

Wallerstein, J. (1983). Children of divorce: Stress and developmental tasks. In N. Garmezy & M. Rutter (Eds.), *Stress, coping, and development in children* (pp. 265–302). New York: McGraw-Hill.

Wallerstein, J., & Kelly, J. (1975). The effects of parental divorce: The experiences of the preschool child. *Journal American Academy of Child Psychiatry, 14,* 600–616.

Wechsler, D. (1967). *Manual for the Wechsler preschool and primary scale of intelligence.* New York: Psychological Corporation.

White, B. (1985). Competence and giftedness. In J. Freeman (Ed.), *The psychology of gifted children: Perspectives on development and education* (pp. 59–73). New York: Wiley.

White, R. W. (1959). Motivation reconsidered: The concept of competence. *Psychological Review, 66,* 297–333.

27

Gifted Adolescents

THOMAS M. BUESCHER   *Mid Coast Mental Health Center, Rockland, Maine*

Gifted and talented learners are constantly challenged to negotiate a difficult passage enroute to adulthood. Most young people with exceptional talents in the arts, in science and letters, and even in athletics usually are first noticed and identified long before they venture into middle school. Yet between the time they are "discovered" and the point at which talents reach productive maturity through self-ownership in young adulthood, numerous obstacles must be overcome. Students are expected to deftly balance the demands of their talents in one hand and the biological and emotional needs of human development in the other, while inching their way along the tightrope across the psychosocial chasm of adolescence. Some travel alone, others are afraid; many carry the hopes and burdens of families, friends, and teachers on their backs. What is surprising is not the danger and intricate complexity of the journey, but rather the tangible success the majority of talented adolescents achieve.

The purpose of this chapter is to briefly explore some of the major issues that challenge talented students, not because of their remarkable abilities, but rather because of their age and stage during the dance of human development. It broadly maps the passage of talented adolescents from the days of identification in later childhood to the proud moments of self-discovery and achievement in early adulthood. The first section reviews the role of adolescence in development, noting its cultural and psychological necessity for young people from the standpoint of biology, relationships, and cognitive structures. The second section explores significant challenges talented adolescents face in balancing their abilities and needs while their identities emerge. Finally, the chapter considers the impact of adolescence and talent on the students themselves as well as their families and schools, suggesting factors that parents, teachers, and counselors must weigh when they work with talented students.

Adolescence, Talent, and Being Normal

Talented adolescents are quite acquainted with one of society's misconceptions: that being gifted and talented and being "normal" are incompatible. Indeed, most highly talented students at one time or another see themselves as being quite different from their peers. It should not be surprising that during adolescence, when so much about the young person is changing and being called into question and comparison, these worries and societal myths gain greater potency. Adolescence itself is a strange enough phenomenon to understand and negotiate without complicating it by discussions of normality and abnormality. Most researchers who study adolescence assert that the only thing normal about adolescence is its lack of predictability about what *is* normal!

One reason for this quandary is "the very questionable, if not bad, reputation adolescence has gained, second only to the terror that the 'terrible two's' elicits in less experienced parents" (Shapiro & Hertzig, 1988, p. 113). The exploits of being a monster at age 2 are forgotten by almost everyone after age 5; however, adults believe they have lucid and conscious memories of their adolescence. They relish the fond memories of being different, even outrageous, as teenagers. Yet what those carefully chosen and favored memories mask are the painful feelings of being ignored, belittled, even rejected by peers for quite unpredictable reasons: appearances, ideas, or self-perceptions. Adults glorify their own adolescence yet seem to fear their own children's teenage years!

Society treats its adolescents in a schizoid manner. It exploits the mammoth commercial impact adolescents can have in the marketplace or at box-office windows while simply ignoring the deep needs these same young people present in trying to understand themselves, their abilities, their relationships with parents and each other, and the world that holds their future.

"Being labeled 'gifted and talented' in America today is a prize that often comes with strings attached" (Higham & Buescher, 1987, p. 26). Exceptional abilities in school or the arts provide many adolescents with recognition and status not attainable by their peers. Often the cost is not hearty acceptance; rather, factors such as increased expectations and opportunities from teachers or jealousy and resentment from friends may create deep channels for separation. Some young people feel dissatisfaction with past and present accomplishments alike, or at times a chronic anxiety about the future. Typical adolescent stresses can be heightened and compounded by the difficulties talented students uniquely encounter. Frustration and disappointment easily become the backdrop for their adolescent passage.

What Is Adolescence?

In describing adolescence, researchers separate the biological and hormonal onset phase, *puberty*, from the ensuing psychosocial process, *adolescence,* that unfolds for many years afterward leading to early adulthood. To young people, adolescence is the first conscious experience of living out and through a *transitional life stage*. Transitional life stages are described as lengthy stretches of human development marked by discontinuity, dissonance, and large-scale change and adaptation at biological, psychological, and social levels. Infancy and midlife changes are similar transitional steps. Adolescence is a blend of upheaval and stability that various writers have tried to capture by amplifying certain kernels. Kestenberg (1980), for example, emphasized the biological and psychosexual aspect of adolescence, focusing on the journey from barren-ness and sterility in childhood to the burgeoning fertility in adolescence. Erik Erikson (1956, 1963, 1968), on the other hand, underscored the central goal of ego identity as the target for adolescence, calling it "the accrued confidence that one's inner sameness and continuity prepared in the past are matched by the sameness and continuity of one's meaning for others in the future" (1956, p. 261). Peter Blos (1967, 1985) saw the necessity of a second and final process of separation and individuation from and within the family of origin by age 19. He observed that adolescents have to create space for new love relationships in which their evolving identity and sexuality can be expressed. Manaster and Powell (1983) highlighted the dilemma all adolescents face in striving to fit in rather than be fused or lost as anonymous faces in adult society. The quest to belong, in their estimation, far outweighs the stereotype society creates of adolescent rebellion.

These clinicians identified elements of the adolescent passage that together form a useful framework of growth: *fertility, identity, individuality, and integrity*. Rapid shifts and changes around these four features are characteristic of adolescence in American society. Daniel Offer (1986; Offer, Ostrov, & Howard, 1981), perhaps one of the most prominent adolescent clinicians and researchers, sees the *transitional* nature of adolescence as setting the stage for other growth points like midlife and old age. Adolescence allows a child to gradually adjust to growth, development, and change. The adolescent transition helps avoid potential crises and allows for more gradual and sustained growth to take place (Offer, 1986).

Progressive Shifts During Adolescence

Adolescence stretches from the onset of puberty at age 11 or 12 to the attainment of early adulthood at 22 or 23. It can be viewed as a complex process involving four major spheres of change: biological growth and maturation, adjustments in peer relationships, shifts in how new learning occurs, and realignments of relationships in the family of origin. As Figure 27.1 shows, the adolescent system is highly

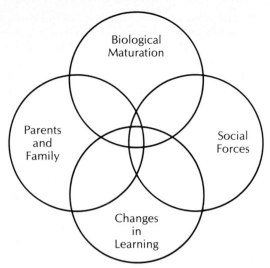

Figure 27.1 Major areas of change during adolescence.

What Changes during Adolescence?

Without sounding simplistic, what puberty and adolescence change is how a young person looks, feels about himself or herself, responds to others, and understands new and often conflicting information about relationships, events, and intentions. For talented young people who prize their mastery of certain areas, progressive loss of control over body image, feelings, and patterns of friendship can be unacceptable. Much has been written about the scope of changes that confront talented and normal adolescents alike (Buescher, 1985; Higham & Buescher, 1987). Several key aspects require brief mention here.

Changes in Appearance. Pubertal onset plays a dominant role in setting the tone for adolescence. Brooks-Gunn and Petersen (1984), in reviewing studies that probed the cognitive and social consequences of menarche in girls, noted that the biological roots of adolescence force systemwide disruptions at all levels. Adolescents need to better understand the powerful role genes and hormones play in the physical images they project to friends and family members. The characteristic growth spurt following on the heels of pubertal onset is a good case. "Young people sense for the first time that their bodies have taken on 'lives of their own,' acting and reacting in concert with unseen, unfelt hormonal commands that they cannot modify much less control" (Buescher, 1985, p. 12).

Certainly the most dramatic result of puberty is sexual maturity. When younger adolescents first realize the power of their sexual selves, society and families usually offer little support—only regulations and worry. The flight to sexual modes of behavior with opposite-sex friends is seldom due to the need for intimacy; it can be an anxious verification of the continued intactness of one's sexual functioning and identity (Chilman, 1980). The apparent wave of sexual activity sought by more than half of all adolescents before age 17 (Hass, 1979; Offer, 1986) certainly poses conflicts for teenagers who have set their sights on long-term career goals after college and before marriage.

interactive and, as a result, quite emotionally charged. While the driving force behind the adolescent transition is *hormonal* (onset of puberty; structural changes in the body; and capacity for sexual behavior, fertility, and reproduction), the observable responses in adolescents are more social and emotional: anxiety, anger, isolation, defensiveness, and an intense desire to both belong and withdraw. Since these four areas of change constitute the dramatic shifts from the previously stable stage of late childhood, they must be seen as the main stage where all adolescents, whether talented or not, work out their own questions about being normal, being acceptable, and becoming an adult (Buescher, 1985).

In one sense, the successes and setbacks young people experience during adolescence rise and fall on the strengths they have to manage change in the four areas of physiology, peers, school, and family. This individual strength to weather the transitions of adolescence seems closely linked to three factors: previous adjustments made as a child, especially before age 5; the consistency of support offered by the family before adolescence; and the young person's desire to move toward a state of equilibrium (Buescher & Higham, 1989; Petersen, 1988).

Changes in Relationships. While parents and other adults seem to focus on how children *look,* teenagers spend greater energy sorting out the new relationships that define how they *feel.* They devote considerable effort to making sure they are accepted and cared for by all the "right" people—both in their families and among friends. Yet the process becomes cumbersome because both their parents and their peers are also experiencing significant changes that sap their emotional resources. Smoothing out new patterns of relationships seems complicated by the fact that those with whom the teenagers need to relate differently are now also changing.

There are predictable troubles as adolescents seem to race to build new relationships while trying to clearly differentiate themselves from their parents. Elkind (1984) observed that adolescents' return to *egocentrism*—seeing themselves as the center of the universe—makes them appear narcissistic, renewing earlier conflicts. As the adolescent member strives to be *separate but connected,* the family system undergoes its own transformation. Its initial vertical organization, in which parents "rule" above their children, is slowly supplanted by one that recognizes more horizontal lines of responsibility for all (Montemayor, 1982, 1983). Perhaps such changes might be more welcome later, but they are initially upsetting to the family system.

Outside the family, adolescents continue the theme of striving to be separate but connected. Sometimes the need to belong to a certain peer group the young person sees as necessary can outweigh most previous expectations about achievement, independence, and self-determination set by parents during earlier years.

Changes in Reasoning and Learning. The cognitive changes accelerated by puberty are potent and long-lasting. Adolescence typically marks the broad emergence of higher levels of intellectual functioning, called *formal operational thinking* by Piaget (1952). Between the ages of 12 and 15, most adolescents improve their ability to understand their world in more abstract terms, to think in a self-consciously deductive manner, and to be able to create hierarchical models in order to explain novel experiences.

Complementary changes ensue in how young people organize the world from a moral perspective. Gilligan (1982) suggested that teenage boys and girls exhibit quite different modes of reasoning about questions of morality that carry over into their own relationships. Most boys but few girls make decisions using firm cognitive frameworks of justice and legal rights. On the other hand, most girls but few boys make their choices based on frameworks of caring responsiveness. Gilligan said that these divergent ways of making choices might be associated with different forms of *self* definition and perhaps reflect different experiences of relationships prior to adolescence.

Gilligan asked if differences in thinking about moral issues might reflect diverse paths boys and girls have pursued in reaching adolescence: boys as unequal competing *individualists,* girls as avowed *equals* who prize interdependence and mutual support. Similar cognitively linked sex differences among exceptionally talented students have been noted. Benbow and Stanley (1983) have conducted several longitudinal studies that map the lower average attainment in mathematics in high school and college by girls compared with boys. Other studies have examined the effects of different modes of thinking on coping, adjustment, and advice giving by talented teenagers in middle school and high school that seem strongly linked to factors like age and sex (Buescher, 1989; Buescher, Olszewski, & Higham, 1987; Buescher & Higham, 1989).

What Is Normal about Adolescence?

Given the great variety of experiences young people encounter and remember as part of their adolescent passages, it is risky to suggest too many commonalities about "normal" adolescence. Adolescence is a transitional process of equifinality: Many roads lead to Rome and also to successful adulthood. Still there are core thoughts, feelings, and actions that characterize all of adolescence, and these can form a useful template for looking at the unique experiences and needs of highly talented adolescents.

Daniel Offer (1986) was among the first to challenge the assumption that adolescence was necessarily a time of *storm and stress*. He argued that the caricatures of tumultuous adolescent growth did not reflect normal adolescents but simply a relatively small portion of the teenage population who had been interviewed or treated by clinical or correctional programs for significant problems. Later studies of *nonpatient* adolescents have shown that it is common for adolescents to be soundly adjusted, getting along well with peers, teachers, and families throughout this time span (Csikszentmihalyi & Larson, 1984). Offer, Ostrov, and Howard (1981) even proposed at least four different normal pathways adolescents might follow enroute to young adulthood. Perhaps adolescence is better understood now as a *transitional* life stage in which young people gradually adjust to biological and emotional shifts within themselves, preparing for more advanced adaptation and functioning as adults in society (Offer, 1986).

Shapiro and Hertzig (1988), combining a wide range of theoretical vantage points, suggested at least eight major themes that can form the framework of the adolescent transition. Stated in no particular order, these include (1) independence–dependence, (2) intellectualized control–free license, (3) family contol and influence–peer control and influence, (4) need for disclosure–need for privacy, (5) idealization of others–devaluation of others, (6) identity–diffusion, (7) comfortable intimacy with sexuality–isolation or panic, and (8) openness–defensiveness (Shapiro & Hertzig, p. 117). While each theme weaves throughout adolescence, various ones are most prominent in the earlier or later stages. For example, struggles about independence, license, and peer control normally occur before the age of 15 or 16; issues of identity and intimacy more often announce the *"launching"* phase of later adolescence at age 19 or 20.

One interesting fact uncovered by numerous adolescent research efforts is that the developmental envelope for adolescent sexuality, identity formation and independence, and experience of intimate behavior has progressively elongated in the past 75 years. Consequently, the length of time young people are

"out of synch" with the expected time line for achieving all the major adolescent tasks prior to adulthood has been stretched, reaching now from about age 11 to nearly 25.

What is normal about adolescence is that it is a long, protracted stage of transition during which a person's body, ego, relationships, skills, and identity are stretched by numerous tasks to prepare for adulthood. No one escapes these changes or challenges; they must be addressed and resolved for progress to be made. Though the central tasks may vary in intensity from one adolescent to another, and quite often are linked to gender, they follow a fairly predictable course.

The next section explores several of the major tasks facing talented adolescents, highlighting the complications and variations most encounter as they use self-discovery to move from the point of being identified and labeled as *talented* in childhood to the destination of talent ownership and development in young adulthood.

Tasks and Issues Facing Talented Adolescents

Talented teenagers must face and overcome all the normal tasks of adolescence; there are no developmental shortcuts or capacities for "stage leaping" when it comes to the adolescent passage. While parents and teachers often remark about the *advanced* reasoning and technical skills of bright children, it is just as likely they will express regret and uncertainty about those same students' lack of progress in social wisdom and maturity during adolescence (Alvino, 1986). One reason for their concern is the marked difference in progress they observe about their talented sons and daughters after puberty. This regression seems alarming. Often the reason for its visibility is the high trajectory the son or daughter had been taking during previous years. When these parents, like many others, expect the same course to even accelerate in adolescence, they are surprised and dismayed at what they see. Adolescence is a regressive process for *all* young people, but for talented youth it seems more noticeable, ushering in some knotty issues that will be examined in the following sections.

Strengths

It would be a mistake to believe that adolescence for talented students is an insurmountable journey undertaken by "weakened" or enfeebled individuals. It is not. In fact, these adolescents bring considerable strength to a fairly rugged adventure. By the age of 13 or so, their accumulated strengths include most of the following:

1. Increased capacity for relationships with adults and peers as well as an ability to learn from them
2. Increased ability to be self-observing and to verbalize strong feelings aptly rather than act them out
3. Greater propensity for deductive thinking
4. Eagerness and excitement for further developing specialized interests and skills while expanding areas of talent
5. Increased needs for both autonomy and cooperation, being better able to resist regressive pulls back into childhood patterns
6. More realistic notions of personal self-esteem that reflect an adequate ego-ideal

These strengths and others arm them for some of the later challenges they will encounter. But no armor is quite strong enough to not be dented and dulled by the assaults of adolescence. One way to gauge this strength is to observe how young people handle both victories and setbacks with family members, friends, and school personnel as they face important tasks and questions.

The next sections will explore important aspects of being a talented adolescent, outlining how normal tasks of adolescence may present particular twists on the journey and probing how most of them eventually cope. Enroute, three broad areas will be considered: (1) self-acceptance, (2) relationships with family members and friends, and (3) unique demands made by the talent itself.

Accepting the Talented Self

The first task every adolescent meets on the road to adulthood is to answer the question *"Who am I?"* Having been defined by their parents for at least 11 or 12 years, by the expectations of teachers or valued mentors, and by the labeling and programming of their school districts, talented adolescents suddenly find themselves landlocked and separated from the open and inviting seas of normal adolescent adventure. Living now in a changing body that seems to be regulated more by hormones and external structures than by its very owner, some talented adolescents feel out of contact with their own past, the sense of being *diffuse* that Erikson (1963, 1968) equated with the earliest experience of adolescence. In this state of flux, any recurrent doubts about the reality, depth, or strength of one's own talent and its acceptability to adults and peers can gain inappropriate weight (Piechowski & Colangelo, 1984). For some young people, early adolescence creates denial or doubt of previously recognized and cherished abilities as well as a loss of direction.

Remembering some of the crucial adolescent tasks that must be worked on before age 15, it is not surprising that denial and doubt about special talents would appear. The need to see oneself as separate from parents and family, for example, can pressure an adolescent to exclude elements of the past that are particularly potent attachments: parental goals and expectations, teachers' priorities and incentives for achievement and mastery, and experiences of being successful or unsuccessful that are historic to childhood. In a broad effort to quickly disconnect from dependence on others, talented adolescents find themselves staring pessimistically at their talents, wondering whether these truly belong to them or to others. No wonder it is so tempting to create a momentary sense of independence by tossing off the talent with the eschewed trappings of childhood: "That was then, this is now."

Put another way, the postpubertal world is less likely to accept talents as unique "gifts"; rather, these are interpreted as signs of being *noticeably different*. Younger adolescents in particular are intensely preoccupied with their appearances and images, whether real or imagined. Regardless of what they say or do, being different to them means being *inferior*. Not to see oneself as conforming is difficult to accept. In a large study of talented adolescents that explored how teenagers coped with feeling different or set apart because of a combination of talents and educational programming, a wealth of coping strategies were uncovered (Buescher & Higham, 1989). Having exceptional ability ceases to be an asset when young people feel compelled to work so hard to cover it up. Often the need to camouflage exceptional talent leads to such lack of acceptance of the ability that later ownership becomes virtually impossible to regain. This extreme result is far more common among highly talented girls under 15 years of age than among boys at the same age (Buescher et al., 1987).

A second formidable obstacle talented adolescents encounter is personal dissonance or dissatisfaction about how well their talents are faring. In many ways, this is simply the reemergence in adolescence of the *perfectionism* displayed by some talented youngsters in childhood. This time, however, the stakes can be more costly to the young person's self-image and self-esteem.

Typically, the propensity to expect more from oneself than talent or ability might actually warrant appears to be compounded by the struggles of adolescence. "Strained by the shifting tides of self-concept, uneven physical maturation, and sometimes hostile peer judgements, it is not uncommon for gifted adolescents to experience some distance between what they have accomplished and how well they *think* they should have done" (Buescher, 1985. p. 14). At issue, of course, is the lack of some objective, nonjudgmental self-awareness of the limitations of the growing edges of their talents. This seems to be fueled at times by the hypercritical expectations of parents, teachers, and even peers who demand consistent high performance from them or else resort to chiding and jeering as motivational or evaluative techniques.

Talented adolescents can be their own worst critics. They set performance standards that reflect some chronic grandiosity and omnipotence that rightfully emerged in childhood.

Parents and peers sometimes unknowingly reward this strained behavior by admiring it, even modeling it. In the end, when the adolescents' performances fall short of unwarranted expectations, they are angry and disappointed, fearing reprisals from those who might have been central to the process. They perceive a widening gulf between talent and performance and in some severe cases completely give up on the further development of their unique abilities.

At the heart of this dilemma is the struggle for self-control against abandonment and license. For some talented adolescents, perfectionism is a defense against losing control and running wild. Some parents even fear that if an adolescent *stops* developing a particular talent area, the son or daughter will take on restless and aimless behavior—in effect, going from rigid self-control, dictated by the talent, to unbridled acting out. What is true, of course, is that every adolescent must work out this tension point for himself or herself. For talented adolescents, the focal point is the talent and its ability to regulate their behavior, relationships, and ultimately, appeal and acceptability. In the final analysis, the successful negotiation of adolescence for these students requires some objective but nurturing evaluation of their personal aspirations and expectations. This can be facilitated by trusted adults who are sensitive to young people's vulnerability. Unchecked, perfectionism among talented adolescents weakens the potential for growth and relationships not only in college but also in early adulthood.

A third major task that typically stumbles both bright and normal adolescents alike is the quest for a satisfactory *identity*. The attainment of one's identity, usually in early adulthood, is a journey of many years, built on necessary failures, losses, and successes. It is far more than a choice of careers; it is a confirmation of personality. The striving to attain that ego-identity, according to Erikson and others, is driven from the earliest stages of a child's development by a need for intimacy and connection, for *belonging* in a significant way. The search for identity, therefore, is necessarily woven into the quest for intimacy (McAdams, 1985).

Two particular phenomena cause difficulty. First, gifted children are typically ambitious, controlling, and *impatient.* Their social interactions with parents and other interested adults throughout childhood predisposes them, to some degree, to be intolerant of ambiguous, unresolved situations. Coupled with the normal adolescent drive to act impulsively, these young people feel compelled to seek closure quickly, to leave no question unanswered. Edward deBono's (1983) characterization of bright, clever students' vulnerability for the so-called intelligence trap appears to become pronounced in adolescence. The intelligence trap, capitalizing on gifted children's impatience with a lack of clear-cut answers, options, or even decisions, drives them to randomly seek answers where none truly exist. Quite humorously, at times, this impatient compulsion to resolve ambiguity even surfaces in complex personal relationships: "Do you love me or not? Let's settle this once and for all." They expect ready acceptance of *their* answers and resolutions to some of the most difficult matters people face. In addition, they expect partners or colleagues to be equally confident and swift in accepting these solutions. As clinicians and parents can attest, the anger, denial, and resentment talented adolescents express when their one-sided resolution falls flat is fierce and bitter.

The second underlying complication in the quest for identity is the reluctance these students have to experience or withstand personal confusion and ambiguity. While the roots of this behavior are not readily grasped, the impact it makes on individual lives is well documented (Buescher & Higham, 1989). The quest for an immediate ego-identity, typically represented by the selection and development of a career path, seems like a natural consequence of a long stretch of precocity. Having experienced marked acceleration of some cognitive and social skills, fairly constant affirmation of being unique and acceptable, and general support for moving full steam ahead into life's greater challenges, some talented adolescents cannot be convinced that identity formation takes a great deal of time, energy, and investment.

To understand what bright adolescents try to do, and why it so often has dramatic repercussions in early adulthood, requires briefly considering how identity is formed during the adolescent passage. Erikson (1963, 1968) was among the first to recognize the central focus of identity achievement for the task of adolescence, but many others have delved deeper into this theme. Using longitudinal research data, Marcia (1966, 1976), Adams and Shea (1979), and McAdams (1985) described differences in the attainment of ego-identity status and theorized how these reflect progressive stages of adolescence. Marcia teased apart Erikson's broader conceptualizations, suggesting that the process moves through four phases during adolescence:

Identity diffusion	(Between ages 11 and 14)
Identity foreclosure	(Between ages 13 and 17)
Identity moratorium	(Between ages 16 and 20)
Achieved identity	(Between ages 19 and 23)

He suggested that all adolescents move through all the stages, but usually in very individualized ways. Older adolescents who were found to not yet have achieved the final stage, achieved identity, lacked signs of attaining mature intimacy with others.

What is compelling about his line of research during later adolescence is its explanation for why particular individuals become stuck at certain points and find it difficult to resolve a more advanced stage of identity (Archer, 1982). For example, four possible outcomes of the process might be considered. The paramount stage is *identity achievement.* Here an adolescent has ventured through significant occupational and ideological questioning or exploration and has been able to make solid commitments to career, values, and beliefs (McAdams, 1985). Less advanced but healthy is the person at the *moratorium* level. He or she has made the exploration of options and beliefs a priority but stands unable to make commitments. Further back in development is the stage of *foreclosure.* These individuals have ignored exploration and instead have made premature commitments to career paths, beliefs, and values. The naive commitment has been superimposed, without exploration, and is held fast beyond doubt.

Identity foreclosure poses perhaps the most serious challenge for talented adolescents enroute to maturity. They seem more disposed than most adolescents, perhaps because of their early identifications with trusted adults, to move quickly to foreclose any risky, unwanted exploration of identity issues. Heeding the freely given recommendations of teachers, counselors, parents, and most importantly, *themselves,* bright adolescents latch on quickly to any semblance of identity, no matter how unsuitable or mismatched to skills, discipline, or talent areas.

While this tendency is not unique to talented students, they appear more likely to maintain the foreclosed identity in the face of mounting troubles. Elkind (1984) warned parents and teachers about the tendency adolescents have to adopt "patchwork selves" or identities as a way to cope with society's increased pressure to grow up and act independent quickly, thereby freeing adults from their caretaker and parenting roles. Apparently, the pressure of competing expectations from adults and the lack of patience felt by talented adolescents fuels their rapid search for a secure identity, convincing them to settle for an unexplored yet foreclosed point of development. The tragedy, of course, is that in accepting a premature identity, they not only shortcut the lengthier, time-consuming process, but they also risk closing important doors to opportunities that might stretch and fortify their multiple talents (Delisle, 1985).

Building Relationships with Others

Adolescence is not an individual, isolated journey. For adolescent actors on the stage of development, it is a large-scale psychosocial process involving multiple scripts, numerous scenes and locations, and more than a fair share of disagreeing directors. While on the one hand the most formidable challenges facing talented adolescents are *intrapsychic,* or internal, the most difficult to understand and adjust to are *relational,* or external to the influence of these young people. Adolescents might be comfortable with their own need for perfectionism, their impatience, and their foreclosed identity. What complicates their lives, however, is the demanding interactions with others.

Family Relationships. Perhaps the most critical task to be completed during adolescence is *individuation:* discovering how one is different from parents, siblings, peers, and intimate others. The process of seeing oneself as separate but connected to family members is a common stumbling block for all young people, but gifted and talented adolescents find it particularly troublesome.

The roots of individuation are in the first years of life and the child's first significant relationships, first with the mother and then with the father (Mahler & McDevitt, 1980). Faced with the dilemma of being fused or merged with parents in such a way that exploration and separation are not possible, or of being quickly separated from them in a way that precludes merger again, every child vacillates and tests. By the first birthday, the child is eager to use newly discovered and perfected legs and arms—to walk away, to touch and grab, to move beyond the extended arms of parental control. By 18 months, most children encounter some panic, try to regress and become less independent, and even become very "clingy" to mothers and fathers. Soothed and reassured, armed with facile language and an intense curiosity, these same toddlers by age 2 are once again on their way to a more settled state of independence.

Much the same process recurs throughout childhood and into adolescence. Children seek wider circles of independence beyond their parents' earlier orbits, but they are prone to panic, seeking reassurance when feeling depreciated or lonely. Peter Blos (1967), one of the eminent adolescent theory builders, suggested that all adolescents use some kind of regression as a way of finally resolving tasks of identity and intimacy. This individuation process for an adolescent includes shedding older family dependencies, loosening the ties of childhood to parents, and accepting a personal role in the lifestream of society. Teenagers most often remember this time as one of being counted as an individual and fitting in for the first time in adult society.

When one knows what individuation encompasses, it is easy to see why this process can be uncomfortable and difficult for talented adolescents. On the one hand, these young people have actually become quite accustomed to acting independently from their parents and family; on the other, a great deal of what they have accomplished is locked into cooperation by parents and family members. As a result, the normal amount of panic felt at long-term separation and individuation can be more intense, less easy to accommodate, or even worse, denied and repressed. These tactics can forestall the attainment of identity and even damage the motivation to further develop talent itself.

Freeman (1981) suggested that the path to differentiation in the family system has at least three different levels: *undifferentiated, reactive,* and *differentiated* (with many transitional points between). Figure 27.2 outlines how most young people emotionally experience these three progressive stages from early adolescence into young adulthood. The *risk* increases for both the adolescent and the family as greater separation and individuality is achieved. But as risk increases, so also does the potential for sustained growth.

This author's clinical experience with talented adolescents suggests some variations on this normal model of individuation. For example, gifted students are often seen as being more differentiated *as children,* more confident and comfortable with their autonomy, and as a result, more open to exploration and risk taking prior to puberty. Adolescence, though, seems to trigger a reversal that moves them far past the *reactive* stage described by Freeman, normal for most adolescents, to the least mature level, the *undifferentiated* phases of childhood. The precocious *pseudodifferentia-*

tion observed among talented youngsters is then revealed for what it has been: a caricature of late adolescent differentiation.

Talented adolescents seem to experience a more jarring separation-individuation process. Not only are past significant attachments severed, but the affirmations and supports contributed by those ties must be renegotiated. For this reason, some talented adolescents, faced with the formidable task of accepting and owning their unique talents *on their own,* choose to drift away from talent development. They use ambivalence and anger to separate themselves not only from their talents but also from previously supportive parents, teachers, and friends.

Talent is strengthened by the gradual forging of ownership. Differentiation opens more doors of opportunity, welcoming in new supporters beyond the family and immediate friends. Naturally, this requires a period of time in which parents, siblings, and former friends are sometimes harshly devalued. The earlier ideals of mother and father, even favorite teachers, give way to a variety of role models, some of them questionable and completely contradictory to previous values. These role models can range from Nobel Prize winners to movie actors and actresses, or range through rock music groups to highly successful artists. A crush on a favorite teacher or the longing to be a superstar of any sort helps adolescents to take the appropriate steps to build strong ego-ideals with which to measure their own personal growth away from the family (Shapiro & Hertzig, 1988).

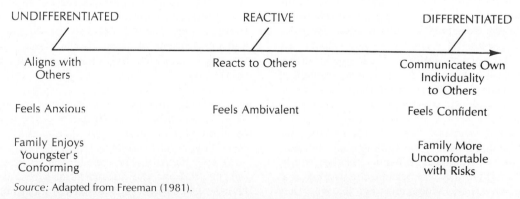

Source: Adapted from Freeman (1981).

Figure 27.2 How adolescents and their families react: Three suggested "waystations" on the road to becoming *differentiated* as a young adult.

Friends and Confidantes. Although the tensions of individuation within the family might be the most prominent, they are not the only social pressures facing talented adolescents. Equally serious are the problems posed by classmates, friends, and chosen confidantes who seem to encourage as well as dismiss adolescents' individuality and sense of ownership of their abilities. One reason for this ambiguous relationship pattern is the competing desires to be noticed and accepted versus being viewed as substantially different and becoming estranged from an important circle of friends. Talented adolescents are quite concerned about the stresses and strains of feeling different; they develop elaborate strategies to cope with any appearance that produces feelings of separation or inferiority. Like all adolescents, these students seek a sense of power in the face of feelings of powerlessness and being controlled. Some even resort to unacceptable social behavior or risky efforts to gain fleeting peer admiration as a way to increase personal status. Others abandon their recognized talents as a way to exert their own power against self or parents, using denial of the talents as a way of asserting control even though the long-term results can be most difficult to remedy.

Associating with friends, confidantes, and cliques presents all adolescents with numerous opportunities for feeling controlled and anxious. Quite naturally, competing feelings of openness versus closedness and defensiveness get triggered. So it is that adolescents develop elaborate unconscious defenses to control these feelings. Talented adolescents are no exception. The only difference might be the degree of subtlety or sophistication in their defensive maneuvers.

The normal pattern of adolescent defensiveness reflects the age and temperament of the individual. More often than not for talented students, whose childhood experiences include a variety of other-centered expectations and directions, there is a marked increase in the defenses of projection, denial, and most certainly, intellectualization. In other words, the *world and others* become the invoked reason why these adolescents act the way they do—rather than their own inner wishes, fears,

or experiments. "Blame is placed outside the individual; responsibility for actions are seen as exterior to and beyond the self" (Shapiro & Hertzig, 1988, p. 120).

Among gifted and talented adolescents there is a natural movement away from the more primitive tactics of projection and denial as the peer group gains prominence, usually by age 14 or 15 (Buescher & Higham, 1989). In their stead are the more potent defenses of intellectualization and asceticism. Talented adolescents adapt these two mechanisms to the ongoing process of talent development that demands discipline, adherence to priorities, and rationalizations about postponing gratifications. Confronted by a need and desire for closer peer contact, but wary at the same time about being lost in the shuffle during the hectic moments of differentiation, bright students become attracted to each other, often in mixed-sex clusters or groupings.

The initial intimacy created by this common bond of talent and purpose often poses another obstacle to be hurdled: privacy versus self-disclosure. Researchers have often noted the difficult conflict adolescents encounter between the normal desire to know and be known and the equally strong need for absolute privacy. Often the two needs openly compete. Adolescents wonder: "What can I say about myself, something private, that will *really* get them to like and accept me?" versus "What can I tell them that isn't private, that isn't sacred to my family or to myself?" Juggling openness and privacy successfully in a relationship requires skill and sensitivity. Talented adolescents, having usually greater verbal fluidity and insight, handle these issues well. Nevertheless, they worry about the consequences and implications of being part of closer relationships in which they experience loss of control.

Securing Intimacy. In Erikson's schema of developmental issues, intimacy is the final capstone of adolescence, gained from the successful negotiation during the journey to locate one's own identity. The capacity for intimacy appears to have the hallmarks of a resolved adolescent passage: mutual caring, emotional closeness, eroticism, and deep trust (Perlman

& Fehr, 1987; Sarrel & Sarrel, 1981). Some experts have suggested that this might be too severe a restriction, pointing out that the two processes, identity achievement and intimacy, are closely related, intertwined spirals in which rebonding, exploratory sexual experiences, and caring relationships all help to foster and establish the adult identity.

Intimacy is one of the least researched areas about talented adolescents. Some of the most promising work has been conceptualized on two fronts. On one, Foster and Mangel (1987) suggested that there are powerful interconnections between intimacy, self-esteem, and productive talent. In their view, intimate relationships, particularly in late adolescence and early adulthood, greatly enhance self-esteem, allowing talents and abilities to be released for some form of *productive excellence*. They believe that the real search for excellence begins with an exploration of intimacy in day-to-day relationships.

On another front, one of the oldest longitudinal studies of life-span facets of highly talented individuals, drawn from the pioneering study begun by Terman and Oden, showed the primary contribution of healthy, sustaining intimate relationships as a crucial feature of productive living (Sears, 1977).

Adolescents' relationships with friends, confidantes, and parents seem to reflect the level of identity achieved as well as the depth of intimacy previously experienced. This capacity to be intimate appears to be slowly titrated from small but always successful experiences of trust, sharing, fantasizing, and exploring one's own sexual capacities and needs with a caring partner (Calderone & Johnson, 1983). While some have argued the importance of pairing, sexual behavior, and bonding as necessary components of the march to identity, evidence is lacking to show it to be a necessity. Most research with adolescents (Petersen, 1988) shows that widespread social and sexual experimentation with many partners is not the norm. Adolescents, particularly those with goals of college, career, and family, seem to work within a narrow band of criteria and options, testing, exploring, and evaluating their newly found sexual feelings and intimate connections with partners who demonstrate not

only *safety* but most important *promise* for the future (Sarrel & Sarrel, 1981).

To summarize, the capacity for caring, symmetrical relationships reflecting intimacy seems strongly linked to the journey toward achieving an ego identity. For most talented adolescents, as with the general population of young people, the end of the identity *moratorium* phase is often announced by a first intimate relationship. Sometimes, but not always, this is accompanied by a sexual experience (Sarrel & Sarrel, 1981). This impetus to act on one's own sexual identity in the search for intimacy signals the approaching closure to adolescence and the temporary resolution of the ego identity. Talented adolescents appear to be more sensitive and resonant to the complex demands of others in their quest for intimacy and identity. As a result, they sometimes achieve this status later but with equal success.

Coping with Talent and Its Demands

The development of exceptional talent is a costly enterprise, bringing financial and emotional burdens to young people, their families, and the schools and programs they attend (Bloom, 1985). It is important to keep these costs in mind when considering how adolescence can, at times, become complicated by the very talents society prizes in its citizens. Talent development, when effective and successful, exacts its own tolls on young people during adolescence. *Talent costs every adolescent something.* This section examines only a few of the major prices adolescents might pay for a "prize with many strings attached."

Talents Demand Time. While parents sometimes recoil at the real and hidden costs of raising, educating, and launching an exceptionally talented son or daughter, their adolescents complain about the excessive *time* talent demands. Productive excellence, whether in the classroom, swimming pool, concert hall, or studio gallery, for example, exacts heavy wages in time and dedication. For the adolescent, time seems both endless and finite. Moments spent with friends or favorite adults are offset by hours and months of focused energy, practice, frustration, and occasional triumph. To most adolescents, time is their own. To very bright students, time belongs to talents and at least one taskmaster—a teacher or mentor both loved and feared. In effect, time is a seductive thief, robbing talented young people of free time, free space, and carefree relationships, always reminding them of the next deadline to be met. It is no wonder that, for many, stress produces dissatisfaction and lack of ownership for further developing the talent area.

Talent Requires Perseverance. Few fruits of talent development are tasted in adolescence. While some exceptional adolescent athletes, musicians, and actors achieve sudden and sustained success, most young people with talent must be disciplined and patient, and above all, learn to persevere. Obviously, adolescents are not a patient group by any norm; they demand results and are often unwilling to walk the lonely, unproductive miles talent development demands. Talented students are not accustomed to this measure of patience and endurance. Even when one considers the accomplishments of somewhat older adults who gain prestigious recognition as Presidential Scholars, Nobel Prize laureates, Guggenheim or MacArthur Fellows, or international winners in the performing arts, the overall image is mixed: solitary dedication and perseverance, but with immense satisfaction and joy.

Gifted and talented adolescents are impatient, used to seeing immediate results and earning praise for their earliest efforts. They look with disfavor on extensive periods of work, study, and preparation as a prerequisite for achievement. That makes the pursuit of productive excellence even more exasperating. Their disenchantment is reinforced by the necessity of postponed gratifications as the months and years pile up.

In a society in which most adults measure their success in salaries and benefits, the elusive prizes for substantially sacrificing time and resources in order to develop exceptional talent seem inconsequential. Young people forget that one of the costs for being trained to be a lawyer, physician, architect, artist, or concert-level musician is a fairly lean, uncomfortable existence for most of the first 10 years *after*

adolescence. In what ways are talented adolescents prepared, counseled, or willing to live on fast food, drive hand-me-down cars, and entertain friends and lovers on discarded family furniture until they achieve not only personal success but also financial stability (Delisle, 1987)? At a time when starting MBAs from some graduate business schools drive late-model cars and live in refined urban luxury before age 25, how well will talented young people endure the enforced poverty of several graduate programs, long hours in community or not-for-profit agencies or clinics, and the constant pressures of being judged, evaluated, or reassigned? Even greater are the binds of marrying, starting a family, and maintaining the momentum of talent development during lean years.

Not all talented adolescents are eager to see their personal lives postponed while the demands of developing exceptional talent are met. Yet despite the obstacles, many *willingly* do—hoping that the loving and successful family, the bigger paycheck, the broad acclaim, or the personal satisfaction will not materialize too late to be enjoyed and will make all the early discipline and sacrifice worthwhile.

Talent Necessitates Coping Strategies. Assuming that one of the most critical tasks of adolescence is learning how one best belongs or fits into adult society, talented teenagers face a critical problem: Will their exceptional abilities foster acceptance or lead to isolation? There seems to be no simple answer. For example, some talents seem to *enhance* an adolescent's being noticed, valued, and accepted by peers and society, while others seem to create separation, difference, and distance (Buescher & Higham, 1989). Varsity athletes in most high school circles merit communitywide attention; elsewhere, being named a finalist in the Westinghouse Science Competition draws front-page coverage in the local newspaper. But how friends and families applaud these efforts varies, based as much on the personality of the talented young people as on the values of the community itself. Some schools prize state basketball championships; others, National Merit scholarships. The difference can be the administrators, the school board, or the constituent parents.

Talented adolescents have been keenly aware of the issues their exceptional abilities raise for peers. They acknowledge employing a range of coping strategies or maneuvers in order to reduce the stresses and strains of feeling different, of not quite fitting in among friends at school (Higham & Buescher, 1987). In a comprehensive study of over 600 highly talented adolescents, 12 to 20 years old, at least eight main strategies were detected and analyzed as part of the search for a general pattern of coping behaviors (Buescher et al., 1987). Table 27.1 lists these strategies in descending order from those viewed as most *positive,* acceptable to the young people themselves and their friends, to those seen as most *negative,* costly in terms of the risk to developing one's own talent fully. It was found that age and gender of the adolescents studied was an important determiner of why certain strategies were favored more by boys or girls at particular ages.

Equally critical, however, was the discovery that how particular talented adolescents adjusted to the feelings of being different was most related to individual personality factors. For example, talented adolescents who were more independent, sensitive, and flexible in temperament generally selected a small number of positive strategies. On the other hand, those young people who appeared to be more rigid, conforming, and apprehensive used a narrow range of *negative* strategies (Buescher & Higham, 1989). The most disturbing finding in these studies was that more boys than girls, even controlling levels of ability and a range of family factors, arrived at age 16 with their talents intact and development well under way. It appears that adolescent girls were more at risk for losing the earlier momentum for talent development.

Talented adolescents face difficult choices about what to do with their exceptional talents. Often it comes down to a stark either–or situation: *Either* expand a circle of friendships in the search for intimacy and identity, *or* withdraw, develop the talent, and hope to rise beyond those developmental needs at a later point. One cannot underestimate the strength of the feelings of being different that can interfere with optimal social acceptance and personal development as a healthy, well-adjusted young adult (Coleman, 1985). Feeling different and not belonging can be greatly magnified by the reactions of the peer group or the less-than-sensitive labeling inflicted even by schools or special programs for talented students. Talents require ways to cope with one's own feelings and the expectations of others.

Table 27.1
Coping Strategies Identified and Used by Academically Talented Adolescents 12 to 16 Years Old

Description of the Strategy
MORE POSITIVE RESULT
Accept and use talents to help peers do better in class.
Adjust language and actions so peers seem unaware of the talent area.
At school choose classes and programs for talented individuals.
Work to achieve better in nonacademic areas *at school* in order to gain a second label.
Use some stereotypic behaviors ("Act like a brain") so larger peer group ignores individual efforts.
Develop closer relationships with other talented students to the exclusion of other peers.
Actively *mask* talents so that no one is aware of them.
Develop talents and excel in performance *outside school* (private lessons, community groups, competitions).
Build closest relationships with adults who are not put off by the talent.
Avoid any programs or opportunities that develop talent.
MORE NEGATIVE RESULT

Source: Adapted from Buescher, Olszewski, and Higham (1987).

Impact Talented Adolescents Make on Family and School

The first two sections of this chapter considered the forces of adolescence that affect talented students as well as some of the complications that being talented can create during the adolescent passage. Bright adolescents appear to be unwilling puppets pulled along by fateful strings. That is not the case. This final portion describes another perspective crucial to understanding talented adolescents in their world: *they* influence a great deal of what happens with and to them, particularly within their own families, at school, and at the hands of teachers and counselors who meet them during the middle and high school years.

Influences on the Family System and Its Response

Talented adolescents have exerted much pressure on their family units during childhood. Parents, brothers and sisters, and even grandparents have felt the needs and controls of a gifted and talented youngster. As noted extensively by Bloom (1985) in his retrospective studies of the early years of talented individuals, the family was not only a core of strong support, both structurally and financially, but it also was increasingly responsive to—perhaps at times even controlled by—the talented child. Family members sacrifice time, money, interests, and a good bit of personal freedom to fuel the furnace of talent development. While some educators and administrators who teach and create services for talented children complain about "pushy parents," in fact the talented students themselves do far more pushing of the system than their parents do (Buescher, 1986; Olszewski, Kulieke, & Buescher, 1987).

None of this changes during the adolescent years. If anything, the influence, commitment, and costs to family members become greater while the tension and conflict linked to talent development increase. The earlier section of this chapter and the more detailed contribution by Linda Silverman about families of the gifted (see Chapter 22 by Silverman) address some of these complications. Several important elements can be emphasized again.

First, families with talented children and adolescents work hard to "level out the resources" among all the siblings; but at face value, that seldom works out successfully. In some families, perhaps because of birth order preferences, parental dispositions, or childhood temperaments, time and money are not equally allocated (Albert, 1980; Bloom & Sosniak, 1981). There are family members who *ask and have,* and other members who seem *ignored and have not.* These differences often crop up when at least some family members are adolescents and are difficult for most families to surmount, particularly if there has been a prior history of unresolved conflicts (Buescher, 1986; Piechowski, 1987). Since adolescence usually strains family emotional and financial supplies, it is important to observe how the family system responds to the pressures of talent development that are focused on an adolescent son or daughter who seeks, among other things, a more powerful relationship with parents and a bigger piece of the family pie to sustain later aspirations (Hackney, 1983).

Another angle on the question of family stress and responsiveness to the needs and demands of talented adolescents was probed by Colangelo (1982). His study showed that family problems and parental conflict were not as significant as matters involving peers, particularly in terms of relationships. Colangelo observed that with increasing age peer influence became a stronger factor in shaping a son's or daughter's behavior while parental influence waned. Yet at no time did these families ever appear to be noninfluential, even into the college years. Talented adolescents both shape and are shaped by their family systems, enjoying influence as well as support; at the same time, though, they always seem to withdraw more than they deposit in their families' emotional vaults.

A second facet of family life influenced by adolescents is the assignment of roles, including in some ways the paths other family members might pursue with their own talents and abilities. While all families undergo some degree of role reassignment in accommodating adolescents, they also experience some reprioritizing of opportunities and interests. Brothers and sisters particularly feel the pressure of not being allowed to compete with talented siblings. Only in less cohesive families is open competition between all family members in the same talent area encouraged, and then the results are disquieting (Buescher, 1986). In most families with talented offspring, roles are assigned based on a child's talents, interests, opportunities, and responsiveness. In such families, for example, the oldest child might stake out sports or dancing as a special interest area, the second child a different area than the first, perhaps music or schooling, and so on throughout the rest of the family.

How have families successfully responded to the unique pressures their talented adolescents might use to overtly influence organization, roles, and functions? Any minor critical change within a subsystem can have a ripple effect throughout the entire family. By observing how families of exceptional adolescents have successfully encountered and mobilized the strong influences of sons and daughters, Csikszentmihalyi (1987) suggested five key aspects they employ: choice, clarity, commitment, prizing intrinsic rewards, and challenge. All lead to a greater sense of motivated ownership for teenagers.

Matters of control are central to families with adolescents. By accepting the responsibility to help the adolescents exercise *choice* and control over activities, parents are able to limit unnecessary pressures and complications talented students experience when spreading themselves too thin. Similarly, working for *clarity* about family rules by providing consistent feedback about expectations and progress allows parents to encourage older sons and daughters toward full individuation. Adolescents seem to be adept at sniffing out parental inconsistency and working to have their own needs met beyond family limits. Demonstrating effective patterns of making choices and being clear enhance the skills talented adolescents will gain to better manage their own lives.

The third critical element, *commitment,* is reflected in a great deal of the activities and influences parents contribute to their talented sons and daughters. It is seen in long-term interest and involvement in the adolescent's area of talent, in the provision of a secure, compassionate relationship and home. Most of all, commitment reflects an abiding trust of par-

ents and adolescents in each other that has been nurtured since early childhood and continues to sustain those relationships despite minor conflicts.

Csikszentmihalyi (1987) noticed that bright teenagers who seemed best motivated to develop their talents had benefited from a family milieu that prized *intrinsic* rewards. Although positive reinforcement or even subtle bribery can effectively influence some young people to change certain behaviors, talented adolescents are more likely to do so because of important internal rewards that are the result of lifelong intrinsic processes. For example, highly talented student musicians, artists, or mathematicians intensely practice and compete for personal satisfaction rather than monetary gain, even though college scholarships might be in the offing.

Finally, families best support their talented adolescents by valuing *challenge:* encouraging reasonable risk-taking behavior and seeking doors of opportunity. There is a difference between pushing young people and sustaining their responsiveness to good challenges. Some talented adolescents severely limit the expansion of their talent areas, honing in on only one or two and leaving many others closeted against opportunity (Buescher, 1985). Parents do an important job when they challenge sons and daughters to action and growth that resonate to identified talents and lay the groundwork for further development.

Influences on the School and Its Response

As much of this current volume attests, a great deal of research and program development has targeted how schools can best respond to the needs of gifted and talented students. For the most part, the way schools have perceived the matter is that *they alone* influence the talented students by offering them suitable programs and opportunities. Something quite the opposite actually occurs: Schools themselves have slowly been shaped by their adolescent students. This has not been an overnight transition; in fact, parents are most often perceived as the key persons who demand responsive change. Yet when one views the kinds of programs that have been created at the middle school and secondary school levels in particular, the handiwork of adolescent needs and thoughts cannot be mistaken. Several major shifts can be considered.

Advanced Placement Programming. Though sometimes shunned as not being in the best interests of young people, programs offering accelerated content, usually individually paced and carrying college credit, were created and improved in response to the real needs of talented adolescents. The ineffectiveness of traditional college preparatory coursework to capture the ability and motivation of exceptionally talented high school students forced educators to draft more radical means of teaching and learning for these young people.

Recognition of Multiple Talents. Another significant influence talented adolescents have had on secondary school and university programs is in fostering the evolution of cross-disciplinary programs that offer more adequate options for them. In trying to meet the needs of exceptional adolescents in our society, schools and colleges have been forced to recognize the desire of many of these young people to develop and use all their talents, their *multipotentialities*. No longer do talented adolescents only consider career paths in the professions. They explore educational experiences that embrace several areas and open numerous doors of opportunity down the road. Major universities, in a deliberate effort to attract and keep the brightest and best of society's adolescents, have developed richer programs of interdisciplinary study that offer multiple options at graduation. Changes of this magnitude can only be effected if young people themselves are at the center of the demand.

Comprehensive Counseling Services. For too many years, talented adolescents were offered minimal counseling services in high school and none at all in the elementary years. Guidance counselors confined their services to the brightest students along two lines: administering career preference measures in preparation for graduation, and then writing obligatory letters of recommendation for college applications. In time, adolescents demanded

more and the institutions ever so slowly responded. With the resurgence of interest in the gifted, on the coattails of mandated special education services in the 1970s, high school counselors gradually expanded their concerns to include brighter students who were not being successful in school (Sanborn, 1979).

With the renewed vigor of adolescent-based research in the late 1970s, more was demanded for exceptional students who were doing well enough in school but whose personal lives seemed less satisfying. Equipped with new conceptual models, provided especially by Marshall Sanborn and Philip Perrone at the University of Wisconsin's Research and Guidance Laboratory, and encouraged by the responses talented adolescents and their families aroused in high schools, counseling programs devoted to the concerns of gifted and talented students gained a foothold even though they lacked financial support (Zaffrann & Colangelo, 1977). Despite convincing studies of the appropriateness of full-scale programs to effectively counsel talented adolescents, much has remained unchanged. More often than not, high schools adopt the philosophy that these students—being both bright and manipulative—will search out and use support systems on their own. No special services are necessary.

One promising development in recent years has been the interest in *peer counseling* programs for the gifted, or in some schools, a *group guidance* experience within a support group setting. These efforts are not without their own dangers and limitations, but they do demonstrate the potent influence talented students can exert on schools to have their own psychosocial needs met (Buescher, 1989).

Conclusion: Enhancing Self-Discovery

Talented adolescents are at constant risk of having their abilities remain undeveloped or, even worse, become completely lost during the adolescent years. Three key factors seem to impose the greatest difficulties on the lengthy passage from identification by others to self-discovery and personal acceptance: (1) inability to accept *ownership* of the exceptional talent, (2) chronic experiences of low self-esteem or emotional neglect, and (3) habits of socializing and seeking acceptance, often linked to one's gender, that minimize the importance of developed talent (Buescher & Higham, 1989). While the driving developmental task of adolescence is learning how to belong and fit into the larger adult society without becoming anonymous or unattached, the real goal is to know and accept one's own true identity. It is a self-discovery process each person must complete. For talented adolescents, this process includes the unquestioning acceptance and ownership of their unique abilities and experiences. To cast off the talent, or to see it go fallow and wither, is to refuse an essential element of their ego and identity. It creates a path of disappointment and frustration that can linger throughout adulthood, affecting their relationships, work, and purpose for living.

This chapter has emphasized how large the challenge to fit in and belong can be for adolescents with remarkable talents. The pressures to fold up one's tent and move in with the severe compromises of the peer group are seldom equalled in later adult life. Yet parents, educators, and counselors still should have quick access in their own memories to how intimidating the wave of conformity was in their own adolescence. Little has changed today. Although most adolescents seem to defend themselves by invoking their uniqueness and acting rebellious, the most seductive defense for talented adolescents is to give up their own talents and individualities and simply blend into the crowd at school or in the community.

While the complications facing most talented adolescents outlined here might seem foreboding and overwhelming, the fact is that a great majority of the gifted young people continue to grow and flourish during adolescence and adulthood. However, the fact that most are successful does not diminish how difficult the journey can be or what it has cost them, their families, and their friends along the way.

The significant difference between talents discovered, developed, and becoming substantially productive at the conclusion of the adolescent passage and those unknown, discarded, and lost en route can often be traced to a few trusting, caring, and supportive adults. While a great deal has been written about the valuable role mentors can play in the drama of talent development, far too little has resulted in substantial programs that carry out the concept. It is no accident that young adults who have seen the first fruits of their productive talents welcomed by others always point clearly to trusted teachers, coaches, parents, and friends for buoying up their courage and sustaining their determination in adolescence (Bloom, 1985).

Talented adolescents are *adolescents* first and foremost. They experience fully the regression, defensiveness, and relational fluctuations of normal adolescence. They feel the tensions created by the long march from sterility to fertility in many aspects of their lives: intimacy, sexuality, identity, and a commitment to talent development. Significant adults who can listen with great care to these young people, respect their attitudes and values, provide sensitive insight for their questions and issues, and above all, sustain involvement in their world make a substantial impact on their future lives and happiness.

REFERENCES

Adams, G. R., & Shea, J. A. (1979). The relationship between identity status, locus of control, and ego development. *Journal of Youth and Adolescence, 8*, 81–89.

Albert, R. (1980). Family positions and the attainment of eminence: A study of special family positions and special family experiences. *Gifted Child Quarterly, 24*, 87–95.

Alvino, J. (Ed.). (1986). *Parents' guide to raising a gifted child*. Boston: Little, Brown.

Archer, S. (1982). The lower age boundaries of identity development. *Child Development, 53*, 1551–1556.

Benbow, C. & Stanley, J. (1983). *Academic precocity*. Baltimore: Johns Hopkins University Press.

Bloom, B. (Ed.). (1985). *Developing talent in young people*. New York: Ballantine.

Bloom, B., & Sosniak, L. (1981). Talent development. *Educational Leadership, 39*, (2), 86–94.

Blos, P. (1967). The second individuation process of adolescence. *Psychoanalytic Study of the Child, 22*, 162–186.

Blos, P. (1985). *Son and father: Before and beyond the Oedipus complex*. New York: Free.

Brooks-Gunn, J., & Petersen, A. (1984). *Girls at puberty*. New York: Plenum.

Buescher, T. (1985). A framework for understanding the social and emotional development of gifted adolescents. *Roeper Review, 8,* 10–15.

Buescher, T. (1986, November). *The effect of family structure and expectations on the performance and adjustment of highly talented adolescents: Selected case studies*. Paper presented at annual meeting, National Association for Gifted Children, Las Vegas.

Buescher, T. (1989). *Natural advice and peer counseling: Developmental factors and implications when talented adolescents counsel each other*. Unpublished master's research paper, Loyola University of Chicago.

Buescher, T., & Higham, S. (1989). A developmental study of adjustment in gifted adolescents. In J. VanTassel-Baska & P. Olszewski (Eds.), *Patterns of influence: Home, self, and school* (pp. 102–124). New York: Teachers College Press.

Buescher, T., Olszewski, P., & Higham, S. (1987, April). *Influences on strategies gifted adolescents use to cope with their own recognized talents*. Paper presented at biennial meetings, Society for Research in Child Development, Baltimore.

Calderone, M., & Johnson, E. (1983). *The family book about sexuality*. New York: Harper & Row.

Chilman, C. (1980). *Adolescent sexuality in a changing American society*. Washington, DC: U.S. Department of Health, Education and Welfare.

Colangelo, N. (1982). Characteristics of moral problems as formulated by gifted adolescents. *Journal of Moral Education, 11,* 219–232.

Coleman, L. (1985). *Schooling the gifted*. Menlo Park: Addison-Wesley.

Csikszentmihalyi, M. (1987, April). *Developing intrinsic motivation in children and adolescents*. Paper presented at annual research symposium, Phi Delta Kappa, Northwestern University Chapter, Evanston, IL.

Csikszentmihalyi, M., & Larson, R. (1984). *Being adolescent*. New York: Basic.

de Bono, E. (1983). The direct teaching of thinking as a skill. *Phi Delta Kappa, 64,* 703–708.

Delisle, J. (1985). Vocational problems. In J. Freeman (Ed.), *The psychology of gifted children* (pp. 178–201). New York: Wiley.

Delisle, J. (1987). Career choices and gifted adolescents: The uneasy alliance. In T. Buescher (Ed.), *Understanding gifted and talented adolescents* (pp. 35–39). Evanston, IL: Northwestern University, Center for Talent Development.

Elkind, D. (1984). *All grown up and no place to go*. Reading, MA: Addison-Wesley.

Erikson, E. (1956). The problem of ego identity. *Journal of American Psychoanalytic Association, 4,* 56–83.

Erikson, E. (1963). *Childhood and society*. New York: Norton.

Erikson, E. (1968). *Identity: Youth and crisis*. New York: Norton.

Foster, W., & Mangel, H. (1987). Work and love: The interaction of intimacy, self-esteem, and productive excellence. In T. Buescher (Ed.), *Understanding gifted and talented adolescents* (pp. 11–16). Evanston IL: Northwestern University, Center for Talent Development.

Freeman, D. S. (1981). *Techniques of family therapy*. New York: Aronson.

Gilligan, C. (1982). New maps of development: New visions of maturity. *American Journal of Orthopsychiatry, 52,* 199–212.

Hackney, H. (1983). Effects of the family: Random or orchestrated? *Journal for the Education of the Gifted, 6,* 30–38.

Hass, A. (1979). *Teenage sexuality: A survey of teenage sexual behavior*. New York: Macmillan.

Higham, S., & Buescher, T. (1987). What young gifted adolescents understand about feeling different. In T. Buescher (Ed.), *Understanding gifted and talented adolescents* (pp. 26–30). Evanston IL: Northwestern University, Center for Talent Development.

Kestenberg, J. (1980). Eleven, twelve, thirteen: Years of transition from the barrenness of childhood to the fertility of adolescence. In S. Greenspan & G. Pollock (Eds.), *The course of life* (Vol. 2, pp. 229–264). Washington, DC: National Institute of Mental Health.

Mahler, M., & McDevitt, J. (1980). The separation-individuation process and identity formation. In S. Greenspan & G. Pollock (Eds.), *The course of life* (Vol. I, pp. 395–406). Washington DC: National Institute of Mental Health.

Manaster, G., & Powell, P. (1983). A framework for understanding gifted adolescents' psychological maladjustment. *Roeper Review, 6,* 70–73.

Marcia, J. (1966). Development and validation of ego-identity status. *Journal of Personality and Social Psychology, 3,* 551–558.

Marcia, J. (1976). Identity six years after: A follow-up study. *Journal of Youth and Adolescence, 5,* 145–160.

McAdams, D. P. (1985). *Power, intimacy, and the life story*. Homewood, IL: Dorsey.

Montemayor, R. (1982). The relationship between parent-adolescent conflict and the amount of time adolescents spend alone and with parents and peers. *Child Development, 53,* 1512–1519.

Montemayor, R. (1983). Parents and adolescents in conflict: All families some of the time and some families most of the time. *Journal of Early Adolescence, 3,* 83–103.

Offer, D. (1986). Adolescent development: A normative perspective. In A. Frances & R. Hales (Eds.), *Annual review, psychiatry update* (Vol. 5, pp. 404–419). Washington, DC: American Psychiatric Association.

Offer, D., Ostrov, E., & Howard, K. (1981). *The adolescent: A psychological self-portrait.* New York: Harper.

Olszewski, P., Kulieke, M., & Buescher, T. (1987). The influence of the family environment on the development of talent: A review. *Journal for the Education of the Gifted, 11,* 6–28.

Perlman, D., & Fehr, B. (1987). The development of intimate relationships. In D. Perlman & B. Fehr (Eds.), *Intimate relationships: Development, dynamics, and deterioration* (pp. 13–42). Beverly Hills: Russell Sage.

Petersen, A. (1988). Developments in adolescent psychology. In C. P. Stone (Ed.), *Annual review of psychology* (Vol. 39, pp. 81–94). New York: Academic.

Piaget, J. (1952). *The origins of intelligence in children.* New York: International Universities.

Piechowski, M. (1987). Family qualities and the emotional development of older gifted students.

In T. Buescher (Ed.), *Understanding gifted and talented adolescents* (pp. 17–23). Evanston IL: Northwestern University, Center for Talent Development.

Piechowski, M., & Colangelo, N. (1984). Developmental potential of the gifted. *Gifted Child Quarterly, 8,* 80–88.

Sanborn, M. (1979). Differential counseling needs of the gifted and talented. In N. Colangelo & R. Zaffrann (Eds.), *New voices in counseling the gifted* (pp. 154–164). Dubuque, IA: Kendall/Hunt.

Sarrel, L., & Sarrel, P. (1981). *Sexual unfolding: Sexual development and sex therapies in late adolescence.* Boston: Little, Brown.

Sears, R. (1977). Sources of life satisfactions of the Terman gifted men. *American Psychologist, 32,* 119–128.

Shapiro, T., & Hertzig, M. (1988). Normal growth and development. In J. Talbott, R. Hales, & S. Yudofsky (Eds.), *Textbook of psychiatry* (pp. 106–122). Washington DC: American Psychiatric Press.

Zaffrann, R., & Colangelo, N. (1977). Counseling with gifted and talented students. *Gifted Child Quarterly, 21,* 305–321.

28

Educating Gifted Girls

BARBARA KERR   *University of Iowa, Iowa City*

◼ Teachers who work closely with gifted students have long observed and lamented the failure of gifted girls to fulfill their early intellectual promise. They watch in frustration as the little girls who were once so eager to demonstrate their intelligence and creativity grow into teenagers who carefully obscure their achievements or who blithely pass up opportunities for special programming designed to nurture their talents. Counselors who work with gifted young women may notice a gradual disengagement with goal setting but are unable to pinpoint exactly what seems to be holding bright females back. Those of us who research characteristics of gifted females have what seems to be a straightforward task: Discover the barriers to gifted females' achievement and investigate means of overcoming them. This was indeed the focus of Lynn Fox's work in the mid-1970s with mathematically gifted junior high school girls (Fox, 1976; Fox, Benbow, & Perkins, 1983); Elyse Fleming and Constance Hollinger's Project Choice (1979) with gifted girls identified according to U.S. Commissioner of Education guidelines (1972) and my own research related to academically talented and high-IQ girls and women (Kerr, 1983, 1985). The results of this earlier work and the findings of the many studies now being published show that the problem of gifted females' failure to realize their potential is complex and the task of guiding gifted girls anything but straightforward. In addition, recent trends in intelligence research, in gifted females' behavior, and in the values of society as a whole have brought about rapid changes in how we perceive, teach, and guide gifted girls.

Females and Giftedness: Recent Changes

First, the concept of giftedness itself is undergoing transformation. New concepts of intelligence such as Sternberg's (1986) information processing approach and Gardner's (1983) theory of multiple intelligences challenge the notion of the unitary IQ score as a predictor of extraordinary intellectual performance (see Chapter 4 by Sternberg and Chapter 5 by Ramos-Ford and Gardner). While these new theories improve our understanding of intelligence, they make the task of identification of giftedness more difficult because instruments are not yet available to measure the abilities they propose. More critical, though, to the problem of female giftedness is that new theories of intelligence have little or nothing to say about gender, and it will probably be decades before a body of research exists on such topics as "gender differences in information processing" or "effects of gender on Gardner's personal intelligences."

A second problem that occurs when we try to summarize the state of the art in educating gifted girls and women is that our subjects are changing before our very eyes. There have been extraordinary changes in the last 5 years in bright young women's career choices and aspirations. Studies in the early 1980s showed gifted adolescent girls and young women to have lower aspirations than their gifted male age-mates (Kerr, 1983). Currently, however, young gifted women are choosing professional careers in almost equal proportions to gifted young men. For example, business has replaced education as the most popular career choice of bright young women (Kerr & Colangelo, 1988).

Changes are occurring in phenomena once thought to be fixed aspects of the psychology of women, such as fear of success and math anxiety. Research studies indicate that many bright girls today simply do not manifest fear of success (Tressemer, 1977), and one recent study of gifted girls could find no evidence of math anxiety (Weiner & Robinson, 1986). Sex role expectations and attitudes are also in flux. Sometimes, parental attitudes change in reaction to findings of psychological research: The highly publicized research of Benbow and Stanley (1983) has affected parental attitudes toward girls' math attitudes in a complex manner, confirming some parents' stereotypes and sending some to the defense of their daughters' abilities (Jacobs & Eccles, 1985). In studying gifted girls and women we are observing a moving target, and our very observations are changing our observed subjects.

Finally, value conflicts about women's roles now pervade society, education, and research. The education and guidance of gifted girls take place within the context of a society that is deeply conflicted in its attitudes toward women's roles. Although the majority of American women now work outside the home, the deep ambivalence about women's rising aspirations is reflected in the many cautionary stories in the media about the dangers of "Superwomen," persistent criticisms and concerns about effects of nonmaternal child care, and the extraordinary interest in biologically based gender differences in abilities.

That societal concerns about women's roles can affect research was made clear to my colleagues and me when the Guidance Laboratory for Gifted and Talented at the University of Nebraska was investigated by a conservative political group and a state senator's office to determine if we were influencing gifted girls to abandon traditional family values. (We were fortunately found innocent of this charge.)

Values conflicts and ambiguities about women's roles are also evident within psychology and education. While most researchers on women's achievement use societally recognized measures of achievement such as educational attainment and occupational status, a number have questioned the practice of measuring women's achievement with male-oriented measures of achievement (Callahan, 1987; Eccles, 1985). Gilligan's (1982) proposal that women experience a different process of moral development than men has led to a broad interpretation of her theory to fit many observed gender differences. The *separate spheres* argument, that is, that men and women are basically different, inhabit different realities, and must be considered and judged within their own spheres rather than in comparison with one another, is one that reemerges every generation, immediately following upon the heels of the equity argument—that is, women and men are more alike than they are different, and should be treated equally in all respects.

Despite rapid changes in women's status in some areas of the economy and changes in particular aspects of the psychology of women, the fact of continued differential socialization of girls and boys can hardly be denied. A few hours spent watching Saturday morning cartoons will bring home the striking differences in society's images of boys and girls. In children's toy commercials, boys continue to be depicted as action-oriented problem solvers, playing with noisy, active toys in outdoor settings, while girls are quiet, pretty nurturers, playing almost exclusively with passive toys that require grooming and dressing, almost invariably in the girls' bedrooms. In the cartoons themselves, boy characters outnumber girl characters, and boys are capable and adventurous while girls are helpful observers. As Sadker and Sadker's (1985) work shows, girls continue to receive less attention than boys throughout their education. In our own laboratory at the University of Iowa, the Counseling Laboratory for Talent Development, we have observed that young gifted women are deeply concerned about their role expectations and often confused and unclear about their goals. Nevertheless, many of our clients feel a need to hide their confusion by claiming impressive-sounding career goals like business management, when in fact they have little interest in that goal or knowledge of how to pursue it.

Young gifted women today seem to feel pressure to be highly achieving and work-oriented but have not learned the deeper lesson of the women's movement: that they are in charge of their own lives.

Perhaps the best approach that can be taken in a subject area fraught with value conflicts is to simply explain one's own biases and move on. As in *Smart Girls, Gifted Women* (Kerr, 1985), my assumption is that gifted women are happiest when they are challenging the limits of their intellectual potential. In addition, it is assumed that the best type of achievement for both men and women is the attainment of one's own dreams and goals. Despite the advice of advocates who desire different standards for measuring the achievements of men and women, traditional measures of achievement of gifted females such as educational degrees and occupational prestige will be explored here, not because they are the only measures of accomplishments, but because they are markers of less measurable qualities of lifestyle, such as autonomy and opportunities for challenge. The use of these measures does not mean that gifted females can only be studied in comparison with gifted males. It is assumed here that gifted females are interesting in themselves.

Reports of gender differences in achievement test scores, educational degrees, occupational prestige, and attainment of eminence tell us little about individual gifted girls, but much about our society. However, our knowledge of these differences provide clues to potential societal restrictions on the freedom of an individual gifted girl to enjoy as many options as she deserves. These restrictions, whether lack of expectations of success, inadequate course taking, or absence of mentoring, can be remedial. The next sections review what is known about gifted girls and gifted female adolescents, followed by suggestions for education and guidance.

Gifted Girls: Trends and Problems

Giftedness is evident in girls at an earlier age than boys because gifted girls are more likely to show developmental advancement (Silverman, 1986). High-IQ girls tend to be taller, stronger, and healthier than girls of average IQ (Terman & Oden, 1935). Nevertheless, gifted girls may feel less physically competent than gifted boys or boys in general (Chan, 1988).

In the moderately gifted range defined by Kerr and Colangelo (1988) as approximately the 95th percentile on IQ and achievement tests, gifted girls are as healthy mentally as they are physically. Studies comparing gifted girls with gifted boys and with average girls and boys consistently show gifted girls to have excellent social adjustment. Whether measured in terms of "social knowledge" (Terman & Oden, 1935), perceived self-competence (Chan, 1988) or absence of behavioral impairments on behavior rating scales (Ludwig & Cullinan, 1984), gifted girls are remarkably free from childhood adjustment disorders. At the very highest levels of ability, gifted girls may experience more adjustment problems. Terman and Oden (1935) and Hollingworth (1926) noted, fairly predictably, that the highest IQ children in general suffered more adjustment problems, probably as a result of their profoundly deviant intellectual abilities. Interestingly, eminent women, in retrospective accounts of their lives, remember feeling either "different" or "special" as children; whether the consequences were negative or positive, eminent women seemed well aware as girls of their deviancy from the norm (Kerr, 1985).

Gifted girls are more similar to gifted boys than to average girls in their interests, attitudes, and aspirations. Gifted girls apparently enjoy a wide variety of play activities, including many of those activities traditionally associated with boys: outdoor activities, adventurous play, sports, and problem-solving activities. They also frequently maintain feminine interests as well, such as playing with dolls and reading girls' magazines (Silverman, 1986; Terman & Oden, 1935). Eminent women remember girlhoods full of exploration, adventure, and voracious reading. As girls, eminent women also spent an unusually large amount of time in solitary activities (Kerr, 1985).

Although sex-role-stereotyped career interests are well established by second grade in the general population of girls and boys, gifted girls may have career interests more similar to those of gifted boys (Silverman, 1986; Terman & Oden, 1935). Young gifted girls have high aspirations and vivid career fantasies: They dream of being paleontologists, astronauts, and ambassadors (Kerr, 1985). Throughout childhood, gifted girls outperform gifted boys in classroom achievement, maintaining higher grades in all subjects. Gifted girls also outperform gifted boys on achievement tests throughout elementary school (Gallagher, 1985).

Adolescence brings changes in gifted girls' aspirations, expectations, attitudes, and achievement. The changes that occur for gifted girls today are more subtle than those that occurred 50, 20, or even 10 years ago. Nevertheless, the direction of change is still the same overall, and it is one of declining involvement with former achievement goals. The changes are most evident in academic achievement test scores, course taking, and other academically related behaviors.

Gender Differences in Achievement and Aptitude Tests

On American College Testing (ACT) exams taken during the senior year of high school, 61% of students scoring above the 95th percentile on the composite score are male; 72% of students scoring in the 99th percentile on the composite score are male (Kerr & Colangelo, 1988). With regard to the four subtests, males outperform females at the highest levels on the ACT mathematics, natural sciences, and social studies. Only on the English subtest do females outperform males. There are 3 times as many males who earn perfect math scores; 5 times as many males earn perfect natural sciences scores; and 2½ times as many males get perfect social studies scores (Colangelo & Kerr, in press).

The lower scores for females on the ACT seem to be strongly related to course taking; Laing, Engen, and Maxey (1987) have provided convincing evidence that much of the variance in ACT scores is accounted for by curriculum. Gifted adolescent females apparently not only take fewer and less challenging math and science courses than gifted males, but also fewer and less challenging social studies courses.

More puzzling, however, are Benbow and Stanley's (1983) findings of extreme sex dif-ferences favoring boys at the highest levels of mathematical reasoning among gifted seventh-graders. Benbow and Stanley's group was made up of seventh-graders who scored at or above the mean for high school seniors on the Scholastic Aptitude Test, mathematical section (SAT-M). Their research is worth examining in some detail because it has been a source of controversy.

Note that the finding of gender differences in mathematical achievement test scores is nothing new; across many cultures, gender differences appear in mathematical measures by about 10th grade (Maccoby & Jacklin, 1974). These differences have been linked in the past to math course taking. Gender differences in math scores generally begin at the point at which girls stop taking math courses.

The Benbow and Stanley results are considered important, first, because the seventh-graders in their study had had similar course experiences, and second, because the makers of the SAT-M consider it a test of mathematical reasoning ability rather than a test of mathematical achievement. Therefore, course taking alone could not account for the large differences in proportions of boys and girls scoring extremely high. There is a possibility that some native reasoning ability above and beyond mathematical operations is brought into play on this test, and that consequently gifted boys were found to be superior in this sort of reasoning. Also, critics of this study (Eccles, 1985; Kavrell & Petersen, 1984) have pointed out that the participants were a nonrepresentative sample of gifted girls and boys; they were all seventh-graders whose school officials had publicized the Talent Search Program that sponsored the testing and whose parents had arranged for their testing on the SAT college entrance exams. It is possible, according to this argument, that some of the most highly mathematically gifted girls did not participate in the talent search. Studies have shown that gifted girls are less likely to enroll in advanced math classes (Benbow & Stanley, 1982), less likely to voluntarily enter a gifted/talented program (George & Denham, 1976), less likely to participate in accelerated math courses (Fox & Cohn, 1980), and less likely to be interested in science and engineering careers even when they are capable of them (Benbow & Stanley, 1984). Therefore, factors other than native ability can discourage even very brilliant girls from participating in the talent search in the first place.

Expectations of success and belief in the value of the task (Eccles, 1985), instrumental and expressive behavior (Hollinger & Fleming, 1988) and "exploratory" behaviors (Steinkamp, 1984) all have been linked to bright girls' achievement. All these are socialized perceptions, attitudes, and ways of approaching problems.

Studies that have explored the relationship of chromosomal patterns (Bock & Kolakowski, 1973) and pubertal hormones (Petersen, 1979) to math ability have produced mixed results. The first line of research has been pretty well disconfirmed; no differences have been found that could be linked to the X chromosome (Boles, 1980). The only study to show an indirect relationship between hormones and math achievement simply compared math scores and body types. Boys with more "feminine" physical characteristics and girls with more "masculine" physical characteristics were found to have higher math scores (Petersen, 1976). This finding would not support masculine superiority in math achievement so much as "androgynous" superiority.

Even if these studies did provide evidence of some biological basis for sex differences in mathematical reasoning, what difference should it make to teachers, parents, and gifted girls themselves? First, Hyde (1981) showed that sex differences, whatever their basis, account for less than 4% of the variance in math achievement. Most of the variability in achievement scores is within genders, rather than between genders. It is likely that differences in math ability are the result mainly of factors within our control, such as the shaping of expectations and confidence, rather than factors out of our control, such as gender. Therefore, the presence of biological differences could hardly be used as an excuse for discouraging gifted girls from mathematical pursuit, when the effect, if it exists at all, is so small.

Second, even the most august and rigorous math-related jobs in the world, for example, theoretical mathematician, astrophysicist, cosmologist, do not necessarily require the most extraordinary mathematical reasoning powers in the land. The vast majority of mathematically gifted girls, certainly all those who qualify by the talent search criteria, have the intellectual capacity for any math-related position existing today if to their intellectual ability they add the training, confidence, expectations, attitudes, and personality characteristics needed to explore the concept of number or the beginnings of the universe.

Career Aspirations

Changes seem to be occurring across society in gifted adolescent girls' career aspirations. Whereas highly gifted girls such as the top 1% of National Merit scholars usually maintained high career aspirations in adolescence (Kaufmann, 1981), until recently moderately gifted girls (those scoring in the upper 5% on IQ and achievement tests) tended to have declining career aspirations during adolescence (Fox, 1976; Kerr, 1983, 1985). More recently, however, gifted adolescent girls have been naming college majors and career goals that are frequently nontraditional for women (Kerr & Colangelo, 1988). Among 12,330 girls scoring in the 95th percentile and above on the ACT, there were about the same proportion of girls as boys choosing majors in premedicine, prelaw, and mathematics. Health professions (17.9%), social science (14.0%), and business (13.0%) were the most popular majors of this group. Sharp disparities continued in only one traditionally male career—engineering, where the proportions were 30.5% males to 7.9% females choosing that major. When gifted adolescent girls were asked to name their career goals, they seemed to aim high. Dolney (1985) observed the same trend in his study of Toronto gifted students' aspirations.

Adjustment and Self-Esteem

There is strong evidence that the majority of moderately gifted girls, like gifted boys, remain well adjusted during adolescence (Janos & Robinson, 1985; Lessinger & Martinson, 1961; Terman & Oden, 1935). That is, on personality inventories, girls and boys identified as gifted are usually similar or superior to average students on psychological characteristics associated with good mental health and adjustment. However, gifted adolescent girls may experience social anxiety and decreases in self-confidence. This was shown most dramatically in Groth's (1969) cross-sectional study that showed an abrupt psychological shift at age 14 from wishes and needs related to achievement and self-esteem to wishes related to love and belonging. Her study showed that gifted younger girls tended to dream about successes in school activities and accomplishments; older gifted girls dreamed of popularity and intimate friendships. Kelly and Colangelo (1984) found that while gifted boys were superior to average boys in academic and social self-concepts, gifted girls were not similarly higher than average girls.

In Kerr, Colangelo, and Gaeth's (1988) study of adolescents' attitudes toward their own giftedness, gifted girls were evidently quite concerned about the impact of their giftedness on attitudes of others. Although most of them believed that there were some social advantages to being gifted, females saw more disadvantages than their male peers to being gifted. There was a deep ambivalence about the label *gifted* as well as concern about negative images others might hold of that label.

Perhaps the most significant work in the area of the adjustment of the gifted adolescent girl has been done by Constance Hollinger and Elyse Fleming (Fleming & Hollinger, 1979; Hollinger, 1983, 1985; Hollinger & Fleming, 1984, 1988). Beginning with over 100 gifted girls identified on the basis of U.S. Office of Education guidelines, Hollinger and Fleming created a career development program aimed at overcoming barriers to gifted girls' achievement. Participants in the program have been followed closely since 1979, and frequent assessments have been made of their self-perceptions, self-esteem, and aspirations.

Of particular interest to Hollinger and Fleming has been the development of social self-esteem, which they believe is central to the realization of potential in gifted girls. Social self-esteem is made up of *instrumentality*, or the belief that one has the ability to act effectively and to make decisions independently, and *expressiveness*, a sense of responsiveness and caring, with instrumentality making the stronger contribution to high self-esteem (Hollinger, 1983, 1985). Social self-esteem seems to protect gifted girls from fears of social rejection that may accompany high achievement and serves to build the self-confidence needed to follow through on high goals. Self-confidence may be a better predictor of adult achievement than high grades or high aspirations (Eccles, 1985).

Hollinger and Fleming (1988) found that from sophomore year of high school through 3½ years after graduation, self-perceptions of instrumentality were predictive of occupational confidence and life satisfaction. Expressiveness, on the other hand, while not being predictive of occupational confidence or life satisfaction, did predict social self-esteem in combination with instrumentality. The results of their research so far seem to show that gifted girls need to be encouraged to develop not only those instrumental characteristics associated with masculinity but also the expressive characteristics associated with femininity if they are to be highly achieving as well as socially confident. Gifted girls need to understand that they do not need to reject the nurturing, caring side of themselves in order to be bold and achieving. More will be said about Hollinger and Fleming's social self-esteem model later.

Good social adjustment in adolescence is not a prerequisite for eminence. Kaufmann (1981), in her study of the extraordinarily talented young women who had been named Presidential Scholars, found that they had received little recognition for their accomplishments in high school and were often perceived as loners. Eminent women often had unhappy, difficult adolescences (Kerr, 1985). For some, social rejection and the status of the "outsider" paradoxically lent them the freedom to develop independent opinions and free-ranging intellects. Therefore, in guiding gifted girls, it seems best to nourish the growth of self-esteem but to deemphasize the pursuit of popularity.

Identification

An early start may be critical to gifted girls receiving an appropriate education. As mentioned earlier, gifted girls are more likely to show developmental advancement than gifted boys and are likely to be ready for kindergarten earlier than gifted boys (Silverman, 1986). Gifted girls do very well as early admittants to kindergarten (Callahan, 1979). Identification of giftedness only becomes a problem when schools require "proof" of giftedness. Although intelligence tests such as the Stanford-Binet, the Wechsler Intelligence Scale for Children—Revised (WISC-R), and the Kaufman Assessment Battery for Children (K-ABC; Kaufman & Kaufman, 1983) have been used with very young children, they are often not reliable measures of giftedness before ages 9 or 10 for children in general. Developmental scales are usually more effective at identifying deficits than advances in development. Nevertheless, an excellent instrument like the Stanford-Binet, administered carefully by a competent psychologist, will pick up the extraordinary verbal skills that are often the earliest signs of giftedness in girls (Silverman, 1986). Whenever possible, however, bright 4- and 5-year-old girls who simply show signs of school readiness—advanced vocabulary, precocious reading, math skills, and an eagerness for school social activities—should be given the benefit of the doubt and admitted early. An early start helps ensure that gifted girls will be challenged, even when no other gifted programming is available. Where schools are locked into an age-in-grade format, early admission to kindergarten may be the *only* window of opportunity available to gifted girls.

In selecting tests for admission into a gifted education program, test bias must be considered (Kitano & Kirby, 1985). Tests that emphasize content that is more familiar to boys than girls, such as word problems about mechanical toys or sports, may be biased against girls. Achievement tests with a heavier weighting of math and science items than language-related items will select more boys, particularly in the upper grades. Intelligence tests that deemphasize verbal skills and emphasize performance, that is, spatial-visual activities, may also be biased against girls who receive much less practice than boys at puzzles and assembly.

Several approaches to identifying gifted girls for particular educational interventions have been found to be effective in predicting performance. One method is the use of different cutoff scores for admission to advanced course work in specific areas. It is very difficult to prove that particular tests are sex-biased. Nevertheless, it is fairly easy to show for some tests that different aptitude scores for girls and boys actually predict the same levels of success in learning in areas such as math and science. For example, a girl scoring 490 on the SAT-M in seventh grade may perform similarly in accelerated mathematics to a boy in seventh grade scoring 530. Therefore, in those subject areas in which gifted boys have generally received higher scores than gifted girls, it is possible that girls receiving scores slightly lower than boys may be able to perform at equivalent levels in the classroom.

A second method for identifying gifted girls is a multidimensional approach (Fleming & Hollinger, 1979). Gifted girls may possess a wide variety of skills and characteristics that contribute as much to their academic performance as aptitude for particular tasks, for example, leadership skills and creativity. A multidimensional approach will help to ensure that girls with potential for high performance are identified above and beyond those who score well on objective tests of intellectual aptitude. The multidimensional approach is most useful in selecting gifted girls for broad-based programs of enrichment or other increased academic challenges. It is also useful for targeting girls who might benefit from specialized career education, guidance, and mentoring.

Finally, although tests and assessment devices are useful in predicting academic performance, few objective measures have been shown to be predictive of adult accomplishment of gifted women. Neither high IQ (Terman & Oden, 1947), high achievement test scores (Kaufmann, 1981), nor high grade point averages (Kerr, 1985) have been found to be associated with women's achievement. Torrance, Bruch, and Morse (1973) found that the Torrance tests of verbal creativity were more predictive of accomplishment in women than any measures of intellectual aptitude. Therefore, any measure of the intellectual aptitude of gifted girls must be used for short-term prediction and with a clear understanding of the many powerful nonacademic factors operating in determining the progress of a gifted girl toward the achievement of her potential.

Increasing Equity in the Classroom

Potential sources of bias need to be removed from the program of study as well as the identification procedures. Ample evidence exists of inequitable instruction in the classroom (Sadker & Sadker, 1985). Boys receive more attention from teachers than girls throughout their education. Boys are called on more often in class than girls. They are more frequently rewarded for calling out answers while girls are more frequently reprimanded for the same response. Boys also receive more informative responses from teachers; Sadker and Sadker found that girls receive more bland "accepting" responses from teachers, whereas boys receive more praise and criticism. Boys receive more instructional attention; they get detailed instructions on the correct approach to tasks. On the other hand, girls frequently are simply given the right answers. These differential teacher responses do not seem to be the result of deliberate discrimination on teachers' parts; even staunchly feminist teachers exhibit similar patterns. Differential instruction seems to be both a response to different behaviors of boys and girls and a reflection of underlying socialized attitudes that are mostly unconscious.

Similar studies have not been done specifically with gifted children or in the context of a gifted education program. Nevertheless, there are some indicators that gifted girls suffer from differential treatment. In the study of attitudes toward gifted students, Solano (1977) found that when teacher attitudes were negative toward gifted students in general, they were more negative toward gifted girls. One study found that female teachers may be more discouraging toward gifted girls' aspirations than male teachers (Cooley, Chauvin, & Karnes, 1984). Fox (1976) found evidence of gifted girls having been discouraged from taking advanced math courses, entering gifted education, and participating in summer opportunities for gifted students.

Although the causes of teachers' differential treatment of girls and boys may run deep, the remedy may not be difficult or complex. Sadker and Sadker (1984) found that most teachers wanted to teach in a nonsexist manner and were anxious to learn how. Even brief training workshops were effective in improving equitable behavior. Teachers can learn to call on girls as often as they call on boys; to give girls informative responses, praising and criticizing in detail; to reward girls' assertiveness in the classroom; and to resist "overhelping" girls by giving them answers or solving problems for them.

Another perspective on equity in classroom instruction is given by Dweck and Licht (1980), who showed that girls learn to attribute the causes of their successes and failures differently than boys. Possibly because of bland teacher responses and overhelping, girls learn to attribute their successes to luck and effort and their failures to lack of ability. This may lead them to avoid course work that they believe requires considerable effort and for which they believe they lack the ability (Eccles, 1985). Therefore, girls need to be taught to have confidence in their abilities and to believe that their efforts are effective. This may translate into teacher behaviors that encourage effort ("I know you can do this" or "I want you to try to solve the problem on your own").

Gifted girls must be given specific information about their superior abilities very early (Kerr, 1985). They should be helped to understand their intellectual strengths and to see how their abilities can help them in their classwork. Gifted girls need to perceive their giftedness not as a mysterious force out of their control, but rather a set of potentials that, when combined with effort, can lead to extraordinary accomplishment.

Changing teacher behavior is only one aspect of removing bias from the education of gifted girls. Boy-centered textbooks, literature, and activities may discourage bright girls from pursuing interests even in those areas in which they excel and which they enjoy. This can be particularly a problem in science and math classes, where experimenters, teachers, and the subjects of study are rarely female or feminine. However, language arts and social studies materials are also sometimes biased against females, and these should be checked for the balance of presentation. Do illustrative pictures have an equal number of males and females? Are female authors represented? Are the roles of women in history and current events represented?

Gifted girls' tendency to be able to read popular adult literature while still very young may occasionally have negative effects; popular novels and magazines are often much more sexist than school materials or age-appropriate materials. Restriction of the amount or type of reading engaged in by gifted girls is almost always a bad idea. However, teachers and librarians should discuss recreational reading materials with bright girls, pointing out stereotypes of women and girls in popular literature. "Inoculating" bright girls against negative portrayals of women with biographies of eminent women and stories about strong, active, courageous girls may be the best approach to combating sexism in print (Kerr, 1985).

What about Single-Sex Schooling?

One hope for "girl-friendly" education may lie in single-sex schooling. Proportionately more women scholars and leaders graduate from single-sex colleges (Kerr, 1985). Fox (1976) was able to maintain girls' interests and aspirations in math in an all-girl, female-led accelerated math class. Mary Baldwin College's Program for the Education of the Gifted (Garrison & Rhodes, 1987) is a new educational program for highly gifted girls that combines high school and college in a 6-year course of study. This program, which emphasizes academic challenge, career guidance, "model women," and individualized instruction, uses all that is known about gifted girls to provide appropriate experiences. The first evaluations of this promising program will tell much about the benefits of single-sex education for gifted girls.

Enhancing Achievement-Oriented Behaviors

Many theories and models have been proposed to explain women's achievement—or lack of achievement. Research-based models of achievement that have been applied to bright girls and women include Eccles's (1985) model of achievement; Hollinger and Fleming's (1988) social self-esteem theory; and Steinkamp's (1984) motivational theory. Each of these contains within it practical implications for educating and guiding gifted girls. In addition, case studies of eminent individuals can help in understanding guidance needs of gifted girls.

Achievement-Related Choices

Jacqueline Eccles's (1985) model of achievement-related choices assumes that many variables contribute to gifted girls' achievement and that these variables are related to one another in complex ways. Two of the most important components of achievement-related choices are *expectation for success* and *subjective task value*. That is, differential socialization of females can affect both expectations for success in sex-role-stereotyped academic plans or career goals and perceptions of how important or valuable particular academic and career goals might be. It is not clear if gifted girls lack confidence in their abilities. Moderately gifted girls (Terman & Oden, 1935; Kerr, 1985) seem to have less confidence in their intellectual abilities than highly gifted, particularly mathematically gifted, girls (Benbow & Stanley, 1982). Hollinger (1983) found a strong relationship between gifted girls' confidence in their math abilities and their plans to pursue math-related careers. Gifted girls may also value achievement goals differently. Like average girls they may be more "people-oriented" than boys and may have different perceptions of sex-role-stereotyped occupations than boys (Fox & Denham, 1974).

Therefore, it may be very helpful for gifted girls to increase both their confidence in their ability to achieve academic career goals and the degree to which they value these goals.

Specific information about relative abilities can help increase the confidence of gifted girls in their goals: "You are probably able to read better than 9 out of 10 children your age"; "Your math skills are as good as those of kids who grow up to be mathematicians and scientists." Teachers should avoid vague or bland confidence-giving statements; they should back up their encouragement with solid facts.

Increasing the task value may be a matter of helping gifted girls to understand the consequences of academic decisions. For example, few gifted girls are aware of the absolute importance of mathematics to their future goals. Frequently, gifted girls drop out of math and science courses for superficial reasons, not realizing that most college majors leading to high-level careers and professions require 4 years of high school preparation in math and science (Kerr, 1985). Teachers need to be careful not to collaborate in gifted girls' plans to take less challenging courses in order to keep up their grade point average; instead they need to emphasize the value of taking the most comprehensive and rigorous curriculum available.

Social Self-Esteem

According to Hollinger and Fleming (1988), social self-esteem, as we noted earlier, is related to achievement and life satisfaction and is the product of two self-perceptions: *instrumentality* and *expressiveness*. Instrumentality, which is central to achievement, is an attitude and a set of self-perceptions related to the ability to act effectively, to make things happen, to have an impact. Women with high instrumentality are decisive, active, and risk taking. Expressiveness is the self-perception of being caring, communicative, and affiliative. Women who are high in expressivity are interpersonally adept and sensitive as well as possessing high levels of self-awareness and self-understanding. Expressiveness seems to protect girls from the social rejection that sometimes accompanies high intellectual ability in girls.

It is possible that instrumentality could be increased through leadership opportunities, development of decision-making skills, and many experiences of success in challenging activities. Even when they are very young, bright girls need to be given the opportunity to lead other girls and boys. They can lead task groups, captain sports teams, and teach skills they possess to others. Many curriculum units on decision making exist; the actual techniques used to teach decision making are probably less important than communicating to girls that their decisions have weight.

Throughout their education, gifted girls need to be encouraged to take risks. This means taking the most challenging course work available, engaging in play activities that are physically challenging and occasionally competitive, and learning to speak out and defend their opinions in groups. To encourage instrumentality in bright girls, teachers may need to reverse the common practice of rewarding quiet, compliant behavior and withdrawing rewards for, or even punishing, noisy and nonconforming behavior. Teachers might experiment with rewarding boisterousness and idiosyncrasies in gifted girls with humorous, approving responses.

Expressiveness is more likely to be gifted girls' strong suit. Nevertheless, it needs to be acknowledged and reinforced. Social skills need to be labeled as such and praised. Friendship skills and considerateness can be reinforced by opportunities to help other children and through cooperative problem solving.

Exploratory Behavior

Marjorie Steinkamp (1984) proposed a theory of motivational style which states that certain *exploratory* childhood behaviors set the stage for adult achievement in science. Exploratory behaviors flourish in an environment free of evaluation, responsibility, and externally imposed challenge. Exploratory behaviors take place in situations of uncertainty and ambiguity. There is evidence that girls are socialized in our society to have a *compliant* rather than exploratory motivational style, according to Steinkamp. Compliant behaviors are dependent on external reward, need external feedback, take place only in the context of society, and function best under external locus of control.

The clear implication of Steinkamp's theory is that gifted girls need help learning self-directed behaviors. They need to learn to work alone, to enjoy ambiguity and uncertainty, and to work without external reward or approval. This, again, may mean reversing the normal socialization processes. Instead of drawing girls who are playing by themselves into a group, teachers should consider leaving them alone. When a girl turns in a project that clearly required exploration of difficult, ambiguous, or uncertain issues, she needs praise and encouragement. In many ways, science experiments and activities provide these latter kinds of experiences. Creative play and schoolwork also seem important. However, Steinkamp warns that it is easy to transform an independent exploratory behavior into a compliant one simply by giving too much help, information, and feedback. It takes sensitive observation and careful reward to discover and encourage exploratory behavior. Finally, there is some evidence that encouraging young women to be exploratory in science may be too little, too late. Interventions to enhance exploratory and decrease compliant behaviors may need to begin very early in the gifted girl's development.

Eminence and the Gifted Girl

Two studies of eminent individuals have important implications for gifted girls. Bloom's (1985) study of talent development in such individuals as concert pianists, Olympic athletes, and sculptors showed that a critical step in the attainment of eminence was the development of an identity. Eminent individuals usually had the opportunity early in adolescence to identify themselves and be identified by others as "the class artist" or "the school athlete." Teachers may be able to help gifted girls toward the achievement of their potential by assisting them in their identity development. "You're the math whiz around here!" and "Lisa, you certainly are a scientist!" are the kinds of statements that can aid the identity development of girls who show strong inclinations toward and enjoyment of those fields.

Eminent women have been shown to demonstrate a great many of the qualities and behaviors that have been discussed here (Kerr, 1985). As children, they spent a great deal of time alone, during which they engaged in a great many exploratory behaviors: reading, trying out new skills, and seeking new ideas. If they were not rewarded for these behaviors, at least they were not punished. They felt "different" or "special" as children depending on their self-concept, and this sense of uniqueness may have made nonconformity possible. In adulthood, they maintained the ability to remain separate from the crowd. In fact, eminent women were frequently perceived as having "thorns"—a dry wit or even a caustic, argumentative style. They took responsibility for themselves, for their tasks, and for accomplishing their life goals, demonstrating instrumentality. In addition, most eminent women created loving partnerships with another, often finding their love relationship through their work. Later, many of them competently integrated a mothering role into their other roles. This seems to be a case of integrating expressiveness and instrumentality, as Hollinger and Fleming (1988) advised.

The educational methods suggested by the experiences of eminent women include early educational experience, learning at a challenging pace, individualized instruction, and mentoring. It may be that these educational strategies interact with one another to enhance achievement-related behaviors. For example, the presence of a supportive mentor may help increase a gifted girl's confidence in her ability to meet the challenge of fast-paced learning. The success of the Mary Baldwin College Program for the Education of the Gifted (PEG) model seems to lend credence to this possibility.

The single most important commonality in the lives of eminent women seems to be that they "fell in love with an idea." Falling in love with an idea means committing oneself to a deeply held value, a theory, or an attitude (Torrance, 1979). It is the discovery of a calling or a vocation. People who have fallen in love with an idea have a deep sense of purpose. Falling in love with an idea seems to protect many women from succumbing to sexism, discrimination, and other pressures to conform to traditional women's roles (Kerr, 1985).

Teachers can help gifted young women in the process of falling love with an idea by encouraging their enthusiasms for particular ideas with related readings and opportunities to explore beyond the treatment of a particular subject in the classroom. As is the case with encouraging the growth of identity, it is important to discover specific talents and "passions" that are unique to each gifted girl. Generalized praise and encouragement may not be as useful as specific comments and observations: "Marie, when you play the violin, I can really see your love for the instrument and your passion for interpreting Bach," or "Your writing lately seems to me to be showing that you are finding your voice as a writer. I can always identify your work by its vivid descriptions and sharp humor."

Sometimes gifted girls and young women may need permission to fall in love with an idea, and sometimes they need help recognizing that they already are in love with an idea. A value-based career counseling intervention developed at the University of Iowa's Counseling Laboratory for Talent Development serves both these purposes (Kerr, 1988). The value-based counseling approach includes group future planning; personality, interest, and values assessment; and intensive individual counseling. Participants are encouraged to imagine in detail their "perfect" future day; to examine roles and relationships; to understand how their interests, needs, and values make them unique; and to understand the importance of choosing a career based on their most deeply held values. Participants in the workshop have been found to increase their sense of identity and their development of purpose as measured by inventories of student development.

Conclusion

Much has been learned since Lewis Terman and Melita Oden first described the gifted girl, but much remains to be learned. Specific educational and guidance programs for gifted girls are few and far between, and many programs lack the information they need to provide optimal conditions or to evaluate what they have accomplished. Nevertheless, the interest in this area is great and growing. For example, the International Symposium on Girls, Women, and Giftedness (Ellis, in press) held in May 1987, brought together for the first time teachers of gifted girls, researchers, and eminent women to discuss all facets of the gifted female. Perhaps that conference, and the research, theory, and practice it produced may mark a new era in understanding and guiding gifted girls toward the realization of their potential.

REFERENCES

Benbow, C. P., & Stanley, J. C. (1982). Consequences in high school and college of sex differences in mathematical reasoning ability: A longitudinal perspective. *American Educational Research Journal, 19,* 598–622.

Benbow, C. P., & Stanley, J. C. (1983). Sex differences in mathematical reasoning ability: More facts. *Science, 222,* 1029–1031.

Benbow, C. P., & Stanley, J. C. (1984). Gender and the science major: A study of mathematically precocious youth. In M. W. Steinkamp & M. L. Maehr (Eds.), *Women in science* (pp. 165–196). Greenwich, CT: JAI.

Bloom, B. S. (1985). *Developing talent in young people.* New York: Ballantine.

Bock, R. D., & Kolakowski, D. (1973). Further evidence of sex-linked major-gene influence in spatial visualizing ability. *American Journal of Human Genetics, 25,* 1–14.

Boles, D. B. (1980). Linkage of spatial ability: A critical review. *Child Development, 21,* 626–635.

Callahan, C. M. (1979). The gifted and talented woman. In A. H. Passow (Ed.), *The gifted and talented: Their education and development* (The 78th yearbook of the National Society for the Study of Education, pp. 401–423). Chicago: University of Chicago Press.

Callahan, C. (1987, May). *Gender and the gifted: A roadmap for reflecting, questioning, and understanding.* Paper presented at the International Symposium on Girls, Women, and Giftedness, Lethbridge, Alberta, Canada.

Chan, L. K. S. (1988). The perceived competence of intellectually talented students. *Gifted Child Quarterly, 32,* 310–315.

Colangelo, N., & Kerr, B. A. (in press). Extreme academic talent: Profiles of perfect scorers. *Journal of Educational Psychology.*

Cooley, D., Chauvin, J., & Karnes, F. A. (1984). Gifted females: A comparison of attitudes by male and female teachers. *Roeper Review, 6,* 164–170.

Dolny, C. (1985). University of Toronto Schools' gifted students' career and family plans. *Roeper Review, 7,* 160–162.

Dweck, C. S., & Licht, B. G. (1980). Learned helplessness and intellectual achievement. In J. Garber & M. E. P. Seligman (Eds.), *Human helplessness: Theory and applications* (pp. 197–221). New York: Academic.

Eccles, J. S. (1985). Why doesn't Jane run? Sex differences in educational and occupational patterns. In F. D. Horowitz & M. O'Brien (Eds.), *The gifted and talented developmental perspectives* (pp. 253–295). Washington, DC: American Psychological Association.

Ellis, J. (Ed.). (in press). *Proceedings of the international symposium on girls, women, and giftedness.* Lethbridge, Alberta, Canada: University of Lethbridge.

Fleming, E., & Hollinger, C. (1979). *Project choice: Creating her options in career education.* ERIC Reproduction Service No. EO185321.

Fox, L. H. (1976, August). *Changing behaviors and attitudes of gifted girls.* Paper presented at the American Psychological Association, Washington, DC.

Fox, L. H., Benbow, C. P., & Perkins, S. (1983). An accelerated mathematics program for girls: A longitudinal evaluation. In C. P. Benbow & J. C. Stanley (Eds.), *Academic precocity* (pp. 113–138). Baltimore: Johns Hopkins University Press.

Fox, L. H., & Cohn, S. J. (1980). Sex differences in development of mathematically precocious talent. In L. H. Fox, L. Brady, & D. Tobin (Eds.), *Women and the mathematical mystique* (pp. 94–111). Baltimore: Johns Hopkins University Press.

Fox, L. H., & Denham, S. A. (1974). Values and career interests of mathematically and scientifically precocious youth. In J. C. Stanley, D. P. Keating, & L. H. Fox (Eds.), *Mathematical talent: Discovery, description, development* (pp. 140–175). Baltimore: Johns Hopkins University Press.

Gallagher, J. J. (1985). *Teaching the gifted child.* Newton, MA: Allyn and Bacon.

Gardner, H. (1983). *Frames of mind: The theory of multiple intelligences.* New York: Basic.

Garrison, C., & Rhodes, C. (1987, May). *Mary Baldwin College's Program for Educating the Gifted.* Paper presented at the International Symposium on Girls, Women, and Giftedness, Lethbridge, Alberta, Canada.

George, W. C., & Denham, S. A. (1976). Curriculum experimentation for the mathematically talented. In D. P. Keating (Ed.), *Intellectual talent: Research and development* (pp. 103–108). Baltimore: Johns Hopkins University Press.

Gilligan, C. (1982). *In a different voice: Psychological theory and women's development.* Cambridge, MA: Harvard University Press.

Groth, N. J. (1969). *Vocational development for gifted girls.* ERIC Document Reproduction Service No. ED931747.

Hollinger, C. L. (1983). Counseling the gifted and talented female adolescent: The relationship between social self-esteem and traits of instrumentality and expressiveness. *Gifted Child Quarterly, 27,* 157–161.

Hollinger, C. L. (1985). The stability of self-perceptions of instrumental and expressive traits and social self-esteem among gifted and talented female adolescents. *Journal of Education of the Gifted, 8,* 107–126.

Hollinger, C. L., & Fleming, E. S. (1984). Internal barriers to the realization of potential: Correlates and interrelationships among gifted and talented female adolescents. *Journal of Youth and Adolescence. 14,* 389–399.

Hollinger, C. L., & Fleming, E. S. (1988). Gifted and talented young women: Antecedents and correlates of life satisfaction. *Gifted Child Quarterly, 32,* 254–259.

Hollingworth, L. S. (1926). *Gifted children: Their nature and nurture.* New York: Macmillan.

Hyde, J. S. (1981). How large are cognitive gender differences? A meta-analysis. *American Psychologist, 36,* 892–901.

Jacobs, J. E., & Eccles, J. S. (1985, March). Gender differences in math ability: The impact of media reports on parents. *Educational Researcher, 14,* 20–25.

Janos, P. M., & Robinson, N. M. (1985). Psychosocial development in intellectually gifted children. In F. D. Horowitz & M. O'Brien (Eds.), *The gifted and talented: Developmental perspectives* (pp. 149–195). Washington, DC: American Psychological Association.

Kaufman, A. S., & Kaufman, N. L. (1983). *K-ABC: Kaufman assessment battery for children.* Circle Pines, MN: American Guidance Service.

Kaufmann, F. (1981). The 1964–1968 Presidential Scholars: A follow-up study. *Exceptional Children, 48,* 2.

Kavrell, S. M., & Petersen, A. C. (1984). Patterns of achievement in early adolescence. In M. W. Steinkamp & M. L. Maehr (Eds.), *Women in science* (pp. 1–36). Greenwich, CT: JAI.

Kelly, K., & Colangelo, N. (1984). Academic and social self-concepts of gifted, general, and special students. *Exceptional Children, 50,* 551–553.

Kerr, B. A. (1983). Raising aspirations of gifted girls. *Vocational Guidance Quarterly, 32,* 37–44.

Kerr, B. A. (1985). *Smart girls, gifted women.* Columbus: Ohio Psychology.

Kerr, B. A. (1988). Career counseling for gifted girls and women. *Journal of Career Development, 14,* 259–268.

Kerr, B. A., & Colangelo, N. (1988). The college plans of academically talented students. *Journal of Counseling and Development, 67,* 42–49.

Kerr, B. A., Colangelo, N., & Gaeth, J. (1988). Gifted adolescents' attitudes toward their giftedness. *Gifted Child Quarterly, 32,* 245–248.

Kitano, M. K., & Kirby, D. F. (1985). *Gifted education: A comprehensive view.* Boston: Little, Brown.

Laing, J., Engen, H., & Maxey, J. (1987). *The relationship of high school coursework to corresponding ACT assessment scores.* (ACT Research Report, 87-3). Iowa City: American College Testing Program.

Lessinger, L., & Martinson, R. (1961). The use of the California Psychological Inventory with gifted pupils. *Personnel and Guidance Journal, 39,* 572–575.

Ludwig, G., & Cullinan, D. (1984). Behavior problems of gifted and nongifted elementary school girls and boys. *Gifted Child Quarterly, 28,* 37–40.

Maccoby, E. E., & Jacklin, C. N. (1974). *The psychology of sex differences.* Stanford, CA: Stanford University Press.

Petersen, A. C. (1976). Physical androgyny and cognitive functioning in adolescence. *Developmental Psychology, 12,* 524–533.

Petersen, A. C. (1979). *Hormones and cognitive functioning: Developmental issues.* New York: Academic.

Sadker, D., & Sadker, M. (1984, March). *Year II, Final Report, promoting effectiveness in classroom instruction.* Washington, DC: NIE Contract 400-80-0033.

Sadker, D., & Sadker, M. (1985, April). *Interventions that promote equity and effectiveness in student–teacher interaction.* Paper presented at the annual meeting of the American Education Research Association, Chicago.

Silverman, L. K. (1986). What happens in the gifted girl? In C. J. Maker (Ed.), *Critical issues in gifted education: Defensible programs for the gifted* (pp. 43–89). Rockville, MD: Aspen.

Solano, C. H. (1977). Teacher and pupil stereotypes of gifted boys and girls. *Talents and Gifts, 19,* 4.

Steinkamp, M. W. (1984). Motivational style as a mediator of adult achievement in science. In M. W. Steinkamp & M. L. Maehr (Eds.), *Advances in motivation and achievement: Women in science* (pp. 281–317). New York: JAI Press.

Sternberg, R. J. (1986). A triarchic theory of giftedness. In R. J. Sternberg & J. E. Davidson (Eds), *Conceptions of giftedness* (pp. 223–243). New York: Cambridge University Press.

Terman, L. M., & Oden, M. H. (1935). *Genetic studies of genius: Vol. 3. The promise of youth.* Stanford, CA: Stanford University Press.

Terman, L. M., & Oden, M. H. (1947). *Genetic studies of genius: Vol. 4. The gifted child grows up.* Stanford, CA: Stanford University Press.

Torrance, E. P. (1979). *The search for satori and creativity.* Great Neck, NY: Creative Synergetic.

Torrance, E. P., Bruch, C. B., & Morse, J. A. (1973). Improving prediction of the adult creative achievement of gifted girls using autobiographical information. *Gifted Child Quarterly, 17,* 91–95.

Tressemer, D. (1977). *Fear of success.* New York: Plenum.

U.S. Commissioner of Education. (1972). *Education of gifted and talented.* Washington, DC: U.S. Office of Education.

Weiner, N. C., & Robinson, S. E. (1986). Cognitive ability, personality and gender differences in math achievement of gifted adolescents. *Gifted Child Quarterly, 30,* 83–87.

29

Ethnic and Cultural Issues

ALEXINIA YOUNG BALDWIN   *University of Connecticut, Storrs*

Ethnic and cultural issues are of crucial importance as we consider appropriate educational programming for gifted students. These issues are subsets of the broader issues of educating the gifted: (1) defining giftedness—whom are we looking for and how do we find them? (2) curriculum—what do we consider the appropriate goals to be? (3) instructional system—how should we help those we have defined as gifted to achieve these goals? and (4) evaluation—how do we judge the attainment of the goals we have set?

A substantive review of the ethnic and cultural issues as they affect education for the gifted requires more than a cursory look at the realities because a proportional representation of minority and ethnic and cultural populations is lacking in programs for the gifted. This chapter provides a perspective on the realities of the problem and proposes some possible solutions.

Ethnic and Cultural Concepts

The concept of *ethnic and cultural issues* as used in this chapter will give the reader a contextual base from which the perspectives on these issues are derived. The terms *ethnic* and *cultural* are used as adjectival modifiers of education, groups, traditions, and so forth. Although they overlap in their meanings, important distinctions are often overlooked. In order to discuss issues related to these terms we first must clarify their meanings.

Banks (1979) defines an *ethnic group* as those individuals who share a sense of group identification, a common set of values, behavior patterns, and other cultural and physical characteristics such as color and facial features. "Its origins preceded the creation of a nation state or were external to the nation

state; e.g., immigrant groups or Native Americans. . . . Ethnic groups have distinct pre–United States or extra–United States territorial bases" (NCSS Task Force, 1976, pp. 9–10, cited in Banks, 1979).

Culture, on the other hand, refers to a set of beliefs and traditions that are unique to a broader group that could include several ethnic groups. Americans, for example, have a set of common beliefs and traditions, yet Americans are made up of several ethnic groups, each of which also has a common heritage, set of beliefs, and so on. Concomitantly, assimilation and acculturation can result in a different set of cultural traditions within an ethnic group. Banks (1979) illustrates in his diagram this broad yet integrative concept of culture (see Figure 29.1).

Banks uses the shaded area to represent the general American culture that is shared by all ethnic groups. "Circles A through D represent ethnic subsocieties such as Anglo-American, Afro-American, Italian American, and Mexican American subsocieties" (p. 11).

The ethnic and cultural issues of this chapter will be addressed in relation to the ethnic minorities that have easily identifiable physical characteristics. This distinction has made these ethnic minorities easy victims of racism, neglect, isolation, and stereotypes because regardless of the cultural patterns they choose, unlike Anglo ethnic groups such as German, French, or Irish, individuals are easily identified and treated as a stereotype instead of as individuals.

Four Basic Issues

Of the four main issues discussed in this chapter, the one most hotly debated is what consti-

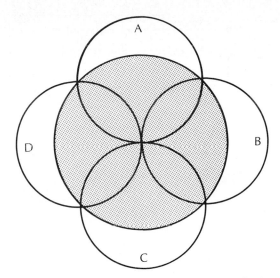

Figure 29.1 Ethnicity and the universal American culture. The shaded area represents the general American culture shared by all ethnic groups. Circles A–D represent ethnic subsocieties.

tutes giftedness and how to identify those characteristics. To resolve this issue we must change our attitudes about what giftedness is and rely less on academic achievement and/or IQ scores as the only indicators of giftedness.

I. Defining the Population

Defining a population as gifted involves the development of a construct of giftedness and sets the stage for designing a process for selecting those whose characteristics are reflected in this construct. These two factors—a definition of giftedness and proper identification procedures—represent the most frequently discussed matters when considering ethnic and cultural concerns.

Several questions that need to be addressed are related to ethnic and cultural issues.

1. Who are the gifted of these ethnic groups? Are they different?
2. What are the intervening variables that influence the display of their giftedness?

3. What are the advantages of multiarea identification for various ethnic and cultural groups?
4. What are the limitations within the regular school setting of the identification of multi-areas of giftedness?
5. What are the advantages and disadvantages of subjective versus objective assessment?
6. What are some answers to research questions regarding the identification of children from different cultures?

On the broader issue of defining giftedness, Hoge (1988) discussed the weaknesses he sees in the definition and measurement of the giftedness construct. Hoge said that "the choice of psychological instruments and procedures to be used in identifying and labeling gifted pupils, and the evaluation of them, should be guided by an explicit statement of the giftedness construct. This construct would incorporate the range of traits, behaviors, or aptitudes that define giftedness or gifted potential in a particular situation" (p. 12).

Baldwin (1985a) proposed the construct shown in Figure 29.2, based on four broad areas of cognitive, creative, psychosocial, and psychomotor gifts, to be used in defining and subsequently identifying gifted students from ethnic or cultural groups. Unfortunately, the weak element of this strategy is the unavailability of assessment instruments that measure these constructs. In lieu of quantitative psychometric evidence for each of the areas, subjective assessment strategies that "flag" gifted potential are used.

In applying this four-part definition the following assumptions guide the process of selection:

1. Giftedness can be expressed through a variety of behaviors.
2. Giftedness expressed in one dimension is equally as important as giftedness expressed in another.
3. Giftedness in any area can be a clue to the presence of potential giftedness in another area.
4. A total-ability profile is crucial in the educational planning for gifted children.

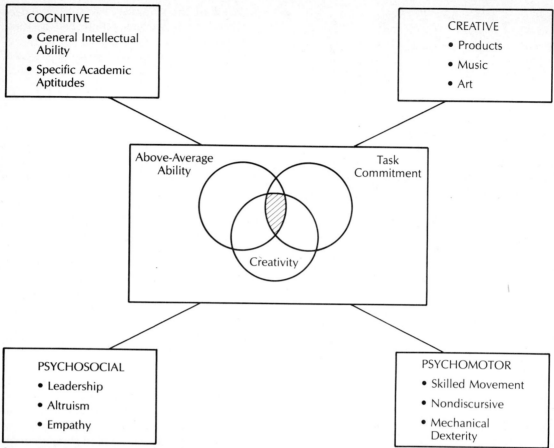

COGNITIVE
- General Intellectual Ability
- Specific Academic Aptitudes

CREATIVE
- Products
- Music
- Art

Above-Average Ability

Task Commitment

Creativity

PSYCHOSOCIAL
- Leadership
- Altruism
- Empathy

PSYCHOMOTOR
- Skilled Movement
- Nondiscursive
- Mechanical Dexterity

Source: From ''Programs for the Gifted and Talented: Issues Concerning Minority Populations'' by A. Y. Baldwin. In *The Gifted and Talented: Developmental Perspectives,* edited by F. Horowitz & M. O'Brien, copyright © 1985 by the American Psychological Association, Washington, DC. Reprinted by permission. The three-ring circle is reprinted by permission from *What Makes Giftedness? A Reexamination of the Definition of the Gifted and the Talented* by J. Renzulli, 1979, Ventura, CA: Office of the Superintendent of Ventura County Schools.

Figure 29.2   Areas of giftedness. Subcategories under each area are not all-inclusive. The diagram shows the areas under which the various aspects of human response to stimuli can be grouped. The three-ring illustration shows that the potential or presence of these qualities should be exhibited in the broad area or any of its subcategories when identifying the child who is gifted.

5. All populations include gifted children who exhibit behaviors that are indicative of their giftedness.
6. Carefully planned subjective assessment techniques can be used effectively in conjunction with objective assessment techniques.
7. Behaviors classified as gifted should be above the average of a broad spectrum of individuals.

Given the preceding sets of proposed questions and assumptions, let us examine their significance for ethnic and cultural minorities.

Recognizing Characteristics of Giftedness. If the assumption that giftedness can be expressed through a variety of behaviors is accepted, then the manifestations of giftedness in a minority ethnic group might be unique to that group and different from the standard accepted by Anglo ethnic groups. In Table 29.1 Baldwin (1985b) summarizes behaviors that might be indicators of giftedness. For example, from behaviors such as those listed under the column titled "Descriptors," we see that giftedness might be exhibited in unique ways.

This table also illustrates problem areas and attendant mental ability processes that can frequently be found among ethnic minority populations. However, it does not mean that every minority child should be judged by these criteria. One can find, for instance, that differences within the black ethnic group can be as diverse as differences between ethnic groups. As Banks (1979) stated so well, "The gross differences that exist within various ethnic groups often make it exceedingly difficult for an ethnically illiterate person to understand why many Japanese Americans are anti-Chinese, why the Nisei [second-generation Japanese] often express disappointment about the values and lifestyles of the Sansei [third-generation Japanese], or why some upwardly mobile Mexican Americans disdain Mexican migrant workers" (p. 65). Further, although Americans tend to understand why a German corporate president would not feel a common bond with a German dishwasher, middle- or high-income Afro-Americans are often considered odd in the eyes of many Anglo-Americans if they know little about life in the inner city. In other words, a minority group has a certain cultural and ethnic commonness, yet has a wide range of cultural experiences, some quite like those of the majority cultural or ethnic group.

Identification Concerns. Teachers or those given the task of identifying the gifted must become more alert to behaviors that indicate high mental ability (Table 29.1). In the case of ethnic minorities, identification has been difficult because inadequate attention has been paid to nonacademic or performance indices of giftedness. Many characteristics that have been deemed characteristics of the gifted can be seen in the behaviors listed in Table 29.1 under "Descriptors" and "Exceptional Characteristics to Look For."

Whereas nonacademic or performance indices of giftedness are not necessary for all chil-

dren from an ethnic minority, the use of such measures enhances the judgments made on the abilities of the child. Biographies of undisputedly gifted members of minorities, extensive literature reviews, and experimental data have shown that observation or knowledge of the above-average quality of certain behaviors can lead to more accurate identification of gifted minority students.

Central to the identification of gifted ethnic minority children is an understanding and recognition of the variables that influence the *functioning level* of the children of this group. Figure 29.3 illustrates the variables and combinations of variables that mitigate against the acquisition of skills deemed important for success in school. Although it is impossible to formulate a composite that describes every minority child, there should be a sensitivity to variables that, as seen in Figure 29.3, affect the display of ability in the traditional sense.

Promising Practices for Identification. Cultural and ethnic minorities might express their giftedness in ways other than those usually expected by school personnel. In such cases the practice of dubbing those who fit the school's criteria as "gifted" implies that those not selected are "not gifted."

Instead, a complete profile of students' abilities is recommended by Baldwin (1985a). This profile shows both strengths and weaknesses of each student. It will also assist in program planning for the child. The selection of assessment data to be used on the matrix is important. Group tests such as the Otis-Lennon School Ability Test (OLSAT) have been found to be less desirable tools for use with minority students. Ortiz and Volkoff (1987), in a study of 65 Hispanic students who had been recommended by their teachers for assessment, found a substantial group mean score difference between the OLSAT and the Wechsler Intelligence Scale for Children—Revised (WISC-R) in favor of the WISC-R. These researchers focused on several points to consider in interpreting test score results for minority students, including the curriculum of the classrooms, the validity of the tests, and issues related to group versus individual testing. Interestingly, they also found that creativity test scores on Williams (1980) divergent test bat-

Table 29.1
The Most Common Descriptors for Children Affected by Cultural Diversity, Socioeconomic Deprivation, and Geographic Isolation

Descriptors	External and Internal Deficit	Possible Environmental Causality	Exceptional Characteristics to Look For	Intellectual Processing Ability Indicators	Horizontal/Vertical Program Adaptation
1. Outer locus of control rather than inner locus of control	1. Inability to attend to task without supervision	1. Discipline does not encourage inner locus of control. Child is given directions. Tradition dictates strict adherence to directions.	1. Academic: good memory	1. Convergent production of semantic units	1. Contract activities; directed level development; counseling for trust–skill development
2. Loyalty to peer group	2. Inability to externalize behavioral cues	2. A need to belong; empathy for those in similar situation	2. Psychosocial: sense of humor; intuitive grasp of situations; understanding of compromise	2. Affective behavior: possible indication of convergent production of behavioral units or classification	2. Group activity, debating, counseling seminars, philosophy, logic, process and skill development
3. Physical resiliency to hardships encountered in the environment	3. Inability to trust or consider beauty in life	3. Environment dictates needs to survive. Anger and frustration increase animalistic desire to survive. Alternatives, solutions are forced.	3. Creative: tolerance for ambiguities, insight, inventiveness, revolutionary ideas	3. Divergent production	3. Creative activities, counseling mentor relationship; process/skill development
4. Language rich in imagery and humor rich with symbolism; persuasive language	4. Perhaps only avenue of communication; standard language skills not used	4. A need to use subterfuge in environment to get message across; a lack of dominant language skills; a need to fantasize through language; acute awareness of environment due to its effect on individual	4. Creative: fluency, flexibility, ability to elaborate, originality Academic: good memory, ability to think systematically	4. Divergent production of semantic classifications, systems relations, and transformations; fluency of thought and evaluation of behavioral consequences	4. Writing and speaking emphases; debating, rhetoric analysis, contemporary and historical literary comparisons; literary product development

5. Logical reasoning; planning ability and pragmatic problem-solving ability	5. Opinions disallowed in school situation	5. Early responsibility related to survival	5. Thinks in logical systems, uncluttered thinking, insightfulness, understanding cause and effect	5. Systems analysis, decision-making skills	5. Exposure to systematically developed strategies for solving problems, logic
6. Creative ability	6. Lack of directed development of ability	6. Need to use items of environment as substitute, e.g., dolls, balls out of tin cans; wagons, sleds out of packing boxes; dolls out of corn husks	6. Flexibility of thinking, fluency, special aptitudes in music, drama, creative writing	6. Divergent production of symbolic transformation, flexibility of thought	6. Special classes in creative aptitudes, independent study, mentor, process and content skills development
7. Social intelligence and feeling of responsibility for the community; rebellious regarding inequities	7. No opportunity to exercise behavior in community without censorship	7. Social reforms needed to help community; high regard for moral obligation to fellow human; religious influence, tradition, survival dictates awareness of social elements related to survival.	7. Intuitive grasp of situations, sensitiveness to right and wrong	7. Affective domain: Kohlberg's upper levels of moral development	7. Leadership seminars, community service participation, counseling, historical antecedents, process and content skills
8. Sensitivity and alertness to movement	8. Lack of training and development	8. Need to excel, toughness of environment, family emphasis on physical prowess to substitute for lack of educational input	8. Hand–eye coordination, physical stamina, skilled body movements	8. Divergent production, convergent production, and behavioral implication	8. Special developmental classes, olympic participation, physical culture classes

Source: Adapted by permission from *Educational Planning for the Gifted: Overcoming Cultural, Geographic, and Socio-economic Barriers,* edited by A. Y. Baldwin, G. Gear, and L. Lucito, copyright © 1978 by the Council for Exceptional Children, Reston, Virginia.

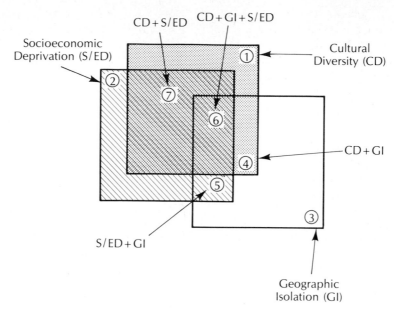

CD+S/ED   CD+GI+S/ED

Socioeconomic
Deprivation (S/ED)

Cultural
Diversity (CD)

CD+GI

S/ED+GI

Geographic
Isolation (GI)

Source: Adapted by permission from *Educational Planning for the Gifted: Overcoming Cultural, Geographic, and Socio-economic Barriers,* edited by A. Y. Baldwin, G. Gear, and L. Lucito, copyright © 1978 by the Council for Exceptional Children, Reston, Virginia.

Figure 29.3 Interrelations between the three variables used to define the gifted child with unique needs. Cultural diversity (CD) is a condition of racial, ethnic, language, or physical differences from a dominant culture. Socioeconomic deprivation (S/ED) is a condition of legal or de facto denial of social interaction combined with substandard housing and jobs. Geographic isolation (GI) is a condition of being geographically located away from the mainstream of society.

tery for these 65 students were comparatively lower than IQ scores on the WISC-R. They called into question the use of divergent thinking scores to identify gifted minority students. As these authors suggested, there must be caution in the interpretation of test scores when dealing with minority students.

Kirschenbaum (1988) recommended the use of ethnographic measures with Native American students, especially those American Indians who live on reservations. Toneman (cited in Kirschenbaum, 1988) classified the characteristics of the gifted Indian student into four categories: aesthetic abilities, acquired skills, tribal-cultural understanding, and personal-human qualities. The Gifted Attitudes Inventory for Navajos by Abbott (cited in Kirschenbaum, 1988) is based on the attitudes of the Navajo Indian toward giftedness and has been

used to identify those characteristics considered to be attributes of giftedness. Abbott indicated that one must recognize cultural behavioral characteristics that show mental processing above and beyond that which is average in this population.

In research by Jensen, Schafer, and Crinella (1981), correlations between various chronometric (reaction-time) techniques and the Raven Matrices have been used to establish further the ability of standardized tests to accurately judge the intelligence level of an individual. Any positive findings in Jensen's research could support the notion that standardized tests can indeed determine (according to constructs of the tests), in an unbiased manner, the ability of an individual. In a study of 50 fourth- and fifth-grade students, using the response time strategy used by Jensen, a low correlation was found between the scores these students made on their IQ and achievement tests and the scores they made on the Raven Matrices and the Response-Time Button Box. Several students who had not been selected for programs for the gifted were discovered. The population studied was 99.5% black and Hispanic (Baldwin & Start, 1987).

The discussion of issues related to defining and identifying the population of gifted ethnic and cultural minority students has drawn attention to the use of subjective processes such as case studies and parent, peer, community, and self-nomination. Renzulli and Smith (1977), for example, found that with inner-city children peer nominations were more effective in identifying gifted minority students than teacher ratings, interviews, or information in cumulative records. The validity of these processes will always be called into question. However, studies have shown that careful development of the items used in the process will lead to the identification of a larger pool of gifted minority students (Bernal & Reyna, 1974; Blackshear, 1979; Cummings, 1979; Dabney, 1983; Mercer, 1971; Nelson, 1982; Renzulli & Smith, 1977).

We cannot risk the loss of a mind as great as that of Einstein who like many minorities would not have been included in a program for the gifted.

2. Curriculum—Where Should We Be Going?

The issue of appropriate curriculum or where we should set the goals for the gifted ethnic or cultural minority student is inextricably tied to the issue of differentiated curriculum for all children who are considered gifted. The questions we must ask ourselves are: Should the curriculum for gifted minority students be different? If so, what content should be included?

Attitudes and Approaches to Consider. There have been discussions regarding the effect of gifted programs on minority gifted students. Fordham (1988) expressed a concern that the established goals of gifted programs tend to rob minority students of their cultural heritage. It is interesting that this concern is

never expressed when Anglo-ethnic groups are discussed. Perhaps the concern is based upon the fact that in these programs too little attention has been paid to the use of ethnic materials as an integral part of the curriculum, thus denying these students an opportunity to explore many of the trajectories their lives might take. If curriculum is defined as the end result to be obtained, then minority students can still attain these goals and not be robbed of the many historical roots and artifacts of their heritage. The curriculum content should include the inventions, explorations, drama, literature, music, and other contributions to civilization by the peoples of the students' culture.

Banks (1979) stated, "The multiethnic curriculum should help [all] students develop the ability to make reflective personal and public decisions. A curriculum focused on decision-making must be conceptual, interdisciplinary, and based on higher levels of knowledge" (p. 93). Banks (1979) has outlined a great untapped source of material that would be invaluable to the teacher or curriculum planner. His book includes a good set of guidelines for evaluating and selecting materials to be used as curriculum.

Research in curriculum adaptations for the minority gifted student is vitally needed. We need to analyze selected materials to determine the concepts that should be learned, the mental processes that can be enhanced, the knowledge to be gained, and the parallels to traditional curriculum materials. The use of this combination of materials will enhance the self-concept of the ethnic or minority student and dispel some of the myths held by the Anglo-ethnic students.

3. The Instructional System—Issues of How to Reach the Goals

The instructional system includes the day-to-day strategies, the appropriate teacher, the appropriate environment, and evaluation processes. Each of these aspects of the instructional system will be discussed.

Teaching Strategies. What the teacher does from day to day can change to fit the needs of the students being taught. The issue of teaching strategies involves research on both learning styles and lesson content that are appropriate for minority students. One question is whether these students should be taught using a single style deemed most appropriate for them, or whether they should have the experience of using several learning styles. This issue becomes critical because people who recommend a particular learning style for certain minority groups fail to note the inherent danger of low teacher expectations and closed options for these students if experience with different learning styles does not occur.

Hale-Benson (1986), a strong proponent of specific culturally related learning styles, theorized that the culture of the black minority individual is distinct and emanates from the African heritage. Her research has led her to theorize that this distinction supports a unique or preferred learning style of black students. Although her emphasis has been on the black ethnic group, she has reviewed research on other ethnic groups and their preferred learning styles. Generally, she suggests that ethnic or minority groups tend to prefer a more relational cognitive style as opposed to an analytic cognitive style.

I do not accept her theory that learning style preferences emanate from heritage; however, I feel that a knowledge of cultural differences or experiences that might influence the students' cognitive approach is important for the teacher of gifted minority students. It is equally important that students be helped to use both analytic and relational styles to their advantage. In America, ethnic or cultural minority students should be helped to master styles of the Euro-American culture as well as those of their respective cultures.

When helping the gifted minority student to overcome his or her skill deficiencies, the teacher should not approach the subject as remedial training. Remediation is often a repetition of small fragments of information in isolation from other activities. However, a bright student who needs to erase a skill deficit can very often assimilate basic concepts with a minimum amount of instructional time without being isolated from enriching activities.

The manner of reaching curriculum goals can be planned to meet the needs and interests of minority students without changing the intended outcomes. For example, the selection of *West Side Story* to develop the concepts of Shakespeare's writings or the use of parallel poems from various ethnic literature sources to teach the mechanics of writing can enhance the self-concept of the minority students and create a feeling of belonging. Both analytic and relational cognitive styles can be used to understand the concepts in Shakespeare's plays.

Another teaching strategy that has not been used effectively is dramatics. Analyzing the attitudes of people during the period of the selected drama, the origins and significance of their costumes, the geography of the setting of the play, the mechanics involved in producing the play, and a myriad of activities can draw upon the creative ability of these children and stimulate cognitive growth.

Research that provides an analysis of the common concepts across various disciplines would help teachers select different routes to help students acquire skills and knowledge. Math, for example, has common concepts that can be learned through music, and vice versa. Meter and the use of fractions to designate timing are examples of mathematical concepts that appear in music. Giftedness expressed in one area can be used as a catalyst for developing ability to manipulate the concepts of another area.

It is important that we focus on the positives of minority students and not the deficits. Frasier and McCannon (1981) suggested that *bibliotherapy*—reading books that contain role models and/or present real-life struggles that were overcome through a belief in oneself—will help the minority student. One such book is *Black Music in America: A History Through Its People* (Haskins, 1987). This book gives a panoramic overview of America from the early 1800s and includes fascinating stories of the extraordinarily gifted men and women who gave the world one of America's truly original cultural gifts. Books of this type can be selected to serve different purposes and can be used by the entire class.

Whereas bibliotherapy helps to enhance the self-concept and plays an important role in counseling, other authors have emphasized teaching inquiry skills through black history content. Additional references for helpful strategies and sources of materials related to various ethnic and cultural groups can be found in Banks (1979) and Tiedt and Tiedt (1979).

The Teacher. The teachers' attitudes and understanding of the history of the students' cultural background are extremely important in working with these gifted youngsters. An example of this can be illustrated in a story told by a minority parent. Her daughter was in a class that was studying American history, and the students were analyzing the realities of the pre–Civil War period. In a burst of enthusiasm, an Anglo student told the minority student that if she [the minority student] had lived in that period, she would have been a slave. The teacher was taken aback, and the minority girl was made to feel uncomfortable. In discussing the event with the teacher, the mother of the minority student suggested that a response to the situation might have been simply to say to the Anglo child that she too could have been a type of slave because during that period there were many indentured servants, both black and white. Conversely, there were many black individuals in this country who were not slaves. Teachers whose educational programs have provided them with accurate historical information on ethnic groups and have helped them develop an appreciation for ethnic differences are better prepared to work with these students.

The Environment. Research by Cox, Daniel, and Boston (1985) resulted in a recommendation that gifted programs for a district have many patterns of organization to serve its gifted population. This is especially crucial when considering the different abilities children of minority groups might bring to the situation. These recommendations include in-class enrichment; evening and Saturday classes; mentors; experts-in-residence; large- and small-group classes; resource rooms; pull-out programs; specialized schools; and self-contained classes.

The environment should be an accepting one in which the ethnic or cultural minority student can feel secure as a risk taker in developing new skills and ideas. Materials that include stories, pictures, and so forth, that feature a variety of ethnic groups should be included among resources used in the classroom. The open classroom environment has been suggested as appropriate for gifted students because the characteristics of an open classroom fit the activity and learning needs of gifted students. Community resources such as banks, retail businesses, churches, or law-making institutions can provide internships, mentors, and the support of the community in the development of the abilities of these students.

4. Evaluation Processes

Evaluation issues include the procedures used to judge the success of students and the effectiveness of processes used to develop the abilities of the minority student. An important question is: Should minority students in gifted programs be judged in the same ways as other students in the programs?

It is important that the evaluation of the ethnic minority student be conducted as carefully as that of the gifted Anglo student. Careful evaluation of student abilities must take into consideration all relevant aspects of the child's background. In this sense all children should be carefully assessed. On the other hand, additional assessment strategies might be required for the minority child. Therefore, the question of whether gifted minority students should be evaluated in the same ways as others cannot be answered with a clear yes or no. *All* evaluation should be related to the objectives set for each child. Evaluation can focus on the originality and scholarship of products created by the student and the level of development in academic areas. Outcomes to be evaluated also include basic skills acquired, strengths developed, weaknesses overcome, and improvements in self-concept and motivation.

In spite of the fact that traditional measures of academic development are part of the regular school setting, it is important that success in the gifted program should not be judged on these criteria only.

Summary

This chapter has focused on issues related to the inclusion of ethnic and cultural minorities in programs for the gifted. The distinction between ethnic and cultural groups must be understood in order to avoid the pitfall of inappropriate categorization. Within an ethnic group cultural differences can exist, and vice versa, so there will be overlap between the two.

The important issues of identification of gifted cultural or ethnic minority students and all aspects of the program-delivery system are dependent upon a change in the perception of giftedness and the traditional methods used to develop the unique abilities of the students selected. We are still groping for the definitive test that can accurately assess the mental capability of an individual; dependence upon present-day achievement and intelligence tests alone for the selection of gifted minority students denies many students a well-deserved opportunity to develop their abilities.

The traditional setting of the school does not always lend itself to the gifted minority student's needs. Materials that include content that is part of the ethnic cultures are important for the development of good self-concepts and for the respect of peers. Organizational program patterns designed to accommodate the needs of minority gifted students also need to be innovative. The use of community resources and the inclusion of parents in the development of programs, as well as in-service training for teachers' own self-development, produces a more accepting and productive environment for minority students.

It is crucial that more qualitative as well as quantitative research be conducted for the purpose of addressing some of the issues of this chapter. Until this is done, however, it is far better to err on the side of inclusion rather than exclusion.

REFERENCES

Baldwin, A. Y. (1985a). *Baldwin identification matrix 2*. New York: Trillium.

Baldwin, A. Y. (1985b). Programs for the gifted and talented: Issues concerning minority populations. In F. Horowitz & M. O'Brien (Eds.). *The gifted and talented: Developmental perspectives* (pp. 223–249). Washington, DC: American Psychological Association.

Baldwin, A. Y., Gear, G., & Lucito, L. (Eds.). (1978). *Educational planning for the gifted: Overcoming cultural, geographic, and socio-economic barriers*. Reston, VA: Council for Exceptional Children.

Baldwin, A. Y., & Start, K. B. (1987, August). *Raven matrices scores and educational achievement of black and underprivileged children*. Paper presented at the meeting of the World Council for the Gifted, Salt Lake City, UT.

Banks, J. (1979). *Teaching strategies for ethnic studies* (2nd ed.). Boston: Allyn and Bacon.

Bernal, E., & Reyna, J. (1974). *Analysis of giftedness in Mexican-American children and design of a prototype identification instrument*. Final report, Contract No. DEC-47-062113-307, USOE. Austin, TX: Southwest Education Development Laboratory.

Blackshear, P. (1979). *A comparison of peer nomination and teacher nomination in the identification of the academically gifted, black, primary level student*. Unpublished doctoral dissertation, University of Maryland, Baltimore.

Cox, J., Daniel, N., & Boston, B. (1985). *Educating able learners: Programs and promising practices*. Austin: University of Texas Press.

Cummings, W. B. (1979). *Using alternative criteria to identify gifted children from among culturally different educational disadvantaged youth*. Unpublished doctoral dissertation, University of California, San Francisco.

Dabney, M. (1983, July). *Perspectives and directives in assessment of the black child*. Paper presented at the meeting of the CEC conference on the Black Exceptional Child, Atlanta, GA.

Fordham, S. (1988). Racelessness as a factor in black students' school success: Pragmatic strategy or Pyrrhic victory? *Harvard Educational Review, 58*, 54–84.

Frasier, M., & McCannon, C. (1981). Using bibliotherapy with gifted children. *Gifted Child Quarterly, 25*, 81–85.

Hale-Benson, J. (1986). *Black children: Their roots, culture, and learning styles*. Baltimore: John Hopkins University Press.

Haskins, J. (1987). *Black music in America: A history through its people*. New York: Crowell.

Hoge, R. (1988). Issues in the definition and measurement of the giftedness construct. *Educational Researcher, 17*(7), 12–16, 22.

Jensen, A. R., Schater, E. W. P., & Crinella, F. M. (1981). Reaction time, evoked brain potentials, and psychometric g in the severely retarded. *Intelligence, 5*(2), 179–197.

Kirschenbaum, R. (1988). Methods for identifying the gifted and talented. *Journal for the Education of the Gifted, 11,* 53–63.

Mercer, J. R. (1971, September). *Pluralistic diagnosis in the evaluation of black and Chicano children: A procedure for taking sociocultural variables into account in clinical assessment.* Paper presented at the American Psychological Association, Washington, DC.

Nelson, H. (1982). *The identification of black and Hispanic talented and gifted students, grades kindergarten through six: In search of an educational standard.* Unpublished doctoral dissertation. Fairleigh Dickinson University, Rutherford, NJ.

Ortiz, V., & Volkoff, W. (1987). Identification of gifted and accelerated Hispanic students. *Journal for the Education of the Gifted, 11,* 45–55.

Renzulli, J. (1979). *What makes giftedness? A reexamination of the definition of the gifted and the talented.* Ventura, CA: Office of the Superintendent of Ventura County Schools.

Renzulli, J., & Smith, L. (1977). Two approaches to identification of gifted students. *Exceptional Children, 43,* 512–518.

Tiedt, P., & Tiedt, I. (1979). *Multicultural teaching: A handbook of activities, information, and resources.* Needham Heights, MA: Allyn and Bacon.

Williams, F. (1980). *Creativity Assessment Packet (CAP).* East Aurora, NY: DOK.

30

Gifted Handicapped

MERLE B. KARNES   *University of Illinois, Urbana-Champaign*
LAWRENCE J. JOHNSON   *University of Alabama, Tuscaloosa*

■ **H**istory tells us that gifted persons with handicapping conditions, given the opportunity to develop their potentials, can make a significant impact on society. Consider, for example, the contributions of Ludwig van Beethoven, Franklin D. Roosevelt, Helen Keller, Vincent van Gogh, Albert Einstein, and Thomas Edison. Unfortunately, attention to the gifted among the handicapped has been sorely neglected. In fact, some of us who have been interested in identifying and nurturing the talents of the gifted handicapped have encountered considerable resistance among educators and representatives of funding agencies. All too often we hear such remarks as, "Yes, there have been and are gifted among the handicapped, but why should we be concerned about these individuals; if they are truly gifted, their giftedness will emerge." We have no idea of the number of handicapped individuals who have gifts that are never maximized because we fail to recognize, support, and nourish their potential.

Data regarding the number of gifted individuals with handicapping conditions are sketchy, at best. Whitmore (1981) estimated that the number of gifted handicapped might be as high as 540,000. Mauser (1980) found that 2.3% of the learning-disabled children he tested in Illinois were gifted. More recently, Whitmore and Maker (1985) asserted that there were no accurate statistics on the incidence of giftedness among the handicapped but estimated conservatively that at least 2% of handicapped children are intellectually gifted. If we believe that there are as many gifted among the handicapped as in any other segment of the population, then we are vastly underserving this segment of our population.

Failure to identify and nurture giftedness among the handicapped is unfair to these individuals and to society. An important aspect of our educational system is the belief that all individuals must be given an opportunity to maximize their potential. Moreover, failing to actualize one's potential creates a breeding ground for frustration and poor mental health. Finally, as a society we are desperately in need of all the gifts that can be made available to us. Failure to identify and serve the gifted handicapped is an indictment against our society and a problem we can no longer tolerate. As Whitmore and Maker (1985) aptly stated:

> It is obvious that appropriate educational programming for these children could release a very significant amount of creative productivity of great value to society and would also reduce the possibility of economic dependence in adult years, as is often the case when suitable employment cannot be obtained. (p. 12)

Gallagher (1988) discussed the leadership role the federal government should take in gifted education. He made a plea for better serving those gifted individuals who are now being underserved. He included the gifted handicapped as one target group that should receive top priority.

In reviewing the literature to determine the status of education of the gifted handicapped, we are struck with the realization of how little has and is being done to serve this group. We do not deny that in isolated instances some of these individuals have been recognized as possessing certain characteristics associated with giftedness and have been served in appropriate ways. But these cases are rare. There has been very little research conducted on the effectiveness of interventions with this group of children. The few reports that exist generally do not include formative or summative data regarding how intervention decisions were made or their outcomes. In addition, interventions are not delineated in sufficient detail to allow others to replicate a seemingly effective model.

The purposes of this chapter are first, to emphasize that there are gifted children among the handicapped and that these children are being underserved and second, to foster a commitment to develop procedures for improving the lives of this subgroup of children. To achieve these purposes, this chapter is divided into the following sections: (1) a historical overview of what has been done to date for gifted handicapped individuals, (2) barriers that have hindered the identification and programming for these children, (3) an example of a promising programming model, and (4) implications of research and experience.

Historical Overview

It is not surprising that we are lagging even further behind in developing appropriate procedures for identifying and programming for gifted children with handicapping conditions than for gifted children in general. In the 1950s, for a short time following Sputnik, we became more interested in gifted children. During this period special emphasis was placed on challenging the gifted, particularly in the fields of math and science. Mass screening to identify the gifted made use of intelligence tests, achievement tests, and teacher referrals. Intelligence test scores were often the chief factor considered when determining whether or not a child was gifted. Special programs were developed, many of which included segregated classes for the gifted.

In the 1960s we became more concerned with culturally disadvantaged and minority children. Head Start was initiated in the summer of 1965 as a crash summer program, and shortly thereafter it was expanded to a full-year program. In the mid-1970s Head Start was mandated to serve handicapped children. Although Head Start made a significant impact, its focus has never been on the gifted, especially the gifted handicapped.

In 1971 Congress requested that the Commissioner of Education, Sydney P. Marland, Jr., determine the status of gifted education.

The Marland Report (1972) revealed that fewer than 4% of all gifted children were receiving special programming. With so little interest in the gifted in general, it should not be a shock to us that the gifted among the handicapped received virtually no attention at all.

The first book devoted entirely to the gifted handicapped, entitled *Providing Programs for the Gifted Handicapped,* was written by Maker (1977). In this book are descriptions of the work by Sanford and Karnes. In 1975 these educators received funds from the Bureau of Education for the Handicapped, now known as the Office of Special Education Programs, for the development and demonstration of models for educating young handicapped and gifted children. Sanford used a conceptual model derived from Bloom's taxonomy (Bloom, Englehart, Furst, Hill, & Krathwohl, 1956) and Karnes used a conceptual model derived from Guilford's (1967) structure of intellect. Karnes's model continues to be used in a program at the University of Illinois. Both programs were successful in identifying the gifted among the handicapped and programming for them. Karnes's program has been disseminated widely and will be presented later.

Of all the subcategories of gifted handicapped, the gifted learning-disabled child has received the most attention. Two books on learning-disabled gifted children have been published in recent years. One is *Learning Disabled Gifted Children,* by Fox, Brady, and Fabin (1983), and the other is *Teaching the Gifted/Learning Disabled Child,* by Daniels (1983). These books deal in depth with such important issues as identification programming characteristics and the role of the counselor.

The most recent book on the gifted handicapped is Whitmore and Maker's (1985) *Intellectual Giftedness in Disabled Persons.* These authors cite Mary Meeker, Merle Karnes, and Anne Sanford as the first educators to concentrate on this population. The book is a valuable resource, with case studies of gifted hearing-impaired, visually impaired, physically handicapped, and learning-disabled children. The needs of gifted children with a certain handicapping condition are delineated, along with identification procedures and the interaction between giftedness and the handicapping condition. The authors emphasize that each gifted handicapped child is unique, and present specific guidelines for dealing with these children. Educational programs for children with the specific handicapping condition also are covered.

The Association for the Gifted, a division of the Council for Exceptional Children, established a national committee of educators of the gifted handicapped. In 1976 and 1977 national conferences were held. The Educational Resource Information Center (ERIC) includes a category of *gifted handicapped,* but submission of manuscripts continues to be low.

The mainstreaming movement, brought about by Public Law 94-142, the Education for All Handicapped Children Act (1977), requires that handicapped children have the right to a free, appropriate education in the least restrictive environment. The damaging effects of labeling and segregating handicapped children has been a grave concern of professionals as well as parents (Hobbs, 1975). An orientation away from a deficit model, emphasizing the handicap, to a model that emphasizes the *strengths* of children with handicapping conditions could greatly enhance our ability to achieve the goals of the mainstreaming movement.

An organization known as Very Special Arts, founded in 1974 by Jean Kennedy Smith, is dedicated to enriching the lives of children, youth, and adults who are handicapped. It is an educational affiliate of the John F. Kennedy Center for the Performing Arts. This organization provides opportunities in drama, dance, music, literature, and the visual arts. In 1984 the international program of Very Special Arts was established, with 50 affiliates around the world and over 1 million persons in 15,000 communities participating. In the United States, Very Special Arts programs and training sessions are conducted in over 1,000 sites in all 50 states.

At the heart of this organization is the Very Special Arts Festival. These are noncompetitive programs for children, youth, and adults with special needs. It gives these individuals an opportunity to share accomplishments in the arts through performances, exhibitions, and workshops. In 1989 there were over 650 festivals. Persons or communities who wish to affiliate with the Very Special Arts organization to enhance the lives and development of handicapped individuals should get in touch with the office of this organization (Very Special Arts Education Office, 1985).

Barriers

A number of barriers hinder or deter identification and appropriate programming for gifted handicapped children. Some of these barriers are described in the following sections.

Inappropriate Identification Procedures

One barrier to identification of many handicapped gifted children is expecting these children to demonstrate the same characteristics and at the same level as the nonhandicapped gifted. It should be recognized that handicapping conditions may obscure or suppress their gifts.

Instruments used in the identification of the nonhandicapped gifted are criticized as being inappropriate for use with the handicapped. It is true that most instruments have been standardized on nonhandicapped children, but the *use* of these instruments is the important consideration. For some handicapping conditions adaptations must be made. For example, when identifying the gifted among the handicapped, these children must be compared with each other.

The procedure of identifying the gifted handicapped on a one-time basis is faulty. Some handicapped children have not had the opportunity to fully develop their potential. If they are given the opportunity, marked progress may occur. Professionals must constantly watch for emerging gifts; identification of gifts must be an ongoing process.

Faulty Expectations

Whitmore and Maker (1985) point out that some of the expectations of typical gifted children may impede identification of the gifted handicapped. For example, gifted children may be expected to "look bright," while some physically handicapped children who are very bright may look dull. This perception could even lead to an assumption of mental retardation. The hearing handicapped child whose language is absent or retarded also may be labeled mentally retarded since, stereotypically, we think of a gifted child as having advanced language skills. These authors also point out that some handicapped children do not display curiosity by physically investigating the environment, as is typical of many gifted children.

Whitmore and Maker (1985) explain that "the most important needs that can be met by both educators and families are high expectations for success and an environment that facilitates achievement" (p. 59). Expectations must be within the capabilities of the child, of course. If a teacher or parent expects very little from a child, the child will produce very little. On the other hand, showing confidence in the child's ability to produce and supporting his or her efforts will bring about positive results.

Developmental Delays

Handicapping conditions may cause developmental delays. Maker (1977) stated that cognitive development and intellectual functioning are delayed when certain handicapping conditions prevent or limit the child's ability to respond to cognitive stimulation and to demonstrate cognitive abilities through expression and problem solving. In many instances gifts are slow to appear, but with encouragement, support, and appropriate programming they will emerge.

Gaps in Information

Gaps in information may be a barrier to identifying the gifted among the handicapped. It is risky to make a hasty diagnosis of a child just because he or she is lagging behind in certain facets of development. Public Law 94-142 tries to safeguard decisions being made about handicapped children without complete information on a child. This law requires a multidisciplinary team including the parents to share all pertinent information about the child that is essential for diagnosis, educational placement,

and programming. When this information is sparse, decisions regarding the child's potential and program needs may be inaccurate and result in inappropriate programming.

Lack of Models and Research

Relatively few models that others might want to adopt have been developed and tested. Likewise, we have a dearth of research findings to endorse or refute the interventions that have been developed and disseminated. When there are no models or research to guide practice, educators often don't know what to do. With few exceptions, most research has been conducted with adults who are gifted and also handicapped (Maker, Redden, Tonelson, & Howell, 1978). Critical questions must be answered by carefully designed research.

Training of Professionals

Personnel working in the field are poorly equipped to identify and educate the gifted handicapped. Special educators of the handicapped may have little or no knowledge about characteristics of gifted children or how to program for them. Furthermore, the orientation of most special educators is to identify deficits and to program for these deficits in an attempt to get handicapped students on an equal par with their nonhandicapped peers. Such an orientation is inconsistent with the identification and nourishment of gifts. On the other hand, professionals in gifted education have little knowledge about handicaps or the effects of a handicapping condition on learning. Finally, mainstream educators have had, as a rule, no formal training in either the handicapped or gifted areas.

In-service training is one way to help professionals obtain the knowledge and skills they need to work more effectively with handicapped students who have special gifts. Such training can also aid communication among members of the child's team.

Pre-service training is another avenue for solving these problems. Hopefully, the day will come when special educators of the handicapped, educators of the gifted, and regular educators will have a greater degree of collaboration and the boundaries that now separate these groups will become less distinct. Special educators should be required to take course work in the field of the gifted; professionals in the gifted area should take course work on handicapping conditions; and regular educators need to be familiar with both fields to effectively accommodate the needs of children with handicaps and special gifts.

Failure to Disseminate Information Effectively

The Council for Exceptional Children is charged with dissemination of information through ERIC. However, much of the printed information available through ERIC is seldom accessed by practitioners. The best practices in working with the gifted handicapped should be more readily available to those who need the information most—the professionals working directly with these children and their parents. Lack of efficient and effective ways of disseminating the latest knowledge is a barrier to improving services to the gifted handicapped.

Lack of Supportive Equipment and Materials of Instruction

Lack of funds for the needed equipment and materials of instruction is another barrier. To meet the special needs of the gifted handicapped a budget must be earmarked for the purchase of equipment and curricular resources. Whitmore and Maker (1985) wrote that "adaptive use of computers perhaps is the most promising single aid to improving instruction of disabled children" (p. 23).

Lack of Appropriate Career Counseling

The cases presented in Whitmore and Maker's (1985) book clearly indicate that the school system did very little to promote the development of these individuals or to provide them with the kind of counseling they needed. As Karnes (1984b) explained the situation for the gifted handicapped, "If handicapped children did develop their gifts or talents, it was almost in

spite of the educational program, not because of it" (p. 18). It was found that customarily the handicapped were counseled into vocational training. Counselors tend to discourage the disabled from pursuing advanced education and professional careers. Gifted handicapped children need to develop a realistic, healthy self-concept and self-esteem; to become as independent as possible; and to have a well-rounded life that includes hobbies, interests, and participation in activities. They need to have an opportunity to explore different careers, to know their strengths and special abilities, and to match career goals with interests and capabilities. Counselors can play an important role in helping the gifted handicapped acquire the knowledge and skills they need to fully actualize their potentials. Unfortunately, as a general rule counselors are ill prepared to provide career counseling for the gifted handicapped.

Inadequate Funding of Education

Schools are being asked to do more and more with less and less. Until education is supported at a level at which it is possible to provide adequate staff; instructional materials and equipment necessary for individualized instruction; and salaries that can help recruit the cream of the crop into the teaching profession (and require them to have the training to work with the gifted handicapped), we are going to find a barrier to meeting the educational needs of the gifted handicapped.

A Promising Practice: The RAPYHT Model

Logic tells us that the earlier we identify potentially gifted handicapped children and provide them with programming to nurture their abilities, the greater will be their chances of fully actualizing their potential. With this belief as a foundation, in 1974 the University of Illinois, under the direction of Merle Karnes, responded to a call from the Bureau of Education for the Handicapped for proposals to develop and demonstrate a viable model in early childhood handicapped. Her project was entitled Retrieval and Acceleration of Promising Young Handicapped Talented (RAPYHT) and received initial funding for 3 years to develop and demonstrate a model for identifying and programming for handicapped preschoolers. In the summer of 1978 this model was funded as a University of Illinois outreach project. It continued as an outreach project until 1986 and during this period was replicated in over 20 states at 89 local sites.

The RAPYHT project was originally developed to train teachers and parents to identify and program for gifted and talented preschoolers with mild to moderate handicapping conditions (Karnes, 1978, 1979, 1984a, 1984b; Karnes & Bertschi, 1978; Karnes & Johnson, 1986, 1987b; Karnes, Shwedel & Lewis, 1983a, 1983b; Karnes, Shwedel & Linnemeyer, 1982). Experience and research with the model reinforced the belief that it is effective in identifying and nurturing the gifts and talents of the potentially gifted handicapped. There are seven components of the RAPYHT model: (1) general programming, (2) talent identification, (3) talent programming, (4) parent involvement, (5) interagency collaboration, (6) transitional procedures, and (7) evaluation.

General Programming

General programming is based on the assumptions that giftedness is not a trait that will emerge irrespective of the environment. A deliberate effort must be made to provide handicapped children with a program that encourages gifts and talents because of the difficulty for these traits to emerge in these children.

General programming includes a set of classroom activities and home activities. Materials are based on Guilford's (1967) structure of intellect model and include activities to develop convergent, divergent, and evaluative thinking skills. General programming allows children to demonstrate their abilities more fully and encourages strengths or gifts to emerge by stimulating creativity, problem solving, and critical thinking. This curriculum is initiated at the beginning of the school year and continues throughout the year. The activities in this curriculum have proved to be challenging and interesting to the children and teachers.

Talent Identification

Talent identification in the RAPYHT model involves the use of the RAPYHT Parent Checklist and Teacher Checklist to identify those children who are potentially gifted. Both instruments focus on children's performance in six areas of giftedness: intellectual, academic (separate subarea scales for reading, math, and science), creativity, leadership, visual and performing arts (art and music), and psychomotor abilities. Each of four items in an area of giftedness is a behavioral indicator of a particular strength or potential talent and is rated on a 4-point scale, with 1 = *rarely* and 4 = *almost always*. Ratings are summed across items to yield a total score for each scale. Possible scores range from 4 (indicating that the area is not a strength for that child) to 16 (an area of strength or potential giftedness). Scores on the two checklists from parents and the teacher are summed and tabulated on the Talent Identification Summary.

Teachers are encouraged to evaluate children separately, ensuring that their scores profile individual strengths. The Talent Identification Summary is examined to identify areas in which the child scores markedly higher than other areas. When scores are approximately equal in all areas, scores on the individual items assessing interest are examined to identify areas of special interest.

When evaluating a child who is potentially gifted, the teacher is encouraged to compare the child with his or her handicapped peers. Decisions regarding potential talent are made by teams comprising parents, classroom teachers, and ancillary staff. It is anticipated that 10 to 20% of the children in a classroom may be identified as potentially gifted. Although it has been generally assumed that the gifted make up 3 to 5% of the population, a wide net approach is used to make sure that potentially gifted handicapped children are not overlooked.

Talent Programming

More in-depth talent assessment, which is linked with programming, involves the administration of a project-developed and field-tested curriculum-based assessment in each talent area. This assessment is based on observation and is conducted with those children identified as potentially gifted by the talent checklists. Results from this assessment are used to develop educational goals and to measure progress. "Naturalistic observation of children is a viable and valuable alternative of formal testing as a means of talent assessment" (Karnes, Shwedel, & Lewis, 1983a, p. 272). There are many times during the day when children have opportunities to demonstrate their talents. If teachers are trained to observe children carefully and know the indicators of giftedness and talent, they will detect such traits and encourage talent development. Teachers trained in the RAPYHT model become very adept at determining, with the help of the assessment instrument, the strengths a child has in a talent area and what should be done to assist the child.

Talent programming begins with the Individual Education Program (IEP) meeting or midyear evaluation. The team determines ways to enhance the classroom environment to stimulate talent areas, for example, grouping children by strength (encouraging interaction between handicapped and nonhandicapped children), enlisting the aid of a mentor, planning field trips, displaying artwork in the classroom, or procuring musical recordings. Advice in specific talent areas may be solicited from members of the interagency advisory committee. Talent programming typically begins in the second half of the year.

Parent Involvement

Parents are encouraged to become involved in all components of the model. Parents participate in the talent identification process, and workshops are held to assist parents in acquiring the knowledge and skills to promote the children's strengths at home. Booklets suggest activities for parents to enhance problem solving, creative and productive thinking, and other types of higher-level thinking in their children. In each of the areas of giftedness, booklets are available that give the parents ideas for activities to enhance a particular talent. Parents are also invited to become members of the interagency advisory committee and to volunteer in the classroom.

Interagency Collaboration

Interagency collaboration is incorporated into the model in two ways. First, an interagency committee including school staff, RAPYHT staff, and parents of handicapped and nonhandicapped children is put in place to promote interagency communication and cooperation. Interagency committee members advise on programming for individual talent areas and adapting activities to meet children's needs and on identifying resources in the community. This group also helps identify consultants for the teachers and mentors for the children.

Transitional Procedures

An important but often overlooked concern in gifted education arises when children move from one program to another. There are several ways the young gifted handicapped child is helped to make a smooth transition from preschool to kindergarten. First, an attempt is made to identify the receiving teacher, and that teacher is invited to visit the child in the preschool program, if possible. A packet of information about the child is also sent to the school where the child will be in attendance. Finally, a meeting is scheduled in the fall among preschool personnel knowledgeable about the child, the principal of the school where the child is enrolled, and the receiving teacher. The preschool personnel make it clear that consultative help is available to the receiving teacher if such services are needed.

Evaluation

Evaluation includes both process and outcome evaluation. Parent and teacher feedback regarding the value of identifying and programming for children's strengths is also collected. Over the years a great deal of research has been conducted and written on the model. The following is a brief summary of some of this research.

Karnes, Shwedel, and Lewis (1983b) evaluated the short-term impact of RAPYHT on 28 handicapped preschoolers identified as having special gifts and talents. A regression-discontinuity analysis (Campbell & Stanley, 1963) was used to determine the impact on achievement motivation, task commitment, creativity, and teacher ratings of talent area performance. Children who had received RAPYHT programming performed higher than would be expected without the intervention. Children made significant gains in their talent area, self-esteem, task persistence, and creativity.

In a second study, Karnes, Shwedel, and Lewis (1983a) investigated the long-term impact of RAPYHT programming. Of the 61 children who received RAPYHT programming between 1975 and 1981, 30 were located. (More were not located because a large group were from military families.) Of the children found, 90% were in regular classrooms. Data from standardized achievement tests indicated that they scored at or above the 50th percentile in reading and math at each grade level. In addition, these children were rated by their teachers as above their nonhandicapped classmates on listening skills, self-assurance, memory, writing, independence, attention span, and willingness to try new activities.

The RAPYHT approach has also been revised and used with Head Start children, 10% of whom have a handicapping condition. A field test conducted with Head Start children (Karnes & Johnson, 1987a, 1987c) revealed that the model had a positive impact on teachers and all of the children, not just those identified as potentially gifted. The experimental children's creativity and problem-solving skills were significantly better than those of a comparison group. Teachers receiving training became more positive toward the children in their classroom. This research supports the contention that it is important to program for all children's strengths, not just those children identified as gifted.

Overall, the positive effect of the RAPYHT model on parents and teachers has been very

encouraging (Karnes & Johnson, 1986). Parents are assisted in identifying children's strengths, developing a Talent Educational Plan, and participating in talent-based activities, thus developing skills and confidence in working positively with their children. Similarly, the model has a positive effect on teachers. As their perceptions of the children change, their teaching efforts improve and they interact with the children more positively. Lastly, our research indicated that if we want children to become more creative and think at higher levels, we must give them opportunities to do so and encourge and reinforce their efforts. Unfortunately, we oftentimes sell short children with handicapping conditions by not expecting enough of them.

Conclusions and Implications of Research and Experience

The findings of research and experience indicate the following:

1. Contrary to the opinion of many, it is possible to identify indicators of above-average abilities and talents among handicapped children.
2. Teachers can be helped to more effectively identify the potentially gifted child among the handicapped if they have an instrument to guide them in observing children's behavior in naturalistic settings.
3. Identifying and programming for the gifted handicapped pay off in terms of how these children perceive themselves. Their self-concepts improve.
4. Handicapped children identified as potentially gifted, after being provided with a special program focusing on their strengths and fostering the development of higher-level thinking and talents, are able to make it in the mainstream of the public school.
5. Implementing a model that emphasizes the strengths or gifts and talents of handicapped children promotes a more positive attitude among teachers toward the handicapped children with whom they work.

6. In identifying the gifted among the handicapped, the most appropriate procedure is to compare one handicapped child with another in dimensions that are associated with giftedness or talent. To avoid overlooking those with potential, the top 10 to 20% of the handicapped population should be viewed as potentially gifted.

7. Children identified as gifted handicapped and provided an appropriate program at the preschool level retain these good abilities over time.

8. Regular teachers need to know more about handicapping conditions and their impact on learning; therefore, in teachers' preservice training, courses in special education of the handicapped should be required.

9. Special educators of the handicapped and specialists in the gifted need to have a better understanding of each other's field and work more closely together for the good of children.

10. Mainstreaming the gifted handicapped with other handicapped and nonhandicapped children, including the nonhandicapped gifted, is important and in keeping with current philosophy. Segregating these children in special classes for the handicapped is not conducive to the full development of these individuals. They need good models, gifted persons who are handicapped and nonhandicapped.

11. There is a scarcity of exemplary programming models for educating gifted handicapped children that have been evaluated on a research basis. Such models are badly needed.

12. Funds should be made available to exemplary programs so they can provide technical assistance to sites interested in replicating their models.

13. More attention needs to be given to training counselors who understand giftedness and handicapping conditions so they are better prepared to help gifted handicapped individuals choose and prepare for suitable careers.

14. Participation of parents in a program that promotes the gifts and talents of the handicapped child has a positive effect on how parents perceive the child.

15. It is important that, in programming for the gifted handicapped, the IEP should be written for both the weaknesses and the strengths of the child.

16. An individualized program for the gifted handicapped fares best if there is a knowledgeable supervisor, coordinator, or administrator who advocates for these children and ensures that they are challenged. These children should be given opportunities to have a well-balanced program and to pursue their interests.

17. An in-service training program for personnel working with the gifted handicapped should include workshops focusing on meeting the instructional needs of these children. Participants should include regular teachers, teachers of the handicapped and the gifted, supervisors and administrators, and ancillary personnel.

18. Gifted handicapped children should have continuity of programming, which means that there must be viable procedures for transitioning children from one level to another and for placing them in classes where teachers are cognizant of the special needs of this subgroup of children and know how to appropriately program for them. Parents must help ensure program continuity for their child.

19. Institutions of higher learning that are training teachers must include in their curriculum courses and practicum experience that will enable regular teachers and teachers of special subgroups (handicapped and gifted) to individualize instruction for every student in their classes.

20. The federal government needs to provide leadership in the identification and programming for the gifted handicapped. Better serving this group of children should be a top priority of the federal government (Gallagher, 1988). When the federal government establishes a priority, states and local school systems usually are influenced to take more responsibility.

21. It is imperative that the fields of special education and gifted education work more closely together to better serve gifted handicapped children. This close collabo-

ration should take place at the federal, state, and local levels.

In summary, we cannot continue to ignore our obligation to handicapped individuals who are also potentially gifted. For the good of society and for the well-being of the gifted handicapped, we must put forth greater effort to alleviate the problem of underserving gifted handicapped children.

REFERENCES

Bloom, B., Englehart, M., Furst, E., Hill, W., & Krathwohl, D. (1956). *Taxonomy of educational objectives. Handbook I: Cognitive domain.* New York: McKay.

Campbell, D. T., & Stanley, J. C. (1963). Experimental and quasi-experimental designs for research on teaching. In N. L. Gage (Ed.), *Handbook of research on teaching* (pp. 171–246). Chicago: Rand McNally.

Daniels, P. (1983). *Teaching the gifted/learning disabled child.* Rockville, MD: Aspen.

Fox, L., Brady, L., & Fabin, S. (1983). *Learning disabled gifted children.* Baltimore: University Park Press.

Gallagher, J. J. (1988). National agenda for educating gifted students: Statement of priorities. *Exceptional Children, 55,* 107–114.

Guilford, J. (1967). *The nature of human intelligence.* New York: McGraw-Hill.

Hobbs, N. (1975). *The future of children: Categories, labels, and their consequences.* Report of the project on classification of exceptional children. San Francisco: Jossey-Bass.

Karnes, M. B. (1978). *Identifying and programming for young gifted/talented handicapped children.* Presentation at the Council for Exceptional Children World Congress, Stirling, Scotland.

Karnes, M. B. (1979). Young handicapped children can be gifted and talented. *Journal for the Education of the Gifted, 2,* 157–172.

Karnes, M. B. (1984a). A demonstration/outreach model for young gifted/talented handicapped. *Roeper Review, 7,* 23–26.

Karnes, M. B. (1984b). Special children . . . Special gifts. *Children Today, 13*(5), 18–23.

Karnes, M. B., & Bertschi, J. D. (1978). Identifying and educating gifted/talented nonhandicapped and handicapped preschoolers. *Teaching Exceptional Children, 10,* 114–119.

Karnes, M. B., & Johnson, L. J. (1986). Early identification and programming for young gifted/talented handicapped. *Topics in Early Childhood Special Education, 6,* 50–61.

Karnes, M. B., & Johnson, L. J. (1987a). Bringing Out Head Start Talents (BOHST). *Head Start Bulletin, 19,* 14.

Karnes, M. B., & Johnson, L. J. (1987b). Bringing Out Head Start Talents: Findings from the field. *Gifted Child Quarterly, 34,* 174–179.

Karnes, M. B., & Johnson, L. J. (1987c). An imperative: Programming for the young gifted/talented. *Journal for the Education of the Gifted, 10,* 195–214.

Karnes, M. B., Shwedel, A. M., & Lewis, G. F. (1983a). Long-term effects of early programming for the young gifted handicapped child. *Exceptional Children, 50,* 103–109.

Karnes, M. B., Shwedel, A. M., & Lewis, G. F. (1983b). Short-term effects of early programming for the young gifted handicapped child. *Journal of the Education of the Gifted, 6,* 266–278.

Karnes, M. B., Shwedel, A. M., & Linnemeyer, S. A. (1982). The young gifted/talented child: Programs at the University of Illinois. *The Elementary School Journal, 82,* 195–213.

Maker, J. (1977). *Providing programs for the gifted handicapped.* Reston, VA: Council for Exceptional Children.

Maker, C. J., Redden, M. R., Tonelson, S., & Howell, R. M. (1978). *The self-perception of successful handicapped scientists.* Albuquerque: University of New Mexico, Department of Special Education.

Marland, S. P., Jr. (1972). *Education of the gifted and talented* (Report to the Congress of the United States by the U.S. Commissioner of Education). Washington, DC: U.S. Government Printing Office.

Mauser, A. (1980). LD in gifted children. *ACLD Newsbriefs, 130,* 2.

Very Special Arts Education Office. (1985). John F. Kennedy Center for the Performing Arts, Washington, DC 20566.

Whitmore, J. (1981). Gifted children with handicapping conditions: A new frontier. *Exceptional Children, 48,* 106–114.

Whitmore, J. R., & Maker, C. J. (1985). *Intellectual giftedness in disabled persons.* Rockville, MD: Aspen.

PART VII

The Future

31

Future Goals and Directions

DONALD J. TREFFINGER   *Center for Creative Learning, Honeoye, New York*

Accepting an invitation to look into the future of gifted education is fraught with peril; it brings with it a new sense of empathy with television weather reporters. First, the history of gifted education is scarcely the kind of straight and true path that makes most formal forecasting methods appropriate or plausible. The field's many zigs and zags make any predictions risky or speculative. For more than three decades, for example, American educational practitioners and scholars have had, as Tannenbaum (1983) and Gallagher (1985) have previously observed, a love–hate relationship with gifted education. Tannenbaum (1983) observed, for example:

> Whenever and wherever human beings excel in endeavors of cultural importance, they invariably arouse some degrees of public interest, suspicion, appreciation, or antipathy, depending on the temperament of their audiences. . . . Broadly speaking, however, humankind has always managed to show more interest in encouraging than in hampering the work of gifted individuals, but it has also had to moderate its support because of persistent undercurrents of suspicion and negativism. (pp. 2–3)

Similarly, Gallagher (1985) asserted:

> There seems to be little doubt that we as a society hold ambivalent feelings about our gifted and talented youth. A strong love/hate relationship seems to exist between the society and the high-ability individual. (p. 73)

We have not seemed certain whether gifted education represented a compelling matter of ensuring instructional equity, or a manifestation and propagation, however subtle, of an exclusive and undesirable educational caste system. We have experienced advocacy based on pleas for nurturing the "best and brightest"

minds; exhortations that the potential world leaders of tomorrow demand our best efforts; and calls (some plaintive and others strident) for school programs to serve our most capable students, rescuing them from the grasp of an educational system perceived as committed to mediocrity. At the same time, there has been opposition to gifted education in which allegations have been made with strong language: elitism, offering some students "special privileges," and creating special opportunities for a few students in "undemocratic" methods. We have seen clearly that, for every proposal, there is an equal and opposite counterproposal.

Second, the nature of the field itself has been characterized by—and continues to experience today—a rapid and accelerating rate of change. This stems, in part, from advances in theory and research in gifted education as such, but equally as much from many other areas in which advances have direct consequences for gifted education. Studies in creativity, intelligence, thinking skills, learning styles, curriculum and instruction, for example, as well as in basic research in developmental psychology, differential psychology, and cognitive science, all have substantial impact on our efforts in gifted education. These are also fields in which there has been great change and rapid growth in their own right. Hence, much of the knowledge that educators need today for success, both in teaching in general and specifically in gifted education, was quite likely not available when they were involved in their initial teacher training programs. We can be confident that much of what we will need to know one decade from now is yet unknown or at least not fully articulated.

Third, it is difficult to forecast future goals and directions for gifted education because it is but one miniscule part—a few bricks and windows in a mile-tall edifice—of the architecture of contemporary education. That larger building is itself buffeted, as if from many directions at once, by cold winds of change. The news media ask who's teaching our children, or how principals should establish discipline. The National Commission on Excellence in Education (1983) tells us we are at risk, and we seek new mandates for school improvement or effective schools or educational reform. We must attend to the pressing needs and concerns of society, address the global community, step in to fill gaps created by changing family structures, deal with new technologies and expanding curricula, and create new structures for governance and leadership within a fiscal structure often taxed beyond its capacity to pay. The ways we will eventually find to deal with these critical areas of concern (and those solutions are not clearly evident at present!) will surely carry over strongly into all other, more specialized concerns in the schools. Gifted education will certainly not be exempt from the impact or consequences of decisions in those areas.

Having now at least attempted to absolve myself of any future responsibility for the accuracy (or lack thereof) of the predictions that follow, and as risky as I may convince you it is even to attempt forecasts for gifted education, I can say that there is also another, more positive dimension of the challenge. Even knowing the risk of being viewed as foolish by later generations, for whom such forecasts will have become history, I believe there are useful and important reasons for attempting to look ahead. To do so is to seek ways to influence those directions, or chart the course, under the belief that the futurists have expressed: "The future isn't just something that happens; we create it." We are now laying the foundation for what will take place in that time we call only *the future*. If our goals, aspirations, or dreams are too timid, our search not sufficiently piercing, our vision too myopic, we will have written our own epitaph. The challenge, then, is almost exactly the same one as confronts any effective problem solver: to achieve a vision that derives from the tension between our view of the current state of events, or the way things are now, and the desired future state, or the way we would like things to be.

For a number of years, while interest in gifted education has grown substantially, there has also appeared to be a degree of consensus among those involved in the field: We have agreed that we are advocates for gifted programming. We also have shared a generally common view of the nature and fundamental conceptions that underlie gifted education. Even though there has been some disagreement on a number of specifics (e.g., whether or not giftedness is well represented by IQ scores), the traditional consensus seemed to be reasonably clear concerning the basic questions with which gifted education should be concerned. Thus, we can describe in Kuhn's (1970) sense of the term, a *paradigm* that characterizes gifted education, and from that paradigm we may find safer footing for our search for new directions and issues. The central premise underlying the well-established paradigm, which has guided both scholarly efforts and practical applications, might be stated thus: A group of individuals, called *gifted students,* can and should be distinguished or differentiated from the larger, "nongifted" population; once identified, the gifted group should receive specialized services.

Structure of the Current Paradigm

This paradigm seems rather strongly rooted in the psychometric tradition, drawing primarily on ability and achievement measures as the primary criteria for identifying "the gifted student." In addition, another root system of the paradigm appears to be the so-called medical model, which is often associated with the field of special education. This dimension of the paradigm asks that we consider *being gifted* as demonstrating a particular, well-defined set of characteristics or "symptoms." The goal is to determine the students' status with respect to the "condition"—seeking to determine (the earlier the better) if the student is "really" gifted or not. This has led us to emphasize that the purpose of identification is to select only those students who truly demonstrate the condition. Taken together, these dimensions have established a paradigm under which being gifted is a fixed condition demonstrated by only a small percentage of students. The goal of identification is to locate those who "have the condition," while excluding those who do not. Improvements in identification are viewed as techniques or strategies that allow *more precise* designations (in or out; gifted, highly gifted, or even severely and profoundly gifted) and more specific quantitative indices or cutoff scores. Once a student has been identified as gifted, the next step of the paradigm is placement in the gifted program, a special instructional opportunity presumably commensurate with the characteristics and needs of the gifted. Much emphasis has been placed on the articulation of principles of a differentiated curriculum, and on developing a carefully defined, well-structured gifted curriculum plan.

Concerns with the Current Paradigm

There are rising concerns, however, that the traditional paradigm may be seriously inadequate in many important respects. Future trends and directions in gifted education will certainly be strongly influenced by theory, research, and serious dialogue through which the paradigm is examined comprehensively and critically. To understand the challenges that must be addressed, let us consider three major areas of concern: the nature of giftedness, the nature of identification, and the nature of the response we call *gifted programs.*

The Nature of Giftedness

Many complex concepts might be defined in either a *stronger* or a *weaker* sense. Referring to the stronger sense, let us consider a term's richest, most powerful connotations—the way the term might be used to provoke thoughtful analysis or serious inquiry, or the way it might convey as fully as possible the essential elements of its meaning to others. The weaker sense refers to the more mundane meaning that a term seems to acquire if it is reduced to stereotypes, caricatures, or jargon. In the stronger sense, for example, *patriotism* speaks to one's deepest, strongest loyalties to homeland, to the strength of one's values and beliefs—even, if need be, to putting one's life

on the line for those values. In the weaker sense, patriotism might be seen merely as whether or not one wears a flag pin on the lapel, or publicly recites a certain pledge. In gifted education, there seems to be a significant problem of having used and defended the term *gifted* for so long that we have come to focus almost exclusively on its weaker sense. The traditional paradigm proposes that giftedness is a category or classification dimension, fixed and defined by specific criteria, a status that one holds by virtue of one's standing on those important criteria. There are numerous limitations in this view, among them the following:

• It is evident from research that many of the cognitive skills (e.g., memory, critical thinking, creative thinking, problem solving, inferences and deductions, analogies, and decision making) and affective skills (e.g., motivation, persistence, confidence, task attention, and metacognitive skills) traditionally associated with intelligence can be nurtured through direct instructional intervention. The dimensions of ability emphasized in defining who is (and also who is not) gifted are thus not best viewed as fixed and predetermined, absolutely present or absent in any person over time and in all circumstances.

• It is also readily evident that creatively productive accomplishments by individuals over an extended period of time in real life are neither predicted very well by the traditional IQ or achievement indices used in orthodox gifted education nor controlled exclusively by the people and circumstances of the school experience (see Chapter 3 by Tannenbaum).

The weaker definition of *gifted* in the traditional paradigm needs to give way, then, to a stronger use of the concept. A stronger meaning of giftedness, building upon a broadened understanding of human talents and abilities, views giftedness as *potential for creative productivity,* considering the person's accomplishments or attainments over a sustained period of time in his or her life, perhaps even over two decades or more (Treffinger, 1988; Treffinger & Renzulli, 1986). This is a more complex, dynamic, and growth-oriented conception of the nature of giftedness. The general nature of the proposed shift for this paradigm is illustrated in Figure 31.1. The change from *photograph* to *collage* in Figure 31.1 entails a shift from conceptualizing giftedness as a fixed, quantifiable event to a long-term pattern of behavior with qualitative dimensions.

Identification: Purposes and Methods

If, in fact, the paradigm for understanding the nature of giftedness begins to change, then a closely related shift must also occur in relation to *identification*. Consider the following:

• Present identification practices are arbitrary and contrived. Even when indicators other than IQ and achievement scores are considered, in an effort to follow the commonly heard plea for *multiple selection criteria,* the additional indicators tend to be items that correlate better with IQ or achievement scores than with anything else, thus adding very little that is original or unique to the screening process. Some indicators are so dubious in validity or reliability that it cannot be asserted with any confidence that they are really measures of anything. It is very common practice for all the available data to be "tortured until it confesses," thus enabling us to obtain a single score by which the student can be declared gifted or not gifted so he or she can then be included or excluded from the school's program. A common tactic for accomplishing these

Giftedness is . . .

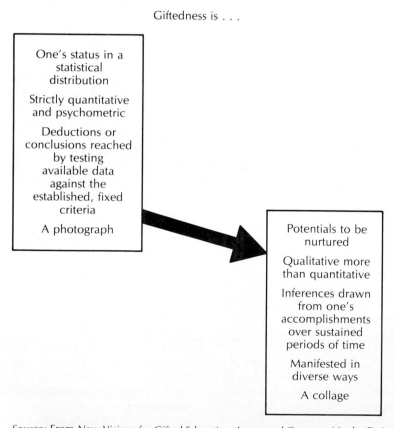

> One's status in a statistical distribution
>
> Strictly quantitative and psychometric
>
> Deductions or conclusions reached by testing available data against the established, fixed criteria
>
> A photograph

> Potentials to be nurtured
>
> Qualitative more than quantitative
>
> Inferences drawn from one's accomplishments over sustained periods of time
>
> Manifested in diverse ways
>
> A collage

Figure 31.1 Dimensions of a new paradigm: Expanding our conception of giftedness.

analyses is to use a matrix, in which interval data are reduced to ordinal data by assigning points for test scores that fall into preset intervals (e.g., if your IQ is 140+ you get 5 points, but if it is "only" 130–139 you get just 4 points, and so on). The logical and statistical deficiencies of this tactic are numerous and have been specifically identified in the literature (Feldhusen, Baska, & Womble, 1981). One of these deficiencies involves treating numerically small differences among students' scores as though they were meaningful (such as a difference of 1 or 2 points between two students on an intelligence test). Others include reducing complex profiles of diagnostic data to oversimplified categories or *point totals* and encouraging educators to add up data from many different sources, creating arbitrary cutoff points for inclusion or exclusion. Nonetheless, the tactic remains popular, and the number of students who have been victimized by it is difficult to determine with precision, but probably quite high. Coordinators and program administrators grasp eagerly any straw that appears to promise simple formulas that produce specific numbers to use for selecting students and for explaining selection decisions to students, parents, or staff.

• Contemporary understandings of the nature and diversity of human talents, and of the individual nature of students' learning styles or preferences, suggest that identification should focus more on the needs of students, to enable us to plan appropriate instruction, than merely an effort to categorize or label the student.

The needed paradigm shift, then, seems to be in the direction of more flexible, inclusive, and instructionally oriented conceptions and away from using identification simply to include or exclude students from a particular category. The proposed shift is illustrated in Figure 31.2.

Understanding the Response:
Gifted Programming

The third major dimension of the shifting paradigm deals with programming, or the instructional response to the changes taking place in defining giftedness and identification. Consider these problems:

• Many present practices rely almost exclusively on providing a single, fixed program to all students labeled gifted. It is most common for the school to preplan a single program that will be offered to all students identified for the program, on the premise that the needs of the gifted are homogeneous and thus can be readily defined and met. Students whose strengths, talents, or interests vary too widely from the anticipated characteristics and needs are removed from programs (often either by being judged not to be gifted after all or by being defined as members of a category not served by the existing program, such as in the frequent explanation, "Our program serves only the academically gifted student").

• Present practices also rely almost entirely on a *pullout, resource room* model for delivering services, in which the designated students are sent to "the gifted teacher" at a designated daily time (or weekly, or even less frequently) to partake of the gifted activities. There is, in truth, very little specific consideration of the individual needs of the students. Further, most lists of principles of the "differentiated curriculum" describe goals, strategies, and activities that are desirable for virtually all students in a strong, contemporary regular school program.

• Separating the gifted program from the larger context of the school's total instructional program offers some teachers a means for justifying lack of any concern or involvement in individualization or making daily instruction more thoughtful and challenging—the gifted teacher takes care of that.

• Educators frequently overlook the powerful learning and thinking tools that can be learned and applied successfully by all students, and which enable many students to become more successful and more creatively productive than would have been predicted on the basis of test scores or prior achievement. We have at our disposal today more information than ever before about powerful tools and processes for creative and critical thinking,

Identification is . . .

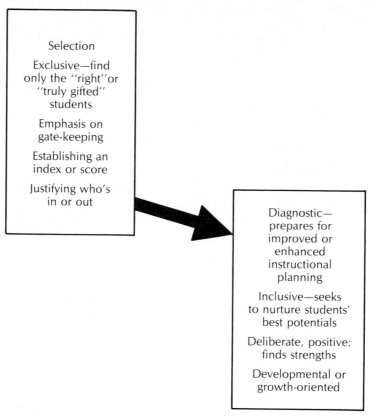

Selection

Exclusive—find only the "right" or "truly gifted" students

Emphasis on gate-keeping

Establishing an index or score

Justifying who's in or out

Diagnostic— prepares for improved or enhanced instructional planning

Inclusive—seeks to nurture students' best potentials

Deliberate, positive: finds strengths

Developmental or growth-oriented

Source: From *New Visions for Gifted Education: Issues and Opportunities* by D. J. Treffinger, p. 17, copyright © 1989 by the Center for Creative Learning, Honeoye, New York. Reproduced by permission of the publisher.

Figure 31.2   New directions for identification.

problem solving, and decision making—tools that can help students to rise above the boundaries created by arbitrary categorizations. We also have more knowledge about individualized teaching, as well as more and more powerful technology at our disposal. It is entirely possible that, given time and competent instruction, many more students will be able to function at higher levels than is envisioned by the dimensions of any traditional gifted programs. We can be prospectors for potentials rather than merely gatekeepers, and we have the opportunity to help students to become more than we thought they were capable of being!

Thus, the paradigm shift that I believe is called for would challenge schools to consider a broad range of instructional responses or services that are designed to challenge all students to a greater degree and to provide many students with new opportunities for higher-level challenges and opportunities in areas of their own greatest potentials and interests. Instead of an emphasis on "programs for the gifted," I believe we need more diverse and varied programming for giftedness. Some of the dimensions of the proposed shift are illustrated in Figure 31.3.

The response is . . .

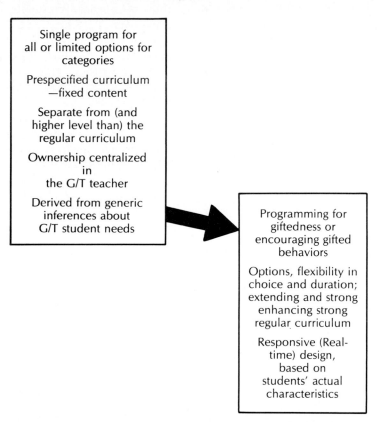

Source: From *New Visions for Gifted Education: Issues and Opportunities* by D. J. Treffinger, p. 22, copyright © 1989 by the Center for Creative Learning, Honeoye, New York. Reproduced by permission of the publisher.

Figure 31.3 New directions for gifted programming.

Implications of the New Paradigm for Research and Practice

Unfortunately, it is not easy to describe the implications of the emerging new paradigm for research and practice, since they are diverse and often integrated with other emphases in ways that do not lead to treatment effects that can clearly be isolated.

Implications for Research

The familiar experimental versus control and pre- versus post-test kinds of designs that most researchers use are often very difficult to apply

to complex, multidimensional programs that occur in busy environments, the effects of which may take long periods of time to observe. The new paradigm does not present us with an easily defined, unidimensional treatment that can be applied with precision and careful control to a specific sample. The new paradigm requires that we look at scholarship from many different subject areas and topics simply to begin to understand its nature and scope. Figure 31.4 illustrates the broad and varied foundations for the new paradigm. It will require great sophistication and imagination as an experimenter to design studies in which these variables are well defined, well controlled, systematically manipulated, and easily operationalized for large groups of students who are randomly assigned to experimental and control conditions.

It seems likely, however, that some important research needs of the field can be broadly characterized in these concerns:

• Studies of program effectiveness will require varied documentation of both the mastery of several higher level skills and complex student products and accomplishments, rather than merely end-of-year comparisons of basic standardized achievement data.

• Since these complex outcomes may require longer periods of time to be manifest, we must plan for long-term investigations rather than seeking only immediate indicators of program impact.

• Complex outcomes are also likely to take many forms of expression, so it seems important to investigate their attainment through the perspectives of many different data sources and disciplines.

• Programming must be described through much more complex processes, perhaps through such means as extended case studies, ethnographic studies, school audit methods, or other more qualitative approaches, rather than through characterizations of collections of content or activities as though they constituted a well-defined treatment or program.

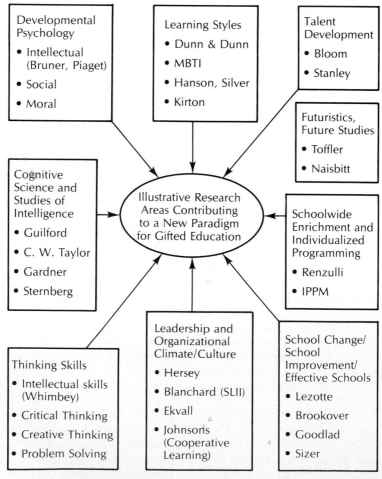

Figure 31.4   Illustrative dimensions of research contributing to a new paradigm.

• Complex multivariate models will surely be required to investigate the multiple factors that contribute differentially to the accomplishments and productivity of various individuals and groups; we cannot think in terms of simple correlational studies. Also, rather than simply using single measures, such as IQ scores, to characterize research subjects as gifted or not gifted, it will be much more important to design studies in which we investigate the differential consequences of programming educational experiences in relation to various sets of student characteristics.

Implications of the New Paradigm for Practice

Meanwhile, what can be suggested for those who are now, or soon will be, working with students in schools on a day-to-day basis? The professional in the school cannot wait for the definitive experiment or the ultimate model. New paradigms for gifted education suggest new opportunities and directions for practice, if not as firm conclusions resting on a solid foundation of research evidence, at least as hypotheses for constructing a working agenda for those who seek to guide learners from potential to productivity.

In addressing elsewhere the need to transcend traditional concepts and practices (Treffinger & Renzulli, 1986) and attempting a forecast for gifted education in the 21st century (Treffinger, 1989a, b), we proposed that one of the most fundamental shifts in the newly emerging paradigm is to view giftedness as *creative productivity,* recognized in the accomplishments of people over sustained periods of time. To help students grow within such a view, it is important for practitioners to seek and respond to students' unique strengths and sustained interests, and to begin to modify identification policies and practices substantially. Also, as educators become increasingly aware of many opportunities to nurture the fundamental ingredients of creative productivity (the abilities, skills, and motivations that underlie creative accomplishment), it will be necessary for them to learn to place greater faith in, and emphasis upon, providing tools (processes, techniques, and skills) for students, rather than merely choosing the proper students. With a broadened conception of giftedness, and increasing emphasis on flexible, diagnostic, developmental identification, there also arises a new emphasis on programming options and services that reach across the total school program, rather than being narrowly limited to predefined individuals or groups (e.g., Renzulli & Reis, 1985; Treffinger, 1986). The new paradigm challenges educators to take seriously, in newer and richer ways, their role as catalysts for creative, productive students and lifelong learners.

REFERENCES

Feldhusen, J. F., Baska, L. K., & Womble, S. (1981). Using standard scores to synthesize data in identifying the gifted. *Journal for the Education of the Gifted, 4,* 177–186.

Gallagher, J. J. (1985). *Teaching the gifted child.* Boston: Allyn and Bacon.

Kuhn, T. S. (1970). *The structure of scientific revolutions* (2nd ed.). Chicago: University of Chicago Press.

National Commission on Excellence in Education. (1983). *A nation at risk: The imperative for national reform.* Washington, DC: U.S. Government Printing Office.

Renzulli, J. S., & Reis, S. M. (1985). *The schoolwide enrichment model.* Mansfield Center, CT: Creative Learning.

Tannenbaum, A. J. (1983). *Gifted children: Psychological and educational perspectives.* New York: Macmillan.

Treffinger, D. J. (1986). *Blending gifted education with the total school program.* East Aurora, NY: DOK.

Treffinger, D. J. (1988, April). Cultivating potentials—Beyond the gifted program. *Teaching K-8,* pp. 54–57.

Treffinger, D. J. (1989a). From potentials to productivity: Designing the journey to 2000. *Gifted Child Today, 10,* 17–21.

Treffinger, D. J. (1989b). *New visions for gifted education: Issues and opportunities.* Honeoye, NY: Center for Creative Learning.

Treffinger, D. J., & Renzulli, J. S. (1986). Giftedness as potential for creative productivity: Transcending IQ scores. *Roeper Review, 8,* 150–154.

Adams, G. R., 389
Adamson, D. P., 182
Adkison, M. R., 184
Adler, D., 15, 224
Aiken, L. R., 33
Alam, S. J., 189
Albert, R. S., 229, 275, 308, 312, 316, 396
Albo, D., 82
Alvino, J. J., 9, 81, 286, 386
American Association of Gifted Children, 274
Amabile, T. M., 34, 230
Anastasi, A., 68–69, 227, 253
Anderson, C. T., 183
Anderson, J. R., 105
Anderson, R. S., 5
Angoff, W. H., 87, 156
Anthony, E. J., 376
Appelbaum, M. I., 376–377
Archer, S., 389
Arendt, H., 256, 262
Argulewicz, E. N., 230
Arthur, G., 337
Asher, J. W., 77
Ashmore, R. D., 368
Atkinson, J. W., 42, 182
Austin, J. H., 41

Bachtel-Nash, A., 18
Backman, M. E., 225
Bacon, M. K., 368
Bagley, M. T., 241
Bahnmuller, M., 183–184
Bailey, H. P., 182
Baird, J., 82, 266
Baker, M., 227
Baldwin, A. Y., 12, 15–16, 416–428
Baldwin, J. W., 84
Ball, O. E., 91, 223, 227
Ballering, L. D., 307, 316
Bamberger, J., 28, 158
Bandura, A., 112
Banks, J., 416–417, 419, 423, 425
Barbe, W. B., 84
Barbee, A. H., 30
Barell, J., 10, 256–270
Barker Lunn, J. C., 182, 184
Barker, W., 224
Barlow, F., 347, 352
Barron, F., 289
Barthelmess, H. M., 182

Bartkovich, K. G., 160
Barton, D. P., 182
Baska, L. K., 445
Baumgarten, F., 352–354
Baumrind, D., 309
Bayley, N., 157, 371, 373, 376
Beattie, O. V., 312
Becker, L. J., 189
Bedell, J., 374
Beery, R. G., 35, 333–334
Begin, J., 72
Belcher, T. L., 225
Belenky, M. F., 294
Bell, M. E., 189
Bellarosa, A., 226
Belmont, J., 18–19
Benbow, C., 9, 15, 17, 32–33, 38–39, 154–165, 166–167, 169–170, 385, 402–403, 405–406, 410
Bennett, W. J., 249
Bensusan, R., 354
Bent, L. G., 189
Bergman, W. G., 183
Berkun, M. M., 182
Berliner, D. C., 102
Berlyne, D. E., 237
Bernal, E., 423
Bertschi, J. D., 433
Bestor, A. E., 7
Betts, G., 9, 142–153
Bicak, L., 182, 184
Bierden, J. E., 187
Bieri, M. D., 374
Biggs, B. E., 334
Billett, R. O., 178–179, 182
Binet, A., xv, 6, 14, 55, 348, 350
Binger, C. M., 374
Birch, J. W., 84, 155
Birns, B., 366
Black, H., 83
Blackshear, P., 423
Bloom, B. S., 3, 15, 68, 71, 74–75, 100, 113–114, 200, 241, 245–247, 249–250, 308–309, 311–312, 325, 331–332, 338–339, 393, 396, 399, 412, 429, 448
Blos, P., 383, 390
Bobbit, B. L., 156
Bock, R. D., 406
Boersma, F. J., 224
Bogner, D., 220

Boles, D. B., 406
Borg, W. R., 179, 182
Borke, H., 291
Borkowski, J. G., 156, 358
Borland, J. H., 350
Boston, B. O., 76, 81, 163, 170, 197, 209, 308, 311, 425
Bouchard, T. J., Jr., 72
Bowlby, J., 285–286, 374–375
Boyer, P. A., 182
Bradley, R. H., 371–372
Bradshaw, G. F., 158
Brady, L., 429
Brandt, G., 82
Branscomb, L. M., 37
Bratton, J. C., 77
Breidenstine, A. G., 182
Bremer, N., 182
Brennan, T. P., 291, 295, 299
Bridges, S., 274, 309
Brill, A. A., 362
Brody, L. E., 38–39, 163, 170
Bronowski, J., 256, 264
Brookover, W. B., 448
Brooks-Gunn, J., 366–367, 373, 384
Brooks, J., 310
Broughton, J., 303
Brower, P., 86, 276, 302
Brown, B. F., 374
Brown, G. W., 374
Brown, M. M., 351
Bruch, C. B., 408
Brucker, S., 76
Bruininks, R. H., 69
Bruner, J., 20, 112, 269, 448
Bryan, M. M., 179
Buescher, T. M., 12, 315, 331, 382–401
Bull, K. S., 236, 238
Burks, B. S., 30, 273, 316
Burns, D. R., 242
Burton, N. W., 167, 175
Busch, J. C., 223
Butterfield, E. C., 156
Byrnes, P., 225

Cain, A. C., 374
Calderone, M., 393
Caldwell, B. M., 371–372
Callahan, C. M., 10, 17, 76, 117, 219–235, 403, 408
Callender, W. M., 374

Campbell, A. L., 187
Campbell, D. T., 246, 435
Carlson, N. A., 220
Carlsson, I., 227
Carpenter, T., 267
Carroll, J., 224
Carson, R. M., 186
Cartwright, G. P., 186
Case, R., 48
Castenell, L. A., 35
Cattell, J. M., 250–251
Chambers, J., 253
Chambers., J. A., 249
Chan, L. K. S., 404
Chandler, M., 15
Chapman, M., 291
Charness, N., 357
Chase, C. I., 224
Chase, W. G., 247
Chauvin, J., 409
Chi, M. T. H., 158
Chilman, C., 384
Chismar, M. H., 186
Chitwood, D. G., 308, 315
Christianson, B. P., 336
Ciabotti, P., 76
Cicchetti, D., 285
Cignetti, M. J., 187
Ciha, T. E., 84
Clance, P. R., 350
Clarizio, H. F., 189
Clark, B., 105, 109, 286, 311
Clark, P. M., 229
Clarke, A. D. B., 372
Clarke, A. M., 372
Clayton, P. J., 374
Cleveland, J. C., 313, 338
Clifton, J., 357
Clinchy, B. McV., 294
Clinkenbeard, P. R., 197
Cluff, J. E., 189
Coates, D. L., 372
Cochran, J. R., 182
Cohen, J., 180
Cohn, S. J., 9–10, 157, 166–177,
    405
Colangelo, N., 3–13, 14, 40, 86,
    309, 311, 314, 316, 272–284,
    288–289, 300, 302, 387, 396,
    398, 402, 404–407
Coleman, J. S., 39
Coleman, L., 395
Coleman, W., Jr., 20
Collins, E. C., 205
Combs, A. W., 274
Cook, D. M., 183
Cooley, D., 409
Cooper, C., 138
Cornell, D. G., 275–276, 315–316
Cornish, R. C., 84
Corno, L., 74
Costa, A., 267

Covington, M. V., 35–36,
    333–334
Cox, C. M., 30, 250–251
Cox, J., 76, 81, 163, 170, 197,
    209, 308, 311, 425
Crabbe, A., 242
Craft, M., 357, 362
Cramer, S. H., 321
Cramond, B., 40
Crawford, R. P., 241
Crinella, F. M., 422
Cronbach. L. J., 68
Cropley, C., 224
Cullinan, D., 404
Cummings, W. B., 423
Cunningham, K., 289
Cunnington, B. F., 221–222
Curtiss, S., 372
Csikszentmihalyi, M., 28, 37,
    105–106, 158, 245, 302, 312,
    354, 362, 386, 397

Dabney, M., 423
Dabrowski, K., 11, 86, 286–287,
    293–300, 302–304, 314
Daniel, N., 76, 81, 163, 170, 197,
    209, 308, 311, 425
Daniels, J. C., 182
Daniels, P., 429
Dark, V. J., 156
Daurio, S. P., 157, 163, 310
Davidson, J. E., 4, 15, 28, 49, 53,
    65, 156, 247
Davis, A., 83
Davis, G. A., 3–13, 14, 69, 99,
    102, 222, 225–226, 228,
    236–244, 329, 333, 337
Davis, K., 372
Davis, J. C., 82
Davis, S. N., 245
Day, J. D., 358
Deats, P., 295
de Bono, E., 240, 389
Deblinger, J., 224
DeGrow, G. S., 186
Deitrich, F. R., 183
Delisle, J. R., 77, 138–139, 274,
    302, 390, 394
DeMars, S. T., 223
Dembinski, R. J., 308
DeMille, R., 241
Denham, S. A., 405, 410
Dennis, W., 372
Dettmann, D. F., 275–276, 280,
    309, 311
Deutsch, R., 275, 309
DeVillis, R. F., 156
Dewar, J. A., 187
Dewey, J., 112, 258
Dewing, K., 312
Dice, M., 225
Dickinson, R. M., 308

Diener, E., 289
Dietrich, F. R., 184
DiPego, G., 242
Dirks, J., 307, 309, 315
Dixon, J., 229
Dolny, C., 406
Domino, G., 222
Donham, R., 228
Donlon, T. F., 156, 168
Doolin, R. B., 189
Douglas, J. W. B., 374
Dowdall, C. B., 278
Down, J. L., 357
Downing, C. J., 48
Drews, E. M., 182, 184
Duckworth, E., 269
Dugas, J., 156
Dunn, K., 448
Dunn, R., 448
Durkin, M. C., 106
Dweck, C. S., 409
Dwinell, P. L., 226
Dyson, E., 184

Eberle, B., 241, 243
Eccles, J. S., 17, 403, 405–407,
    409–410
Eddleman, V. K., 187
Edison, T., 261
Edwards, M. O., 238
Eichenberger, R. J., 222, 225
Eichorn, D. H., 370
Eilber, C. R., 14, 214
Eisenberg, L., 371
Eisendorfer, C., 374
Elardo, R., 372
Elkind, D., 224, 293, 301, 311,
    385, 390
Ellenhorn, J. H., 309
Elliott, G. R., 374
Ellis, J., 413
Ellison, R. L., 82
Emmons, R. A., 289
Engen, H., 405
Englehart, M. D., 100, 200, 241,
    247, 429
Ennis, R. H., 204
Enright, M. K., 371
Enzmann, A. M., 188–189
Erickson, G. R., 184
Erickson, M. E., 374
Ericsson, K. A., 247
Erikson, E., 285, 383, 387, 389
Espeseth, C., 183
Essen, J., 182
Evans, E., 266
Evans, E. D., 189, 224
Eysenck, H., 15

Fabin, S., 429
Fagan, J. F., 366–367
Falk, R. F., 34, 289

Faloon, S., 247
Farles, J. E., 228
Farley, F. H., 237
Fast, I., 374
Favazza, A., 160
Fehr, B., 392
Feiring, C., 372
Fekken, G. C., 228
Felder, R. M., 312
Feldhusen, J. F., 10, 18, 77, 105, 139, 197–208, 224, 228, 445
Feldman, D. H., 11, 28, 31, 55, 60, 77, 158, 314, 347–364
Felton, G. S., 334
Feltovich, P., 158
Fennema, E., 267
Ferrari, M., 65
Ferris, T., 264
Fick, W. W., 182, 184
Findley, W. G., 179
Fine, M. J., 309, 313, 315, 332–333
First Official U.S. Education Mission to the USSR, 7
Fischer, A., 368
Fischer, J. L., 368
Fitzgerald, D., 227
Flair, M. D., 182
Flavel, J. H., 362
Fleet, J., 266
Fleming, E. S., 402, 406–408, 410–412
Floyd, B., 224
Fogelman, K., 182
Follis, H., 197
Ford, M. E., 69
Fordham, S., 423
Foster, W., 73, 393
Fowler, W., 361
Fox, L. H., 17, 33, 102, 159–160, 166–167, 169, 351, 402, 405, 409–410, 429
Fraenkel, J. R., 106
Frasier, M., 15–16, 424
Frazier, A., 330
Freeman, D. S., 391
Freeman, J., 315, 366–367, 370, 376
French, J. L., 330, 337
Frensch, P. A., 50
Friedman, F., 224
Furst, E. J., 15, 100, 200, 241, 247, 429
Fuson, K. H., 209

Gabriel, C. L., 331–332
Gaeth, J., 86, 275, 407
Gage, N. L., 249
Gagné, F., 8, 65–80
Galaburda, A. M., 359
Gallagher, J. J., 3, 7, 14–23, 197, 275, 405, 428, 436, 441
Gallagher, R., 16

Galton, F., 6, 362
Gamoran, A., 39
Gandhi, M. K., 291–292
Gardner, B., 83
Gardner, H., 8, 15, 27, 32, 55–64, 69, 86, 113, 147, 158, 291, 303, 354, 402, 448
Gardner, J. W., 3–4
Gardner, M. R., 83
Garmezy, N., 376
Garrison, C., 410
Gaskill, B., 328
Gastel, J., 50
Gauss, K. F., 245
Gear, G., 421–422
Gear, G. H., 84, 90
Geller, L., 299
George, W. C., 157, 160, 166, 168–169, 405
Geschwind, N., 359
Getzels, J. W., 40–41, 105–106, 245, 302
Ghiselin, B., 264
Giaconia, R. M., 249
Gibb, L., 17
Gilligan, C., 280, 385, 403
Ginsberg, G., 308
Glaser, R., 18, 48, 78, 156, 158
Glass, G. V., 179–180
Goddard, H., 6
Godwin, L. J., 224
Goertzel, M. G., 38, 146, 308, 331
Goertzel, T. G., 38, 308
Goertzel, V., 38, 146, 308, 331
Goldberg, M. L., 4, 179, 183–184, 330
Goldberger, N. R., 294
Golden, M., 366
Goldman, B. A., 223, 226
Goldsmith, L. T., 354–355, 361
Goldstein, K., 357–358
Goleman, D., 82
Good, H. G., 5
Goodchild, F., 266
Goodenough, F. L., xv
Goodlad, J., 20, 448
Goolsby, T. M., 83
Gordon, W. J. J., 241–242
Gottfredson, L. S., 321–324
Gottshalk, L., 136
Gough, H. G., 227
Gowan, J. C., 274
Grant, B. A., 289, 291, 300
Gray, H. A., 189
Graybeal, S., 223
Green, D. R., 186
Green, K., 332
Greene, M., 257–259, 262
Greeno, J., 18
Greif, E. F., 280
Grossberg, I. N., 315
Groth, N. J., 407
Grout, C., 183

Gruber, H. E., 158, 245
Gubbins, E. J., 76, 138
Guilford, A. M., 367
Guilford, J. P., 15, 27, 32, 55, 69, 82, 100, 222, 240, 365, 368, 433, 448
Gustafson, S. B., 158

Hackney, H., 316, 396
Hagen, E., 27, 92, 351
Hague, W., 298
Hainsworth, J., 77
Hale-Benson, J., 424
Hall, L. K., 229
Halliwell, J. W., 186
Hamblin, D. G., 361
Hamburg, D., 374
Hansen, J. B., 197, 204
Hansen, M., 87
Harrah, D. D., 187
Harrell, J., 275
Harris, R., 84
Harrison, C. H., 308
Hart, R. H., 186
Harter, S., 285, 315
Hartill, R. W., 183
Hartman, R. K., 76, 117, 230
Haskins, J., 424
Hass, A., 384
Hatch, T., 60
Hattie, J. A., 224, 227, 229
Havighurst, R. J., 245
Hawkins, D., 269
Hayes, J., 259, 263, 372
Hedges, L. V., 180, 249
Heidegger, M., 262
Herbig, M. P., 10, 245–255
Hermelin, B., 358
Herr, E. L., 321
Hertzig, M., 382, 386, 391–392
Hess, K. K., 241
Hesse, P., 285
Hetherington, E. M., 374, 376
Hickok, L., 297
Hiebert, E. H., 39
Higham, S. J., 315, 383–385, 388–389, 392, 394–395, 399
Hill, A. L., 357
Hill, W. H., 15, 100, 200, 241, 247, 429
Hinze, R. H., 189
Hiskey, M., 337
Hobbs, N., 275, 430
Hocevar, D., 225, 227, 229
Hoffman, B., 83
Hoffman, C., 84
Hoffman, J. L., 336
Hoffman, L., 291
Hofstadter, R., 4
Hogarty, P. S., 370, 373, 376–377
Hoge, R. D., 113, 417
Holland, J. L., 82, 84, 227, 321, 324–325

Hollinger, C., 402, 406–408, 410–412
Hollingworth, L. S., xv, 6–7, 189, 273–274, 308–309, 315–316, 347–352, 356, 404
Holmes, T. H., 374
Holt, K. S., 374
Holy, T. C., 183
Hom, H. L., Jr., 328
Honeywell, L., 222
Honzik, M. P., 371, 373, 377
Hoover, S. M., 77, 205
Horner, M. S., 350
Horowitz, F. D., 418
Houtz, J. C., 224
Howard, K., 383, 386
Howell, R. M., 431
Howell, W. J., 189
Howieson, N., 223
Howley, A., 99–100
Howley, C. B., 99–100
Hoyt, D. P., 82
Hultgren, H., 310, 315
Hunt, J. M., 157
Hunt, J. McV., 370, 372
Hunter, J. E., 180
Hurlburt, N., 373
Hurwitz, W., 87
Hutchins, M., 328
Hyde, J. S., 406
Hyman, M. B., 171

Illingworth, R. S., 374
Imes, S. A., 350
Ingram, V., 186
Inhelder, B., 362
Institute for Behavioral Research in Creativity, 228
Isaksen, S. G., 240, 242
Ivey, J. D., 189

Jacklin, C. N., 17, 405
Jackson, G. B., 180
Jackson, N. E., 71, 156, 312
Jackson, R. M., 313, 338
Jacobs, J. C., 84
Jacobs, J. E., 403
Jacobsen, T. S., 82
James, W., 112, 301
Janos, P. M., 16, 310, 315, 351, 407
Jaskir, J., 371
Jay, G., 274
Jensen, A. R., 422
Jensen, D. W., 30, 273, 316
Jensen, L. R., 220
Johnson, B., 105
Johnson, D. W., 448
Johnson, E., 393
Johnson, L. J., 12, 428–437
Johnson, R., 256
Johnson, R. A., 81
Johnson, R. T., 448

Johnston, F., 214
Johnston, H. J., 183
Jones, D. M., 187
Jones, J. C., 186
Jones, R., 275
Judson, H. F., 264
Justman, J., 179, 183–184

Kagan, J., 372
Kaltsounis, B., 222, 226
Kamin, L. J., 83
Kaplan, S. N., 105, 143
Karamessinis, N. P., 274
Karnes, F. A., 205, 409
Karnes, M. B., 12, 189, 428–437
Karweit, N., 187
Katz, A. N., 229
Katz, E. L., 315
Katz, I., 35
Kaufman, A. S., 408
Kaufman, M., 225
Kaufman, N. L., 408
Kaufmann, F., 406–408
Kavrell, S. M., 405
Kearney, K., 309–310, 314, 316, 351
Keating, D. P., 156–157, 160, 166–167, 169, 351
Kellas, G., 156
Kellog, R. M., 189
Kelly, J., 375
Kelly, K. R., 40, 274–275, 407
Kerr, B. A., 12, 86, 273–275, 279, 402–415
Kestenberg, J., 383
Khatena, J., 221–222, 225–226
Kierstead, R., 186
Kilpatrick, A., 224
Kirby, D. F., 250, 408
Kirk, M. K., 32
Kirk, S. A., 19
Kirkland, J., 224
Kirschbaum, R. M., 374
Kirschenbaum, R. J., 228, 422
Kitano, M. K., 250, 408
Klausmeier, H. J., 183
Kline, R. E., 183
Klineberg, O., 83
Knapp, J., 142
Koch, A., 307, 316
Koestler, A., 264
Kogan, N., 224, 229
Kohlberg, L., 279–280, 301, 362–363
Kohlberg, L. A., 322
Kolakowski, D., 406
Kolloff, P. B., 10, 14, 209–215
Kolodny, A., 265
Koluchova, J., 372
Koontz, W. F., 183
Koopmans-Dayton, J. D., 197, 204, 207
Koukeyan, B. B., 189

Krasney, N., 35
Krathwohl, D. R., 15, 100, 200, 241, 247, 429
Krupnick, J. L., 374
Krutetskii, V. A., 158–159
Kuhn, T. S., 159, 441
Kulieke, M. J., 35, 331, 396
Kulik, C. C., 10, 39, 157, 178–196
Kulik, J. A., 10, 39, 157, 178–196
Kulp, M., 225
Kurtines, W., 280
Kush, J. C., 230

La Rossa, C., 362
LaFontaine, L., 358
Laing, J., 405
Langley, P. W., 158
Larsen, R. J., 289
Larson, R., 386
Lash, J. P., 292, 295, 297
Lefkowitz, M. M., 374
Leming, J. S., 280
Lenihan, E. A., 374
Leroux, J., 22
Leroux, J. A., 301
Lessinger, L., 407
Lewis, G. F., 433–435
Lewis, M., 11–12, 310, 365–381
Lezotte, L., 448
Licht, B. G., 409
Liebmann, R., 261, 267
Lindzey, G., 373
Linnemeyer, S. A., 433
Lipman, M., 240, 265
Lissitz, R. W., 224
Loeb, R. C., 274
Loehlin, J. C., 373
Long, R. G., 189
Loomer, B. M., 183
Louis, B., 11–12, 365–381
Lovell, J. T., 183
Lowe, B., 330–331, 333
Lubart, T. I., 53
Lucito, L., 421–422
Ludwig, G., 404
Luttrell, J., 189
Lutz, S. W., 227
Lyman, L., 183–184
Lynch, M. D., 225
Lysy, K. Z., 289

Maccoby, E. E., 405
MacDonald, L., 357
Machado, L. A., 85, 93
MacKenzie, B., 372
MacKinnon, D. W., 69, 253, 312, 316
Madow, W., 87
Maehr, M., 35
Mahler, F. L., 189
Mahler, M., 390

Maker, C. J., 9, 16–18, 99–110, 103, 201, 237, 428–432
Malkus, U., 60
Manaster, G., 383
Mangel, H., 393
Marascuilo, L. A., 183–184
Marcia, J., 389
Marken, D., 189
Marland, S. P., Jr., 81, 147, 309, 429
Martin, C. E., 40
Martin, W. B., 183
Martinson, R. A., 189, 351, 407
Marzano, R., 256, 264
Maslow, A. H., 237–239, 286–287, 298–299, 303
Mauser, A., 428
Mauser, A. J., 308
Maxey, J., 405
Mayer, R., 256
McAdams, D. P., 388–389
McCall, R. B., 370, 372, 373, 376–377
McCall, W. A., 189
McCannon, C., 424
McCarthy, D., 370
McCauley, C., 156
McCown, G. W., 189
McCoy, G., 189
McCuen, J. T., 313
McCurdy, H. G., 250
McDevitt, J., 390
McDonald, R., 189
McDonnel, R. C., 9, 81, 286
McGaw, B., 179
McGillicuddy-Delisi, A. V., 368
McGrath, S. K., 366–367
McGreevy, A., 122
McGuire, W. J., 274
McGurk, H., 373
McIntosh, D. K., 186
McKee, M. G., 227
McNaughton, A. H., 106
McNemar, Q., 32
McPeck, J., 265
McSweeney, M., 183–184
Meckstroth, E. A., 138, 273, 286, 351, 361
Mednick, S. A., 225
Meeker, M., 18, 91
Meeker, R., 91
Mchrens, W. A., 68
Mercer, J. R., 423
Merenda, P. F., 313, 338
Merrill, M. A., 370
Merton, R. K., 247
Messick, S., 27
Meyer, A. E., 5
Mezynski, K., 160, 170
Michalson, L., 310, 366–367, 370
Michelmore, P., 65
Mikkelson, J., 188–189

Miller, A., 82, 289–290
Miller, L. P., 83
Miller, N. B., 298
Mink, O. G., 313
Minor, L. L., 33
Mirels, H. L., 229
Mitchell, J. W., 39
Monroe, W. S., 187
Montemayor, R., 309, 385
Montour, K., 362
Moore, J. W., 186
Moorhouse, W. J., 186
Moran, J. D., III, 224
Morelock, M. J., 11, 347–364
Morgan, E. F., Jr., 186
Morgan, H., 40, 142–143
Morgenstern, A., 183–184
Morse, J. A., 408
Mortlock, R. S., 189
Moses, P. J., 183
Mulholland, T. M., 48
Mumford, M. D., 158
Munday, L. S., 82
Murray, H. A., 221, 227
Mussen, P. H., 339
Myers, I. B., 314
Myers, R. E., 238, 240
Myers, R. S., 274

Nairn, A., 83
Nathan, C., 307
National Assessment of Educational Progress, 264–265
National Commission on Excellence in Education, 3, 14, 20, 328, 441
National Education Association, 179
National Science Board, 159
Neihart, M., 145, 152
Nelson, H., 423
Nevin, D., 170
New York State Department of Education, 82
Newbold, D., 183
Newland, T. E., 5, 337
Newton, I., 245
Nichols, N., 186
Nichols, R., 227
Noble, K., 317
Nurius, P. S., 274
Nyiregyhazi, E., 352–354

O'Brien, M., 418
O'Bryan, K., 224
O'Connell, P., 20
O'Connor, N., 358
O'Connor, P., 182
Oakes, J., 178, 191
Oden, M. H. xv, 6, 15, 17, 27, 30,

32, 273, 404, 407–408, 410, 413
Offer, D., 383–385
Office of Technology Assessment, 159
Ogburn-Colangelo, M. K., 314
Oglesby, K., 3, 197
Olenchak, F. R., 139
Olkin, I., 180
Olson, L., 60
Olszewski-Kubilius, P., 35
Olszewski, P., 331, 385, 395–396
Omelich, C. L., 35–36
Ortiz, V., 419
Osborn, A. F., 237, 241–243
Osborne, W. L., 223, 227
Oscanyan, F. S., 240
Ostrov, E., 383, 386

Pace, T. M., 274
Page, B. A., 307
Parke, B. N., 225
Parker, M., 274–275, 309
Parkes, C. M., 286
Parnes, S. J., 18, 100, 237–238, 240, 242–243
Parrilla, R. H., 374
Parron, D., 374
Passow, A. H., 179, 183–184, 330
Paul, R., 265
Pearce, N., 77
Peck, R. F., 300
Peck, V. A., 156
Pegnato, C. C., 84, 155
Pellegrino, J. W., 48
Pendarvis, E. D., 99–100
Perkins, D. N., 15–16, 225, 263–265
Perkins, J. A., 313
Perkins, S., 402
Perlman, D., 392–393
Perrone, P., 11, 274, 321–327, 398
Petersen, A., 384, 393
Petersen, A. C., 405–406
Peterson, D., 275
Peterson, P. L., 267
Peterson, R. L., 183–184
Pfleger, L. R., 274
Pfouts, J. H., 316
Phenix, P. H., 37, 112
Piaget, J., 57, 285, 353, 362, 385
Piechowski, M. M., 11, 34, 86, 285–306, 312, 314, 361, 387, 396
Pitts, R., 313, 333
Platz, E. F., 183–184
Plomin, R., 14, 70
Pollins, L. M., 163
Post-Kammer, P., 324
Potter, M., 84
Powell, P., 383

Poze, T., 241–242
Pressley, M., 266–267
Price, P. B., 82
Provus, M. M., 183
Prugh, D. G., 374
Pulvino, C., 273
Purdom, T. L., 183
Putbrese, L. M., 187

Quilling, M., 183
Quinton, D., 374

Rabinowitz, M., 18, 156, 158
Rabkin, J. G., 374
Radin, N., 339
Radke-Yarrow, M., 291
Rahe, R. H., 374
Ramos-Ford, V., 8, 55–64, 402
Rand, D., 17
Rankin, P. T., 183
Rapaport, D., 69
Raphael, B., 375
Rasher, S. P., 331–332
Raven, J., 249
Raymond, B. A., 224
Rebhorn, L. S., 197
Redden, M. R., 431
Reis, S., 9, 17, 20, 69, 77,
    111–141, 238, 242
Reisman, F. K., 224
Renzulli, J. S., 9, 16, 19, 28, 34,
    65, 69, 71–72, 76–78, 81–82,
    86, 99, 111–141, 143, 219,
    228, 230, 238, 242, 370, 423,
    443, 448–449
Resnick, D. P., 176
Resnick, L. B., 176, 261–262,
    265, 267
Rest, J., 362
Revesz, G., 352–354
Reyna, J., 423
Reynolds, C. R., 227
Rhodes, C., 410
Richards, R. L., 229
Richards, J. M., 227
Richardson, T. M., 163
Richert, S. E., 9, 81–96, 286
Riegel, T., 227
Rifkin, B., 48
Riley, H. W., 186
Rimland, B., 357, 362
Rimm, S. B., 3–4, 11, 16, 69, 99,
    102, 226, 239, 241–242, 278,
    328–343
Rist, R., 275
Robinson, A., 275
Robinson, H. B., 32, 71, 157–158,
    163, 312
Robinson, N. M., 16, 157, 315,
    351, 407
Robinson, R. E., 28, 158, 354, 362
Robinson, S. E., 403

Robinson-Wyman, A., 197
Rodgers, B. S., 189
Roe, A., 33–34
Roedell, W. C., 71, 286, 301,
    310–312, 315
Roeper, A., 86, 290–291
Rogers, C. R., 237, 239, 274
Rogers, H. J., 229
Rogers, M. T., 307
Roid, G., 91
Rolfe, L., 356
Roosevelt, E., 291–293, 296–299,
    304
Root-Bernstein, R. S., 32–33
Rorschach, H., 222
Rosen, B. C., 34–35
Rosencrans, T., 331–332
Rosenthal, A., 223
Rosenthal, R., 180
Ross, A., 274–275, 309, 315
Ross, A. O., 275, 308–309
Ross, J. M., 374
Rothman, E., 357–358
Rothman, S., 30
Rothney, J., 189, 273
Rothrock, D. G., 186
Roweton, W. E., 228
Ruckman, D. R., 197
Runco, M. A., 229
Russell, D. H., 186
Rutherford, E., 339
Rutter, M., 371–372, 374–375
Ryle, G., 258, 261, 263, 266

Sadker, D., 17, 403, 409
Sadker, M., 17, 403, 409
Saint-Exupery, 298
Salvatore, L., 76
Sameroff, A., 15
Samuda, R. J., 83
Sanborn, M. P., 273, 308, 398
Sanders, J., 17
Sandler, A.-M., 285
Sandler, J., 285
Sands, H. H., 374
Sarrel, L., 393
Sarrel, P., 393
Sarthory, J. A., 184
Sato, I. S., 105, 142–143
Sattler, J., 351, 377
Sawyer, D. M., 182
Sayler, M. F., 197
Scarr, S., 70
Scarr-Salapatek, S., 372
Schaefer, C. E., 222, 226–227,
    253
Schaefer, R. A., 157
Schafer, E. W. P., 422
Schaffer, H. R., 374
Scheerenberger, R. C., 357
Scheerer, M., 357–358

Schiever, S. W., 9, 16, 99–110,
    237
Schlichter, C., 114
Schmidt, F. L., 180
Schrepfer, R. M., 274
Schwartz, W. P., 189
Seagoe, M. B., 348
Sears, P. S., 30
Sears, R. R., 30, 393
Sebring, A. D., 307–308
Seddon, G. M., 229
Seeley, K. R., 201
Selby, C., 20
Selfe, L., 357
Seligman, M. E., 334
Selman, R. L., 303
Seymour, D., 290–291
Shakhashiri, B., 159
Shallcross, D. J., 241
Shapiro, T., 382, 386, 391–392
Sharp, A. M., 240
Shaw, M. C., 313
Shea, J. A., 389
Shields, J. M., 187
Shwedel, A. M., 433–435
Siegler, R. S., 48
Sigel, I., 261, 267
Silverman, L. K., 11, 34, 86, 92,
    109, 274, 286, 289, 291,
    307–320, 350–351, 361, 396,
    404, 408
Simmons, R., 15–16
Simon, H. A., 158, 246–248
Simon, T., 6, 55, 348
Simonton, D. K., 40–41, 158,
    246, 250, 312, 350
Simpson, H. R., 374
Simpson, R. E., 189
Sisk, D., 16, 201–202
Skapski, M. K., 186
Skaught, B. J., 138–139
Skowron, C., 265
Slavin, R. E., 39, 178, 185, 187,
    191
Sloane, K. D., 38, 316
Smith, E., 238
Smith, G. J. W., 227
Smith, J. K., 430
Smith, L. H., 76, 111, 117,
    123–124, 134, 423
Smith, M. A., 298
Smith, M. B., 299
Smith, M. L., 179
Smith, S. B., 360–361
Smith, W. M., 187
Smolowe, J., 66
Snow, R. E., 68, 70, 74, 158
Snyder, S., 362
Snyderman, M., 30
Snygg, D., 274
Sokol, L., 197
Solano, C. H., 166, 169, 409

Solomon, F., 374
Sosniak, L. A., 3, 245, 312, 325, 339, 396
Soward, W., 189
Spearman, C. E., xv, 32, 365
Spence, E. S., 187
Spencer, H. L., 228
Spitz, H. H., 358
Springer, K. J., 312
Spuhler, J. N., 373
Sparling, S., 17
Sroufe, L. A., 285
Stanish, B., 238, 240–243
Stankowski, W. M., 65
Stanley, J. C., 6, 15, 17, 32–33, 77, 154–160, 163, 166–170, 175–176, 209, 212, 214, 310, 351, 385, 402–403, 405–406, 410, 435, 448
Starko, A. J., 138
Start, K. B., 423
Staub, E. M., 374
Steinkamp, M. W., 406, 411–412
Sternberg, R. J., 4, 8, 15, 18, 27–28, 31, 45–54, 65, 69, 86, 113, 156, 228, 246–247, 263, 266, 402, 448
Sternberg, S., 48
Stevenson-Hinde, J., 286
Stilwell, W., 223
Stone, A., 17
Straughan, R. R., 280
Streuning, E. L., 374
Strop, J., 315
Stucker, G. R., 186
Sudman, S., 87
Sunderlin, A., 316
Sutton, D. H., 183
Svensson, N.-E., 183
Swanson, L. W., 182
Swartz, R., 265

Taba, H., 106, 108–109
Taft, R., 312
Talmadge, G. K., 87
Tannenbaum, A. J., 7–8, 27–44, 72, 82, 86, 143, 145–146, 441, 443
Tarter, B. J., 225
Tarule, J. M., 294
Tauber, M. C., 184
Taylor, C. W., 77, 82, 114, 448
Tegano, D. W., 224
Terman, L. M., xv, 6, 14–15, 17, 29–32, 55, 250–251, 273, 316, 348–351, 370, 404, 407–408, 410, 413
Tesiny, E. P., 374
Thomas, T., 3, 197
Thompson, G. W., 183
Thompson, J. M., 186
Thorkildsen, T. A., 207

Thorndike, E. L., 365
Thorndike, R. L., 27, 32, 351
Thurstone, L. L., 32, 55, 69, 365
Tibbenham, A., 182
Tidwell, R., 274
Tiedt, I., 425
Tiedt, P., 425
Tisak, M. S., 69
Toffler, A., 448
Tolan, S. S., 138, 273, 286–287, 351, 361
Tollefson, N., 332
Tolstoy, L., 294–295, 304
Tonelson, S., 431
Torrance, E. P., 18, 69, 83–84, 86, 91, 112, 138, 143–144, 221–227, 229–230, 238, 240, 408, 412
Treffert, D. A., 357–359, 361–362
Treffinger, D. J., 12, 18, 113, 197, 204–205, 224, 228, 231, 240, 242, 441–449
Tremaine, C. D., 188–189
Tressemer, D., 403
Trotman, F. D., 38
Tsai, S.-L., 247, 331–332, 343
Tuckman, B. W., 225
Tyska, C. A., 297, 299

Udall, A., 16
U.S. Commissioner of Education, 402
U.S. Department of Education, 83
Uzgiris, I. C., 372

Vakos, H. N., 183
Van den Daele, L., 321–323, 325
Van Devender, F., 186
Van Tassel-Baska, J., 19, 101–102
VanderVen, K., 292
VanEerdewegh, M. M., 374
Vernon, P. E., 32, 69
Very Special Arts Education Office, 430
Volkoff, W., 419
Von Oech, R., 238
Vowles, R. W., 187

Wachs, T. D., 372
Waddington, C. H., 372
Wagner, R. K., 50
Waitzkin, F., 362
Wakefield, J. F., 226
Walberg, H. J., 10, 30, 245–255, 331–332
Walesa, L., 250
Walker, L., 300

Wallace, A., 362
Wallace, T., 30
Wallach, M. A., 158, 224–225, 229
Wallas, G., 240
Wallen, N. E., 187
Wallerstein, J., 375
Walters, J., 56, 158
Ward, V. S., 111–112, 138
Ward, W. C., 225
Wardrop, J. L., 183
Wasson, F. R., 336
Waterman, A. S., 299
Waters, J. L., 308–310, 315
Way, B., 239
Webb, J. T., 138, 273–274, 286, 351, 361
Wechsler, D., 14, 351, 370
Wechsler, L., 250
Weeks, M., 226
Weinberg, R., 14
Weiner, B., 334
Weiner, N., 362
Weiner, N. C., 403
Weinstein, T., 331–332
Weisberg, P. S., 312
Weiss, P., 3, 197, 275
Wertlieb, D., 351, 362
Wexler-Sherman, C., 60
Whipple, G. M., 178
White, A., 117
White, A. J., 76
White, B., 366–368, 370, 376
White, R., 266
White, R. W., 370
Whitehead, A. N., 112
Whitmore, J., 16, 18, 278, 286, 309, 313, 330, 333, 351, 428–432
Wicas, E. A., 313
Wiener, N., 362
Wilcox, J., 183–184
Willcutt, R. E., 183–184
Willhoft, J. L., 224
Williams, F. E., 100, 114, 228, 419
Wilson, C., 84
Winne, P., 274
Witty, P. A., 308, 348–349
Wleklinski, D. J., 228
Wolf, D. P., 60
Wolf, R., 37–38
Wollersheim, J. P., 189
Womble, S., 445
Wong, B., 274
Wong, P., 16–17
Wong, S., 16–17
Wood, C. T., 87
Woodlands, M., 274
Worlton, J. T., 183
Wright, D., 226
Wrightsman, L. S., 296

Wu, T. H., 223
Wyman, A. R., 105

Yamamoto, K., 229
Yarborough, B. H., 81
Young, G., 310
Yussen, S. R., 280

Zaffrann, R. T., 274, 288, 398
Zahn-Waxler, C., 291
Zajchowski, R., 265
Zappia, I., 16
Zegas, J., 230
Zehrbach, R. R., 189
Zessoules, R., 60

Ziehl, D. C., 189
Zilli, M. J., 313, 330
Zonderman, A. B., 32
Zuckerman, H., 158
Zweibelson, I., 183–184
Zytkow, J. M., 158

Ability grouping, 10, 178–191
  between class, 180–184
  within class, 181, 186–188
Acceleration, 9, 33, 38–39, 99–110, 154–163, 190, 310
  Research on, 101–102
  (*see also* Study of Mathematically Precocious Youth)
Achievement Identification Measure, 337
Achievement Identification Measure-Teacher Observation, 337–338
Adjective Check List, 222
Adolescents, gifted, 382–401
  appearance, 384
  coping strategies of, 394–395
  effects of labeling, 383
  identity formation of, 387–390
  reasoning and learning of, 385
  relationships of, 385, 390–393
  self-concepts of, 387–390, 398–399
  strengths of, 387
  tasks and issues facing, 386–395
Advanced Placement program, 159, 169
Advanced placement programs, 19, 100, 398
  in residential high schools, 212
Affective domain, 287 (*see also* Emotional development)
  in children, 366–368
ALM (*see* Autonomous learner model)
Alpha Biographical Inventory, 227–228
American College Testing Program, 157, 279, 405–406
American Men and Women of Science, 250
Analytic giftedness, 45
Anti-intellectualism, 4
Arthur Adaptation of the Leiter International Performance Scale, 337
Artists, 251–252
Arts Propel, 60
Association for the Gifted, 430
Attachment theory, 285–286
Attribute listing, 241
Autonomous learner model, 9, 142–153
  definition of gifted, 147
  enrichment-activities dimension, 151–152
  goals of, 145
  individual development dimension, 150–151
  orientation dimension, 149–150
  seminars, 152
  social skills in, 143

Bandura, Albert, 112
Bayley Scales of Infant Development, 371, 376
Beethoven, Ludwig van, 428
Bibliotherapy, 424
Biographical Inventory-Creativity, 227
Black Music in America: A History through Its People, 424
Blind Learning Aptitude Test, 337
Bloom's taxonomy (*see* Taxonomy of educational objectives)
Bohr, Niels Henrik David, 264
Brainstorming, 241
Bruner, Jerome, 20, 112, 269, 448

Calendar calculators, 347
Canalization, 372
Career counseling, 279
  of handicapped gifted, 432
Career development, 11, 321–327
  environmental conditions, 325
  Gottfredson's theory of, 321–324
  Holland's theory of, 324–325
  psychocreative factors in, 326
  psychological factors in, 326
  social factors in, 326
Carter, Jimmy, 241
Carver, George Washington, 33
Catastrophe theory, 102–103
CEEB (*see College Entrance Examination Board*)
Ceiling effect, 156, 205
Center for Academic Precocity, 171, 175
Center for Talent Development, 156
Center for the Advancement of Academically Talented Youth, 156, 175
Certification, 19
Challenge for Youth—Talented and Gifted, 155, 157, 161–163
Chance, 40–42
Characteristics of gifted:
  adolescents, 384–399
  children, 366–369
  females, 404–406
  minority students, 418–423
Checklist technique, 242
Children, young gifted, 365–381
  affective skills of, 366–368
  characteristics of, 369
  creativity in, 368
  definition of, 365–366
  environmental influences on, 371–373
  parental beliefs about, 368–371

Children, young gifted *(cont.)*
  social skills, 368
  stress on, 373–375
Christ, Jesus, 291, 296–297
Churchill, Winston, 40
Cicero, 295
Co-incidence theory, 354
  and prodigious achievement, 355–356
Cognitive Development, Van den Daele's stages in, 321–322
Cognitive Research Trust, 240
College Entrance Examination Board, 167
Compacting, curriculum, 123–126
Componential theory of intelligence, 46–49
Connie Belin National Center for Gifted Education, 274
CoRT, 240
Council for Exceptional Children, 430, 432
Counseling, 10–11, 273–284
  career, 279
  family, 307–320
  gifted adolescents, 398
  moral development, 270–282
  with parents, 275
  school program for, 282–283
  underachievement, 278–279
Counseling Laboratory for Talent Development, 412
Creative atmosphere, 237
Creative Attitude Survey, 226–227
Creative attitudes, 239–240
Creative Behavior Checklist for Disadvantaged Children, 227
Creative problem-solving model, 237, 242–243
Creative Process Inventory, 228
Creativity, 10, 18, 263–264, 443
  abilities, 240–241
  adolescent, 252–253
  assessment of, 219–235, 368
  developing talent, eminence, and, 245–255
  in gifted children, 368
  and giftedness, 219
  improving student understanding of, 240
  individual differences in, 236–237
  and intelligence, 229
  motivation in, 237
  self-actualized, 237–238
  special talent, 237–238
  teaching for, 236–244
  teaching goals in, 238–243
  techniques, 241–242
  viewing giftedness as, 449
Creativity Assessment Packet, 228
Creativity consciousness, 239–240
CTY (*see* Center for the Advancement of Academically Talented Youth)
Cupertino Program for Highly Gifted Underachievers, 313
Curriculum for the gifted, 105–110, 423–426, 445–446

in Purdue Saturday and summer programs, 199–202
in residential high schools, 213
thinking skills, 267–269
CY-TAG (*see* Challenge for Youth—Talented and Gifted)

Darwin, Charles, 6
Definitions, 8, 28–29, 63, 65–80, 81–82, 85–86, 245, 308, 417–418, 443
  in autonomous learner model, 147
  of eminence, 245
  of gifted children, 365–366
  of gifted savants, 357, 362
  of minority gifted, 416–418
  pluralistic, 93–94
  of thinking, 256, 261–262
  U.S. Office of Education, 219
  (*see also* Models, instructional)
Detroit Public Schools Creativity Scales, 225
Developing giftedness, 53 (*see also* Acceleration; Enrichment; Models, instructional)
Developmental curriculum, 93
Dewey, John, 112, 258
Diagnostic testing-prescriptive instruction model, 160–161
Disadvantaged gifted (*see* Ethnic and cultural issues)
DT-PI (*see* Diagnostic testing-prescriptive instruction model)

Early childhood (*see* Preschool giftedness)
Early entrance:
  to college, 100–101
  to kindergarten, 100–101
Eberstark, Hans, 360–361
Edison, Thomas, 3, 40, 261, 428
Educational Wastelands, 7
Effect size, 179–189
Egbert, Dallas, 146, 274
Einstein, Albert, 40, 264, 428
Elitism, 4, 81–82, 85, 441
Eminence, 245–255
  childhood conditions for, 250–251
  definition of, 245
Emotional development, 11, 285–306
  characteristics of, 300–303
  Dabrowski's theory of, 11, 86, 286–287, 293–300, 302–304, 314
  levels of, 293–299
Emotional giftedness, 285–306
Enrichment, 99–110
Enrichment triad model, 99, 111–113, 127–137
  research on, 137–139
Environmental influences on gifted children, 371–374
Ethnic and cultural issues, 83, 416–428
  characteristics, 418–423
  curriculum, 423–426
  definitions, 416–418

Ethnic and cultural issues *(cont.)*
  evaluation, 425–426
  identification, 419–423
Evaluation, 448
  with handicapped gifted, 434–435
  with minority gifted, 425–426
  in Purdue Saturday and summer programs,
    202–207
  in residential high schools, 214–215
  in schoolwide enrichment model, 121–122
Experience, role of, 49–50

Family counseling, 307–320
Females, gifted, 12, 17–18, 20, 402–415
  career aspirations of, 406
  characteristics of, 404–406
  identification of, 408–409
  math abilities of, 405–406
  problems of, 404–405
  self-concepts of, 406–407, 411
  social adjustment of, 406–407
Fischer, Bobby, 362
Fleming, Sir Alexander, 41–42
Font, Louis Paul, 295–296
Frontiers of Faith, 295
Future of gifted education, 12, 21, 441–449
Future problem solving program, 242

Gandhi, Mahatma, 291–292, 296, 299, 304
Genetic Studies of Genius, 30
Genetics *(see* Nature versus nurture)
George and Charles, 347
Gifted Attitudes Inventory for Navajos, 422
Gifted Child Development Center, 274, 310, 312,
    316
Gifted Children Speak Out, 274
Gifted Education Resource Institute, 197
Gifted Kids Speak Out, 274
Girls *(see* Females)
Group Achievement Identification Measure,
    337–338
Group Inventory for Finding Creative Talent, 226,
    331
Group Inventory for Finding Interests, 226, 331
Grouping *(see* Ability grouping)
Guidance Institute for Talented Students, 273–274
Guidance Laboratory for Gifted and Talented, 274,
    403

Handicapped gifted, 12, 20, 83, 428–437
  barriers to, 430–432
  identification of, 430–431, 433, 436
  parents of, 434
  programming for, 434–436
Harvard Project Zero, 55
Hearthstone Traveler, 242
Heinecken, Christian Friedrich, 347
Heredity Genius, 6
Hidden talent, 73
High schools, residential, 10, 14, 209–215
  benefits of, 213–214

characteristics of, 211–213
  issues in, 213–214
  (see also Secondary education programs)
Hippogriff Feathers, 242
History of gifted education, 5–7
Hollingworth Center for Highly Gifted Children,
    361
*Home Observation for Measurement of the
    Environment,* 371
Hunt, Governor James B., Jr., 210

Identification, 8–9, 45, 63, 75–76, 81–96, 308–309,
    444–446
  criticisms of, 442–445
  of gifted females, 408–409
  of gifted handicapped, 430–431, 433, 436
  of minority gifted, 419–423
  principles of, 85
  in Saturday and summer programs, 198–199
  in schoolwide enrichment model, 114–119
  self-nominations in, 91–92
  in SMPY, 155–157
  in talent search, 168–169
  (see also Intelligence; Testing; Models,
    instructional)
Illinois Mathematics and Science Academy, 212,
    214
Imagination Express, 242
Individual education programs, 434
Information processing, 15, 21
Institute for the Study of Child Development, 372
Intellectual Giftedness in Disabled Persons, 429
Intelligence, 14–15, 29–31, 69
  analytic, 8, 45
  bodily-kinesthetic, 57
  in children, 365–377
  components of, 46–49
  and creativity, 229
  environmental effects on, 371–375
  gender differences in, 405–406
  interpersonal, 57–58
  intrapersonal, 58
  linguistic, 56–57
  logical-mathematical, 57
  multiple, 8, 55–64, 402
  musical, 57
  practical, 8, 46
  and social class, 37–38
  spatial, 57
  stability of, 373, 375–377
  synthetic, 8, 45–46
  (see also Precocity, extreme)
Interest-A-Lyzer, 122
Inventory of Emotional Style, 289
Issues, 14–23

James, William, 112, 301
John F. Kennedy Center for the Performing Arts,
    430
Joplin Plan, 181, 185
Judging Criteria Instrument, 222, 225

Kaufman Assessment Battery for Children, 408
Keller, Helen, 428
Kepler, Johannes, 33, 264
Kissinger, Henry, 295
Klein, Wim, 360

Labeling, effects of, 275–276, 383, 445
Learning disabled gifted, 83
Learning Disabled Gifted Children, 429
Learning styles, 123, 445
Learning Styles Inventory, 123
Lederberg, Joshua, 264
Lemke, Leslie, 358–359, 361
Lister, Joseph, 32–33
Liszt, Franz, 241
Louisiana School for Math, Science, and the Arts, 211–212, 214–215

MacArthur Fellows, 311
Magnet schools, 310
Mainstreaming, 430–431
Making It Strange, 242
Mary Baldwin College Program for the Education of the Gifted, 410, 412
Mathematical ability, 86, 154–165
    gender differences in, 405–406
Mathew effects, 247–248
McCarthy Scales of Children's Abilities, 370, 372
Metacognition, 265–267
Metalearning, 36
Midwest Talent Search, 175
Minority gifted, 12, 15–17, 20, 416–428
Mississippi School for Math and Science, 211
Models, instructional, 9–10, 97–215
    differentiated, 65–80
Moral development, 279–282
Morphological synthesis, 242
Motivation, 34–35, 71–72
    achievement, 34
Mozart, Wolfgang Amadeus, 347, 361
Multidimensional Stimulus Fluency Measure, 224
Multiple intelligences, 8, 55–64, 402
Multipotentiality, 398

Nation at Risk, 3, 14
National Aeronautics and Space Administration, 363–364
National Report on Identification, 81, 83–90
National Research Center for the Gifted and Talented, 20
Nature versus nurture, 14–15, 36–37, 67, 70, 72–73
Nebraska Test of Learning Aptitude, 337
New Voices in Counseling the Gifted, 288
Newton, Sir Isaac, 264
North Carolina School of Science and Mathematics, 210, 214–215
Nyiregyhazi, Erwin, 352–354

Odyssey of the Mind, 242
On Being Gifted, 274
Oppenheimer, J. Robert, 33

Origin of the Species, 6
Otis-Lennon School Ability Test, 419
Overexcitability, 34

Parents:
    counseling with, 275
    gifted, 316
    of handicapped, 434
    and school interactions, 276–278
    and underachievement, 332–333
Pasteur, Louis, 32–33
PCCP/NOVA program, 199, 201
Peer group influence, 39–40
Peer relations, 315
Perceived Competence Scale for Children, 315
Perfectionism, 313–314, 335, 388
Planck, Max, 33
Plato, 5
Practical giftedness, 46
Precocity, extreme, 347–364
Preschool giftedness, 11–12, 18, 20
Prisoners of Childhood, 82, 289–290
Problem finding, 134–135
Problem solving, 105–109, 256–270
Prodigies, child, 11, 28, 347–348, 352–354, 359–360, 362
    Baumgarten's nine, 353
    in China, 5
    family relationships of, 356
    social and emotional concomitants of, 356
    (*see also* Precocity extreme)
Project Choice, 402
Project for the Study of Academic Precocity, 166–176
Project Spectrum, 60–63
Providing Programs for the Gifted Handicapped, 429
PSAP (*see* Project for the Study of Academic Precocity)
Public policy, 19–20
Pullout programs, 19, 197, 310, 445
PULSAR/PALS program, 199, 201

Quick Test of Intelligence, 229

RAPYHT, 432–435
Raven Matrices, 422–423
Reagan, Ronald, 241
Remediation, 51
Remote Associates Test, 224–225
Resource room programs, 197
Resurrection, 294, 304
Retrieval and Acceleration of Promising Young Handicapped Talented, 432–435
Revolving door identification model, 111, 137 (*see also* Schoolwide enrichment model)
Risk taking, 82
Rocky Mountain Talent Search, 156, 175
Roosevelt, Eleanor, 291–293, 296–299, 304
Roosevelt, Franklin, D., 428
Rorschach Inkblot Test, 222, 227

Saturday and summer programs, 10, 197–208
    identification in, 198–199
    curriculum of, 199–202
    supervision in, 202–204
    teacher selection and training for, 200–202
Savants, idiot, 11, 357–362
    characteristics of, 357–358
    definition and description of, 357, 362
    explanations of, 359
Scales for Rating the Behavioral Characteristics of Superior Students, 117, 230
Scholastic Aptitude Test, 155–157, 161–162, 166–175, 205, 405
    nature of, 168–169
    predictive value of, 169
Schoolwide enrichment model, 9, 111–141
    identification system, 115–119
    service delivery components, 119–121
    theory underlying, 113–115
Secondary education programs, 19 (*see also* High schools, residential)
Self-actualization, 286, 296–300, 303
    and emotional giftedness, 299–300
Self-concepts, 35, 274–275, 302–303, 315
    of gifted adolescents, 387–390
    of gifted females, 406–407
Self-nominations, 91–92
SEM (*see* Schoolwide enrichment model)
SENG, 146, 274
Shakespeare, William, 241, 264, 267
Simulated situation, 121
Single-sex schooling, 410
SMPY (*see* Study of Mathematically Precocious Youth)
Social class, 37–38
Social psychology of giftedness, 8, 27–44
Socrates, 290
Something about Myself, 222, 225–226
South Carolina Governor's School for Science and Mathematics, 211
Soviet Commitment to Education, 7
Special classes, 19
Spiral model of thinking, 103–109
Sputnik, 3, 7
Stanford-Binet Intelligence Scale, 7, 205, 273, 337, 348, 370–372, 376, 408
STAR program, 199, 201
Sternberg Triarchic Abilities Test, 51–52.
Structure of intellect model, 222, 433
Student Product Assessment Form, 137–138
Study of Mathematically Precocious Youth, 9, 33, 38–39, 154–163
    identification in, 155–157
    Math Clinic, 162
    program options in, 159–161
Styles:
    learning, 123
    working, 59
Summer programs (*see* Saturday and summer programs)
Sunflowering, 242
Super Saturday program, 199, 201

Supporting the Emotional Needs of the Gifted, 146, 274
Synectics methods, 242
Synthetic giftedness, 45–46

Talent development, 3, 15, 71, 74, 245–255
Talent Identification Program, 156–157, 175
Talent pool, 115, 122
Talent search, 154–163, 166–176, 405–406
    educational alternatives in, 169–170
    goals of, 167
    history of, 167
    identification in, 168
Talent Search Project, 175
Taxonomy of educational objectives, 99, 114, 200, 247, 429
Teacher nominations, 115, 117
Teachers of the gifted, characteristics of, 200–202
Teaching Is Listening, 242
Teaching, research on, 248–249
Teaching the Gifted/Learning Disabled Child, 429
Test of Standard Written English, 168–169, 199
Testing, 6, 45, 51–52, 58–59, 83–89, 308–309
    creativity, 219–235
    criticisms of, 27, 83–85
    cultural, racial, socioeconomic bias, 230
    handicapped, 89
    learning disabled, 89
    out-of-level, 170
    (*see also* Identification; Intelligence; Tests)
Tests:
    appropriate, 86–87
    (*see also* Creativity, assessment of; Intelligence; Testing)
Texas Academy of Mathematics and Science, 211, 214
Thematic Apperception Test, 221, 227
Thinking Creatively in Action and Movement, 224
Thinking Creatively with Sounds and Words, 221, 224
Thinking skills, 10, 256–270, 443
    teaching, 267–269
Thinking:
    causes of, 260–261
    definition of, 256, 261–262
    process of, 261–267
Three-ring conception of giftedness, 112–114
Torrance Tests of Creative Thinking, 91, 220, 222–224, 230–231, 240
    with gifted females, 408–409
Triarchic theory, 8, 45–54

Underachievement, 11, 16, 20, 83–84, 278–279, 311–313, 328–343
    characteristics of, 333–334
    home environments, 330–331
    model identification in, 339–340
    reversal of, 334–342
    school environments, 329–330
    trifocal model, 335–342
Underachievement Syndrome: Causes and Cures, 335–336, 341

Van Gogh, Vincent, 428
Very Special Arts, 430

Wechsler Intelligence Scale for Children—Revised:
   with gifted females, 408
   with minority gifted, 419, 422
   with underachievers, 337

Wechsler Preschool and Primary Scale of
   Intelligence, 370, 372
What Kind of Person Are You?, 222, 225–226
What Works, 249
Whitehead, Alfred North, 112

You Learn by Living, 292, 299
Your Style of Learning and Thinking, 227